The End of the Jihād State

SUNY Series in Medieval Middle East History
Jere Bacharach, editor

The End of the Jihād State

The Reign of Hishām Ibn 'Abd Al-Malik and the Collapse of the Umayyads

Khalid Yahya Blankinship

State University of New York Press

Published by
State University of New York Press, Albany

Printed in the United States of America

For information, address State University of New York Press,
State University Plaza, Albany, NY 12246

Production by Bernadine Dawes • Marketing by Bernadette LaManna

Library of Congress Cataloging-in-Publication Data

Blankinship, Khalid Yahya
The end of the jihād state : the reign of Hishām ibn 'Abd al-Malik and the collapse of the Umayyads / Khalid Yahya Blankinship.
p. cm. — (SUNY series in medieval Middle East history)
Includes bibliographical references (p.) and index.
ISBN 0-7914-1827-8 — ISBN 0-7914-1828-6 (pbk.)
1. Islamic Empire—History — 661–750. I. Title. II. Series.
DS38.5.B58 1994
909'.09767101—dc20 93-26126
CIP

10 9 8 7 6 5 4 3 2 1

Contents

Acknowledgments ix

Explanations, Symbols, and Abbreviations x

Introduction 1
The Importance of the Umayyad Caliphate and Its Collapse / 1
The Problem of the Reign of Hishām / 4

1 Jihād and the Caliphate before Hishām 11
The Doctrine of Jihād / 11
An Outline of the History of the Jihād State 2–132/623–750 / 19
The Madīnan State and the First Expansion 2–35/623–56 / 21
The First Civil War and the First Hiatus 35–40/656–61 / 23
The Sufyānid Umayyad State and the Second Expansion 40–63/661–83 / 24
The Second Hiatus and the Second Civil War 63–76/683–92 / 26
The Marwānid Umayyad State and the Third Expansion 73–99/692–718 / 28
The Third Hiatus and ʿUmar II 99–101/718–20 / 31
The Marwānid Umayyad State and the Fourth Expansion 101–22/720–40 / 34

2 Administrative Geography and Tribal Identity under Hishām 37
The Administrative Geography of the Caliphate in 105/724 / 37
Tribal Identity in the Administration and the Army / 42

3⁓ The Individual Provinces of the Caliphate 47
Syria, the Metropolitan Province / 47
The Jazīran Superprovince / 50
The Iraqi Superprovince: The 'Viceroyalty of the East' / 57
The North African or Western Superprovince / 67
The Southern Zone: The West Arabian Backwater / 73

4⁓ Administrative Policies and Ideology at the Beginning of Hishām's Reign 77
The Caliph Hishām and the Caliphal Office / 77
The Central Administration of the Caliphate under Hishām / 79
Caliphal Fiscal Policy at the Start of Hishām's Reign / 81
Ideological Centralization / 92

5⁓ The Challenges of Internal and Foreign Opposition to Hishām's Caliphate 97
The Internal Opposition under Hishām / 97
The External Strategic Situation in 105/724 / 102
The Byzantine Empire / 104
The Caucasian Principalities / 106
The Khazar Khanate / 108
The Turgesh Khanate and Transoxiana / 109
Sijistān / 110
India / 110
The Franks / 112
The Berbers / 113
Other Parts of Africa: Nubia and Abyssinia / 114

6⁓ The Beginning of the Military Crisis 105–11/724–29 117
The Building Crisis / 117
The Byzantine Front 105–11/724–29 / 117
The Caucasus 105–11/724–29 / 121
Transoxiana 105–11/724–29 / 1255
Sijistān 105–08/724–27 / 129
India 104–08/723–27 / 131
Egypt 105–11/724–29 / 135
North Africa and the West Mediterranean 105–11/724–29 / 136
Spain and the Franks 105–11/724–29 / 140

7. The Climax of the Military Crisis 145
A Sudden Turn for the Worse / 145
Sijistān 108–14/726–32 / 146
India 108–13/726–31 / 147
The Caucasus 112–14/730–32 / 149
Transoxiana and Khurāsān 111–15/730–33 / 155
The Byzantine Front 112–14/730–32 / 162
The Frankish Front 112–14/730–32 / 163
Egypt and North Africa 112–14/730–32 / 165

8. The Continuation of the Policy of Expansion 115–22/733–40 167
Lull and Resumption / 167
The Byzantine Front 115–22/733–40 / 168
The Caucasus Front 115–23/733–41 / 170
Transoxiana and Khurāsān 115–23/733–41 / 176
Sijistān 115–25/733–43 / 185
India 113–22/731–40 / 186
Khārijī and Shīʿī Revolts in Iraq and the East / 190
Egypt 115–22/733–40 / 192
North Africa 115–22/733–40 / 193
Spain and France 114–22/732–40 / 196

9. The Collapse of the Expansion Policy 122–25/740–43 199
The Berber Revolt and the End of Expansion / 199
The Byzantine Front 123–25/741–43 / 200
The East, Including Sind 122–25/740–43 / 202
The Great Berber Revolt 122–25/740–43 / 203
Causes of the Revolt / 204
The Beginning of the Revolt 122–23/740–41 / 206
ʿAbd al-Malik b. Qaṭan al-Fihrī's Coup in Spain 123/741 / 208
The Brief Governorship of Kulthūm b. ʿIyāḍ 123–24/741 / 209
The North African Governorship of Ḥanẓala b. Ṣafwān al-Kalbī 124–27/742–45 / 213
The Caliphal Twilight in Spain 124–25/742–43 / 218

Conclusion 223
Final Results of the Destruction and Scattering of the

Syrian Army / 223
The Yamanī-Sponsored Reform Program: Rationale and Result / 225
General Conclusions / 230

Maps 237

Appendix A: Sources for the Reign of Hishām b. 'Abd al-Malik 247
Historical–Critical Considerations / 247
Some Aspects of Methodology / 251
The Nature of the Sources / 254
The Limitations of the Material Evidence / 257
The Muslim Literary Sources and Their Geographical Limitations / 258
Christian Literary Sources / 265
Social and Structural Limitations in the Muslim Literary Sources / 267
Modern Scholarship / 270

Appendix B: On the Population of the Umayyad Caliphate 273

Glossary of Arabic Technical Terms 275

Notes 279

Bibliography 353

Index 369

Map Index 395

Acknowledgments

I would like to thank all those who contributed to the writing of my dissertation and to its thorough revision for publication as the book you now hold before you. First, I would like to thank the editors and staff at the SUNY Press for their excellent work and their patience when my revision and editing were going more slowly than I would have liked owing to reasons beyond my control. I include in this the readers who recommended the dissertation for publication with criticisms that I hope I have dealt with. I would especially like to thank Professors Jere L. Bacharach, my dissertation supervisor, and Carol G. Thomas, Arther Ferrill, and Farhat J. Ziadeh, members of my committee, for their guidance, insights, and suggestions made on the original dissertation. Furthermore, I want to express my appreciation to Professor Hussain Monés of Cairo University, without whose training and help at the Master's level this book would scarcely have been possible. In addition, I wish to credit the late Professors Muhammad al-Nowaihi and Muḥammad Ḍiyā' al-Dīn al-Rayyis for their important contributions to my training. I also extend my thanks to Yasir Sakr for helping me to revise the maps. My thanks also go out to my wife, who patiently bore my engrossment in the preparation and revision of this work and actively encouraged me to hasten its completion. Whatever faults may remain in the work are my own.

Explanations, Symbols, and Abbreviations

The Arabic transliteration used in this book is that generally in use among scholars. However, the final *tā' marbūta* is not represented by an 'h' or any other symbol, except when it is the first element of a construct (*idāfa*), in which case it is shown as a 't'.

Throughout the text, dates are given according to both the Muslim *hijri* calendar and to the common era, the *hijri* dates come first, followed by both common era dates; thus, 105–25/724–43, not 105/724–125/743. In all cases, the two dates are separated by a slash mark (/).

Complete references for the sources cited in the notes are found in the bibliography. Citations in the notes give the author's short name as alphabetized in the bibliography and the page number of the reference. In case more than one source by a particular author is cited, a short title is also given to indicate which of the author's works is meant. Volume numbers are given in capitalized Roman numerals; Qur'ānic *sūra*s are indicated by small Roman numerals.

I have used very few abbreviations for references in the notes that cannot be found explained in the bibliography. Probably the most significant of such are *EI*^{1} and *EI*^{2}, which refer respectively to the first and second editions of *The Encyclopedia of Islam*.

Most names on the maps represent those contemporary with the reign of Hishām b. 'Abd al-Malik. Some modern names on the maps are printed in italics. This is especially the case in the map of India, map 7. But many of the names common to modern Western usage, such as geographical terms like 'Mediterranean Sea,' or the names of French cities, still occur in ordinary type. On the whole, I have tried in the maps to represent the medieval names actually used by the sovereignty ruling a place. Thus, most names in Anatolia (map 4) are transliterated from the Greek, although they may have Arabic equivalents occurring in Arabic texts. Likewise, French names are shown for France, including Narbonne (Ar. Arbūna), Arabic names for Spain. For India, I have given such Arabic names as occur in the texts, supplementing these with transliterated Indian names where the Arabic terms are unknown or unavailable.

Introduction

The Importance of the Umayyad Caliphate and Its Collapse

The early Muslim state or caliphate, first centered in al-Madīna and then in Syria, constituted one of the largest unitary empires that mankind has ever known. Starting from small beginnings in western Arabia, the Muslim state rapidly grew enormous, uniting a territory stretching from Spain to China and from Yaman to the Caucasus under the rule of the Muslim caliph within a single century. As a result of this expansion, the Muslim caliphate surpassed the Roman and Chinese empires in land area, perhaps being exceeded only by that of the Mongols in pre-modern times. Although precise information for its population is lacking, the Muslim state also undoubtedly would rank high on the list of pre-modern states in that regard as well, owing to its sheer size.[1]

Like all other multinational empires, the Muslim state reached its greatest extent through a series of military campaigns. These are referred to in Muslim literature as "the openings" (*al-futūḥ* or *al-futūḥāt*). This terminology is directly comparable to the American expression "opening up," as in "the opening up of the West" in reference to the extension of Euro-American conquest and settlement westward to the Pacific Ocean in the nineteenth century. In this case, as in those of the Romans, the Mongols, the Spanish, and others including the Muslim Arabs, expansion became an ideological imperative justified on moral grounds.[2] In the case of the Muslim caliphate, this imperative was the establishment of God's rule in the earth, for that was the sole legitimate sovereignty. God's rule was to be established by those kinds of efforts that He had ordained, which included armed struggle in His path. Such armed struggle became known as *jihād*[3] and remained the most salient policy of the caliphate down to the end of Umayyad rule in 132/750. Most significantly, the *jihād* called for a mass mobilization of Muslim manpower that played an important role in the caliphate's success.

Indeed, the persistence of the Muslim movement forward on all fronts, for nearly a century, can only be explained if this basic doctrine of early Muslim ideology is taken into account. Many other peoples have shared the desire for wealth and the wish to escape poverty and overpopulation, insufficient explanations which have been offered for the astonishing rapidity and extent of the early Islamic conquests. Such a persistent dedication to armed struggle as exhibited by the early Muslims required an ideological belief to back it, even if worldly expectations also played a role. After all, the Muslim fighters, especially in the earliest period, were not professional soldiers but, nevertheless, carried out the *jihād* continuously, despite numerous debacles and defeats.

Being partly inspired by a belief is not, of course, unique to the Muslims. For example, the Mongols, from an early stage in their conquests, were also propelled by the belief that they were destined to rule the whole earth.[4] However, in the case of Islam, the work of conquest through *jihād* was first for God, second for the reward of the other world for those who sacrificed their property and their lives in God's path, and only third for worldly rewards for God's warriors who survived.[5] Unlike the Mongols, whose empire was founded by a warrior chieftain, the Muslims did not fight to establish the rule of a particular person or his family, for Islam was taught by a spiritual leader who was, above all, a prophet rather than a warrior.

While the Muslims' inspiration for fighting in God's path had spiritual roots, it is clear that the material success of their early conquests in this world helped to strengthen their belief in the rightness of their pursuit of *jihād*. Fighting in God's path succeeded brilliantly against an exhausted Sāsānid Persia, a seriously divided East Roman or Byzantine empire, a weak Visigothic Spain, and a Sind alienated from its rulers when the early Arab Islamic strength had not yet spent itself. The great amounts of booty gained, helped finance the continuing struggle to advance on various fronts. As a result, the Islamic state grew accustomed to financing itself through booty to a considerable extent.

However, despite the enormous size of the caliphate and the ideology of *jihād* that supported it, the universal caliphate did not endure for centuries like the Roman and the Chinese empires, but suffered a sudden and unexpected disruption after which it was never reconstituted. This came about before the end of the rule of the Umayyad family in 132/750. Because of this disruption, which began with the civil wars of 122–32/740–50 and culminated in the replacement of the Umayyads with the 'Abbāsids, three major results emerged.

First, the political unity of Islam and the Muslims, which is strongly insisted upon in the Qur'ān,[6] was immediately and forever sundered after 122/740. Although the 'Abbāsids continued the caliphate and maintained the unity of most of the caliphal domain, 'Abbāsid rule never extended far west of modern Tunisia,[7] so that the lands in the modern countries of Algeria, Morocco, Spain, and Portugal were lost. While most of these lands had been acquired by the caliphate under the Umayyads only forty or so years earlier, their separation nevertheless constituted a huge loss. Furthermore, they were not simply lost to the caliphate but immediately became Muslim states outside of it. This decisively ended the political unity of the Muslims and undermined the legitimacy of the 'Abbāsids by denying the universality of their rule, thus contributing to the eventual disintegration of their domain. 'Abbāsid rule was eventually replaced with an ever-shifting kaleidoscope of separate Muslim polities that prevail to this day.

Second, the *jihād* stopped on all frontiers, also from 122/740, with only a couple of exceptions. Just as the Umayyad collapse spelled the end for Muslim unity in a single state, so it also meant the end of the universal *jihād*, immediately and forever. Under the Umayyads, the Muslim caliphate had rarely concluded even temporary truces with non-Muslim polities; under the 'Abbāsids, such truces would become frequent, leading in time to exchanges of embassies, and finally a diplomatic mosque in Constantinople.[8] Under the Umayyads, the frontiers had frequently been expanded right through the time of the caliph Hishām (105–25/724–43), but the 'Abbāsids made only minor local frontier expansions, and otherwise suffered from continuous territorial losses to new, parochial Muslim entities that presaged the political division of the medieval Muslim world. This political division created a doubt about who could authorize and lead *jihād*, which, as a universal campaign to claim the earth for God's rule, ended with the fall of the Umayyad caliphate.

Third, the end of the Umayyad state fundamentally changed the way Muslims looked at the world, thus helping to shape the future course of Islam. Without expansion as a main cause, the Muslims had to turn their attention inward to the internal ordering of their own society. The principle of the equality of the believers of all different origins and stations in life was strengthened.[9] Although the establishment of an Islamic government remained an ideal, respect for the actual rulers continued to dwindle, as the 'Abbāsids discovered to their chagrin, and the Muslim religious leadership became more and more dissociated from the government in fact, if not in theory. With the failure of the universal war *jihād*, more emphasis began to be placed on the peaceful spiritual quest,[10] even though the concept of religiously sanctioned warfare remained "on the books," to be invoked if needed. By this peaceful transformation, the doors were opened for the already extant spiritual element of Islam to undergo a continuous elaboration persisting to this day, a development which has greatly enhanced the attractiveness of Islam to non-Muslims and thus facilitated its spread in the world.

In view of its spectacular and defining importance, we must carefully consider the causes of the downfall of the Umayyad caliphate. Although these causes have been seen in the internal situation in the caliphate, in tribal or ethnic conflict, regional rivalry, and schismatic religious movements, the external context of the caliphate must also be, as it has not usually been, taken into account. In particular, it is necessary to scrutinize in greater detail the reign of Hishām b. 'Abd al-Malik, who witnessed with frustration the end of his family's venerated *jihād* policy in his own lifetime, and to pay special attention to the little-studied external relations of his reign.

The Problem of the Reign of Hishām

Most modern historical opinion considers the reign of Hishām to have been one of the more successful in the Umayyad period.[11] This opinion owes mainly to the belief that, as a personally sober, serious, and apparently hardworking ruler, Hishām delivered his enormous realm undiminished and undamaged to his successor, despite severe pressures on it from many sides. In fact, he even enlarged it on several fronts; for example, the Muslims reached farther than ever before in France, the Caucasus, and India during his rule. Likewise, the Muslim tradition about Hishām has pictured him as a conscientious and efficient, if severe and tightfisted, administrator.[12] And, medieval Muslim historians unite with the moderns in concurring that, rather than the rule of Hishām, it was more the brief rule of the prodigal al-Walīd b. Yazīd (125–26/743–44) that exacerbated underlying problems, leading to a series of revolutions and civil wars which ended with the collapse of Umayyad rule altogether. Thus, the modern historian Hugh Kennedy has stated, "It should not be thought that collapse was inevitable or that another Hishām could not have sustained the empire,"[13] and, "The Umayyad regime had never been as strong as it had been under Hishām only a decade before the final collapse."[14]

Others have sought longer-term causes for the Umayyads' fall in the social conditions of the times rather than in the personal qualities of the caliph. But, it is worthwhile to note that modern western, as well as medieval Muslim historical opinion has been sufficiently impressed by the apparent zenith of Islamic expansion under Hishām to look for these deeper reasons almost entirely in the internal problems of the Islamic state: tribal, regional, and sectarian. Outwardly, this appears reasonable enough, for after all, the Syrian Arabs of the metropolis did start the civil wars of the Third *Fitna* (126–34/744–52) by killing al-Walīd II. Then, while the Syrians fought among themselves to establish power, the 'Abbāsids relied on provincial Khurāsānīs who had responded to their call for the government of a righteous imam.

Most modern historical analyses expand on these bits of information. Thus, Wellhausen found the dissatisfaction of the growing class of non-Arab Muslims with their second-class status, especially in Khurāsān, to have been the prime cause of the Umayyads' downfall, along with the tribal strife among the Arabs themselves.[15] Shaban has emphasized the assimilation of the Arab tribes in Khurāsān to local interests as providing a model for solving the problem of equitable integration for all Muslims in the state, a process which led the newly integrated revolutionaries to oppose the Umayyads' Arab tribal state, leading to its downfall.[16] Crone considers the main cause of the Umayyads' fall to be the appearance of a class of generals who no longer needed the dynasty's tribally based regime.[17] Curiously, all three of these share a social explanation for the entirely military events of the civil wars of the Third *Fitna*.

However, a close examination of the evidence suggests quite another view that also takes into account the structure of the relations of the Umayyad caliphate, but also looks at those relations outside its borders as well as within. The various internal problems which beset the Umayyads, including tribal strife, regionalism, and revolutionary movements with a religious coloring, were mostly long standing. Though severe, these previously had been and still might have been compassed, deflected and overcome, even in Hishām's reign, given enough time, concentration of effort, and political wisdom. But what made that impossible was an unprecedented series of military disasters inflicted on the caliphate by outside powers during this reign. It was mainly this combination of spectacular military defeats that started the Umayyad rule hurtling toward its sudden downfall, rather than any new or worsening set of internal problems. Even the sage Hishām was incapable of doing much to remedy the situation and gradually lost control over the course of events, though it was left to his successors to feel the full force of the deluge.

If reponsibility is to be assessed with the benefit of hindsight for this outcome, it may best be assigned to the unbending Umayyad adherence to their traditional policy of expansion through war against the non-Muslims, a policy that was entirely continued by Hishām,[18] though now with disastrous results. The expansion policy was a fundamental pillar of the state ideology, informed as it was by the belief in *jihād*, the military struggle against the non-Muslims until they either embraced Islam or agreed to pay tribute on their persons in exchange for protection (*jizya*), a belief derived originally from the Qur'ān itself[19] and pursued ever since, almost without a break, by the successive caliphal governments.

By the time of Hishām, the Muslim state not only faced a growing reluctance to fight on the part of some of its own troops, who preferred to settle down to enjoy the many fruits of victory.[20] But also, it faced, more ominously, a wall of strong peoples on all sides, against whom the caliphate unavailingly hurled its troops in the renewed campaigns to advance the frontiers that followed the death of 'Umar II. They faced not only a reinvigorated Byzantium shorn of most of its non-Greek provinces, but also relatively unurbanized, poor, and unorganized peoples at the fringes of civilization, the Central Asian Turks, the Khazars, the Berbers (these had never been completely islamized), and the Franks. Besides these, they also faced an important front against several civilized kingdoms in India.

Fighting against all these opponents turned out to be materially unrewarding. Each of these except the Franks had been partially subdued by the earlier blows of the first Muslims they had encountered. Each seemed to have learned from adversity in the interim and now dealt the Islamic state one or more severe defeats during Hishām's reign. The Turks and the Khazars even forced the Muslims onto the defensive. It would appear, in fact, that the reaction of each of these peoples to the Muslim onslaught reached its peak at the same time, overburdening the capacity of the Muslim state to respond.

Of course, it is true that the military debacles of Hishām's reign did not precipitate the downfall of the Islamic state itself. The caliphate's central areas remained safe and unravaged. In fact, the caliphate actually succeeded in overcoming its external opponents to some extent, renewing the offensive even before the end of Hishām's reign against the Turks, Khazars, and Berbers and keeping up warfare against the Byzantines and the Indians. This persistence is what has given a false impression of the effects of these campaigns on the state. Since the caliphate did not disappear but instead continued to triumph for a while over certain of its foes into ʿAbbāsid times, it is assumed that the wars of Hishām were merely further stages in the hard but steady process of Muslim military success. Since the results of Hishām's debacles were not immediately fatal to the Muslim state, their possibly dominant role in the dynasty's downfall has not been considered. But actually, though Hishām's hard-fought wars did not directly bring about the Umayyads' downfall, they nonetheless immediately created three fatal difficulties.

First, the expense of carrying on continuous warfare and replacing lost military units brought huge new burdens to a state treasury that had to some extent depended on a steady flow of booty from campaigns, a flow which had by then been greatly curtailed because new conquests had stopped. The state's dependence on booty was compounded by the lack of a sufficient administrative infrastructure that would enable it to tax its subjects efficiently. As a result of this situation, the increased military burdens contributed to an unexampled financial crisis which compelled the state to impose severe methods of financial retrenchment, including various forms of stricter accounting and taxation as well as cost-cutting measures and restrictions on spending. Naturally, these fiscal measures created a good deal of discontent, provoking violent resistance in many areas within the caliphate. Furthermore, the stricter financial measures were often ineffective, or at least insufficient, so that the financial crisis persisted.

Second, the continuous harsh campaigning and accompanying military disasters had, to a considerable extent, weakened the enthusiasm of the troops for fighting. This was especially the case when the fighting was not only unrewarding in material terms, but also militarily useless or, worse, disastrous, as was usually the case with campaigning under Hishām. Just as success had strengthened the spirit of *jihād* earlier, failure now weakened the will to perform it. This unprecedented weakening of the will to carry out the principles of the state ideology first showed itself on those fronts where the fighting had been the hardest, particularly Khurāsān, where it is best documented. But, it was present on other fronts as well. Naturally, as the men began to feel bitter over their hard lot, they increasingly made invidious comparisons about how their situation was worse than that of troops on other fronts who received the same pay but had it easier. Under Hishām, the reluctance of such troops to go out on campaigns at all forced the caliph to introduce Syrian troops to defend the various provinces. This made the local troops even more hostile to the central government, because it introduced interlopers who threatened to make the locals superfluous and to take over their locally privileged positions.

But, while some of the provincial troops thus became furious about the Syrian domination, the dominant group, the Yamanī Syrians, themselves bore the greater losses in the military catastrophes of Hishām's reign, especially those that occurred later. By upsetting the two-party tribal balance in the empire between the Yaman and the Muḍar in favor of the latter, the Yaman's losses created the third fatal weakness in the Umayyad state, the collapse of the dynasty's main support, that of the Syrian army units identified with the Yaman tribal grouping. In particular, the severe losses suffered by the Yamanī Syrians in North Africa from 122/740 undermined the Yaman's claim to be the basis of Umayyad power, a claim which they had maintained since their victory over the Muḍarī Qays grouping at Marj Rāhiṭ in 64/684.

Their losses also appear to have created a military vacuum in Syria at the end of Hishām's reign. Though the Syrian army continued to exist, its remaining forces were now almost entirely dispersed, especially in North Africa. This situation greatly enhanced the position of the geographically unified Jazīran army adjacent to Syria on the Byzantine front. This force was now probably more dominated than ever before by Jazīran Muḍarī units. This Muḍarī dominance of al-Jazīra stemmed from the loss of many Syrian Yamanīs in Ādharbayjān with al-Jarrāḥ al-Ḥakamī in the disaster of 112/730, as well as to the subsequent withdrawal of the Syrian Yamanīs of Ḥimṣ from the Byzantine front, along with some Muḍarīs of Qinnasrīn, for service in North Africa. Furthermore, their disastrous losses may have given the surviving Syrians less stomach for further fighting.

These Syrian military reverses, as well as the regime's fiscalism, strengthened the resolution of the Syrian Yaman tribes to further elaborate their own political program, first clearly adumbrated in the caliphates of Sulaymān and 'Umar II. These tribes pushed furiously for its adoption, even by violent means, partly out of belief in reform for its own sake, and partly in a desperate effort to save themselves from the weakness of their position by broadening their power base.

From this resolve issued the killing of Hishām's successor al-Walīd II, who had stuck unrepentantly to the outmoded traditional policy of the Umayyad house but had nevertheless managed to alienate even its members. Once the Umayyads' legitimacy once destroyed by the Yaman's military coup against al-Walīd II, it was left to the only two significant surviving army groups in the empire, the Jazīran and the Khurāsānī, to fight it out to see whose preferences would dominate. The Khurāsānīs' victory established the 'Abbāsid regime. The isolated Syrian Yamanī remnants in Spain and North Africa were thereby left out in the cold, while Spain, Morocco and Algeria were forever sundered from the caliphate as a result of the 'Abbāsids' victory elsewhere.

To summarize, at the outset of Hishām's reign, it could not have been expected that the Umayyad state would unravel so quickly. By the end of the reign, the deterioration was nakedly exposed for all to see. Therefore, as far as the Umayyads are concerned, it was in the reign of Hishām that their fate was decisively sealed rather than before or after it. The Muslim power with its united state survived, but the dynasty did not, except as an exile state in Spain with an entirely different elite. This outcome stemmed, above all, from an unprecedented series of military defeats inflicted on the caliphate mostly by non-Muslim outside powers during Hishām's reign. These defeats overburdened the Islamic state's military capacity, which led, in turn, to a serious financial crisis, a weakening of the will to fight in the provincial armies, and huge losses in the Yamanī-dominated Syrian army, until then the main prop of the state. This situation exacerbated pre-existing tribal and provincial rivalries which had only just been controlled, causing them to break out again with a renewed virulence that swept away the Umayyad dynasty itself.

∴ 1 ∾

Jihād and the Caliphate before Hishām

The Doctrine of Jihād

More than any polity that had existed before it, the early Muslim caliphate was an ideological state, that is, a state directed toward a single, unified ideological goal. In general, the caliphate's ideology was the religion of Islam or the submission to God's will, as revealed in the Qur'ān to the Prophet Muhammad. Whether or not the Qur'ān contains clear prescriptions for an Islamic state, it is certain that the Prophet himself did in fact establish a charismatic polity based both on the enlightenment of God given to him by revelation, and on his own personal leadership. The sole official purpose of this polity was to teach and transmit the ideology of Islam.[1] After the Prophet's death, the caliphal state carried on this purpose, finding clear ideological expression for it in the doctrine of *jihād*, the struggle to establish God's rule in the earth through a continuous military effort against the non-Muslims until they either embraced Islam or agreed to pay tribute (*jizya*) on their persons in exchange for protection.[2] The idea of *jihād* was derived from the Qur'ān itself and had been applied by the Prophet Muḥammad perhaps as early as Ramaḍān 1/March 623.[3] From that time forward, for more than a century and almost to the end of the Umayyad caliphate, despite a few interruptions, the policy of *jihād* was applied unswervingly. Indeed, the policy of *jihād* constituted one of the main ideological underpinnings for the institution of the caliphate from the beginning; since the struggle to expand Islam's realm had been continuous from the time of the Prophet, there was an obvious need for a central political and military leadership to control and coordinate that effort.

The emphasis put on *jihād* from the earliest times is one of the best attested facts of early Muslim history and therefore has been less challenged by doubts that have been raised by certain scholars about the value of the Muslim historical corpus, than have other aspects of the received tradition. This is because the existence of the *jihād* is abundantly evidenced from many sources, including contemporary ones, both Muslim and Christian. Therefore, the early *jihād* is evidenced not by the elaboration of its theoretical doctrine in ʿAbbāsid and later legal texts so much as in the historical record. In fact, the earliest reference to the Prophet Muḥammad in a non-Muslim source, the *Doctrina Iacobi nuper baptizati* of c. 13/634, already mentions the military aspect of his teaching.[4] The *jihād* is also emphasized by the Armenian pseudo-Sebêos, who wrote shortly after 40/661.[5] Of course, the *jihād* also enjoys prominent display in the Arabic Muslim sources. Although the Muslim wars of conquest in the caliphal period are not always referred to in the sources using the term *jihād*,[6] they are, nevertheless, plentifully documented.

Above all, the doctrine of the *jihād* is clearly spelt out in the Qur'ān. Muslims are required to go out to fight in God's path against unbelievers[7] or, to make monetary contributions to the war effort.[8] Such contributions are a loan to God that God will repay manyfold.[9] Only those who either fight or spend in God's path are the truly sincere.[10] Those holding back are threatened with both divine and worldly punishments and denounced as hypocrites.[11] From this, we can conclude that we have here an example of mass mobilization with universal conscription.[12] Fighting in God's path is portrayed as a commercial exchange by which the believers purchase paradise by sacrificing themselves.[13] Great rewards in the afterlife are specified for those killed. It is beleived that they will go straight to paradise without any further reckoning of their doings in their worldly life.[14] Others who fight are also promised rewards in the hereafter, while shares of the booty are laid out for them if they prove victorious.[15] Of this booty, the troops should get four-fifths of the total.[16]

The purposes of the *jihād* are also laid down clearly in the Qur'ān. At first, *jihād* is ordained to be waged defensively, so that the worship of God may be pursued freely in the earth.[17] Then, it is also enjoined in retaliation against those who fight against the Muslims[18] or have driven the believers out of home and family.[19] But, it eventually takes on a more general definition. Muslims should fight those opposing them until all religion is devoted to God alone.[20] Indeed, God sent Muḥammad so that the religion of truth would triumph over all [other] religion.[21] Opponents are usually characterized as oppressors both in the Qur'ān and in the historical tradition, which often refers to an opposing monarch as a tyrant (*ṭāghiya*).[22] Therefore, wars against them are wars of liberation.

When those opposing cease their opposition, their desire for peace must be accepted.[23] However, this concession eventually is only made in consideration of a payment (*jizya*), which symbolizes their submission.[24] Presumably, this payment then belongs to the reward of the Muslim fighters, who should receive four-fifths of it.[25] *Jizya* should only be taken from peoples of the book, Jews, Christians, Sabeans, and perhaps Zoroastrians,[26] while idolaters may be slain wherever they are found and must be fought unless they accept Islam.[27] On the other hand, non-Muslims are not to be forced to embrace Islam.[28] Muslims are not to fight against one another.[29]

The Qur'ān even advises the Muslims on military tactics. Especially, they are not to flinch or become weak when the fighting gets rough, but to endure patiently.[30] They should fight in a solid battle formation (*ṣaff*).[31] This verse suggests the use of military tactics quite different from those of the stereotypical raiding traditions of nomadic Arab tribes. The causes for the near defeat at the Battle of Uhud in 3/625 are analyzed in some detail.[32] But the emphasis is most strongly on ideological commitment to fighting in God's path, a doctrine highlighted by the repeated promises of otherworldly rewards.[33]

The second main source of Islamic religious and legal practice, the *ḥadīth* traditions attributed to the Prophet, supports what the Qur'ān says on the *jihād*. Even though the authenticity of their attribution to the Prophet has been challenged by some Western scholars, it is hardly disputable that the *ḥadīth* corpus is relevant to the reign of Hishām, at which time much of it must have been in circulation, and at least beginning to be recorded in writing, if indeed that process was not already considerably advanced. Certainly, as the *ḥadīth* represents what the Islamic community chose to remember about the Prophet's words and deeds, it also must reflect, on the whole, the norms of that community, at least by the end of Umayyad rule. Also, the tone of the *ḥadīth* concerned with *jihād* certainly fits what is known of the *jihād* of the Umayyad period better than it does that of the 'Abbāsids.

According to the *ḥadīth*, waging *jihād* in God's path is specifically defined as a duty which every able-bodied Muslim [male] must either perform or try to perform. In particular, a Muslim must respond to the call to arms if called upon.[34] The Prophet is said to have drawn up a list of all male Muslims for military purposes,[35] suggesting universal conscription, or at least the possibility of it. However, spending to support the *jihād* effort is equated with actual participation.[36] Certain other nonmilitary types of *jihād* are also acknowledged by the *ḥadīth*. Thus, performing the pilgrimage to Makka is equated with performing the war *jihād*.[37] The women's *jihād* is the pilgrimage,[38] though women may also go out to the *jihād* with the men in noncombatant roles with equal spiritual reward implied, but without shares in the spoil.[39] Building a mosque to transmit the knowledge and religion of Islam is called the best kind of *jihād*.[40] Finally, in a tradition which spiritualizes and dematerializes the concept, the true fighter in God's path (*mujāhid*) is described as he who struggles against himself by himself.[41] A noncanonical tradition even calls this the greater *jihād* in comparison to the military one, which is lesser.[42] However, the overwhelming majority of *ḥadīths* refer to the military struggle when they use the term *jihād*.

Other *ḥadīths* state that the reward of going forth to fight in God's path is either paradise if one is killed or dies, spiritual reward for the effort and hardship involved, or spoil that is won from the enemy.[43] But the greatest reward is paradise for martyrs, that is, those killed while struggling in God's path, about which there are many *ḥadīths*.[44] These include the famous *ḥadīth* that paradise is in the shadow of swords.[45] Dying as a martyr completely wipes out one's sins.[46] Other *ḥadīths*, however, suggest that the moral state of the martyr at death also determines his degree in paradise.[47] Both a warrior in *jihād* who dies later in bed or a person who migrates for the sake of God and dies peacefully can also be considered martyrs.[48] Boring military duties such as garrison and guard duty also bring great spiritual rewards even if they involve no fighting.[49] A Muslim who dies from plague,[50] abdominal disease, drowning, or a collapsing building, also dies a martyr.[51] Other versions add to this list those who are burnt alive, fall off a mountain, or are eaten by carnivorous beasts, and women who die as virgins, when pregnant, or in childbirth.[52]

Jihād is the third most important duty of a Muslim after regular worship and filial piety,[53] or the second after regular worship.[54] Elsewhere, however, it is considered the very best work.[55] Holding back and cowardice are reproved.[56] *Jihād* is to be waged only to exalt God's word; other motives either detract from an effort or disqualify it from being real *jihād*.[57]

As for unbelievers, they must be combatted until they accept God's unity, the cardinal tenet of Islam.[58] Such people do not necessarily have to be Muslims, however, but can keep their religions if they are people of the book. Other traditions suggest, though, that the struggle must be kept up until they also perform *ṣalāh* (Islamic worship) and pay *zakāh* (a tax paid only by Muslims).[59] Polytheists should not be left in Arabia.[60] In other versions, Christians and Jews also should not be left there.[61] Opponents should be invited to embrace Islam before the Muslims launch any assault.[62] Another version adds that they should be given the choice between Islam, payment of the *jizya*, or fighting.[63] Treaties or agreements must be scrupulously observed.[64] Moral limits are to be observed in warfare, including avoidance of killing noncombatants such as the elderly, women, and children and of destroying fruit trees, livestock, and buildings.[65] These limitations are further elaborated in the Islamic law.[66] Extensive rules are also established in the *ḥadīth* for dividing the spoil, with one-fifth going to the government, as outlined in the Qur'ān.[67]

As in the Qur'ān, tactical advice is also given in the *ḥadīth*. The Muslims should fight in close ranks. They should be patient and persistent.[68] They must avoid trying to grab the spoils prematurely,[69] which was a serious temptation for medieval armies. Troops should make sure they have adequate provisions.[70] They must also, at all times, obey their commanding officer, unless he orders something in contravention to the divine law.[71] Thus, the individual free-for-all of bedouin raiding was out; disciplined, committed order was in.

In general, the impression of the *jihād* that one gets from the Qur'ān and *ḥadīth* is of a highly motivated mass ideology directed toward a single goal. Indeed, the ideology of Islam anticipated modern ideologies in its mass appeal and means of creating enthusiasm. This enthusiasm was probably contagious and did not strictly rely either on promises of paradise or expectations of worldly gain, though both of these were present to help ignite the movement at the first, and both continued to play a role. Nothing that had gone before had ever resembled the Muslim mobilization methods, especially as far as the Arabs were concerned. No wonder the non-Muslim empires of the time were outclassed and tended to be easily dominated and defeated for over a century.

Not only the teachings embodied in the Qur'ān and *ḥadīth*, but even the structure of the communal worship required of Muslims five times a day reflected the military commitment and helped to maintain the enthusiasm for the *jihād*. Except perhaps for details, the structure of this worship must be early and therefore reinforces our evidence from the Qur'ān about the paramount importance of the *jihād* in earliest Islam. Muslim males assemble in the mosques; females stay at home. The men line up for worship in rows, as if in a battle formation. Being in the first row is considered more meritorious than the back rows, as in battle.[72] The word used for row in worship is *ṣaff*; exactly this word is used in the Qur'ān for a battle rank or formation.[73] During worship services, absolute obedience to the leader (*imām*) is required, as well as the imitation of all his actions in unison. Just as the pews in a church are sometimes said to represent the benches of the oarsmen in a galley, all pulling in unison, so the rows in the mosque represent the Muslim battle ranks in the struggle to establish God's rule in the earth. According to Jandora, the communal worship "must have inculcated discipline and teamwork, as does modern close order drill."[74]

In addition to the worship itself, the physical layout of the early mosque building reflects the military mission of the *jihād*, as well. The earliest known mosques were large, much larger than most later ones, even though the number of Muslims at the beginning was less than later on. Probably, the mosques in each city were designed to accommodate all the Muslim fighters located there. Thus, the great mosque in al-Kūfa was over one hundred meters square,[75] enclosing a space of over ten thousand square meters, enough to accommodate nearly twenty thousand worshipers closely packed together. Such a number would represent at least a substantial proportion, if not all, of the troops stationed at al-Kūfa when that city was founded.[76] Therefore, it would appear that attendance at mosque was mandatory, which conforms to the military image, just as close-order drills are also mandatory.

Furthermore, there was at first only one central mosque in each military settlement.[77] This kept the troops in the same place, bringing all the tribes and clans together for communal worship, rather than allowing them their own separate mosques.[78] That there was originally only one congregational mosque in each place is suggested by the Shīʿī tradition still in force to this day, which says that Friday worship was only to be held in one place of worship in each locale. Among Sunnīs, the same is suggested by the designation of one great mosque in each city as the *masjid jāmiʿ*, or the congregational mosque for worship on Friday (*al-jumʿa*), as in India. Having only one major mosque in a settlement enabled it also to function as mobilization center and parade ground. Additionally, the mosque could provide a military redoubt if necessary, much like a fortified Roman camp, which also tended to be square or rectangular, like the early mosque. Indeed, the fact that the original mosque of al-Kūfa was surrounded by a trench rather than a wall perhaps suggests a military purpose of basic fortification, particularly in view of the use of the trench in defending al-Madīna in 5/627.[79] The exhortations of the Friday sermon to self-sacrifice in God's path were paralleled on the battlefield by the *quṣṣāṣ* and *qurrāʾ*. Their role was to encourage the troops to seek the reward of paradise by either winning or else dying as martyrs, and they recited Qurʾānic verses to that effect in a loud voice.[80] Finally, the early mosque was always associated with the house of the *amīr* or governor, who, as military commander, most naturally had to be available to his troops at a moment's notice.[81]

Actually, a number of interesting parallels exist between the mosque-governor's palace complexes in al-Kūfa, al-Baṣra, and Jerusalem on the one hand, and Roman legionary fortresses of the imperial period on the other. Just as governor's palace and mosque were joined in the early Muslim cities, the Roman commander's palace, called the *praetorium*, was directly adjacent to a building for the assembly and review of the troops, called the *principia*.[82]

The *principia* consisted of a very large enclosed courtyard surrounded by a colonnade, like the early mosques. The courtyard might be covered with gravel, as in the early mosques.[83] On the side adjacent to the commander's palace stood a basilica with three naves that ran the width of the courtyard; this is analogous to the covered part of the mosque near the *miḥrāb*.[84] Its space was just large enough for most of the troops to crowd together in it, just as the early mosques were able to hold most, if not all, of the troops of the locale. In both cases, the dimensions of the building might be on the order of one hundred meters square.[85] In the *principia*, the troops were assembled to hear edifying speeches, and it was there that the commander dispensed justice, just as in the early mosques.[86] In both cases, it was the military commander who spoke to the troops from a raised platform (*tribunal*) or pulpit (*minbar*). Also, the troops would be assembled to swear allegiance to new rulers in just such places.[87] The religious symbols of the Roman legion were stored in its *principia*, where some religious ceremonies also probably took place. In addition, the treasury of the troops was kept in the *principia*, as apparently was the case with the earliest Muslim mosques.[88] The Roman and the Muslim troops probably received their pay respectively in the *principia* and mosque, as well. Likewise, the mosque was the religious center of the city. While there is no evidence that the Muslim complexes were inspired by Roman models, the parallels do at least point to probable shared military functions.

Beyond worship and mosque, the Muslim troops in the former lands of the Roman and Persian empires, from the beginning were quartered in new military camp cities called *amṣār* or were assigned quarters in existing towns that performed the same function. Such cities kept the troops together in a strange and possibly hostile environment, so that they could respond immediately to any emergencies. Significantly, ʿUmar is said to have commanded that these cities be located so that no water separated any of them from Arabia.[89] This was clearly a military consideration, as the Muslim Arabs, especially the Madīnan leadership, did not consider themselves adept at seafaring and, in particular, lacked control of the sea until 34/655, at least in the case of the Mediterranean. Thus, al-Kūfa and al-Baṣra were situated on the south side of the Euphrates, al-Fusṭāṭ on the east side of the Nile, and the Syrian military camps in cities by the desert, rather than the coast. Indeed, none of the cities was on a coastline.

Inside these camp cities, the troops were organized on clan lines into regiments which were then grouped into larger divisions. These camp cities became the metropoleis of Islam and served both as bases for military activity and as administrative centers for the collection of taxes supporting the military activity, precisely the dual functions over which the caliphs presided.[90] Indeed, these two functions, the struggle to make God's religion victorious over all, and the necessity of funding that struggle, also dictated the structure of the caliphal state itself. Despite their geographical extent and the sophisticated urban populations they contained, the Rāshidūn and Umayyad caliphates were rather simple affairs. Their institutions consisted largely of the citizen army of able-bodied adult male Muslims, and a tax-gathering apparatus to provide material support for the army. The caliph presided absolutely over both as supreme military commander, albeit one who rarely took the field himself.

In view of its ideology, the simplicity of its functions directed by its ideology, and the actual course of its history, it makes sense to designate the early Islamic state through Umayyad times *the jihād state* par excellence. From 2/623–122/740, for a period of over a century with only three interruptions (35–40/656–61, 64–73/683–92, 99–101/718–20), the Muslim state was more or less engaged in hostilities against all those who did not have a specific treaty with it. Although in the first few years, the Muslims had to be careful not to provoke opponents they could not yet afford to face, the policy gradually changed with the victories in the Prophet's own lifetime. From 9/631 at the latest, the Muslim polity was engaged in a struggle with all who would not offer submission to it.[91]

Other examples of the policy of perpetual war until domination is achieved exist in history, of course. The Assyrians, like the Romans under the republic, used to take to the field every year against someone.[92] Frequently, if a treaty did not exist, a state of war was assumed. Even the United States and its allies in modern times have preferred a policy of obtaining the unconditional surrender of the enemy where possible, as in the Second World War. But perhaps never before or since was such a campaign waged on so many fronts simultaneously for so long a period as happened in the case of the early Muslim state. This could scarcely have occurred without the ideological motivation provided by Islam, however much other factors may have played a role as well.

An Outline of the History of the Jihād State 2–132/623–750[93]

The history of the *jihād* state of the Prophet and the early caliphs, to the end of the Umayyad dynasty, may be conveniently divided into eight periods: four expansions each followed by a hiatus, the last of which was to become final. The first expansion lasted 2–35/623–56. It accomplished the original establishment of the state at al-Madīna, followed by the subjugation of Arabia and then the Fertile Crescent lands of Syria, Iraq, Egypt, and Iran. This expansion was ended by the first civil war or *fitna*, which lasted 35–40/656–61. During this time, all conquests were stopped and a truce was concluded with the Byzantines.

The second expansion then came 40–63/661–83. In this period, most of Tunisia and Khurāsān came under more permanent control and settlement, although afterwards, Tunisia was lost again for a few years. This expansion was ended by the second civil war of 63–73/683–92, during which all conquests were again suspended and another truce was concluded with the Byzantines.

The third wave of expansion lasted 73–99/692–718 and witnessed the conquest of North Africa, Spain, Transoxiana, and Sind. This time, the Muslim expansion was thwarted by the external defeat of 98–99/717–18 inflicted by the Byzantines at Constantinople, rather than internal discord. The succeeding hiatus of 99–101/718–20 consisted of a voluntary cessation of hostilities ordered by the caliph ʿUmar II in view of that defeat. Such a voluntary lull was unprecedented.

Soon, though, the caliphate embarked on yet another expansion, the fourth, 101–122/720–40, which is the main subject of this book. This attempted expansion was a failure on nearly all fronts. It was finally and decisively stopped by the outbreak of the great Berber revolt in North Africa in 122/740, which led to the permanent end of Muslim political unity and contributed to the subsequent collapse of the dynasty in 132/750. The period 122–32/740–50 constitutes the fourth and final interruption in the expansion policy, caused by military exhaustion and the third civil war of 126–32/744–50. As the unity of the state was destroyed with the end of the

Umayyads, the 'Abbāsids were never able to resume the universal *jihād* on all fronts, nor indeed, to expand the boundaries of the caliphate much at all. Therefore, I have not considered the 'Abbāsids' attempts to campaign against the non-Muslims, principally the Byzantines, as a resumption of the same kind of *jihād* that was practiced in the early and Umayyad periods.

Although the point should not be pushed too far, lest it produce a periodization that is too schematic, the ebb and flow of expansions followed by hiatuses form a kind of rhythm in early Muslim history. The first expansion lasted for twenty-three solar years, the second for twenty-two, the third for twenty-six, and the fourth for twenty, periods of strikingly similar length. Each of the first three were ushered in by a completely new regime. First was the primitive state of the Prophet and the early caliphs, which was nondynastic, followed by the Sufyānids, followed by the wholly different rule of their cousins, the Marwānids. Only the fourth expansion saw a continuation of the same Marwānid ruling group that had dominated the third. This successful carryover of the third expansion's overseers into the fourth period was perhaps a factor in the violent destruction of the Marwānids in the disastrous civil wars that followed the fourth and final expansion, for they faithfully kept to the outmoded policy of expansion on all fronts for too long.

Like the expansions, the hiatuses tended to follow certain patterns. The first hiatus was caused by a civil war and lasted for five years. The second was also caused by a civil war and lasted for nine years. The third was caused by an external defeat and lasted for only two years, while the fourth was caused by external defeats, led to a civil war, and lasted for ten or more years.[94] With the exception of the first hiatus, each break followed on the heels of a severe defeat or humiliation inflicted by the Byzantines. Thus, the second followed the disastrous destruction of the fleet retreating from Constantinople in 58/678, as well as the Mardaite campaigns in Syria. The third came after the disastrous defeat of 98–99/717–18 at Constantinople. And the fourth followed the serious defeat at Akroinon in 122/740, which came on top of the numerous other military disasters of Hishām's reign. The coincidence of military disasters with political change in the caliphate certainly suggests that the prestige of the *jihād* state was, to an important extent, bound up with military success, any cessation of which tended to bring change, among other consequences.

Indeed, each hiatus brought or attempted to bring a new regime to power. In the first hiatus, 'Alī, though a Qurashī himself, presided over an attempt to overthrow the Quraysh and establish a more broadly based government centered in Iraq. In the second, 'Abd Allāh b. al-Zubayr attempted to revive the fortunes of the old believers of the Ḥijāz, but faced a more dangerous revolutionary rival in al-Mukhtār in Iraq. In the third, 'Umar II, though an Umayyad, completely reversed the policies of his house, also signalling a more broadly based regime in his appointments. His rule forms a clear break in the Marwānid regime between the third and fourth expansions. In the fourth hiatus, Yazīd III enunciated a radical program for a limited caliphate which was swept away by his rivals.

Generally, the movements that emerged in the hiatuses were characterized by a tendency to try new policies that included a broader sharing of power. They were mostly led by a parade of failed revolutionaries, who often left behind them sweet memories and pure reputations, whether deserved or not, that the execrated Umayyads did not enjoy. In the first hiatus, 'Alī became the first hero of Islam after the Prophet, a status he retains today among both Sunnīs and Shī'īs. Though 'Abd Allāh b. al-Zubayr left only a mixed memory, al-Ḥusayn b. 'Alī, whose slaying just before the second civil war helped to precipitate that strife, also became an everlasting hero and martyr among nearly all the Muslims. In the third hiatus, 'Umar II was the only Umayyad to achieve such wide approval that he is often called "the fifth of the rightly guided caliphs," even to this day. Significantly, it was improbably reported that he was poisoned,[95] so that he too became a martyr in the cause of righteousness. The fourth hiatus produced no permanent heroes of like stature; perhaps they were precluded by the founding of the 'Abbāsid regime, which censored such attempts. However, to some extent Zayd b. 'Alī, who led an abortive Shī'ī revolt in al-Kūfa in 122/740, just before the fourth hiatus, fulfills the role of hero-martyr for his time and is venerated to this day, especially among the Zaydī Shī'a of Yaman.

Thus, this eightfold periodization of early Muslim history turns out not only to be of relevance to the military campaigns, but also to the internal history of the caliphate. Now it behooves us examine each of these periods in greater detail.

The Madīnan State and the First Expansion 2–35/623–56

The first stage of expansion, which I have dated 2–35/623–56 according to the initiation and cessation of external military campaigns, may be conveniently referred to as the period of the Madīnan state, for the capital remained at al-Madīna throughout this period. From 1/622, when the Prophet moved to al-Madīna, the Muslim state immediately began to take shape. While it remained virtually a city-state until the Muslims defeated the siege of 5/627, it then went from strength to strength and quickly became a large territorial state in western Arabia. Although the Prophet's conquest of Arabia is often contrasted with the early caliphs' conquests outside of Arabia immediately after his death in 11/632, the actual picture is not so clear cut. By 11/632, the Prophet had only yet certainly been able to subdue western Arabia; great areas of the north, east, and south continued to escape his control. However, at the same time, the Prophet had already initiated a military thrust toward Byzantine Syria to the northwest with several campaigns, one of which, the Mu'ta expedition, is said to have met and fought the Byzantines east of the Dead Sea, 850 kilometers north-northwest of al-Madīna, as early as the year 8/629.[96]

The Prophet's death in 11/632, though it required the new political arrangement of the caliphate, did not at all interrupt the sending of military expeditions against the non-Muslims on all sides. The expedition which the Prophet had prepared to send to Syria was sent out under the same commander without delay. Therefore, no distinction in policies need be drawn between those of the Prophet and his immediate successors, the first three Rāshidūn caliphs, Abū Bakr, 'Umar I, and 'Uthmān (11–35/632–56). However, it was under these rulers that the early *jihād* achieved its greatest success by bringing the present Islamic heartland of Egypt, Syria, Iraq, and Iran under Muslim control. These early conquests were achieved mostly in the reign of 'Umar I (13–23/634–44) and were entirely made at the expense of the Sāsānian Persian and Byzantine empires. The first was swallowed whole by the Muslim caliphate, while the second was shorn of its disaffected and alien Near Eastern provinces. Significantly as well, control of the Mediterranean Sea was wrested from the Byzantines at Dhāt al-Ṣawārī in 34/655, a feat which put those opponents of the Muslims on the defensive until 58–65/678–85, for the defense of the Byzantine capital of Constantinople ultimately depended upon naval forces.

These early Muslim conquests were greatly facilitated by the quick collapse of the previous non-Muslim regimes, which were apparently not popular with most of their subjects, at least not in the areas taken over by the Muslims. Nevertheless, the conquests were not easy but involved numerous battles and took years to complete.

Once Muslim rule was established, however, it faced little active resistance from the inhabitants. Partly, this was because the Muslims literally stepped into the shoes of the territories' earlier rulers, whose subjects had long ago become accustomed to submit peacefully to distant and often alien rulers. This was especially true of the large peasant populations of the great river valleys and plains, such as the Aramaeans of Iraq and Syria, and the Copts of Egypt. It was principally mountain peoples who maintained long, fervent, and sometimes permanent opposition, such as the inhabitants of the Lebanon and Amanus Mountains,[97] the Armenians, the Berbers, and the inhabitants of Zābulistān near modern Kabul, many of these never having been digested by an imperial system before.

The First Civil War and the First Hiatus 35–40/656–61

It was not, however, external opposition that stopped the smooth outward rhythm of the first wave of Muslim expansion. Rather, opposition to the ruling Quraysh tribe, which was also split in itself, coupled with dissatisfaction caused by pay differentials in the army and other inequities, led to a revolution in al-Madīna which overthrew the government, killing the third caliph 'Uthmān (24–35/644–56) in the process. The revolutionaries were not, however, able to establish their rule in Syria, so that a civil war developed between the Iraqi and Syrian army groups. The latter was victorious, but only after the fourth caliph, 'Alī (35–40/656–61), had also been slain by an assassin. These disturbances are known as the First *Fitna* or civil war, which was exactly coterminous with the period of 'Alī's caliphate.

Owing to the civil war, military campaigns against non-Muslims immediately ceased on all fronts for the duration of the strife. On the Syrian front, the Umayyad governor even concluded a pact with the defeated Byzantine empire by which the Muslims were required to pay tribute to the Byzantines in exchange for a truce.[98] This constituted the first hiatus or temporary cessation of the external *jihād*, and was especially humiliating because the Muslims had to pay tribute to a non-Muslim potentate, a situation that was not supposed to occur.[99]

Out of the civil war emerged the basic geographical, political, and religious splits that would continue throughout the history of the Umayyad caliphate. Aside from the Umayyads themselves, ensconced in their Syrian stronghold, these included the unreconciled supporters of 'Alī's caliphate, called the Shī'a, who were most strongly centered in al-Kūfa, the *khawārij*, or rebels, who were prominent in eastern Arabia, al-Baṣra and al-Mawṣil, and the Zubayrids, who supported the family and relatives of the first caliph, Abū Bakr (11–13/632–34). The Umayyads naturally depended on the Syrian Arab army units to support their rule. The Shī'a found a following among the dissatisfied Yaman Arabs of al-Kūfa. The *khawārij* increasingly came to be drawn from the eastern Arab nomad groups of the Tamīm and the Rabī'a, especially the latter. These groups had largely been excluded even from local power. The Zubayrids had considerable local support in al-Baṣra and more in the Ḥijāz, the original homeland of Islam.

The Sufyānid Umayyad State and the Second Expansion 40–63/661–683

The Syrian victors moved the capital to Damascus, the center of their province. The new rulers were of the Umayyad family, which was bitterly attacked by the other parties because its members had fought the Prophet and resisted Islam until the conquest of Makka in 8/630, when all remaining pagan Qurashīs became Muslims. As they were descendants of Abū Sufyān, the Prophet's former nemesis, they are known as the Sufyānids, and their rule is coterminous with the second wave of Muslim expansion.

The new caliph, Mu'āwiya (40–60/661–80), lacked legitimacy because he had taken power by force against much opposition and because the office of the caliphate in general, and the Sufyānid caliphate in particular, lacked deep roots. Mu'āwiya tried to compensate for this in several ways. First, he attempted to accord himself legitimacy by continuing the development of the claim that he was God's chosen deputy who must by obeyed.[100] To help establish Islamic credentials, he gave attention to the reconstruction of several mosques.[101] He also tried to improve the organization of the Muslim troops in the military cities such as al-Kūfa and al-Baṣra. More importantly, he sought mildly to reconcile all of his opponents to his rule by relying on personal ties with the Arab tribal chiefs. He did not seek vengeance for what had occurred in the civil war, so that irreconcilable opponents such as Qays b. Sa'd b. 'Ubāda were able to die peacefully in their beds. Such policies gave him a reputation for generosity and crafty forbearance.[102] On the other hand, he kept a tight grip on all offices, bestowing most to members of his immediate family and dependents, or on Syrian army commanders. This lack of equitable distribution of offices, as it was perceived in the other provinces, especially Iraq, remained a serious grievance.

Most crucially, though, Mu'āwiya resumed the military offensive on all fronts, attacking North Africa, East Khurāsān, and especially the Byzantines. Although achieving few new permanent conquests, these campaigns produced a great deal of booty that kept the army supplied and in good spirits. Of the areas involved, North Africa, where a new forward military city of al-Qayrawān was established around 50/670, was the most notable new territorial accession. While much of North Africa had previously been nominally Byzantine, it contained great masses of unsubdued Berbers who resisted fiercely for decades. Naturally, it was the previously Byzantine areas, mostly in Tunisia, where the Muslims first established themselves, but even here their presence was strongly contested and the conquest was not completed, as Byzantine Carthage held out. Rather, the reverse happened; with the death of the conqueror 'Uqba b. Nāfi' al-Fihrī about 62/682, the whole territory was lost. Thus, the second wave of Muslim expansion on the North African front ended in defeat.[103]

The situation in Khurāsān offered similar contrasts between the early successes of the first expansion and the difficulties faced by the second. Areas that had been under the Sāsānians had fallen easily in the first expansion, but the small Hephthalite principalities, further east, now put up a furious resistance.[104] As a result, the Muslim frontier was not advanced by the second expansion in Central Asia either. However, Marw was turned into a major Muslim military city like al-Qayrawān by the transfer of a reported fifty thousand troops and their families to it in 51/671. Unlike al-Qayrawān, which was later lost, the new settlement at Marw was not lost again to non-Muslims under the Umayyads.

On the Byzantine front in Anatolia, the Muslims opposed an ancient, organized empire, but one which had also, by now, become mostly united in language and powered by a highly charged Orthodox Christian ideology that was far from losing its vitality. Nevertheless, the Muslims continued to put much emphasis on campaigns against the Byzantines, attacking the Aegean and the vicinity of Constantinople by sea while campaigning in Anatolia by land. To facilitate the sea campaign, Rhodes was occupied as the Muslims' main forward base in 52–53/672–73.[105] The Muslims also raided the area near Constantinople from a further base at Kyzikos, but the idea that a "siege of Constantinople" took place is a great exaggeration.[106]

Although the sources are obscure, these campaigns ended disastrously with the destruction of much of the Muslim fleet, so that Muslim seaborne campaigns ceased from 58/678.[107] Apparently the Muslims had lost control of the sea, for in about the same year, the Byzantines launched a furious seaborne counteroffensive in Syria, where they could rely on local Christian support, and carried on a war there in the Umayyads' own metropole until 65/685.[108] This compelled Yazīd I (60–64/680–83) to suspend all offensive operations and concentrate on the fight in Syria. The Muslims were forced to demolish their base in Rhodes and withdraw from there, as well.[109] These setbacks cannot have enhanced the prestige of Mu'āwiya and his son and successor Yazīd I, especially among the Syrian troops upon whom they depended. It suggests, to some extent, that Mu'āwiya's reign, usually considered a success, should be reevaluated as I now propose to reevaluate the reign of Hishām, and that Yazīd I stepped into a difficult if not impossible situation much like what befell al-Walīd II after Hishām.

Perhaps the most interesting aspect of the second expansion is the coordinated effort to plant permanent new military cities beyond the Fertile Crescent, thus overturning 'Umar I's command not to let water separate the *amṣār* from the capital. In the space of three years, new cities were successively founded at al-Qayrawān, Marw, and Rhodes, indicating a planned permanent occupation of the surrounding territory in each case. Each new base was populated with troops and their families, incentives being given to encourage recruitment for these distant frontiers.[110] This represented a definite step forward, even if it did not really bear fruit until the period of the third expansion.

The Second Hiatus and the Second Civil War 63–73/683–92

Even though the external campaigns of the second expansion continued until 63/683, the death of Mu'āwiya and the accession of Yazīd I in 61/680 brought growing disaffection and strife. The atmosphere was poisoned for the Sufyānids almost immediately by the revolt and death of the Prophet's grandson al-Ḥusayn b. 'Alī, which undoubtedly disturbed many, especially the Iraqis. The unpopularity of the regime meant that all the tendencies that had emerged in the first civil war and subsequently been repressed or masked under Mu'āwiya's regime of conciliation now burst forth afresh.

The second civil war commenced with the revolt of al-Madīna, the old capital city. Although the rebels were rather easily defeated, the deaths of so many prominent Muslims from early Muslim families added another shock to the death of al-Ḥusayn.[111] This was followed almost immediately by Yazīd I's own death, which led to disarray in the Syrian camp and the end of Sufyānid rule.

Meanwhile, 'Abd Allāh b. al-Zubayr, representing the Qurashī "old believers,"[112] established a backward-looking anticaliphate that remained stubbornly rooted in Arabia. Nevertheless, at first he enjoyed wide support or acquiescence, if only because he offered an alternative to the discredited Sufyānid regime. He even received some recognition in Syria in the confusion following the death of Yazīd I. But another branch of the Umayyad family, the Marwānids, asserted their claims to represent the Umayyad cause and to be considered God's deputies in 64/684. Their claimant, Marwān I (64–65/684–85), was only Mu'āwiya's second cousin, while he was the first cousin of the third caliph, 'Uthmān. Therefore, his claims were considered flimsy, even inside the Umayyad house. But, then, no one's claims were very strong, so that his chances were as good as others if he could drum up enough support, which he started to do in Syria. He then decisively defeated his Syrian opponents at Marj Rāhiṭ in 64/684, establishing the first basis for Marwānid rule. At the same time, Egypt was recovered from Ibn al-Zubayr, who had been acknowledged there as caliph briefly. Shortly thereafter, the Zubayrid regime became bogged down fighting a major Shī'ī revolution that was directed against it in the Iraqi metropolis of al-Kūfa (65–67/685–687).

Even after securing much of Syria and recovering Egypt, the Umayyads' circumstances were still quite serious. But the Marwān I's son and successor in Syria, 'Abd al-Malik (65–86/685–705), though at first seeming to dispose fewer resources than some of his opponents, was eventually able to defeat all of them and establish the Marwānid caliphate on a firm basis. To cover himself, he signed a ten-year truce with the Byzantines that required him to pay three hundred sixty-five thousand gold pieces, one thousand slaves, and one thousand horses per annum, an onerous and completely humiliating pact. In return, the Byzantines withdrew twelve thousand Mardaites (native Syrian Christian fighters) to Byzantine Armenia (Armenia IV).[113] How 'Abd al-Malik could have afforded this burden and still had enough cash to pay armies big enough to defeat his various opponents is unclear. Some of the wealth probably had been hoarded up from campaigns of the Sufyānid period; perhaps the possession of the wealthy province of Egypt was another important factor. In any case, once free of possible Byzantine interference, he was able gradually to recover Iraq and Arabia, finishing off his opponents in both Arabia and Khurāsān in 73/692.[114]

The Marwānid Umayyad State and the Third Expansion 73–99/692–718

The most immediate need of the Marwānid regime was to establish some ideological justification for itself once it had prevailed against all its Muslim opponents in the civil war. Although the ideology of Islam itself was already well established, the Marwānids were still very insecure, both internally and externally. In particular, they had suffered a bad scare from the great Byzantine counteroffensive and Mardaite war of 58–65/678–85. That had been the first time that any of the defeated peoples had come back to challenge the Muslims' dominance. Most disturbingly, the native Christian majority in Syria had proven unreliable. While the native Christians did not generally rise against the Syrian Muslims, the possibility that such a rising could occur was brought dramatically to the Marwānids attention by the Mardaite incursions.

Thus, the Marwānid caliphate set itself to respond to the Christian counterthrust on ideological as well as military fronts. Until the time of 'Abd al-Malik, Byzantine gold coins had continued to be the coin of the realm. These were now replaced by an independent Islamic coinage. First, one with the caliph's picture emphasized his role as spiritual and military head of the Muslim community. That was replaced a short time later by an imageless epigraphic series with statements of Islamic religious creed adapted from the Qur'ān. Concomitant with the new coins was the inscription of the Muslim testimony of the faith in Greek on papyrus sheets exported to the Byzantines. Also, the caliph decreed the replacement of Greek with Arabic as the official chancery language used in Syria and Egypt. Furthermore, Christian religious processions and the display of crosses were restricted, and a great mosque expansion and construction program, including inscriptions apparently directed against the Christians, was undertaken. These steps will be more fully discussed in the context of ideology in chapter 5 below, but for the moment we must note that they began to be adopted immediately after the Mardaite war and thus were probably connected with it.

The ideological measures were not aimed only at the Christians, of course. They were also, perhaps mainly, aimed at the numerous Muslim opponents of the Umayyads. The Umayyad victories in both the first and second civil wars had been military, not ideological; their opponents were repressed, but far from eliminated. Rather, it was the opposite. Greater repression simply led to a more deeply felt opposition, one that continued to break forth in frequent if poorly organized violence. To meet this, with ideological measures largely unavailing, the Marwānids used ever-increasing force, especially in Iraq. This policy has become attached to the name of al-Ḥajjāj b. Yūsuf al-Thaqafī, the longtime governor of the East (75–95/694–714). Syrian troops were quartered in a newly established garrison town, Wāsiṭ, halfway between the old garrison cities of al-Kūfa and al-Baṣra. The Iraqi population was largely demobilized and dropped from the military rolls. Iraqis could only obtain a military stipend by going out to remote and dangerous frontier provinces such as Khurāsān, Sijistān, and Sind. The Marwānids constantly sought to expend the excess energy of the Muslim troops in external military campaigns.

Thus, on the military front, the Marwānid regime in the third expansion renewed the great early conquests of the first expansion. Although fighting continued throughout the entire twenty-six-year period, especially on the Byzantine front, the most dramatic Marwānid conquests were accomplished in the reign of al-Walīd I (86–96/705–715), a period of only ten years, as North Africa, Spain, Transoxiana, and Sind joined the empire as new and quickly subdued provinces. These conquests, at last, seemed to bring back the magic of the first Muslim conquests, brought in great wealth, did credit to the *jihād* policy, especially in the eyes of the troops, and had much to do with the stubborn continuation of that policy under Yazīd II and Hishām in the period of the fourth expansion.

While many of the earlier Muslim campaigns had been difficult, some of the great conquests of the third expansion seemed quite easy, especially at first. Around the same time that the Byzantines were finally being driven out of North Africa (79/698), the Berbers, who had furiously resisted the Muslims for forty years, suddenly embraced Islam, and even provided the caliphate with troops for further expeditions. This appears, in large part, to have owed to the tolerant policy of the governors Ḥassān b. al-Nu'mān and Mūsā b. Nuṣayr, who, unlike their counterparts elsewhere in the caliphate, enrolled the non-Arabs in the army in units of their own.[115] This policy was probably dictated by the small numbers of Arabs in North Africa and the impossibility of making headway against the Berbers any other way. But whatever its motivation, it was most effective in spreading Islam. It also planted the seeds of the future disruption of the unity of the caliphate under Hishām, as we shall see.

The most immediate result of the accession of North Africa to the caliphate, however, was the conquest of Spain, where an unpopular Visigothic aristocracy ruled over a Hispano-Roman population. In such a situation, the kingdom fell after a year's campaigning during which time the king was killed.[116] Continuing military operations were required, but the situation was under control. At almost the same time, nearly seven thousand kilometers away, at the other end of the realm, the kingdom of Sind, where a Brahmin Hindu king ruled over a largely Buddhist population, was also falling to the Muslims. Here, as in Spain, when the king was killed after a few battles, the kingdom fell.[117] Interestingly, both the targets were counterpoised at extreme opposite ends of the caliphate, and getting to them involved some leapfrogging past poorer areas yet unsubdued in North Africa and Makrān. This suggests that the motive in targetting them may have had more to do with financial rather than other considerations. Like Sāsānian Iran and the Near Eastern and North African Byzantine provinces taken over in the first expansion, these two kingdoms were relatively organized, urbanized states in lands that had been civilized for centuries.[118] This not only made them attractive targets because of the amounts of booty that could be expected, but also meant that they tended to collapse as soon as their centralized leadership, personified by their kings, had been overthrown.

By the end of al-Walīd I's reign in 96/715, the easier conquests of Spain and Sind were essentially complete. Indeed, in one other theater, Transoxiana, the famous general Qutayba b. Muslim had been slogging away against great resistance from the local princes, who, because of their lack of prior assimilation into a single empire, had to be reduced one by one. Nevertheless, considerable wealth was obtained as the entire area was subdued. However, that this type of campaigning was disliked by the soldiers is strongly suggested by the precipitateness with which Qutayba's army mutinied against him and murdered him.[119] Perhaps forewarned by Qutayba's fate, Yazīd b. al-Muhallab undertook only the mopping up of a small area previously bypassed in Jurjān and Ṭabaristān in 98/716–7 rather than attempt a new extension of the outer bounds of the caliphate. But this campaign too proved difficult.

Even on the Byzantine front, where the Muslims had not been notably successful since they had first seized control of the sea in 34/655, the Marwānid caliphate enjoyed some success. No new territory was gained from the Byzantines, although on the flank, Armenia was at last better secured than previously. But, despite the lack of new territory for Islam, the Byzantine empire was severely devastated. In light of Byzantine successes on land and sea in the Mardaite war, the emperor Justinian II had even tried to act haughtily, tearing up the ten-year truce prematurely in 73/692. But he soon suffered reverse after reverse in war, which with other factors eventually cost him his throne, ending the Heraclian dynasty that had been present when Islam had first appeared on the scene. After that, the Byzantines suffered an ever-increasing anarchy that continued throughout the third expansion of the caliphate. With the Byzantines much weaker, the Muslims saw the chance for a change of goal in their struggle on that front, and under Sulaymān (96–99/715–17) and 'Umar II all resources were marshalled for a great campaign to conquer the Byzantine capital of Constantinople itself, the only such campaign ever undertaken by the caliphate.[120]

The Third Hiatus and 'Umar II 99–101/718–20

The caliph 'Umar II has usually been considered by Muslim and western historians alike as an unusual and innovative ruler, and justly so. Desiring to put the *jihād* state on a more regular basis, and one more in line with both the spirit and letter of the Qur'ān, he embarked on a dramatic program of reforms that sharply distinguishes his incumbency from that of both his predecessors and successors. His most important reform was the decision to equalize the treatment of non-Arab Muslims (*mawālī*) with that accorded to the Arabs. This issue was especially acute in the army, where non-Arab troops were often not allowed the same rights to spoil, land, and pay that were granted to Arabs. But it also affected the position of noncombatant Arabs and *mawālī* by extension. After the reforms, no Muslims would have to pay the *jizya* that had continued to be collected from the *mawālī* up to this point. The special status already enjoyed by the North African Berbers perhaps provided a model. In taking these steps, 'Umar II was seeking to put the caliphate on the basis it would have to have if it ever ceased being a *jihād* state and became, rather, a settled state among states.

Besides improving the status of the *mawālī*, 'Umar II also sought to establish more equality between various Arab groups in the caliphate. On one level, he is often believed to have sought to give more offices to the disadvantaged Yaman tribes. By the same logic, since the rival Muḍar group had tended to hold more than their share under earlier rulers, they might thus be expected to oppose 'Umar II's changes. But, in fact, he gave no consideration to the eastern Yamanī leader Yazīd b. al-Muhallab, a general associated with the Marwānid regime just as his father had been. Rather, it appears that 'Umar II appointed relative unknowns whose ideological commitment to his reform program he could count on, altering the previous policy of sending out Syrians or others closely associated with the Umayyad house to govern.[121] The degree of interest that these men showed in Islam seems to have played a role in their selection.[122]

In order to head off the disunity that might result from these changes, and perhaps in order to mollify or outmanuever the conservatives, 'Umar II increased the ideological charge of Islam that had already been building under the earlier Marwānids. Measures taken to distinguish and separate Muslims clearly from followers of other religions are attributed to him. Through such discriminatory steps, the group feeling and loyalty of the Muslims to their caliphal benefactor might be enhanced. He also implemented a Muslim iconoclasm that eventually issued in the iconoclastic decree of his successor Yazīd II requiring the destruction of all images throughout the caliphate. In an ideological gesture, he sent a letter to the Byzantine emperor Leo III seeking to persuade the latter to embrace Islam.[123] Elsewhere, the former crown prince of Sind had half of his kingdom restored to him after agreeing to embrace Islam.

Internally as well, 'Umar II made ideologically charged reforms meant to demonstrate his sincerity to the Muslim people at large, especially those out of power. Thus, he publicly denounced the repressive policies of the previous Umayyads. Further, to show his earnestness, he ordered the cessation of the cursing of 'Alī b. Abī Ṭālib in the Friday sermon. He also returned estates that had been illicitly usurped by Umayyads to their rightful owners. He generally made himself available to hear complaints. At the same time, he increased the pay of the troops, including the ubiquitous Syrians, which indicates what a thin line he may have been treading.[124]

These steps were also encouraged by 'Umar II's startling reversal of military policy, for he gave up the external war *jihād* upon which the Umayyads' self-legitimation had hitherto rested. Up to this point, Muslim strategic thinking had been almost entirely concentrated on the offense, with little consideration of defensive strategy. There had been virtually no questioning of the aggressive policy, though it had twice had to be put aside until internal disputes were settled in the civil wars that had caused the first and second hiatuses. Now under ʿUmar II, however, the third lull in the Muslim expansion occurred, this one more by choice than by direct necessity. This showed the birth of defensive thinking among the Muslims and revealed important policy disagreements for the first time at the highest levels of the caliphal administration. But the new policy of military retrenchment was put into effect at the insistence of the caliph himself. Not only did he command the wars of conquest to cease. He also wanted actually to withdraw from the relatively new conquests of Spain and Transoxiana, as well as the frontier posts in Kilikia, including the important town of al-Maṣṣīṣa (Mopsuestia), which would thereby bring the Byzantine frontier all the way back to Antioch.[125]

Modern scholars have disagreed on the motivation for this dramatic reversal in military policy. Wellhausen attributes ʿUmar II's new attitude toward conquest to his piety, but by itself this is insufficient, as one man's decision could hardly be enforced unless it met with some wider approval.[126] Shaban suggests that the new policy was because the Yaman party was now in power. The Yaman were, Shaban says, the party of settlement and assimilation, who hated the continuous military expeditions that required them to be away from their homes. Though he states that the Yaman's first plank in their program was greater social justice for the *mawālī*, he does regard ʿUmar II as virtually a Yamanī radical in his policy of stopping the wars of conquest.[127]

There is, however, an alternative to Shaban's view that ʿUmar II's change of heart owed to Yamanī anti-militarism. The reason that a policy as successful as aggressive expansion had come to such an abrupt halt may have had a greater cause than the mere resentment of the troops at being kept in the field more than one season (*tajmīr al-buʿūth*). As important as this was, such complaints had been made for many years.[128] The sources record that ʿUmar II's desire to withdraw from Spain and Transoxiana was motivated by fears of what the enemies, presumably the Byzantines and the Turks, might do. But why should this have worried the caliphate at the very zenith of its expansion?

The answer might lie in the terrible defeat suffered by the Muslims in the unsuccessful siege of Constantinople of 98–99/717–18.[129] The magnitude of this debacle is quite graphically portrayed by the Byzantine historian Theophanes, quoting from a contemporary Byzantine source,[130] as well as by Michael the Syrian,[131] though the Muslim historians are naturally more reticent.[132] If the defeat was as great as it appears, then the Muslims may have lost control of the sea,[133] making 'Umar fear that the Muslims in Spain might be cut off just as Xerxes feared being trapped in Greece in 480 B.C.E. if the Greeks cut his bridges at the Hellespont. In both cases, it was an overreaction caused by defeat, but nevertheless, the fears were real. 'Umar may have thought of withdrawing troops from Transoxiana to defend the Umayyads' home province, metropolitan Syria. Certainly, his anxiety to bring the Anatolian frontier positions back as far as Antioch and Malaṭya, thus abandoning Kilikia, was motivated by fear of a Byzantine counterattack.[134] Summer campaigns against the Byzantines were suspended following that of the summer of 99/718. That expedition was sent only to help facilitate the Muslim army's escape from Constantinople. No more expeditions took place under 'Umar II.[135]

Now, however, it was time for those who favored the forward policy to grumble. 'Umar's policy of retrenchment would have left large numbers of troops who were accustomed to booty and to regular stipends with little to do. One of the standard planks of Umayyad policy toward the turbulent troops of the *amṣār* had always been to dispatch as many as possible to the frontiers to absorb their energies in fighting.[136] That did not always please the troops, as the revolt of Ibn al-Ash'ath shows.[137] But it nonetheless had generally been quite successful on the whole, as that is how the bulk of the conquests had been executed in the first place. To those favoring the traditional policy, it seemed unnecessarily dangerous to stop fighting the non-Muslims on all the frontiers. Their argument was finally clinched by the inability of the Byzantines to take any advantage of the Muslims' disaster at Constantinople. Neither Muslim nor Byzantine sources record any military efforts at all by the Byzantine state at this time, other than a couple of naval raids. Thus, it must have appeared quite safe to the new caliph, Yazīd II, and his brother Hishām, to resume the forward policy.

The Marwānid Umayyad State and the Fourth Expansion 101–22/720–40

Thus began the fourth great wave of Islamic forward movement against the non-Muslims. It began slowly, owing to the need to suppress the revolt of Yazīd b. al-Muhallab first, in 101–2/720–1.[138] Having done this, the caliphate renewed aggressive campaigning on all frontiers. The campaigns in North Africa, the Caucasus, and

Transoxiana began to run into difficulties at once, however. The difficulties stemmed from the new strategic situation, which had already worsened since the beginning of ʿUmar II's reign only a few years before. Under Yazīd II (101–05/720–24), the great *jihād,* now resumed on all fronts, did not immediately encounter any disastrous difficulties. But under Hishām (105–25/724–43), the fourth wave of Muslim expansion encountered an unexpected and catastrophic series of defeats that put an end to both the universal *jihād* and to the universal caliphate that presided over it.

2

Administrative Geography and Tribal Identity Under Hishām

The Administrative Geography of the Caliphate in 105/724

To understand the background of Hishām's turbulent reign, it is necessary first to examine the geographical setting of the caliphate in his time, with special attention to its internal administrative arrangements and to the foreign states which it bordered. The caliphate at the beginning of Hishām's reign in 105/724 enjoyed a geographical extent unattained by any previous empire the world had seen to that time. It stretched from recently conquered Spain in the west to the border of Xinjiang (Chinese Turkistan) in the east, and from the Caucasus Mountains in the north to Yaman in the south. The surface of this huge area was on the order of five million square miles, larger by far than either its contemporary, T'ang China, or the earlier Roman Empire. This is important to keep in mind, for it should not be thought that the trials of this state and its ultimate disintegration are indications of failure. Rather, it is more impressive that this enormous territory remained united under one rule for as long as it did.

On the other hand, it must be admitted at once that the Muslim caliphate contained vast areas of uninhabited desert, so that its population, according to what can be only very rough guesses, was somewhat less than that of the Roman or Chinese empires. According to very speculative estimates by J. C. Russell, the total population of the early 'Abbāsid caliphate, excluding Umayyad Spain, amounted to over twenty-three million.[1] C. McEvedy raises this number slightly to about thirty million inhabitants, something like two-thirds the population of the Roman Empire at its height and three-fifths that of the Chinese of Hishām's day.[2] However, adding the figures displayed on McEvedy's graphs for individual countries yields a slightly higher figure of about thirty-three million for

105/724, the beginning of Hishām's reign.[3] Though these figures must be approached with a great deal of reserve, even in relative terms they make the Umayyad caliphate one of the most impressive states in size that the world had seen up to that time.[4]

Indeed, in 105/724, at the beginning of Hishām's rule, the caliphate was nearly at its maximum. The conquests of Morocco, Spain, Transoxiana, and Sind had all taken place simultaneously in the reign of al-Walīd I (86–96/705–15), only a few years before. These had culminated in the great Muslim effort to take Constantinople and to put an end to the Byzantine Empire in 98–99/717–18, an effort which nearly succeeded. The subsequent peaceful policy of 'Umar II, followed by the renewal of the forward policy by Yazīd II, had not diminished the caliphate's territorial extent. Thus, on coming to power, Hishām found many areas which had been only recently annexed and never fully pacified. Indeed, it is likely that the mountainous recesses of farther North Africa, like those of Ṭabaristān, Zābulistān (Central Afghanistan) and Makrān, remained virtually untouched by Muslim campaigns in spite of their nominal inclusion in the Islamic state on the map.

The administration of the caliphate's vast territory had been developing for a century by the time of Hishām. Though there is little information for the earliest period, it is reasonable to assume that the provincial administration of the Islamic state began by keeping to the arrangements of the defunct Byzantine and Sāsānian regimes. This is attested to by coins, which maintained distinct types in the former Sāsānian provinces from those produced in the former Byzantine provinces until the coinage reform of 'Abd al-Malik in 74–79/693–98.[5] It is also attested to by papyri, which continued to use Greek as the official government language in Egypt until the change to Arabic made by al-Walīd I in 87/706. It is not known when exactly this reform was implemented in each province; it may be that it was delayed in some areas well into Hishām's reign, as in Khurāsān, where the change is attested to in 124/742.[6] But the point is that independent Muslim administrative arrangements with their own precedents were increasingly being established by Hishām's time, even though these arrangements had not yet become absolutely fixed.

Like any governmental hierarchy, ancient or modern, the Islamic state was divided into administrative units, which were in turn divided into smaller, subordinate units, which were subdivided into still smaller units, and so on. This system was mostly adapted from those of the defunct empires, especially in the case of the medium and smaller-sized units.[7] Naturally, we have the most information for the highest-level units in the hierar provinces (*wilāyāt*), less about the middle-sized units (*ku* still less about the smaller units (*rasātīq*).[8] These are the on of terminology about administration that can be clearly distinguished in the sources for the reign of Hishām. This terminology designating the level of units in the administrative hierarchy, however, is used somewhat loosely.[9] Usually, a *wilāya* consisted of a geographically well-defined area containing a number of cities or towns with their hinterlands. Its governor was known as a *wālī* or *amīr*, but if a *wilāya* was subordinated to a greater *wilāya*, the subordinate *wilāya* might be known as an *'amal*, governed by an *'āmil*.[10] However, the subordinate governors of *kuwar* and *rasātīq* were also known as *'āmil*s (pl. *'ummāl*) and their districts as *'amal*s (pl. *a'māl*), possibly even down to the level of administrators of mere villages.[11] The term *amīr* was also in use at all levels. A further difficulty is that both the official governors and their usually subordinate fiscal administrators are described by the terms *'āmil*, *wālī* or *amīr*.[12] The picture is further confused by changes that occurred from time to time in the boundaries between provinces and in their degree of subordination to one another.

But the ambiguity of some of the terminology in our sources should not obscure the fact that a well-defined, many-levelled administrative hierarchy existed. For the reign of Hishām, three or four levels of administration generally can be distinguished for any area for which enough information exists. First, the entire caliphate tended to be divided into four or five superprovinces, sometimes called viceroyalties, but known in Arabic only by the terms *wilāyāt* or *a'māl*. These were in addition to the metropolitan province of Syria, which had its own separate administration. Each of these superprovinces naturally contained a number of ordinary provinces, known by the same terms, with their metropoleis. These ordinary provinces, usually distinct geographical units, constituted the second level of administration, though they might vary tremendously in size. Thus, a large province of this second level, such as Khurāsān, Ifrīqiya, or Ādharbayjān might contain a number of cities, each of which would be the capital of a subordinate division of the third level. On the other hand, districts of the third level, which were known as *a'māl* or *kuwar* and their governors *'ummāl*, generally would be established around a single city.[13] The third-level provinces were then divided into country districts, known as *nawāḥī* or *rasātīq*, each centered around a town or large village. These were the fourth level in the administration.

This view of the administrative system of the Islamic state is generally similar to that described by the tenth-century geographer al-Muqaddasī (d. 375/985). According to him, at the highest level was the *iqlīm* or region, which had a *miṣr* for its capital. He then identifies fourteen *iqlīms* (their capitals are given in parentheses): Arabia (Makka and Zabīd), Iraq (Baghdad), al-Jazīra (al-Mawṣil), Syria (Damascus), Egypt (al-Fusṭāṭ), North Africa and Spain (al-Qayrawān and Qurṭuba), Khurāsān (Naysābūr and Samarqand), al-Daylam (Barwān), Armenia and Ādharbayjān (Ardabīl), al-Jibāl (Hamadhān), Khūzistān (al-Ahwāz), Fārs (Shīrāz), Kirmān (al-Sīrjān), and Sind (al-Manṣūra). Each *iqlīm* is divided into a number of *kuwar*, each of which is administered from a *qaṣaba*. Each *kūra* is then divided into *nāḥiyas*, each governed from a town (*madīna*). The *nāḥiyas* are then divided into villages (*qurā*). Al-Muqaddasī then gives an exhaustive list of seventy-seven subordinate *qaṣabas* along with the towns belonging to them.[14] Despite a number of changes in his list from the known arrangements of Hishām's time, it is likely that the basic elements of the Umayyad system were preserved, for it is certain that it consisted of a hierarchichal administration arranged in tiers. As we shall see, both the contemporary and literary evidence for Hishām's reign support a picture much like that painted by al-Muqaddasī.

In fact, the arrangement of the caliphate into superprovinces under Hishām is strikingly confirmed by numismatic evidence. After the year 106/725, Hishām is said to have made Wāsiṭ the sole mint for silver dirhams.[15] The source, however, can only be referring to the Iraqi superprovince, whose coinage was indeed centralized at Wāsiṭ after that. But the Jazīran superprovince to the north struck dirhams at Irmīniya (Armenia) and at al-Bāb, the Western superprovince at al-Qayrawān in Ifrīqiya and at Qurṭuba in al-Andalus, and the Khurāsānī superprovince at Marw until 110/728 and then at Balkh from 111/729. No dirhams were struck in Khurāsān while it was attached to the Iraqi superprovince, until 109/727 and in 117–20/735–8. In each case, dirhams were struck at only one place in each superprovince, except for the West, which had two mints, revealing its looser structure.[16]

This system had evolved gradually and continued to develop under Hishām. In its earliest days after the initial Muslim outpouring from Arabia, the Muslim administration was mainly confined to the Muslim military cities (*amṣār*),[17] to each of which were attached vast country districts left under native administration following the usage of the defunct empires. But the spread of Muslim settlement away from the large military towns, coupled with the entry of more and more non-Arabs into Islam, required direct Muslim administration to be set up in many more places than the few original *amṣ* The large number of provinces thus created needed to be grou into larger units for administrative convenience.[19] At the same time, the old *amṣār* did not want to give up their claims to territory they regarded as theirs by right of conquest. Both these factors helped to build up the concept of superprovinces, each dominated by one or more of the *amṣār*, at the top of the administrative hierarchy.

The administration of each unit, at each level except perhaps the lowest, was carefully divided between separate military and fiscal authorities. Although the former official was usually in charge overall, the fiscal governor was not always under his control, being sometimes appointed by the caliph himself. In one well-attested case, 'Ubayd Allāh b. al-Ḥabḥāb, the fiscal governor in Egypt, even though a *mawlā*, virtually supplanted the military governor,[20] a portentious development foreshadowing the attempts of the 'Abbāsid caliphs to exert more direct control over the provinces and especially to derive more income from them for the central treasury. This two-headed military-fiscal administrative system seems mainly to have originated from the desire of the early Muslim governors to get money to pay their troops without the necessity of collecting taxes on their own. The financial administration was left in the hands of the non-Muslim natives, many of whom at the higher administrative echelons soon embraced Islam, becoming *mawālī*.[21] Thus, by the time of Hishām, a system of parallel military governors almost always Arabs,[22] and fiscal governors nearly always *mawālī*, was firmly developed.[23]

Generally, tenure of office was brief under the Umayyads, a year or two being a common term for a governor, though no fixed terms were established. Probably this reflected a desire to keep the appointees from becoming too well-rooted in the provinces of the far-flung empire. However, under Hishām the tendency was quite the opposite for most provinces. Governors were kept in office for as long as possible and were often promoted or moved from one province to another.[24] This bespeaks a large degree of mutual trust and loyalty between the caliph and his governors, as well as possibly a mistrust of other, untested notables who may have been clamoring for office.[25] In some cases, it may also indicate the need to keep seasoned military commanders in governorships where hard campaigning was expected, though the many debacles and the sources' frequent sarcasm about the military abilities of the governors tend to contradict this.[26]

Nevertheless, the relations of the caliph with the provincial governors also seem to disclose a certain lack of administrative tradition and development. In the first place, appointments of governors to various provinces appear to have been on an ad hoc basis, involving little planning and depending heavily on personalities.[27] The first qualification for office was loyalty to the caliph. This meant that, whatever their abilities, governors were usually outsiders, often belonging to tribes with little influence, so that they would be reliable creatures of the caliph.[28] However, the caliphs frequently came to dislike or fear governors with too great a military reputation or popularity, which led to the second outstanding feature in relations between the two sides. Governors frequently were cashiered, deprived of their often presumably ill-gotten wealth,[29] and even tortured.[30] This repeated and seemingly disorderly process hardly indicates stability or sophistication in the system.[31] It does appear that Hishām went out of his way to mitigate the excesses of this process,[32] but the number of governors cashiered, stripped, and tortured in his reign shows that it was still the normal way of doing business.

Tribal Identity in the Administration and Army

The organization of the caliphate was also strongly affected by the identification of its Muslim citizens with tribal groupings of pre-Islamic Arabian origin. This identification appears to have been especially strong in the army, which was organized into divisions (*arbā'*, *akhmās*, etc.) and regiments (*katā'ib*) strictly on tribal lines. The Arab tribal system identifies members of a group by their shared patrilineal blood descent from a common ancestor. This trait is characteristic of tribally organized peoples in general and nomadic groups in particular, rather than a shared residence in a specific locale, a form of identification more common among settled peoples. Though the majority, probably by a large margin, of the Arabs who established the Islamic state were not nomads,[33] all the inhabitants of the Arabian peninsula identified with one or another tribe of alleged common ancestry.[34]

Although once more the terminology is very fluid, the basic unit of the Arabian tribal system was the *baṭn* or *'ashīra*, which was a clan, that is, a collection of families united by claimed descent from a common ancestor as well as by more practical political ties that put the members under a single agreed leadership usually derived from the clan's generally recognized leading family (*ahl al-bayt*).[35] This was the highest level at which political cohesion existed in the pre-Islamic period, and even at so petty a level there was often rivalry over leadership and nobility (*sharaf*). The *buṭūn* or *'ashā'ir* were in most cases unified genealogically into larger tribes (*qabā'il*), but these had only fleeting political reality, if any, in the period before Islam. Even when several *buṭūn* were united in an alliance, often rationalized by the "discovery" of descent from a common ancestor into a single "tribe," that alliance often did not last long, though it might leave some trace on the genealogies of the constituent *buṭūn*. The point is that the clans at the level of *buṭūn* generally retained a great deal of cohesion as the fundamental tribal identities of their members, while the larger groupings were to a large extent ideal or fictitious.[36]

It comes as no surprise, then, that in the early Islamic state the entire army was organized into regiments (*katā'ib*) based on the *buṭūn*. Even originally non-Arab units like the Persian *Asāwira* were adopted into the army upon their embracing Islam as if they were individual tribal *buṭūn*.[37] Usually the tribal regiments based on the *buṭūn* would have only a few hundred warriors each.[38] Though the *buṭūn* probably varied widely in size, it was normally impossible to balance the regimental enrollment by transferring some recruits from larger regiments to smaller ones they did not belong to. This was because of the frequent mutual hostility and suspicion among the clans and their dislike of outsiders. An outsider who joined a clan was known as an interloper (*dakhīl*) until enough time had passed so that the genealogy he was given in that clan was believed.

However, the genealogical works indicate that some *buṭūn* allowed the addition of extraneous elements to their ranks. This is expressed by the words, "Clan X entered into (*dakhal fī*) Clan Y," in which the dominant clan Y would retain its name.[39] Why such events took place is not usually made explicit. In pre-Islamic times, a smaller clan might perhaps have sought protection with a larger one. The smaller group would change its genealogy, subordinating itself to the larger group in order to ratify its new position as a part of the larger group. But it is probably to Islamic times that most of the changes recorded by the genealogical works refer. One possible motive, then, for such changes could have been the need to balance and equalize tribal regiments of diverse sizes for the sake of military efficiency. This was effected by adding very small *buṭūn* that could not stand on their own to larger *buṭūn* in order to make up a full-sized regiment. Alternatively, several small *buṭūn* combined could form their own new regiment of sufficient size.[40] However, smaller clans also may have joined the very largest ones for still better protection, thus increasing the differences in size among the various regiments instead of reducing them. Usually, *buṭūn* that were combined with others came from the same original areas in Arabia so that they might get along more easily. After a time, the new combination would win total acceptance as a single descent group, especially as it reflected the reality of a functioning military unit.

There seems to be no evidence as to whether the caliphate directed or encouraged these combinations of genealogically separate clans into one regiment, or whether, as is perhaps more likely, they arose out of the need of the participants to be in larger units. Probably the government had the ability, at least in theory, to limit or adjust the size of individual regiments by setting only a fixed number of stipends for each one. But it is not clear that the Umayyad government ever used this means to control regimental size, and it is perhaps unlikely that it did so, given the instability of the army owing to continuous warfare, internal and external. Replacements had to be obtained wherever and from whatever groups they could, which would not have allowed examining each recruit's clan origin and then juggling the numbers around to come up with regiments of the same size.

On the other hand, the larger army divisions to which the regiments belonged were indisputably creations of the government, as at al-Kūfa, where Ziyād b. Abī Sufyān's establishment of the fourths (*arbā'*) is well-attested.[41] Though these larger divisions were based on pre-existing tribal associations of the alliance type,[42] they had less cohesion than the *buṭūn* owing to their artificiality and perhaps to their being government sponsored. Generally, each division seems mostly to have consisted of those clans in each of the *amṣār*, or military settlements, which derived from the same well-defined area of the Arabian peninsula. The clearest example of larger units' homogenous geographical origins is found in the *akhmās* of al-Baṣra and Khurāsān.[43]

The larger divisions each had a centralized command,[44] a feature necessary to a large, well-organized regular army but certainly foreign to pre-Islamic tribal federations. Competition over command of these large divisions was a major source of strife among the *buṭūn* constituting them, which may have been pleasing to the government, as it lessened the threat of revolt.[45] Minor or marginal groups tended to get shoved aside in the struggle for leadership and thus were open to resentment. Plenty of rivalry went on inside the divisions, but as time went on, they gradually gained greater cohesion and *esprit de corps*, especially as military units, as they were no longer merely temporary tribal alliances, but rather the real basis for army organization. This is demonstrated by the glorification of the large divisions in poetry as well as by their cohesion in battle, both against non-Muslim enemies and against each other. Also, as there is strength in numbers, it finally began to be more reassuring to identify with a larger unit that would protect its members' rights.

This gradual building up of loyalty to ever-larger units culminated at the highest level in the famous Qays versus Yaman, or, more accurately, the Muḍar versus Yaman-Rabīʿa split, which became general across the Islamic state and was in full bloom under Hishām. The source of this split is obscure. The extant Arab tribal genealogies derive all the Arab tribes from one or the other of two primordial ancestors, ʿAdnān and Qaḥṭān.[46] Scholars used to think that although these eponyms were mythical, they represented a real primordial cleavage between northern and southern Arab tribes.[47] However, the view developed by Goldziher and Wellhausen, which continues to dominate scholarly opinion, posits that the split originated entirely in the context of the Islamic state and that the pre-Islamic Arabs had no consciousness of any such general twofold divide.[48] The latter opinion holds that the existing genealogical books reflect a situation that gradually developed under the Umayyads, and that these works in any case are full of contradictions and ambiguities which reveal the very process of the slow crystallization of the Muḍar and Yaman supergroups.[49] A subsidiary question raised by certain believers in the lateness of the appearance of the Muḍar-Yaman split is whether the two groupings were more akin to seventeenth-century English political parties[50] or the expediency-based, ruthless factions of the late Roman Republic.[51]

It would appear more profitable to look upon the various levels of tribal allegiance as a more enduring phenomenon. While certain changes in tribal allegiance took place up to the beginning of Umayyad times, the great Arab genealogical scheme became nearly fixed thereafter, the last major modification occurring in 64/685,[52] and its major lineaments are probably older. The creation of the army rolls by ʿUmar I, who listed recruits under their tribal clans, probably also required some greater, overall placement of the clans in relation to one another.[53] While this may have been partially artificial at the level of the broadest groupings in the beginning, it became a believed reality when it was applied in practice over a long period. Just as the Muḍar and Yaman factions may have come into existence somewhat earlier than is generally acknowledged, possibly by the outset of Islam or during the early conquests, the two groups also proved more enduring than has been admitted by certain scholars, particularly Crone.[54] It is true that Arab tribal identity became politically less and less important in the caliphate, especially after the ʿAbbāsids' advent.[55] Certainly, disadvantaged and marginal groups would grow to hate the tribal system, and an evolution was going on continuously. But these facts do not imply that the system was moribund or that its future decline would have been visible at the outset of Hishām's reign even to the discerning eye.

It was, rather, the opposite, for Hishām's reign in many ways represented the zenith of tribal feeling, especially at the level of the tribal army divisions. Tribal loyalty and feeling are persistent themes in Islamic history, particularly in its Arab chapters. They may be observed even today, if only on a small scale in Upper Egypt, with its blood-feuds and strong family identification. The persistence of the Qays-Yaman split among Syro-Palestinian villages down to modern times is well known.[56] More relevant perhaps are indications of tribal group loyalty and feeling that thoroughly permeate the ancient Arabic sources for Hishām's reign. They are abundantly attested to in the contemporary poetry of al-Farazdaq, Jarīr, and al-Kumayt, not to mention in the surviving fragments of numerous other poets.[57] Whatever the date of the origin of the Muḍar-Yaman cleavage, it was certainly a strongly believed reality in the time of Hishām.

The practical effects of the Muḍar-Yaman cleavage appear to have been mostly pernicious. Their empirewide distribution exacerbated a polarization that gradually subsumed lesser conflicts. The rivalry of the two groups led to an ever-increasing cycle of violence as each side strove to monopolize all the offices in a superprovince where the governor was one of their men, to the exclusion of the other side.[58] By the time of Hishām, the mutual enmity of the Muḍar and the Yaman was a clearly defined, discordant fact throughout the Islamic state. The geographical distribution of the two tribal groupings became a fact of paramount importance in determining the outcome of their conflict and must not be omitted from a geographical survey of the caliphate's provinces.

3

The Individual Provinces of the Caliphate

Syria, the Metropolitan Province

At the pinnacle of the administrative hierarchy was the seat of the caliphate, greater Syria, extending from the border of Egypt in the south to the Euphrates River in the north (see map 3). Ever since the final triumph of Mu'āwiya with his firm establishment as caliph in 40/661, Syria had been not only the location of the capital but also the dominant province in the empire. Ultimately, this dominance owed to the superior strength of the Syrian troops more than it did to native wealth, trade, population, or geographical position, though it should be noted that Syria's central position was probably helpful in controlling such a far-flung empire. The Syrian dominance of the state through force, became even more open after the Second *Fitna* of 64–73/683–92, which led to the first introduction of Syrian troops into Iraq in 77/697 and their military occupation of it from 82/701.[1] Later, Syrian troops were sent to most of the other provinces as well.

In view of the military domination of the Islamic state by the Syrian army, it is not surprising that Syria's administrative units were military districts from their inception. Even their name, *al-ajnād* (sing. *jund*), which was unique to Syria as a designation for administrative divisions, indicates their military function, as it virtually means "army division."[2] As geographical expressions, each *jund* delineated an area for whose defense a particular army division was responsible and from which that army division drew its pay and provisions.[3] It also geographically defined that division's possible recruitment pool.

There were five *ajnād* in Syria: from south to north, Filasṭīn, al-Urdunn, Damascus, Ḥimṣ, and Qinnasrīn. A glance at the map shows that their capitals, al-Ramla, Tiberias, Damascus, Ḥimṣ and Qinnasrīn, which were not only their administrative centers but possibly at the outset, mobilization centers as well, were nearly evenly spaced from each other, as befits a system of military defense trying to cover and protect a large area (see map 3).[4] Unlike the Roman and Byzantine administrative centers of Antioch and Caesarea Palaestinae, none of these capitals was located on or even near the coast, apart from al-Ramla in the extreme south. This suggests a desire to keep the mobilization centers away from any immediate danger of Byzantine seaborne attack.

The boundaries of the *ajnād* are given by geographers of the late third/ninth century and later. Though these show some slight differences from each other, which suggest that their borders might have changed from time to time, as is common with administrative divisions, it is nonetheless likely that they were essentially the same as those of Hishām's time. It can be seen, for example, that the *jund* of Filasṭīn is substantially the same as the Roman-Byzantine province of Palaestina Prima, while the *jund* of al-Urdunn shares some of the boundaries and the general shape of the province of Palaestina Secunda. Farther north, the parallels are less exact. Nonetheless, the *jund* of Damascus contains most of the territory of Phoenice Prima and Phoenice Libanensis, as well as Arabia. Ḥimṣ has most of Syria Secunda, and Qinnasrīn contains most of Syria Prima and Euphratensis.[5] It should also be noted, however, that Qinnasrīn was only separated from Ḥimṣ some time after the establishment of the first four *ajnād*, under Mu'āwiya or Yazīd I,[6] probably owing to mutual hostility between the dominant Arab tribal groups in each of the two regions.

It can also be seen from the map that, despite the somewhat even spacing of the *ajnād*'s capitals, their areas vary greatly in size. Thus, Filasṭīn appears relatively small and al-Urdunn quite tiny, while the massive territory of Damascus, which includes the district east of the Jordan River known as al-Balqā',[7] stretches around them in an L-shape embracing both. But this does not necessarily mean that they were all so unequal in terms of wealth and population. Indeed, Filasṭīn is accounted, by the tax figures given in certain sources, to have been the richest *jund*.[8] It is difficult to assess the exact relative importance and wealth of the five *ajnād* under Hishām, as no figures dating from his reign have come down to us. The closest in time to his reign appear to be those claimed by al-Ya'qūbī and al-Balādhurī respectively, to belong to the reigns of Mu'āwiya (40–60/661–680) and 'Abd al-Malik (65–86/685–705), and those cited by al-Jahshiyārī and Qudāma which are attributed respectively to the reigns of al-Rashīd (170–93/786–809) and al-Ma'mūn (198–218/813–33).[9] These are given in the following table. Figures are in dinars. Payments in kind are omitted, as these are apparently only mentioned sporadically by the sources.

Table 1 TAX INCOME OF THE SYRIAN AJNAD

	Ya'qūbī	Balādhurī	Jahshiyārī	Qudāma
Filasṭīn	450,000	350,000	320,000	295,000 or 195,000
al-Urdunn	180,000	180,000	96,000	109,000
Damascus	450,000	400,000	420,000	110,000
Ḥimṣ	350,000	800,000 or 700,000	320,000	118,000 or 218,000
Qinnasrīn	(included in Ḥimṣ)		490,000	360,000

These figures seem reasonable enough in their degree of magnitude as well as in their evolution over time. The lowness of the Qudāma's figures presumably reflects the unsettled conditions caused by the Fourth *Fitna* of 193–212/809–27. The beginning of Hishām's reign would fall perhaps thirty years after the date of the data given by al-Balādhurī, if accurately attributed to 'Abd al-Malik's time, and about seventy years before the figures given by al-Jahshiyārī for the reign of al-Rashīd.

If we rely especially on those figures which in their origin are closest in time to Hishām's reign, it appears that the *ajnād* were all nearly equivalent to each other in cash income, except for the tiny *jund* of al-Urdunn, which appears rather small in this regard as well. It is likely that Arab settlement was more heavily concentrated at first in Filasṭīn and al-Urdunn, which must have been able to recruit sufficient troops for each to form a full division from smaller territories than could the other *junds*. Probably the *jund* of al-Urdunn, despite its heavier concentration of Muslim Arabs,[10] gradually lost in importance as the larger, more northerly *ajnād* became more secure from the Byzantines and hence, more attractive. It seems likely that at first there was a relative reluctance to settle on exposed lands near the Byzantine frontier, which would explain why that area alone was dominated by the relatively latecoming Qays tribes.[11] It is also possible that the larger areas of the northern *ajnād* helped them to increase in importance as the Byzantine threat receded, especially after about 76/695, and their Muslim populations expanded. Perhaps too, those on the frontier kept up more of a fighting ethos than those now peacefully living far behind the front lines to the south.

Part of the reason for the superiority of the Syrian army over other forces in the caliphate was probably its size. The troops of the Damascus *jund* alone are said to have numbered forty-five thou-

under al-Walīd I (86–96/705–15).[12] It is likely that not all of e were effectives, and that not all the effectives were combat troops, but, even allowing for the greater size of the Damascus *jund* compared to the other *ajnād*, it would appear that the Syrian army rolls must have held at least one hundred seventy-five thousand names, exclusive of those of the related Jazīrans.[13] This figure contrasts sharply with the total for Khurāsān of fifty thousand in 51/671[14] and fifty-four thousand, including seven thousand *mawālī*, in 96/715.[15] It also explains how the Syrians were able to post garrisons all over the caliphate sufficient to dominate the various provincial armies. Further, it is important to keep the figure of one hundred seventy-five thousand or so in mind to judge the seriousness of losses suffered by that force in campaigns under Hishām.

The tribal composition of the Arabs in Syria, though more homogenous than some other provinces, was nevertheless quite varied. Basically, it consisted of three groups: the Quḍā'a, many of whom were already there before Islam,[16] and the more recently arrived Yaman from the far south of Arabia and Muḍar from its desert heart.[17] The Quḍā'a, whatever their earlier ties—and these do appear to have been to the Muḍar through the Ma'add—combined with the Yaman from 64/685 onward, as we have seen. This led to the complete discomfiture in Syria of the Muḍar, who became as a result a small, dominated minority in the four southern *ajnād*. Only in the *jund* of Qinnasrīn, hard against the Byzantine frontier, did the Muḍar maintain their position of absolute dominance. The newly combined Syrian Yaman, having absorbed the Quḍā'a, should have been able comfortably to control Qinnasrīn and the empire, if not for the presence just across the Euphrates of the great province of al-Jazīra, which was almost exclusively populated by Muḍar tribes. With the Muḍar of Qinnasrīn, these formed a solid counterweight to the Syrian Yaman which was a most significant fact of life throughout Hishām's reign.

The Jazīran Superprovince

The Muḍarī-populated province of al-Jazīra and its dependencies was politically the next most important province after Syria (see map 3). This province consisted of Upper Mesopotamia, the lands between the Euphrates and the Tigris Rivers above the narrow waist of central Iraq. Its political weight was derived mainly from its possession of a powerful army that did not tire of campaigning, as well as from its proximity to the seat of caliphal power in Syria.

As time passed, the Jazīran element had become steadily more important in caliphal politics. This is graphically demonstrated by the movement of the caliphal capital north and east toward al-Jazīra, as if it were drawn that way by an irresistible force. Officially, the capital remained at Damascus, where Hishām went to be formally installed as caliph, but it seems that after al-Walīd I the caliphs preferred to govern from elsewhere, mostly in the north.[18] Sulaymān had built al-Ramla in Filasṭīn when he was governor there, but spent his caliphate in Qinnasrīn, where he died.[19] 'Umar II ruled from various places in Qinnasrīn.[20] Moving the caliphal seat back to his own estates in the south, Yazīd II preferred al-Balqā' and died in it at Irbid.[21] But after that, the trend was clearly more toward the northeast. Hishām's choice of al-Ruṣāfa near the Euphrates, in territory probably associated with the Ḥimṣ *jund*,[22] for his actual administrative capital is more likely to have owed to necessity than to chance. Al-Walīd II preferred to live near his father's center of power in al-Balqā' or al-Urdunn, but even he was killed to the north near Palmyra, probably while trying to flee to the Jazīran army.[23] Had he lived nearer to the Jazīran army, he might not have been trapped by the reformist rebels of the Damascus *jund*, who cut off his escape. Marwān II then took the natural step of moving the capital still further to Ḥarrān in Diyār Muḍar across the Euphrates, where his power wholly lay. Thus the effective caliphal capital had already moved considerably away from Damascus long before the 'Abbāsids moved it officially to Iraq.

The administrative arrangements for al-Jazīra varied over time. At first separate, it was added to the Syrian governorship of Mu'āwiya by 'Uthmān (24–35/644–56) and thus became part of the metropolitan province until Mu'āwiya's death in 60/680. This association with Syria continued the previous longstanding Romano-Byzantine arrangements, as Syria and al-Jazīra had formed the Roman Diocese of the East. But al-Jazīra nevertheless remained a somewhat separate entity owing to its different Arab tribal composition, and this was recognized by 'Abd al-Malik when he separated it from Syria in 73/692 and made it a province on its own, perhaps giving it the status of a *jund*.[24] It may be that this was part of the peace settlement he made in 71/691 towards the end of the Second *Fitna* with the Jazīran tribes, who had not yet become reconciled to his rule.[25] After that, al-Jazīra remained a separate province, but one enjoying an unusual status owing to its nearness to Syria as well as its military activity on the prestigious Byzantine front.

The province of al-Jazīra was divided into two parts, Diyār Muḍar in the west along the Euphrates, and Diyār Rabī'a in the east along the Tigris. These divisions were strictly along tribal lines according to the groups that dominated them. That they bore the names of Arab tribal groupings suggests that the Arab element in the population was large. This could account in part for the frequently demonstrated military strength of the province, as it would then have had a larger recruitment pool for the army than other provinces. As with Syria, a considerable Arab population already existed before the Islamic conquest.[26] The divisions of Diyār Muḍar and Diyār Rabī'a also suggest, perhaps significantly, pre-Islamic administrative precedent. The district of Diyār Muḍar coincides fairly closely with the old Romano-Byzantine province of Osrhoene. This province had existed as an independent kingdom under an Arab line of kings some centuries earlier and also was a center of learning and culture for Monophysite Christianity. It may have retained, therefore, a sense of separate identity which may have come to affect somewhat even the Arab ruling group.[27] The territory of Diyār Rabī'a, on the other hand, was larger, less well-defined, and had been the zone of greatest confrontation between the Byzantine and Sāsānian Empires before Islam.[28]

Al-Mawṣil is sometimes reckoned a part of Diyār Rabī'a, even to the extent of being considered its capital,[29] but under Hishām al-Mawṣil constituted a separate province not joined to Diyār Rabī'a. However, while remaining apart under its own governor, al-Mawṣil did tend to become a dependency of al-Jazīra at different times. This seems to have been the case about 102–06/721–25, when the Jazīrans were riding high in the whole East after their defeat of Ibn al-Muhallab. After that, Hishām seems to have restored al-Mawṣil's independence. Certainly, it was not subordinate to al-Jazīra while his wife's nephew al-Ḥurr b. Yūsuf was governor.[30] Thus, it became a small exception to the general prevalence of superprovinces, as it appears to have been on its own most of the time.[31] However, as it was not a frontier province and thus had no major military base or troop concentration, it had slight importance in the power politics of the caliphate.

More indicative of the power and influence of al-Jazīra than any tenuous ties it may have had with al-Mawṣil is the subordination of Armenia and Ādharbayjān to it. The three units of al-Jazīra, Armenia, and Ādharbayjān, when put under a single governor, constituted the Jazīran superprovince. This step was definitively taken by 'Abd al-Malik in 83/702, when Armenia and Ādharbayjān were added to his brother Muḥammad's Jazīran governorship.[32] Jazīran control over Armenia and Ādharbayjān thereafter was broken for the first time under Yazīd II by the introduction of Ḥimṣī and other

Table 2   TAX INCOME OF THE JAZIRAN SUPERPROVINCE

	Ya'qūbī	Jahshiyārī	Qudāma	Ibn Khurdādhbih
Diyār Muḍar	} 55,000,000	34,000,000	{ 6,000,000	5,600,000
Diyār Rabī'a			4,635,000+ 4,100,000 or 6,200,000[36]	7,700,000
Tarīq al-Furāt[37]			2,900,000	
Al-Mawṣil	45,000,000	24,000,000	6,300,000+ 6,650,000 or 6,850,000[38]	4,000,000
Armenia		13,000,000	4,000,000+ 100,000[39]	
Ādharbayjān	30,000,000[40]	4,000,000	4,000,000	

Syrians in 103/721–22.[33] Probably the Jazīrans had to give up control of Armenia and Ādharbayjān in exchange for being allowed to take up the much more lucrative task of governing Iraq and the East. After Hishām had removed the Jazīrans from the Iraqi provinces in 105/724, however, he restored their position in Armenia and Ādharbayjān in 107/726, possibly as a consolation to keep them satisfied. Later, probably to meet the military crisis brought on by the Khazar threat, he gave Armenia and Ādharbayjān back to the Syrian Yamanīs (in 109/727), but the destruction of the latter's army at Ardabīl in 112/730 ended their power there for the most part and required bringing the Jazīrans back to stay. The whole of the Jazīran superprovince, al-Jazīra, Armenia, and Ādharbayjān, became a separate power base for Marwān b. Muḥammad b. Marwān from 114/732.[34]

The relative importance of al-Jazīra and its dependencies may be indicated to some extent from their tax figures. All figures are given in dirhams rather than dinars, though the kharāj of the former Byzantine territories probably had been calculated in dinars at first. The figures from al-Ya'qūbī refer to the time of Mu'āwiya; those of al-Jahshiyārī to that of al-Rashīd; those of Qudāma to that of al-Ma'mūn; and those of Ibn Khurdādhbih (also cited by Ibn al-Faqīh) to 250/864.[35]

Compared to those cited for Syria, the figures given for the Jazīran superprovince show much less coherence. If correct, they eloquently portray a disastrous sinking of central tax-collecting power in 'Abbāsid times. Unfortunately, the earlier figures, especially those cited by al-Ya'qūbī, are in very round figures and hence, may be mere guesses or exaggerations. However, if the figures for al-Jazīra given by either al-Ya'qūbī or al-Jahshiyārī are even approximately correct, the economic importance of that province by itself must have been of nearly the same order of magnitude as that of all of Syria together. This is all the more so if the tax figures cited for Ādharbayjān and Armenia are included.

The relative similarity of the the two regions' incomes from taxes implies that the two regions' military strengths might also be comparable, because the income determined the number of the troops who could be maintained. Since the number of troops in the Jazīran army still numbered sixty thousand in 133/751 even after their defeat by the 'Abbāsids,[41] they probably had numbered at least seventy-five thousand under Hishām,[42] compared to about one hundred seventy-five thousand Syrians. These possibilities also point to the growing influence of al-Jazīra and its Muslim inhabitants in late Umayyad times.

Indeed, so large an army as the Jazīran was not important only for its size, but also gained prestige and influence from the number of active war fronts it maintained against the non-Muslim powers. The most important of these was the Byzantine front, because the Byzantine Empire remained the caliphate's chief nemesis, as indeed it had been from the beginning. Besides the considerable prestige that accrued to Muslim warriors on this front, fighting on it had also probably brought in considerable booty since the Muslims had reassumed their offensive stance in 75/694,[43] while it was the Byzantines' turn to sink into a time of troubles (76–98/695–717).[44] Al-Jazīra's influence was further extended by its acquisition of Ādharbayjān, with its front against the Khazars. The Khazar kingdom, though ultimately neutralized by the Muslims, was to prove a most formidable enemy under Hishām.

The most spectacular element in the increasing power of the Jazīrans, however, was the peculiar arrangement of Arab intertribal relations in the province. Like most other provinces, the tribal composition of the Arabs of al-Jazīra was not homogenous, though it revealed fewer cleavages than existed elsewhere. Like many provinces of the caliphate, al-Jazīra held two distinct and antithetical groupings, each mostly concentrated in its own district: the Muḍar, locally represented by their branch of the Qays, and the Rabī'a. What was peculiar about al-Jazīra, though, was the overwhelming, unmitigated superiority of the Muḍar in the whole province, a superiority so pronounced that al-Jazīra can be regarded as the true blue Muḍar stronghold par excellence.[45] Yet Diyār Muḍar was a smaller area than Diyār Rabī'a and, at least according to the much later figures in table 2 above, produced significantly less income. How then did the Muḍar/Qays of the province exert so much influence and the Rabīʿa so little?

The answer lies in several factors. As for the Qays, as Wellhausen pointed out, they were the first to form a tightly knit group consciousness (*ʿaṣabiyya*) that became prevalent across the whole empire. Thus, they were better organized at an earlier date than the other groups. Wellhausen attributed this to the dominant position of the Thaqīf, an important tribe of the Qays, who held a number of famous early governorships and thus were able to organize their tribal party better by taking advantage of their possession of the government machinery.[46] One might add that the majority of governorships under the Umayyads in general were held by Qaysī or other Muḍarī appointees.[47] There is no doubt that being in possession of the government helped the Muḍar.

But another possibility is that the continuous fighting with the Byzantines annually, almost without a break from the very beginning of Islam, except during Muslim civil wars, created the power of the Jazīran army. First, the fighting against the venerable, strong, and well-organized Byzantine state must have required a tremendous commitment of manpower. Muḍarīs, and especially Qaysīs, tended to concentrate with their fellow tribesmen in the Muḍarī frontier area, namely Diyār Muḍar, which had an excellent strategic location at the apex of the Fertile Crescent. This led to the permanent establishment of a large force.

Second, the maintenance of this force was necessary most of the time owing to a possible Byzantine threat, for the Byzantine Empire was resilient even though it was often weak. Therefore, arrangements had to be made for the Jazīran army's pay and supply, which required putting more territories under it in its superprovince, so that it could enjoy the income derived from them. Third, from as early as 75/694 and throughout most of Hishām's reign, the Muslims were able to keep the initiative and stay on the offensive on the Byzantine front. This meant at least some booty and some periods of easy raiding with fewer really difficult wars. Fourth, the constant fighting provided excellent training and experience for the troops so that they became seasoned warriors with a considerable advantage over adversaries equal to them in other respects. From experience, they could imitate Byzantine tactics and military technology.

In contrast, the Rabīʿa were among the most backward of Arab groups in fighting ability, though they often did not lack in valor. Weaker than either the Muḍar or the Yaman, they were often shoved into marginal roles wherever they were found. They had to be satisfied with second or third place, or else nothing. Scattered widely in the East, they were unrepresented in the metropolitan province of Syria and thus had no one to speak for them to the caliph. Indeed, they were held in considerable contempt.[48] They expressed their rage at the way they had been treated, and at the same time sought protection for themselves, in an alliance with the Yaman, though genealogically they were linked to the Muḍar through the Nizār.[49] Except for a part of their elite, they rarely supported the Umayyad government but became its most radical enemies as *khawārij*.[50] Like the ʻAbbāsid and Shīʻī movements, the *khawārij* were supposed to have cut across tribal lines by uniting groups as antithetical as the Rabīʻa and the Tamīm, their former archenemies, but except for the earliest period, the *khawārij* in the East were mainly of the Rabīʻa.[51] This was especially true under Hishām.[52] Thus they impotently vented their righteous rage, usually to their own detriment.

Probably another factor that strongly contributed to the weakness, humiliation, and rebelliousness of the Rabīʻa was their clinging to Christianity. Not only were the Taghlib, who made up a substantial portion of the Rabīʻa in the Jazīra, Christians, but so were many of the Bakr.[53] As Christians, they had no role in the Muslim military and thus did not enjoy the benefit of the long experience in large, organized units that the Qays had. What fighting abilities they had were limited to the individual heroics and small-time raiding of nomadic warfare so characteristic of the *khawārij*. It is unclear how long the Rabīʻa Christians remained true to their religion. Under Hishām, many Muslim Rabaʻīs are found from various tribes, including the Taghlib. But the Taghlib had a special right to remain Christians while paying an extra tax, and the Jazīran Taghlibī court poet al-Akhṭal (d. c. 91/710) remained a Christian as late as the reign of al-Walīd I, despite obvious inducements to embrace Islam.[54] These facts, added to a citation from the Tamīmī Jarīr of unknown date,[55] suggest that Christianity remained prevalent among the Taghlib under Hishām. But whenever it was that most of the Rabīʻa became Muslims, it is likely that they found all of the important positions in the army already filled and thus closed to them, which deprived them of all influence and provided another inducement to rebel as *khawārij*.

On the other hand, though the Jazīran Qays had been worsted at first in the series of conflicts that had led to the establishment of Marwānid rule by Marwān I and ʻAbd al-Malik, a government they did not help to set up and had indeed resisted, the Qaysīs made a rapid and spectacular comeback after they had accepted the new Marwānid regime. Under it, their influence and position steadily improved, owing to the caliph's need for more and more loyal troops, especially since Iraq continued to prove indifferent or rebellious. Probably their proximity to Syria, their close genealogical relationship with the Qaysī tribes of the Syrian *jund* of Qinnasrīn, and their absolute indispensability as wardens of the Byzantine frontier also all weighed heavily in their favor. After they were called on to provide the main forces that defeated Ibn al-Muhallab in 102/720, they even enjoyed a few years of total dominance in the East under Yazīd II. From 105/724, the new caliph Hishām moved to restore the balance by cutting back the Qaysī influence, but the Jazīran Qays remained one of the main factors in caliphal politics until the 'Abbāsid era.

The Iraqi Superprovince: the 'Viceroyalty of the East'

By far, the greatest and best-known of the provinces of the Umayyad caliphate were those subsumed under the huge eastern superprovince, especially Iraq, with its famous cities of al-Kūfa and al-Baṣra, and Khurāsān, though the superprovince also included in its territory many other areas: al-Rayy, al-Jibāl, Jurjān, Qūmis, al-Ahwāz, Fārs, Kirmān, Sijistān, Sind, al-Yamāma, al-Baḥrayn, and 'Umān (see map 1).[56] Thus, it amounted to roughly half of the caliphate and produced more than half of the income.[57] The reason so many areas were put under the Iraqi superprovince principally was that these areas had been originally conquered from either al-Kūfa or al-Baṣra and maintained their ties with their mother city. The two Iraqi centers carried great demographic as well as cultural weight throughout the Umayyad period, judging by the number of their tribes and scholars. Nevertheless, they singularly lacked any significant political influence at the caliphal level and hence nursed a strong, unassuaged sense of grievance against the Umayyads that was the most significant aspect of their role under Hishām.

Of the two *miṣrs*, al-Kūfa was by far the more volatile. This was largely because of its background and history. After the initial conquests, immigration by Arab tribesmen to Egypt, Syria, al-Jazīra, al-Baṣra, and their subordinate provinces was limited only to certain groups, most often those which had arrived first. Thus, Egypt was the exclusive preserve of certain Yamanīs and Quḍā'īs,[58] Syria had the three elements of the Yaman, Quḍā'a, and Qays,[59] al-Jazīra received, with very few exceptions, only the Qays and Rabī'a, while al-Baṣra received the Qays, Tamīm, Rabī'a, and Azd.[60] Though the Baṣran group seems quite a mixture, it must be remembered that the last three tribal groups named all came from eastern Arabia, near the Gulf. On the other hand, al-Kūfa ended up receiving all groups that were unwanted elsewhere and thus contained representatives of virtually all Arab tribal elements.[61] Nor does this reveal the different nature of al-Kūfa sufficiently, for although most of its main tribal groups were also found elsewhere, many *buṭūn* which had been involved in the *Ridda* wars had not been allowed to settle anywhere else when they initially chose to migrate.[62]

However, tribal diversity alone still might not have rendered al-Kūfa so volatile, if not for other factors that intervened. Quite apart from elements of compulsion that may have contributed to its tribal variety, al-Kūfa's geographically central position in the caliphate and its surrounding rich agricultural lands quite naturally attracted the largest number of immigrants. But, at the next stage of Islamic expansion, much to their chagrin they found nothing to take on but the mountain districts of western Iran and Ādharbayjān, which were populated by fractious mountaineers who were often hard to subdue and still harder to extract any booty from. This was at a time when Arab immigrants to the other centers of Egypt, Syria, al-Jazīra, and al-Baṣra had found rich fields for the taking of booty, so important in this period.[63] When the newly conquered lands became settled provinces, the Kūfans then found their patrimony smaller than those of the other *amṣār*. This imbalance in income and opportunity, more than any other single factor, contributed to the relatively greater degree of disaffection at al-Kūfa.

Furthermore, the Kūfans did not enjoy the profits of the Iraqi lands they had conquered earlier, as these went to the government to be distributed to the fighting men only as stipends. In the Kūfans' case, however, they were quite miniscule, because the stipends were assigned according to the earliness of one's entry into Islam (*sābiqa*).[64] The practice of granting estates to Umayyad princes and other favorites out of Iraqi lands that by rights should have belonged to the conquerors also rankled. Thus, a background of poverty and envy exacerbated already extant tribal differences.

Kūfan discontent caused by these factors culminated in a series of revolutionary explosions whose echoes have continued to reverberate throughout the course of Islamic history. The Kūfans rose again and again in major revolts against the Qurashī regime they detested and held responsible for their woes, first against 'Uthmān, then against Mu'āwiya, Yazīd I, and 'Abd al-Malik (twice). The rule of Mu'āwiya established Syrian control. The continuing revolts led to the definitive introduction from 77/697 of Syrian troops,[65] which were perceived by the Iraqis, particularly the Kūfans, as foreign occupiers. The nature of Syrian rule was clearly underlined by the construction between 81/700 and 84/703 of the new *miṣr* of Wāsiṭ, a mainly Syrian military colony placed between al-Kūfa and al-Baṣra in order to keep a watch on both and possibly to be a rival to them.[66]

At about the same time, the Kūfans and other Iraqis were demilitarized owing to their unreliability and rebelliousness.[67] Not only did their demilitarization deprive them of the means to defend their patrimony and inflict upon them great humiliation by equating them with the *mawālī* and the *'ulūj* (non-Muslim subjects), but it also deprived the state of a significant pool of fighting men. Having lost control over their own destiny, their rebellions usually crushed with great bloodshed and followed by numerous executions, the Kūfans were forced to channel their considerable energies elsewhere.

The most important effect of the Kūfans' political humiliation and subordination was that they developed a degree of political and religious sophistication and consciousness that the other Muslim centers, even metropolitan Syria, mostly lacked. This sophistication owed directly to their sense of long suffering from Umayyad domination. It expressed itself through the wide spectrum of political-religious movements recorded in the sources, but especially in revolutionary Shī'ism, for which al-Kūfa was the crucible par excellence.[68] Most significantly, while other centers stumbled along blindly toward ever-greater tribal conflicts, al-Kūfa gradually inclined toward Islamic universalism, which hitherto had not been much applied. Shī'ī doctrines of the universal rule of a righteous imam, already adumbrated by al-Mukhtār al-Thaqafī in his revolt (65–7/685–7), clearly implied such universalism.[69] It is worthy to note that the implementation of such doctrines in the 'Abbāsid revolution, in which tribal affiliations were officially downplayed, was inspired and supported by men of mainly Kūfan origins or connections.[70] Another important plank in the Kūfans' program was, naturally, that the Umayyad caliphate was illegitimate. This doctrine was elaborated in a proliferation of anti-Umayyad propaganda that the Umayyads proved incapable of eliminating, whether by force of argument or of arms.

The second important consequence of the Kūfans' subordination flowed quite naturally from the first: the Kūfans' greater sophistication led to an outpouring of scholarly study and literature which began and led the long process of the elaboration of the Islamic religion.[71] Partly, this was a reaction to the perceive imacy of the Umayyad caliphate; alternative institutio needed until a righteous rule could be established. As a re

Islamic law and heritage were recorded independently of any official supervision. Though this process took place in the various Islamic cities at the same time, al-Kūfa, by far, led all other centers in influence and output. The scholarly and literary works produced were not written in isolation from society, however, for they played a large role in undermining the legitimacy of Umayyad rule in the minds of a broad spectrum of the public. Even more importantly for us, it was al-Kūfa that, as a part of its scholarly pursuits, provided the vast majority of the written source material that has come down to modern times. Because the Kūfan writers held preconceived views and were mainly interested in only certain issues, there has been a continuing tendency to view Islamic history through Kūfan spectacles. This has had an incalculable effect on modern historians from Wellhausen on down.

The other great Iraqi city, al-Baṣra, played a less dramatic role than its more northerly sister in the course of Umayyad history. While it felt most of the same grievances that exercised the Kūfans, it was always more concerned with its own internal tribal strife, which was often violent, partly owing to the large bedouin element represented particularly by the division of the Tamīm.[72] This tribal group engaged in a long and bloody strife with the Rabī'a, who were later helped by the Azd, for control of the city.

On the other hand, despite its internecine strife among its own inhabitants, al-Baṣra's relatively greater access to provincial wealth reduced its people's tendency to rebel against the Umayyad caliphate. Though al-Baṣra did have native political movements, they were either ideologically vague like the Zubayrids, who mainly offered a different family as rulers than the Umayyads, were quiescent like the Murji'a, or, if violent, were small-scale and easily driven from the city like the *khawārij*. Al-Baṣra's one great revolt (101–02/720–21), that of Yazīd b. al-Muhallab al-Azdī, which took place just before the reign of Hishām, was singularly devoid of new political content, was heartily opposed by important elements in the city population for reasons of tribal loyalty, and failed ignominiously.[73] Even though the Baṣrans were demilitarized like the Kūfans, they expressed little resentment openly at any rate, as they caused Hishām no trouble throughout his long reign and later contributed almost nothing to the 'Abbāsids' triumph over the Umayyads.

Although the two *miṣrs* of al-Kūfa and al-Baṣra had originally been administered separately, they were combined into a single governorship in the reign of Mu'āwiya, who gave both to Ziyād b. Abī Sufyān in 50/670,[74] and they mostly remained united after that.[75] Each city retained its own local governor, however, who, in the absence of the higher governor, exercised full power. The new foundation of Wāsiṭ, which became increasingly important under the later Umayyads, had its own local governor under the overall control of the higher governor. The higher governor of the whole superprovince seems not to have always resided in one place, that is, he did not necessarily keep to the Syrian center of Wāsiṭ. This suggests that Wāsiṭ's main role was military rather than administrative. Under Hishām, the governor Yūsuf b. 'Umar could be found at al-Ḥīra,[76] and Khālid al-Qasrī was not always at Wāsiṭ.[77]

Of the enormous territories dependent on Iraq, only a few belonged to al-Kūfa, while the vast majority were dependencies of al-Baṣra. I have already mentioned this imbalance as the major cause of the greater dissatisfaction of the Kūfans. The reason for this inequality lay in rights of conquest; the fruits of each outlying province belonged initially to the *miṣr* which had conquered it.[78] In 30–31/651–52, the Baṣrans had beaten the Kūfans in the crucial race for Khurāsān and thus cut off the Kūfans from further expansion toward the east entirely.[79] By default, all lands further east fell to al-Baṣra. Especially in the earlier period until the reign of al-Walīd I,[80] this sometimes meant that the Baṣrans exclusively enjoyed the income from their vast conquests. But far more importantly, it meant that the Baṣrans had many more areas to which they could immigrate freely to seek their fortunes and still feel at home, while the Kūfans lacked such an outlet. As if this were not enough, in early Umayyad times the Kūfans also apparently lost to the Jazīrans Ādharbayjān, in whose conquest they had participated.[81] Thus, the Kūfans found themselves continuously losing contests with neighboring Arab groups.

The lands left to the Kūfans outside of Iraq were small and produced relatively less income than those ruled from al-Baṣra. The nearest region to al-Kūfa consisted of the mountains of western Iran known as al-Jibāl.[82] Just beyond this lay the considerable city of al-Rayy in the plains at the foot of the Elburz Mountains. For their efforts to get to Khurāsān first, the Kūfans in the East had only mountainous Ṭabaristān and the insignificant provinces of Qūmis and Jurjān to show,[83] and even these were not fully subdued until much later.[84]

The poorness of the Kūfans' patrimony contrasts startlingly with the inflated Baṣran superprovince. Al-Baṣra's earliest Iranian conquests were already larger than al-Kūfa's and included al-Ahwāz, Fārs, parts of al-Jibāl, Kirmān, and Sijistān. But much more was to come. The conquest of Khurāsān by the Baṣran governor in

30–31/651–52 represented not merely the acquisition of another ordinary province, but rather a territory almost as large as all of al-Baṣra's other provinces combined. Further expansion added the extensive territory of Transoxiana, which remained a part of Khurāsān throughout Umayyad times. Khurāsān proved too big to remain al-Baṣra's alone, however. As early as 51/671, al-Rabīʿ b. Ziyād al-Ḥārithī brought fifty thousand men with their families from Iraq to settle in Khurāsān.[85] Although the sources allege that these derived in equal parts from al-Kūfa and al-Baṣra, in fact they were overwhelmingly from al-Baṣra, as shown by their tribal affiliations, which are nearly always Baṣran.

Indeed, it is doubtful whether any Kūfans at all came to Khurāsān before the reign of ʿAbd al-Malik,[86] and they always remained a minority of the province's Arabs even after they had begun to arrive. The continued dominance of original Baṣrans in Khurāsān illustrates the persistence of the rights of a province's original conquerors to that province under the Umayyads. Some Kūfans, escaping from the failure of Ibn al-Ashʿath's revolt, seem to have reached Khurāsān in 83/702 and were integrated into the Baṣran units, beefing up the Azd and the Bakr.[87] But separate Kūfan units were evidently first introduced only in 95/714.[88] In 96/715, these Kūfan troops numbered only seven thousand against forty thousand Baṣrans.[89]

Also, it would seem that the Kūfans were unwelcome in Khurāsān, for in 98/716–17, Yazīd b. al-Muhallab, as governor of Khurāsān, had to conquer lands in the Kūfan zone, namely Jurjān, to assign to the Kūfans in his army.[90] He also brought much larger numbers of Kūfans to Khurāsān as part of the continuing Umayyad policy to move troops out of Iraq, a place where they only contributed to the discontent, to an active war front where they could fight usefully.[91] Politically downtrodden but experienced from their sufferings in Iraq, the Kūfans helped to spread the ideology of revolution epoused by the ʿAbbāsids in Khurāsān and had far more to do with that ideology's success there than did the original Baṣran elements. Thus, the Kūfans eventually exerted some influence in Khurāsān, but only through an anti-Umayyad revolutionary movement, and it may be that their dissatisfaction with the Baṣran element's dominance of the province had much to do with their revolutionary fervor.

Another great appendage of al-Baṣra under Hishām was the freshly conquered province of Sind along the Indus River in India. The earliest attempts to conquer it by Baṣrans marked it out as Baṣran territory.[92] As in Khurāsān, the Kūfans in Sind were probably subordinate to the Baṣrans, though both groups participated in its final conquest by Muḥammad b. al-Qāsim in 93–95/712–14.[93] The subsequent transfer of most of these Kūfans in 95/714 to Khurāsān allowed the province to take up a mostly Baṣran character like the rest of the East. Shown by the names of those playing big roles there, most of the early Muslims in Sind had either a Baṣran or a Syrian origin.[94] The governors there were, with few exceptions, Syrians from the start.[95]

Last in al-Baṣra's long list of dependencies comes Eastern Arabia, including the two provinces of al-Yamāma, with al-Baḥrayn, and 'Umān. These were apparently attached to the Iraqi superprovince in the time of al-Ḥajjāj (75–95/694–714), if not earlier.[96] Their Baṣran connections are shown by the number of Baṣrans who governed them to the general exclusion of Kūfans.[97] In any event, they would be connected with al-Baṣra rather than al-Kūfa owing to the affinity of shared tribal identities; all the East Arabian *buṭūn* were represented in al-Baṣra, only a few, marginally, in al-Kūfa.

The persistent identity of the Baṣran half of the Iraqi superprovince as a unit, opposed to the Kūfan half, is illustrated by the longstanding roles played by the two great Baṣran families of the Muhallabids and the descendents of Muslim b. 'Amr al-Bāhilī. Members of these two families held office as local governors at various times in al-Baṣra, al-Ahwāz, Sijistān, Khurāsān, Sind, and 'Umān, as well as occasionally elsewhere, far into 'Abbāsid times.[98] Perhaps significantly, no families of similar prominence derive from al-Kūfa.

Though space does not permit a detailed analysis of the tax figures for the East, a general idea of the relative income derived from different provinces can be gained by a brief review of them. The sources used are al-Ya'qūbī, referring to the reign of Mu'āwiya, al-Jahshiyārī, referring to the time of al-Rashīd (170–93/786–809), and Qudāma, referring to the time of al-Ma'mūn (198–218/813–33).[99] All figures are given in thousands of dirhams.

These figures, at first glance, seem to show a certain parity of income between the two *miṣr*s, or even the superiority of al-Kūfa, but if certain facts are considered, they actually suggest the greater wealth of al-Baṣra. Certainly, al-Kūfa had its greatest advantage in its initial possession of the lion's share of the Sawād, the rich agricultural plain of Iraq. But its other territories were much inferior in both number and wealth, a situation which is not reflected in the tax figures given by the various sources cited above. Particularly suspect are the figures for the distant eastern provinces. These were tightly controlled by the central authority under Hishām, but al-

Table 3 TAX INCOME OF THE EASTERN SUPERPROVINCE

	Ya'qūbī	Jahshiyārī	Qudāma 1	Qudāma 2[100]
Kūfan Territories[101]				
Sawād[102]	120,000	95,580	114,457 or 180,457	130,200
Takrīt			700	900
Kūfan Jibāl[103]	70,000	38,150	31,278	31,258
Jurjān-Qūmis		13,500	5,150	5,150
Subtotals	190,000	147,230	151,585 or 217,585	167,508
Baṣran Territories				
Kaskar[104]		11,600		
Kuwar Dijla	10,000	20,800		
Baṣran Jibāl	20,000	21,350	23,700	24,300
Ahwāz	40,000	25,000	18,000	23,000
Fārs[105]	70,000	27,000	24,000	24,000
Kirmān-Makrān		4,600	7,000	7,000
Sijistān		4,600	1,000	1,000
Khurāsān		28,000	38,000	37,000
Sind		11,500		
East Arabia	15,000		12,150	12,150
Subtotals	155,000	154,450	123,850	128,450
Ṣawāfī in Iraq	100,000			
Totals	445,000	301,680	275,435 or 341,435	295,958

Ya'qūbī ignores them in his list, perhaps because they were not yet producing much regular income under Mu'āwiya. On the other hand, by the period to which al-Jahshiyārī's and Qudāma's figures presumably refer, the central government's hold on its outer territories was becoming tenuous, so that they may have produced less income then than they did under Hishām. Thus, the figures for Khurāsān and possibly Sind may be too small. It is difficult to imagine that the income of Khurāsān, including Transoxiana, was only comparable to a part of al-Jibāl, or that Khurāsān's income was only a little over twice that of the relatively tiny province of Jurjān, as al-Jahshiyārī would have it, given the number and reported extent of the Khurāsānī cities.[106]

Another drawback to using these tax figures is that, while giving the impression of a regular, steady income from each province, a condition that generally may not have obtained under the Umayyads to the end of their rule, they give no inkling of a second, possibly important, source of income: booty. While regular tax income went partially to defraying the costs of administration and hence was only partially disbursed to the troops in the form of stipends, booty did not go through the government at all, but was divided on the spot, except for the fifth that had to be sent to the caliph. Thus, while the tax figures can give some idea of the relative financial contribution made by each province, it must be remembered that they are only part of the picture.

Actually, booty may have been more important to the average warrior than his stipend, because it offered the men in the ranks their best opportunity to make good. The importance of booty can be documented from a number of sources which, unlike the tax figures given, do correspond to late Umayyad times. When Muḥammad b. al-Qāsim conquered Sind in 93–95/712–14, he is reported to have sent an astronomical figure of one hundred twenty million dirhams in booty to al-Ḥajjāj in Iraq.[107] Such an amount is approximately equivalent to the whole annual *kharāj* of Iraq. Assuming the amount forwarded to al-Ḥajjāj was only the prescribed fifth, as is actually stated in *Fatḥnāmah-i Sind*, the total takings would have been six hundred million dirhams, not to mention thirty thousand slaves.[108] Even if the government managed somehow to forward more than the prescribed fifth of the spoils to al-Ḥajjāj, the total amount disbursed to the troops must have been very impressive indeed. Shortly after this, when al-Junayd al-Murrī, who governed Sind for Yazīd II and Hishām, raided deep into India, he took eighty million dirhams, representing the state's fifth alone, in addition to a grand total of six hundred fifty thousand captives.[109] The total cash booty for al-Junayd's campaigns would seem to amount then to four hundred million dirhams, another astronomical sum.

The value of frontier service to the individual is exemplified by the case of Bukayr b. Māhān, a *mawlā* and 'Abbāsid partisan. Coming to Sind in about 104/723 to claim a great inheritance from his brother, who had probably been a soldier there, Bukayr not only received the legacy but significantly added to it while working as a translator for the governor, apparently only for a short period, about 104–05/723–24.[110] This seems to show, first of all, that fortunes could be made out of fighting on active war fronts and, second, that an enterprising man could also find other enriching opportunities that might not have been available back home.

Taking another example, in 98/716–17 Yazīd b. al-Muhallab reported to the caliph that six million dirhams represented the government's fifth of the booty from his campaign in Jurjān and Ṭabaristān.[111] Since he had little success in Ṭabaristān, nearly all the booty must have come from Jurjān. This implies a value of thirty million dirhams from a single season's campaigning in one small province and is far in excess of the annual reported income from that province. Such examples confirm the probable centrality of booty as a goal in the frontier warfare of late Umayyad times, a goal particularly important to the troops. The importance of the booty factor in making caliphal foreign policy under Yazīd II and Hishām should not be underestimated.

Also, the relatively greater access of the Baṣrans to booty should not be overlooked as a factor in the continuing rebelliousness of the Kūfans and their uncooperative attitude toward the Umayyad government. Indeed, except for the war fronts of Jurjān and Ṭabaristān, which were minor compared to Khurāsān, Transoxiana, and Sind, the Kūfans seem to have had no warlike frontiers at all, while the Baṣrans faced the Turks on the very large and important Khurāsānī-Transoxianan frontier as well as the Indians on the Sindī front. Each of these fronts had been significantly rewarding in terms of booty in the few years just before Hishām's reign.

As for the tribal composition of the Iraqi cities and their dependencies, it is too complicated to go into much detail here. However, certain salient characteristics may be noted. Al-Kūfa, though containing a significant number of Muḍar tribesmen, held a far larger proportion of Yamanīs, making it the chief center for the Yaman grouping.[112] The Muḍar, though keeping up their tribal *ʿaṣabiyya*, as exemplified in the poetry of al-Kumayt,[113] nevertheless went along with Yamanī causes, even sometimes Shīʿism,[114] as well as the ʿAbbāsid cause.

The Yaman themselves, however, took a very long time to get united, while for its part, the Umayyad government was usually successful in playing off the Yaman's traditional leaders against those with revolutionary inclinations. The Umayyads were also helped in this, perhaps, by the fact that some of the tribes (*buṭūn*) that formed al-Kūfa's inhabitants were also found among the privileged Syrians. These included the Ḥimyar, Hamdān, and even Kinda, all inveterate, original Yamanīs, as well as a few Quḍāʿa subtribes such as the Juhayna and Kalb. It is difficult to assess the persistence of tribal loyalty over that greatest of social gaps, the gulf between the Kūfans and the Syrians. But it is perhaps indicative of the strength of tribal relations that the vindictive Yūsuf b. ʿUmar, when he came secretly to Iraq to depose Khālid al-Qasrī in 120/738, unhesitatingly stayed in the Kūfan quarters of his own subtribe, the Thaqīf, where he could expect loyal service and aid.[115]

In al-Baṣra, the continued strength of original tribal loyalties is well-documented in the poetry of the Baṣrans Jarīr and al-Farazdaq. Scarcely a page of their *dīwāns* is devoid of some reference to tribal particularism. Because the Tamīm, the division to which both poets belonged, was large in al-Baṣra and strongly inclined to oppose the Yaman, the Baṣran tribes could never get together against the government and hence posed little threat in the time of Hishām. Also, the energy of the Yaman there, in particular the 'Umānī Azd, was absorbed to a large extent in the Baṣran lands to the east.[116] The Rabī'a divisions of Bakr and 'Abd al-Qays, though bitterly opposed to the Tamīm, were never willing to press a revolution, except ineffectively as *khawārij*. Therefore, the Umayyads were able to easily maintain control in al-Baṣra by balancing the different mutually hostile groups against each other.

The North African or Western Superprovince

The third great superprovince was that beginning at the frontier of Africa with Asia and extending westward, including three geographically well-defined main provinces: Egypt, North Africa (al-Maghrib), and Spain (al-Andalus) (see maps 2, 9). Despite its vast extent, the western superprovince seems to have played a much lesser role in shaping the fate of the caliphate than the eastern areas. To some extent, the Islamic West's apparent marginality may simply be an impression gained from the tendencies of the sources; al-Ṭabarī, for example, consigns the region to oblivion by hardly ever mentioning it. However, the West may also have had less effect on caliphal politics owing to a relative dearth of Arab settlers in the region under the Umayyads.[117] But again, matters of relative demographic weight are highly speculative. Certainly, the Islamic West played a more insignificant cultural and religious role than the East in Umayyad times, judging by the numbers of the two regions' respective scholars recorded in biographical dictionaries. Furthermore, those North African works on the early period which survive, though they do enable us to obtain a picture of what transpired in the region under Hishām, are inevitably shorter, less detailed, and dated later than those produced in the East.

Perhaps the most salient characteristic of the Islamic West under the Umayyads is the unusually large political role played by the native non-Arab Muslims, the Berbers of North Africa. The Berbers are conventionally described as a Hamitic people, linguistically related to the Arabs, but less closely than the Syriac speakers of the Fertile Crescent, who were also Semites like the Arabs. The majority of the Berbers embraced Islam enthusiastically within a generation or two of their being conquered, were enrolled massively in the army, and made the largest contribution to the conquest of Spain. They did this in spite of their being mountain dwellers who were traditionally hostile to intrusive political authorities. Elsewhere in mountainous districts, as in Armenia, Ṭabaristān, and Zābulistān, the Arabs fought bitter wars only to find these areas still wholly or partly unsubdued by the end of Umayyad times, while the religion of Islam made little or no progress in them. But in North Africa, the Berbers became the first non-Arab people to accept Islam widely. This process had perhaps reached its greatest fruition only shortly before Hishām's time, in the reign of 'Umar II, who sent out a number of missionaries.[118] It is hard to imagine that many of the Berbers could have deeply absorbed the Islamic faith and teachings in only a couple of years. Nevertheless, Berber politics were henceforth entirely within the framework of Islam.

Entry into Islam in the case of the Berbers implied privileges that were not usually bestowed on non-Arabs elsewhere. As part of the army, the Berbers enjoyed similar, if not the same, rights as those of the Arab troops, including the significant right to booty as well as the right to claim lands in new conquests. To be sure, the granting of these privileges to the Berbers was resisted by the Arabs in the army, but unsuccessfully, owing in part to the huge size of the Berber contingents. Since the army was organized on tribal lines, the Berbers were duly enrolled according to their own tribes, which were then at least sometimes furnished with spurious links back to Arab tribes of both the Yaman and the Muḍar.[119] They were the only group to receive this distinction, aside from certain Sāsānian military formations.[120] Thus, the full-scale induction of the Berbers of North Africa for military service in the West was unusual and perhaps reflects Arab numerical weakness there.

Another possibly related and unusual feature of Islamic rule in North Africa is that the political and military governors were, as a rule, not Arabs.[121] This does not mean that they were Berbers, though. In the few cases which are known, they were *mawlās* from the East, Jazīran, or Iraqi natives.[122] It is highly unusual to find *mawālī* commanding Arabs in the Umayyad period at all. The fact that this occurred in North Africa almost as a rule is difficult to explain but at the very least implies that the number of Arabs there must have been relatively few.

Administratively, the three western provinces appear to be a classic example of pyramidal subordination. At the top stood the metropolitan province of Syria. Egypt had been conquered from Syria and received its governors directly from the Umayyad caliph residing in Syria. North Africa had been conquered from Egypt and was sometimes subordinate to the governor of that province.[123] Troops based in North Africa had conquered Spain, whose governor was usually appointed by the governor of North Africa.[124] This system resembled the concentric rings of subordination also found in the Jazīran and Eastern superprovinces, where, for example, Khurāsān was subordinate to Iraq which was subordinate to the caliph in Syria.

Such a system would not seem at first glance to be the most efficient but rather to reflect the historical circumstances of the conquests. However, the subordination of the provinces in such a series of concentric circles might constitute a reasonable administrative scheme in view of the distance of those provinces from the caliph. In such a far-flung empire, it may have seemed better to have the next highest authority nearby.[125] Also, the caliphs may have feared the independence of distant governors who had become too proud and powerful, as demonstrated by the many cases of such governors who fell into caliphal disfavor.[126]

Actually, the system of uniting the West in a single superprovince was applied with less uniformity than that which characterized developments in the East. In particular, Egypt was separate more often than not. The superprovince uniting Egypt and North Africa, though often implied by the common heritage of many of the Arabs settling in them and by the interchangeability of some governors, actually only seems to have been under a single paramount governor in 47–62/667–82 (when al-Qayrawān was as yet only an isolated outpost), 69–85/688–704, 102–05/721–24, and 124–27/742–45, and to some extent 116–23/734–41, when Ibn al-Ḥabḥāb oddly retained fiscal but not political control over Egypt from North Africa through the agency of his sons. It would appear that sometimes the united superprovince was ad hoc and dependent on the personalities and prestige of the individuals involved. Thus, Mūsā b. Nuṣayr until 85/704 had been clearly subordinate to ʿAbd al-ʿAzīz b. Marwān, the crown prince and brother of ʿAbd al-Malik, but refused to obey his successor ʿAbd Allāh b. ʿAbd al-Malik, preferring instead to correspond with the caliph directly.[127]

As for the individual western provinces, Egypt, the one nearest to Syria, had long been a model of stability in the caliphate by the beginning of Hishām's reign, having suffered no disturbances while contributing a steady stream of tax money to the Umayyad coffers since the start of the Marwānid period. Egypt's *miṣr* was al-Fusṭāṭ, one of the earliest *amṣār,* founded in 21/642.[128] Though al-Fusṭāṭ was the mother city of the entire western superprovince, the military importance of both city and country had declined owing to the advance of the active war fronts to other areas.[129] Egypt's economic importance, however, remained undiminished, while its prosperity was facilitated by the hardworking and politically quiescent Copts, the native Christians who still formed the overwhelming majority of Egypt's population.

Egypt's loss of military prominence was North Africa's gain. The latter had been rising in importance, as demonstrated by the fact that several governors of the combined western superprovince under Hishām based themselves in North Africa rather than Egypt.[130] At the outset of Hishām's reign, North Africa appeared to have remained peaceful since the reign of al-Walīd I, which might have further enhanced its value. By then it had at least two *miṣr*s. The main one was al-Qayrawān in Tunisia, founded in 51–55/671–75.[131] A secondary one was at Ṭanjā (Tangier) in Morocco, founded in 89/708 as a jumping-off place for the conquest of Spain.[132] Its continuing importance is attested to by its frequent mention later. Tripoli in Libya may possibly have been a third North African *miṣr,* as it certainly was the home of some Arab troops and receives frequent mention under Hishām, but it is never specifically designated as a military town by any source.[133]

The third and most recently acquired western province was Spain, where the Muslims now controlled virtually the entire peninsula. Its relationship to the caliphate was something like that of Transoxiana at the other end of the empire, which was also subordinate to three successive superior layers of administrative hierarchy.[134] Showing his apprehension at the distance of Spain and Transoxiana from the center of the caliphate, ʿUmar II had wished to withdraw from both provinces.[135] Conquered only in 92–97/711–16, Spain had scarcely been pacified by the outset of Hishām's reign, though there remained little active military opposition.[136] The Muslims had made Cordoba (Ar. Qurṭuba) their *miṣr* there only in 97/716.[137] Owing to the recentness of the introduction of Islam in Spain, it had as yet hardly made any progress among the native Gothic and Roman populations.

The value of the *kharāj* of the western provinces was perhaps

 # firmmil ? no not like Basra (silk spice trade)

needed mill to feed an army in N Africa

less than that derived from the East, but reliable totals are harder to find for the West. The best documented province is Egypt, which is said to have produced an annual revenue of two million and later four million dinars in the reign of 'Uthmān.[138] Under Mu'āwiya, Egypt's revenue is reported to have been three million dinars.[139] Egypt's taxes were raised by Hishām,[140] under whom the *kharāj* of Egypt is reported to have reached four million. In another version about Hishām, the amount sent to the caliph after the deduction of expenses is said to have been 2,723,839 dinars.[141] Later, it is reported to have produced in 'Abbāsid times 1,920,000 under al-Rashīd,[142] but another version for the same reign reports that 2,280,000 was provided after the deduction of expenses, which may have been considerable.[143] For the time of al-Ma'mūn, which followed a period of civil war, the Egyptian income was 1.5 million dinars.[144]

These figures show a general consistency that makes them likely to be close to the truth. They reveal Egypt to be a most valuable province, with an income greater than all of Syria put together and equalling a bit under half the income of Iraq. Still, it was far less valuable than all of the East together. It appears that a much greater proportion of the income than the fifth was sent to Syria, perhaps because the Yamanī tribes in Egypt were the same as those in Syria, so that Egypt's *kharāj* in particular may have helped to support the Syrian army.[145] The figures also show a decline in 'Abbāsid times as is the case with the other regions, suggesting that revenue fluctuated considerably, as one would expect.

Much less is known about the income of North Africa and Spain. For North Africa, al-Balādhurī gives a figure of 2.5 million dinars as the amount of the supposed annual payment by the original peace agreement.[146] Al-Jahshiyārī states that this income had fallen to a mere thirteen million dirhams for North Africa in the reign of al-Rashīd, when the province was already slipping from 'Abbāsid control.[147] Probably the monetary value of the province in Hishām's reign was somewhere between those very wide limits. However, it appears that much of the tribute from North Africa was not monetary. Rather, the Berbers seem to have paid tribute mostly in slaves, as evidenced by direct reports relating to Umayyad times[148] as well as by the rather large number of luminaries born in late Umayyad times who had Berber mothers.[149] Naturally, it would be nearly impossible to measure the monetary value of this tribute, even if some idea of the numbers involved were available.[150] This tribute in persons did, however, have a terrific impact on Arab-Berber relations in North Africa, and to a lesser extent in Spain, as we shall see.

For Spain itself, under the Umayyads no data seem to be available. Probably the province produced only an irregular tribute, as it had not yet been really pacified, and matters had not yet settled enough to allow peaceful tax collection, though Hishām did strive to introduce orderly taxation there.[151] Indeed, the Muslims in Spain remained turbulent, fighting over land and booty, the main goals in the early period of conquest rather than the production of a regular cash income.

In fact, it could be argued that the West's greatest contribution to the caliphate's history was as a battlefront. By Hishām's time, the front against the Christians had been rolled from Spain all the way across the Pyrenees into southern France. It is this spectacular Muslim advance, which seemed to menace the heart of what was left of Western Christendom, that has concerned many European scholars. For Islam, it was merely one of many fronts, and certainly not the most important one. Still, it meant that a large number of fighting men were drawn to the Spanish theater of action.

But the most crucial war front, as it turned out, was that against the Berbers, especially those farther west in the rugged mountains of Morocco. It is difficult to determine if it was exclusively a front against recalcitrant or rebellious Berbers who had already become nominal Muslims, or rather, if some or possibly many of the Berbers had not yet embraced Islam at all, which seems more likely. In the latter case, we would have to view the Berber front in Hishām's time as being, at least in part, like the other war fronts: the Arab Muslim army comes up against non-Muslim tribal peoples who are without a centralized organization and are therefore difficult to subdue. Regardless of the extent to which the Berbers had embraced Islam and absorbed its teachings by the reign of Hishām, the Umayyads could not trust the Berbers to remain completely loyal and thus had to keep fairly large forces in North Africa at the *amṣār* of al-Qayrawān, Tangier, and Tripoli.

North Africa did have another war front in conjunction with Egypt, namely the sea front against the Byzantines. In earlier times, this had largely been concentrated in Egypt, where the navy was built and manned by Copts.[152] However, with the retreat of the Byzantines after 76/695 on the one hand, and the failure of the Muslim attempt on Constantinople by 99/718 on the other hand, Muslim naval efforts seem to have shifted to the west, especially against Sicily.[153] The naval front probably involved large numbers of Arabs or Muslims only as troops carried on the ships, not as seamen or perhaps even as naval commanders. Like many other land powers including the Romans of the Republic, the Arabs preferred to let others handle their ships for them. This tended to decrease the prestige and importance attached to the naval as opposed to the land-based raiding and warfare, as evidenced by the relatively little mention devoted to naval warfare by the sources.

The internal tribal makeup of the West, having been heavily based on the original Yamanī groups that had migrated to Egypt, was fairly homogenous and less prone to civil violence than elsewhere. Partly, this was because the wars against the Berbers left little time or energy for internecine struggles. This Arab homogeneity was eventually altered, especially in North Africa and later in Spain, by the occasional introduction of new forces needed to subdue or balance the Berbers. Therefore, despite the prominence of the Yaman group, a large number of Muḍar were organized as the Ahl al-Madīna, those Qurashīs and others who began migrating to North Africa with 'Uqba b. Nāfi' al-Fihrī about 50/670 and whose numbers further increased after the Battle of al-Ḥarra in 63/683. However, they seem to have mixed well, perhaps owing to their fewness and their need for unity in the face of the Berbers. The only other significant Arab element to enter North Africa under the Umayyads was that of the Syrians, who came late in Hishām's reign, in 122/740.[154] Interestingly, it is shortly after their arrival that the Yaman-Muḍar split makes its appearance in the West, and then only in Spain, to which the Syrians had retreated. Before that, the only important split in Muslim ranks was that between the Arabs and the Berbers.

The Southern Zone: the Western Arabian Backwater

The remaining Arabian territories, namely West Arabia, including the Ḥijaz and Yaman with Ḥaḍramawt, did not constitute a super-province and were not governed together, at least in Hishām's reign. At the beginning of the Islamic state, the Ḥijaz had constituted the metropolitan province, but it had soon lost this distinction when the Caliph 'Alī moved the capital to al-Kūfa in 36/656. It had suffered a second blow at the Battle of al-Ḥarra in 63/683, when al-Madīna's attempt to regain its earlier prominence was definitively defeated by the Umayyads. After that, though al-Madīna retained a certain prestige, most notably in the areas of religious tradition and poetry and song,[155] its political power was ended, and with it the political power of the rest of the Ḥijaz.

Yaman, including Ḥaḍramawt, was in a slightly different situation. It had never been the center of strength in the caliphate and had mostly remained politically docile. This probably owed to a huge exodus of emigrants to the various *amṣār*, where they received stipends and were more likely to have political influence through their participation in the army. In this situation, Yaman, despite its populousness, sank into the role of a geographically isolated backwater.

In fact, geographical isolation may well have been why Yaman was not included in any of the superprovinces. Instead, it appears clearly to have retained its administrative independence as a separate province directly under the caliph.[156] The Ḥijaz likewise retained its independence, partly perhaps as a concession to its former glory and its historic role in Islam and partly as a politically unimportant but prestigious plum to be given out to the caliph's relatives. Its capital was al-Madīna, while Makka and al-Ṭā'if constituted a separate district together that was usually administered from al-Madīna but sometimes was under an independent governor.[157]

What is known of the income derived from the West Arabian provinces confirms the impression that they were less important than many other areas of the caliphate. In the case of Yaman, however, it appears that the province had a fair value. In Mu'āwiya's reign, it is reported to pay an annual *kharāj* of nine hundred thousand or 1.2 million dinars.[158] Much later, under al-Rashīd, its payment amounted to eight hundred seventy thousand dinars.[159] Under al-Ma'mūn or his successors, its *kharāj* had dwindled to only six hundred thousand dinars.[160] These figures show a fair consistency and indicate that Yaman had not ceased being a productive and valuable area in early Islamic times. The Ḥijaz was less valuable, but still managed to produce a *kharāj* of three hundred thousand dinars under al-Rashīd,[161] which fell to one hundred thousand under al-Ma'mūn.[162] Thus, the total value of West Arabia's contribution to the state coffers was less than half that of Egypt alone.

Arabia also had become a backwater with regard to active fighting fronts. It contained none, being surrounded by relatively safe seas on the south, with little mention in the sources of any interaction with Abyssinia, the only country in that direction likely to be a menace. The fact that political prisoners were regularly relegated to the Dahlak Islands off Abyssinia's coast seems a fair indication of the great security felt by the Umayyads in that direction, for if any serious confrontation had existed, the Abyssinians would have been able to liberate and exploit the relegated opponents of the Umayyads.[163] Otherwise, the only occasionally active front was the internal one against revolts of *khawārij*, and these too never reached the dangerous proportions of the various revolts in other areas.

The tribal groups in Yaman and the Ḥijaz were mixed, but were largely Yamanī. However, none of them were enrolled in the Umayyad army, so they did not enjoy stipends, fight the non-Muslims, or engage in any but local politics. The only exception to this general isolation and nonparticipation was that sometimes victims of political persecution fled to the Ḥijaz to hide out or seek protection.[164] It may be supposed that the troops in the tribal regiments in the *amṣār* kept up a gradually weakening connection with their relatives in the old country, but there is little evidence of this in the sources for the Yamanīs, although the attachment of the great Tamīmī Baṣran poets to their original desert homelands suggests that similar ties may have persisted elsewhere as well. Nevertheless, both West and East Arabia had become backwaters in most respects by the time of Hishām and had little direct influence on the great events and developments that fell in his reign.

4

Administrative Policies and Ideology at the Beginning of Hishām's Reign

The Caliph Hishām and the Caliphal Office

At the pinnacle of the administrative hierarchy stood the caliph, the effective representative of God and executive expression of His sovereignty on the earth. Although the office is not sanctioned by the Qur'ān, where the usages of the word *khalīfa* are not necessarily complimentary,[1] and although the office under the title *khalīfa* is also practically absent from the *ḥadīth*, it nevertheless possessed a considerable aura of officially promoted sanctity throughout the Umayyad period.[2] While Islamic law devotes little attention to the office of caliph, perhaps because of pietistic dissent owing to the arbitrary and often oppressive character of Umayyad and 'Abbāsid rule, several major principles may be culled from the *ḥadīth*, which may be cited to show the view of the caliphate prevailing in traditionist circles under Hishām.

The caliph (referred to usually as *amīr* or *imām*) is portrayed primarily as the executor of God's unchangeable will.[3] His main prerogative is the power to command and be obeyed, as in a military hierarchy.[4] His manner of selection is not specified, but he must be from the tribe of Quraysh,[5] a condition that could apply equally well to the early caliphs, the Umayyads, the 'Abbāsids, the 'Alids, and the Zubayrids. He is inaugurated with an oath of allegiance (*bay'a*) to which all the faithful must subscribe.[6] Various oaths sworn to the Prophet provide possible models.[7] Especially relevant, perhaps, are the forms of oath attributed to the inaugurations of 'Abd al-Malik b. Marwān and 'Uthmān b. 'Affān, the latter significantly requiring the ruler not only to uphold the *sunna* of God and His Prophet, but also of his predecessors as caliph.[8]

Once the ruler is installed in office, the caliph must be obeyed loyally,[9] unless he orders anything unlawful to be done or otherwise acts against the law.[10] Rebellion is condemned as a capital crime.[11] Even if the ruler is sinful or unjust, he must be borne,[12] at least as long as he upholds Islamic worship,[13] but it is a virtuous act to condemn his actions or challenge him verbally in such a case.[14] If a second caliph arises as a challenger, he should be killed.[15] The caliphs must be given their just due,[16] whatever that may be. None of this suggests a stable constitution or institutional authority, nor any machinery to check the caliph's unfettered exercise of his power, except for the threat of divine punishment should the ruler behave oppressively or fail to carry out his responsibilities.[17]

However, in actual practice, though the Umayyad caliphs usually enjoyed the support or at least the acquiescence of most of the Muslims in their rule, they also faced frequent revolts by Muslims rejecting their legitimacy. Such movements were especially threatening in the first and second civil wars (35–40/656–61 and 64–73/683–92). The pious fount of Muslim tradition in al-Madīna remained outside the realm of power and thus generally hostile to their rule, especially after the terrible massacre of its inhabitants at al-Ḥarra in 63/683. The mere claim by the Umayyads to God-given authority also did nothing to stem the more significant opposition of demilitarized Iraqis to both their legitimacy and rule. Thus, the Umayyads suffered from what might be described as the crumbling of their charisma. Once having established and exercised their power, their regime was emptied of any claim to spirituality in the eyes of the ruled because of its need to rely on the harsh exercise of force to maintain itself and because of its resulting inability to keep to the minimum standards of ethical behavior expected by the Islamic law and the Muslim community.

To fight back against the religious circles that already had them on the run at the very outset of their rule, which, it must be remembered, originated in a military triumph, the Umayyads responded with programs designed to vindicate their religious claims. One part of this was the many Islamizing reforms undertaken by ʻAbd al-Malik, his sons including Hishām, and their cousin ʻUmar II. In addition to these reforms, the caliph Hishām specifically made a point of cultivating the rising class of religious scholars, among them Ibn Shihāb al-Zuhrī, who served as tutor to his sons, and Abū Zinād.[18] But above all as a justification for their rule, the Umayyad caliphs' role in presiding over the *jihād* stood out. Except under ʻUmar II, the *jihād* policy was faithfully continued by all the Umayyad caliphs through Hishām, and even ʻUmar II's retrenchment had partially owed to the defeat of his forces at Constantinople in 99/718. The *jihād* policy had worked rather well for the Umayyads by concentrating attention at the distant frontiers, keeping the troops employed, dispersing discontented elements, and, above all, by legitimating Umayyad rule, as the proportion of the earth claimed for God's rule grew ever wider.

Hishām came to the caliphal throne at the age of thirty-three well prepared for it. Though he had only been nominated as successor by his immediate and short-lived predecessor Yazīd II, he had long been initiated into the ways of power and its judicious exercise. Unlike certain of his predecessors, he was sober rather than self-indulgent in his personal habits. His chief personal fault was said to be avarice,[19] but some of that tradition about him may simply express the financial stringency of his times.[20] Thus, he may have rewarded poets only parsimoniously as a cost-saving measure,[21] and his reputation may have suffered as a result. On the other hand, the story about how he commanded his governor of Iraq to withhold his grain from the market until the caliph's grain had sold has some plausibility.[22] Otherwise, he is usually shown as a competent monarch who was always active and careful in affairs of state, frequently exerting a personal supervision or interfering.

Finally, the utter disaster of Hishām's reign was largely not his responsibility, but owed to circumstances completely beyond his control. If he is to be faulted, it is his unswerving persistence in the application of the Umayyad doctrine of the universal *jihād* that must be blamed. But he cannot be held entirely culpable, even though it did result in the total ruin of his family. The outcome could not have been foreseen, especially to a generation weaned on glorious victories as Hishām's had been. And the prestige of the Umayyad house had hitherto heavily rested on the continuation of the *jihād*. The course of events was, in any case, beyond his control, and his personality perhaps made little difference to the end result.

The Central Administration of the Caliphate under Hishām

As we have seen in dealing with the provinces, the Umayyad caliphate, though theoretically a unitary state under the absolute authority of the caliph in the metropolitan province of Syria, was actually a somewhat loose conglomeration, where much allowance was made for local conditions. In fact, none of the superprovinces were much alike. The inequalities between different areas inside each superprovince were also clear for all to see. There really was no "typical province," except to the extent that Iraq may have usurped that role for itself through its later dominance in the sources.

This regional diversity comes as no surprise if one considers the relative recentness of the Islamic state's formation in relation to the time of Hishām. For example, it could hardly be expected that the old Byzantine-Persian border in al-Jazīra, which had existed since the first century B.C.E., would be swept away overnight without leaving a trace.[23] Thus, the Byzantine and Sāsānian administrative systems were mostly left intact until the time of 'Abd al-Malik, even down to the coinage. The application of Arabic as the official language of the administration was only completed in 124/742, near the end of Hishām's reign, if then.[24]

But it was not only the persistence of old traditions and administrative divisions that hampered the centralization of authority. The caliphal government at its beginning had only a very rudimentary bureaucracy, and it took time to develop bureaucratic traditions. By the time of Hishām, after almost a century of Islamic rule, a certain amount of centralization, sometimes said to derive from Sāsānian models, had taken place.[25] This centralization made much more progress under Hishām. But the fact that a certain amount of development was taking place should not keep us from perceiving the continuing simplicity of the central caliphal administration.

A few points suffice to show the continuing nonbureaucratic, informal character of the Umayyad rule of Hishām and even of his successors. The caliph governed mostly from his personal estates, usually located in desert areas, not from cities, because he neither had nor deemed necessary a large administrative infrastructure.[26] Since these estates were personal, each new caliph, upon taking office, simply moved the capital to one of his own castles. Usually, each caliph was based in a different *jund* of Syria; 'Abd al-Malik and al-Walīd I in Damascus, Sulaymān in Filasṭīn (though he spent his caliphate in Qinnasrīn), 'Umar II in Qinnasrīn, Yazīd II in al-Balqā' or al-Urdunn, Hishām in Ḥimṣ, al-Walīd II in al-Balqā', Yazīd III in Damascus, and finally Marwān II in Diyār Muḍar. Other senior princes were also widely scattered, the influential 'Abbās b. al-Walīd I being in Ḥimṣ[27] and Maslama b. 'Abd al-Malik in Qinnasrīn.[28] The frequent moving of the capital, which always took place at each new accession from Sulaymān on, suggests that whatever records may have existed must have been relatively simple.

Furthermore, although it is well-attested that various officials, almost always non-Arab *mawālī,* were in charge of the different departments of the central caliphal administration by the reign of Hishām, it appears that these departments themselves must have been quite small. Thus, although Sālim b. 'Abd al-Rahmān is rat grandiosely described as being "in charge of the correspondence department" (*'alā dīwān al-rasā'il*),[29] stories describing his activity make it clear that he worked nearly alone, with, perhaps, one assistant and a couple of slaves to help out.[30] Other stories describing visits of delegations to Hishām give no impression of elaborate protocol or court ceremonial at all; rather, quite the opposite.[31]

A glance at the departments listed by the sources also reveals their fewness and lack of specialization and development, especially noticeable when compared with the contemporary and very complex central administration of the militarily inferior Byzantine state. Ibn Khayyāṭ lists for Hishām departments of security (*al-shuraṭ*),[32] correspondence (*al-rasā'il*), taxes and military rolls (*al-kharāj wa al-jund*), (great) privy seal (*al-khātam*), treasury (*al-khazā'in wa buyūt al-amwāl*), lesser privy seal and private estates of the caliph (*al-khātam al-saghīr wa al-khāṣṣa*), in addition to the offices of commander of the guard (*al-ḥaras*)[33] and chamberlain (*al-ḥājib*).[34] To these al-Jahshiyārī adds Hishām's well-known chief adviser, al-Abrash al-Kalbī, who is never given a proper title but is most commonly described as being the most influential person around Hishām (*ghāliban 'alayh*).[35] He also adds to the list of departments another tax department (*al-ṣadaqa*) and a department in charge of producing official robes (*al-ṭuruz*).[36] These offices seem to have increased in number under Hishām, as several of them which had been combined with each other under his predecessor, Yazīd II, were now separated.[37]

From this list of governmental departments, one can see that the caliphate had two primary concerns. The first, represented in the departments of security and military rolls, was to keep the frontier armies in the field while maintaining internal peace by force, if necessary. The second was to secure the financial means to support the armed forces, as well as to provide a modicum of extra income for the maintenance of the court. These two concerns were normally central in ancient states. How then did the caliphate deal with them under Hishām?

Caliphal Fiscal Policy at the Start of Hishām's Reign

Aside from its military concerns, the main interest of the central caliphal administration was financial. This concern too, though, was mainly connected with the military problem, as much of the state income went to support the troops. Try as it might, the state never had enough income to support its large military establishment, which at its height under Hishām may have numbered as many as four hundred thousand.[38] Earlier rulers had managed to get along, often largely through letting the troops be satisfied with the booty they obtained from raids or new conquests. This had frequently flowed in liberally, especially at the beginning under 'Umar I and 'Uthmān. In other cases, when attacks were unsuccessful, large losses might mean fewer stipends to pay anyway.

After the caliphate was reorganized following the Second *Fitna*, however, matters rapidly became unbalanced in the third phase of expansion (73–99/692–718), leading to serious fiscal stringency in Hishām's reign. The great new conquests of Spain, Transoxiana, and Sind in the latter half of the short reign of al-Walīd I had brought in enormous amounts of booty, the like of which had not been seen since the days of 'Umar I, if then. This surfeit naturally whetted appetites for more and led to expectations that the new riches would continue to flow.

Responding to these expectations, al-Walīd I embarked on a huge public works and social welfare program certainly unprecedented in the caliphate. This included the rebuilding of the congregational mosques of Makka, al-Madīna, al-Ṭā'if, Damascus, Jerusalem (al-Aqṣā), and probably others, on a far more magnificent scale.[39] It also included land reclamation, digging wells along the roads, lighting in the streets, and public aid and servants for the handicapped.[40] Not all the expenses were borne by the caliphal treasury, however. The Damascene and possibly other Syrian army divisions had to forfeit a quarter of their pay for nine years to pay for the Damascus mosque.[41] This shows that the government felt that the Syrian troops were paid well enough that they could be taxed safely, and not that the government was already impoverished.

Among those with the highest hopes and expectations of a continuing increase in wealth were the various Umayyad princes, who were best positioned to get their share. Even those outside of the Marwānid lineage, and even those who did not campaign, received large grants from the government to their personal accounts. Often this took the form of land grants (*iqṭā'*),[42] although at other times they received cash, as well.[43] From grants of relatively valueless land into which they put a capital investment in the form of land reclamation, they could increase their wealth. Certainly such lands in princely hands were not taxable.

Evidence of these estates is plentiful. Sulaymān, Hishām, Maslama, and Sa'īd, the sons of 'Abd al-Malik, as princes each built up private estates of reclaimed land complete with irrigation canals.[44] Muḥammad b. 'Abd al-Malik also had an estate, possibly bestowed on him by Hishām, at Raysūn in the *jund* of al-Urdunn.[45] It is likely that 'Umar II also had estates in Qinnasrīn before becoming caliph,[46] as well as in Ḥawrān.[47] Al-'Abbās b. al-Walīd I had been granted an estate in Ḥimṣ by his father.[48] Al-Ghamr b. Yazīd II had extensive estates at Ḥarrān, which had been granted to him out of the state lands (*ṣawāfī*), while 'A'isha bt. Hishām was granted an estate by her father at Ra's Kayfā.[49] That the princes' estates were private is indicated by the fact that they were inherited by blood heirs.[50] Successful generals were also granted estates that they passed on to their heirs, and these were also probably tax free.[51]

The literary evidence for these princely estates is corroborated by the extensive amount of physical remains of large, sumptuously decorated palaces scattered mostly along the edge of the desert in Syria and Jordan.[52] These have been plausibly dated to the period from al-Walīd I through al-Walīd II (86–126/705–44).[53] Though a couple of them have been attributed to specific caliphs on the evidence of inscriptions,[54] it is uncertain whether these commemorations indicate more than the date at which they were built. Possibly a much larger number of such places existed originally, especially in more settled areas where all trace of them is now effaced. It is reasonable to suppose that most of these estates belonged only to various princes,[55] not to the caliph, who after all was only a first among equals as far as the Umayyad family was concerned.

It is difficult to know how heavily princely extravagance weighed on the exchequer, as no further evidence for it is available. Indeed, it is tempting to dismiss it as only a superficial contributor to the financial crisis. Naturally, the Umayyads' enjoyment of luxury would tend to be resented by those less fortunate, namely nearly everyone else, even the Syrian troops. The extent of their extravagance then might be seized on and exaggerated by their many enemies for use in the latter's propaganda.

On the other hand, the new wealth under al-Walīd I certainly provided the caliphs with an opportunity to show off their unstinting generosity toward their relatives, while at the same time fulfilling the requirement of both Arabic custom and Islamic practice to help or take care of the less fortunate among them.[56] Also, the steadily increasing numbers of young princes growing up with expectations of enjoying the same wealth as their fathers meant that there were ever more prospective recipients of such generosity, contributing to an increasing drain on the treasury.[57] Certainly, the demands that both princely constructions and stipends stop formed an important part of the reform program of the rebel caliph Yazīd III.[58]

Nevertheless, it is probable that the expense of equipping and sending out military expeditions was a greater cause for the worsening of the financial crisis. One case points to this conclusion. When al-Ḥajjāj sent Muḥammad b. al-Qāsim to conquer Sind, the expedition cost sixty million dirhams, while the booty forwarded to the central treasury was one hundred twenty million dirhams.[59] This indeed shows that booty could be a profitable source of revenue, but the conquest of Sind was one of the most successful expeditions ever and therefore hardly typical. Rather, one is struck by the enormous size of the cost.

The disastrous Constantinople expedition of 98–99/717–18 was probably much more expensive than the conquest of Sind, owing to the huge number of ships outfitted.[60] Because of their size and the workmanship they required, outfitting ships was far more expensive than equipping land forces. Also, while infantrymen and cavalrymen could sometimes partly equip themselves, creating the huge fleets that sailed to Constantinople was not a task that could be carried out privately. Therefore, the destruction of the Constantinople expedition and its fleet was not only a severe setback for the troops, their morale, and the government's military policy, but also constituted a financial blow that may have practically wiped out the gains made under al-Walīd I. While a single such blow could be endured occasionally, a series of expensive, profitless setbacks could lead to a serious financial crisis in a state with huge fixed military expenditures and no way of satisfying them, except for booty.

Other factors also contributed to the crisis. The occupation of Iraq, for example, involved an enormous expense as well as a considerable waste of manpower, for troops so used could not be said to be gainfully employed, as they produced nothing. The construction of Wāsiṭ as a garrison town is likely to have cost much and produced little in return. As an economizing measure, and also to remove the threat of Iraqi military force, the Umayyads seem to have reduced the native Iraqi *jund*s in size. Thus, the demilitarized Iraqis of al-Kūfa and al-Baṣra were probably no longer receiving stipends, except when they took the field occasionally against rebels or were enrolled to be sent to the frontier. Though this step saved some money, perhaps, it was at the price of alienating the demobilized *muqātila,* who had come to see the stipends as their right. Furthermore, the hostility of the Iraqis may have made tax collecting difficult, as even the severe al-Ḥajjāj was not able, apparently, to obtain a satisfactory amount of revenue.[61] This problem also reflected the ever-present reluctance of the provinces to forward a fifth of their income to the central government. Any leniency on the part of the government in this regard tended to be seen as weakness by the provincials and an open invitation to send nothing.

The budding fiscal crisis, like the related military crisis, was dealt with drastically by 'Umar II. His remedy involved a large cut in the main area of expenditure, the military. This is indicated by his curtailing or altogether stopping the wars of conquest on all fronts.[62] This almost certainly meant a demobilization of some of the armed forces. Such a step is also suggested by his withdrawal of the Syrian garrisons from Iraq.[63] It also appears that he began a reduction in the armed forces by limiting the size and number of stipends that could be received by the children of the troops.[64] He also evinced a desire that the troops be paid only by booty.[65] His desire to withdraw from Spain, Kilikia, and Transoxiana can also be seen in a context of military retrenchment.[66] The same goes for restoration of the deposed Chach dynasty of Sind to its throne so that that province could partially police itself.[67]

'Umar II also economized on the extravagant stipends and grants that had been given to the various Umayyad princes by al-Walīd I and others. In fact, it appears that these were virtually cut to nothing,[68] while some that had been granted previously were withdrawn.[69] As a money-saving measure, this was doubtless a much-needed and popular step, except with the Umayyad family, many of whom were mere rentiers without much political influence.[70] The money saved helped 'Umar II to finance his reforms.

But 'Umar II's attempt to separate the state finances from the caliph's private wealth is also significant as an attempt to put the state finances on a regular, constitutional basis instead of the existing informal one. Previously, there had been little distinction between the state treasury and the private purse of the caliph. This is demonstrated not only by caliphal land and money grants to relatives, but also by the extravagant prizes awarded to poets. 'Umar II perceived that in order for the state finances to be put on a stabler basis, the private wealth of the caliph would have to be distinguished from the state treasury, and the caliph's access to the latter would have to be limited by certain rules, including perhaps distribution of grants based only on need.[71] He set an example by refusing to grant his immediate family even small sums from the treasury.[72] He also refused gifts from governors, considering them a form of bribery. Here again, we see the tendency to separate the caliph's property from that of the state.[73] Though most of 'Umar II's reforms were immediately reversed by his successor, the concept of differentiating the state wealth from the private wealth of the caliph was an idea that continued to develop under Hishām.

However, the biggest challenge made by 'Umar II to the received fiscal policy related to the treatment of the *mawālī*. 'Umar II decided that all Muslim subjects of the caliphate should be treated equally. Therefore, he abolished the practice of continuing to take the personal capitation tax (*jizya*) from non-Arab Muslims.[74] All Muslim landholders would have to pay the land tax (*kharāj*), however. *Mawālī* who fought in the Arab armies were to be paid stipends on a scale equal to that of the Arabs.[75] Previously, the *mawālī* had not been paid at all.[76]

The motivation for these changes may have arisen out of a desire of the pious caliph to apply Islam fairly, as God had intended. But it should be noted that these policies also accord with the principle of reducing government expenditures through reducing military burdens. If the government could gain greater popular acceptance through more egalitarian policies, it could count on the local Muslims in each province, who now were beginning to include a greater number of *mawālī*, to undertake a larger share of the security needs and to defend the Islamic state with more enthusiasm.[77] However, although 'Umar II seems to have striven to reduce military spending, he continued many of the public works and social welfare programs begun by al-Walīd I[78] and also built way stations on the roads for travelers.[79]

It is hard to know how well 'Umar II's reforms would have worked out, because they were applied only for a very short period. The main complaint of the opposition to them was that the state income would drop severely as a result of removing the disabilities from the *mawālī*. It is questionable, however, how important this complaint was outside of Khurāsān, for which alone we have adequate information. Possibly the *mawālī* were not numerous enough elsewhere, with the important exception of Berber North Africa, to cause a fiscal crisis when freed from the capitation tax, provided that military spending was also reduced.

But this was precisely the goal in 'Umar II's program that could not be achieved. In fact, there is little evidence of direct opposition to 'Umar II in his reign exactly because there is little evidence that he tried to reduce the size of the army through demobilization. Perhaps he intended to do it in very small steps, possibly by retiring the old or the exhausted without recruiting new men.[80] Elements favoring the traditional forward policy may have accepted the need for a recovery period after the Constantinople defeat and thus did not press for any new expeditions immediately. That the most obvious champion of the traditional policy, Maslama b. 'Abd al-Malik, was in some eclipse after presiding over the Constantinople defeat also may have chastened the military party and counselled them to be patient.[81]

But as soon as 'Umar II was dead and the rebel Yazīd b. al-Muhallab was out of the way, 'Umar II's reforms were put aside and the forward policy was enthusiastically resumed. One might have expected to find Maslama and his Jazīran protege, 'Umar b. Hubayra al-Fazārī, who had also been involved in the Constantinople debacle and had in fact commanded the ill-starred Muslim fleet there,[82] in permanent disgrace. But now, both were restored to commanding positions by Yazīd II.[83] Iraq was subdued and again garrisoned with Syrian troops. Reforms favoring the *mawālī* in Khurāsān were revoked and expansion resumed. Increases in the Egyptian *dīwān*, presumably those involving the Egyptian sailors of the Muslim fleet, were cancelled.[84] The same may have occurred under Yazīd II in Sind, however, the dating is uncertain. On the Khazar front, a great war broke out. Raids against Byzantium were resumed. Extravagant grants to Umayyad princes were resumed.[85]

We may assume that these steps were taken to renew the flow of booty to enable the traditional forward policy to support and keep the troops occupied, if not contented, as well as to win support of factions within the ruling elite. However, easily captured booty was becoming scarce and was entirely inadequate to provide sufficient income to maintain the large forces at the caliph's disposal. Therefore, the caliphal administration began seeking other remedies, which turned into a broad policy of financial retrenchment under Hishām.

The first step in the new policy was to increase the flow of money into the central treasury through the appointment of more trustworthy, thoroughgoing, and responsible governors. As we have seen, the provinces tended to try to avoid forwarding the caliphal fifth to the treasury at every possible opportunity. Also, many governors were accused of embezzling funds that were the central government's by right. It is true that the new caliphal policy found its origin in that of al-Ḥajjāj, who was honest, scrupulously loyal to the caliph, and merciless in collecting taxes. Therefore, it is possible to speak of a reversion to the policy of al-Ḥajjāj under Yazīd II.[86] But this policy was now applied to all areas of the empire, including some, such as Khurāsān, Sind, North Africa, and Spain, where they had not really been applied before. Included in the new policy was a return to the idea that the *mawālī* must pay the *jizya*.

However, the attempt to return to the policy of al-Ḥajjāj in the interests of financial stringency immediately came up against hard realities. Maslama, the conqueror of Yazīd b. al-Muhallab, was rewarded with the governorship of Iraq and the East, but then removed almost immediately in 102/721 for failing to forward any money to the caliph.[87] As Maslama was a senior prince and had a large military following in al-Jazīra, he could not be constrained, but only removed from office. His removal virtually ended the practice of employing Umayyad princes as governors, because greater central control over the provinces was needed, and Umayyad princes with minds, and especially forces, of their own could not be easily controlled. Indeed, the subsequent development of an independent power base in al-Jazīra by Marwān b. Muḥammad, another of Maslama's proteges and an Umayyad prince in his own right as well, emphasized the necessity of removing such princes from positions of power. Even so, Maslama was replaced by a non-Umayyad Jazīran protégé of his, 'Umar b. Hubayra.[88]

In Khurāsān, the new policy was carried out by another Qaysī associate of Maslama, Sa'īd b. 'Amr al-Ḥarashī from Qinnasrīn, the governor from 103–04/721–22.[89] His enthusiastic enforcement of full *jizya* payments on the rebellious Transoxianans led immediately to a war in which his early striking successes belied the true gravity of the situation.[90] Interestingly, he was removed from office for failing, despite his victories, to forward any of the *kharāj* to the central government.[91] He was succeeded by the son of an associate of al-Ḥajjāj, Muslim b. Sa'īd al-Kilābī, also a Qaysī, who was left to reap the results of the resumed war policy.[92]

The same policy was also reapplied in Sind in the time of Yazīd II. Although the historical chronology of Sind for this period is unclear, it best can be reconstructed from the governors' lists in Ibn Khayyāṭ, which are more complete than those in other sources. From these lists, it would appear that the succession of Qaysī governors was begun on the recovery of the province from the Muhallabids in 102/721 but that the new policies, including the resumption of the taking of the *jizya* from the *mawālī*, began to be applied firmly only under al-Junayd b. 'Abd al-Raḥmān al-Murrī, who was appointed by Yazīd II in 104/723 and whose governorship continued for two years into Hishām's reign.[93]

But it was in North Africa, where the *mawālī* element in the army was the strongest, that the return to al-Ḥajjāj's policies failed most signally. Here, Yazīd II appointed as governor in 101/720 the scrupulously honest Yazīd b. Abī Muslim Dīnār, the *mawlā* of the Thaqīf, who had been al-Ḥajjāj's secretary in charge of the *kharāj* in Iraq. This man tried to restore things as they had been, perhaps even before the governorship of Mūsā b. Nuṣayr fifteen years earlier when the Berbers were still largely resisting Islam and had been liable to pay the capitation tax, which was levied in persons.[94]

But by now, many, perhaps most, of the Berbers were at least nominal Muslims. Thus, they naturally resented having to pay taxes prescribed only for non-Muslims and, moreover, had the strength needed to enforce their objection. Even before any general revolt could take place, however, Ibn Abī Muslim offended his own Berber guard by insisting that they be tattooed, presumably to show his ownership and their subordination. Enraged, they rose and killed him in 102/721. Furthermore, they forced Yazīd II to accept their act and temporarily their choice of successor to the governor.[95] This was a shocking example of the approaching bankruptcy of the policy of maintaining the traditional Arab domination without compromise. It also showed the opposition that could be expected to a policy of fiscal stringency that meant harsher tax collecting and denying the rights of Muslims. Though a new governor sent out in 103/722 by Yazīd II restored a semblance of central control and executed one of the alleged perpetrators of Ibn Abī Muslim's murder, the latter's harsh policies against the Berber Muslims were not tried again.[96]

That the new, harsher tax-collecting policy was also applied in Spain is shown by a report saying that 'Anbasa b. Suḥaym al-Kalbi, who was governor for Yazid II, doubled the amount of the *kharaj*. This led to considerable discontent. His successor under Hishām, Yaḥyā b. Salama al-Kalbi, tried to ameliorate conditions of taxation and returned property that had been improperly seized to its rightful owners. Nevertheless, the Spanish *Continuatio Isadori* contains an unusual outpouring of invective against Hishām's regime, whose rapacity was unexampled in previous history.[97]

Besides attempts to increase its income through a more loyal and thoroughgoing provincial administration, the central government also sought to reduce military expenditures while maintaining full strength. This meant not a policy of cutting back existing forces, but rather of supporting them more economically. Thus, the rules of military stipends began to be enforced more strigently, with stipends being actually reduced whenever and wherever possible.[98] Naturally, any reduction in their stipends was bound to be furiously opposed by the troops, so that the government had to resort to chicanery to get its will carried out. This is visible in the attempt in Hishām's reign about 117/735 to reduce the grain ration of the troops in Egypt. The latter resisted and smashed the new grain measures which had been made to the standard of the new ration size.[99] The attempt to persuade the troops to make do with less is also perhaps shown in the ascetic lifestyles among some of the new governors, such as the ill-fated Yazīd b. Abī Muslim, who refused to take more than a modest three hundred dirhams a month as al-Ḥajjāj's secretary in Iraq, saying that if he could not make do with three hundred, then thirty thousand would not be enough.[100] It may be doubted how efficacious such steps to reduce military spending were in fact.

The attempt to run a more efficient administration also explains the reform of the coinage and its centralization at Damascus and especially Wāsiṭ, where it could be kept under tighter supervision than when it was scattered among many provincial mints. The first step in this direction seems to have been taken in 99–100/718–19, the coinage of silver dirhams issuing from only ten mints in 99/718 and six in 100/719, compared with nineteen mints in 98/717, the last year of Sulaymān's rule. It would certainly appear that this centralization of minting was connected with the reform program of ʿUmar II. Unlike others of his reforms, the centralization of the coinage lasted and was further developed under Hishām. By 112/730, dirhams were being minted at only four places: Damascus, Wāsiṭ, Ifrīqiya (al-Qayrawān), and al-Andalus (Qurṭuba).[101] According to al-Maqrīzī, in 106/725 Hishām ordered that dirhams be minted only at Wāsiṭ,[102] but this is not strictly correct, as examples exist from other mints, usually from one mint at a time in each superprovince.[103] At the same time, coin styles were unified, which also shows centralization. This, perhaps, can be seen in the dated copper *fulūs* of 101/720, with their identical legends emphasizing honesty and justice.[104] Furthermore, western variations of legends on gold coins were replaced by those used in the east at least by 114/732. Even mere graphic variations had been standardized by 122/740.[105]

Hishām also commanded the dirham's weight to be increased by from six to seven *dāniqs*. This remained in force under Khālid al-Qasrī until 120/738, when the lighter weight was restored by Yūsuf b. ʿUmar.[106] Increasing the dirham's weight might indicate prosperity, but it also may have been done as a sop to public opinion for the introduction of some other unpopular measure. The later reduction in weight, however, probably owed to the financial stringency exacerbated by the defeats the caliphate had suffered in the preceding few years. However, the quality of the silver in the dirham remained high throughout Hishām's reign, and extraordinary measures were taken to prevent loss through theft.[107] The centralization of the mints under ʿUmar II and especially Hishām helped to save the caliphate money by making the mint operation more efficient and by allowing for an easier accounting to be made of the precious metals that went into the coins. By these means, purity was improved and maintained.

Another possible supplement to state income was in the profits derived from the caliph's private estates, though it is impossible to determine whether the caliph gave some support to the state budget out of his own pocket. It is perhaps unlikely that he did so, especially as the development of big estates and the construction of palaces by the caliphs were two of the prominent complaints treated in the reform program of Yazīd III in 126/744, which implies that the profits of these estates were of no benefit to the public. Still, even though the private estates of the caliph did not devolve on his successors in office, but rather on his children, they probably had a quasi-official status, bearing some comparison with the imperial *res privata* in the Later Roman Empire.[108] This is shown by the existence of a government department in charge of the lesser privy seal and the caliph's private estates (*al-khātam al-saghīr wa al-khāṣṣa*).[109] This department seems to have been created sometime under Hishām, which clearly demonstrates the rising importance of the caliphal estates in that reign.[110] Indeed, the Caliph Hishām is especially known for his estates, both in Syria and in Iraq, and these produced an enormous income for him, said to have exceeded the total income of the state from all taxes.[111] It would seem likely that some of this income might have been devoted to certain state needs in times of financial hardship.

To be part of the state apparatus, the caliph's private estates did not have to fund the official budget, of course. They could still have plenty of impact as a source of patronage for retainers. This is most dramatically displayed by the case of the Waḍḍāḥiyya[112] and especially the Dhakwāniyya, the five-thousand-man or larger private army of Sulaymān b. Hishām, the caliph's son. This latter force, though privately recruited out of his own *mawālī*, and perhaps supported by the prince's own funds that he had received from his father, still fought for the state. But they were also available to the prince for his own account in time of internal disorder.[113] The Dhakwāniyya have been quite properly singled out as a portentious development heralding the replacement of the Muslim citizen army based on tribal ties with forces of retainers having only personal ties of loyalty to their commander.[114] Their creation does not necessarily suggest distrust of the reliability of the citizen army by the Umayyads so much as the inability of the state to provide adequate funding for its traditional armed forces through its existing tax-gathering machinery.

Ideological Centralization

However, the caliphs also had some difficulty establishing their legitimacy in the eyes of the Muslim community. As the Muslims' supreme ruler, who ultimately derived his authority from God, the caliph was expected by the Muslim body politic to adhere to and to enforce the Islamic norms established by the Qur'ān and *sunna*.[115] The human failure of the caliphs to meet the expected standards, both in their personal behavior and in their application of the law, especially when the vital interests of large groups of people were at stake, led inevitably to internal opposition in some circles. Because the rule of the caliph was supposed to be based on divine law, both he and his opponents tended to see political questions in terms of absolute right and wrong. This tendency to see matters in black and white reduced the room for political compromise between the government and its opposition, and contributed to many revolts and civil wars. Each new conflict brought the opposition to a greater degree of ideological sophistication, to which the government had to react.

This process is clearly demonstrated already very early in Islamic history. The Caliph 'Uthmān's (24–35/644–56) opponents demanded that he step down on account of his errors, which were tantamount to immoral behavior in thier opinion. 'Uthmān rather emphasized that he had a right to absolute obedience as God's appointee.[116] After 'Uthmān had been killed and 'Alī defeated in the First *Fitna*, Mu'āwiya had to look for some basis on which to claim legitimacy for his rule. He chose a policy of currying the favor of the prestigious leaders of all the tribes, while at the same time acting clemently and trying to prevent renewed bloodshed.[117] The failure of Mu'āwiya's policy was shown as early as in 51/671 by the continuance of pro-'Alid revolutionism in al-Kūfa[118] and further emphasized by the bloodshed associated with the Second *Fitna* that followed on the death of his son Yazīd I in 64/683.[119] Repeated *khārijī* outbreaks also revealed the failure of Mu'āwiya's attempt to build a consensus about the legitimacy of his rule.[120]

Moreover, the opposition to the Umayyads during the Second *Fitna* showed a greater degree of political and religious sophistication, especially as revealed in the beliefs in a divinely guided imam propagated by al-Mukhtār al-Thaqafī.[121] The renewed attempts of the Zubayrids to restore the pristine caliphate of earlier days also was accompanied by a greater ideological emphasis. Although the Umayyads were successful again against their opponents, their triumph was entirely a military one, and their control of most of the provinces, especially those in the East, now depended on force. Because their rule now relied mainly on their loyal army, and because that army was a parochial one localized in Syria, it became more necessary than ever before for the Umayyads to have a coherent religious policy to deflect opposition and to justify their claims of divine sanction for their authority, if they were to have any chance of enduring in the long run. The islamizing program adopted by the Marwānids represented just such an attempt to occupy the higher ground in terms of Islamic authenticity and legitimacy, even as the Muslim rank and file increasingly questioned the dynasty's possession of these qualities.[122]

But it was not only internal opponents who compelled the Umayyads to insist more firmly on the Islamic basis of their rule. The increasingly ferocious contest with the Byzantines after the Second *Fitna* also developed an important ideological dimension. Partly, this may reflect the beginning of the defection of the Middle Eastern Christians to Islam, which may have alarmed the Byzantines and caused them to take countermeasures to put their own internal front on a firmer footing. This, in turn, made necessary a Muslim response. Thus, the islamizing program of the Marwānids also represented a policy of action in the ideological controversy with the Christians. Indeed, judging by the content of the program, it would appear more to have been aimed at the Christians both inside and outside the caliphate than at Muslim opponents.[123]

Although the Umayyads' attempts to claim religious sanction for their rule have received little attention from scholars, owing to the worldliness of the Umayyads in the received tradition about them, these efforts can be clearly traced in the policies of the Marwānids. They are plainly revealed in the program of islamization adumbrated first by the Caliph 'Abd al-Malik b. Marwān and steadily continued with greater urgency by his successors al-Walīd I, Sulaymān, 'Umar II, Yazīd II, and Hishām. Adding to the urgency of the situation, the renewed campaigns on all fronts led to previously unknown and unexpected military and financial problems. This further increased pressure on the Umayyad government to adopt a clearer ideological stance against both internal and external opponents.

Under 'Abd al-Malik, a new religious concern is already apparent in the building of the Dome of the Rock on a magnificent scale even before the end of the Second *Fitna*. While this building, completed in 72/691, was once considered to have been built to offset Ibn al-Zubayr's advantage in holding the Great Mosque of Makka during the civil war,[124] the Qur'anic inscriptions it contains seem rather to be directed at the Christians.[125] It should be noted that the decoration of the Dome, while continuing a Byzantine tradition of mosaic, with some Sāsānian themes, eschews all figural representation, which is interesting in light of the greater Byzantine insistence on the use of religious images, as codified at the Quinisext Council of 73/692.[126] Further, it is reported that as early as 67–70/686–89 all crosses in Egypt were destroyed and the doors of churches made to bear the Islamic inscription, "Muḥammad is the great apostle of God, and Jesus also is the apostle of God. But truly God is not begotten and does not beget."[127] 'Abd al-Malik also apparently applied a policy against public display of Christian images, judging by a story connected with the death of al-Aṣbagh b. 'Abd al-'Azīz, who died in 86/705.[128]

Perhaps the most salient part of the new islamizing program under 'Abd al-Malik, as well as that most clearly directed against Byzantium, was the reform of the coinage. Previously, the Muslims had struck their own silver coins but had employed Byzantine gold solidi imported from Constantinople as their standard gold currency. Probably following the iconophile decree of the Quinisext Council in 72–73/691–92, a bust of Christ replaced the cross on one side of the solidus. The Muslims, perhaps taking umbrage at such an unexampled display of a Christian holy figural portrait, rejected the new coins and instead began a gold coinage of their own showing on one side the caliph standing and on the other a mere pole in place of the cross that had been on the coins struck by the Byzantines. These Muslim coins date from 74–77/693–97. But the caliph's image evidently proved little more palatable than Christ's had been, and the gold coinage was dramatically changed to an imageless, wholly epigraphic form in 77/696–97. The same reform was applied to the silver coinage in 79/698–99, ending the traditional display of the former Persian king's visage.[129]

Soon after the coinage reform, 'Abd al-Malik in 81/700 ordered that public records, which had hitherto been kept in Greek in the former Byzantine provinces of the Islamic state, henceforth be kept in Arabic, which thus became the sole official language.[130] Also in the reign of 'Abd al-Malik, the Islamic statement of belief in Greek was put on the otherwise blank papyri exported to the Byzantines.[131] This is important not only because it shows the thoroughgoing nature of the islamizing reforms of 'Abd al-Malik's time, but also in that it indicates an effort to display or preach Islam to the Byzantines in their own country using their own language. Thus, already in 'Abd al-Malik's time, the Muslim-Byzantine struggle was tending to produce an out-and-out ideological conflict. At the same time, the islamizing reforms gave the caliphate a more ideological and programmatic coloring it had previously lacked.

The islamizing measures continued to be applied with undiminished intensity under 'Abd al-Malik's successors. Al-Walīd I embarked on a considerable mosque-building effort, which included the construction of the famous Umayyad Mosque in Damascus, built on part of the enclosure of a church. Sulaymān, not to be outdone, built the congregational mosque of Aleppo. 'Umar II promulgated laws regulating and restricting the behavior of non-Muslims, particularly Christians, including an order to destroy crosses.[132] Most interestingly, he also wrote a famous letter to the Byzantine Emperor Leo III (98–123/717–41) inviting the latter to embrace Islam.[133] 'Umar's successor, the supposedly worldly Yazīd II, brought Muslim iconoclasm to its climax in the well-known iconoclastic decree of Muharram 103/July 721 or 104/722–23 in which he commanded the destruction of all images of humans and animals in the territory of the caliphate.[134] Physical proof of the image-smashing work of 'Umar II and Yazīd II is shown by church mosaics in Jordan in which the pictures literally have been torn out and the holes patched over with floral or geometric patterns.[135] In one case, the repair work is dated to 101/719–20.[136] The destruction seems to have extended to synagogues and, therefore, was not directed only at the Christians.[137]

Under Hishām, the islamization of the caliphate seems to have taken a new turn, for he is reported to have been favorable toward the Christians, even though certain of his governors were not. On the other hand, two of his governors, Khālid al-Qasrī and Ḥanẓala b. Ṣafwān al-Kalbī had Christian mothers.[138] The former built a church for his mother and was extensively denounced for his Christian ties. But perhaps we should not make too much of this, for both these men had served previous caliphs as well. Hishām may have enjoyed a better reputation with the Christians simply because he did not introduce new restrictive measures, the iconoclastic part of the islamization being essentially complete.

Nevertheless, Hishām showed great concern for Islam. Publicly, he cultivated a pious demeanor and a reputation for justice,[139] while in private he did not drink wine.[140] That he was worried about his reputation is indicated by the report of the extraordinary measures he took to ensure that no one found out that he listened to singers or comedians in private.[141] He rewarded poets only parsimoniously.[142] He punished one of his sons for contravening the Islamic law to beat a *dhimmī*.[143] His conservative lifestyle was implicitly ridiculed by his more free-living successor, al-Walīd II, with whom he was on bad terms.[144] Nevertheless, the fact that his main wife, Umm Ḥakīm, was a famous wine-bibber, author of wine-drinking poetry (*khamriyyāt*), and possessor of a famous cup legendary for its size suggests that his sumptuary measures inside his family and private life were to some extent cosmetic.[145]

However, his concern with Islam most significantly manifested itself in his efforts to cultivate Islam and its pious scholars. Throughout his reign, he maintained a good relationship with the famous Muḥammad b. Muslim b. Shihāb al-Zuhrī (d. 124/742),[146] as well as with Abū Zinād ʻAbd Allāh b. Dhakwān (d. 130/748), another important scholar.[147] It might be supposed that their reputations would have become somewhat tarnished later, owing to their association with the Umayyads. However, the fact that they nonetheless remained trusted transmitters, and that al-Zuhrī was still considered the leading scholar of his day, suggests that Hishām had in fact won over an important part of the religious element. Hishām seems to have worked assiduously to this end, leading the pilgrimage in person to inaugurate his reign,[148] leading the prayers over pious scholars lately deceased, treating the Qurashī scion and religious transmitter al-Qāsim b. Muḥammad b. Abī Bakr with great respect,[149] refusing to curse ʻAlī, at least personally,[150] and trying, as we have seen, to keep a pious demeanor. This effort on Hishām's part to cultivate the religious leaders may have been partly a response to the propagation of a more carefully articulated *khārijī* position by missionaries throughout the empire under the Marwānids.[151]

In sum, the conflict with non-Muslims, especially the Christians, as well as constant internal pressures, caused the Marwānid caliphs to adopt a stricter and more programmatic ideological policy. Although the warfare on the frontiers began anew and continued to intensify from the reign of ʻAbd al-Malik on, it is likely that the injection of a greater ideological element into the conflicts helped to increase both their ferocity and their unresolvability, as neighboring states that might have been willing to pay some tribute resisted giving in to the Muslims' ideological insistence. At the same time, the Muslims, right up to their highest leadership, were so thoroughly imbued with the idea of carrying on the *jihād* against non-Muslims that they found it hard even to reduce, much less end, their military expeditions, even when these became prohibitively costly. Thus, they stuck stubbornly to a failing policy in the reign of Hishām. Moreover, the greater pressure from the outside demanded a strengthening of the internal front, meaning a greater enforcement of orthodoxy within Islam and a greater control over and even discouragement of Christianity among the non-Muslim subjects.

5

The Challenges of Internal and Foreign Opposition to Hishām's Caliphate

The Internal Opposition under Hishām

Having considered the nature of the administration under Hishām, it behooves us next to discuss the internal opposition he faced, for it is usually such internal opposition of one form or another that has hitherto been credited with the responsibility for the downfall of Hishām's dynasty shortly after his death. Our discussion will best be brief as much, possibly too much, attention has already been devoted to this internal opposition elsewhere.[1] The fact is that despite the attention paid in the sources to various rebellions against the caliph, these were not very important in Hishām's reign. This is probably why the anonymous author of the pro-Umayyad *al-Imāma wa al-siyāsa* denies that there were any disturbances in Hishām's reign at all,[2] which is not quite true even for the East and certainly not for the West. Nevertheless, a general internal quiet did prevail, which is probably also one of the main reasons some modern scholars regard the reign as a success.[3]

However, lack of revolts alone is not a sufficient criterion of success against an opposition, particularly when the state in question suffers a complete overturn shortly afterward. Thus, the Umayyads may have faced relatively little visible trouble under Hishām, but it would seem that the 'Abbāsid revolutionaries who came to power a mere seven years after his death must have already sown the seeds of their movement in a fertile field during his long reign. It is true that dissatisfaction stemming from Hishām's reign in particular played a major role in undermining the Umayyad caliphate. But this dissatisfaction owed more to the bankruptcy of the traditional military policy on the frontiers than to the inherent strength of the internal opposition. Indeed, the opposition under Hishām was neither innovative nor effective, as can be seen by reviewing each segment of it separately.

One form of opposition alleged to have been decisive was tribal. The Arab tribes, which, as we have seen, formed the basis of army organization, were turbulent and difficult to subordinate in a hierarchical system. Tribal war between the Qays and Yaman in Syria had earlier rocked the caliphate to its foundation in the Second *Fitna*. Under Yazīd II and Hishām, the Qays-Yaman struggle returned, but was now empirewide. Each group, upon succeeding the other in a governorship, promptly removed all the officials of the other party and frequently put them under torture to extract embezzled funds from them.[4] The Arabs had a custom of blood-revenge for wrongs inflicted, a custom moreover sanctioned in Islam as well. This led to a revolving cycle of violence gaining in ferocity under Hishām and supposedly culminating in the murder of al-Walīd II in revenge for the Yamanī leader Khālid al-Qasrī.[5] Added to this, according to Shaban, the Yaman had a political program, adumbrated by 'Umar II, that had been brusquely pushed aside by pro-Qays caliphs.[6]

However, on closer inspection, these arguments prove less persuasive. Undoubtedly tribal feeling was important, everpresent, and ready to break out given a suitable opportunity. But it was not new and had been successfully managed and overcome before, as in the Yaman-Qays compact engineered by 'Abd al-Malik.[7] There were no wholly pro-Yaman or pro-Qays caliphs. Each caliph tried as best he could to balance the two tribal groupings. While scholars have devoted most of their attention to which party was in power in the East at a given moment, the opposite party's power in the West at the same time has often gone overlooked. For example, Hishām is seen as moderately pro-Yaman until 120/738 because he left Khālid al-Qasrī in power in the East,[8] but the fact that for much of this period Qaysī governors were in office in Egypt and the West is usually not mentioned. Most importantly, though there was rivalry, there are no recorded cases of Yaman-Qays violence inside the dominant Syro-Jazīran army under Hishām. The outbreak of violence shortly after his death owed mainly to the military imbalance brought about by the scattering and destruction of the Yamanī army units in external wars, as I hope to show.

A variation of the tribal impact theme is that of provincial rivalry. As we have seen, the Umayyad caliphate was clearly dominated by the Syrian army, which by Hishām's reign may well have made up over half of the armed forces. This dominance was resented elsewhere, especially in Iraq, and in the Iraqi dependency of Khurāsān, from which came the 'Abbāsid revolution. Iraqi resentment expressed itself in large revolts, such as those of Ibn al-

Ash'ath and Ibn al-Muhallab.[9] Grievances included inequitable taxation, the forwarding of tax money to Syria, and especially the garrisoning of Syrian troops in the provinces, a practice much extended by Hishām, which seemed to the provincials to be like an occupation.[10] The sense of grievance was especially acute in the frontier provinces of Khurāsān and Ifrīqiya, where the tribal regiments felt that their efforts to hold back the non-Muslims were unappreciated and unrewarded.

These arguments are not without a grain of truth but again are exaggerated. Provincial resentment against central control had manifested itself violently already in 34/655 when the ever-turbulent Kūfans expelled the Caliph 'Uthmān's governor.[11] Repeated revolts and opposition, though requiring much caliphal effort to control, had remained totally ineffective. Furthermore, tribal ties were more important than local ties. Even late in Umayyad times, when outsider Arab troops, even Syrians, were introduced to a province, they usually found a warm reception from their tribal cohorts in the province, especially if they were members of the same subtribe.[12] Also, the 'Abbāsid revolution, which tried to paint itself as above tribal differences, was actually hotly pro-Yaman and anti-Qays until firmly ensconced in power, whereupon it took up the tribal balancing policy of the defunct Umayyad regime.[13] The ability of the Khurāsānīs to overwhelm the Jazīrans in the revolution owed to the imbalance introduced into the system by the scattering and destruction of the Syrian army under Hishām. Only this gave the Khurāsānīs their opportunity to step into the power vacuum thus created.

Another often-emphasized cause of the Umayyads' downfall is the dissatisfaction of the increasing numbers of *mawālī*, non-Arab Muslims, whose role was subordinate in the state.[14] Generally, the new non-Arab Muslims, just like their countrymen who had not embraced Islam, had to pay taxes in exchange for protection from hostile attack from outside the caliphate and from arbitrary seizure within it, but were not allowed to join the army or receive stipends. The exceptions were the frontier provinces of Khurāsān and Ifrīqiya, where the *mawālī* were allowed to fight, presumably as 'volunteers', but received no pay for their efforts other than a right to share in the booty. When this lessened under Hishām owing to defeats, disaffection was bound to appear. As the *mawālī* became more numerous, they pressed their grievances more fully, aided by some descendants of Arabs who had intermingled with them.[15] However, their demands for redress were resisted by conservative caliphs and opposed by the Arab troops, who saw that any extension of privileges to the *mawālī* would not only reduce the state tax income but also limit their own share of the tax pie through the introduction of more stipend recipients into the military rolls. The frustrated *mawālī* thereupon had no recourse but to rebel in North Africa and to support the 'Abbāsid revolution in Khurāsān, and it was they who provided the masses of troops necessary for these successful revolts.

Again, while there is some truth in this view, the role of the *mawālī* in the Umayyads' downfall was secondary. This is demonstrated most clearly in two ways. First, it is extremely doubtful that the *mawālī* contribution to the revolutionary forces was that important. In the case of Khurāsān, the *mawālī* never amounted to more than a minority of the troops,[16] and some of them remained loyal to the Umayyads during the revolution even in Khurāsān.[17] Interestingly, both Ṭukhāristān and Transoxiana, the region in Khurāsān that apparently contained the largest number of *mawālī*, contributed little to the 'Abbāsid revolution, which leads to the conclusion that it was rather the partly demobilized old Arab *muqātila* around Marw that provided the backbone of the revolutionary forces.[18]

As for North Africa, it is doubtful to what extent the Berber rebels were *mawālī* assimilated to Islam at all. It is likely that most of the Berber *mawālī* in the army were in Spain, where they did not revolt until that province had been already cut off from the rest of the caliphate.[19] The North African rebels may have had leaders with some military training in the Muslim armies, as indicated by their names,[20] but it is perhaps unlikely that the most of the ranks had ever seen any such service. Indeed, it is possible that the khārijī Berber rebels may have actually spread Islam further among those more inaccessible Berbers who had never hitherto been exposed to Islam at all. In this event, the 'Berber revolt' is more a continuation of a war of pacification against an external enemy than a disturbance inside the Muslim body politic, despite the veneer of Islam the rebels had acquired.

Furthermore, the '*mawālī*' did not exist as a group united against second-class treatment that they received from the government. They consisted of many different tribes, nations, and language groups that had not yet had time to coalesce into any mass resistance movement. Where there was some *mawālī* resistance, it was usually local. It was only later, through arabization and islamization, that any unity was realized through Islam. Besides this, many *mawālī* had begun to find their way to high positions in the government, prefiguring the later institution of the 'Abbāsid ministries.[21] These progovernment *mawālī* were not inclined to go out against the government, but rather may have encouraged their fellows to be loyal to the Umayyad caliph. Thus, all in all, *mawālī* opposition to the government, though present in varying forms and degrees, was not that crucial in determining the outcome of Hishām's rule.

A fourth source of opposition was found in religious dissatisfaction with the Umayyads. This is often considered to have been of great significance, as the rebels inevitably identified with persons or trends looked upon as founders of later Islamic religious groupings. The *khārijī* Berbers and the Kūfan 'Alid rebel Zayd b. 'Alī are obvious examples. Especially the latter and his son Yaḥya became martyrs to the 'Abbāsid cause and were used widely to stir up passions against the Umayyad dynasty.[22]

But, while the religious beliefs of the rebels were undoubtedly a factor, especially perhaps the fear of God's judgement against them for failing to rebel against an evil *imām*, the actual expression of the rebel movements was in fact mainly political. In a state where the caliph constantly reiterated that he was "God's deputy,"[23] political dialogue necessarily had to take a religious course.[24] This was because the caliph's claims to absolute religious authority could only be opposed by being negated and denied. The gap between the ideal of a rightly guided caliph and the reality of worldly one-man rule provided plenty of ammunition for the opposition, which even held up "God's deputies" to ridicule for their lack of perfection.[25] Inevitably, rebellion against the caliph would have to be based on some positive principles as well, if only the substitution of one ruling family for another. This in itself would quite naturally develop into a religious claim. But meanwhile, behind the religious claims, political purposes clearly formed a large part of the rebel motivations, especially for those movements appearing in the reign of Hishām.

To take the largest group of religious rebels, it would appear that the motivations of the *khawārij* were mainly political.[26] The *khawārij* of 100/719–20 who debated with 'Umar II carried on an entirely political discussion concerned mainly with which attitude was to be adopted about the righteousness of particular past rulers. As the party out of power, they naturally adopted a severe attitude toward those in office. For them, the main political as well as religious question was about who should be obeyed.[27] Bahlūl, the famous Mawṣilī *khārijī* of Hishām's reign, is shown to have been motivated by a personal affront probably connected with tribal group feeling.[28] No religious beliefs, scruples, or connections are given. The North African *khawārij*, though possibly inspired to adopt Khārijism by a disaffected Berber *mawlā*,[29] mainly embarked on a national war against what they saw as political oppression. Their only unique religious expression was the substitution of their own caliph for the distant Umayyad, but that is hardly a basis for calling them a separate sect.[30] They may have drawn some of their organizational inspiration from contact with the caliphate, but that is another question.

The "Shī'ī" movement of Zayd b. 'Alī in al-Kūfa perhaps offers a more creditable example of religious influence, as exemplified in his stated program. But it still must be identified more as a political than a religious movement. Most of the articles in Zayd's program are political in nature and are only religious to the extent that they claim that the Umayyad caliphate was a failure and illegitimate. No new religious doctrines were propounded.[31] There is no reason the movement of Zayd should be seen as sectarian while that of Yazīd III, whose program is actually much more radical in suggesting limitations to the caliph's powers, is merely political.[32] Moreover, despite his extensive preparations,[33] the movement of Zayd was of little consequence because of its ineffectiveness. It did not generate much enthusiasm nor require a major effort to suppress.[34] While it undoubtedly revealed the dissatisfaction of the Kūfans, their disaffection was not new. The 'Abbāsids demanded revenge for Zayd and his son through the mediacy of the Khurāsānī army. The downfall of the Umayyad caliphate was not caused by Shī'ism or religious schisms.

Although the various kinds of internal opposition were important during Hishām's reign, it must be emphasized that such opposition was old and had been managed well enough before. It was only when the external military reverses suffered by the caliphate under Hishām put a strain on the budget and scattered the Syrian army that the opponents of Umayyad rule had a chance to press violently for a redress of their various grievances.

The External Strategic Situation in 105/724

The desire of the caliphs Yazīd II and Hishām and their chief advisers to get on with renewed campaigning on all fronts collided head-on with a new situation, brought about not by the Muslims' weakness or failure, but rather by their very success. On the maps (maps 1 and 2), it can easily be seen that the Muslim caliphate by 101/720 was a sprawling geographical entity. This was a direct result of the continuous expansion it had long enjoyed, which had accustomed its leaders to ignore defensive thinking and planning, at least until 'Umar II. Rather, they had looked for targets of opportunity in order to increase the size of the wealth and territory under their control. This generally meant following the course of least resistance.

Thus, the caliphate had come to consist mostly of lands of four previous kingdoms, Sāsānian Iran, the Byzantine Empire's Near Eastern provinces including eastern North Africa, Gothic Spain, and Sind, which had each fallen quickly, usually after a few decisive battles.[35] Territories inhabited by independent mountain peoples, proving difficult to subdue, tended to be bypassed. Not only did the caliph's realm have some holes created by such islands of resistance, but also it was stretched out far more along its east-west axis than on the north-south one. Spain and Sind, being at extreme opposite poles in the West and East, naturally tended to draw less central attention than areas nearer to the caliphate's core, except when they momentarily took the center stage by providing immoderate amounts of booty, usually only for a short period. In fact, the caliphate's appearance on the map was more one of a distended archipelago of holdings rather than a unified mass, an impression which increases when one considers the discontinuities caused by deserts.

The easier targets having been conquered by Hishām's reign, along with the one more difficult area of the Transoxianan principalities, nothing was left except still farther away lands never before subdued. These lands, far from being devoid of independent power, contained half a dozen large states which loomed like a wall around the caliphate. From the West, following the caliphate's northern perimeter, they included Frankish Gaul, the Byzantine Empire, the Khazar Turkish Khanate of the Caucasus, the Turgesh Turkish Khanate beyond the Jaxartes, and various Hindu kingdoms beyond Sind, especially those of the Gurjara-Pratiharas in central India and of the Chalukyas on India's west coast.[36] Besides these, the imperfectly subdued Berbers of North Africa virtually constituted an independent external enemy, especially those farther to the west, who had had the least contact with Islam. Also, several smaller unconquered mountain fastnesses remained inside the caliphate's general boundaries.[37]

In choosing which theaters to concentrate on, the caliph had to consider the geography of his own territories and their natural division into a West and an East. The western zone consisted of a long, narrow string of territories stretching along the shores of the Mediterranean from Syria through Egypt and North Africa and curling up into Spain. The West's long sea front made naval strength essential, but the Arabs of the Umayyad period preferred to avoid using the sea whenever possible. This greatly curtailed the Arabs' interest in the West. The eastern lands of the caliphate, on the other hand, fronted on a few mostly landlocked seas and contained the only large, compact mass of territory in the caliphate, namely that between Syria and Transoxiana. As we have seen, the eastern lands were also much more valuable than the western. Thus, it was only natural that the caliphate put more emphasis on the eastern fronts, especially in the struggles with the Byzantines, Khazar Turks, and Turgesh Turks, all of whom were nearer to the Muslim bases in the *amṣār* of the Fertile Crescent than the Berbers, Iberians, and Franks were. In these struggles against the Byzantines and Turks, the Muslims showed more persistence than they did in those with the Franks or the Indians.

To sum up, besides Arabia, the caliphate mainly consisted of five areas whose complete conquest had been relatively swift and easy: The former territories of Sāsānian Persia, the Byzantine Near East including eastern North Africa (Tunisia and Libya), Gothic Spain, Transoxiana, and Sind. Now, under Yazīd II and Hishām, it faced a cordon of six formidable adversaries of unimpaired strength: the Byzantines, the Khazar Turks, the Turgesh or Central Asian Turks, the Hindus, the Franks, and the Berbers. Against this array of powers, relying on a tried and tested aggressive policy that had so far failed only against Constantinople,[38] the caliphs blithely threw their forces into renewed expeditions on all fronts. In order to understand fully the implications of this policy, it is necessary to examine the various theaters in detail.

The Byzantine Empire

The Muslims' first strategic concern and worry was their chief nemesis, the venerable Byzantine Empire, which was the only truly ancient, highly developed, and organized enemy confronting the caliphate under Hishām. Shorn of many of its scattered possessions by this time, the Byzantine state had virtually been reduced to its Greek-speaking areas. These same areas for the most part subscribed to Constantinopolitan orthodoxy in religion. Geographically, it was now a compact mass, mainly consisting of Anatolia and a few enclaves in Greece and Italy, including the important island of Sicily. Anatolia (see map 4), surrounded on three sides by sea and well protected by the Taurus and Pontic mountains on the east, as well as by a generally mountainous terrain throughout its large extent, was an excellent defensive redoubt. Behind the Bosphorus, Constantinople sat on its peninsula, well defended by its venerable walls, a virtually unconquerable last refuge for the empire.[39]

After its numbing defeats in the seventh century CE, and especially after the utter failure of Justinian II's attempt to renew offensive warfare against the caliphate in 74/693,[40] the Byzantine Empire steadfastly followed a defensive strategy, allowing the Muslims to invade Anatolia without retaliatory raids on the caliphate, which would have left the Byzantine forces open to attack.[41] While this situation does indicate a certain Byzantine weakness, it also bespeaks a conscious choice of defensive strategy because of the extraordinary danger the empire was in, owing to the proximity of the powerful caliphate. After all, the empire was not without forces, as shown by its triumphant defense of Constantinople in 98–99/717–18. It simply did not want to risk losing them in a decisive final battle that might lead to its downfall.

The advantages gained by the empire's policy are plain. Though the rugged landscape of Anatolia was exposed to some ravaging, the Muslims were made to fight far from their bases, on terrain and on terms usually of the Byzantines' own choosing. This was particularly true in the great siege or blockade of Constantinople, during which the Muslims did not even come close to taking the city. Both Muslim and Greek historians make it abundantly clear that the first cause of the Muslims' failure was logistical. They were simply too far from their bases to maintain so large a force.[42] As a result, their supplies ran short and they starved. Then, the distance from their bases worked against them again in another way: it was much farther to escape. This caused the substantial destruction of the expedition.[43]

One other factor that strongly favored the Byzantines was their navy, which was always present in some force. Although the Muslim fleet at Constantinople seems to have been larger, possibly much larger,[44] it was operating too far from its bases. Again, it was the Byzantines who could choose the site of the combat and could operate from ports all around Anatolia. The Byzantines, thus, could usually protect their coasts adequately from all but the largest Muslim fleets. Besides this, the Muslim fleet was largely manned by Egyptian Christians who evidently were not entirely trustworthy in the expedition against Constantinople.[45] The disaster suffered by the Muslim naval forces may have exceeded that suffered by the land forces in that expedition.[46] No wonder the Umayyad caliphate never again sent a fleet so far from its bases! But the failure of the Umayyads to use their navy in Anatolian waters after that meant that those waters had virtually been conceded to the Byzantines by default, meaning that only the narrow, mountainous land frontier offered itself as a possible invasion route for Muslim troops. Losing command of the sea thus meant that Constantinople could not be conquered after that, even in theory.

The Caucasus Principalities

Farther east, a desperate, seesaw struggle was going on in the eastern Caucasus against the Khazars. The fact that we are less well informed about this front than about Transoxiana, owing to the paucity of information on it in the sources, does not mean it was less important than Transoxiana. Indeed, the Muslims very likely viewed the Khazar front as the most immediately dangerous and pressing military theater, owing to its proximity to the heart of the caliphate and to the possiblity, never to be entirely discounted under Hishām, that the Khazars might eventually be able to make effective use of their alliance with the Byzantines to stage a military breakthrough in an area that really mattered.

The actual Caucasus front (see map 5) was a rather narrow one, mostly confined to the present-day territories of independent Azerbaijan and Russian Dāghistān, though neighboring areas also seem to have been involved. The main points of conflict were the two passes of Darband (Bāb al-Abwāb or simply al-Bāb) and the Darial (Bāb al-Lān), otherwise known as the Caspian and the Alan Gates. These had been important even in antiquity as invasion routes leading from the plains in the north to those in the south, and their defense had been one of the Sassanid king's greatest responsibilities, for the Caucasus range otherwise formed an almost unbreachable wall against northern invaders from the Caspian to the Black Sea. In Hishām's reign, however, there is curiously little evidence of static front fighting to hold these positions. Rather, both Muslims and Khazars seem alternately to range over the others' territory on the mountains' opposite slopes without much impediment.

To the west, Muslim Caucasia fronted on Georgia (Jurzān) and Armenia, two distinct Christian lands, each of which, theoretically, had a state of its own but were actually divided among feuding princes. Georgia, the farther of the two from Muslim settlements, had generally retained its independence up to Hishām's reign. Meanwhile, most of Armenia was a Muslim province. While the Byzantines controlled the much smaller western portion of Armenia, the Muslims had inherited the dominant Iranian position from the Sāsānids. The border between the Muslims and the Byzantines, which ran east of the districts of Ta'iq and Theodosiopolis down to the Euphrates, appears to have remained much the same as it had been between the Sāsānids and the Byzantines before the arrival of the Muslims.

Curiously, the Caucasus front did not link up with the Byzantine front through Armenia, despite the continued Byzantine presence. Several reasons explain why. The Muslims, for their part, preferred to avoid the extremely rugged mountains of Byzantine Armenia, which they mainly seem to have left alone at this period. At the same time, the Byzantines were reluctant to waste any strength on so distant an area. The Byzantine Armenians appear not to have provoked the Muslims by any hostile actions and were thus left alone. But the decisive factor was the large bulk of the Armenians under Muslim rule. As a numerous, heavily armed mountain people steeped in a tradition of fighting, they were entirely capable of discomfiting the Muslims with Byzantine help or the Byzantines with Muslim help. Thus, both sides tended to leave them alone to a large extent, being satisfied with tribute and pro forma submission.

Unable to disarm the Armenians, the Muslims had continued the tradition of local autonomy in their part of Armenia. Though the Armenians had to pay tribute, they had largely been left to govern and defend themselves, despite occasional hostilities. This situation was upset by the intensification of the struggle between the Byzantines and the caliphate after 74/693. From about 81/700, the Muslims, under their governor of Ādharbayjān, Muḥammad b. Marwān, renewed the effort to effect a real annexation of Armenia. Armenian leaders called on the Byzantines to intervene, after which the Muslim subgovernor and some thousands of Muslim troops were slain about 84/703. However, Muḥammad b. Marwān returned to defeat the Byzantines and Armenians and, to make sure such problems were not repeated, slew the rebel Armenian princes about 86/705. Muḥammad's successor after 92/711, 'Abd al-'Azīz b. Hātim al-Bāhilī, rebuilt Dabīl (Dvin), the capital, to hold a Muslim garrison. This represented a watershed in the history of Armenia, for it meant a somewhat more direct Muslim control, though it was still not as strong nor as direct as that in lowland provinces. Owing to these steps and to the policy of 'Abd al-'Azīz, the rebel Armenians became reconciled to the caliphate. To effect the reconciliation and show his sincerity, the rebels' most important prince sacked the important Byzantine town of Poti in Colchis, which the Byzantines had entrusted him with, and returned to Muslim territory (92–8/711–7).[47]

Despite the acquiescence of Armenia to rule by the caliphate, Islam had not yet made much headway among the inhabitants, and the same applies to the rest of Transcaucasia as well. Transcaucasia was mostly a mountainous region where the Muslims controlled only the plains, as shown by the governor al-Jarrāḥ's need to campaign right around the Muslim *miṣr* of Ardabīl in the officially secure heart of Ādharbayjān as late as 112/730. The smallness of the area actually under direct Muslim control tended to limit their ability to manuever freely, for the Muslims could not trust the mountain dwellers not to ambush them. But, when faced with the invasions of the seminomadic Khazars from outside the area, the Muslims found the Georgians and the Armenians to be willing allies, for the Khazars tended to plunder these peoples just as much as they did the Muslims.

The Khazar Khanate

Unlike the divided Caucasian principalities, the Turkish Khazars possessed a powerful state like the Byzantines, though one more of a tribal rather than urban character. The Khazar Khanate existed north of the Caucasus Mountains and extended to the lower courses of the Volga and Don Rivers and beyond. Though the Khazars were already in their historical homeland by 569 C.E. and formed an independent khanate with the downfall of the West Turkish Khanate 36–37/657,[48] the Khazar realm probably received new impetus and "civilizing" influences owing to close contacts with the Byzantines from the beginning of the eighth century C.E..[49] Despite occasional conflicts with the Byzantines, a virtual alliance existed with them during most of the century. Their intention not to fall into the Byzantine sphere, however, is indicated by their *khāqān*'s and their nobles' adoption of Judaism as a religion c. 122/740.[50] The Khazars were to prove difficult opponents for the Muslims, perhaps partly because their state was not highly organized and thus did not have a center whose fall would bring about a sudden collapse and rapid surrender. Their nomadic character meant that they were highly mobile and used to fighting.

Although they had fought intermittently before,[51] Muslim-Khazar hostilities did not seriously intensify until the campaign of Maslama b. 'Abd al-Malik to establish a Muslim presence at al-Bāb north of the Caucasus in 96/715.[52] The war went on thereafter with increasing ferocity. Probably the cause of Khazar involvement should be sought in the politics of Byzantine-Muslim conflict. The

Khazars were allied with the Byzantines, an alliance that had been sealed by the unusual marriage of the emperor Justinian II to the sister of the Khazar *khāqān* by 86/705.[53] The Khazar attack, then, was probably at the suggestion of the Byzantines, who were under severe pressure from the onslaught of the third wave of Muslim expansion.[54] If indeed the Khazars initiated hostilities with the Muslims, that would help explain the subsequent persistence of the Muslims in wreaking retribution on the Khazars, despite the difficulty of campaigning against them and despite the relative smallness of the gains in prospect owing to the poverty of the Khazar realm. In any case, by the beginning of Hishām's reign, a serious war had been fully in progress on the Caucasus front with the Khazars for some time.

The Turgesh Khanate and Transoxiana

To the east of the Khazars, the Muslims faced another Turkish state, the Turgesh Khanate. However, the Turgesh realm was even less of a settled state then the Khazar Khanate, as it had no cities and its troops were those of a typical Central Asian nomadic force, highly mobile and having no fixed targets to defend. Although reputed by Chinese sources to have had two hundred to three hundred thousand fighting men,[55] which is probably an exaggeration, the Turgesh's strength likely lay more in mobility and fighting qualities than in numbers.

The powerful Turgesh state was the successor to the West Turkish Khanate which had been destroyed by the Chinese in 36–37/657. Although the Turgesh were only one among many West Turkish tribes, they came completely to dominate the others under their leader Sülü (97–120/716–38), who had been acclaimed *khāqān* or supreme ruler, though he was apparently not of royal lineage.[56] As is often the case with nomad states, the Turgesh Khanate mushroomed into a powerful empire in a very short time.

However, the Turgesh were not free to pursue an offensive policy against the caliphate immediately, because the Chinese, who regarded the West Turks as a part of their traditional sphere of influence, opposed the rise of Sülü.[57] Their opposition occupied him fully for some years and intermittently thereafter, so that the caliphate had still not fought the nomadic Turks nor felt the full force of their arms by the beginning of Hishām's reign, except for the very difficult evacuation of Qaṣr al-Bāhilī in 102/720, which gave a taste of problems to come.[58] Nevertheless, the situation was extremely unstable on the Transoxianan front, because the settled natives, including the Sughdīs and other groups, many of which may have been Iranian with a Turkish ruling class, had not really been pacified and were desperately looking for a chance to escape Muslim rule. This is indicated dramatically by the tenor of the appeals they sent to the Chinese emperor in 101/719, asking him to send troops to drive out the Muslims, or at least to command the Turgesh *khāqān* to march to their aid.[59] Thus, in Transoxiana the Muslims not only faced the threat of renewed Turgesh power, but also the doubtful loyalties of their own recently acquired Transoxianan subjects.

Sijistān

A sideshow of the Transoxianan front was the isolated desert backwater of Sijistān, which faced the mountainous region of Zābulistān that the caliphate had repeatedly failed to conquer.[60] Here peace reigned, although the Zunbīl, the ruler of Zābulistān, steadfastly refused to pay any tribute to the caliphate.[61] The failure of the Muslims to do anything about this contumacious principality, which had eqivocally signalled its submission in a token way earlier, probably means that their attention had been diverted elsewhere and that they had insufficient forces to spare for a minor, unthreatening front. Zābulistān continued until ʿAbbāsid times to be a salient extending westward from the Tibetan massif into the Muslim lands, thus interrupting the direct line of communication between Transoxiana and Sind.[62]

India

The fourth major theater of operations for the caliphate was further south in India (see map 7). Here the province of Sind, like Transoxiana, had been only recently subdued and was not yet wholly pacified. Though Sind was a significant province for the caliphate, it was quite marginal in the vast Indian subcontinent, which otherwise was untouched by the Muslims. However, it provided a convenient base for further operations in India, constituting as it did a kind of Muslim salient into the subcontinent.

On the Hindu side, India in 105/724 was very fragmented politically, consisting of a constellation of many kingdoms small and large. Altogether, it was far vaster than the patchwork of small principalities in Transoxiana.[63] Owing to their own internecine warfare, the Indian kingdoms represented little threat to the Muslim position in Sind. Nevertheless, some of the Hindu kingdoms may have been individually comparable in military strength to certain of the caliphate's other main opponents. Our knowledge about India, however, is limited by the total lack of native historical narratives for this epoch. Therefore, it is fortunate that the general outline of the structure and history of the Indian states has now been worked out from inscriptions and chance references in Hindu religious and poetic works.[64]

The Indian kingdoms facing the Muslims may be divided for convenience into northern, central, and southern groups. Access to North India from the Muslims' base in Sind was across the Punjab, where Muslim holdings reached at least as far as Multān. Beyond this, to the north, lay the vigorous Kashmiri kingdom of the Karkotas.[65] To the east of the Punjab in the Ganges valley was a large state ruled from Kanauj (Kanyakubja) by Yasovarman, a ruler of unknown antecedents and possibly a military adventurer. This state enjoyed some preeminence, as it held the core territory of the greatest earlier Indian empires. But it was not in its most glorious period in the second/eighth century.[66]

South of the Punjab, Sind was separated from central India by the Great Thar Desert. Nevertheless, a considerable interaction went on between Sind and the many principalities in Rajputana just to the east. These were known as the Gurjara states. They recognized the paramountcy of the prince of Bhillamala.[67] Around and mostly beyond Bhillamala to the east lay its vassals, some of whom, like the important prince of Malwa, with his capital at Ujjayini, claimed to be of Gurjara descent.[68] It was this latter principality that was destined to give rise to the imperial Pratiharas, the next great Indian dynasty. Other vassals of Bhillamala, like the Mauryas of Chitor (Chitrakuta),[69] the Guhilots west of Chitor,[70] and the Bhattis of Jaisalmer,[71] were not Gurjaras, however. Another group, the Chahamanas, ruled from an uncertain location between Chitor and Broach and were dependent on the Gurjara prince of Malwa. They may have been established by that prince after the Muslim invasions under Hishām, and thus may not have been on the scene yet, at the outset of his reign.[72]

To the south lay many more states in what is now Gujarat. Nearest to Sind was the principality of Cutch (Kaccha), on what was then virtually an island. Beyond that, on the Kathiawar Peninsula, were several states, foremost among which was the Maitraka principality of Valabhi.[73] In the far west of Kathiawar lay the new Saindhava state of Saurashtra at Bhumilka.[74] East of Kathiawar were the Chapas (also Chapotakas) with their capital at Anahilapataka.[75] South of these were two separate dynasties in Broach: the Gurjaras of Lata, with their capital at Nandipuri,[76] and the Chalukyas of Lata, a cadet branch of the imperial Chalukyas.[77] These latter were Kanarese with their capital far to the south at Badami (Vatapi) in Karnataka, and they constituted the largest state in India with which the Muslims had to deal under Hishām. A great and venerable dynasty with several branches, they were nevertheless past the peak of their power.[78] They counted among their vassals the Rashtrakutas of Berar, whose base was nearer the theater of conflict with the Muslims in the north.[79]

The great disadvantage, to the Muslims, of campaigning in India, apart from Sind's remoteness from the homes of most of the troops, was that it was virtually endless. As a result, no matter how many forces they brought to bear, the Muslims were bound to be worn down in the end. Indeed, even after a millenium, when a substantial proportion of the total population of India had become Muslims, the latter were still unable to subdue the whole subcontinent, suggesting that even a fraction of such a task would be impossible to carry out in Hishām's reign. On the other hand, unlike the harsh Turkish frontiers, India offered great cities, treasuries, and temples capable of producing a rich booty. But that reward would inevitably exact a heavy price to obtain.

The Franks

At the opposite end of the Islamic realm stood the other distant opponent of Muslim expansion, the Merovingian Frankish Kingdom, now under the effective control of the so-called "mayors of the palace" of the line of Pepin of Héristal. This kingdom, because it is seen as representing the heritage of Western Europe, has received far more than its share of attention in relation to its actual importance at that time. Owing to this, a more recent contrary trend has tended to belittle the effect of the Frankish resistance to Islam on history. However, while the Franks were very remote from Damascus in the second/eighth century, they still exerted some influence on the course of affairs.

After reaching its nadir under the Merovingian *"rois fainéants"* of the first/seventh century, the Frankish Kingdom grew more unified and powerful again under Pepin of Héristal (68–96/687–714) and especially Charles Martel (98–123/717–741), whose dominion over Aquitaine near the Spanish border was recognized by that province's duke in 100/719. The Frankish Kingdom ruled over a considerable amount of Western Europe, larger perhaps than any single one of the multiplicity of states covering the Indian subcontinent. But it was at the same time a loosely joined proto-feudal state, without cities and with local barons actually exercising a great deal of independence.[80] As a result, it would never have been easy to conquer, even under the best of circumstances.

The Muslims' contact with the Franks came later than that with most of their other adversaries. It first occurred in 100/719 when the Muslims crossed the eastern end of the Pyrenees to take possession of Septimania, a province which had belonged to Spain's Gothic kings for centuries. This advance made the Muslims neighbors of Duke Odo (Eudo) of Aquitaine. Basing themselves in Narbonne, they proceeded to attack the duke's territory, besieging Toulouse in Dhū al-Ḥijja 102/June 721. Here they suffered a severe defeat, however, in which the Muslim governor of Spain was killed.[81] This reverse indicated that even on this remote frontier, the traditional policy of military advance was going to face a hard test.

The Berbers

The situation of the North African Berbers was unlike that of any of the caliphate's other adversaries whom we have already met. This is because the Berbers straddle the definitions of internal and external opponents. Viewed as part of the Muslim body politic, their situation was quite anamalous. They constituted the only ethnic people in Umayyad times to embrace Islam wholesale, aside from the Arabs, yet they consistently proved the most persistent and troublesome rebels. Perhaps it would be more profitable to view them, or at least the opponents of the caliphate among them, as external enemies. Seen in this light, they fit the pattern of several of the caliphate's other enemies: a people without any centers to capture, or fancy hierarchical organization to easily overthrow, or cities rich with loot to plunder, and who as a consequence required many difficult, unrewarding campaigns to overcome. The only difference was that, as Muslims, they felt doubly aggrieved by the denial of their rights, which they knew about perfectly well, whatever else they may have known about Islam.

Although some of the sources aver that all the Berbers had become Muslims by the time of Hishām,[82] it is very doubtful that this was the case. More probably the area of Tunisia and some of the coastal towns farther west were the quickest to submit and join Islam. After all, these areas had been held by the Byzantines and were more accustomed to a settled rule. On the other hand, those areas of the distant High Atlas which had never been touched even by the Roman Empire at its height and had hardly been seen by the Arabs except in a couple of sweeps through their main valleys, probably remained fully outside the bounds of the caliphate, whatever its claims that they were included within them. This would put the efforts of 'Ubayd Allāh b. al-Ḥabḥāb to subdue those more remote areas in a different light, for they would then represent a continuation of the conquests rather than the supression of rebels. Nevertheless, it must be admitted that the Berber leadership in these wars was wholly Islamic, although *khārijī*.

In particular, it was the terrain of North Africa that gave the caliphate its worst strategic problems in this quarter. From Tunisia westward, North Africa seems like an endless succession of difficult mountain ranges interspersed with a few relatively small plains. The task of initially conquering, let alone holding and pacifying, such a region was enormous and was one that even the Romans had balked at undertaking, for their forward lines had enclosed only Tunisia, eastern Algeria, and a little bit of Morocco. Without considerable cooperation from significant elements among the native population, the effort could scarcely be contemplated.

That help had been forthcoming when the Berbers embraced Islam, however little they may have understood of its nuances. Not only had North Africa effectively joined the Islamic state, except perhaps for its more remote regions, but Spain was also conquered with the Berbers' help. As their just reward, the Berber troops expected to be treated on an equal footing with their Arab comrades. That had seemed to be in the offing under 'Umar II. But Yazīd II's governor, Yazīd b. Abī Muslim, attempted to treat them like conquered subjects and to revert to levying the *jizya* from them in both cash and persons, probably mostly the latter. His murder in 102/721 at the hands of his outraged Berber guard bode most ominously for the future, though the province had returned to an appearance of calm before the outset of Hishām's reign.[83]

Other Parts of Africa: Nubia and Abyssinia

Two other fronts in Africa had seen some activity earlier but were quiescent under Hishām. The first of these was the Nile frontier above Aswān, inhabited by Christian Nubians, who gave the caliphate little trouble and in return were seldom bothered by it after the campaign of 31/652, when a tribute of slaves was imposed on them. However, it is unclear how regularly the terms of this truce (*hudna*) were enforced, as another report states that it broke down in the very next year and was restored again as late as the reign of al-Mahdī (158–69/775–85).[84] The fact that 'Umar II confirmed the pact suggests that it had not always been in force.[85] Nevertheless, no further campaigns are noted. According to al-Balādhurī, the reason for the Nubians' immunity from the regular *jihād* was their extreme fierceness in war.[86] Probably more important was the difficulty of provisioning an army in the Nubians' extremely arid and desolate country. There the Nile Valley narrowed[87] to a canyon with only a few patches of plain wide enough for agriculture here and there, while the many Nile cataracts prevented navigation above Aswān. Nor was much booty to be expected in that quarter.

Second was the sporadically active overseas front of Abyssinia, which, despite its close proximity to Arabia and the holy cities, also did not face any concerted Muslim military campaign. This has been attributed to friendly relations that long persisted because the Abyssinians had given refuge to the early Muslims, and the Prophet, in response, had forbidden *jihād* against them.[88] However, this is scarcely possible, as war with Abyssinia had occurred intermittently, and the caliphate would hardly have returned to peaceful relations without obtaining a total victory once war had commenced.

In particular, the Abyssinians are said to have raided the Hijāz coast as early as the time of the Prophet in the year 9/630,[89] and 'Alqama b. Mujazzaz is said to have been killed on a counterraid in 20/641 or 31/652, after which 'Umar I forbade overseas expeditions due to the danger.[90] This is the only reason given in the sources for Abyssinia's immunity, and it probably is the most logical one, coupled with the fact that Abyssinia was also a mountain fastness, the type of terrain the Muslim warriors were least enthusiastic to take on. A further reason not to attack Abyssinia could have been the lack of any large concentration of Muslim forces in a nearby *miṣr* on the opposite shore of the Red Sea. The whole momentum of Muslim expansion rolled forth toward the north, west, and east out Arabia. Abyssinia was not in its path.

In Muslim eyes, Abyssinia may have seemed isolated and lacking in strategic importance. Almost all other warfronts were strategically connected with others. From France to India, the caliphate faced adversaries on the north side. In the struggle for strategic position, even difficult mountain fronts might become important. Thus, the Muslim campaigns in distant North Africa struck, first of all, at the caliphate's chief nemesis, the Byzantine empire, while control of Zābulistān would round out the eastern frontier and eliminate a dangerous salient that could be a staging area for opponents seeking to drive the Muslims from both Sind and Transoxiana. Abyssinia, isolated and alone, was not particularly dangerous and thus did not warrant immediate attention.

On the other hand, the apparent rareness of Muslim clashes with Abyssinia may simply reflect a dearth of source material. Muslim disinterest, owing to a lack of success on that front, coupled with a complete lack of Ethiopian sources for so early a period, may have left some expeditions unrecorded. The Abyssinian port of Adulis may have suffered ruin and eclipse during this period as a result of one of these. The one certain instance of such warfare is the surprise Abyssinian sack of Jidda in 83/702, which seems to have provoked the Muslims to occupy the Dahlak Islands.[91]

∴ 6 ∴

The Beginning of the Mili Crisis 105–11/724–29

The Building Crisis

When Hishām became caliph in Sha'bān 105/January 724, considerable military struggles already were taking place on most fronts. Though the perpetual war with the Byzantines now burned only slowly, serious warfare was going on with the Khazars in the Caucasus as well as with the new Turgesh power in Transoxiana. In addition, the cancellation of 'Umar II's reforms favoring the *mawālī* had provoked protests and actual revolts in North Africa, Transoxiana, and Sind, the latter of which had only just been recovered by the caliphate at the beginning of Hishām's reign. However, defeats suffered under Yazīd II in the Caucasus, Transoxiana, and Sind had already been avenged in that caliph's reign, and the Muslim armies were finally poised everywhere to resume the cherished offensive policy. The first six years of Hishām's reign witnessed continuous, tedious campaigning on the external fronts as well as a fair amount of internal difficulties. But by the end of 111/729, the caliphal armies, though they had managed to avoid total disaster, had wearied from the continuous campaigning and were, if anything, in a worse position than they had been at the outset of the reign.

The Byzantine Front 105–11/724–9

Until the reign of 'Umar II, the Byzantine front had generally been the pre-eminent war theater for the Umayyad caliphate, both because Byzantium was the largest and probably the richest and most powerful state bordering the caliphate and because the Byzantine border fronted directly on the Umayyads' metropolitan province of Syria.[1] After the catastrophe of the failed second siege of Constantinople of 98–99/717–18, however, the Umayyads for the time being abandoned any hopes they may have had of conquering the Byzantines and directed most of their energies elsewhere. This remained true even when the advocates of expansion came back to power under Yazīd II.

Nevertheless, the renewed policy of expansion was applied on the Byzantine front as well, albeit to a lesser extent than it had been in earlier times. Now the policy was expressed more in the form of raids seeking booty than in any serious attempts at conquest, as no attempt seems to have been made to hold on to any captured territory beyond the Taurus mountains under Yazīd II or Hishām. This might have owed to the difficulties and expense involved in trying to hold onto any such conquests, more than an unwillingness to undertake them at all.

Usually, the Muslim expeditions into Anatolia occurred with great regularity every summer. Frequently, there were two separate summer expeditions. One of these, known as "the expedition on the left" owing to its muster point being near the left end of the Muslim border with the Byzantines, departed from Kilikia and consisted of troops from Ḥimṣ and possibly Qinnasrīn (*al-ṣā'ifa al-yusrā* or *al-ṣughrā*). The other summer expedition, called "that of the right" since its base was farther to the right on the border, mustered at Malaṭyā and consisted of Jazīrans (*al-ṣā'ifa al-yumnā* or *al-kubrā*).[2] The latter, as indicated by its alternative name, seems to have been the larger of the two, suggesting that the Jazīran troops were more numerous than the Syrians on this front.[3] Sometimes a naval expedition was added, though the scene of most naval activity now moved to the West Mediterranean. There was also supposed to be an annual winter expedition,[4] though this does not always seem to have been undertaken in this period.

The general picture of the areas of Anatolia raided by the Muslims accords with the land-based nature of their power in the Mediterranean region. While the coastal areas of the south, the west, and especially the north of the peninsula were left virtually untouched, the central plain and its adjoining valleys were systematically devastated. As more and more towns were devastated, those left containing any worthwhile quantities of booty became harder to find. Rarely was a town devastated twice, which shows that once one was ruined, it did not immediately recover.[5] As the Muslim expeditions ranged over ever wider areas, much of the population of central Anatolia may have fled. As a result, the Muslims were drawn by the ease of their passage through deserted countryside to attack farther and farther west. Such deep penetration tended to get them too far from their bases, threatening them with renewed disaster despite the lessons of Constantinople. On the other hand, the Byzantine Empire reacted rather supinely, as if it had no military forces left at all. This was the result of a studied and deliberate defensive policy rather than actual impotence, however, for the countryside was studded with fortresses.[6]

Under Yazīd II, summer raiding was renewed by al-'Abbās b. al-Walīd I. He invaded Paphlagonia, is said to have carried off twenty thousand captives, and took Dabasa, probably the Byzantine Thebasa, in 102/721. In the same year, 'Umar b. Hubayra, representing the Jazīrans and in command of the right flank of the front, defeated the Byzantines in Armenia IV, taking seven hundred prisoners.[7] In 103/722, Marwān b. Muḥammad led the greater of the two summer expeditions, while 'Uthmān b. Ḥayyān al-Murrī led the lesser. They succeeded in taking a fortress, apparently Dalisandos in Kilikia. Al-'Abbās b. al-Walīd I is again reported to have campaigned as well, suffering losses among the raiding parties.[8] Perhaps he carried on a winter campaign. In 104/723, 'Uthmān b. Ḥayyān al-Murrī led the left and 'Abd al-Raḥmān b. Salīm al-Kalbī led the right summer expedition, taking Sibora[9] in Armenia I and Qaysara, the latter a fortress and thus probably not the city of Kaisareia Mazaka in Cappadocia.[10] In 105/724, Marwān b. Muḥammad is reported to have commanded the summer expedition on the right and to have captured Qūniya, which is Ikonion, and Kamakh, the Greek Kamakhon.[11] There is mention of a raid by al-'Abbās b. al-Walīd which occurred in 104–05/722–23 and took a fortress called Shīza or Sīza, but this could be a repeat of one of al-'Abbās's earlier raids, as it seems unlikely that he would have undertaken as many as three in Yazīd II's short reign.[12] Most of the expeditions under Yazīd II seem to have taken place near the border, revealing a pattern of trying to reduce the Byzantine frontier defences to open up the interior for raiding and conquest. However, their importance was perhaps not too great, for the Byzantine historian Theophanes does not notice any of them except the last, which was a disaster for the Muslims.

Under Hishām, the expeditions continued and increased somewhat in importance. In 106/724, Marwān b. Muḥammad commanded the summer expedition on the right, consisting of Jazīran and Syrian troops, and captured and destroyed a Byzantine fortress called Mawāsā, near Malaṭyā on the Upper Euphrates.[13] The caliph's brother Sa'īd b. 'Abd al-Malik also led an expedition against the Byzantines consisting of Syrians, probably the summer left flank, but suffered large losses.[14] Apparently, the lost troops were in a detachment under Kathīr b. Rabī'a which was annihilated, though Kathīr himself escaped with a few others.[15] Al-Ya'qūbī's lone claim that the caliph's son Mu'āwiya b. Hishām led the summer campaign of 106/724 is probably only a doublet of his actual campaign in the following year.[16]

In 107/725, Muʿāwiya b. Hishām led a huge summer expedition including four thousand Ḥijāzī conscripts as well as a special force of *mawālī* called the Waḍḍāḥiyya, and penetrated deeply into Anatolia, taking many fortified places and captives, devastating the land, and finally reaching as far as Dorylaion. At the same time, the Jazīran Maymūn b. Mihrān, the *mawlā* of the Naṣr, led a sea expedition to Cyprus. In the same year, Maslama b. ʿAbd al-Malik embarked on a winter expedition from Malaṭyā, taking Kaisareia Mazaka, the capital of Cappadocia, by storm on 4 Ramaḍan 107/13 January 726. This last expedition is noted by many sources and appears to have been a signal success.[17]

In 108/726, Maslama b. ʿAbd al-Malik led the summer expedition on the right, while ʿĀṣim b. ʿAbd Allāh b. Yazīd al-Hilālī, a Jazīran general, led that on the left. Hishām's uncle Ibrāhīm b. Hishām, though governor of al-Madīna, is also reported to have campaigned against the Byzantines in this year and to have taken one of their fortresses.[18] An expedition by Muʿāwiya in this year is also reported by Syrian sources to have taken many fortresses and returned with many captives.[19] If so, it must have been a winter raid.

In the winter campaign of 109/727, Muʿāwiya penetrated again deep into Anatolia. ʿAbd Allāh b. ʿAmr (or ʿAmr b. ʿAbd Allāh)[20] al-Baṭṭāl, in charge of Muʿāwiya's vanguard, captured the important city of Gangra in Paphlagonia, sacking it and destroying its walls. Then, the forces under Muʿāwiya, taking the road to the west captured the fortress of Ateous or Ṭataya in Bithynia on the Sangarios River at or near the modern Geyve. Troops from Antioch in Muʿāwiya's forces are said to have suffered considerable losses. After that, the Muslims went on a little farther to besiege the famous and important city of Nikaia for forty days, the Byzantine inhabitants fleeing before them in their ships. However, the ships came back with reinforcements which saved the city. The importance of the expedition is confirmed by the detailed accounts of it in Christian sources.[21] For the same year, Ibn Khayyāṭ reports the capture of al-ʿAṭāsīn or al-Ghaṭāsīn, which appears to be an unidentified place east of Nakoleia in Phrygia.[22] In the same year, ʿAbd Allāh b. ʿUqba b. Nāfiʿ al-Fihrī campaigned by sea, showing that the Muslims were now rebuilding their naval strength in the East Mediterranean.[23] But al-Fihrī's expedition was probably of limited scope.

These expeditions signal a considerable intensification of military effort on this front, owing to their size and to their attacks on the important cities of Nikaia and Kaisareia. The depth of

Mu'āwiya's successful penetration as far as Nikaia, virtually on the doorstep of Constantinople, is especially spectacular. Unfortunately for the caliph's offensive policy, his son's expedition was to prove to be a unique achievement without lasting results, as Umayyad armies never would push so deep into Anatolia again. These two expeditions of 109/727–28 were undertaken during a lull when troops were not needed on most other fronts, especially the vital Caucasus, which was defended by the same Syro-Jazīran army that regularly fought the Byzantines.

In 110/728, Mu'āwiya b. Hishām captured the two fortresses of Semalouos or Ṣamāluh and al-Mawa.[24] Either 'Abd Allāh b. 'Uqba al-Fihrī or 'Abd al-Raḥmān b. Mu'āwiya b. Ḥudayj al-Sakūnī led the summer seaborne expedition.[25]

In 111/729, Sa'īd b. Hishām led the summer expedition on the right, penetrating to, but presumably not taking, Kaisareia Mazaka, while his brother Mu'āwiya b. Hishām led the summer campaign on the left and was able to return safely. This wording suggests that his campaign may not have been a great success.[26] 'Abd Allāh b. Abī Maryam, the *mawlā* of the Anṣār, led the seaborne expedition.[27] Three successive seaborne expeditions suggest that Muslim naval power had somewhat recovered since the debacle at Constantinople, though their extent is unknown and no brilliant exploits are recorded.

Through this period, the Muslims certainly retained the initiative on the Byzantine front, showing surprising vigor in their ability to keep mounting both summer and winter campaigns. But few of these seem to have been a striking success, with the notable exceptions of the captures of Kaisareia and Gangra by Maslama and al-Baṭṭāl respectively. Indeed, most of the Muslim expeditions we have information about seem to have attacked obscure and today mostly unidentifiable fortresses near the frontier. After the failure of the great Constantinople expedition and with more troops sent to other fronts, more modest targets nearer at hand may have seemed better prospects.[28] But these more modest goals may have appeared unrewarding for the remaining troops that had to fight for them, though it is also likely that the long struggle with the caliphate's traditional main adversary may have helped keep the spirit of *jihād* alive on this front longer than on others.

The Caucasus 105–11/724–29

The Caucasus bid to be the worst of the various warfronts the Muslims faced at the outset of Hishām's reign, for he found it already aflame. As in Transoxiana, the Muslims had suffered a defeat in the Caucasus under Yazīd II. In this battle, a large Khazar army had routed the forces of the Ḥimṣī Miʿlaq b. Ṣaffār al-Bahrānī, the governor of Ādharbayjān and Armenia, in Ramaḍān 103/February–March 722 in Armenia, south of the Caucasus and therefore inside the boundaries of the caliphate. As the Muslims complained of the severity of the winter, it seems that this battle was the culmination of a winter war rather than the beginning of an early spring campaign. What was most significant about this defeat, however, was that severe losses of Syrian troops were involved, for the Caucasus front had been entrusted to the Syrians.[29]

To avenge the reverse, another army of Syrians, totalling at least twenty-five thousand was sent marching to the rescue in 104/722 under the famous al-Jarrāḥ b. ʿAbd Allāh al-Ḥakamī, another Syrian Yamanī who replaced Miʿlaq as governor. Al-Jarrāḥ not only recovered al-Bāb and drove the Khazars north of the Caucasus, but also carried the war into their homeland there, taking their capital of Balanjar on 3 Rabīʿ al-Awwal 104/21 August 722.[30] But the main Khazar forces, apparently forewarned well in advance, highly mobile like the other Turks, and not dependent on cities for supplies, eluded the Muslims and remained in the field, where their threat forced al-Jarrāḥ to withdraw to Warthān to the south of the Caucasus. Another factor in the withdrawal was the lack of pacification of the recently hostile territory around the Caucasus Range that al-Jarrāḥ had left in his rear. Al-Jarrāḥ also felt compelled to ask for additional troops from Yazīd II, which suggests that the campaign may have been less of a success than it is painted by Ibn Aʿtham.[31]

However, it appears that al-Jarrāḥ undertook still another campaign, this time against lands beyond Balanjar, in 104–05/723 before Hishām came to the throne. As this is scarcely noticed by the sources, it cannot have amounted to much.[32] Following this, the Khazars crossed the Caucasus to raid Armenia, but al-Jarrāḥ defeated them in the lands between the Kur and Araxes rivers south of the Caucasus in Ramaḍan 105/February 724, in a battle that went on for days.[33] The date of this, similar in season to that of Miʿlaq's defeat, would seem to imply that while the Muslims took the offensive only in summer as a rule, the Khazars, like their Turkish counterparts in Transoxiana, would campaign in any weather.

Though Hishām at first kept al-Jarrāḥ in office and promised him more Syrian troops, he appears not to have sent any, suggesting that the limits of the Syrian army to undertake further campaigns were already being reached. Nevertheless, in 106/724, al-Jarrāḥ took Tiflīs in Georgia and imposed the *kharāj* on its people, granting them a kind of charter in exchange.[34] Though it may not have been the first time the Muslims captured Tiflīs, it was the first time they established their rule there successfully.[35] Then al-Jarrāḥ campaigned against the Alans[36] of the Central Caucasus and imposed the *kharāj* on them too, though the Khazars remained unsubdued. He became the first Muslim commander to return from north of the Caucasus via the Darial Pass.[37] His campaign against the Alans is reminiscent of his contemporary Asad b. 'Abd Allāh's tendency to lead expeditions against smaller peoples in Khurāsān while avoiding a showdown with the major opponent of the Muslims, the Turgesh *khāqān*. However, al-Jarrāḥ's campaign against the Alans was also perhaps part of a strategy of blocking a possible Khazar threat to Muslim Ādharbayjān through Georgia while at the same time opening up the Darial Pass as a second attack route for the Muslims against the Khazars. As the Alans lived astride the Darial Pass, their homeland was very strategically located.

In any event, in 107/725 al-Jarrāḥ was replaced by the caliph's aggressive brother, Maslama b. 'Abd al-Malik.[38] The reason for this step was possibly to quiet the Jazīrans' displeasure at having lost the governorship of the Eastern superprovince to the Yaman tribal grouping in 105/724. Under Yazīd II, the Western superprovince as well as Ādharbayjān and Armenia had been held by Syrian Yamanīs while the East had been under the Jazīrans. Now, after removing the Jazīrans from the East, Hishām may have returned Ādharbayjān and Armenia to their control to quiet their complaints and to maintain his official neutrality with regard to the different provincial and tribal army groups. However, uniting Ādharbayjān and Armenia to al-Jazīra eventually had the unfortunate effect of creating on the very border of metropolitan Syria a strong provincial power base which could become a threat to the central authority.

At the time, however, Maslama still found substantial Syrian Yamanī forces on the Caucasus front. Therefore, while he himself remained on the Byzantine front, he delegated the actual campaigning in the Caucasus to the Yamanī al-Ḥārith b. 'Amr al-Ṭā'ī, who only attacked districts in the Kur valley south of the Caucasus,[39] al-Lakz and Khasmadān,[40] in 107/725. As with al-Jarrāḥ's campaign against the Alans, al-Ḥārith's effort seems to represent the consolidationist policy of the Yaman rather than the aggressive expansionism espoused by the Muḍar. Of course, al-Ḥārith achieved nothing against the Khazars by such mopping up work behind the front lines.

Part of the reason for al-Ḥārith's relative inactivity at this time may have been the census of the inhabitants of Armenia and the survey of its lands, which was being carried out for tax purposes as part of an empirewide reassessment. This was followed by a substantial increase in the level of taxation.[41] There is evidence for a reassessment and subsequent tax increase about this time in Spain and France (c.106–07/724–25), Egypt (106/724), and Khurāsān (c. 106–07/724–25)[42] as well as in Armenia. These steps were ordained from the top and reveal the caliphate's search for more money to finance its extensive military campaigns. They also indicate Hishām's continued complete adherence to the traditional policy of the expansion of the caliphate's domains.

But as far as the Caucasus was concerned, the campaign of the very next year, 108/726, suddenly revealed the gravity of the situation, as the Khazars are found once more south of the Caucasus, ravaging Ādharbayjān and even besieging the city of Warthān south of the Araxes, despite the victories claimed over them in the previous years. Al-Ḥārith is said to have defeated them, driving them back across the Araxes. But the Khazars were not subdued, and their use of mangonels in the seige shows that we are dealing with a militarily sophisticated nation, not a mere disorganized pack of barbarians.[43] Thus the Muslims seem to have been put on the defensive again.

In 109/727, the same year in which Ashras al-Sulamī began his difficult career as governor of Khurāsān, the situation in Ādharbayjān had deteriorated enough for Maslama to take the field in person. Presumably, the great general brought fresh troops with him. If so, they were probably Qaysī Jazīrans and Qinnasrīnīs. In accordance with his impetuous nature, he immediately went on the offensive, recovering the Darial Pass, which had been lost, and crossed the Caucasus to fight the Khazars in their homeland, before returning to winter in Ādharbayjān.[44]

But it appears that the efforts of the great Maslama had made little impression, for in 110/728 the performance had to be repeated. However, this new campaign seems to have turned into a near disaster, like the Battles of Baykand and Kamarja in Khurāsān in the same year. Before finally 'defeating' the Khazar *khāqān* on 7 Jumādā II 110/17 September 728, or perhaps rather only breaking off the engagement, Maslama's forces are said to have fought for a month or forty days. The main recollection of the Muslims in this campaign was that of slogging miserably through the mud while it rained continuously. Maslama's army was also ambushed as he retreated across the Darial Pass. Michael the Syrian even says the Muslims abandoned their baggage train and fled. In both campaigns of 109/727 and 110/728, Maslama is said to have been faced by the Khazar *khāqān* himself, campaigning in person for the first time, which would show the intensification of the struggle, just as in Khurāsān at the same time. That Maslama's persistent campaigning was hardly a success is indicated by the fact that the Khazars invaded Muslim Ādharbayjān again in 111/729, when al-Ḥārith b. 'Amr again repulsed them.[45]

At this juncture, Maslama was removed from office by Hishām, who may have been influenced by the fallout from his brother's 'victory' over the Khazars in 110/728 and felt that the time had come to retire the old general. On Maslama's watch, the Muslim position had again deteriorated on the Caucasus front. Years of campaigning against the Khazars had brought no tangible result. The Muslim sources are silent about large amounts of booty and captives, as well as unusually reticent about the victories claimed. It is of great significance that at the outset of Hishām's reign the Muslims were in a strong position and firmly in control of all the territory up to the Caucasus, at least in eastern Transcaucasia. But, by 111/729, despite the presence of Maslama and the repeated dispatch of more troops, the Muslims had been put on the defensive and pushed back to Ādharbayjān. On the Caucasus front, the situation was, if anything, graver and probably more worrisome to the caliph by 111/729 than that in Transoxiana, owing especially to the former's closer proximity to Syria and Iraq.

Transoxiana 105–11/724–29

Transoxiana is the front whose campaigns we are best informed about, thanks to the care with which the 'Abbāsids preserved the traditions of the province on which their power was based. The relatively greater amount of information available for Transoxiana does not necessarily mean that it was the most menacing front, however. Indeed, it is likely that conditions prevailing there were also generally the rule on other fronts. Nevertheless, a serious challenge to the Muslim armies under Hishām developed on the Transoxianan front. Under Yazīd II, attempts to reimpose the *jizya* on the new Muslims in Transoxiana had so angered the latter that some of them had rebelled against the Muslim government. Though these had been brought to heel by a severe campaign, the Transoxianans also seem to have repeated their appeals to the Turgesh *khāqān*, which they had first made a few years earlier, to come to save them from the Muslims.[46]

From this point on, it was the Turgesh Turkish Khanate that led the battle against the Muslims in Transoxiana, though the local princes usually sided with the Turks and offered them some help. The Turkish onslaught, which began in 102/720 with the sudden, unexpected attack on the outpost of Qaṣr al-Bāhilī,[47] probably near Samarqand, lasted until the defeat of Sülü in 119/737. The continuous warfare of this long period was both difficult and unrewarding from the Muslims' point of view. Since the Turks were horse-riding nomads operating in arid plains, they had a decided advantage in mobility that is noted by the Muslim authors for several battles in which the Turks surprised the Arabs by appearing out of nowhere or by overtaking them. This was despite the fact that the Arabs themselves had a significant horse cavalry divided into light (*mujarrada*) and armored units (*mujaffafa*). The nomadic character of the Turks also meant that there was little booty to be had even in case of victory, except what the Turks may already have plundered from the Muslims or their subjects. Furthermore, the nomadic Turks could not be expected to provide any significant amount of tax money if the Muslims ever did succeed in conquering them.

Nevertheless, at first the Muslims reacted with characteristic alacrity to the Turkish challenge. The garrison at Qaṣr al-Bāhilī was evacuated with difficulty and Sa'īd b. 'Amr al-Ḥarashī, a famous general from Qinnasrīn, was appointed to be the new governor of Khurāsān. Sa'īd led the Muslims to the offensive, crushing the revolt of the Sughdīs in the vicinity of Samarqand and then carrying his arms to the Jaxartes to conquer the large town of Khujanda (103/722), which had previously submitted to Qutayba b. Muslim but then had been lost. In this way, Sa'īd nearly restored the boundaries reached by Qutayba, except perhaps for the far district of Farghāna, which nevertheless probably made at least a formal submission. But this he achieved only at the cost of alienating the Sughdīs, who had been suppressed by force and massacre.[48]

As Sa'īd would not forward sufficient tax money to Iraq, the governor of the Iraqi superprovince, 'Umar b. Hubayra, replaced him with Muslim b. Sa'īd al-Kilābī (104–06/723–25),[49] of the Baṣran branch of a subtribe based mainly in al-Jazīra. Muslim was thus in office when Hishām began to reign. At the end of 105/724, Muslim led his forces out to campaign beyond the Jaxartes into Farghāna. At the outset, there was some difficulty getting the troops out to campaign, especially the Yaman faction, of whom four thousand refused to set out with Muslim in anticipation of his dismissal by the new governor of the Eastern superprovince, Khālid b. 'Abd Allāh al-Qasrī.[50] Muslim's army ran straight into major Turkish forces while besieging the main city of Farghāna.[51]

What followed was the classic disaster known as the Day of

Sijistān 105–08/724–27

A minor front that had never ceased to give the caliphate problems was that facing the Zunbīl of Zābulistān from the Muslim province of Sijistān. While the Zunbīl posed no offensive threat to the caliphate, the high mountain fastnesses of his principality in the Hindū Kush of eastern Afghanistan constituted some of the most forbidding terrain faced by the Muslim armies. Nevertheless, the caliphate had often committed large forces before in its attempts to subdue the Zunbīl. These had never achieved much success, and the expeditions of 61/681, 74/693, and especially 78/697 had ended in notable disasters. In several cases, the Muslims had even had to pay tribute or ransom to the Zunbīl![62] Without doubt, the serious revolt of Ibn al-Ash'ath, which began in the Kūfan army sent to Sijistān in 79/698, was partly motivated by the feeling of the troops that the notorious governor of Iraq, al-Ḥajjāj, by sending them against the Zunbīl, was putting them on a suicidal mission deliberately in order to destroy them.[63] Even the mighty Qutayba b. Muslim, the conqueror of Transoxiana, had accepted the rather minimal tribute offer by the Zunbīl and preferred not to fight, calling Sijistān an "ill-omened front."[64]

However, by Hishām's reign, the Sijistān front had long ceased to be so volatile, owing to the wise decision to give up trying to conquer so impregnable an area. No fighting had occurred for a generation. Unfortunately, Muslim quiescence led the Zunbīl to refuse sarcastically to pay even a token tribute.[65] Such a situation was theoretically intolerable, as it had been customary for the caliphate to make war on whoever would not accept Islam or pay tribute. Not only did the idol-worshipping Zunbīl refuse to pay tribute, but he had also practically annihilated several Muslim armies without suffering much in return. Such a situation clearly called for severe retribution, especially with the expansionist party back in power.

Nonetheless, under Yazīd II, nothing was done to exact such retribution, as no additional forces were yet available to send to Sijistān. The provincial governors continued to belong to either the Tamīm or the Rabī'a, the two major tribal groupings that had settled in Sijistān.[66] As in other provinces, the local Muslims who knew how hard it would be to subdue the Zunbīl were the least enthusiastic to carry out such a forbidding assignment. As long as they or their tribal kin from elsewhere held the governorship, no aggressive policy could be implemented.

But as soon as Hishām became caliph, the policy began to

change. Apparently Khālid al-Qasrī in Iraq first appointed as governor in 106/724 Ḥīla b. Ḥammād al-Ghaṭafānī, who was most likely a Syrian. Very likely, he came to the province accompanied by at least a guard consisting of his own tribesmen. In early 107/spring 725, Khālid replaced Ḥīla with Yazīd b. al-Ghurayf al-Hamdānī, who was a Syrian from the *jund* of al-Urdunn.. Yazīd at last resumed the campaigns against the Zunbīl by sending an army under Bilāl b. Abī Kabsha, but it returned without obtaining anything from the Zunbīl. However, at least he avoided a repetition of earlier disasters.[67]

Yazīd was most unpopular among the Arabs settled in Sijistān.[68] His unpopularity may have been caused by his trying to impose a standard Umayyad provincial system, including more efficient taxation, on the unruly province. But it is at least equally possible that the local troops did not want to face the Zunbīl because they knew how unprofitable and deadly any encounters with that enemy were likely to be. Therefore, Yazīd's resumption of the war with that enemy may have been responsible for his unpopularity.

Whatever the case, owing to the tension in the province, Yazīd's security chief was assassinated by a band of *khawārij*, who also slew as many of his men as they could. This was probably politically rather than religiously motivated, however much it may have been perceived in a religious light, especially if the victims were Syrians or other outsiders to the province. Yazīd was either dismissed or perished in the revolt, while the caliphate lost control of the province to the *khawārij*. In 108/726, Khalid sent out a new governor, al-Aṣfaḥ b. 'Abd Allāh al-Kalbī, to restore order.[69] Al-Aṣfaḥ, a Syrian like his two predecessors, probably was accompanied by at least some Syrian troops to fulfill his mission.

Though Sijistān was a relatively minor province, it caused quite a bit of trouble for the Umayyad caliphs. More than that, it was to some extent a bellwether for the future, as its troubles prefigured those of Khurāsān and other areas. Expansionist policy first led to hardship for local troops, who became increasingly reluctant to fight against external enemies. Their refusal forced the introduction of some Syrian troops to stiffen the backbone of the locals, but this step also led to a new dimension of tribal rivalry as well as the feeling that the Syrians, who had to obtain their stipends from somewhere, were responsible for mulcting the provincial income that rightly belonged to the locals. Pressure to obtain more tax money also increased on the governors because of the expense of continuous military campaigns. Though the evidence for this process is not great for Sijistān, the increasing troubles there suggest that these are reasons for provincial dissatisfaction that one should keep in mind when looking at developments in other provinces.

India 104–08/723–27

Though the Indian front has been but little considered by historians, it actually had great importance, especially during the reign of Hishām. But the course of the Muslim campaigns there is difficult to trace comprehensively, owing both to the overall incompleteness of the information in the sources, which leaves one feeling that some expeditions may have been lost to history altogether, as well as to the lack of chronological data for the campaigns which are reported. Nevertheless, it is possible to establish that the Muslims enjoyed a large measure of success early in Hishām's reign, perhaps even larger than the Muslim sources would mostly seem to imply. Later, however, the same problems that plagued them elsewhere also hurt them on the Indian front.

At first, the situation in Sind did not look promising for renewed military conquest, as a peaceful policy had taken over. 'Umar II's governor, 'Amr b. Muslim al-Bahili, is reported to have campaigned, perhaps in the area of Jullundur, where Jaysinh[70] b. Dāhir, the heir of the former Chach dynasty of Sind, was staying.[71] Soon thereafter, when 'Umar II implemented his reconciliation policy toward non-Arab Muslims, he restored the lands on the east bank of the Mihrān River, the Indus' central branch, to Jaysinh's rule and granted him virtual taxfree autonomy in exchange for his embracing Islam. Thus, the Arabs continued their direct rule only of the lands west of the Mihrān. These steps would appear consonant with 'Umar II's retrenchment policy of withdrawing from areas that could be cut off from behind by naval attack.[72]

As soon as 'Umar II had died, the rebel Yazīd b. al-Muhallab seized the province, appointing Waddā' b. Ḥumayd al-Azdī as governor (101/720). But, after the collapse of Ibn al-Muhallab's revolt, Hilāl b. Aḥwaz al-Māzinī quickly recovered the western part of Sind for Yazīd II (102/720), slaying many of the Muhallabids at Qandabīl. Hilāl was succeeded by 'Ubayd Allāh b. 'Alī al-Sulamī, another Jazīran appointed by 'Umar b. Hubayra in 103/721. Nothing whatever is known of al-Sulamī's governorship, except that Jaysinh remained a Muslim at peace with the caliphate but not paying tribute throughout this period. Then, about 104/723, 'Umar b. Hubayra appointed as governor of Sind, al-Junayd b. 'Abd al-

Raḥmān al-Murrī (c. 104–08/723–26), a man who was to leave a lasting impression on Hishām's reign in Sind and Khurāsān, and sent him there with a large army.[73]

On arriving in Sind, al-Junayd first went to Daybul to secure the province's port, on which it mainly depended for communication with the rest of the caliphate,[74] and then marched to the banks of the Mihran River, intending to cross to the east. Jaysinh refused to allow him to pass, considering it a breach of the autonomy guaranteed to him by 'Umar II. Moreover, al-Junayd summoned Jaysinh to pay the *jizya* once more, which the prince also refused, as he was already a Muslim. It was bad enough that the government take the *jizya* from new Muslims elsewhere, but in Sind it was even worse to try to impose it on a considerable kingdom that had for several years been guaranteed the right not to pay it. At this considerable provocation, Jaysinh is said to have renounced Islam and prepared for war, which probably confirmed al-Junayd in the belief that Jaysinh's Islam had been a mere opportunistic sham. Alternatively, this could be a mere justification falsely alleged by al-Junayd or subsequent transmitters of the story. Jaysinh's alleged apostasy occurred about 105–06/724, after the start of Hishām's reign. A war of unknown length ensued. After defeating Jaysinh in a naval battle on the Indus River, al-Junayd captured and executed him. When Jaysinh's brother Chach attempted to go to Iraq to complain about al-Junayd's unfair treatment of the Sindi Muslims, al-Junayd captured him by a ruse and executed him too. The Sindi kingdom east of the Mihrān was again annexed.[75]

Possibly al-Junayd's reconquest of East Sind for the caliphate did not take very long, for al-Junayd next embarked on spectacular invasions of India that must have taken up the rest of his governorship. These invasions should not be considered mere raids, but rather a deliberate attempt on a grand scale to conquer much of Northwest India and Gujarat.[76] In confirmation of this, the sources state that al-Junayd sent out subgovernors (*'ummāl*) to collect taxes in various districts, which shows that permanent conquest was envisioned.[77] Unfortunately, it is impossible to trace these attempted conquests chronologically, so that we will have to deal with them geographically.

Perhaps the first of al-Junayd's efforts was that directed to the north against al-Kīraj, possibly to be identified with Kīra or the Kangra Valley near Dharmsala in the present-day Himachal Pradesh.[78] This area, along with Kashmir, had previously been raided by Muḥammad b. al-Qāsim[79] and 'Amr b. Muslim al-Bāhilī.[80] As no campaigns against places between al-Kīraj and Sind are mentioned by the sources, it must be assumed that these territories, including much of the great plain of Punjab, were regularly a part of Sind and therefore presented no obstacle to al-Junayd's progress. In alliance with the rising kingdom of Kashmir, al-Junayd took the capital of al-Kīraj by storm. This seems to have effectively put an end to the kingdom of al-Kīraj.[81]

However, al-Junayd concentrated most of his efforts farther south in Rajasthan and Gujarat. A justification for his offensive was that both the Gurjara confederacy and the Maitrakas of Saurashtra in Kathiawar had previously paid tribute to Muḥammad b. al-Qasim but then apparently stopped.[82] In Jurz or Gurjaratra, the present-day Rajasthan, al-Junayd attacked and subdued Marmad (Maru-Mala, modern Jaisalmer and North Jodhpur) and al-Baylamān (Bhillamala or Vallamandala, the modern Bhinmal or Barmer in South Rajasthan near Jodhpur), which was the capital of the Gurjara confederacy. In modern Gujarat, he subdued Qaṣṣa (Kaccha, modern Cutch), al-Mandal (near modern Ahmadabad), Dahnaj (unidentified), Surast (Saurashtra in Kathiawar), and Barūṣ or Barunj (Broach). Beyond these, he sent forces as far as Uzayn (Ujjayini), the capital of Mālaba (Mālava or Malwa), in present-day Madhya Pradesh. The Muslims seem not to have captured Ujjayini itself, though they burnt the outer city of Baharīmad nearby.[83]

Al-Junayd's Indian conquests were perhaps even more extensive than this list from Muslim sources would suggest, for it appears from Hindu literature that many of the small kingdoms of South Rajasthan and Gujarat received blows from which they never recovered. Those kingdoms weakened or destroyed include the Bhattis of Jaisalmer, the Gurjaras of Bhillamala, the Mauryas of Chitor, the Guhilots of Mewar, the Kachchhellas of Cutch, the Maitrakas of Saurashtra, and the Gurjaras of Nandipuri near Broach.[84] Others who left no trace may also have succumbed. On the other hand, al-Junayd seems to have striven to erect a new province, as he sent his agents to gather taxes in Marmad, al-Mandal, Dahnaj, Barūṣ or Barunj, Surast, al-Baylamān, and even Mālaba.[85] This means the boundaries of the new province would have included western and southern Rajasthan, nearly all of Gujarat, and a small part of Madhya Pradesh.

It is notable that most of these places are near the sea, none being farther inland than Jodhpur, Chitor, and Ujjayini. Owing to the concentration of reports about Cutch, which was then an island, and various states in or near Kathiawar, which was then more surrounded by water than it is today, it would seem that a good part of the Muslim effort was naval or seaborne. Probably this effort required a considerable reliance on local seafarers from Sind, Cutch, and Kathiawar.[86] The concentration of military effort on areas near the seacoast of western India was later repeated by al-Junayd's successor al-Ḥakam, as we shall see.

Financially, as well, al-Junayd's Indian campaigns were a considerable success for the embattled caliphate. While his claim to have taken six hundred fifty thousand captives must be exaggerated, it nevertheless reveals that India was then a populous and thus probably wealthy land.[87] According to al-Balādhurī, al-Junayd sent forty million dirhams to the treasury, while keeping another forty million in his house, aside from what he distributed as largesse to visitors.[88] Al-Ya'qūbī probably conflates the two figures when he says al-Junayd sent eighty million dirhams to the treasury, besides having distributed many times that amount to the troops as booty.[89] Al-Junayd's generosity and distribution of largesse were long remembered and celebrated in contemporary poetry.[90] Even if we minimize the likely total amount of booty to around two hundred fifty million dirhams, the figure is still stupendous. It must be remembered, though, that most of this went straight to the troops in the field and thus was not at the caliph's disposal.

While the booty gained from al-Junayd's conquests in India may have given a much needed shot of cash to a financially strapped caliphate, the cost of such conquests in both financial and human terms is unknown, but was probably considerable.[91] Therefore, despite al-Junayd's apparently total success, his campaigns may have added yet another strain on the overextended resources of the caliphate. This is perhaps especially true of the manpower resources, for it is likely that many of the Muslim troops campaigning in India were Syrians. As in the case of al-Kīraj, where the Karkota king of Kashmir assisted the Muslims in their conquest,[92] al-Junayd may have relied on subject allies as much as possible, but they proved not to be enough and always required the balancing presence of a large number of Arab troops to keep the enterprise under effective caliphal control.

Al-Junayd's conquests in India were to be the last success of the traditional Umayyad policy of expansion. Because they turned out to be ephemeral, al-Junayd has been deprived of the place among famous Muslim generals he perhaps deserves. Never had a foreign empire based outside the subcontinent region penetrated so far into India before. Though the course of the conquests cannot be established with certainty, they remained at their maximum extent at least until al-Junayd left office about 108/726, so that it was left to his successors to reap the results of his rapid advance.

Egypt 105–11/724–29

Though the province of Egypt was not normally a theater of war at this time, being in the interior of the caliphate, there was one front where some activity did take place. This was against the Cushitic Red Sea people called the Buja or Beja who inhabited the desert east of the Nile Valley extending as far as Ethiopia. Although no military action is directly mentioned, the terms of the cited peace agreement are unfavorable enough for the Buja to discern that military force was probably employed. In any case, the treaty made with the Buja by 'Ubayd Allāh b. al-Ḥabḥāb, the fiscal governor of Egypt, was the first of the Muslims with this people. Interestingly, the treaty is said to have required an annual tribute of slaves, resembling the attempt to reimpose a tribute in slaves implemented by Ibn al-Ḥabḥāb later in North Africa with disastrous results. Why Ibn al-Ḥabḥāb, who was never the political and military governor of Egypt, but only the fiscal one, should have made such a treaty and possibly undertaken a campaign is unclear. But he did enjoy the personal confidence of the caliph Hishām, somewhat put the political governors into the background, and went on to become political governor of North Africa, a very exalted station for a *mawlā*. Perhaps this was because the Buja country contained gold mines directly connected with the treasury.[93]

More immediately, Ibn al-Ḥabḥāb also managed to create a small military problem in Egypt itself by helping to provoke the Coptic revolt of 107/725. The Copts, though frequently complaining about the harshness of the Umayyad governors,[94] had been politically quiescent since the first entry of the Muslims into Egypt. But in 106/724, as a part of Hishām's policy of greater fiscal stringency, Ibn al-Ḥabḥāb raised the land taxes by one twenty-fourth. He also drafted Copts for forced labor, which amounted to another form of taxation. These steps precipitated some of the Copts in the eastern Nile Delta into rebellion for the first time, forcing the political governor, al-Ḥurr b. Yusūf, to stay three months at Dumyāṭ to organize the suppression of the revolt.[95] The revolt evidently failed to reverse the raising of the tax rate, and Ibn al-Ḥabḥāb indeed may have raised taxes again, this time by an eighth, after 112/730, which caused a deflation and added hardships for the Copts.[96]

Probably in response to the revolt, Ibn al-Ḥabḥāb in 109/727 asked Hishām to authorize the settlement of three thousand Muḍari Arabs on the eastern edge of the Delta, in the same area that the Copts had risen, although the reason cited in the sources was Ibn al-Ḥabḥāb's desire to increase the power of the faction with which he was associated. These troops could have been used better elsewhere and added a new burden to the Egyptian provincial treasury, which had to provide for them. Owing to the financial difficulties then present, however, these troops were encouraged to engage in trade on the side in order partially to support themselves. Despite the authorization to raise three thousand troops, by the end of Hishām's reign only fifteen hundred had been settled, all of them new recruits from northern Arabia.[97] This shows the difficulty the caliphate had in raising new forces from the Arab tribes.

The Coptic revolt, small though it was, brought out certain limitations of the caliphal policy of expansion. First, the revolt clearly showed that the government could hardly solve or even palliate its financial problems by raising the taxes of the non-Muslims, for if the latter revolted, the expense of their suppression quickly would exceed any possible gains in the amount of revenue. Second, it revealed that the armies controlling the vast territory of the caliphate were already stretched thin, and that sufficient reserves of manpower might not be available from the traditional sources, in the event of a crisis.

North Africa and the West Mediterranean 105–11/724–29

As we have seen, Muslim North Africa was an anomalous province in the caliphate, in that it contained the first significant group of non-Arab Muslims, the Berbers. These had contributed greatly to the army in the West, especially in the recent conquest of Spain, but also formed the most dangerous potential rebel force inside the body of Islam owing both to their numbers and to the ruggedness of their country. However, their position did not at first differ too much from that of the Transoxianans or the Sindī princes who had nominally embraced Islam, for the Muslim armies used such allied local forces whenever possible. The difference arose from the inability of the relatively few Arabs in North Africa to control the vast numbers of Berbers and from the Berbers' continued enthusiastic adherence to Islam despite discrimination and obstacles that were put in their way.

That the Umayyads would no longer be able to treat North Africa as they treated the other provinces first became manifest in 102/720. At that time, Yazīd II's choice for governor, Yazīd b. Abī Muslim, the *mawlā* of the Thaqīf and former secretary of al-Ḥajjāj, tried to restore the practice of taking the *jizya* from the *mawālī*, as was being done elsewhere in the caliphate, apparently as a matter of centrally dictated policy. But Ibn Abī Muslim was almost immediately assassinated by his Berber guard. Though his discriminatory mistreatment of the guard was the immediate occasion for the assassination, it is clear from the subsequent trend of events in North Africa that the attempt to reimpose the old policy of discrimination toward the *mawālī* in general had been rejected by the Berbers and thus failed.[98]

As a result, a kind of compromise was reached which remained in effect for much of Hishām's reign. First, the caliphal government would henceforth concentrate its control and taxation in North Africa itself on the more easterly and coastal regions that had formerly been part of the Byzantine Empire, and which the Berbers had not regarded as their own territory. This is shown by the fact that places mentioned as having been settled or occupied by Arab troops by late Umayyad times are entirely in the former Byzantine zone.[99] Places outside that zone are mentioned only as centers for Berber rebels.[100]

Second, the Berbers would be left as nominally Muslim and nearly autonomous subject allies who might be called on to provide troops but would pay no capitation tax. This is demonstrated by the total lack of mention in the sources of any actions by or against the Berbers 102–22/720–40. If the Berber's new Muslims had been forced once more to pay tribute during this period, there surely would have appeared some opposition. These policies that were acquiesced in by Yazīd II and continued by Hishām almost exactly resemble 'Umar II's solution in Sind, where the native prince Jaysinh had been left to handle the exposed and difficult part of the province more or less unfettered.

In exchange for their autonomy, the Berbers submitted to Islam and its outward practices, which they probably had to keep up at least while on campaign with the Arab Muslims. Although it appears that the caliphate made some effort to instruct the Berbers in Islam, sufficient teachers were not available. Thus, Mūsā b. Nuṣayr is said to have sent twenty-seven Arabs to teach twelve thousand Berber troops the Qur'ān and the religion of Islam at Tangier, while 'Umar II is said to have provided ten missionary instructors.[101] These would hardly have been sufficient to make much of an impression on the several million people that may have then inhabited North Africa.

However, it seems that at least from the reign of 'Umar II a vigorous campaign to teach the Berbers Islam was carried on by freelance missionaries who were at odds with the Umayyad government. These especially may have included Berbers who were former slaves of famous religious personalities in the Arabia or the East, men who had imbibed the message of Islam deeply at its source. The most dramatic example is 'Ikrima, the Berber *mawlā* of Ibn 'Abbās, who is said to have undertaken missionary activities for Khārijism throughout the caliphate, especially in his North African homeland.[102] However, this only means that he opposed the continuation of the Umayyad family rule, a mainly political question, though viewed in religious terms. Through the preaching of such individuals, the Berbers came to embrace the Islamic identity with great persistence, even if it took a long time for them to absorb the teachings of Islam more thoroughly.

Inside the bounds of the province of Ifrīqiya controlled by the caliphate, the governors tried to enforce the same policies in effect elsewhere, with a special eye to collecting more money. Thus, Bishr b. Ṣafwān al-Kalbī (102–09/721–27) confiscated the property of the family of the earlier conqueror of North Africa and Spain, Mūsā b. Nuṣayr, on the excuse that it was embezzled state property. Bishr was ordered to appear before Yazīd II in 105/723 and set out loaded with 'gifts' for the caliph. After setting out, he found Yazīd II dead and Hishām on the throne. Therefore, he forwarded the gifts to the latter. Hishām appears to have been satisfied with Bishr's gifts and the amount of tribute he had brought, as well as with his performance generally, for he allowed him to return to his province in 106/724.[103] According to one report, his pursuit of the wealth of Ibn Nuṣayr intensified after his return from Hishām. Bishr also typically tortured Ibn Nuṣayr's former appointees in order to make them disgorge their wealth, a method widely used by new governors against their predecessors under the later Umayyads.[104]

After Bishr's death, Hishām appointed 'Ubayda b. 'Abd al-Raḥmān al-Sulamī governor of Ifrīqiya (110/728). 'Ubayda began his rule much as Bishr had, entering al-Qayrawān unannounced, arresting and imprisoning Bishr's officials, fining them, and torturing some of them.[105] Somewhat later, 'Ubayda became furious with his governor of Spain, 'Abd al-Raḥmān b. 'Abd Allāh al-Ghāfiqī, because the latter had captured a particularly valuable piece of furniture inlaid with precious stones, and had smashed it up in order to divide it among the troops with the rest of the booty, while only sending the customary fifth to his superior, the governor of Ifrīqiya. Rather, 'Ubayda thought 'Abd al-Raḥmān should have forwarded so valuable a treasure to him whole.[106] Such apparently greedy behavior as that of Bishr and 'Ubayda, so often repeated, may have resulted from financial difficulties caused by the policy of renewed offensive campaigning on most fronts around the caliphate and thus not necessarily from personal avarice. Not only did the caliph increasingly try to obtain more income from the provinces, but the provincial governors had to look for ways to employ and pay their ever-needy troops.

As the Berber front needed to remain at peace from the Arab point of view, because of the unpalatability and likely unprofitability of a war against the Berbers, the energies of the North African Muslim troops, both Arab and Berber, had to be absorbed elsewhere. The Byzantine-held islands in the West Mediterranean, especially Sicily and Sardinia, presented a convenient and tempting target. Though little is known of Sicily under the Byzantines, apparently it had not been seriously ravaged since the fifth century C.E.[107] Sardinia may have been in a similar state. While the Muslims had been defeated before Constantinople and had to some extent lost control of the sea in the East Mediterranean, their capacity for naval warfare in the West Mediterranean was unimpaired and had been greatly enhanced by their construction of a naval base at Tunis with the help of Egyptian Christians.[108] In addition, attacking Byzantine Sicily and Sardinia would help keep the Byzantines off balance and too busy to think about campaigning against the caliphate's Syrian metropole.

Despite a few earlier raids against Sicily and Sardinia,[109] the campaign against the islands really began in earnest in 102/720 with an expedition to Sicily led by Muḥammad b. Aws al-Anṣārī.[110] After the murder of Ibn Abī Muslim, the campaign against the Byzantine-held islands was fully continued by his successor, Bishr b. Ṣafwān al-Kalbī (102–09/721–27). In 103/721, Yazīd b. Masrūq al-Yaḥṣubī campaigned against Sardinia.[111] 'Amr b. Fātik al-Kalbī led the seaborne expedition of 104/722 against an unknown objective.[112] In 106/724, Muḥammad b. Abī Bakr, the *mawlā* of the Jumaḥ, campaigned against Corsica and Sardinia.[113] Bishr, the governor of Ifrīqiya, himself apparently led the sea campaign of 107/725 against Sicily. Although he took many captives, he lost a great part of his army, which suggests why such expeditions often may have proven to be unprofitable, despite an outward appearance of success.[114] In 108/726, Qutham b. 'Awāna al-Kalbī led the expedition, whose goal is again not specified.[115] In 109/727, Ḥassān b. Muḥammad b. Abī Bakr, the *mawlā* of the Jumaḥ, led the expedition against Sardinia.[116]

From 110/728 the next governor, 'Ubayda b. 'Abd al-Raḥmān al-Sulamī, a Qaysi, intensified the campaign against the Byzantines begun by his Yamanī predecessor. In 110/728, 'Uthmān b. Abī

'Ubayda al-Fihrī, with only seven hundred troops, raided the Sicilian capital of Syracuse itself and is claimed to have captured the Byzantine patrician or governor.[117] But in 111/729, a larger expedition led by al-Mustanīr b. al-Ḥārith al-Ḥarashī (or al-Ḥuraythī) consisting of 180 ships met with disaster. According to the sources, al-Mustanīr tarried too long besieging some place until winter came, whereupon his fleet sank in a storm while trying to return. Only seventeen ships managed to get back safely. 'Ubayda mercilessly punished al-Mustanīr, whose ship had reached Tripoli, for his failure and humiliated him publicly once a week.[118] This is hardly surprising, considering that ships were then, as now, the costliest of all equipment of war.

Thus, as in the Caucasus and Transoxiana, the period we are examining ended on a rather sour note in North Africa as well, despite the many apparently successful raids that had been undertaken in earlier years. Even the successful expeditions had involved considerable expense. While the Muslims kept the initiative throughout, the Byzantines' defensive efforts may have improved with practice, as shown by their ability to hold off al-Mustanīr and delay his return, leading him into a classic military disaster. It is also likely that each successive expedition found less available, movable booty than its predecessor. Most of what could be carried away already had been taken before, while what had been left behind by previous expeditions was by this time better hidden or protected by the inhabitants. It is not clear why the Muslims did not try to settle in Sicily as they had earlier done in Spain. A possible reason is that owing to a lack of manpower they could not even begin to contemplate such a step. Fear of becoming trapped across a broad sea from their North African base may have been another factor. On the other hand, the one bright point in North Africa remained the quiescence of the Berbers. Here alone, the ghost of 'Umar II continued to show the wisdom of his policy.

Spain and the Franks 105–11/724–29

Last, and perhaps least important, of the fronts facing the caliphate under Hishām was that in Spain and France. Though Spain had been quite a prize when it had fallen, those areas that remained unsubdued now consisted of mountain fastnesses in the north where fighting was difficult and unrewarding. Although details are lacking, the governors of this period, nevertheless, probably had to spend much of their time consolidating the conquest of Spain. This is confirmed by the fact that Galicia and the northern mountains had not been pacified yet or perhaps even conquered for the first time, nor were they ever completely subdued.[119]

Otherwise, the next step was across the Pyrenees to France, and it was toward that goal that the Muslim governors of Spain now directed themselves. The Muslim advance in South France, though it may have seemed promising at first, did not accomplish any lasting conquests. Soon after the Pyrenees had been crossed in 101/719 and Narbonne had been captured, the governor al-Samḥ b. Mālik al-Khawlānī was slain before Toulouse by Duke Odo of Aquitaine (Dhū al-Ḥijja 102/June 721). The defeat and death of al-Samḥ stemmed the Muslims' progress westward from Narbonne into Aquitaine.[120]

Al-Samḥ's successor, 'Anbasa b. Suḥaym al-Kalbī (103–07/721–25), had to delay any retaliation for the defeat and al-Samḥ's death, however, for he faced difficulties in Spain itself. Early in his governorship, he had to campaign against the Christian remnants in the mountains of Asturias, where a Gothic leader named Pelayo (Pelagius) was carrying on resistance. Probably in late 103/spring 722, 'Anbasa dispatched an expedition under a certain 'Alqama. According to the main source for these events, the *Chronicle of Alfonso III*, for whom Pelayo is a hero, 'Alqama was defeated and killed.[121] Muslim sources imply rather that Pelayo, though unable to face the Muslim forces in the field and for a time reduced to desperate straits, was a tenacious guerilla fighter whose remote redoubt seemed too insignificant to go after at the time and, hence, was left alone.[122] The conquest of Spain being almost complete, 'Anbasa is also reported to have doubled the amount of *kharāj* payable by the non-Muslims in territories under his control.[123]

Furthermore, 'Anbasa is said to have campaigned vigorously against the 'Romans' (*al-Rūm*).[124] But his only recorded expeditions seem to have taken place near the end of his governorship, one when he took Carcassonne by storm in 107/725.[125] Continuing north, he received the surrender of Nîmes. Captives, who seem to have been a goal in many of these early campaigns, were transferred to Barcelona.[126] His other campaign, if not merely a continuation of the first one, was the farthest-reaching and boldest Muslim raid into France yet. In it, 'Anbasa plundered Autun far up the Rhône Valley (Rabī' II 107/August 725), in alliance with Duke Odo of Aquitaine.[127] Returning from this campaign, 'Anbasa died (Sha'bān 107/November–December 725).[128]

Afterward, 'Anbasa's successor, Yaḥyā b. Salama al-Kalbī (107–09/726–27), did not campaign at all, which suggests that

'Anbasa's campaigning may have been less than a complete success.[129] However, another reason for Yaḥyā's policy was his concentrating on domestic affairs, particularly in forcing the Muslims to return the possessions they had taken unjustly from the Christians. These seem to have been considerable.[130] This naturally could have made him unpopular with the local Muslims. Interestingly, the fact that Yaḥyā was implementing this policy at the western end of the empire at nearly the same time (109/727) that Ashras al-Sulamī was trying to implement a similar policy in the Khurāsān and Transoxiana shows that this was almost certainly a policy approved centrally by Hishām. Likewise, its revocation may have been centrally approved, as indicated by Yaḥyā's removal from office and Ashras' backtracking on it after a short time.

After 'Anbasa's death, the Muslim position in Spain may have begun to suffer some of the same deterioration that was also occurring elsewhere in the caliphate, as shown by the increasing political turmoil that affected the province. In particular, this possibility is reflected in the bewildering succession of governors in the years 107–12/725–30, when six men held the post.[131] All of these held only very brief tenures because of political dissension among the various parties in Spain, which included Berbers as well as Arabs, with the latter subdivided into Muḍar and Yaman factions. There was also rivalry between Syrian and other Arabs.[132] The latter dissension was particularly caused, perhaps, by the efforts of the Umayyad government to establish more effective administrative control over the first conquerors in order to extract more tax money from the province, a policy that was naturally opposed by the local Arabs.[133] Such divisions, which would blaze forth in full brilliance at the end of Hishām's reign, probably helped to curtail campaigning into France. Except possibly for local raids launched by the Arabs of Narbonne, no general campaigns against France took place again until 113/731.[134] Rather, the governor of Spain campaigned in 111/729 against a rebellious Berber leader in the Pyrenees who had made a marriage alliance with Duke Odo of Aquitaine. Although details are sketchy, this effort seems to have gone unrewarded until after 'Abd al-Raḥmān al-Ghāfiqī took office in 112–13/730–31.[135]

Muslim settlement in Spain under Hishām was still new, weak, and divided, while the Frankish front remained a sideshow. Being so far away at the end of the long axis of the caliphate, this front naturally would receive less attention when the other fronts became active and threatening. In any event, the Muslims' first aim in crossing the Pyrenees was probably mainly to secure the territory around Narbonne, which had belonged to the Spanish Gothic kingdom they had succeeded. This was the only territory in France they held for long. Otherwise, despite their few far-ranging raids, the Muslims in France were a long way from even trying to establish a new province, as their brothers were attempting in the far more important theater of India, though they might have eventually tried if they had remained unchecked. Most importantly, the Muslim expeditions into France in this period appear to have been quite costly in view of the deaths of one or two governors on the field of combat there.

7

The Climax of the Military Crisis 112–14/730–32

A Sudden Turn for the Worse

Despite the setbacks of the first six years of Hishām's reign, and despite the tension caused by the continuous military effort, the situation of the caliphate near the end of 111/729 looked far from hopeless. The Byzantine front, source of the most immediate threat, was well under control. The struggles in the Caucasus and Transoxiana, though they had been going somewhat badly, were by no means lost. Western India appeared to be a promising field for further expansion. The Berbers were quiescent, and Spain, if disorderly, was not threatened. Also, there was little internal threat to the caliph's sovereignty.[1] If we consider the large increases in taxation early in Hishām's reign to be signs of financial difficulty,[2] the financial situation probably did not look as good. But it apparently remained under control, for the issue of dirhams continued regularly at the mints as before and there is no sign that the caliphate could not meet its financial obligations.

On the other hand, the troops were still reluctant to remain far from home on long campaigns for extended periods, as we have seen in the cases of those wanting to return from Spain and India. This extended even to the Syrians of the metropolitan province, despite their long loyalty to the Umayyad house and their having benefitted from its generosity in return. Such a situation suggested that a change in military policy, perhaps accompanied by a reform of the military system, would be necessary, but nothing had happened yet to bring such a necessity to the attention of the military leadership and the caliph.

However, in a period of a couple of years, 112–14/730–32, the situation changed dramatically in several military theaters at once, as the caliphate suffered an unprecedented series of unexpectedly disastrous defeats at the hands of its external adversaries for the first time. The fronts affected were India, the Caucasus, Transoxiana,

Asia Minor, and France. These massive defeats actually led to a considerable loss of territory, but their most important impact was on the morale of the troops. In particular, certain provincial armies, especially that of Khurāsān, were heavily hit and subsequently had to be stiffened by reinforcements consisting of Iraqi and Syrian forces. But the Syrians themselves, especially the Yamanīs, also began to be exhausted, as they had to bear many of the casualties as well. This was a chief cause of the thinning of the Syrian Yaman's ranks and the weakening of their will to fight. The Muḍarī Jazīrans, who were responsible for fronts nearer to their own homes, were not as affected.

Incredibly, despite the seriousness of these military disasters, the caliphate went ahead with its traditional policy of perpetual advance until victory, as if little had happened. Probably this caliphal nonchalance has affected the sources, causing them to emphasize internal as opposed to external difficulties, which has led to the latter's importance being overlooked. In fact, it was Umayyads' failure to respond to the clear signs on all sides that broke the regime and precipitated its fall. Even though it could recover somewhat by clinging to its former policy with a grim determination, underlying facts had changed in such a way that required responses which were not forthcoming from the ruling family until too late.

Sijistān 108–14/726–32

The next military catastrophe of Hishām's reign after the Day of Thirst seems to have occurred in the minor province of Sijistān. Few details are available, but that does not mean that the defeat was minor, for the sources often pay little attention to defeats. The new Syrian governor of Sijistān, al-Aṣfaḥ b. ʻAbd Allāh al-Kalbī, embarked almost at once on an ambitious policy of campaigning against the Zunbīl. His first expedition was in 108/726. When he set out for a second time in late 109/727–28, the Sijistānīs who were with him warned him that he should not campaign against the Zunbīl in the winter, especially in the mountain defiles. Al-Aṣfaḥ somewhat arrogantly brushed aside their advice and advanced deep into the mountains. There, according to al-Yaʻqūbī, the Zunbīl surrounded al-Aṣfaḥ in narrow places and totally annihilated his force: "the army was killed; not a single person escaped." However, the more detailed *Ta'rīkh-i Sīstān* reports that al-Aṣfaḥ, though wounded, managed to get back to Sijistān, where he expired. In any case, al-Aṣfaḥ was the first provincial governor to fall in the line of duty under Hishām, but he would not be the last. More importantly, large numbers of Muslims were killed or taken prisoner in the battle, which was a major defeat for the forward policy.[3]

Hearing of the disaster, Khālid al-Qasrī next sent another Yamanī, Muḥammad b. Ḥujr al-Kindī, of a tribe prominent in al-Kūfa but also found elsewhere, to be governor of Sijistān (109–11/728–29). He apparently gave up the war with the Zunbīl and did not campaign. Muḥammad was succeeded in Sha'bān 111/November 729 by 'Abd Allāh b. Abī Burda b. Abī Mūsā al-Ash'arī, of a blue-blooded Baṣran family closely associated with Khālid al-Qasrī.[4] 'Abd Allāh was popular according to the Sijistānī tradition. He constructed a large congregational mosque. But he undertook no campaigns, perhaps because of the continuous activity of the *khawārij*, who gave the province no rest.[5]

Although the Zunbīl was unable, as far as we know, to take advantage of his annihilation of al-Aṣfaḥ's army, the defeat was still a heavy one, and only the first in a series of blows that the caliphate would receive on various fronts in the next few years. Remaining a marginal province for the Islamic state, Sijistān had already caused considerable harm by consuming so many Muslim troops, who in the case of al-Aṣfaḥ's army were also Syrians, without producing any commeasurate return on the caliphate's investment in blood and treasure.

India 108–13/726–31

Apparently the first front to suffer a breakdown, as complete as it was catastrophic, was India, recently the scene of the Umayyad caliphate's latest and last success. As usual for this region, details are sketchy. The victorious governor al-Junayd al-Murrī, having been so successful in conquering Gujarat and part of Rajasthan, as well perhaps as al-Kīraj and Punjab, was appointed in 111/729 to Transoxiana to deal with the deteriorating situation there.[6] That al-Junayd would be entrusted with Transoxiana, which seemed on its way to becoming the worst front for the caliphate, implies that he left India with his conquests undiminished.

After al-Junayd had left, India was entrusted to Tamīm b. Zayd b. Ḥamal al-Qaynī (c. 108–13/726–31), a Syrian Yamanī.[7] His rule must have been secure at the beginning at least, for he either forwarded the eighteen million Ṭāṭarī dirhams that al-Junayd had left in the provincial treasury to Hishām or distributed them immediately to the troops. By this last act or others, he also gained a reputation for generosity.[8]

But trouble was brewing for the Muslims in India, as shown by the story of a Syrian mother's plea to the poet al-Farazdaq to help get her only son back from the Sindi front, where his unit was being kept in the field (*mujammar*). She had already made a request through official channels but had been turned down, and so had no recourse except to the poet. Al-Farazdaq responded by writing a poem requesting Tamīm b. Zayd to send the young man back to his mother. The governor quickly complied with the request. Finding the man was serving in Takkayān (Punjab), he had him sent forthwith to al-Farazdaq.[9] This story contains much interesting information. First, it exemplifies how much the troops hated to be held in the field beyond their assigned year. It shows, especially, how service in India was disliked and the lengths to which some persons might go to avoid it. It also provides our only evidence of a Muslim presence in Punjab under Hishām.[10] This also indicates that the extended Muslim province of Sind was still holding up in the north.

Some time later, complete disaster struck the Muslims in India. Unfortunately, almost no details are available about what happened. The Indians must have revolted, possibly even in Sind, which was the Muslims' main base. Probably the rebels were aided by some of the larger surviving Hindu states in India, which included, in particular, Kanauj of Yasovarman, Malwa under the Gurjara-Pratiharas, and Karnataka under the Chalukyas. After wars of long duration including many campaigns, the Muslim position collapsed entirely. The Muslim troops abandoned all of India except for Cutch and Sind. One gets the impression that the Muslims were not driven out by the Indians. Rather, it appears that most of the troops refused to remain in their posts and insisted on leaving the province, refusing to ever go back.[11] Abandoning even Daybul, on which considerable sums had been spent in order to develop it as a Muslim town, Tamīm, the governor, fled west with the departing troops, only to die at a desert water hole. A grimmer picture could hardly be imagined.[12]

Thus, in a few short years the work of al-Junayd had come to nought and the very continuance of Sind as a province was called into question. Exactly what the Arabs continued to hold is unclear, but they seem to have still held Cutch and probably some fortresses in Sind. Now, however, they faced opponents who knew better how to deal with the Arabs' often successful methods of fighting, especially east of the Thar Desert, where the large Indian kingdoms were determined to resist. Most importantly, besides the huge financial loss implicit in their defeat, the Arab forces had suffered enormous losses in men, many of them Syrians. These losses would be difficult to replace, especially from the strained Syrian manpower pool.

The Caucasus 112–14/730–32

The next military catastrophe befell the Muslims in the Caucasus, where the situation had been deteriorating for some time. After Maslama b. ʻAbd al-Malik was removed from office in 111/729, al-Jarrāḥ b. ʻAbd Allāh al-Ḥakamī was returned to the front as governor of Armenia and Ādharbayjān for the second time, with the hope that he would achieve better results. But unfortunately for the caliphate, he presided over one of the worst disasters of Hishām's reign.

In the campaign of 112/730, we find al-Jarrāḥ crossing through Tiflīs to attack the Khazars via the Darial Pass. Also, he is improbably said to have raided the far-distant Khazar capital of al-Bayḍā' on the Volga. Later, he is at Bardha'a in Arrān on the south side of the Caucasus, to which he may have retreated to hold back the Khazar army under a general named Tharmach.[13] The Khazars either came over the Darial Pass,[14] or by way of the Caspian Gates,[15] or perhaps both. It appears that the Khazars outmanuvered al-Jarrāḥ in the field by managing to get around him and besiege Ardabīl, the relatively defenseless capital city of Ādharbayjān. As the base and military center for all the Muslim troops in Ādharbayjān, Ardabīl was the biggest possible strategic prize for the Khazars. At this time, Ardabīl is said to have been inhabited by thirty thousand Muslim troops and their families. As in other difficult frontier provinces, all the Muslims were concentrated in a single place for security and quick mobilization. But unfortunately, the troops were in the field with al-Jarrāḥ.[16]

To save his capital and base, not to mention the families of his men, al-Jarrāḥ made a spectacular retreat that can be traced from Bardha'a through al-Baylaqān, Warthān, and Bājarwān to Ardabīl. But he was nevertheless defeated and killed in a three-day battle ending on 22 Ramaḍan 112/9 December 730 on a plain called Marj al-Sabalān outside the city, while his army, presumably about twenty-five thousand strong, was annihilated,[17] except for seven hundred or fewer men who escaped.[18] Agapius reports the Muslim losses at twenty thousand killed and twice that number taken prisoner, which could be nearly right if the figure for prisoners includes civilians captured at Ardabīl and elsewhere later in the campaign.[19] The date of the battle shows that once more, while the Muslims moved north against the Khazars in the summer, the Khazars pushed south against the Muslims in the winter. Slain along with al-Jarrāḥ was his ally, the Zoroastrian *dihqān* of Ādharbayjān, Mardān Shāh, which shows that here, as elsewhere, the Arabs used native troops.[20] Some Muslim presence seems to have been left in the area, as al-Jarrāḥ's brother al-Ḥajjāj, the subgovernor of Armenia, was nearby and succeeded in command.[21] But as no exploits are credited to him, it seems he either fled or also was defeated.

The totality of al-Jarrāḥ's defeat is shown by its immediate sequel, for the Khazars laid seige to Ardabīl, brought mangonels against its walls, and took it by storm, killing all the troops within the city, enslaving their women and children, and sacking the place.[22] Many of the forty thousand Muslim prisoners reported by Agapius must have been taken in Ardabīl.[23] To appreciate the magnitude of this catastrophe, it has to be remembered that no equivalent Muslim *miṣr* had ever before been captured by an enemy. Besides their capture of a Muslim provincial capital, the Khazar cavalry ranged over the whole province of Ādharbayjān to plunder. They attacked al-Baylaqān and Bājarwān.[24] They sacked Ganza in Arrān[25] and even reached the vicinity of al-Mawṣil in northern Iraq.[26] No enemy had ever penetrated so deeply into the heart of the caliphate before. The Khazars also plundered the district of Zarawand northwest of Lake Urmiya.[27] Only a few fortified towns held out, such as Warthān.[28]

News of al-Jarrāḥ's disaster precipitated the Caliph Hishām, as well as many other Muslims, into a state of almost hysterical shock.[29] On consulting his advisers, he quickly appointed the veteran Qinnasrīnī Qaysī Sa'īd b. 'Amr al-Ḥarashī, a successful general, to take charge. Sa'īd was at hand nearby at Manbij, not far from the caliph's seat at al-Ruṣāfa. After giving him as a standard a lance said to have been used at Badr,[30] Hishām sent him forth to mobilize, at al-Raqqa, whatever miniscule forces could be found at the moment. Hishām also promised to send him a steady stream of reinforcements as they came in. The caliph further gave Sa'īd one hundred thousand dirhams to help him recruit Jazīrans for his army as he passed through their country on his way to the front. When at Arzān, he met survivors of al-Jarrāḥ's disaster fleeing toward Syria. He had to pay each man ten dinars (or roughly one hundred fifty dirhams) to get them to join him and go back to the war.[31] Probably it was difficult to mobilize many troops in the winter, for his army was small.[32] Alternatively, the manpower pool may have already become stretched. Apparently, Hishām also commanded him to adopt a defensive posture until reinforcements arrived.[33]

Marching through Armenia, Sa'īd found the Khazars holding Akhlāṭ on Lake Van. After recovering that place, he may have driven the Khazars from Zarawand. Then he went on until he reached Bardha'a, hoping to cut off the Khazars while the latter were loaded down with their loot. Turning south, he passed through al-Baylaqān and then raised the Khazar seige of Warthān. About twenty-four kilometers from Bājarwān, he is said to have defeated the *khāqān*'s son who had sacked Ardabīl, to have killed most of the Khazar army of ten thousand, and to have rescued most of the Muslim prisoners, said to number five thousand households. This might mean, however, only those Muslim prisoners who happened still to be with the *khāqān*'s son. The Muslims also took the Khazars' standard, which was afterwards used as the regimental colors of the Ḥarīsh, Sa'īd's clan. The Khazars fled north across the Mughān Steppe and the confluence of the Kur and Araxes Rivers. Sa'īd pursued them as far as Sharwān.[34]

However, Sa'īd had not been given the governorship of Armenia and Ādharbayjān. That went to Maslama b. 'Abd al-Malik, brought back to command so soon after his having been retired a year earlier. Maslama set out with Jazīran forces in Shawwāl 112/early January 731. At that time, he also sent a letter to Sa'īd, removing him from office and appointing 'Abd al-Malik b. Muslim al-'Uqaylī, a Jazīran, to govern the province for him instead. On taking office, 'Abd al-Malik imprisoned Sa'īd at Qabala. Maslama arrived with a much larger army. When he reached Bardha'a, Maslama summoned Sa'īd before him and condemned him for failing to wait for Maslama's reinforcements and for recklessly endangering the Muslim army. Then he imprisoned Sa'īd, but Hishām ordered his release.[35] Lewond states that Maslama was enraged at al-Ḥarashī because the latter had already won the war, taking the booty and the slaves that were to be had, and that he wanted to kill him as a result, but could not do so for fear of al-Ḥarashī's tribal group.[36]

Maslama then moved forward through Sharwān, which resisted his advance. He severely punished the people of Khaydhān, after which all the eastern Caucasus up to al-Bāb quickly surrendered.[37] At al-Bāb, Maslama found one thousand Khazars settled in the city with their families. These held out in the citadel and he chose to bypass them for the moment. Leaving al-Ḥārith b. 'Amr al-Ṭā'ī to supervise the building of a new military base at al-Bāb, Maslama carried the war north into the Khazars' territory, in spite of rain and snow.[38] Clearly, the caliphate was not about to abandon its forward policy, especially against enemies who failed to recognize its superior power. Unfortunately for the Umayyads' plans, however, warfare against the Khazars remained most unrewarding and ultimately unsuccessful.

The war continued into 113/731. Maslama continued his campaign in the north, taking Khamzīn, Balanjar, and Samandar in Khazaria, all of which had been abandoned by the highly mobile and partly nomadic Khazars in their retreat. Then, he encountered the Khazar *khāqān* himself, who turned the tables and compelled the Muslim forces to make another of their spectacular retreats, in which they are reported to have burnt their baggage train. Probably the details of this campaign have been confused with that of 110/728. It was in the campaign of 113/731 that the son of the *khāqān* was supposed to have been killed, though this must remain doubtful. Finally out of the steppes and nearer to home at al-Bāb, Maslama stopped and dug a defensive trench, defeating the *khāqān* when he assaulted it.[39] Perhaps this was the same as the occasion when Maslama defeated a Khazar seige of Ghazāla.[40]

After this, Maslama managed to expel the one thousand Khazars from the citadel at al-Bāb by poisoning their water supply, which caused them to flee. Then he concentrated on the establishment there of the new military settlement, which he divided into separate quarters for the divisions of Damascus, Ḥimṣ, Filasṭīn, and al-Jazīra, the last being lumped together with the other Syrians, no doubt their Qinnasrīnī kin.[41] The names of these divisions indicate that Maslama's army still contained a large number of Syrians. Perhaps more of the troops that settled for garrison duty were Syrians, while the favored Jazīrans and Qinnasrīnī Qaysīs mostly were allowed to go home. It is certain that the bulk of Maslama's forces were Jazīrans and Qinnasrīnīs.[42] The new settlers in al-Bāb numbered twenty-four thousand troops, which must have represented a considerable drain on the available manpower pool.[43] On the whole, Maslama's record suggests a rather limited success, while we are ignorant of the Khazar version.[44] Furthermore, Maslama was removed from his governorship by Hishām on 1 Muharram 114/3 March 732 and was not to serve in the field again.[45] Indeed, Hishām is said to have sarcastically rebuked his brother later for his lack of success in comparison to Marwān b. Muḥammad.[46]

After Maslama withdrew from north of the Caucasus in 113/731, the Khazars and their allies returned to the places from which they had fled. Therefore, in 114/732, the new governor Marwān led an army of forty thousand to Balanjar and beyond into the

Khazar lands, taking herd animals as booty and returning safely to al-Bāb. However, this expedition was also bogged down by rain, which sounds like a doublet (or treblet) of Maslama's 'campaign of mud' in 110/728, so that it is doubtful what its true nature was and how much it may have achieved.[47] Ibn Khayyāṭ reports that Marwān only crossed the al-Ramm River just north of al-Bāb and attacked the 'Slavs,' surely not real Slavs, but rather some other, nearer peoples lumped together under the term.[48] This version may be more accurate. Marwān then passed the winter of 114/732–33 at al-Bāb, in seeming fear of a winter campaign by the Khazars according to their previous practice.[49]

Marwān also introduced important reforms in Armenia in 114/732. Owing to the severity of the Khazar depredations, the Armenians had grown more willing to play an active role as allies. On his entry into the region as governor, Marwān was enthusiastically received by the Armenian princes in Dabīl. On that occasion, he appointed Ashot Bagratouni as 'patrician' and virtual governor of Armenia. This step was opposed by the scions of the rival Mamikonian house as well as Ashot's cousins, sons of the previous ruler who naturally saw themselves as the rightful heirs. Marwān obliged Ashot by having them arrested and sent to the caliph, who exiled the Mamikonians to Yaman while keeping the rival Bagratids in Syria.[50]

The appointment of Ashot, which was approved by the caliph, nearly amounted to a grant of autonomy, which suggests that the caliphate was desperately in need of support to face the Khazars. This possibility is confirmed beyond doubt by Ashot's subsequent visit to the caliph. Hishām not only loaded him with honors, but also agreed to pay three hundred thousand dirhams in arrears due to the Armenian troops who had been fighting alongside the Muslims for three years and to provide the Armenian cavalry with regular pay during their participation in any future campaigns.[51] And this from a regime known for its stinginess! It seems clear from these details that the newly installed Armenian leader was in a position to drive a hard bargain. That the Muslim caliphate, hard on the heels of its reemphasis of Islam's idol-smashing ideology, would pay Christian Armenians to fight for it, shows that the caliphate desperately needed more troops, not only in the Caucasus but also in general.

While the Muslims were lining up allies in the Caucasus, the Byzantines were also not idle. In the same year, 114–15/732–33, the Byzantine Emperor Leo III betrothed to his young son Constantine V the daughter of the Khazar *khāqān*. For the occasion, she embraced Christianity, taking the name Irene.[52] This important event sealed an alliance that had already been developing between the two powers, based on the communality of their struggle against Islam. Probably both Byzantines and Khazars acted under the immediate impact of the Islamic offensives they were facing, for it was unusual for a Byzantine emperor to marry a barbarian woman. Her son later became Emperor Leo IV (158–63/775–80).[53] The marriage of Constantine and Irene further strengthened a link in the wall of powers surrounding the Islamic state.

Thus, the Muslims were able to make a comeback on the Caucasus front that to some extent compensated for the disaster of al-Jarrāḥ at Ardabīl. Nevertheless, the defeat and death of al-Jarrāḥ had many serious implications. It was a terrible humiliation for a governor to be killed in the field, for a provincial capital to be sacked, and for Muslim families to be carried off into captivity, all by a people regarded as backward. The threat to the heart of the empire and the possibility of cooperation between the Khazars and the Byzantines were dangers that the caliph must have pondered. The continuance of such perils required the recruitment of replacement troops for the army, which further strained the already overtaxed caliphal budget. Worse, the caliphate still could not accept such a defeat and needed to avenge it, so that much treasure was spent on new expeditions on a large scale and on the building and peopling of al-Bāb, an entirely new *miṣr*. Also, the aggressive expeditions into Khazaria had little to show for them, and it is doubtful whether they were necessary to deter the Khazars.

But perhaps the worst fallout for the caliphate from al-Jarrāḥ's defeat lay in its cost in lives. Not merely had a governor been killed but a whole army had been destroyed. That army consisted mainly of Yamanī Syrians,[54] who had up to this point been the mainstay of the Umayyad dynasty. Such Yamanī Syrians did not exist in unlimited numbers. But any recruitment of other elements to replace them, such as the demilitarized but highly politicized Iraqis, would lead to unacceptable political consequences, namely, demands for reform and a redistribution of political influence. Therefore, the easiest course was to bring back the Muḍari Jazīrans to dominate Armenia and Ādharbayjān once more, while mobilizing even Christian Armenians, a potentially hostile force, as allies. And the growth of Jazīran power at the expense of the Syrians was most ominous for a regime whose power had always been based in Syria and to whom the Jazīrans had hitherto been only junior partners.[55]

Transoxiana and Khurāsān 111–15/730–33

While the caliphate was expending its troops and treasure fighting the Khazars in the Caucasus, it was also engaged in an equally momentous struggle with the Khazars' relatives, the Turgesh Turks, in Transoxiana. As in the Caucasus, where a successful general had been appointed in 111/729 in hope of better results, a famous commander, al-Junayd al-Murrī, with whom we have already met as a conqueror in India, was made governor of Khurāsān in late 111/early 730. Like al-Jarrāḥ in the Caucasus, al-Junayd was destined to preside over a military catastrophe of the first rank, from which the Khurāsānī army would never recover. This, in turn, would require the overburdened Syrian army to take up yet another military responsibility.

When al-Junayd arrived in his province, his predecessor Ashras al-Sulamī was still fighting the people of Bukhārā and al-Sughd, in a war that seems to have gone on all winter. Al-Junayd was afraid to cross over to Transoxiana at Āmul even with a force of five hundred men. Therefore, he waited for Ashras to send him an escort of seven thousand cavalry. The cavalry escort got into trouble between Bukhārā and Āmul, allegedly being attacked by the Turgesh *khāqān*. Al-Junayd then went forward, but the Turks fell on him about twelve kilometers from Baykand. The ensuing battle was very difficult, although the Muslims finally triumphed. After taking command of Ashras' forces, al-Junayd met the *khāqān* near Zarmān. By now it was the summer of 112/730. Here, al-Junayd seems to have had more success, as he captured the prince of al-Shash and the *khāqān*'s nephew, whom he sent to the caliph. Having concluded his summer campaign, he returned to Marw. He had left the situation somewhat better than he found it, for, apparently, he had reopened the road to Samarqand and relieved the beleaguered garrisons. Then he returned to Marw for the winter, his men no doubt being eager to get home after prolonged campaigning.[56]

Late in the winter, in late 112/early 731, al-Junayd mobilized his forces once more to face rebellions which had broken out in Ṭukhāristān, south of the Oxus. This territory had been pacified twenty years earlier, unlike Transoxiana, which had never been fully pacified. The spread of resistance to the rule of the caliphate to a previously quiescent region like Ṭukhāristān was an ominous sign, for it further overburdened the already fatigued Muslim army. To deal with the various revolts, al-Junayd camped outside Balkh and sent out twenty-eight thousand men in different directions, thus scattering a large part of his forces.[57]

By now, the year 113/731 had begun. At this point, the *khāqān* marched on Samarqand to the north, beseiging its defenders inside the city walls. Sawra b. al-Ḥurr al-Abānī, the commander of the Samarqand garrison, sent al-Junayd an urgent plea for help. Al-Junayd began to recall his troops but was also prepared to go immediately to the rescue himself. However, he was opposed in this by al-Mujashshir b. Muzāḥim al-Sulamī, an important leader of the Khurāsānī Arab troops, who declared, "The holder of Khurāsān should not cross the Oxus with less than fifty thousand men. . . . Wait (for the rest of the troops) and do not hurry."[58] This shows how exhausting and dangerous the campaigns against the Turks of the previous few years had been, as the Khurāsānīs, unless they enjoyed a comfortable superiority in numbers, had grown reluctant to face them.

Al-Junayd insisted on setting out immediately despite the Khurāsānis' reluctance. After they had reached Kishsh, al-Mujashshir persuaded him to take the shortest route over a steep pass through the mountains, possibly hoping the Turks would not expect him to come that way. Some Khurāsānīs began to desert at this point owing perhaps to their fear of being trapped in the pass. Al-Junayd, nevertheless, pressed forward with twenty-eight thousand men. About twenty-four kilometers from Samarqand, the main Turkish army under the *khāqān*, supported by the armies of al-Sughd, al-Shāsh, and Farghāna, fell on al-Junayd's army.[59]

The ensuing battle, known as the Battle of the Defile (*yawm al-shi'b*), is by far the best-documented one to occur during Hishām's reign.[60] Though it is not possible to follow its course precisely, its exact site remaining unidentified, its general outline and result are clear. Al-Junayd's army suffered terrific casualties and was threatened with annihilation.[61] He even had to plead for Sawra to come out of Samarqand to save him by acting as a decoy. The rescuer needed to be rescued. Sawra and his men were inclined to disobey al-Junayd's order, knowing that they might well perish, but al-Junayd sent a threatening message, whereupon Sawra declared, "My lamb will not be removed from the oven until I go."[62] Sawra set out with twelve thousand men, who were wiped out only six kilometers from al-Junayd's camp. Only one thousand escaped.[63] Despite Sawra's sacrifice, al-Junayd still had to fight his way into Samarqand with what was left of his army. The battle had lasted about three days.[64]

Not only was the Battle of the Defile a military catastrophe of the first rank for the Muslims, but it was also a crucial turning point in the history of the Transoxianan front.[65] In numbers, the Muslim army was decimated to a far greater extent than the loss of eleven thousand men with Sawra, though certain sources give the impression that that was the main part of the loss.[66] A poet claims fifty thousand Muslims were slaughtered,[67] which emphasizes the magnitude of the disaster, even allowing for exaggeration. Ibn A'tham gives a minimum of twenty thousand dead, out of a total of forty-three thousand or forty-eight thousand.[68] On receiving news of the battle, the Caliph Hishām dispatched twenty thousand hitherto demobilized Iraqis to Khurāsān and ordered al-Junayd to enroll fifteen thousand more Khurāsānīs.[69] If these were mainly replacements, this suggests that the Muslims killed could have been in the neighborhood of twenty-five to thirty thousand. Hishām also sent thirty thousand shields and thirty thousand lances to al-Junayd, presumably to equip the new troops al-Junayd was supposed to raise.[70] This must have involved considerable expense.

Such numbers suggest that the losses from the Defile would probably exceed even those of the previous year's disaster of al-Jarrāḥ. And indeed, the Battle of the Defile immediately invited comparison with the disaster of al-Jarrāḥ. On seeing the battle develop, al-Junayd is reported to have cried out, "(It is) a night like al-Jarrāḥ's night and a day like his day!"[71] Also, al-Junayd is supposed to have said during the battle, "O people, it is hellfire!"[72] On hearing news of the Defile, Hishām is said to have exclaimed, "The disaster of Sawra b. al-Ḥurr in Khurāsān and of al-Jarrāḥ at al-Bāb!"[73] These lamentations point out, first of all, that the results of these two battles were extremely serious and a real worry to the caliph. Secondly, the conjoinment of al-Junayd's disaster with al-Jarrāḥ's in these phrases shows that the Battle of the Defile, though supposedly a victory, was actually no less a disaster than the acknowledged catastrophe of Ardabīl.

There is plenty of other evidence about the impression this battle made on the Muslims. Al-Mujashshir al-Sulamī is reported to have said to al-Junayd on the eve of the battle, "It used to be said that certain of the troops of Khurāsān would perish at the hands of a luxury-loving man from the Qays. We now fear that you may be he."[74] This seems to be a retrospection after the fact, indicating that the losses were high, especially among the Khurāsānīs. The latter, in any case, made up the overwhelming bulk of the army, as large Syrian contingents had not yet been sent to Khurāsān. Seeing the way the battle was going, an Azdī told al-Junayd, "If we win, it will be for your benefit; if we perish, you will not weep over us."[75] This shows the resentment felt by the Khurāsānīs forced to fight continuous, unrewarding campaigns for the benefit of vainglorious generals on one of the caliphate's worst fronts, by a central government whose special Syrian army had not hitherto, in the Khurāsānīs' opinion, faced similar hardships.

Another indication of the results of this battle and of the struggle with the Turks in general is found in the terror the Turks inspired in the Muslims. It should be remembered that the sources do not usually emphasize the weak points of their own side, so that they are being exceptionally candid in describing this terror. When al-Junayd sent forth a messenger to inform Hishām of the battle, the man was too frightened to go out from Samarqand and asked to be relieved of his mission.[76] Terror of the Turks was widely in evidence in the months following the battle.[77]

Most damning of all is the evidence of the Khurāsāni poems on the battle, more of which exist than for any other battle and none of which have a kind word to say about al-Junayd.[78] Al-Shar'abī al-Tā'ī, for example, said:[79]

> When the *khāqān* moved and his troops went forth,
> deaths overwhelmed us at that time.
> There, Hind, we did not amount to half of them,
> nor did we have, O Hind, any hope in overcoming the enemy. . . .
>
> To God I complain about a shrinking in their[80] hearts
> and a terror which fills their insides and is spreading.
> Who will carry from me a written letter
> to Khālid[81] before we are divided up as booty:
> That, like our remnants, our commander,
> if we even consider him, is the humiliated one brought low.
> They[82] made the *khāqān* and his soldiers greedy for us;
> would we not better have been dry, broken grass shaken [by wind]?

In this poem, which is most valuable as evidence as it is contemporary with the event, the poet raises several points of interest. First, he clearly represents the fear of the Turks felt by the troops. Second, he pinpoints one reason for this. The Turks have nothing the Muslims want, that is, no prospective booty. Rather, it is the Muslims who stand to lose. Third, al-Junayd is a complete failure. Fourth, the leadership, possibly including the caliph himself, are responsible for the disaster. This lament over defeat is almost unique in surviving Umayyad poetry, which is more wont to celebrate victories. It might be possible to regard it as an aberration if not that many other Khurāsānī poems contain the same ideas.

Ibn 'Irs al-'Abdī is still more biting when he addresses al-Junayd about the Battle of the Defile. Because of its unusual directness and relevance in nearly every line, I will quote his poem extensively:[83]

Formerly, our strength used to be feared,
 when we threw back defeated enemy ranks on those advancing,
Until we were tried by that which blemished us,
 after having had mighty, overwhelming strength.
Like he who hocks his camel by never reining in from the first,
 through his fury and urgency,
You split open a thing whose breach could not be repaired
 (even) with an abundantly numerous, assembled army.
You weep because of war when it has shown itself:
 may you be mutilated and cut up as a commander!
You abandoned us, like pieces of a slaughtered beast
 which the slaughterer divides for a round-breasted girl.
Drawn swords rose high,
 chopping off arms at the elbow.
Heads fell continuously from their blows
 between two wings flashing with lightning, thundering,
While you were like an infant girl in her women's tent,
 not ever knowing the trick of the plotter.
We are a people whose war is difficult:
 it blasts both the standing and the sitting.
Samarqand and its contingents have become
 the talk of both those who were not there and those who were.
How many a resolute warrior is buried in the Defile,
 robust of powers, strong, and praiseworthy,
Who sought relief in the disaster and engaged blindly in combat
 neither fearstruck, feeble, nor holding back!
If only you had been on the Day of the Defile in a pit
 covered over with hard, dry mud!
War and its sons play with you
 as hawks play with quails coming to water.
Your heart flew, owing to the battle, out of fear;
 your flying heart will not return.
You should never have thought the fight on the day of the
 forenoon to be like your drinking tangy wine with ice. . . .

Fifty thousand were slain after losing their way,
while you cried out for them like a shepherd for lost sheep.
Do not press at all to meet with battle;
you are not to be praised in rushing upon the enemy.

The devastating portrait of the battle in this poem leaves no room for doubt about the nature of its outcome. The Muslims suffered terrific losses, for which al-Junayd is fully blamed. He is accused of abandoning his troops to the enemy, which means that he doesn't care about their fate. His attitude toward war is flippant. He understands little of war. And this is addressed to the conqueror of western India! Most important, his act of blindly rushing into battle is most severely condemned. This seems to be a criticism not only of al-Junayd personally, but also of the traditional expansionist policy of the Umayyad government. The rejection of the government's leadership implied in the poem represents a most ominous turn of affairs for the Umayyad regime.

After the Battle of the Defile, al-Junayd himself remained at Samarqand for four months (about Rabī' II-Sha'bān 113/July–October 731) to give his army a chance to recuperate and to await some of the reinfocements promised by Hishām. Meanwhile, the Turks had gone on to beseige Bukhārā, the other big Transoxianan center. Al-Junayd, ever the gallant exponent of the forward policy, insisted on rushing to the rescue once again, despite vocal opponents who favored a more circumspect course. Al-Junayd could only persuade a minimal garrison of eight hundred men to stay in Samarqand by offering a high bonus for so risky a duty. Since over twelve thousand had not been enough to securely hold Samarqand before, it is doubtful that al-Junayd expected the smaller garrison would be able to do more than delay the Turks if they attacked again. He then marched carefully towards Bukhārā, where he was able to beat off Turkish attacks between Karmīniya and al-Ṭawāwīs on 1–3 Ramaḍān 113/6–8 November 731, with a combination of caution and luck. The Turks then withdrew, apparently leaving al-Junayd in possession of the field.[84]

Al-Junayd went to his winter quarters in al-Ṣaghāniyān, just north of the Oxus. It was there that the reinforcements sent by Hishām finally reached him. He detailed some of these fresh troops to evacuate the Muslim dependents from Samarqand and escort them to safety in Marw, thereby showing his lack of confidence in his ability to defend Samarqand, though he left its garrison in place.[85]

Superficially, this campaign looks like a success, as had al-Junayd's campaign in 112/730. After putting forth a tremendous effort, the Muslims had once more made the Turks withdraw north of the Zarafshān Valley. Though the Muslim losses were high, the Turks must have also suffered large numbers of casualties.[86] But al-Junayd's 'victory' had in fact weakened the Muslim defences. No further campaigns undertaken by governors of Khurāsān are mentioned until 117/735. The years 114–15/732–33 are almost completely blank,[87] though al-Junayd is said to have campaigned in al-Ṣaghāniyān.[88] This, in itself, is an indication of defeat, as al-Ṣaghāniyān was the most loyal bit of Transoxiana. Having had to campaign there would mean that al-Junayd held little else north of the Oxus.

However, the lack of reported military activity in these years does not suggest, as Gibb thought, that neither the Turks nor the Muslims campaigned in them,[89] but rather that the Turks were on the offensive. Samarqand was lost by the Muslims at an unknown date, because the next time it is mentioned, in 117/735, the Turks are in possession of it.[90] This could easily have taken place as early as 113/731, when it was still probably defended by only eight hundred men. And despite the reinforcements which had arrived, the Muslim position remained shaky in what was left of Muslim holdings in Transoxiana, as well as in Ṭukhāristān. In Transoxiana, the Muslims probably only held onto Bukhārā, Kishsh, and al-Ṣaghāniyān.[91]

Thus, the outcome of al-Junayd's governorship of Khurāsān was disastrous in nearly all respects, providing a matching, if not yet worse, sequel to the contemporary disasters in the Caucasus. The caliphate's frontier was actually pushed back. No booty at all was gained. Enormous numbers of troops were killed, to the extent that the Khurāsānī frontier army was partly destroyed and had to be reinforced with remilitarized Iraqis, hitherto the most dangerous opponents of the dynasty. The surviving Khurāsānīs were increasingly disaffected, as indicated in their sarcastic poetry. The Turkish threat had not been removed. The caliphate had been forced to bear great financial burdens, such as the expense of equipping new forces, with nothing to show for its outlays of cash. This could all be borne by a great empire such as that of the Umayyad caliphate once, twice, perhaps several times, but not indefinitely before requiring major changes in the governing system.

The Byzantine Front 112–14/730–32

Despite the severe deterioration taking place all at once on the Indian, Caucasus, and Transoxianan fronts, the caliphate persisted in making annual expeditions against the Byzantines, while the latter, for their part, continued their defensive policy. However, the Muslim raids on Anatolia seem to have become somewhat less successful. The setbacks on the Byzantine front thus added, if marginally, to the caliphate's military woes.

In 112/730, Mu'āwiya b. Hishām, leading the summer expedition on the right from Malatya, took Kharsianon and burned Farandiyya[92] in Kappadokia.[93] Theophanes claims the fortress of Kharsianon was taken by Maslama, rather than Mu'āwiya, by treachery between Jumādā II 112/September 730 and Jumādā II 113/August 731.[94] Thus, since the summer of 112 ended in September 730, Kharsianon appears to have fallen about Jumādā II–Rajab 112/September–October 730, judging by synchronization of the Muslim and Greek chronologies. This is one of the few cases where a clear synchronization of the same event appears in both Muslim and Greek histories.

In a report probably referring to 113/731, al-Ya'qūbī asserts that Mu'āwiya b. Hishām was unable to enter Byzantine territory and hence merely guarded the frontier from al-'Amq near Mar'ash.[95] This is the only year missing from the series of regular expeditions mentioned by the sources. It is tempting to conclude that the shocks of 112–13/730–31 had been so great on the other fronts that too few troops could be spared in this year for any significant expeditions against the Byzantines commanded by princes of the Umayyad house. However, an expedition of some sort in 113/731 was commanded by 'Abd Allāh al-Baṭṭāl. This campaign evidently failed and led to considerable losses, but became chiefly famous for the death in battle of the hero 'Abd al-Wahhāb b. Bukht.[96] This might have occurred under the auspices of Mu'āwiya b. Hishām in the winter.[97]

In 114/732, Mu'āwiya b. Hishām, assisted by 'Abd Allāh al-Baṭṭāl, led the summer expedition on the left against the Byzantines and is reported to have penetrated as far as Aqrun (Akroinon) in the west of Anatolia. Al-Baṭṭāl defeated a Byzantine detachment and captured a Byzantine commander, Constantine, in battle. This could possibly have resulted from an attempt by the Byzantines to undertake a more active policy by once more meeting the Muslims on the field. A Syrian source says that after Mu'āwiya had departed for home with Byzantine captives, the Muslims he left behind were destroyed. This probably refers to the same battle as that of al-Baṭṭāl and Constantine. Meanwhile, Mu'āwiya's brother Sulaymān led the summer expedition on the right, reaching the vicinity of Kaisareia Mazaka, but achieving no significant success.[98]

The caliphate's military policy on the Byzantine front thus remained completely unchanged despite the disasters occurring everywhere to the east. Nevertheless, the continuation of the policy here too may not have been free of troubles, as evidenced by the possible need to curtail the expeditions of 113/731, contributing to a defeat, and by the indication of growing Byzantine resistance in 114/732. Even so, the Byzantine front continued to give the caliph less cause for worry than other theaters.

The Frankish Front 112–14/730–32

Besides the disasters in India, the Caucasus, and Transoxiana, and the minor check on the Byzantine frontier, the Muslims suffered one more significant military disaster in the short period of 112–14/730–32, that being in France. This battle, variously called the Battle of Poitiers or Tours, has been long considered one of the most decisive engagements in Western history, as it supposedly saved France and Western Europe from islamization.[99] In fact, the battle did inflict yet another blow on the caliphate and its military policy, though its impact was less severe or direct than that of the battles farther east.

In Ṣafar 112 or 113/April–May 730 or 731, 'Abd al-Raḥmān al-Ghāfiqī took up his duties as governor of Spain, having received his appointment from 'Ubayda b. 'Abd al-Raḥmān al-Sulamī, the governor of North Africa. However, he had difficulty with his superior over a piece of furniture inlaid with precious metals and jewels that he had captured but not forwarded, instead choosing to smash it up in order to divide it among his troops. Taking umbrage at 'Ubayda's threats to him, 'Abd al-Raḥmān set out to campaign in France, where he was killed fighting the Franks, possibly in early Ramaḍān 114/late October 732, in a battle called the Field of Martyrs.[100] This is all the Muslim sources have to tell us of this famous battle. Their very reticence to speak about it may indicate that it was a considerable defeat. The main sources we must rely on then are contemporary Spanish and Frankish works, written in late Latin.[101] These have been repeatedly sifted by European scholars, among whom Gabrieli exhibits a salutary reticence.

Perhaps from the beginning of his governorship, 'Abd al-Raḥmān was opposed by a Berber commander named Manūsa in Cerritania (Cerdanya) in the Pyrenees. This Manūsa, having heard his fellow Berbers were oppressed in North Africa, had made an unauthorized truce and even a marriage alliance with Odo, Duke of Aquitaine. This contumacy was tantamount to rebellion and led to a campaign against him, which may have begun as early as 111/729, as we have seen. This culminated in Manūsa's death, which immediately preceded 'Abd al-Raḥmān's expedition north of the Pyrenees.[102] While Gabrieli questioned certain details of this story, particularly the possibly romantic motif of a marriage alliance between an apostate Berber and an Aquitainian duchess,[103] it can scarcely be doubted that Manūsa's revolt has a basis in fact, as it is recorded not only by the earliest source, the *Continuatio Isadori*, but also by Muslim sources. Furthermore, it indeed reflects the Berber complaints of unfair and unequal treatment by their Arab brethren in both Spain and North Africa. Certainly, it is an ominous harbinger of the great Berber revolt that broke out a few years later.

What does seem more certain is the route of 'Abd al-Raḥmān's invasion of Aquitaine. He crossed the Pyrenees at their west end, through Navarre, which no Muslim commander had previously done. He then advanced rapidly through Aquitaine to Bordeaux, which he took by storm, killing the commander of its garrison. Continuing his victorious advance northward, 'Abd al-Raḥmān defeated Duke Odo on the Garonne or Dordogne River, wiping out most of the latter's forces. This caused the duke to appeal to the Frankish leader Charles Martel, who mobilized as large an army as possible to meet this severe threat to the Frankish realm. Meanwhile, the Muslims began to despoil northern Aquitaine, perhaps especially the rich monasteries. Now heavily loaded down with booty, 'Abd al-Raḥmān marched to Poitiers and perhaps reached Tours, though this last is less certain and somewhat unlikely, as it is not vouched for by the best sources.[104]

Near Poitiers occurred the decisive battle of the campaign, perhaps in Ramaḍān/October 732. Unfortunately, we have few reliable details except that, after a difficult fight with the army of Charles Martel, 'Abd al-Raḥmān was slain. His army abandoned its camp and booty to flee south by night. The Franks were too exhausted to pursue them. It was the deepest raid of the Muslims into France, but the cost was considerable. As Gabrieli points out, no reliable information exists on either the exact size of 'Abd al-Raḥmān's force or of the Muslim losses.[105] Nevertheless, these were possibly very large. The best Frankish source suggests that 'Abd al-Raḥmān's army was practically annihilated.[106] Furthermore, the battle is even mentioned by the remote Byzantine historical tradition, which had also noted the very real disaster of al-Jarrāḥ in the Caucasus, though missing that of al-Junayd in Transoxiana.[107] Also, it is impressive that in scarcely a dozen years, two governors of Spain had been killed fighting in France: al-Samḥ and ʻAbd al-Raḥmān. This probably indicates that there were high casualties in the ranks as well.

Egypt and North Africa 112–14/730–32

While the caliphate faced severe defeats on several fronts at once, Egypt and North Africa remained quiet in the wake of the Copt revolt of 107/725. There was no new violent outbreak. In North Africa, the Berber front was absolutely quiet, indicating that the previously established *modus vivendi* between the Arabs and Berbers continued in effect.

A further sign of internal peace in this sector was the regular continuation of sea expeditions against the Byzantine-held islands, despite the disaster of al-Mustanīr in 111/729. In fact, in 112/730, Thābit b. Khaytham, of the Syrian *jund* of al-Urdunn, led a successful plundering expedition to Sicily.[108] In the next year, ʻAbd al-Malik b. Qaṭan al-Fihrī led an expedition against Sicily, while Abū ʻImrān al-Hudhalī led another to an unnamed objective.[109]

In 114/732, ʻAbd al-Malik b. Qaṭan again led a successful campaign against Sicily, while ʻAbd Allāh b. Ziyād al-Anṣārī led one against Sardinia.[110] This is the first time both islands are reported to have been attacked in a single year, which suggests an intensification of campaigning. The Byzantine resistance seems to have been especially passive on this front, no retaliation being mentioned by either Byzantine or Muslim historians.

8

The Continuation of the Policy of Expansion 115–22/733–40

Lull and Resumption

Incredibly, the massive defeats on several fronts at once in 112–14/730–32 were no more effective a deterrent than the hard campaigning of previous years had been to the caliphal government's traditional policy of aggressive expeditions aimed at booty and territorial expansion. Though it permitted lulls or unofficial temporary truces on some fronts in order to allow its forces to recuperate somewhat, the caliphate soon tried to resume its old policy of throwing its forces enthusiastically against its adversaries on nearly all the recently active frontiers at once.[1] Thus, the wars against the Byzantines, the Khazars, the Turgesh, the various states of India, and the Franks were all pursued almost without letup by the caliphate during most of this period. Only on the Khazar and Turgesh fronts did it take the caliphate some time to build up a new momentum of conquest after the disasters of 112–13/730–31.

Also, after having learned certain military lessons, in this final period of the full forward policy the Muslim state avoided a repetition of the disasters of 112–14/730–32 and achieved a certain measure of recovery and success. The enormous resources available to the caliphate were still able to overwhelm most of its opponents. As a result, by 122/740, final victory seemed within reach on some of the fronts. The Turgesh Khanate unexpectedly collapsed on the Transoxianan front, where the Muslims had been doing the worst. The Khazar Khanate saw its capital sacked and may have seemed ready to meet the same fate. Despite the repeated disasters in India, the caliphate's position was better established in Sind than ever before. On the Byzantine front, the Byzantine Empire still engaged in only defensive warfare.

But the constant campaigning finally wore down the Umayyad Caliphate. Despite the striking success of some of its final efforts, it ended the period a hollow shell, ruined by the expense its military excesses claimed in lives and wealth. When the very hour of victory had arrived on some fronts, the caliphate found itself unable to exploit it. Rather, it awaited only the *coup de grāce* from a fresh opponent to send its whole structure crashing to earth.

The Byzantine Front 115–22/733–40

The same type of campaigning was kept up against the Byzantines as before. But now there were fewer successes and more failures owing to the slow improvement of Byzantine defensive tactics. It is notable that in this period, in total contrast to earlier times, the Muslims generally ceased to capture fortresses or towns in their campaigns. Previously, from 102/721 to 112/730, they had taken Dabasa, Sibora, Qaysara, Mawāsā, Ikonion, Kaisareia Mazaka, Gangra, Ateous, al-ʻAṭāsīn, Semalouos, al-Mawa, Kharsianon, and Farandiyya, as well as two or more unnamed fortresses. From 113/731 to 122/740, an equal number of years, they took only the town of Ankyra and the fortresses of Sideroun and Maṭāmīr plus perhaps an unnamed town. This stark new reality meant that they could now only raid the countryside and could not count on taking the supplies laid up in a captured city for provisions. It also meant less booty. Furthermore, Muslim raiders, especially those deep in Anatolia, would be subject to greater danger of attack from the Byzantines in their fortified strongholds, as these now had less to fear from a siege. Nevertheless, nothing daunted, the caliphate went ahead with its annual expeditions as if nothing had altered.

In Ramaḍān 115/15 October–13 November 733, Muʻāwiya b. Hishām engaged in an expedition which reached Paphlagonia, taking many prisoners and possibly capturing and burning an unnamed town.[2] In 116/734, Muʻāwiya led the summer campaign.[3] In his summer campaign in 117/735 on the left, Muʻāwiya b. Hishām, continuing his search ever farther afield for places containing booty, reached Sibora, which had previously been taken in 104/723, while one of his raiding parties reached Sardis in the far west of Anatolia. So far-ranging a raid is hardly an indication of military success, however, for no towns or fortresses were taken. In the same year, Sulaymān b. Hishām led the summer expedition on the right from al-Jazīra and sent out raiding parties in different directions.[4]

In 118/736, Muʻāwiya led an expedition against Anatolia. Sulaymān b. Hishām led an expedition, possibly the summer one on the right, to Armenia but accomplished nothing.[5] Also in this year, the Byzantine fleet, after long inaction in the eastern Mediterranean, made a dramatic reappearance, intercepting and defeating a Muslim seaborn expedition led by Nāfi' b. Abī 'Ubayda al-Fihrī.[6] In 119/737, Mu'āwiya apparently led the summer expedition on the left, reaching Balūniya, while his brother Sulayman led the summer expedition on the right. Mu'āwiya died falling from his horse while hunting on the way back.[7] Al-Walīd b. al-Qa'qā' al-'Absī, a Qinnasrīnī, also led an expedition against the Byzantines.[8]

After this, the Muslims achieved somewhat better results for a couple of years. In 120/738, Mu'āwiya b. Hishām's brothers Maslama and Sulaymān led expeditions against the Byzantines. Sulaymān captured the fortress of Sideroun, taking many prisoners, including Eustathios the son of the patrician Marianos.[9] In 121/739, Maslama b. Hishām led the summer expedition.[10] Maslama captured the area of Maṭāmīr in Byzantine Kappadokia[11] and also besieged and captured the important town of Ankyra.[12] This was the last time the Muslims took a Byzantine fortress or town under the Umayyads.

Finally, as late as 122/740, the caliphate prepared the most massive expedition against the Byzantines in Hishām's reign. Though Muḥammad b. Hishām led a summer expedition and Maslama b. Hishām may have commanded a separate expedition in this year, it was their brother Sulaymān who was in charge overall. Theophanes reports this expedition in unusual detail. Sulaymān sent al-Ghamr b. Yazīd b. 'Abd al-Malik ahead with ten thousand lightly armed troops to reconnoiter and surprise the Byzantines in western Asia Minor. These were followed by twenty thousand cavalry under Mālik b. Shu'ayb, the subgovernor of Malaṭya, and 'Abd Allāh al-Baṭṭāl, who reached Akroinon. Behind them, Sulaymān came with sixty thousand men to Kappadokian Tyana.[13] This number of the rear force, about which Theophanes would naturally know the least, is probably inflated.

Probably Sulaymān's strategy was to protect his lines of communication the whole length of the invasion route with huge numbers of troops, as logistical problems had played a large role in previous disasters on this front. However, it did not work. Though al-Ghamr's and Sulaymān's forces escaped mishap, returning to Syria after wreaking great devastation on man and beast, they failed to capture any towns or fortresses, a signal failure for so great an expedition. Faring even worse, Mālik and al-Baṭṭāl were surrounded by the two Byzantine emperors, Leo III and his son Constantine V, campaigning in person. Mālik and al-Baṭṭāl were killed, presumably near Akroinon, with 13,200 of their men, while sixty-eight hundred managed to get away to Synnada and then to rejoin Sulaymān. It was probably these forces which suffered from severe hunger and high prices for food at either Akroinon or Synnada or both. Nevertheless, upon their escape to Syria, they were rushed to join the army of Kulthūm going to face the Berber revolt in North Africa.[14] According to Agapius, the Byzantines took over twenty thousand Arab prisoners.[15]

Thus, even on this most felicitous of fronts, so close to Syria that it did not require keeping the troops away from their homes for more than a campaigning season and so well known to the Syro-Jazīran army, the aggressive military policy of the caliphate finally led to yet another enormous, classic disaster. There is every probability that the lost troops were mostly Syrians rather than Jazīrans, owing to the massive size of the mobilization and to the absence of the Jazīran governor, Marwān b. Muḥammad, in the Caucasus. In any case, it was yet another severe blow to the manpower pool of the troops the caliph could most rely on.

Finally, the Byzantines began to exhibit a cautious return to the policy of waging aggressive raids themselves. They naturally tended to choose first the medium in which they held a lead over the Muslims in general: the sea. Though it is not recorded as a raid by any source, the Byzantines caused some kind of 'incident' (*ḥadath*) on the Syrian coast about 122/740, which required the mobilization of at least some of the reserve troops of the Damascus *jund*.[16] This must have been a naval raid on the coast belonging to that *jund*, roughly the coast of present-day Lebanon. Such a raid will possibly have come as an unwelcome surprise for the Muslims, as the Byzantines had sent no naval expeditions against Syria since that aimed at al-Lādhiqiyya in 100/719, almost a generation earlier. Any renewal of Byzantine activity was an ominous sign for the caliphate.

The Caucasus Front 115–23/733–41

The Caucasus front against the Khazars, up to this point, had been one of the worst facing the caliphate. It was possibly the one place from which a general invasion of the caliphate's heartlands was feared, if only for a brief time in 112/730.[17] With the coming to office of Marwān b. Muḥammad on 1 al-Muḥarram 114/3 March 732, however, the situation had begun to change for the better.[18] After the campaign of 114/732, an unexpected lull in serious warfare occurred. There were no further Khazar penetrations south of the Caucasus as the Muslims held the line at al-Bāb. Eventually, operations against the Khazars and their allies north of al-Bāb were also attempted, but once again, the cost was high and, except for one instance, the booty little.

In the spring of 115/733, Hishām removed Marwān and reappointed Sa'īd b. 'Amr al-Ḥarashī as governor of Armenia and Ādharbayjān. Perhaps the disappointing results achieved by the two Umayyad princes Maslama and Marwān in 112–14/731–32 caused the caliph to turn once more to the undefeated Qinnasrīnī general. If so, his expectations were disappointed again, for the formerly aggressive general undertook no campaigns in 115/733 and 116/734 at all. This is probably because of the exhaustion of the Muslim troops, now forced into a defensive posture, rather than any weakness on Sa'īd's part. Interestingly, no campaigns were undertaken in Transoxiana in 114–16/732–34 either. Apparently, after their recent massive defeats, the caliphal forces needed some time to recuperate, at least on these two fronts, despite the official desire to resume the offensive policy. Probably in early 117/735, Sa'īd is said to have resigned owing to the loss of his sight.[19]

Though Marwān returned to the Caucasus front in time for the campaign of 117/735, he apparently did not have sufficient forces with him to undertake any but local expeditions in the North Caucasus for a couple of years. This is clear from the orderly documentation of his annual campaigns by Ibn Khayyāṭ, though other sources compress these campaigns, giving the impression that Marwān was able to fight the Khazars immediately. In fact, it appears that no conflict took place between the Muslims and Khazars during 115–18/733–36 at all. The existence of such a lull would tend to verify the report in Michael the Syrian and Agapius that the Muslims made peace with the Khazars.[20] Indeed, Ibn al-Athīr mentions that Marwān made negotiations for a truce with the Khazar *khāqān* in order to gain time until his great expedition against the Khazars was ready. Although the historian gives the impression that this was only a brief trick, perhaps a longer truce in fact occurred.[21] Naturally, the historical tradition formed in the Umayyad era would prefer not to admit to the Muslims that the Umayyads had made a long-lasting truce with the pagan Khazar enemy. This is especially true of the semilegendary tradition, so favorable to the Jazīrans, represented by Ibn A'tham, who makes no mention of any truce.

Nevertheless, Marwān did campaign. In 117/735, he sent two expeditions into the Caucasus Range. One of these captured three fortresses in al-Lān, while the other captured the North Caucasian prince Tūmān Shāh, whom Marwān sent to the caliph, who, in turn, sent him back to his principality.[22]

In 118/736, Marwān campaigned against Wartanīs, a prince in the North Caucasus, from three directions. Wartanīs fled towards the Khazars, but the people of Khamzīn cut off his head and sent it to Marwān. Marwān slew the defenders of Wartanīs' castle despite their surrender and enslaved their dependents.[23]

In 119/737, it appears Hishām was finally convinced to end the Khazar threat once and for all with a massive expedition. Probably Marwān, the leader of the Jazīran army, persuaded him that he could accomplish the mission if given the chance, perhaps paying a special visit to the caliph for this purpose.[24] Marwān is said to have mobilized an army of one hundred twenty thousand, an unlikely figure, but one which indicates that, whatever its true size, this was the largest force ever sent against the Khazars. This number is said to have included Syrians, Iraqis, and Jazīrans, both paid official troops and volunteers who fought only for Islam and a share of the booty. To reach such an enormous number, he is said to have equipped even all of the servants and camp followers. As before, non-Muslims took part as well, for some of Marwān's troops were Armenian cavalry under their prince, Ashot Bagratouni. Marching through Armenia, Marwān reached Kasāk or Kasāl, a place about two hundred forty kilometers west of Bardha'a and one hundred twenty kilometers south of Tiflīs. In order to secure his rear, from this base he subdued Armenia, taking all of its castles.[25] Since Ashot Bagratouni was already his ally, this must refer to the castles of the hostile Armenian faction led by the Mamikonians and the rival Bagratids, the sons of Smbat. Not only did Marwān subdue Armenia, but he made a major campaign into western Georgia to wreak retribution on the Khosroïds, who had fled to Abkhazia in Byzantine-protected territory. He laid siege to Anakopia there, but had to withdraw owing to an epidemic of dysentery which afflicted his army.[26]

Next, Marwān unleashed his great campaign against the Khazars. Ordering his commander in al-Bāb, Asīd b. Zafir al-Sulamī, to advance north with his thirty thousand troops along the Caspian seacoast to meet him at Samandar, deep in Khazaria, Marwān crossed the Darial Pass from Armenia and descended on Samandar from the west. Asīd had with him many 'allied' troops levied from the Caucasian principalities. From Samandar, Marwān went on with his combined force until he reached al-Bayḍā' or Itil on the lower Volga, the Khazar capital, a spectacularly deep penetration.[27] But for what? Itil at this time was probably hardly more than a nomadic camp, as it was still almost such in the time of Ibn Faḍlān and al-Iṣṭakhrī about two hundred years later and had certainly not been more highly urbanized or built up in Hishām's time.[28]

From this point, we only have the account of Ibn A'tham and those derived from it. According to this version, Marwān went through the whole land of the Khazars, then raided the Slavs, and is said to have taken twenty thousand households or forty thousand persons captive. He sent a detachment of forty thousand men across the Volga under al-Kawthar b. al-Aswad al-'Anbarī, his security chief. Al-Kawthar's reluctance to obey shows that another disaster was feared so far from home. In this case, however, the Muslims were successful in surprising the Khazars in a swamp, where they slew ten thousand and took another seven thousand prisoners. This is the only battle that seems to have taken place between the Muslim and Khazar forces in this campaign.[29]

At this point, the *khāqān* supposedly sued for peace and even accepted Islam, requesting a delegation to inform him about the religion. Marwān responded by sending two missionaries, who were successful in persuading the *khāqān* to give up wine and improperly slaughtered meat.[30] Unfortunately, from a text in al-Balādhurī, it can be seen that the original version of the story in Ibn A'tham refers not to the *khāqān*, but to some Khazar noble, who not only embraced Islam but was also taken south by Marwān to be the local ruler of the captured Khazars whom Marwān settled in al-Lakz.[31] This shows that Marwān had to take such Khazar Muslims as may have existed away to safety indicating that the *khāqān* did not seriously consider embracing Islam during Marwān's invasion of his domains. Thus, no authentic Muslim version of an attempt to convert the Khazar *khāqān* himself to Islam exists.

However, there is some other evidence, mostly from Jewish sources, that the Khazar court, after a religious disputation between the Muslims, Christians, and Jews, embraced the Jewish faith, and that this occurred about 122/740.[32] That the Khazars should embrace Judaism at this time would not be in the least surprising in view of the highly ideological nature of the wars of Islam, as we have seen previously in the case of the Byzantine Empire, which was forced into an iconoclastic clean-up of its Christian ideology in order to better fend off the Muslims. Thus, the Islamic onslaught may have eventually strengthened the Khazar Khanate by forcing it to adopt a more thoroughgoing, ideological religion than its earlier paganism. Also, the Khazars' choice of Judaism rather than either Islam or Christianity seems to indicate an intention to remain a politically and culturally independent entity and shows an understanding of the danger of falling under some other empire's ideology. If indeed the Khazar court did embrace Judaism at this time, it would be one more indication of how the caliphate's expansion policy created its own nemesis by forcing their opponents to better organize for resistance, in this case by adopting a contrary ideology.

The outcome of Marwān's Khazar expedition can hardly have been very pleasing to the Muslims. Indeed, it seems that Marwān's campaign may actually have been far less of a success than claimed, if we follow only the bare report of Ibn Khayyāṭ. Though he may have reached Itil and perhaps beyond, he was unable to eliminate the highly mobile, seminomadic forces of the Khazar *khāqān*. Although it is true that the Khazars did not succeed in attacking south of the Caucasus again in Umayyad times, it would be mere speculation to suppose that Marwān's campaign gave them a blow from which they took a long time to recover. Other, unknown forces may have intervened to produce such an outcome, if indeed the Khazars' fortunes had suffered much of a setback from Marwān's campaign at all. Their continued participation in Byzantine politics through their alliance with the Greek empire showed the Khazars' vitality remained still. However, the Muslim campaigns from 112/730 to 119/737 still may have helped to discourage any further Khazar invasions of Islamic territory.

In any event, Marwān returned to al-Bāb and then proceeded to Bardha'a, settling his captives, the Khazars between the Samūr River and al-Shābarān in al-Lakz and the Slavs in Khākhīṭ to the west. The Slavs killed their local governor and tried to escape, but Marwān caught up with them and slew them.[33] These prisoners were all the Muslims had to show for the campaign, for the caliph's forces never again reached Itil or campaigned against the Khazars.

Marwān's remaining campaigns were an anticlimax, as Dunlop asserts.[34] In 120/738, Isḥāq b. Muslim al-'Uqaylī, his loyal lieutenant, invaded and ravaged the lands of Tūmān Shāh and captured his fortresses.[35] This would seem to imply that Tūmān Shāh had stopped paying the tribute agreed to in 117/735, just three years earlier.

In 121/739, Marwān renewed his offensive in the North Caucasus against recalcitrant local princes. He attacked al-Sarīr, Ghūmīk, and Khīraj or Khīzaj.[36] He besieged the fortresses of al-Sarīr and ravaged its countryside for a summer and a winter, until its prince agreed to submit.[37] Marwān then left this prince in possession of his domain.[38] Marwān's frequent apparent leniency toward the conquered suggests that he often succeeded only in extracting a single payment from them in order to make him go away. This would mean that his many campaigns accomplished no permanent conquests but really amounted only to plundering raids. Rather than constituting military successes, these raids may instead imply that Marwān was anxious to find employment and pay for his troops.

This probably brings us to 122/740. Then Marwān again came to Tūmān, which agreed to pay tribute,[39] as did Zirīkarān.[40] After this, he besieged a castle in Khamzīn for a month while ravaging the countryside until they also paid.[41] He also collected tribute from Sindān,[42] Layzān or al-Lakz,[43] Ṭabarsarān,[44] and Fīlān.[45] Marwān also subjected Sharwān[46] and attacked al-Didūwāniyya.[47] All these are around al-Bāb, mostly to the west and south. Thus, these campaigns hardly represent more than local raiding. It was very tedious and probably unrewarding for the troops, and none too successful in obtaining more than temporary tribute, judging by the three campaigns against Tūmān Shāh in 117/735, 120/738, and 122/740.[48] Though Marwān's campaigns seem from this long list to have been quite extensive, most seem to have been no more than demonstrations that involved little or no fighting. Still, these campaigns may have been spread over a number of years, but no text clearly implies a date later than 122/740.

After this, Marwān undertook one last expedition in 123/741 against Jīlān and Mūqān, areas south of the Araxes River far behind the Muslims' main front lines.[49] This probably indicates that the Khazar front was quiet. It also shows, however, that near the end of Hishām's reign Marwān was reduced to waging very minor campaigns that most of the sources have not even deigned to notice. Perhaps such raids were the only way Marwān could think of to get tribute to spend on his troops. No further offensive campaigning in the Caucasus region was ever undertaken by the Muslims under the Umayyad dynasty.

Thus, by 123/741, the situation in the Caucasus had considerably stabilized. A solid frontier base had finally been established at al-Bāb. The Khazars had become quiescent, as they had suffered great losses too. Marwān could finally devote some attention to local pacification. But the Caucasus Mountains were not a wealth-producing plain like Iraq, nor did they contain rich temples and cities like India. Nor was the Muslim control very effective except on the Caspian coast and in the valley bottoms. The effort to maintain control of this unrewarding area had cost the Muslim state dearly in lives and treasure. But its worst effect was that, even after these costs had been borne, it continued to be a drain on the strength of the Syro-Jazīran army, requiring as it did twenty-four thousand to thirty thousand troops on duty at al-Bāb all the time.

Transoxiana and Khurāsān 115–23/733–41

While resources were being burnt up futilely in Anatolia and the Caucasus region, an even stranger situation was developing in Khurāsān and Transoxiana. The disaster at the Battle of the Defile seems to have virtually stopped all campaigning while the Khurāsānī troops were recovering and being partly replaced by the newly introduced and equally unreliable Iraqis. Despite the disaster, al-Junayd al-Murrī was kept on as governor until his death from dropsy in al-Muḥarram 116/February–March 734. However, one report indicates that the caliph had been planning to drop him anyway. Though this is attributed to al-Junayd's marriage to a daughter of the rebel Ibn al-Muhallab, it is possible that Hishām was dissatisfied with his poor performance as a governor and military leader as well, for it is also suggested that Hishām wanted him dead.[50]

Why al-Junayd was retained as governor for two-and-a-half years after the disaster of the Defile is not clear. However, it would seem that unsuccessful generals were not always cashiered. The prime example, above all, is Maslama b. ʿAbd al-Malik, who, despite his reputation for aggressiveness, seems to have failed more often than not under Hishām and before.

Al-Junayd was temporarily succeeded by his deputy and cousin, ʿUmāra b. Ḥuraym al-Murrī, but his official replacement, the Jazīran commander ʿĀṣim b. ʿAbd Allāh al-Hilālī, had already been appointed by Hishām and was on his way. On arriving, ʿĀṣim imprisoned and tortured ʿUmāra and his officials.[51] He also sent Naṣr b. Sayyār to arrest and replace al-Junayd's local governor in Balkh.[52]

Meanwhile, shortly after al-Junayd's death, a most serious revolt of Khurāsānī troops broke out in Ṭukhāristān under the Tamīmī al-Ḥārith b. Surayj, a Muḍarī from Khurāsān. Al-Ḥārith called for the application of the Qur'ān and *sunna*,[53] which means that he felt the government was not applying them. He is also said to have been of the Murji'a, a pietistic trend in early Islam about which little reliable information is available.[54] However, a poem satirizing al-Ḥārith's beliefs by his adversary Naṣr b. Sayyār gives us some idea of them, revealing that al-Ḥārith probably wanted to hold the rulers responsible for un-Islamic conduct and, thus, force them to conform to Islamic principles. His program may possibly have included a less aggressive policy against the non-Muslims, for in the poem Naṣr calls on al-Ḥārith to fight the unbelievers, including those in Muslim territory, as well as hypocrites and rebels among the Muslims.[55]

Besides reforms in other government operations and policies, al-Ḥārith's movement also sought reforms in favor of the *mawālī*. Specifically, al-Ḥārith sought that no *kharāj* (here meaning capitation tax) be taken from any Muslims, that the non-Muslims as well be treated according to their Qur'ānic and treaty rights, and that no one be oppressed.[56] From this program, it is clear that al-Ḥārith's movement had its roots in the abortive reform movement of six years earlier, in 110/728, under Ashras al-Sulamī, which still earlier had first adumbrated its views to the Caliph 'Umar II. Moreover, the ties of many of al-Ḥārith's followers to the earlier reform movement prove beyond any reasonable doubt that the later movement was a continuation of the previous one. The same coalition of forces, including the same elements of the Khurāsānī Tamīm, Azd, Rabī'a, and *mawālī* that existed in 110/728 is also in evidence in al-Ḥārith's movement.[57]

Such a rebellion as that of al-Ḥārith, among troops on a war front, especially those facing a ferocious enemy like the Turgesh *khāqān*, was unprecedented. No such rebellion of Arab troops in Khurāsān had happened since Marwānid rule had been established. In fact, Muslim revolts against the Marwānids had hitherto been quite rare, except in Iraq. But, curiously, the Iraqis who had been dispatched to Khurāsān seem to have had no hand in this revolt.[58] Therefore, the grievances usually associated with Iraq, specifically the complaint about Umayyad oppression, may not have been had much influence in al-Ḥārith's revolt. Rather, so unusual a movement must have been the product of extreme tensions of local provenance. These may have included both complaints about the treatment of the *mawālī* and irritation at the failing, costly, and aggressive war policy.

Al-Ḥārith's revolt, which started at a small military outpost at al-Nukhudh in Lower Ṭukhāristān, began to spread widely as soon as 'Āṣim arrived at Marw, revealing the extent of rage at the Umayyad government and its policies. 'Āṣim showed a conciliatory mood, reflecting the weakness of his position from the outset, by sending a delegation, including a religious leader, to al-Ḥārith, but the latter imprisoned them. Al-Ḥārith, having gathered a force of four thousand, then turned to secure Balkh, the capital of Ṭukhāristān, driving out Naṣr b. Sayyār, the local governor, who had a force of ten thousand. Significantly, Naṣr offered only feeble resistance to al-Ḥārith, despite his disapproval of him, and gave no help at all to 'Āṣim, the Umayyad governor. After this, al-Ḥārith advanced on Marw itself, where he had support as well. Seeing the Khurāsānīs preparing to desert him, 'Āṣim threatened to abandon the capital and flee to Naysābūr, in loyal Qaysī country and astride the road to the west, where he could await the ten thousand Syrian troops he said he would summon to his aid. At this, the Marw Khurāsānīs gave him oaths of their allegiance, so that he stayed and prepared to face al-Ḥārith.[59]

Meanwhile, by picking up many *mawālī* volunteers on the way, al-Ḥārith's force had swollen to a reported sixty thousand. As this army drew near to Marw, 'Āṣim went out to face it. But he was still having trouble with his troops, for when he gave each a dinar, "the men spoke evil of him," so that he had to give each three more dinars. It was a serious situation when he had to pay his troops extra to fight, as they already were receiving stipends. Having the weaker force, 'Āṣim took up a defensive position at Zarq behind a canal, destroying the bridges across it. Al-Ḥārith's men repaired the bridges, but about two thousand of them went over to 'Āṣim, evidently out of fear of the overwhelming numbers of Iranians in al-Ḥārith's army. When the battle took place, 'Āṣim's defensive strategy proved successful, for al-Ḥārith was defeated, many of his men drowning in the canals.[60]

After this, the *mawālī* who were with al-Ḥārith went home, reducing his force to only three thousand loyal followers once more.[61] But al-Ḥārith remained very much in the field. As Shaban has pointed out, the men of Marw had fought for 'Āṣim mainly because of their fear of the large proportion of Iranians with al-Ḥārith.[62] Now that this was no longer a concern, they abandoned 'Āṣim, who was left only with his own guard of one thousand Syrians and Jazīrans. 'Āṣim again worsted al-Ḥārith in a battle at al-Dandanqān near Marw.[63]

But now events took a strange course. Apparently under pressure from the neutral or pro-Ḥārith elements at Marw, 'Āṣim signed a truce with al-Ḥārith and agreed to send a joint letter to Hishām asking the caliph to obey the Qur'ān and the *sunna*! If he refused, they were to join together against him. As was observed by an Umayyad supporter, "This is rebellion against the Commander of the Faithful!"[64]

There seems to be no compelling reason to doubt the veracity of the story of 'Āṣim's agreement with al-Ḥārith in view of its being reported by the best sources, though Shaban rejects it.[65] After all, at the time 'Āṣim held only part of Marw and the Qaysī region of Naysābūr.[66] It appears that, owing to the weakness of his position, 'Āṣim made some public gesture to al-Ḥārith like the reported agreement, but that at the same time he sent in his resignation, warning Hishām to place Khurāsān once more under the governor of Iraq and to send Syrian troops from Iraq to quell the rebellion.[67] In effect, it seems 'Āṣim made the agreement as a political maneuver to buy time and to remove al-Ḥārith from Marw. Nevertheless, the Syrian troops actually with 'Āṣim still felt any agreement with al-Ḥārith was ignoble and opposed it, despite their unfavorable military position.[68] This indicates that the Syrians still possessed the will to fight for the caliph.

However, the implications for the Umayyad caliphate of the situation in Khurāsān at the end of 'Āṣim's governorship were extremely serious. In spite of being worsted twice in the field, a provincial rebel, using as his banner the accumulated grievances of the Khurāsānī Arabs and *mawālī*, had practically driven the Umayyad governor from his province. This was most ominous, for the only analogous situation in Islamic history had been the expulsion of the Caliph 'Uthmān's governor by the Kūfans shortly before that caliph's bloody overthrow. Although 'Āṣim had not quite been driven from the province, the Umayyads could derive little satisfaction from that fact, for the shallowness of any loyalty felt by most of the Khurāsānī army to the regime had been nakedly displayed. Not only the indigenous Khurāsānīs, both Arabs and *mawālī*, but apparently also the twenty thousand Iraqis, or what was left of them, who had been sent to Khurāsān only four years previously, refused to come to the governor's help. That meant no reliance could be put on further mobilizations of Iraqis to meet the manpower shortage on the Khurāsānī front. Only one solution was left, the one suggested by 'Āṣim: more Syrian troops.

To implement this solution, Asad b. 'Abd Allāh al-Qasrī became governor of Khurāsān for the second time in late 116/734 or early 117/735.[69] Asad entered Khurāsān with a large, mostly Syrian army, twenty thousand strong.[70] That it was mostly Syrian can be deduced from the fact that all the campaigns of his second governorship were fought mostly or entirely by Syrians and that the divisions of the five Syrian *ajnād* now make their appearance in Khurāsān for the first time.[71] Interestingly, no Jazīran divisions are named as being with Asad.

On arriving, Asad first arrested 'Āṣim for embezzlement and failure to campaign.[72] Then he went forth with his fresh forces to quell al-Ḥārith's revolt. The war was costly, one hundred fifty Syrians falling in a single battle.[73] As Asad had one success after another, the Khurāsānīs began to return to the Umayyad fold. Asad, being a Yamanī fighting against a Muḍarī, may have helped to attract some of the Yaman tribal grouping back to the Umayyad standard. A significant part of the Rabī'a, the old tribal archenemies of al-Ḥārith's Tamīm, came over to Asad.[74] Al-Ḥārith's revolt collapsed, while he himself retreated farther and farther up the Oxus.[75] Thus, it was still possible for the Umayyads to control revolts by a judicious application of force coupled with the exploitation of traditional tribal rivalries that enabled them to divide and rule.

Having reduced the threat from al-Ḥārith, Asad tried to recover Samarqand from the Turks. Significantly, he had to pay the troops a double stipend to get them to go to Samarqand at all. It is unclear whether this applied to his Syrian troops, to the surrendering Khurāsānīs whom he was now reintegrating into the caliphal army, or to both. In any case, he was unable to make any headway at Samarqand. From there, he returned to Balkh, which he intended to be the new quarters for his Syrian army.[76]

In the next year, 118/736, Asad sent forces against al-Ḥārith's remnants in the remote mountains of Upper Ṭukhāristān and Badakhshān. These were mostly successful in destroying what was left of al-Ḥārith's forces, but al-Ḥārith himself eluded them.[77]

After this, Asad campaigned in 119/737 in al-Khuttal,[78] an area whose rulers had given the Muslims trouble before and who had generally supported both al-Ḥārith and the Turks. While Asad's army was scattered around in al-Khuttal ravaging the land, the *khāqān* finally took the field once more at the invitation of the local ruler in order to meet the renewed Muslim threat. Asad had enough warning to send ahead the baggage train, containing the choicest of the spoils from al-Khuttal.[79] But as the Turkish army, said to number fifty thousand,[80] drew near, it precipitated the Muslims into one of their famous flights, much like the Day of Thirst in 106/724 or the Caucasus campaigns of 110/728 and 113/731.

Asad's force rushed to the Oxus, barely ahead of the Turkish army. There followed scenes of virtual panic, as Asad ordered each man to carry a sheep across the deep and frigid stream. Though it created much confusion, as the men struggling with the sheep were bowled over by the swirling waters, Asad's order is actually less ludicrous than it appears, for the sheep were his army's provisions, through which they could stay in the field, while at the same time he had to deprive the *khāqān* of that provision. But the sheep had to be abandoned as the army struggled to save itself. Asad remained calm, but some of his troops were practically hysterical for fear of the Turks. And indeed the Turks badly mauled the rear guard, which had been left on the north bank and seems to have consisted of Khurāsānīs.[81]

The Muslims south of the Oxus had felt themselves safe, but the Turks crossed right over after them and beseiged their camp. In the morning, Asad found that the Turks had left, which alarmed him, as he knew they were making for his baggage train, which was encamped some distance away. The Turks savaged the defenders of the baggage and made off with the loot, though Asad was able to arrive in time to rescue some of the Muslims that had been with the baggage. The Turks attacked Asad once more on 1 Shawwāl 119/1 October 737, then both sides withdrew to their winter quarters, the *khāqān* remaining in Ṭukhāristān in possession of the field, while Asad retreated to Balkh.[82] At this point, al-Ḥārith b. Surayj, who was also in Upper Ṭukhāristān, joined the *khāqān*.[83]

This campaign only added to the string of Muslim disasters on the Transoxianan front, which had now been pushed south of the Oxus for the first time. The Syrians so far had fared no better than the Khurāsānis before them. Though Asad had saved the bulk of his army, his losses were still probably severe. The ambiguous Persian verses describing a complete defeat of Asad more likely refer to this battle than any other.[84] One version goes:

From Khuttalān you have come,
    With a destroyed face you have come.
A fugitive you have come back,
    Lowly and emaciated you have come."

These lines would seem to indicate a worse outcome for the Muslims in the campaign than is indicated by the prose narrative. It should also be remembered that the sources are normally kinder to the Yamanī governors like Asad than to the Qaysīs such as Muslim b. Sa'īd, Ashras al-Sulamī, al-Junayd al-Murrī, and 'Āṣim al-Hilālī, each of whom we have shown was responsible for some disaster on the Transoxianan front. Thus, it is likely that Asad's defeat was also significant.

Nor did the Muslim troops get any rest after their retreat, for like the Khazars, the Transoxianan Turks could campaign all winter. Thus, the Turks scattered out to raid the country around Balkh in early Dhū al-Ḥijja 119/December 737. However, Asad acted resolutely, mobilizing his Syrian troops. He had to pay each man twenty dirhams to go out to fight. He refused at first to allow any Khurāsānīs to take part, even the loyal ones, which shows how unreliable he considered them. But he eventually relented. This gave him a force of seven thousand. Meanwhile, the *khāqān* had bypassed Balkh and gone on to Lower Ṭukhāristān, where the farthest point reached by the Turkish raiders was Marw al-Rūdh. This marked the lowest point for the Muslims on this front since the

Marwānids had come to power. The *khāqān* allowed his men to scatter for raiding and forage, perhaps partly because supplying a large force in so cold a land in the winter was problematical. Thus it was that Asad caught him with less than four thousand men at Kharīstān.[85]

The ensuing battle is painted as the decisive turning point on this front, but one must agree with Gibb that it hardly amounted to more than a skirmish.[86] The Turks, seeing they were outclassed, ran, abandoning their camp, including their spoils of one hundred fifty-five thousand sheep. However, not only did the *khāqān* and al-Ḥārith both escape, but Asad also was unable to pursue them for more than a short distance.[87] Nevertheless, the fact that Asad had been able to capture the *khāqān*'s camp astonished the Caliph Hishām, who at first could not believe it.[88]

Despite the apparent smallness of its immediate outcome, the Battle of Kharīstān marked the end of the Turkish offensive in Transoxiana and Khurāsān. Whether the *khāqān*'s prestige was seriously injured by this setback is hard to say. Asad's victory at least saved the Muslim position from further deterioration. But, the *khāqān*'s subsequent assassination at the beginning of 120/738 owed more to old internal rivalries stirred up by the Chinese than to any action by the Muslims.[89] The Turgesh Khanate then totally collapsed as the Turks fell to fighting among themselves.[90] Thus, in another dramatic reversal of fortune, one of the most serious threats to the caliphate was suddenly removed.

However, the Muslims were rather slow to take advantage of the opportunities offered, which shows how much the twenty-year war with the Turks had worn them down. Asad died only two months after his victory, in Ṣafar 120/February 738.[91] After an interregnum lasting several months, during which the Ḥimṣī general Ja'far b. Ḥanẓala al-Bahrānī was temporary governor, Hishām appointed the old Khurāsānī leader Naṣr b. Sayyār as governor in Rajab 120/July 738.[92]

Though Naṣr was a Muḍarī, the appointment of a local Arab to the highest position in Khurāsān was unprecedented and showed the extent to which the Umayyads now had to go to control the situation there.[93] Hishām probably thought Naṣr's appointment would conciliate some of the Khurāsānī troops, especially the Muḍarī element that had previously shown the most loyalty to the Umayyad house. With Naṣr in command, the Syrian troops' presence might seem less heavy-handed and oppressive to the local population, and the caliph could not now withdraw the Syrians. Though he had failed sufficiently to resist al-Ḥārith b. Surayj or to help the governor, ʿĀṣim, Naṣr had adequately proven his loyalty to the caliphate and his fighting abilities on numerous other occasions. The evident partisanship of Naṣr for the Muḍar may have also weighed in his favor, as it helped to keep the Khurāsānīs' attention on their tribal-factional dispute.[94]

Despite the favorable situation following the collapse of the Turks, Naṣr did not campaign in 120/738. Probably, it was too late in the season to begin a campaign. Also, Naṣr had to work to consolidate his position, send out his appointees to take charge of the various districts, and so on, all of which took some time.[95] Since his appointment as governor represented a change in caliphal policy, it may have been somewhat unexpected. Therefore, he also might have needed time to plan a campaign. On the other hand, it is also possible that he thought it best to let the troops continue to recuperate from the harsh campaign of 119/737.

However, in the next year, 121/739, Naṣr set about restoring Muslim rule in Transoxiana in earnest. His first step, after setting out from Balkh to secure the area around al-Ṣaghāniyān once more, was to move the capital back to Marw. There, Naṣr proclaimed at last the long-overdue financial reform that had been sought by the movements of Abū al-Ṣaydāʾ in 110/728 and al-Ḥārith in 116–7/734–5. Specifically, he ordered that the *jizya* be taken from every non-Muslim and removed from every Muslim. As a result, it is said that thirty thousand Muslims were freed from the *jizya*, while eighty thousand non-Muslims who had been illegitimately exempted had to start paying it. Naṣr also began collecting the *kharāj* of the land according to the peace treaties various places originally had made with the Muslims.[96] This generally lightened the burden of the *kharāj*.[97]

Armed with these reforms, Naṣr set out to resubjugate the parts of Transoxiana that had been lost. This appears to have been in 122/740, as it is described as his second campaign. He recovered Samarqand,[98] apparently without a fight, as Gibb suggests.[99]

In 123/741, Naṣr set out from Marw on a more ambitious campaign against al-Shāsh, in order to recover even the most distant conquests of Qutayba, lands that the Muslims had not set foot in for almost twenty years. First, he passed through Ushrūsana, receiving the submission of its prince.[100] On reaching the Jaxartes, he finally met resistance, for Kūrṣūl (Köl-chür), who had assassinated the *khāqān* Sülü and tried to hold together his empire, massed fifteen thousand troops to prevent Naṣr from crossing. Also, al-Ḥārith still fought on the Turkish side. Though the Muslim tradition records that Kūrṣūl was captured in an ambush and killed, which caused the Turks to lose heart and flee,[101] Chinese records show that he was actually executed by the Chinese in 126/744.[102] The Muslim account has probably substituted Kūrṣūl's name for that of a lesser chieftain.[103]

It seems that Naṣr neither was able to subdue nor to ravage al-Shāsh, for we hear only that the prince of al-Shāsh made an agreement with Naṣr to send al-Ḥārith to Fārāb, away from the caliphate's borders.[104] However, according to another version, it was the *khāqān* who had already given al-Ḥārith Fārāb as a principality for him and his followers.[105] So, it is doubtful that Naṣr's expedition caused any trouble for al-Ḥārith. This also casts doubt on the whole tradition that Naṣr led a victorious campaign. Naṣr may also have collected some tribute from al-Shāsh, for he is said to have sent an agent there.[106] Perhaps the main part of the settlement with al-Shāsh involved the return of Sughdī exiles who had been with the Turks under the *khāqān*, and had gone to live in al-Shāsh after his assassination. Now these came back to their homes in Samarqand, Naṣr undertaking not to punish them for their apostasy nor to try forcibly to recover Muslim captives they held except by judicial order. Naṣr was severely criticized for making an agreement the likes of which his predecessors never would have made. Hishām disliked the agreement but felt compelled to approve it anyway.[107]

At the same time, Naṣr seems to have sent a delegation consisting of only ten men to collect tribute from Farghāna. These returned with considerable treasure as well as Iranian noble subjects of the caliphate who now either agreed to return or were forced to do so.[108] After this, Naṣr sent a stronger force against Farghāna that ravaged the countryside and is reported, probably by exaggeration, to have taken thirty thousand captives.[109] Though there is one report of a minor battle in Farghāna, another tradition suggests that the Muslims were more anxious than the Farghānans to keep the peace.[110] Therefore, it seems unlikely that Naṣr undertook or achieved any significant conquests in the regions beyond Samarqand.

After this, there were no further campaigns against the non-Muslims in Transoxiana and Khurāsān under Umayyad rule.[111] The great Umayyad offensive juggernaut had broken down here as elsewhere. But on the surface, the caliphate's position in Transoxiana seemed vastly improved over that of ten years earlier. The great Turkish khanate had utterly disappeared. No new threat from the steppes appeared in the offing.[112] Muslim rule in Transoxiana had at last been restored as far as Samarqand and perhaps some tribute levied from farther out. The reconquest had been almost without a battle, except for the efforts of the Turks and Shāshīs at the Jaxartes.

The inhabitants, judging by the lack of resistance, seemed reconciled to Muslim rule at last. To effect this, the caliphate through Naṣr had finally conceded the long-delayed taxation reform. Therefore, in Transoxiana, the caliphate appeared stronger than ever.

But even though the caliphate had nearly reached its earlier maximum boundaries once more, the victory had been bought at too dear a price. Tired of constant campaigning, especially after the Day of the Defile, the Khurāsānīs had decisively rebelled against the Umayyads and could no longer be trusted. Their rebellion had required the introduction of a large Syrian army of twenty thousand, which further exacerbated relations between the caliphate and most Khurāsānīs. The Syrians, as well as those Khurāsānīs still in the army, continued to suffer large numbers of casualties through 119/737. As the Syrian troops were not numerous enough ever to enforce their will totally on the Khurāsānīs, and as more Syrians could not be spared because of crises elsewhere, the caliph finally had to hand over the province to a Khurāsānī Arab governor. This was an unprecedented move that meant a considerable loss of control for the caliphate, threatened to fracture the caliphate on regional lines, and also presaged the ʻAbbāsid revolution. Thus, the apparent victories on the Transoxianan front were not what they seemed. Like almost everywhere else, the scene had been set for the Umayyads' downfall.

Sijistān 115–25/733–43

Except perhaps for Khārijite activity, Sijistān remained quiet throughout the latter part of Hishām's reign. ʻAbd Allāh b. Abī Burda remained as governor for almost nine years until the downfall of Khālid al-Qasrī in Iraq in 120/738. As one of Khālid's associates, Ibn Abī Burda was dismissed and succeeded by Muḥammad b. Ḥijr b. Qays al-ʻAbdī, probably a local officer who was only interim governor very briefly. He is mentioned only by Ibn Khayyāṭ and, as a member of the Rabīʻa would never have received an appointment from Yūsuf b. ʻUmar, Khālid al-Qasrī's extreme Qaysī successor. ʻAbd Allāh's official successor, who arrived to take office in Rajab 120/July 738, was Ibrāhīm b. ʻĀṣim al-ʻUqaylī, a Qaysī Jazīran commander who had been with Asad in Khurāsān. Ibrāhīm arrested Ibn Abī Burda and packed off him to Iraq, where his wealth was confiscated and he was executed by Yūsuf b. ʻUmar. Ibrāhīm died in office about 125–26/743–44 and was succeeded by another interim governor, this time a Qaysī Jazīran from his entourage, Ḥarb b.

Qaṭan b. Qabīṣa b. Mukhāriq al-Hilālī, whose tenure is also only noted by Ibn Khayyāṭ.[113] If nothing else, the rather long tenures and blank records of Ibn Abī Burda and Ibrāhīm al-'Uqaylī suggest that the instability that had hitherto plagued Sijistān had been, to some extent, controlled. On the other hand, it appears that such an achievement of quiet and control was only possible because no campaigns were undertaken against the Zunbīl.

India 113–22/731–40

After the death of the ill-starred Tamīm b. Zayd al-Qaynī, al-Ḥakam b. 'Awāna al-Kalbī, a Syrian commander, was appointed governor of Sind (c.113–22/731–40). Unfortunately, very little is known of his long governorship, despite the fact that his son 'Awāna was a famous historian. Al-Ḥakam's first work must have been to restore order in Sind and in Cutch, where some Muslims had been holding out. After rescuing them by retaking Cutch, al-Ḥakam returned to Sind, where he drove out the enemy forces after a difficult war. Thereafter, the province of Sind enjoyed a period of internally peaceful rule.[114]

Al-Ḥakam's biggest accomplishment was the founding at last of a definitive Muslim base in Sind, the *miṣr* of al-Maḥfūẓa, near Brahmānābād, the second native city of Sind after al-Rawr. The establishment of al-Maḥfūẓa repeats the pattern, better documented in the case of al-Bāb in the Caucasus, of establishing new forward bases on the frontiers. The motivation given in the sources for the founding of al-Maḥfūẓa is that, when al-Ḥakam came to Sind, he found the Muslims had no places where they were safe,[115] which shows again that almost the whole country had been lost under Tamīm. That al-Maḥfūẓa was set near Brahmānābād further suggests that the latter city may have been a major source of trouble. Al-Maḥfūẓa was apparently meant to replace the ill-omened and abandoned Daybul on the Indian Ocean. That the Arabs would move their settlement inland may indicate a greater confidence in their ability to maintain control over Sind. Or, their decision could have owed to a desire to have their base in a more strategic, central location. Possibly, the muggy coastal climate did not suit them. Additionally, they may have preferred to distance their base from their crucial seagoing allies, the Meds. A short time later and during al-Ḥakam's governorship, his deputy 'Amr b. Muḥammad b. al-Qāsim al-Thaqafī founded the city of al-Manṣūra opposite al-Maḥfūẓa.[116] No precise dates are given for either foundation, but it would seem reasonable that al-Maḥfūẓa was for the Yamanī troops, as it was founded by a Yamanī, while al-Manṣūra was founded by a Qaysī and may have been for the Muḍarī units.[117] If this is the case, both may have been built at nearly the same time, perhaps near the beginning of al-Ḥakam's rule.

Having established a secure base, al-Ḥakam invaded India to restore the conquests of al-Junayd. The most certain of his campaigns are those into Gujarat to the southeast, where most of al-Junayd's wars had also taken place. Muslim sources say nothing about al-Ḥakam's efforts, but inscribed Indian commemorative plates do reveal the progress as well as the failure of al-Ḥakam's campaigns. Plates of the Gurjara prince of Nandipuri, Jayabhata IV, show this ruler defeating the Muslims in Valabhi in Kathiawar, the capital of his probable overlords, the Maitrakas, in the year 117–18/735–36.[118] However, Jayabhata's victory was unavailing, for the Muslim advance continued. Plates of the Chalukyas dated 120–21/738–39 prove that some time shortly before, the Muslims had plundered the Saindhavas of Bhumilka in West Kathiawar, the Kachchellas of Cutch, the Maitrakas of Saurashtra, the Chavotakas of South Rajasthan, the Mauryas of Chitor, and the Gurjaras of Bhillamala.[119] This list strongly resembles that of the territories conquered by al-Junayd a dozen years earlier and subsequently lost. Since these conquests had been lost under Tamīm b. Zayd, and since the Muslims had again reached the southeastern corner of Gujarat by 121/739, we must conclude that al-Ḥakam or his lieutenants had indeed reconquered all these territories and that the repetition of reports is not a doublet. Probably, this reconquest occurred early in al-Ḥakam's governorship, perhaps taking a number of years.

The Muslim invasion continued to press south, reportedly with the intention of subduing all the southern kingdoms of India.[120] But it was decisively stopped when the Chalukya prince of Lata, Pulakesirāja, defeated a Muslim army at the southern extremity of Gujarat near Navasarika in 120–21/738–39, thus winning appreciation from the Chalukya emperor Vikramāditya II[121] as well as the title 'the repeller of the unrepellable,'[122] an honor whose wording casts an interesting light on the Chalukyas' view of the Muslim *jihād*. The Rashtrakuta prince Dantidurga also played an important part in the battle, receiving thanks from the Chalukya emperor at the same time.[123] So deep an advance into India can hardly have been achieved without the Muslims first having resecured much of the territory of Gujarat to their rear, probably in concert with some of the Indians. The victory of Pulakesirāja has been considered a decisive battle in history, for it marked the farthest penetration into India the caliphate would ever achieve.[124]

Indeed, the Muslims were not only stopped but pursued out of India following their defeat at Navasarika. For example, in Chitor, the Guhilot Bappa drove out the Muslims after the latter had put an end to the local Maurya dynasty.[125] Yet another Indian prince claimed victory over the Muslims in an inscription: the Pratihara Nagabhata I of Malwa (c. 112–39/730–56). As the inscription is undated, it is uncertain where it should be placed chronologically. But it seems most likely that this prince would seek to take credit, like the others, for the final expulsion of the Muslims from India in the governorship of al-Ḥakam, especially since he seems to have been active in the very region of southeastern Gujarat where the decisive battle took place.[126] From these many claims to victory over the Muslims, it can be seen that the Muslim invasion was a major event that made a strong impression on the Indians.

To the north, al-Ḥakam may have sent an expedition against Kanauj and Kashmir, for in 118/736 these appealed to the Chinese emperor for help.[127] But the threat against Kanauj and Kashmir also may have come from the Tibetans, so that the evidence for al-Ḥakam's activity in this quarter is slight. Another possible evidence of Muslim campaigning in the north is the victory of Yasovarman of Kanauj over the Parasikas claimed in a literary text. If the Parasikas are identified with the Muslims, as alleged by some Indian scholars, such a battle with Yasovarman might fit in a northern context.[128] Despite the absence of much historical evidence for North India at this period, it is not impossible that al-Ḥakam was active there as well, for we would know nothing of the extent of his expeditions to the south if not for Indian inscriptions.[129]

The caliphate spared no resources in its effort to conquer Gujarat, as shown by the sending in 119/737 of Syrian reinforcements under an unnamed Qaynī[130] to fight there for al-Ḥakam. While these forces were passing through Iraq, Khālid al-Qasrī gave them an opportunity to fight a *khārijī* rebel instead, in exchange for extra pay and the right to return home if they were successful. Despite the *khawārij*'s reputation for being ferocious fighters, the Syrians jumped at the chance. The incentive was not the extra pay so much as the exemption from having to go to India, for the troops hated service there, not only because it was so far away, but also because it was so dangerous and disaster-prone. It appears that these Syrians consisted of only six hundred men, which may be an indication of how strained the manpower resources of the Syrians already were becoming, if reinforcements had to be sent in such small increments.[131] It is also interesting how this episode immediately precedes the disaster at Navasarika in 120–21/738–39. Probably, al-Ḥakam sorely needed whatever reinforcements he could get, and the failure of the caliphate to get them or others through to him may well have contributed to the disaster in Gujarat.

Al-Ḥakam's regime stumbled from one disaster to another. After Navasarika, as we have seen, various Indian princes expelled the Muslims from Valabhi and Chitor, and probably from other areas as well. Al-Ḥakam was finally slain in 122/740 fighting the warlike, seafaring Meds of North Saurashtra.[132] Loss of control of the sea may have further contributed to the Muslims' final disaster. The Meds were perhaps subject allies who revolted in light of Navasarika and the subsequent disasters. Thus, it seems the Muslims had already lost all of India except their original province of Sind by the time of al-Ḥakam's death. The claim that al-Ḥakam went out blindly to die a martyr's death after hearing how the new governor of Iraq was dealing with Khālid al-Qasrī's subordinates,[133] of whom he was one, cannot be seriously entertained, for unlike Khālid's other subgovernors, al-Ḥakam had been retained in office.

The period of al-Ḥakam's governorship had spectacular results. Like the previous governorship of Tamīm b. Zayd al-Qaynī, it was an unmitigated disaster for the caliphate. Another massive attempt to subdue Gujarat had ended in a far more conclusive failure than the earlier effort of al-Junayd. Losses in manpower continued to be huge, judging by the nature of the defeat at Navasarika. Al-Ḥakam himself became at least the fourth provincial governor to die in the line of military duty under Hishām.[134] He was not to be the last, though. The Syrian troops became increasingly reluctant to serve on the ill-omened Indian front, which seemed, after so many failures, to be well on its way to becoming the worst front.

Meanwhile, the Indians had begun to grow more accustomed to the Muslims after the first shock of their initial encounter with them and, from their experience, more able to deal with them. At the same time, easy booty was probably now less available, as the Indians began to take better precautions. More importantly, the Muslim offensive completely upset the constellation of principalities that had previously existed in the attacked regions of Gujarat and Rajasthan, destroying many and weakening others. These were now replaced by larger, more powerful states, especially the Rashtrakutas, who for a short time conquered Gujarat and then overthrew their Chalukya overlords.[135] These more powerful states were better able to resist any further Muslim invasions of India than their predecessors and were more capable of stirring up trouble for the Muslims in Sind itself. Thus, the last of the Muslim invasions of India not only caused the caliphate a loss of resources, especially troops, that it could ill afford. But it also helped to create stronger Hindu kingdoms that could be potentially harmful to the caliphate's interests.

Khārijī and Shī'ī Revolts in Iraq and the East 113–22/731–40

I have made little mention of the obviously important province of Iraq to this point, owing to the peaceful conditions that prevailed there early in Hishām's reign and the resulting scantiness of information about it. Much of what we know of the province relates to the massive irrigation and land reclamation projects there undertaken by the governor Khālid al-Qasrī, both on his own account and on that of the caliph. Such projects were of no benefit to the local Iraqis, particularly the Muslims, who alone had any political input. In fact, they were actually harmful, for the big official estates tended to raise prices through manipulation of the markets.[136] Therefore, it is no surprise that some Iraqis, such as the outspoken poet al-Farazdaq, already opposed these projects early on.[137] But, despite the consternation they caused, there is no indication that the big agricultural projects led to open revolts. Rather, they were merely another grievance to add to an already long list.

However, new *khārijī* revolts, a traditional barometer of discontent, ominously began to break out in the East as the reign of Hishām wore on. Typically, these began first in Khurāsān, where they may have been motivated by the hostility of the Rabī'a to the Tamīm.[138] But in Iraq, a whole series of *khārijī* outbreaks is reported for 119/737, just before Khālid al-Qasrī's downfall. Though the sources attribute these to various trivial or personal motives of the rebels, the revolts nevertheless may be seen as a loss of confidence in the regime.[139] While they would seem to have had little chance of success in any case, the revolts may have been encouraged by the knowledge that the Syrian troops were being stretched thin in the wake of the numerous earlier disasters, as well as the growing need to garrison the frontier provinces with Syrians. Though the revolts were put down quite easily in most cases, the sympathy with which the traditions view the rebels indicates that the latter had an influence disproportionate to their small numbers.

The most important of all these revolts was that of the 'Alid Zayd b. 'Alī b. al-Ḥusayn in al-Kūfa at the outset of 122/740, though it, too, ended in miserable failure. Ever loyal to the house of the Prophet, many Kūfans had pledged their support to the effort of this great-grandson of ʻAlī to overthrow Umayyad rule. However, the governor of Iraq, by acting fast, was able to outmanoeuver Zayd and kill him. Thus, no immediate war requiring many troops occurred.[140] But the impact of Zayd's death was nonetheless very extensive. It was the first time that the Umayyads had had to kill an ʻAlid since the disastrous massacre of al-Ḥusayn and his family sixty years before.[141] The Umayyad government considered Zayd's rebellion serious enough to send his severed head to Egypt, presumably as well as to other provinces, to be displayed as an example to would-be rebels.[142] The killing of Zayd had a shattering effect on the Umayyads' pretentions to legitimacy. This can be seen especially in Khurāsān, where the ʻAbbāsid propagandists amply exploited it as an example of Umayyad perfidy.[143]

Aside from his effect in increasing the unpopularity of the Umayyads, Zayd also put forward an interesting political program. In it, he proposed the redress of the kind of grievances that ʻUmar II had striven to deal with. These included some of the same grievances which had exercised al-Ḥārith b. Surayj and his followers in Khurāsān, particularly the need for equitable division of the tax income among those deserving it. This, coupled with general appeals to the Qur'ān and *sunna* that had also been made by the earlier movements in Khurāsān, leaves little doubt that a fairer treatment of the *mawālī* was envisioned, including the removal of the *jizya* from them.[144] Zayd's forward-looking program, despite its vagueness, and despite his own defeat and death, probably increased the pressure on the Umayyads and their Syrian supporters for reform.

Nevertheless, on the whole, Iraq exerted relatively little influence on the course of events at this point, despite its theoretical contribution to the revolutionary Shīʻism of the ʻAbbāsids and its demographic weight. The Umayyads under Hishām were not only able to crush the various Iraqi rebellions easily, indeed more easily than they had Iraqi revolts in the past, but also, they did not feel the need quickly to implement the reforms the Iraqis were asking for. The reason for this Iraqi weakness was that Iraq was a mostly demilitarized interior province without the force to back up its demands. Though the effort required to occupy Iraq and keep it in line was a continuous drain on the resources of the caliphate, it was not a new factor. The decisive strength to budge the Umayyads from their seeming intransigence and, indeed, to bring their regime crashing down, would have to come from elsewhere, even at this late date, after the many expensive defeats already suffered in the course of Hishām's reign.

Egypt 115–22/733–40

Iraq was not alone among the previously peaceful interior provinces that began to give Hishām trouble. Egypt, too, underwent severe strains in the period of the renewed offensive on the frontiers. Though scarcely any disorders had occurred there in the period preceding Hishām's reign, two new revolts now added themselves to the outbreak of 107/725, which I have already discussed. The first of these two was an alleged *khārijī* outbreak among the Yaman in the capital, al-Fusṭāṭ, in 117/735. It gave the governor, a Qaysī, considerable trouble before he was able to suppress it.[145]

Apparently in the same year, the caliph sent new standard wooden grain measures to Egypt, for use in measuring out the troops' rations that were a part of their pay. This was an economizing step, as the new measures would have reduced the amount each man received. It was again among the Yaman that the new measures were first resisted, by a Ma'āfirī Yamanī who smashed them to bits. This simple act of resistance must have been widely imitated, for it caused the government to withdraw the idea.[146] Not only does this episode show that the government was even trying to save money by cutting the troops' pay, but also, it indicates that the troops would resist any reduction in their privileges.

In 118/736, Nāfi' b. Abī 'Ubayda b. 'Uqba al-Fihrī commanded a seaborne expedition of Egyptian troops against some place under Byzantine rule.[147] After unsuccessfully besieging the place, the expedition was intercepted by a Byzantine fleet on its return and defeated. When the news reached Hishām, he removed the governor of Egypt, who was considered too soft in military matters. The reappearance of the Byzantine fleet raised the specter of Byzantine raids against Egypt once more, causing Hishām to send a clearly military man as the new governor of the province.[148]

The third rebellion in Egypt of Hishām's reign in Egypt was another revolt of the native Copts, this time in Upper Egypt, in 121/739. It appears to have been chiefly directed against the exactions of the tax collectors (*ḥārab al-Qibṭ 'ummālahum*). The rebellion was of short duration, but it required the intervention of regular troops, probably sent from al-Fusṭāṭ, and led to high casualties among the Copts.[149]

Thus, reports from the interior province of Egypt during the period of renewed offensive on the frontiers were not that encouraging. Economizing fiscal measures and increased taxes were resisted. Revolts seemed to be occurring with a slowly increasing frequency. Even the Byzantine enemy threatened to become more active. If this was how things were going on the interior, how could affairs on the frontiers be?

North Africa 115–22/733–40

In North Africa, affairs seemed to be going better than anywhere else, by virtue of the longstanding peaceful relations with the Muslim Berbers. Owing to the peacefulness of these relations, little can be found in the sources to elucidate what was going on internally in North Africa at this time. However, it may be supposed that in the period between the much greater spread of Islam among the Berbers, encouraged by the policies of 'Umar II and the beginning of the Berber revolt twenty years after his death, a considerable islamization of the Berbers was taking place, through which they came to learn of the unpopularity of Umayyad rule from pious missionaries dissatisfied with the caliphs on several grounds. I have already spoken above about the case of one such missionary, 'Ikrima, the Berber *mawlā* of Ibn 'Abbās.

But no disturbances were yet visible on the surface, so that the continuous seaborne campaigns against the Byzantine-held islands of the West Mediterranean command the most attention. These became, if anything, greater in scope than before, indicating a supreme, final effort of the *jihād* state here as elsewhere. Also, as elsewhere, these expeditions became increasingly less successful, providing another motive for dissatisfaction with the government somewhat different from the *mawālī* complaints of oppression and unfair taxation.

In 115/733, the Muslim expedition sent by the governor of North Africa, 'Ubayda b. 'Abd al-Raḥmān al-Sulamī (110–15/728–33) against Sicily, under the command of Bakr b. Suwayd, came to grief at Drepana (mod. Trapani) in the west of the island when the Byzantine defenders destroyed much of the Muslim fleet using Greek fire.[150] This may have been part of the reason for Hishām's removal of 'Ubayda from his governorship in the same year.[151] 'Ubayda was ordered to proceed to the capital laden with gifts. Such forced 'gifts' provided a way for the caliph to get more of the often-withheld provincial tribute. One report says that 'Ubayda's gifts included twenty thousand slaves.[152] Another report numbers the slave girls alone at only seven hundred, while also mentioning other slaves, eunuchs, horses, pack animals, gold, silver, and vessels.[153] The prominence of slaves in North Africa's tribute, as before, indicates that the practice of taking payment in slaves from the Berber subjects of the caliphate to cover their *kharāj* assessment, which was a major Berber grievance, had not ceased.

In fact, it seems most likely that 'Ubayda's removal was connected with a desire to implement a new policy ending the special status of the Berbers in the caliphate, for the new governor was none other than 'Ubayd Allāh b. al-Ḥabḥāb,[154] the former fiscal governor of Egypt who had provoked the first Coptic revolt there by his implementation of the caliph's new taxation policy in 106–07/724–25. Ibn al-Ḥabḥāb's star had been in the ascendent in Hishām's favor ever more, like that of Khālid al-Qasrī in the East. Before leaving Egypt, the fiscal governor had become the military governor as well, an unprecedented advance for a *mawlā*. On moving to North Africa, he lost that office, but his son al-Qāsim took over the post of fiscal governor of Egypt, maintaining his father's influence there.[155] For the first time, the rather loosely connected western provinces took on the aspect of a superprovince under one governor, like that of the East.[156]

Ibn al-Ḥabḥāb greatly intensified the offensive expeditions against the non-Muslims, although with mixed results. The expedition to Sicily in 116/734 under 'Uthmān b. Abī 'Ubayda al-Fihrī was apparently a considerable disaster, as the Byzantine fleet again intercepted the Muslims at sea on their return, capturing 'Uthmān's two sons and other Muslim nobles.[157] Ibn al-Ḥabḥāb's other expedition under Ḥabīb b. Abī 'Ubayda al-Fihrī was far to the west, to the valley of al-Sūs in southern Morocco and to the 'Land of the Blacks' beyond, areas very far from the nearest Muslim base in Tangier. It was successful, returning with much gold,[158] as well as many captives.[159] Apparently, al-Sūs was one Berber region that had not yet embraced Islam, or at any rate had not yet submitted fully.[160] That such an expedition was sent out indicates that Ibn al-Ḥabḥāb was seeking to implement the *jihād* on all his frontiers. It also perhaps reveals the need to raise cash through taking booty. Though details are lacking, it appears that the more distant regions of Morocco played a role in North Africa analogous to Transoxiana in the province of Khurāsān. Like Transoxiana, Morocco was more recently conquered and less well pacified than the older part of the province to which it was attached. Like Transoxiana, Morocco would spearhead the resistance to caliphal rule in its province.

In 117/735, Ibn al-Ḥabḥāb sent the same Ḥabīb b. Abī 'Ubayda against Sardinia, where he succeeded in storming and plundering a town.[161] The following year, 118/736, Qutham b. 'Awāna al-Kalbī, a Yamanī commander, took Ūliya (Lilybaion, modern Marsala) at the western extremity of Sicily. Though Byzantines then surrounded him, he was able to make good his escape.[162] In 119/737, this same Qutham captured a fortress in Sardinia but drowned on his return with many of the Muslims.[163] No offensive campaign from North Africa for 120/738 is recorded, and for 121/739, Ibn Khayyāṭ specifically states that no expeditions were sent out from North Africa.[164] The last expedition sent under the Umayyads against the Byzantine islands was that under Ḥabīb b. Abī 'Ubayda that went against Sicily in 122/740 after a four-year hiatus. The expedition obtained booty but failed to take Syracuse, the island's capital. More significantly, the absence of Ḥabīb's army in Sicily hampered Ibn al-Ḥabḥāb in dealing with the great Berber revolt that broke out in North Africa at the same time.[165]

To some extent, the cessation of campaigning on the part of the Muslims must be attributable to the growing unrest there that was soon to break out in the great Berber revolt. But, one wonders if the increasing record of disasters on the naval front with the Byzantines did not also make the troops, Arabs as well as Berbers, reluctant to participate in further expeditions, much like the Khurāsānīs at the other end of the empire. From 115/733 through 119/737, only the expedition of 117/735 is described in wholly positive terms, and that one achieved the rather limited victory of taking a *qarya*, which means a town or village. It appears that the Byzantine defenses, particularly on the sea, were steadily improving. Thus, it may be that the troops were already growing disaffected with campaigning. If, as it seems likely, a large number of those employed in such campaigns were Berbers, their dissatisfaction with the offensive military policy can be added to their indubitable homegrown complaints as a cause behind the Berbers' great upheaval.

As a result, even on the North African front, which hitherto had had one of the best records of success in *jihād* as well as in keeping the internal peace, matters had begun to look ominous. Quite aside from any threatening signs of Berber disaffection that the caliphate may or may not have been aware of, the offensive military campaigns here too had ended in failure and could not be continued. This created an inevitable problem of where to find the cash needed to pay the troops, and the frontiers where they could be gainfully employed to both their satisfaction and that of the government, so that they might not be tempted to turn their spears against their rulers.

Spain and France 114–22/732–40

After the recent military setback on the Frankish front, the governors of Spain began to concentrate on reducing the remaining unsubdued areas inside the Iberian peninsula. Following 'Abd al-Raḥmān al-Ghāfiqī's death in battle at Poitiers in 114/732, the remnants of the Muslim army were led back to Spain by 'Abd al-Malik b. Qaṭan al-Fihrī, a local Muslim leader like his predecessor. He obtained official recognition for his governorship and in 115/733 led the sole expedition with which he is credited against al-Bashkuns (Vascones or Basques) of the western Pyrenees. Though the Muslim sources record a victory, the Christian *Continuatio* states that he accomplished nothing, but lost many of his troops when the Christians drove him back from the narrow mountain defiles. This campaign shows that the northern mountains of Spain remained unpacified. During his rule, 'Abd al-Malik also gained a reputation for being harsh and oppressive, that is reflected in both the Muslim and Christian sources.[166] Probably, 'Abd al-Malik's fiscal measures were directed against the wealthy Christian natives in favor of the early Muslim settlers, of whom he was one. He also failed to forward any money to North Africa.[167]

Spain's administrative independence was ended when Hishām created the new Western superprovince for 'Ubayd Allāh b. al-Ḥabḥāb in 116/734. The latter chose as governor of Spain 'Uqba b. al-Ḥajjāj al-Salūlī, who did not arrive to take up his duties there perhaps until Dhū al-Ḥijja 117/December 735–January 736.[168] The new governor undertook a sweeping fiscal reassessment and reform that was fairly administered but which also oppressively raised taxes.[169] This is not only consonant with the policies of 'Uqba's patron Ibn al-Ḥabḥāb, but with the need of the caliphate to raise more revenue internally. These policies of oppressive taxation coupled with its more equitable distribution may have alienated not only the native Spanish population, but also the Arab and Berber settlers in Spain, whose approval was needed for 'Uqba's administration to be a success.

However, 'Uqba was best remembered for his enthusiasm for *jihād*, which he expressed in military campaigns, pursuing the policy of renewed offensives on all possible fronts to the limit. It was only now that Muslim rule reached its maximum extent in the peninsula, overcoming all resistance. 'Uqba carried one campaign to Narbonne while mopping up the eastern Pyrenees and also conquered Galicia, Ulya,[170] and Pamplona, settling Muslim troops in them. Nothing was left unconquered in Galicia except the remote mountain redoubt of Pelayo near Oviedo.[171]

'Uqba also resumed the offensive in France. Apparently in 117/735, the new subgovernor in Narbonne advanced to and crossed the Rhône River. Arles surrendered to the Muslims on terms, but other cities and the Arelate generally were plundered and despoiled for four years (117–21/735–9). The northward extent of the Muslim conquest and raiding is unknown. This advance represented the Muslim high-water mark on the Frankish front, for the Muslims actually annexed Arles and its province and held them for this period.[172] They were possibly able to do this only at the invitation of and in alliance with Maurontius, the Patrician of Provence, who was worried about Frankish expansionism from the north.[173]

However, this advance brought the Muslims once more into conflict with Charles Martel, who now took the opportunity to conquer the Rhône Valley permanently for the Frankish Kingdom. In 118/736 Charles began to advance southward.[174] It was apparently not until 121/739, however, that he took Avignon, ending the Muslim presence in the Arelate, crossed the Rhône, and blockaded Narbonne itself. Hearing of this, 'Uqba sent an army, possibly consisting of Syrians, to the rescue, but this force was defeated and mostly destroyed on the Buerre River in 121/739.[175] From the Arabic sources, we know that the situation was serious enough to merit 'Uqba's presence in person at Narbonne in 121/739.[176] The Muslims' defeat may have seriously weakened 'Uqba's position internally as well as on the front with the Franks, particularly if it was the Syrians, on whom he had been relying for support, that were defeated.

Though Charles was forced to withdraw from Septimania by a revolt raised in his rear, so that Narbonne for the moment was saved for the Muslims,[177] the defeat he inficted on 'Uqba may have been among the factors that led the Muslim troops native to Spain to depose 'Uqba as governor shortly afterward.[178] While specific evidence is lacking, owing to the spareness of the sources, it is probable that the same complaints being made in Khurāsān were those which activated resistance in Spain. The most serious of these complaints was the suffering of the troops caused by constant and unrewarding campaigning being carried on against tough enemies. Such complaints will have been brought to the fore by 'Uqba's emphasis on campaigns in South France far from the Andalusian homes of most of the troops. The defeat of 121/739 inflicted by Charles Martel near Narbonne may have been the crowning blow on the Frankish front.

9

The Collapse of the Expansion Policy 122–25/740–43

The Berber Revolt and the End of Expansion

During the great military efforts before 122/740, the caliphate's strength had been steadily exhausted. The constant campaigning had killed many of the troops while disaffecting others. Recruitment of replacements was difficult without upsetting the balance of Syrian predominance. Also, it may have been hard simply to find any replacements for unrewarding campaigning against tough enemies. Local populations, both Muslim and non-Muslim, were annoyed by the need to find more money for the central treasury to finance the raising of needed troops and bear the cost of war equipment. This sentiment began to create the feeling in many quarters that local interests should override those of the Umayyad caliphate.

Of the war fronts themselves, some had shown no progress at all, such as the perennial Byzantine cauldron, where the enemy's defenses seemed to be improving and where the Byzantine navy was regaining control in both the East and West Mediterranean. India had remained chronically disastrous. On the other hand, the sudden improvement on both the Caucasus and Transoxianan fronts seemed to offer hope. The caliphate's boundaries were in most cases nearly at their maximum limits, which might be thought to represent the high noon of the Islamic state. But this expansive extent only masked the exhaustion and weakness which were now at last exposed by the great Berber revolt of 122/740, causing the permanent loss to the caliphate of all territory west of al-Qayrawān in Tunisia. Less conspicuously, the revolt also helped bring all offensive military activity to an end, for the vaunted and cherished expansion policy came to an amazingly sudden halt from 122/740, as a brief examination of the different fronts will disclose.

The Byzantine Front 123–25/741–43

On the various fronts of east of the Mediterranean, it was only against the Byzantines that the caliphate continued an aggressive military policy after 122/740. This was because of the prestige involved for the Syro-Jazīran army on the premier front so close to its home. Alternatively, the sudden, complete collapse of offensive campaigning on all other fronts may mean that it was only the Syro-Jazīrans who were still willing to fight for the caliphate. Although Syro-Jazīran forces were also present on the various provincial fronts, on these they had to take the wishes of the local Muslim troops into account as well, in order to be able to count on their loyalty and enthusiasm in battle. Whatever the case, the sudden restriction of the offensive policy to the Byzantine front suggests that the Umayyad regime was already verging on collapse while Hishām was still living.

Even the Byzantine front, where offensive Muslim campaigns continued, underwent a surprising change for the worse. After the disaster of Akroinon in 122/740, followed by the dispatch of many of the surviving Syrian forces to Africa to face the Berber rebels, the caliphate was in no condition to mount another such major expedition into Anatolia. Nevertheless, in 123/741, Sulaymān b. Hishām led a summer campaign which turned into yet another disaster, though probably on a smaller scale than that of the preceding year. He besieged a fortress in Anatolia, but the plague decimated his army,[1] famine raged, possibly owing to lack of supplies, most of his troops' horses died, and the Byzantines killed a large number of his forces. So, he fled back to the Muslim lines. Remarkably, the Christian historian Agapius even reports that a great number of the Muslim troops fled to the Byzantines and became Christians because of their misery.[2]

A far more important disaster for the Muslims in the same year was the Byzantine assault on the Muslims' base at Malaṭya, with an army of twenty thousand. Apparently, the Byzantines came upon the town when its forces were away, for the Muslim women showed themselves on the battlements armed and wearing turbans to deceive the enemy. The Byzantines' surprise raid, which must have been most unexpected after their many years of inactivity, impelled Hishām himself, for the only time in his reign, to put on his sword and lead whatever forces he could collect to rescue Malaṭya. Then he refortified the walls of the town, which had probably been neglected in the long period of Muslim offensives and

Byzantine passivity.[3] Though it failed to take the town, the Byzantine expedition pillaged and devastated the whole countryside of Malaṭya, carrying off the booty to their own territory.[4] This campaign represented the beginning of a new series of offensives by the Byzantines that would continue for a number of years. It also clearly demonstrated the defeat and downfall of the Muslim offensive policy even on this most vital front.

It was also in 123/741 that the caliph Hishām ordered his son Sulaymān to execute all the Byzantine prisoners held by the Muslims. These were put to death in various cities in Syria. According to the *Chronicon ad 1234*, he became incensed on hearing a false report that Leo III had commanded the killing of all Muslim prisoners held by the Byzantines.[5] Whatever the case, the report brings out the choleric temper of the caliph, which was now exacerbated by many defeats, especially Akroinon on the Byzantine front, and the Byzantine assault on Malaṭya.

However, in the very next year, 124/742, the Byzantine threat momentarily receded owing to the civil war that wracked the Byzantine empire for a year following the death of Emperor Leo III. The Byzantines' internal trouble enabled Sulaymān b. Hishām to lead an expedition deep into Anatolia for the last time He met no opposition and reached Paphlagonia, where he took many prisoners. Doubtless greatly exaggerating, Agapius even says that Sulaymān slew fifty thousand men.[6] This expedition is hardly noticed by the Muslim sources, however, which must raise questions about the degree of its importance and success.

In 125/743, after Hishām's death, the new caliph al-Walīd II's brother al-Ghamr b. Yazīd b. 'Abd al-Malik led the last Umayyad expedition against Byzantine territory, which Theophanes says also took many prisoners.[7] But it should be remembered that, despite the mention of prisoners, none of the expeditions undertaken by the caliphate on the Byzantine front after Akroinon seems to have captured any fortresses or made any significant achievement.

Like Sulaymān's expedition of the previous year, al-Ghamr's raid was probably facilitated by the Byzantine civil war. In fact, each party in the civil war even sent a delegation to al-Walīd II seeking an alliance against the other side. This same situation earlier on might have helped the Muslims to make great gains against their traditional nemesis.[8] But this time, al-Walīd II was unable to take advantage of the situation, as he had no major forces at his disposal. When the Byzantine civil war ended on 22 al-Muḥarram 127/2 November 744,[9] less than two years after Hishām's death, the Muslim state was already in utter disarray.

Though the expedition of al-Ghamr fell after the end of Hishām's reign, it is noteworthy as the only offensive expedition of al-Walīd II's reign on any front, for the caliphate was by then rapidly collapsing. Al-Walīd II also transferred many of the inhabitants of Cyprus to Syria. Most likely, those evacuated were Muslims. They were resettled on the Syrian coast.[10] In any case, their transfer seems to indicate Muslim fear of increasing Byzantine power, especially at sea. For only if the Byzantines were becoming more active, would the Cypriot Christians have dared to cooperate against the Muslims. That al-Walīd II felt compelled to take this step even when civil war was raging in the Byzantine empire, eloquently expresses the utter military weakness of the caliphate at this point after the destruction of many of its forces.

The East, Including Sind 122–25/740–43

Farther east, the end of the offensive policy before Hishām's death is even more dramatic. The last expeditions in the Caucasus and Transoxiana, the two fronts where the caliphate's erstwhile nemeses had so precipitiously weakened and collapsed, date to 123/741 and have already been dealt with above. No offensive activity is reported on the Sijistān front either.

As for India, the death of al-Ḥakam b. 'Awāna fighting in Gujarat in 122/740 had effectively ended the Muslim presence in the subcontinent except in Sind. Al-Ḥakam's eventual successor, 'Amr b. Muḥammad b. al-Qāsim al-Thaqafī (122–25/740–43), had little opportunity for offensive campaigning. The Sindīs revolted, perhaps with help from other Indian states, elected a king, and besieged 'Amr in al-Manṣūra, his capital. 'Amr wrote desperately to his superior Yūsuf b. 'Umar, the governor of Iraq, to seek help. Yūsuf sent him four thousand men, perhaps including Iraqis and Jazīrans. This relatively small number were all the forces that could be spared. Nevertheless, they proved sufficient to defeat the enemy and expel them from Sind, so that at least the original Muslim province was saved.[11]

Among these new troops was Marwān b. Yazīd b. al-Muhallab. That a rehabilitated son of the Muhallabī rebel Yazīd would be restored to the army, even on a front as remote as Sind, truly shows the desperation of Hishām to recruit new manpower for the army at the end of his reign. Yazīd's dangerous rebellion had raged only twenty years before.[12] Soon after the native Sindī revolt had been crushed by 'Amr, however, Marwān tried to rebel against that governor and was killed.[13] This latter episode showed the risks involved in sending Iraqi troops to a front dominated by Syrians and explains why the Umayyads faced such a manpower shortage despite the large number of Muslims in Iraq. No subsequent offensive activity by 'Amr b. Muḥammad is known. However, his successor under al-Walīd II is reputed to have carried out eighteen campaigns.[14] If so, they were probably insignificant, for the sole source reporting them gives no details, and the Muslims did not expand beyond Sind again under the caliphate.

The Great Berber Revolt 122–25/740–43

There can be no doubt that the Berber revolt was one of the chief events of Hishām's reign, if not indeed the single most important development. Not only did the revolt break the political unity of the Muslims forever by achieving the first successful secession from the universal caliphate, but it also marked the end of the *jihād* state with its set policy of expansion to establish universal Islamic dominion. Never again would the caliphate summon nearly all its neighbors to choose between total surrender and war. The end of internal unity and peace and the cessation of the universal *jihād* probably had a great impact on the Muslims of the time. Compared to the breakup of Muslim political unity and the end of the universal *jihād*, the actual downfall of the Umayyad dynasty and the rise of the 'Abbāsids seems relatively trivial.

Of course, not all of this can be blamed on the Berber revolt alone. We have already seen how the caliphate's armies were decimated by earlier disasters; how the expense of waging war was tending to impose heavier taxation; how the provincial armies were tired of fighting tough enemies; and how the *mawālī* were demanding better treatment in exchange for fighting. By 122/740, the situation was already seriously deteriorating for the Muslims on the Byzantine front. The Caucasian front was static and reduced to relatively small-scale police operations against recalcitrant mountain tribes. Gujarat had been lost definitively following another disaster, and the Muslim base at Narbonne in France was being threatened by the Franks. Following so many defeats, the Berber revolt came then, not as an isolated occurrence but as the crowning blow in a series of reverses that had been going on throughout Hishām's reign. As the last and perhaps the largest of the military catastrophes of Hishām's reign, the Berber revolt provided a violent and fitting end for the traditional policy of *jihād* that had been so long and so successfully applied by the Marwānids. Neither the caliphate nor the policy would recover from the blow.

Causes of the Revolt

Several main causes seem to have been behind the outbreak of the Berber revolt. The first and most immediate of these causes was the shortsighted policy of 'Ubayd Allāh b. al-Ḥabḥāb, the North African governor, or at least some of his subgovernors. A fifth of some of the Muslim Berbers were taken as slaves on the premise that they were originally booty and that the caliph had never gotten his share.[15] It also seems that the Berbers' property was threatened, because another of the accusations against 'Ubayd Allāh was his wasteful slaughter of pregnant sheep while seeking an especially soft wool from the pelts of unborn lambs to send to the caliph and his sons. Had the sheep been the property of the state, this is not likely to have been so important a complaint.[16]

It was felt, possibly, that Berbers who were Muslims but did not serve in the military should pay tribute instead, even if that meant tribute in persons as well as in property. In seeking to apply this dramatic policy change, Ibn al-Ḥabḥāb presumably thought that the Berbers could be overawed by a sufficient display of force as the Copts had been during his fiscal governorship of Egypt. Or it may be his arrogant and imperious sons who thought so.[17] In either case, it was a fatal miscalculation.

It seems, however, that this policy had also been applied before. It is implicit in the acts of Yazīd b. Abī Muslim which led to that governor's assassination in 102/721, an event I have already discussed. It is also sometimes mentioned that a constant tribute in slaves, particularly girls, was sent to the caliph.[18] Indeed, al-Ṭabarī asserts that the most beautiful Berber girls were taken arbitrarily to be slaves although they were Muslims.[19] It is uncertain how widespread this was or whether it was centrally authorized. But it seems likely that it was so and certainly constituted a great grievance.

Those Berbers who then embraced Islam avoided tribute, at least until Ibn al-Ḥabḥāb's administration.[20] But they took up another burden instead: military service. It is quite likely that a large minority of the troops used in the seaborne campaigns against Sicily and Sardinia were Berbers. Perhaps most of the militarized Berbers ended up in Spain, however, which may partly account for the caliphate's rather weak position there. On occasion, the Muslim Arab commanders deliberately exposed the Berber troops to greater dangers, as for instance during sieges, while keeping the Arab troops safely in the rear. Such treatment did not go unnoticed, nor was the explanation that it gave the Berbers more opportunity to participate in the *jihād* convincing to them.[21]

These Berbers were generally not paid stipends like the Arab tribesmen, but had to rely on their share of the booty alone for income. Sometimes, at least, they were denied even this.[22] Such discrimination, which was imposed by fiscal considerations above all, naturally became a major grievance among the Berber *mawālī*, as it did as well among the *mawālī* in Khurāsān. Although it only affected the militarized Berbers, their complaint strongly helped to nurture the will to revolt, for many of the revolutionary leaders had Arabic names, which probably indicates that they had served in the caliphal armies.

In fact, the various grievances were so important that Maysara, the initial leader of the Berber revolt, is said to have gone in a delegation to the Caliph Hishām seeking redress. This action tends to confirm that Maysara al-Madgharī was a member of the caliphal army in North Africa. As he was the initiator of the revolt, the planning for it then started in the Berber units of the caliphal army. In this way, out of its need for troops, the caliphate had created a monster for itself by arming and training a large number of Berbers, while at the same time denying them equal rights. The Berber delegation was not even received by the caliph. This affront provided yet another immediate cause for the rebellion.[23]

Yet a further cause of the rebellion could perhaps be seen in the activities of the disgraced family of Mūsā b. Nuṣayr, the *mawlā* of the Lakhm. It had been Mūsā b. Nuṣayr who had been originally the leader most responsible for the special position of the *mawālī* in North Africa, owing to his mass arming of the Berbers to help in the invasion of Spain. Nowhere else in the caliphate were there such large numbers of armed *mawālī* organized into their own army units. It was their position of military strength that had enabled the Muslim Berbers to get away with killing Yazīd b. Abī Muslim and to avoid the reimposition of tribute as had happened in Khurāsān.

The family of Ibn Nuṣayr remained closely connected with the cause of the Berbers. When Yazīd b. Abī Muslim came to North Africa, he executed a son of Ibn Nuṣayr and wanted to take a fifth of the *mawālī* of Ibn Nuṣayr as slaves for the caliph.[24] This shows that when the Berbers had first been conquered, Ibn Nuṣayr had accepted their Islam immediately. It must not be assumed that 'the *mawālī* of Ibn Nuṣayr' means only a few thousand persons, for in early Islam people became *mawālī* of those who had brought them to the religion. Thus, the *mawālī* of Ibn Nuṣayr may have included much of the Berber population of North Africa. Therefore, far more was at stake than the mere private estate of Ibn Nuṣayr.

After this, the family of Ibn Nuṣayr was persecuted relentlessly by the governors. This may have been partly because they were trying to protect their *mawālī*, as good patrons should, according to Arab codes of loyalty. Naturally, the governors disliked the family of Ibn Nuṣayr because of their popularity among the Berbers, as well. Later, certain *mawālī* of Ibn Nuṣayr show up in the Berber revolutionary leadership,[25] which suggests that some of the party of Ibn Nuṣayr, so long out of power, may have encouraged the revolution, much as the Khuzā'a and their *mawālī* did for the 'Abbasid revolution in Khurāsān.

A different cause which must be discussed is the spread of *khārijī* doctrines, especially Ṣufrī ones, among the Berbers. However, though the rebels are described as Ṣufrīs, the main motivation behind the revolt was political, albeit politics seen in religious terms of absolute right and wrong. The Umayyad government was regarded by the Ṣufrī Berbers as an unholy abomination owing to its unfairness in continuing to take tribute from the Muslims and in failing to pay stipends to Berber troops as it did to the Arabs, the same two reasons I have already discussed. The differences among Ṣufrīs, Azraqīs, Najdīs, and other sundry *khawārij* seem mostly to concern what is permissible and not permissible when fighting others claiming to be Muslims. No other distinctive doctrine is visible yet, at all.[26] 'Ikrima, the *mawlā* of Ibn 'Abbās, seems to have obtained his reputation as a Ṣufrī from his connection with North Africa and his opposition to the Umayyad government. Otherwise, he was later revered enough among Sunnī circles to be considered a reliable transmitter of *ḥadīth*. 'Ikrima probably would not have kept so good a reputation among Sunnīs had the Ṣufrīs really constituted a separate Islamic sect at the time of the Berber revolt. So much for the supposed sectarianism of the Berber rebels.

The Beginning of the Revolt 122–23/740–41

Ibn al-Ḥabḥāb showed no inkling of suspicion that the Berbers were planning to revolt. Rather, in 122/740 he resumed the seaborne campaigns that had been suspended for two years in the wake of earlier disasters by sending Ḥabīb b. Abī 'Ubayda al-Fihrī against Sicily. Ḥabīb's expedition may have been quite successful, for he is reported to have extracted tribute from the island's capital of Syracuse and to have ravaged the whole island.[27] He is also said to have intended to stay to make the conquest permanent.[28] If true, this means he must have taken large forces with him.

But at the same time, when they were sure that Ḥabīb had crossed over with the North African army to Sicily, the Berbers in western North Africa, both Muslims and non-Muslims, began their revolt.[29] With Ḥabīb gone, the Berbers could be sure that there would be an extra delay before Ibn al-Ḥabḥāb could send effective forces against them. The revolt broke out on 15 Ramaḍān 122/15 August 740 in several places at once, as prearranged.[30] Its quick success shows that it was carefully planned and that its secret had been well kept. The rebels rendered the oath of allegiance to Maysara al-Madgharī as their caliph.[31]

First, ʻAbd al-Aʻlā b. Jurayj al-Ifrīqī, a Greek *mawlā* of Mūsā b. Nuṣayr and a collaborator of Maysara, led the rebel forces against ʻUmar b. ʻAbd Allāh al-Murādī, the governor of Tangier, who came out of the city to fight and was immediately killed with most of his troops.[32] According to another version, it was Maysara himself who defeated the governor.[33] The Berbers then occupied Tangier, which it will be remembered was the chief military base for the western half of North Africa. They are reported to have killed its inhabitants, who were probably mostly Arab troops and their families.[34] Maysara confirmed ʻAbd al-Aʻlā as the governor of Tangier, while he himself marched south to al-Sūs, which was governed by Ismāʻīl b. ʻUbayd Allāh b. al-Ḥabḥāb.[35] Ismāʻīl sent an army against him, but Maysara defeated it and then attacked the Umayyad forces' camp at night, slaying Ismāʻīl.[36] At this point, the rebels had control of all of modern Morocco, most of which was not to see rule by the universal caliphate again.

Upon receipt of the news of the revolt and the killing of the two subgovernors, one of whom was his son, Ibn al-Ḥabḥāb recalled Ḥabīb al-Fihrī from Sicily and also immediately sent forth an expedition under Khālid b. Abī Ḥabīb al-Fihrī against the rebels. Khālid forged ahead to the vicinity of Tangier, where in a heavy battle he evidently worsted Maysara, who withdrew inside the city.[37]

At this point, the rebels became discontented with Maysara, perhaps because of his conduct of the war, and slew him. In his stead, they set up as caliph Khālid b. Ḥumayd al-Zanātī, another Berber whose Arabic names probably also indicate previous service in the regular Muslim army, as was the case with Maysara.[38] Emerging from Tangier, Khālid b. Ḥumayd totally annihilated Khālid b. Abī Ḥabīb and his army, so that, according to one report, not a single man escaped. The battle became known as the Battle of the Nobles (*ghazwat al-ashrāf*) owing to the many men of noble Arab lineage who fell there.[39] This fresh disaster occurred on the Kadar River in about al-Muḥarram 123/December 740.[40] It is highly probable that the destroyed army consisted of a major part of the available Arab forces in North Africa, for the Berbers could no longer be trusted after the revolt.

To prevent the Berbers from advancing east, Ibn al-Ḥabḥāb sent 'Abd al-Raḥmān b. al-Mughīra al-'Abdarī to hold Tilimsān, which was now on the front line. 'Abd al-Raḥmān began the to slaughter the "Ṣufrīs," whom he may have had trouble distinguishing from the general population, and he earned the nickname "the Butcher." The "Ṣufrīs" then rebelled against him, driving him out.[41] That they only rebelled after he began slaughtering them seems to show that they had not been in revolt to begin with. This not only shows how loosely the sources use terms such as *khārijī* and Ṣufrī to describe rebels against the caliphal authority, but also how the Arabs' overreaction to the initial Berber revolt drove many hitherto neutral Berbers into the rebel camp.

By this time, Ḥabīb b. Abī 'Ubayda had returned from Sicily and reached the vicinity of Tilimsān, where he stayed camped on the Wādī Tilimsān, from which he did not move for the rest of Ibn al-Ḥabḥāb's governorship.[42] Clearly, the North African Arabs, in dealing with the revolt, were tired of the aggressive policy that had brought them nothing but severe losses. At Tilimsān, Ḥabīb found Mūsā b. Abī Khālid, the *mawlā* of Mu'āwiya b. Ḥudayj, who had gathered around him the surviving forces loyal to the caliphate in the area, apparently after the expulsion of 'Abd al-Raḥmān al-'Abdarī a short time before. Despite Mūsā's show of loyalty, Ḥabīb accused him of treason and cut off his hand and leg.[43] Whatever the background of this story, it shows disarray in the caliphal ranks.

'Abd al-Malik b. Qaṭan al-Fihrī's Coup in Spain 123/741

When the Muslims in Spain heard of the Berber revolt, the governor 'Uqba al-Salūlī immediately went from Saraqusṭa, where he was recovering from the defeats inflicted on his forces by Charles Martel the year before, to Ṭarīfa on the Strait of Gibraltar, whence he crossed into North Africa. After accomplishing nothing there, he returned to Spain.[44] Curiously, his intervention is only mentioned in the Christian *Continuatio* and does not show an obvious correspondence with the Muslim sources. However, his intervention must be dated to 122/740. Possibly, he arrived to find Khālid b. Abī Ḥabīb defeated and thus was forced to withdraw.

The disaster of Khālid b. Abī Ḥabīb proved to be 'Uqba's undoing as well,[45] for shortly afterward, in Ṣafar 123/January 741,[46] the latter was overthrown by a revolt of the 'old settler' Arab troops led by 'Abd al-Malik b. Qaṭan al-Fihrī, who usurped his place.[47] 'Abd al-Malik's role in Spain was somewhat analogous to that of Naṣr b. Sayyār in Khurāsān. This usurpation reflected the dislike of the Spanish Muslims for the governors appointed by the caliph. It also meant a definitive break with any real adherence to the caliphate, though the caliph continued to be formally recognized. For his part, the mighty Caliph Hishām was forced to recognize 'Abd al-Malik's usurpation. This became apparent when the new caliphal governor in North Africa commanded 'Abd al-Malik to bring him troops and supplies to aid him in the fight against the Berbers. 'Abd al-Malik seems to have ignored the summons, revealing his real independence, though he came with his forces to al-Jazīra al-Khaḍrā' (Algeciras) to await developments.[48] The universal caliphate was not to rule again in Spain, except for a brief and ephemeral restoration.

With the destruction of Khālid b. Abī Ḥabīb and his army, followed by 'Uqba's overthrow in Spain almost immediately afterward, the whole caliphal position in the West seemed to suddenly crumble. For these momentous events were followed by, and perhaps caused, the parallel overthrow of Ibn al-Ḥabḥāb at al-Qayrawān, which may have happened about the same time. News of these increasingly disastrous developments caused the Caliph Hishām to utter his famous sentence, "By God, I will most certainly rage against them with an Arab rage, and I will indeed send against them an army whose beginning is where they are and whose end is where I am!" Then Hishām ordered Ibn al-Ḥabḥāb to return from North Africa, and the latter set out from al-Qayrawān in Jumādā I 123/March–April 741.[49] Meanwhile, conditions in North Africa continued to deteriorate, for we find Ḥabīb's army, which had been stationed on the Wādī Tilimsān, falling back to the ford over the Wādī Shalaf considerably farther east.[50]

The Brief Governorship of Kulthūm b. 'Iyāḍ 123–24/741

In Jumādā II 123/April–May 741,[51] Hishām appointed the Damascene Kulthūm b. 'Iyāḍ al-Qushayrī (or al-Qasrī of the Bajīla)[52] as the new governor of North Africa and equipped him with a mighty army to suppress the Berber revolt. He also provided him with expert advisers on the region.[53] The sources give contradictory information about the size and composition of this army. The most detailed and probably most accurate account is that of *Akhbār majmū'a*, which asserts that Kulthūm went forth with twenty-seven thousand Syrians, six thousand from each *jund* except Qinnasrīn, which contributed only three thousand.[54] This means that the army consisted overwhelmingly of Yamanī troops, with relatively few Muḍarīs. Other valuable information is contributed by Theophanes, who tells us that the sixty-eight hundred survivors of the Akroinon disaster of the previous year were now dispatched as part of the army of the Damascene.[55] Other accounts give a smaller total number of Syrians, but are probably based on the number of Syrians who eventually reached Spain and not on the number who actually set out with Kulthūm.[56]

In addition to the Syrian forces, which were supposed to make up the tough core of the army, Hishām commanded all the governors along Kulthūm's route from Syria to North Africa to join him with their forces. Thus, he picked up the forces of Egypt, Barqa, and Tripoli on the way.[57] It does not appear, however, that all the governors joined him, for Ḥanẓala b. Ṣafwān remained in Egypt. However, Kulthūm picked up three thousand regular troops in Egypt, which may represent the majority of that province's forces. Their addition brought Kulthūm's regular troops to an even thirty thousand.[58] Any forces that may have joined him in Barqa and Tripoli probably were very small.

Kulthūm reached North Africa with his army in Ramaḍān 123/July–August 741.[59] Hishām already had commanded the North African governor to obey Kulthūm and to place all his forces at the latter's disposal. These came out in large numbers. Kulthūm put them under the command of the *mawlā* advisers whom Hishām had sent with him.[60] This subordination to outsiders, even ones originally from North Africa, may have greatly irritated the native North African Muslims, who probably felt that the caliphate's aggressive policy was disastrous, especially to themselves.

Still, Kulthūm tried to please. He avoided entering al-Qayrawān, the capital, perhaps in order to save time, but also so as not to annoy the North African Muslims, whose cooperation was vital to the success of the expedition, for al-Qayrawān was their *miṣr* and home. Instead, he stayed a day's journey away at Sabība, where he was still on 1 Shawwāl 123/19 August 741. It was bad enough having Syrian troops come to North Africa at all, without having to mix them cheek by jowl with the local Muslim Arabs. To further mollify these local Muslims, Kulthūm appointed North Africans, 'Abd al-Raḥmān b. 'Uqba al-Ghifārī and Maslama b. Sawāda al-Fihrī, as deputies to take charge of the administration and garrison in al-Qayrawān. However, the commander of the vanguard, Balj b. Bishr al-Qushayrī, who was Kulthūm's nephew or cousin, treated the North Africans insultingly by sending them a circular letter demanding that they receive the Syrians hospitably and billet them in their houses.[61]

Owing to the high-handed behavior of the Syrians and perhaps to the fear that they might stay, the North African Arabs did not welcome their 'rescuers' from the east at all. Possibly, they preferred the relative independence they had enjoyed for several months since Ibn al-Ḥabḥāb's downfall. Only this can account for the reported reaction of Ḥabīb b. Abī 'Ubayda, who was commanding the North African troops on the Wādī Shalaf, to Balj's rudeness, for Ḥabīb sent Kulthūm a threatening letter. In response, Kulthūm apologized for Balj.[62]

On arriving, Kulthūm found his fears confirmed, for Balj now cursed Ḥabīb in front of others, including Ḥabīb's son 'Abd al-Raḥmān. This incident is supposed to have caused the army to divide into two hostile sides who armed themselves against each other. One of these consisted of the North Africans, who were also joined by the three thousand Egyptians who had come with Kulthūm. The other was made up of Kulthūm's twenty-seven thousand Syrians. Only after negotiations, were relations restored. This mutual hostility of the two halves of the army was widely regarded as the cause of Kulthūm's subsequent failure.[63] However, it may be that this incident has been exaggerated, as it is not likely that Kulthūm would have embarked on an offensive campaign against dangerous rebels had the rift in his army been so serious. More likely, as in Khurāsān, the native Muslims bore the presence of the unwelcome outsiders resentfully but mostly silently. After all, the North African Arabs, however much they may have disliked Syrian intervention in their province, were still hostile enough to the Berber *khawārij* to go out to fight them.

Passing by way of Tilimsān,[64] Kulthūm then pressed ahead with his combined force, said to have reached seventy thousand, until he reached Baqdūra in Wādī Sabū near the present city of Fās in Morocco.[65] Meanwhile, the Berbers had split into two factions. One of these was led by Maysara's successor Khālid b. Ḥumayd. The other was under Sālim Abū Yūsuf al-Azdī. It is uncertain whether, and perhaps unlikely that, the latter had actually declared himself caliph in addition to Ibn Ḥumayd. However, the two groups united to face the threat of Kulthūm.[66]

Probably about Dhū al-Ḥijja 123/October–November 741,[67] Kulthūm met the Berbers at Wādī Sabū in a dramatic and fatal battle. It was, in fact, the decisive battle of the war and ranks with Ardabīl and the Defile among the first-class military disasters of Hishām's reign. Like the other battles of the time, it is not really possible to reconstruct what happened in much detail. Kulthūm sent Balj with the cavalry to surprise the enemy by night. But he only found them in the morning, and they drove him back discomfited. Balj himself was wounded.[68] The Berbers pelted Balj's cavalry with large numbers of stones thrown with slings of some kind. This made the Arab horses balk, forcing the riders to dismount and causing the Arabs to lose the edge they had enjoyed owing to their cavalry. Balj, with seven thousand cavalry, charged through the Berber lines, thus becoming separated from the main Arab army, which the Berbers then attacked furiously. The North African Arabs broke first. The Berbers then virtually annihilated the caliphal army, killing Kulthūm, Ḥabīb, and a host of other nobles.[69]

The losses are hard to estimate. According to one report, one third of the caliphal troops were killed, one third were captured, and one third managed to escape.[70] However, this is too schematic. After this catastrophe, the surviving remnants of the North Africans, including some of the Egyptians, retreated toward al-Qayrawān, while the forces with Balj, numbering about ten thousand, fled north.[71] Only a handful of Syrians escaped to Syria.[72] It appears from these facts that about eighteen thousand Syrians were killed in the battle or taken prisoner, for Balj's surviving forces also included some Egyptians and probably others. There is no way of estimating the North Africans' losses, but they must have been very great, perhaps in the neighborhood of twenty thousand. The North Africans were unable afterwards to protect even the core area of their homeland in Tunisia very well.

The strategic results of the Battle of Wādī Sabū were as important as the losses suffered by the caliphal forces. Balj's escaping Syrians were trapped in Sabta (Ceuta) and had no further influence on events in North Africa, but eventually crossed to Spain, where they took control for a while after a long struggle. More importantly, the Berber revolt was victorious and western North Africa was lost to the Umayyad caliphate and its 'Abbāsid successor forever.

The North African Governorship of Ḥanẓala b. Ṣafwān al-Kalbī 124–27/742–45

The news of the disaster of Kulthūm deeply shocked the Caliph Hishām and the Yamanī Syrian leaders with him. He regretted that he had sent out a Syrian army without sending with it Iraqi or other troops who could have shared the losses. Now, he feared his own special troops had been reduced too much in number.[73] This report reveals the magnitude of the disaster to the Syrian forces, in particular. For, although a substantial number with Balj had escaped destruction or capture, they were as good as lost for all the help they could offer the caliph now in their distant isolation. It also uncovers the extent to which the Umayyads were afraid of the Iraqis, for Hishām had not sent any Iraqi forces to North Africa even though it had been clear that the task of Kulthūm's army was a difficult one.

Nevertheless, the caliph still vowed to continue his uncompromising policy, fully but impractically in tune with the Umayyad tradition of *jihād*. He promised that he would send armies against the Berbers for as long as he lived until they surrendered. First he would send one hundred thousand regular troops, all on stipends, then one hundred thousand more, then more, until, even if none were left except he and his sons, he would cast lots with them and fight himself if the lot came out against him.[74] Of course, hundreds of thousands no longer existed to be sent out. Nor could he raise a substantial army without mobilizing the Iraqis. And the treasury could no longer easily afford to pay stipends for so many troops, had they existed, in view of the increasing fiscal stringency that characterized the reign.

In order to salvage what he could, in Ṣafar 124/December 741–January 742[75] Hishām commanded Ḥanẓala b. Ṣafwān al-Kalbī, the governor of Egypt since 119/737, to go immediately to North Africa. It is said he set out with an army of thirty thousand and that Hishām sent twenty thousand more to him shortly afterwards.[76] These figures seem rather exaggerated in view of the smallness of the results achieved and in view of the fact that Ḥanẓala had to rely on local North Africans in his battles. But if such forces were indeed sent, it only further serves to demonstrate how the North African drain left a military vacuum in Syria.

However, Ḥanẓala probably took at least some Egyptian Arab or Syrian troops with him, for his need for troops seems to have put a further strain on the available manpower reserves from which the army traditionally had been recruited. This is suggested by the fact that Ḥanẓala's successor as governor of Egypt had to restore the troops' stipends in his province to the level at which they had been before, even though the various military emergencies required economizing on expenditures.[77] That the troops could insist on the restoration of their former higher level of pay suggests that recruits may have been in short supply, as Egypt had practically been emptied of regular forces for the disastrous North African campaigns. The ability of the remaining troops and recruits to press for more pay also constitutes a threatening sign of military disaffection for the Umayyad dynasty.

The destruction of Kulthūm left his deputy 'Abd al-Raḥmān b. 'Uqba al-Ghifārī in sole charge at al-Qayrawān.[78] But he was almost without forces. As a result of this government weakness and in addition to the victories of their brethren farther west, most of the Berbers in the rest of North Africa also broke out in revolt. Nothing is said in the sources about the long stretch of territory that is now Algeria. Presumably, it was lost by default with Kulthūm's defeat and never regained.

Farther to the east in Tunisia, confusion reigned as the caliphate had to fight a long, difficult war against the local Berbers in order to hold onto even that small remnant of its former North African province. Near Qābis, south of al-Qayrawān, 'Ukkāsha b. Ayyūb al-Fazārī had already rebelled after Kulthūm had passed on to the west but before he and his army met disaster. Although 'Ukkāsha's rebel forces were Berbers, he himself is surprisingly described as the commander of the advance party of Syrian troops who had come with 'Ubayd Allāh b. al-Ḥabḥāb,[79] apparently about 116/734. That would make him not only a Syrian, but a Qaysī Syrian at that. The same mutilated text of al-Raqīq describes him further as a Ṣufrī, suggesting anti-Umayyad ideological motivation as well. Perhaps in his service in North Africa, he became influenced by the justice of the Berber cause. In any case, his defection not only shows that some of the Syrian troops themselves were tired of the burden of holding the caliphate together by their own sacrifices, but also that the Berber rebels significantly relied on background and experience they had gained in the Muslim caliphal army.

'Ukkāsha sent his brother to try to capture Sabrat near Tripoli, where Arabs were evidently settled, but the attempt did not succeed.[80] After this, Maslama b. Sawāda al-Fihrī (or al-Judhāmī), whom Kulthūm had left in charge of the forces at al-Qayrawān, set out to fight 'Ukkāsha. Maslama reached Qābis, where, after a fierce battle, 'Ukkāsha utterly defeated him, pursuing him right up to the gates of al-Qayrawān.[81] At this point, the future of the North

African Arab capital itself looked very bleak. Sa'īd b. Bajra al-Ghassānī took over from Maslama and put al-Qayrawān in a state of defense, while 'Ukkāsha withdrew to al-Jamma twelve miles north of Qābis.[82]

Meanwhile, marching supposedly to join Kulthūm, who by now was already battling in the west, the governor of Tripoli[83] reached Qābis with his forces. This encouraged Sa'īd b. Bajra, the new governor in al-Qayrawān, to go out with his forces to Qābis, perhaps in order to save that place. But the governor of Tripoli went home with his troops, leaving Sa'īd alone to face the Berbers.[84] 'Ukkāsha then tried to take Qābis by siege, even setting up mangonels against it, but still could not capture it. The use of mangonels shows that the Berber rebels enjoyed a degree of military sophistication that suggests that at least some of them had served in the caliphal army before. Finding no success at Qābis, 'Ukkāsha raised his siege and invested Qafṣa instead.[85]

At this point, the remnants of Kulthūm's army, mostly native North Africans, returned to al-Qayrawān. Wishing to make immediate use of them, 'Abd al-Raḥmān al-Ghifārī himself led them against 'Ukkāsha, whom he totally defeated in Ṣafar 124/December 741–January 742. This probably means only that 'Ukkāsha's rebels were dispersed, for his revolt continued. While 'Ukkāsha fled west to Ṭubna in al-Zāb,[86] 'Abd al-Raḥmān returned to al-Qayrawān.[87] 'Abd al-Raḥmān's victory gave the North African Arabs a needed breathing space.

Next, Ḥanẓala b. Ṣafwān, the new governor of North Africa, having set out from Egypt on 7 Rabī' II 124/19 February 742,[88] arrived in al-Qayrawān in Rabī' II 124/February–March 742[89] or Jumādā I/March–April.[90] Though Ḥanẓala wanted to put his own clansman and fellow Syrian, Abū al-Khaṭṭār al-Ḥusām b. Ḍirār al-Kalbī, in charge of the fight against 'Ukkāsha, the troops clamored for the North African 'Abd al-Raḥmān al-Ghifārī, and the governor had to give way.[91] This indicates that Ḥanẓala's army probably consisted of a majority of North Africans. Though no longer friendly to the caliphate and unwilling to serve far from home, these troops were willing enough to defend their own lands in Tunisia.

'Abd al-Raḥmān then set out, defeating 'Ukkāsha at al-Faḥṣ al-Abyaḍ, perhaps near al-Qayrawān.[92] This victory at least gave northern Tunisia peace for about six months, during which it was mostly safe from further Berber attacks. After this, 'Abd al-Raḥmān went to al-Zāb, the region which was the source of 'Ukkāsha's revolt, in order to reduce it once more to submission. He remained in al-Zāb during Ramaḍān 124/July–August 742. Meanwhile,

'Ukkāsha went west to seek aid from the Berber caliph Ibn Ḥumayd, with whom he had previously been unconnected. On the way, 'Ukkāsha encountered 'Abd al-Wāḥid b. Yazīd al-Hawwāri al-Madhamī, whom Ibn Ḥumayd had dispatched to attack al-Qayrawān.[93] The two agreed to cooperate but marched east toward al-Qayrawān by different routes from al-Zāb, probably because of the difficulty of supplying their large forces. 'Ukkāsha took a valley route while 'Abd al-Wāḥid marched over the mountains to the north.[94]

Ḥanẓala ordered 'Abd al-Raḥmān al-Ghifārī to stop 'Abd al-Wāḥid's advance. The two armies met near Ṭubna in eastern Algeria on 15 Dhū al-Qa'da 124/21 September 742. 'Abd al-Raḥmān was defeated and killed along with several other prominent commanders, while his surviving troops fled to Ḥanẓala in al-Qayrawān. After this, 'Abd al-Wāḥid stopped to take Ṭubna and possibly other places. Ḥanẓala sent out yet another army under Thābit b. Khaytham, a Syrian commander from the *jund* of al-Urdunn with previous North African experience. Thābit met 'Abd al-Wāḥid on 1 Ṣafar 125/4 December 742 but was defeated and killed.[95] This is the defeat which Ibn al-Athīr describes, in which the Muslims lost many men as well as twenty thousand horses because of lack of fodder.[96] According to al-Raqīq, the defeated commander was an unnamed Lakhmī probably identical with Thābit, whom Ḥanẓala had sent forth with forty thousand troops to stop 'Abd al-Wāḥid, who had three hundred thousand men! The two sides faced each other in trenches for a month at Bāja in northwest Tunisia before the defeat. There was a shortage of fodder. The Muslims lost twenty thousand horsemen in the battle and retreated to al-Qayrawān with only twenty thousand.[97]

At these fresh disasters, Ḥanẓala wrote to al-Mustanīr b. al-Ḥārith al-Ḥarashī, the subgovernor of Tūnis, which was the Muslim naval base against Sicily, telling him to evacuate the city and come to al-Qayrawān if he thought he could not hold out. Al-Mustanīr indeed did not feel he could and removed his troops and their families to al-Qayrawān.[98] This information plainly reveals the extent of the caliphate's weakness in North Africa. Apparently Ḥanẓala had very few troops left, only enough to man the defenses of the North African capital. That was not even enough to save the naval base which had witnessed so many proud annual raids against the Byzantines. It would appear that this was the nadir of Ḥanẓala's fortunes until his abandonment of the province two years later. He seems to have held little except al-Qayrawān. But he did not now appeal for more troops, as he must have known none would be forthcoming.

'Abd al-Wāḥid now occupied Tūnis. At this point, flushed with his victories, 'Abd al-Wāḥid appears to have proclaimed himself caliph in rivalry to Ibn Ḥumayd in Tangier. The latter dispatched 'Abd al-A'lā Zurzur, another *mawlā* of Mūsā b. Nuṣayr, to take away 'Abd al-Wāḥid's standard and take over his command.[99]

Meanwhile, Ḥanẓala mobilized all the forces he could find. He even armed noncombatants and women and also dug a trench around the city. He decided to attack 'Ukkāsha first, before the latter united with 'Abd al-Wāḥid. When Ḥanẓala saw the size of 'Ukkāsha's army, he is said to have wanted to retreat and write to the caliph for reinforcements. The Qayrawānīs were in a state of despair. But partly owing to their fear and desperation, under the commander Muḥammad b. 'Amr b. 'Uqba, they were able to defeat and kill 'Abd al-Wāḥid at al-Aṣnām of Jarāwa, about a day's march from the city. 'Abd al-Wāḥid's army was slaughtered. Meanwhile, before 'Ukkāsha had even had time to hear of 'Abd al-Wāḥid's death, Ḥanẓala fell on his army, defeating him as well, at al-Qarn, a site visible from al-Qayrawān.[100] According to al-Raqīq, who has the most detailed rendition, 'Ukkāsha was defeated first, then 'Abd al-Wāḥid, both by Ḥanẓala. Al-Raqīq greatly emphasizes the triumph over 'Abd al-Wāḥid.[101] Thus, al-Qayrawān, at least, was saved from the Berbers. Ḥanẓala was soon able to round out his victory by getting hold of 'Ukkāsha, whom he immediately executed. Ḥanẓala's victories must have occurred in Rabī' I 125/January 743, for news of them reached the Caliph Hishām, pleasing him shortly before he died on 6 Rabī' II 125/6 February 743.[102]

After the defeat of 'Abd al-Wahid and 'Ukkāsha, Ḥanẓala was able to devote some energy to local mopping up. He ordered the governor of Tripoli[103] to end the rebellion of the Berbers in Nafzāwa. The governor defeated the Berbers but was slain. At this, Ḥanẓala sent his clansman and fellow Syrian Zayd b. 'Amr al-Kalbī to lead the Tripolitans back to their base.[104]

The rest of Ḥanẓala's governorship remained stormy. But it was the collapse of the caliphate in Syria that finally undercut his position in North Africa, leading to his departure in Jumādā I 127/February–March 745, two years after Hishām's death.[105] Though it is an impressive achievement that Ḥanẓala had succeeded in restoring to Umayyad rule the easternmost part of the North African province, comprising most of modern Tunisia and western Libya, the Umayyads could take only cold comfort in his victories. Western North Africa was simply lost forever, not only to the Umayyads but also to the universal caliphate and to Islamic political unity. It had been possible to enlist the cooperation of the Arabs settled in the area of al-Qayrawān to defend their homeland. But there could be no question, after so many disasters in so short a span of time, of making any further efforts to recover lost territory farther west.

However, the worst effect of Ḥanẓala's governorship for the Umayyads had not been the loss of most of North Africa. Rather, it was the movement of the last Syrian Yamanī forces to a distant frontier where they were dispersed, lost, and could no longer have any influence on events in the Syrian metropole. Their absence was an important factor in impelling the few Yamanī remnants in Syria to press violently for the adoption of their reform program in order both to broaden their power base and to save the caliphate from itself by overthrowing the traditionalist regime of Hishām's successor, al-Walīd II. His regime seemed bent on continuing previous policies as if nothing had happened. The absence of the Syrian Yamanī troops also helped the Jazīrans to overcome Yamanī Syrian opposition to the rule of Marwān II easily.

The Caliphal Twilight in Spain 124–25/742–43

Balj's force, escaping from the disaster of his uncle Kulthūm at Wādī Sabū, was hotly pursued by the two Berber leaders Ibn Ḥumayd and Abū Yūsuf. But the commander of Balj's rear, Ḥassān b. Ghunāba or 'Atāfa, turned on the pursuers, defeated them, and killed Abū Yūsuf.[106] Free then to proceed unmolested, Balj tried first to enter Tangier, but found it firmly in Berber hands. Thereupon, he led his forces into Sabta. Inside Sabta, the Syrians were trapped. While safe from direct Berber assault because of Sabta's impregnable position, they had no way of escaping. However, they are reported to have defeated repeated Berber attempts to conquer them. Then the Berbers resorted to a scorched-earth policy, burning and destroying the land around Sabta so that the Syrians would find no supplies even by foraging. Soon, the latter had to eat their horses to stay alive.[107]

Balj pleaded with the governor of Spain, 'Abd al-Malik b. Qaṭan, who, it will be recalled, was practically an independent ruler, to allow him and his men to come to Spain. But 'Abd al-Malik was naturally reluctant to let a foreign armed force into his realm. His ideas were confirmed by the North African 'Abd al-Raḥmān b. Ḥabīb, who had escaped the disaster at Wādī Sabū separately from the others and managed to cross over to Spain. Ibn Ḥabīb strongly warned 'Abd al-Malik against admitting Balj and the Syrian remnants to Spain. Therefore, the Syrians languished where they were, and 'Abd al-Malik would not even send them supplies. They might have perished altogether if a certain Muslim Arab in Spain had not privately sent them what he could. Even so, they were finally reduced to eating grass and herbs.[108] But their tale of woe may be exaggerated, and in any case did not last long.[109]

However, a revolt of the Spanish Berbers, encouraged by the success of their brethren in North Africa and in alliance with them, soon broke out. The Spanish Berbers drove the Arabs from Galicia, including Asturqa (Astorga), Mārida (Mérida), and Ṭalabayra (Talavera) near Ṭulaytula (Toledo). Thus, the Berbers seem to have held most of western Spain. This caused the Arabs in Spain, from fear of being slaughtered, to withdraw toward their main bases in the center and south. They abandoned all the frontiers except that of Saraqusṭa in the northeast, where the Arabs had a majority. 'Abd al-Malik sent out armies to the rebelling frontier zones, but they were soundly defeated.[110]

This turn of events made 'Abd al-Malik fear that the Arabs in Spain might soon meet the same fate as those in North Africa. Thus, he was forced to reconsider his treatment of Balj. Reversing himself, 'Abd al-Malik sent the latter supplies at long last and speedily negotiated a treaty with him. He stipulated that the Syrians be brought over and maintained for one year, during which they were to fight for 'Abd al-Malik. At the end of that period, they would leave Spain. 'Abd al-Malik would provide ships to transport them as a group back to Ifrīqiya, meaning Tūnis, where they would be far from the center of the Moroccan Berber revolt. To guarantee their abiding by the agreement, 'Abd al-Malik received ten hostages from among the commanders of each of the six *ajnād*.[111]

As soon as the Syrians had arrived in Spain, 'Abd al-Malik sent them to fight a Berber force at Wādī al-Fatḥ by Shadhūna (Sidonia). The Syrians captured enough booty to get them out of their previous miserable condition.[112] Then 'Abd al-Malik commanded them to go out with his two sons to rescue Ṭulaytula from the Berbers, who were about to attack it. He mobilized, for the occasion, all the Arab troops in Spain except those in Saraqusṭa and beyond, on the northeast frontier against the Franks. The Arab army defeated the Berbers at Wādī Salīṭ near Ṭulaytula, nearly annihilating them. The Syrians, furious from their defeat and subsequent suffering in North Africa, fought especially well. Ibn 'Idhārī calls Wādī Salīṭ "the greatest defeat" of the Berbers. Following this battle, the Syrians carried out a general attack on the Berbers in many parts of Spain, slaughtering large numbers. Then they returned to Qurṭuba.[113]

Their work done, 'Abd al-Malik now asked the Syrians to withdraw. They agreed, requesting only that he transport them to North Africa as stipulated. 'Abd al-Malik said he lacked the ships to transport them altogether, but he could send them in waves. The Syrians rejected this, probably fearing that those left behind could easily be robbed or killed by the Spanish Arabs. Then 'Abd al-Malik offered to transport them back to Sabta, but they said they would sooner be thrown into the sea as face the Moroccan Berbers again.[114]

'Abd al-Malik's attempts to get rid of the Syrians, on terms other than those agreed to, made them doubt his motives. They rose up against him, drove him from the governor's palace in Qurṭuba, and set up Balj in his stead, thus reversing the coup 'Abd al-Malik had, himself, carried out only a little over a year before.[115] One might think that this coup would have restored caliphal rule. But it is striking that the Syrian troops trapped in Spain carried it out only in their own interest, without a thought for the Caliph Hishām, though they continued formally to acknowledge him, as had 'Abd al-Malik. 'Abd al-Malik's sons escaped to Mārida and Saraqusṭa to continue the resistance of the local Arabs (*ahl al-balad*), thus reigniting civil war.[116] Interestingly, neither side is reported to have even bothered to appeal to the caliph for legitimation. Military support was of course out of the question, as the caliph had no more troops to spare. Balj's victory appears to have been accompanied by a plundering of the property of the defeated local faction.[117]

Though Balj now wished to conciliate the local faction, his own Yamanī supporters forced him to execute 'Abd al-Malik in revenge for past wrongs. This caused 'Abd al-Malik's clansman 'Abd al-Raḥmān b. Ḥabīb, Balj's nemesis, to join the dead governor's sons, who were gathering their forces in the northeast. They were joined by the governor of Narbonne and his forces. Their withdrawal left the Frankish frontier bare of troops. The anti-Syrian front also convinced the recently defeated Berbers to join them and to take their vengeance out on the Syrians. The Berbers agreed to this in exchange for a share in the government. The total forces gathered by this alliance are said to have numbered one hundred thousand, an improbable figure that perhaps only indicates that they were very large.[118]

Though the Syrians would have preferred to flee when this mass marched against them in Qurṭuba, they had no choice but to stand and fight. Thus, they went out twelve thousand strong to a place called Aqwā Burtūra, where they defeated the coalition of the local Arabs and Berbers. However, Balj died shortly afterwards, possibly of wounds suffered in the battle. This was in Shawwāl 124/August 742.[119] The battle was a great disaster for the Muslims in Spain, as eleven thousand are said by Ibn 'Idhārī to have been killed.[120] Though Balj is credited with a rule lasting eleven months, this apparently includes his stay at Sabta of undermined length. For, as we have seen, the Battle of Wādī Sabū dates to approximately Dhū al-Ḥijja 123/October–November 741. Tha'laba b. Salāma al-'Āmilī succeeded him.[121]

Soon, the local Arabs and Berbers, mainly the latter, regrouped near Mārida. Tha'laba set out to fight them, but immediately had to withdraw to the citadel of Mārida, where they besieged him. However, he was able to emerge on 10 Dhū al-Ḥijja 124/27 October 742 to defeat and drive them back. To make an example of them, Tha'laba then enslaved one thousand local Muslims whom he had made prisoner and ten thousand of their families and dependents. This was done even though the enslaving of Muslims was contrary to received and accepted Islamic practice, as can be seen from the outrage at this act that is reported in the sources. These he began to sell in a humiliating public auction where the winning bid was the lowest.[122]

To stop the factional warfare and restore peace and sanity, certain Spanish Muslims now appealed to Ḥanẓala b. Ṣafwān, the governor of North Africa, to send them a governor for Spain who would unite the local and Syrian factions. They promised to obey the new appointee and pledged loyalty to the caliph. That they stressed such loyalty indicates that neither faction had been paying anything but lip service to that ideal. Ḥanẓala sent them his clansman Abū al-Khaṭṭār b. Ḍirār al-Kalbī.[123] According to al-Maqqarī, he arrived from Tūnis in al-Muḥarram 125/November 742.[124] Thus, caliphal authority was at last restored in Spain. But it depended on the pleasure of the local and the Syrian factions, for Abū al-Khaṭṭār apparently had no troops of his own.

Nevertheless, for a while Abū al-Khaṭṭār was rather more successful in Spain than Ḥanẓala had been in North Africa. He was accepted by both factions, and upon his arrival he freed all prisoners. He expelled to North Africa a number of leaders whose continued presence was inimical to the peace, including Tha'laba b. Salāma and 'Abd al-Raḥmān b. Ḥabīb. He also permanently settled the six Syrian and Egyptian *ajnād* that had come with Balj in defined territories.[125]

Despite these accomplishments, the days of caliphal authority were numbered in Spain, for Abū al-Khaṭṭār was destined to be the last Umayyad governor.[126] The province contributed nothing to preventing the final Umayyad collapse, though it had indirectly helped to make that collapse possible by trapping and holding a significant number of Syrian troops. These troops' lack of loyalty to the caliphate is striking. Despite their alleged preference for returning to Syria, it is interesting that they passed up the opportunity when they held power. Perhaps they preferred holding the valuable country they had fought for and won, to facing an uncertain future in the East, where the caliph was sure to order them to undertake more unprofitable campaigns.

Given this attitude, which was born out of the sufferings of years of hard fighting for an abstract ideal and a distant master, it is little wonder that the Syrians eventually became disobedient. And once the ancient loyalty of the Syrians to the Umayyad house was broken, it is not surprising that Hishām's successor found no troops to defend him from a coup. Nor is it strange that, once the caliphate had begun to collapse in the center, the various Muslim groups in Spain, including the Syrians, simply removed the last caliphal governor in order to put the rule of the province into their own hands.

Conclusion

Final Results of the Destruction and Scattering of the Syrian Army

Hishām's nephew and successor, al-Walīd II, inherited a tottering throne. Al-Walīd tried to govern in the traditional manner, but it was now too late for that. After the catastrophes of Hishām's reign, the caliphate was so weak militarily that he was only able to mount a single expedition during his entire reign of fourteen months.[1] That was against the Byzantines, who were in the throes of a civil war. Elsewhere, he was militarily helpless, and his helplessness had nothing to do with personal incompetence.

Furthermore, al-Walīd II was severely strapped for cash. Courting popularity, he unwisely had restored certain financial benefits to the Syrians that had been rescinded by Hishām.[2] That these were a strain on the treasury can be seen from the celerity with which al-Walīd II's successor, Yazīd III, abolished them on taking office.[3] Al-Walīd's step may have eliminated whatever cash Hishām left on hand. Besides this, al-Walīd II undertook to build more of the extravagant desert palaces that had especially become a perquisite of the station of caliph under Hishām.[4] More important than these expenses, al-Walīd II almost certainly needed cash for the army in light of the recent military catastrophes of Hishām's reign.

To raise money to cover these expenses, al-Walīd II resorted to expedients which show that the overall financial picture in his reign was not so good. He dismissed several governors, summoning them to come to court laden with extravagant, specified 'gifts' for him.[5] He also sold the great Damascene Yamanī leader Khālid al-Qasrī to the latter's enemy for fifty million dirhams, although he must have known the effect this would have on the Yaman, especially when the enemy killed Khālid under torture.[6] The rising factional tensions between the Muḍar and the Yaman, which had given rise to Khālid's execution or murder and to the Yaman's ensuing need for blood revenge, are often cited as an important cause contributing to al-Walīd II's downfall.[7] However, while it is undoubtedly the case that factional tensions played a role, it behooves us to examine the specific background of these tensions in the time of al-Walīd II to better understand them.

The Syrian Yamanī army, on which Marwānid rule had been

based since the Syrian Yaman's decisive victory over the Qays at Marj Rāhiṭ in 64/683, was broken and ruined by the end of Hishām's reign. Enormous numbers of Syrian troops had been uselessly immolated in profitless battles on many of the frontiers. The most outstanding of these, as far as we know, were the disasters of Ardabīl in 112/730 (over twenty thousand killed), Akroinon in 122/740 (over thirteen thousand killed), and Wādī Sabū in 123/741 (twenty-seven thousand killed, taken captive, or cut off).[8] It is likely that the many other less known battles, such as those in India, may have had an even more destructive impact on the Syrian army.

Just as importantly, the Syrians' surviving units had been scattered to the four corners of the empire, leaving no reserves in the center. Many Syrians had been sent to India, from which few had returned. Some remained in Khurāsān. Twenty-four thousand troops, mostly Syrians, were permanently stationed at al-Bab in the Caucasus. The last reserves of Syrian manpower had been spent, mostly consumed uselessly, in North Africa. Survivors of Kulthūm's army, clearly tired of fighting for the caliph, preferred to start new lives in Spain. Whatever last Syrian forces had been sent out to al-Qayrawān with Ḥanẓala were now stuck there. None of these forces on the various frontiers could much influence caliphal politics. The different armies were isolated from each other, had to keep their arms pointed outward owing to the danger from the various external enemies of the Muslims, and were perhaps growing weary of fighting. This situation created a vacuum and dearth of military power in the center of the caliphate.

Indeed, judging by the forces ranged for and against al-Walīd II during the coup that overthrew him, it appears that there were only a few thousand troops left from the once mighty *jund* of Damascus,[9] which had only recently carried forty-five thousand men on its rolls.[10] A similar situation apparently prevailed also in the neighboring Syrian *ajnād*.[11] Wellhausen observed drily, "Evidently the government of Syria had not any great number of soldiers ready."[12] Indeed it did not, but the point needs more emphasis! And in addition to the losses, probably the disasters had caused a demoralization, making men less eager to be available for service than before.

But there was one significant exception to this situation: the two *junds* of al-Jazīra and Qinnasrīn, both of which were Muḍarī. Unlike the scattered Syrians, the Jazīran army, with the Qinnasrīnīs, remained mostly intact in a compact body, as it was in charge of the Byzantine frontier.[13] Though it may have suffered its share of disasters in Anatolia, it apparently did not share so much in the great catastrophe of Akroinon in 122/740, for the losses there appear to have been of Syrians, not Jazīrans. Indeed, while the Jazīrans who participated in that campaign on another front had been pleased to go home to their families to fight again another day, the Syrian survivors were almost immediately posted to North Africa, where they faced horror upon horror.[14] The Syrians' being widely scattered meant that the Jazīrans had the only large reserves of manpower left, directly adjacent to the metropolitan province of Syria.

The power vacuum in Syria must have seriously alarmed the leaders of the few Syrian Yamanī troops still there. For, as military men, they knew how much their political power relied on force. The position of the Jazīran army just across the Euphrates will have particularly frightened them, for it represented the same rival party they had discomfited and elbowed aside at Marj Rāhiṭ sixty years before. Without military power as a basis for support, the Syrian Yaman could not trust the caliph and his court to continue to acknowledge their status. The sale of Khālid al-Qasrī to his enemies and the Syrian Yaman's own inability to prevent it may have confirmed their suspicions that their status as the main ruling group, aside from the Umayyad family, was likely to be ignored increasingly in the future, which thus looked bleak from the Syrian Yamanī point of view.

The Yamanī-sponsored Reform Program: Rationale and Result

Despair of their situation led the previously conservative Syrian Yamanīs to seek a radical solution. The only step they could take to save the Umayyad regime, in which they enjoyed such a dominant influence, was to initiate the reforms that were being widely demanded throughout the empire in order to win enough popularity to outweigh the military strength of the Jazīrans. These reforms, which we have mentioned above, in particular, consisted of establishing an equal treatment of all Muslims, whether Arab or *mawālī*, especially in the matter of stipends. It also consisted of using the revenue of each province for the benefit of the Muslims in that province. As adopted by the Yaman party, the reforms were aimed at winning the support of the Iraqis as well as of the frontier provinces.[15] They, therefore, amounted to a popular appeal to the Muslims of the whole empire. I will discuss this reform program here because it is a direct result of the Yaman's weakness stemming from the destruction and scattering of their forces under Hishām.

In fact, such demands had been heard before. Arabs assimilated to the provinces in which they lived, as well as their *mawālī* brethren, had already pressed for such reforms in areas as diverse as Khurāsān and Spain much earlier in Hishām's reign.[16] Then the great Berber rebellion had broken out owing to the inability to obtain redress for the same type of grievances. In his failed revolt in al-Kufa in 122/740, the 'Alid rebel Zayd b. 'Alī presented a program which was somewhat vague but specified a number of points, as follows.[17] Zayd promised to:

1. Apply the Qur'ān and *sunna*.
2. Wage *jihād* against oppressors.
3. Defend the weak.
4. Provide for the deprived.
5. Equally divide the income from Muslim property by right of conquest (*fay'*) among those deserving it.
6. Satisfy complaints.
7. Bring back those held in the field on campaigns for more than one year.
8. Support the 'Alids against those resisting or denying their rights.

Points one, three, and six of Zayd's program are general and ambiguous. Point two presumably means it is a sacred duty to fight against the Umayyads. Point four, possibly, might mean to provide military stipends for those who had been deprived of them, namely, the demilitarized Iraqis, especially the Kūfans. Point five is of crucial importance, for it incorporates the earlier demands that *mawālī* warriors receive equal pay and that the income of a province be divided among that province's Muslim troops. However, it is ambiguous as stated. Probably Zayd wanted the support of the beneficiaries of the existing system as well as those suffering from it. Point seven, another old demand, as previously mentioned, would end the practice of keeping troops away from their families. Point eight shows an insistence on absolute charismatic rule by the descendents of the Prophet.

In their effort to win popularity and to save their rule, the Syrian Yamanīs now adopted a considerably more radical and much more detailed program, though it incorporated certain of Zayd's points. This was the revolutionary program announced by al-Walīd II's successor, Yazīd III, on taking office. Its points are as follows.[18] Yazīd III promised on taking office:

1. Not to build any buildings of stone or brick, nor to dig any canals.
2. Not to hoard wealth.
3. Not to give wealth to wives or children.
4. To transfer wealth from one province to another only after adquately paying the first province's troops and taking care of its needy.
5. To send any surplus to the nearest province and divide it among those most in need of it.
6. Not to keep troops in the field more than one year, because that would tempt both the troops and their families to immorality.
7. Not to lock out petitioners, which would allow the powerful to eat up the weak.
8. Not to put such high taxes on the non-Muslims that would caus them to flee their lands and not to reproduce.
9. To give all Muslim troops in all provinces equal annual stipends and monthly provisions.
10. To acknowledge the right of the Muslims to reproach the caliph if he fails to carry out this program and to remove him from office if he does not heed the reproach.
11. To acknowledge the right of the Muslims to replace the caliph with another who will carry out the same program.

This program is redolent of irritation with the policies of Hishām as well as those of al-Walīd II to a lesser extent. It also sharply contrasts with the program of Zayd on essential points. The first three points concern princely extravagance.[19] This problem was not mentioned by Zayd, except perhaps obliquely in his rather ambiguous fifth point. The Syrians' first point means that no more monumental works, especially palaces, would be constructed. Although al-Walīd II was guilty of this, Hishām's reign undoubtedly saw much such construction, as at Qaṣr al-Ḥayr al-Sharqī and al-Gharbī. The part forbidding canals seems especially aimed at Hishām's irrigation works. These were not only wasteful and unfair, as they were private estates built up from state money, but also diverted money from the military budget. The second point reminds us of Hishām's famous avarice. Even when faced with the military crises of his reign, he still insisted on piling up wealth.[20] Point three is also aimed at Hishām, who is known to have given an estate to his daughter and probably distributed many to his sons.[21] Points four and five restrict the spending of provincial tax money much more thoroughly than does Zayd's rather vague point five.

Point six is the same as Zayd's point seven, but in the case of the

Syrian Yaman constitutes a promise by the Syrians themselves to withdraw from the various provinces of the empire they are stationed in, or else to assimilate to the local population.[22] This is because it would be difficult to rotate troops annually from Syria to places as far away as Spain, Khurāsān, and Sind. This point indicates that the Syrian army was now ready to reduce its bearing of the empirewide burdens that had led to its exhaustion. It also means a virtual end to the policy of universal *jihād* on all the frontiers. For local Muslim forces faced with difficult enemies had usually proven unwilling to fight, as in Sijistān and Khurāsān. Probably this point was not meant to end the *jihād* in theory, but it might well have done so in fact, had it been applied.

Point seven of Yazīd III's program is a more precise restatement of Zayd's rather vague and ambiguous point six, that the caliph should be accessible to all. This, again, seems aimed at Hishām, who refused to hear the complaint of the Berber delegation before the great Berber revolt, if he was even aware of their presence.[23] Perhaps the Yaman also remembered Hishām's refusal to see Khālid al-Qasrī after the latter's dismissal.[24]

Point eight, which is missing from Zayd's program, is also aimed at Hishām's policies. Here, the merciless taxation policies applied by 'Ubayd Allāh b. al-Ḥabḥāb and others are criticized for driving the non-Muslims to despair and for thus being counterproductive by lowering the non-Muslims' output. This point seems to contain a recognition of the non-Muslims as human beings with feelings that must be respected. It also may imply that a caliphate which relied less on military force would need a better relationship with its non-Muslim subjects. The problem of unfair taxation of the *mawālī* apparently had been solved near the end of Hishām's reign by a fiscal reform carried out in Khurāsān by Naṣr b. Sayyār, and perhaps elsewhere by others, and is therefore not mentioned.[25]

Point nine also indicates that the Syrian army would no longer be maintaining its dominant role in all the provinces. Instead, the people of each province would be responsible for their own defense. All the different provincial armies would now achieve equality, so there would be no need to revolt. This was as much as the proud Syrians could maintain of their previously superior position in the empire: that they be acknowledged only as equals, keeping solely the distinction of having the seat of the caliph in their province. That this point should be pushed by the Syrians themselves suggests that their military position was weak owing to the destruction and scattering of the Syrian army, and that they were looking for support elsewhere.

It is points ten and eleven, however, that are most impressive. Rather than require obedience to a rightful imam of 'Alī's house, as in Zayd's program, the Syrians propose to make their reform program superior to the will of the caliph himself, who must follow it to stay in office. Point eleven not only implies election of the caliph, a principle already established in particular by the consulative electoral committee (*shūrā*) set up by 'Umar I,[26] but also the right of recall of the incumbent even if he is fit for the office. Like some of the previous points, these would strongly suggest that the Syrians were seeking a much broader base of support and ratification of their program than had previously ever been the case, as indeed does the whole program. In fact, had the Syrian army not been destroyed and dispersed under Hishām, the Syrians probably would never have made such an appeal to the rest of the empire nor pressed violently for the adoption of so radical a program.

The only problem with the program was that the Syrian Yaman had no way of putting it into effect as long as al-Walīd II was in office, for he would never accept any limitation on his powers. This was shown by his autocratic insistence on the succession of his two minor sons instead of any of his cousins or even any of his brothers, despite the opposition of much of the Umayyad house, who felt they had more right to rule than any minors.[27] By dividing the Umayyad house, al-Walīd's change in the succession made some princes willing to cooperate with the Syrian Yaman revolutionaries.[28] But these needed to act quickly, lest the Jazīrans notice their weakness and step in to fill the vacuum in Syria. This fear perhaps accounts for their impatience. Another factor may have been the hopelessness of their position while their remnants remained scattered in places as diverse as Spain, North Africa, Syria, Iraq, the Caucasus, Khurāsān, Sijistān, and Sind. They may have thought that if they could buy time with their program, they could repatriate all their remnants to Syria within one year,[29] and thus at least be able to protect their home province and their rights to keep the seat of the caliph in it.

Therefore, only fourteen months after al-Walīd II took office, the Syrians overthrew him in a bloody coup. Having received some warning, al-Walīd made for the safety of the Jazīran army, but was intercepted and killed.[30] Referring to the killing of al-Walīd II, Shaban succinctly says, "For all practical purposes, this was the end of Umayyad rule," for, contrary to the Syrians' hopes, their coup destroyed whatever legitimacy was left to the Umayyad caliphate.[31] Though they heaped calumnies on al-Walīd II to justify their rebellion, ludicrously accusing him of shooting the Qur'ān with arrows, bathing in wine, and being a homosexual and apostate,[32] their unique and original reform program was read only as a sign of weakness in most of the provinces, and troubles began to break out everywhere. With the sudden death of Yazīd III after only six months in office, it was brushed aside, as the Jazīrans under Marwān II and later the Khurāsānīs under the 'Abbāsids battled for dominance. The triumph of the latter, with their pseudo-Shī'ī imamate and messianic claims, snuffed out whatever hopes there may have been for official limitations on the powers of the caliphal office.

General Conclusions

Looking back over the military reverses of Hishām's reign and their results, his rule should have been considered generally a disastrous failure from the Muslim point of view. Hishām and his advisers cannot be exculpated from blame for the debacle. Their unswerving pursuit of the traditional policy of expansion on almost all the frontiers at once, coupled with their refusal to modify or to abandon it after it had shown its bankruptcy in changed circumstances, led directly to the fatal weakening of the Umayyad caliphate that caused its collapse. It was not so much that the total casualties of the Muslim armies were so high that the Muslims were fatally weakened and threatened with collapse as a whole. Rather, it was the decimation and scattering of the Syrian troops on whom the caliph's main support had been based that undermined the Umayyad regime.

Once the Syrians' military superiority in manpower and fighting ability had been ended by defeats inflicted by the various external enemies and Berber rebels, it was only a matter of time before the various provincial armies, especially the nearby Jazīrans, would be tempted to intervene. In a last desperate effort to prevent that, the Syrians themselves killed a caliph in order to implement a radical reform program and appeal for broader support. But it was too late. Indeed, the killing of al-Walīd II mainly destroyed whatever legitimacy was left to the Umayyad caliphate and, if anything, may have hastened its downfall.

The most decisive element in this process of breakdown was the series of external military defeats suffered by the Muslims, both Syrians and others, in Hishām's reign. Naturally, losses of Syrian troops directly weakened the main pillar of military support for the caliph. But the losses suffered by other caliphal armies, such as that of Khurāsān, also weakened the caliph by requiring him to send more of his precious Syrians to hold the frontiers and to spend more money to mobilize, equip, and maintain them.

Nevertheless, it had taken a very long series of reverses, lasting almost throughout Hishām's reign, before the Syrians were weakened enough, in both numbers and resolve, to become vulnerable to overthrow. In fact, the Umayyad caliphate's ability to recover from its defeats was almost as spectacular as the series of defeats themselves. But the defeats continued, building up finally to the crescendo of losses in the Berber war. By the end of Hishām's reign, the series of disasters had clearly overloaded the state's military capacity, decimating its army and creating a financial crisis that led to ever more severe exactions on the populace in order to pay for replacements. In particular, the army losses almost certainly would have to be made up from new sources of recruitment to the east of Syria, such as Iraq and Khurāsān. Such a change in the nature of the army would lead to incalculable political consequences, as indeed happened with the rise of the 'Abbāsids to power.

In this work, I have tried to trace the stages in this process of military breakdown with some precision. In the earliest part of Hishām's reign, about 105–11/724–29, the wars of expansion resumed by Yazīd II continued on virtually all the frontiers, even the remote and chronically disastrous Sijistān front against the Zunbīl of Zābulistān. This period was characterized by hard fighting punctuated by a few disasters, especially those of Muslim b. Sa'īd in Transoxiana and al-Aṣfaḥ b. 'Abd Allāh in Sijistān. After this, in 112–14/730–32, events took a turn for the worse, as the caliphate suffered at least four major defeats in the Caucasus, Transoxiana, India, and France. In the Caucasus in 112/730, a major Syrian army was annihilated for the first time. The Transoxianan disaster of 113/731 not only caused a considerable decline in the morale of the provincial army owing to the destruction of so many of its fighters, but also forced the caliph to mobilize potentially rebellious Iraqis to bolster the frontier.

After these concentrated disasters, a relative lull ensued from 115–21/733–39. This period, nevertheless, saw many more disasters, especially on the sea in the western Mediterranean and in India, where the front totally collapsed. Possibly these new disasters did not warrant so much attention as they fell in more marginal areas and as the losses of Syrians in them may not have been so great as those of other groups. But in the final period of Hishām's rule, 122–25/740–43, the number of disasters increased dramatically and finally threatened to destroy the Syrian army altogether.

The disasters suffered by the Muslims under Hishām have been arranged for comparison in table 4. The column entitled 'Fate' gives the fate of the Muslim commander in the battle. Of course, the fact that a commander survived the battle does not imply that the reverse suffered was minor. But it is dramatic how many commanders fell in battle, and especially how the number increased sharply toward the end of Hishām's reign. Many of the slain commanders were provincial governors, their disasters inviting comparison with those suffered by Roman consular armies in the Second Punic War. The column marked 'Troops' shows the predominant element among the Muslims in each battle. For some obscure battles, these identifications are only probable. From this column, it can be seen that the Syrians' burdens and disasters also increased dramatically as the reign wore on. The column entitled 'Losses' gives the best estimate available where there is any basis for an estimate from the sources. Those battles for which numbers are given were probably among the worst disasters. Though medieval numbers must always be carefully assessed, those I have given seem most reasonable. For evidence about this and other aspects of each battle mentioned in the table, the reader should refer to the text above.

Not only did the cost of these disasters in money and, especially, in lives begin to erode support for the caliph's war policy, but also the Muslim armies' continual lack of success in the field turned the Muslim warriors and others into opponents of that policy. The caliphate's military failures under Hishām were highlighted by actual territorial losses. In India, the caliphate gained nothing and was barely able to hold onto an unspecified proportion of Sind. Elsewhere, the Byzantines became more organized and posed a real threat by the end of Hishām's reign, inflicting a major disaster on the Muslims at Akroinon in 122/740 and besting the Muslims repeatedly on the sea. For a state which derived its military success from divine approval, these were ominous signs. But worse was to come as the Berbers dealt the caliphate one catastrophic defeat after another in a short period, pushing the caliphate's boundaries all the way back to al-Qayrawān in Tunisia and practically cutting off Spain. Only in the Caucasus and Transoxiana was the caliphate able to triumph over its Turkish opponents. But even these victories brought little territorial gain or booty.

The inability of the Umayyad caliphate to recover from the various disasters probably helped to undermine its legitimacy. The caliphate constituted the *jihād* state par excellence. Its main reason for existence, aside from maintaining God's law, was to protect Islam and to expand the territory under its control, and its reputation was strongly bound to its military success. Not only did military success bring greater power to Islam as well as other material benefits, but it must have seemed a sign of divine approval. Despite

Table 4 MUSLIM MILITARY DEFEATS UNDER HISHĀM

Date	Place	Commander	Fate	Troops	Losses
106/725	Transoxiana (N. of Jaxartes)	Muslim b. Sa'īd	safe	Khurāsānīs	unknown
107/725	Sicily	Bishr b. Ṣafwān al-Kalbī	safe	N. Africans	unknown
109/727	Transoxiana (al-Sughd)	Asad b. 'Abd Allāh al-Qasrī	safe	Khurāsānīs	unknown
109/728	Sijistān (Zamīndāwar)	al-Aṣfaḥ b. 'Abd Allāh al-Kalbī	died	Sijistānīs, some Syrians	unknown
110/728	Caucasus (Darial Pass)	Maslama b. 'Abd al-Malik	safe	Syro-Jazīrans	unknown
111/729	Sicily (at sea)	al-Mustanīr b. al-Ḥārith	safe	N. Africans	163 ships
112/730	Caucasus (Ardabīl)	al-Jarrāḥ b. 'Abd Allāh al-Ḥakamī	killed	Syrians	24,000
c.113/731	India	Tamīm b. Zayd al-Qaynī	safe	Syrians, Iraqis	unknown
113/731	Khazaria	Maslama b. 'Abd al-Malik	safe	Syro-Jazīrans	unknown
113/731	Transoxiana (Samarqand)	al-Junayd b. 'Abd al-Raḥmān	safe	Khurāsānīs, few Syrians	20,000+

Table 4 *(Continued)*

Date	Place	Commander	Fate	Troops	Losses
113/731	Anatolia	ʻAbd Allāh b. ʻAmr al-Baṭṭāl	safe	Syrians	unknown
114/732	Central France (Poitiers)	ʻAbd al-Raḥmān b. ʻAbd Allāh	killed	Spaniards	unknown
115/733	Sicily (off Drepana)	Bakr b. Suwayd	safe	N. Africans	unknown
116/734	Sicily (at sea)	ʻUthmān b. Abī ʻUbayda al-Fihrī	safe	N. Africans	unknown
118/736	E. Mediterranean (at sea)	Nâfiʻ b. Abī ʻUbayda al-Fihrī	safe	Egyptians	unknown
118/736	Kathiawar (Valabhi)	unknown	unknown	Syrians, others	unknown
119/737	Transoxiana (Upper Oxus)	Asad b. ʻAbd Allāh al-Qasrī	safe	Syrians, Khurāsānīs	unknown
119/737	Sardinia (at sea)	Qutham b. ʻAwāna al-Kalbī	sunk	N. Africans	unknown
121/739	S. Gujarat (Navasarika)	unknown	unknown	Syrians, Sindis	unknown
121/739	S. France (Buerre R.)	ʻAmr b. Khālid	unknown	Spaniards	unknown

Date	Place	Commander	Fate	Troops	Losses
122/740	Anatolia (Akroinon)	ʻAbd Allāh b. ʻAmr al-Baṭṭāl Mālik b. Shuʻayb	killed	Syrians, Jazīrans	13,200
122/740	Kathiawar (Meds)	al-Ḥakam b. ʻAwāna al-Kalbī	killed	Syrians, others	unknown
122/740	Tangier	ʻUmar b. ʻAbd Allāh al-Murâdî	killed	N. Africans	unknown
122/740	al-Sūs al-Aqṣā	Ismāʻīl b. ʻUbayd Allāh	killed	N. Africans	unknown
123/740	Tangier (Kadar R.)	Khālid b. Abī Ḥabīb al-Fihrī	killed	N. Africans	unknown
123/741	Anatolia	Sulaymān b. Hishām	safe	Syro-Jazîrans	unknown
123/741	Fās (Wādī Sabū)	Kulthūm b. ʻIyāḍ al-Qushayrī	killed	Syrians, Egyptians, N. Africans	18,000 Syr. + c.20,000 N.Af.
124/742	al-Zāb (Ṭubna)	ʻAbd al-Raḥmân b. ʻUqba al-Ghifārī	killed	N. Africans, some Syrians	unknown
124/742	Qurṭuba	Balj b. Bishr al-Qushayrî	died	Syrians vs. Spaniards	11,000
125/742	N. Africa (Tunisia)	Thābit b. Khaytham al-Lakhmī	killed	N. Africans	unknown

occasional earlier military failures, the caliphate had never before suffered such a series of repeated defeats as it saw under Hishām. Especially shocking were those inflicted by the Berber *khawārij*, who were considered heretics because of their rebellion against the caliph. These setbacks must have shaken confidence in and respect for the state, or at least its present rulers.

Another factor as important as the disastrous losses of men and territory that also contributed to the weakening of the Syrian army and its hold on power was the scattering of the surviving Syrian units across the face of much of the empire. When Hishām came to the throne, there were Syrians only in Syria, Iraq, the Caucasus, and probably to a very limited extent, in Sind. By the end of his reign, while the Syrian troops had almost disappeared from Syria itself, they were found in Iraq, the Caucasus (where a large, permanent force of twenty-four thousand had been sent), Transoxiana, Sijistan, Sind, Egypt (if we count the Muḍarīs settled by Ibn al-Ḥabḥāb), North Africa, and Spain, that is, in virtually every province. Thus spread out, the Syrians may have found it difficult to communicate with each other. More importantly, they probably found themselves diluted everywhere by being mixed with local troops whose interests were not those of the Umayyad caliphate. Even though they may have continued to remember their ties of loyalty to their Syrian brethren elsewhere, as well as to the Umayyad house, they had to consider the feelings of the local Muslim divisions in each place where they were stationed, in order to avoid strife.

The Umayyad caliphate lost its main support with the destruction and the scattering of the Syrian army. Thus, it was more the unprecedented series of defeats at the hands of external enemies than internal problems that led to the weakening and downfall of the Umayyads. Though there were plenty of internal divisions, tribal, regional, and religious, they were of long standing and had always been controllable. There is no evidence that any of these internal divisions had become so intense by itself that it threatened Umayyad rule. On the other hand, the resistance of the external powers who stood in the way of the caliphate's wars of expansion, in addition to the Berber revolt, became acute and highly destructive to the Muslim state under Hishām. Indeed, it is this outside resistance more than internal problems that constitutes the main fact of his reign from the political point of view.

Maps

Map 1: The Eastern Caliphate

Map 2: The Western Caliphate

Map 3: Syria and al-Jazīra

Map 4: The Byzantine Front

Map 5: The Caucasus

Map 6: Khurāsān and Transoxiana

Map 7: India

Map 8: Egypt

Map 9: North Africa, Spain, and France

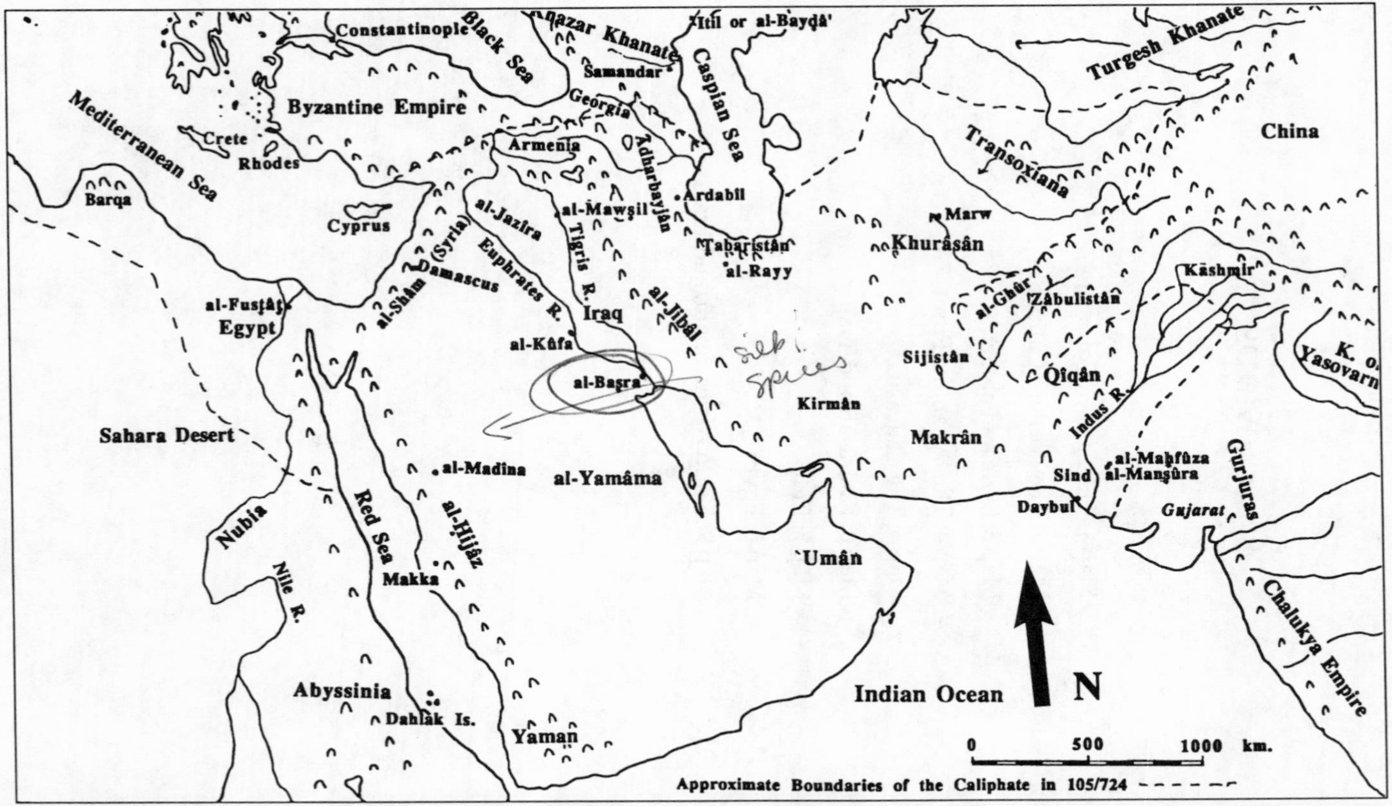
Constantinople
Black Sea
Khazar Khanate
Itil or al-Baydâ'
Caspian Sea
Samandar
Georgia
Byzantine Empire
Mediterranean Sea
Crete
Rhodes
Armenia
Âdharbayjân
Ardabil
Barqa
Cyprus
al-Jazira
al-Mawṣil
Tabaristân
al-Rayy
al-Shâm (Syria)
Damascus
Euphrates R.
Tigris R.
al-Jibâl
Iraq
al-Fusṭâṭ
Egypt
al-Kûfa
al-Baṣra
Kirmân
Sahara Desert
al-Madina
al-Yamâma
Nubia
Red Sea
al-Ḥijâz
Makka
Nile R.
'Umân
Abyssinia
Dahlak Is.
Yaman
Indian Ocean
N
0 500 1000 km.
Approximate Boundaries of the Caliphate in 105/724
Turgesh Khanate
China
Transoxiana
Marw
Khurâsân
al-Ghûr
Zâbulistân
Kashmir
K. of Yasovarm
Sijistân
Qîqân
Indus R.
Makrân
Sind
al-Maḥfûza
al-Manṣûra
Daybul
Gujarat
Gurjuras
Chalukya Empire

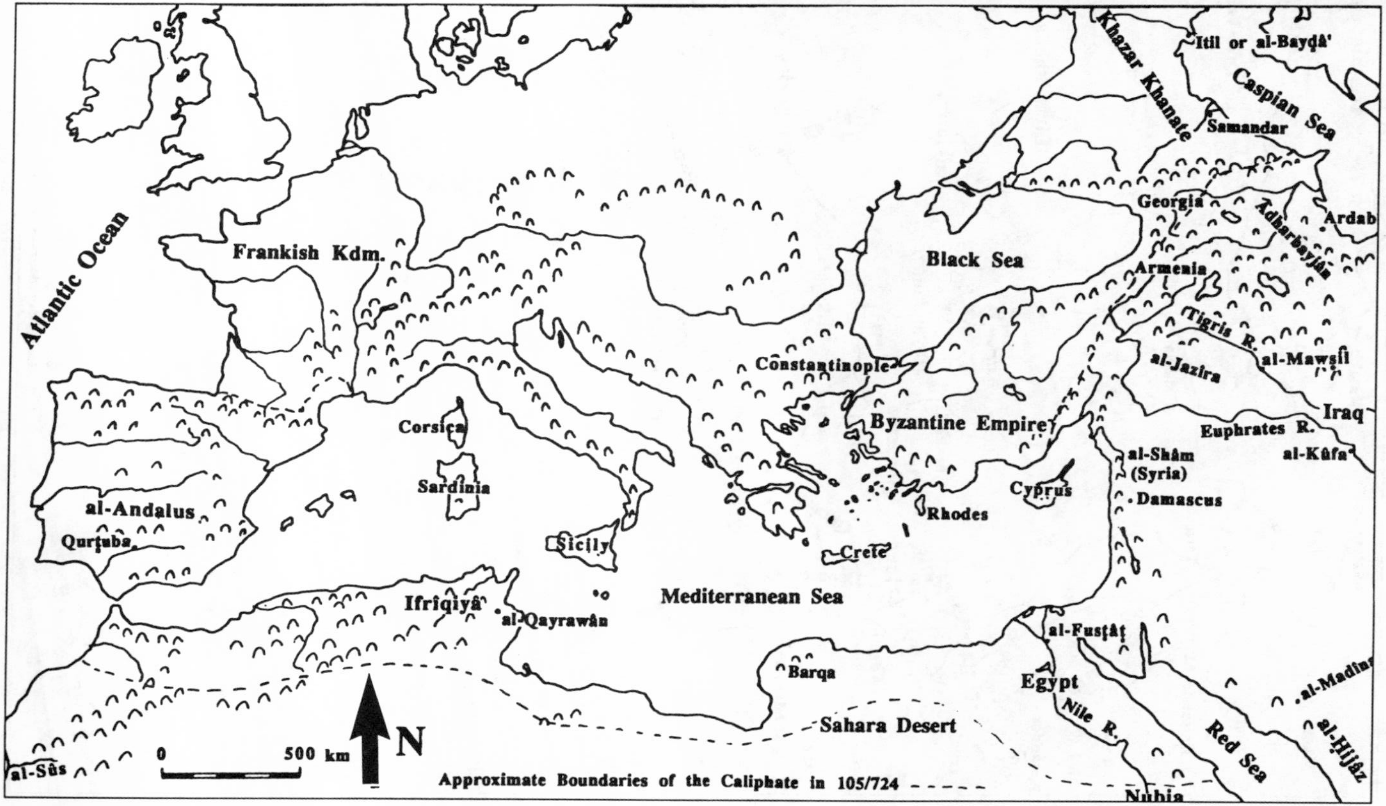

Map 2: The Western Caliphate

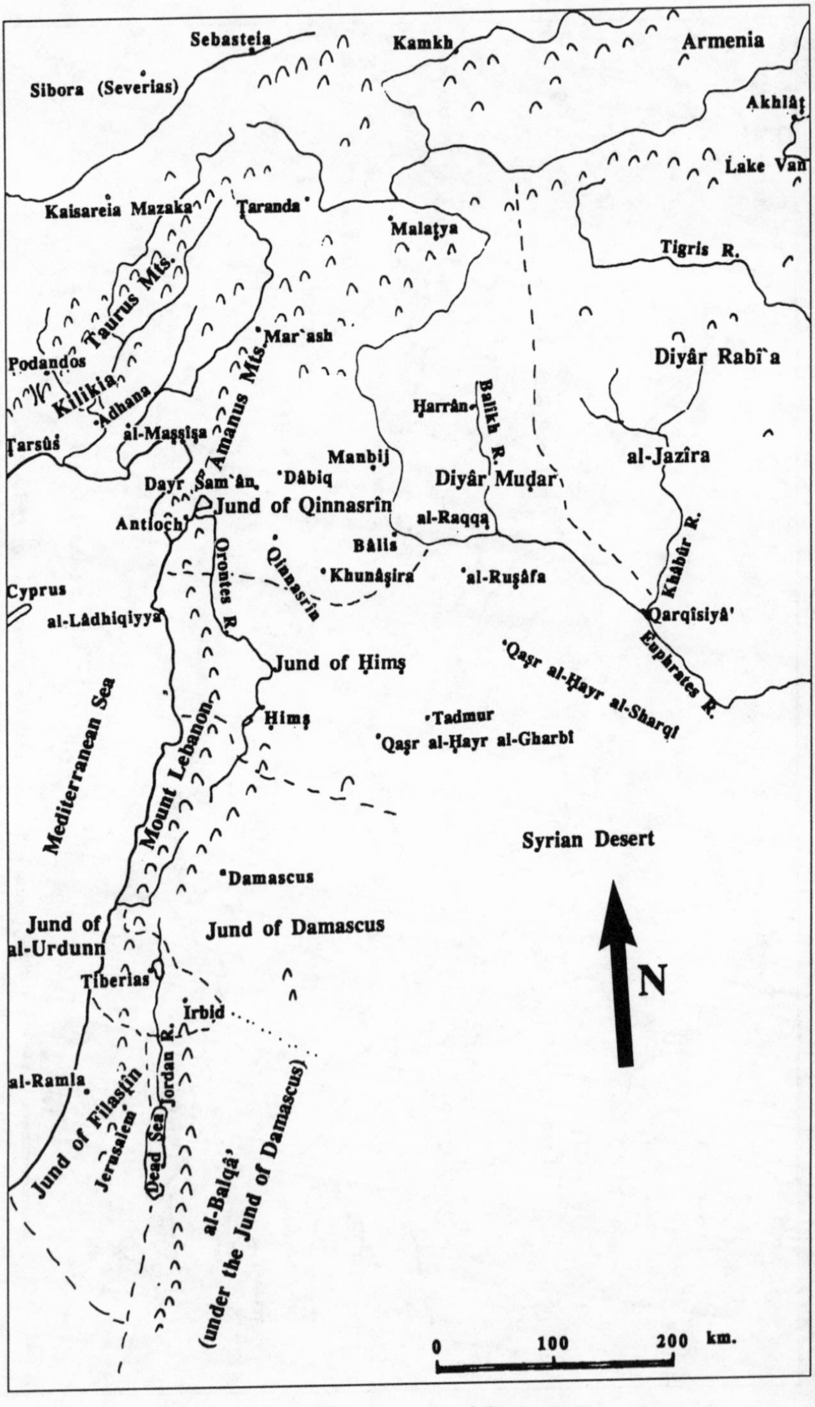

Map 3: Syria and al-Jazīra

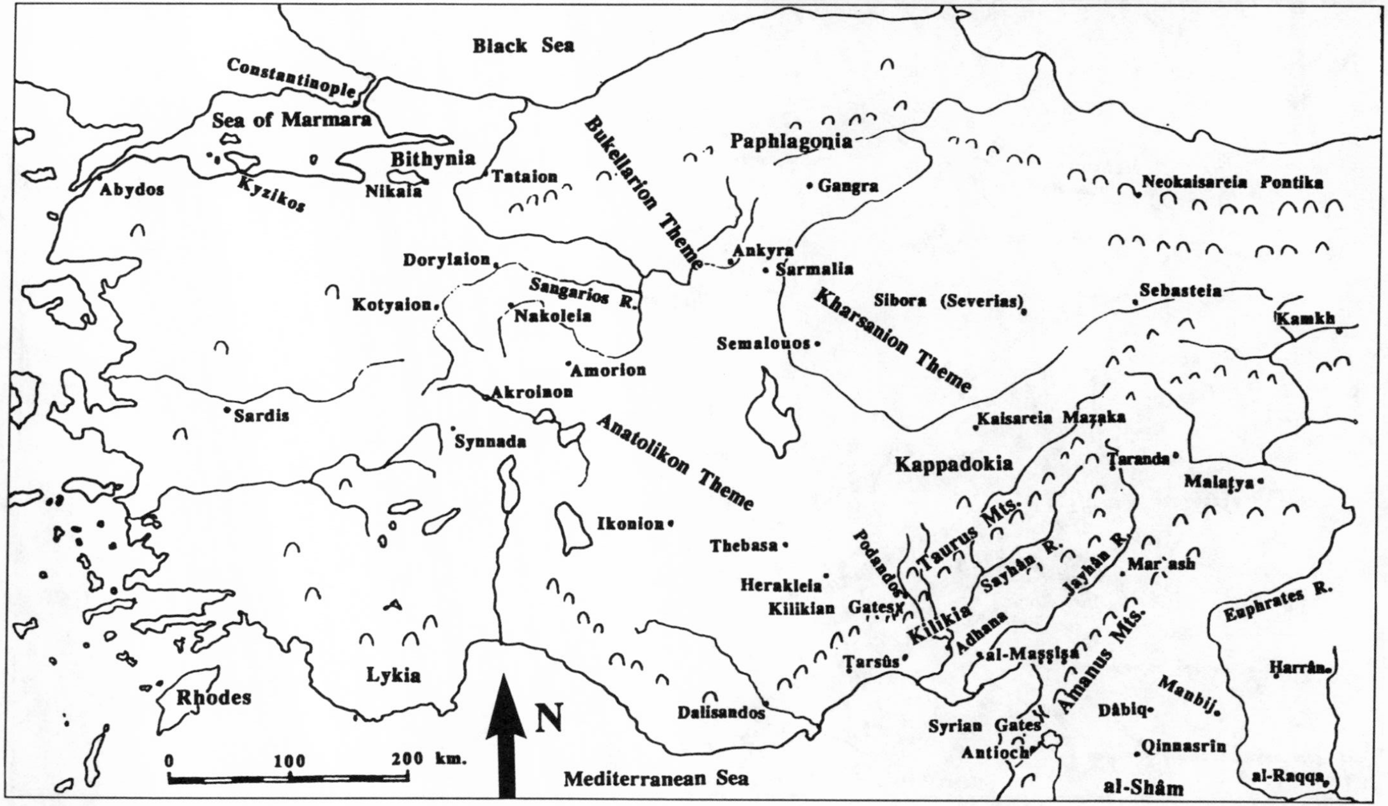

Map 4: The Byzantine Front

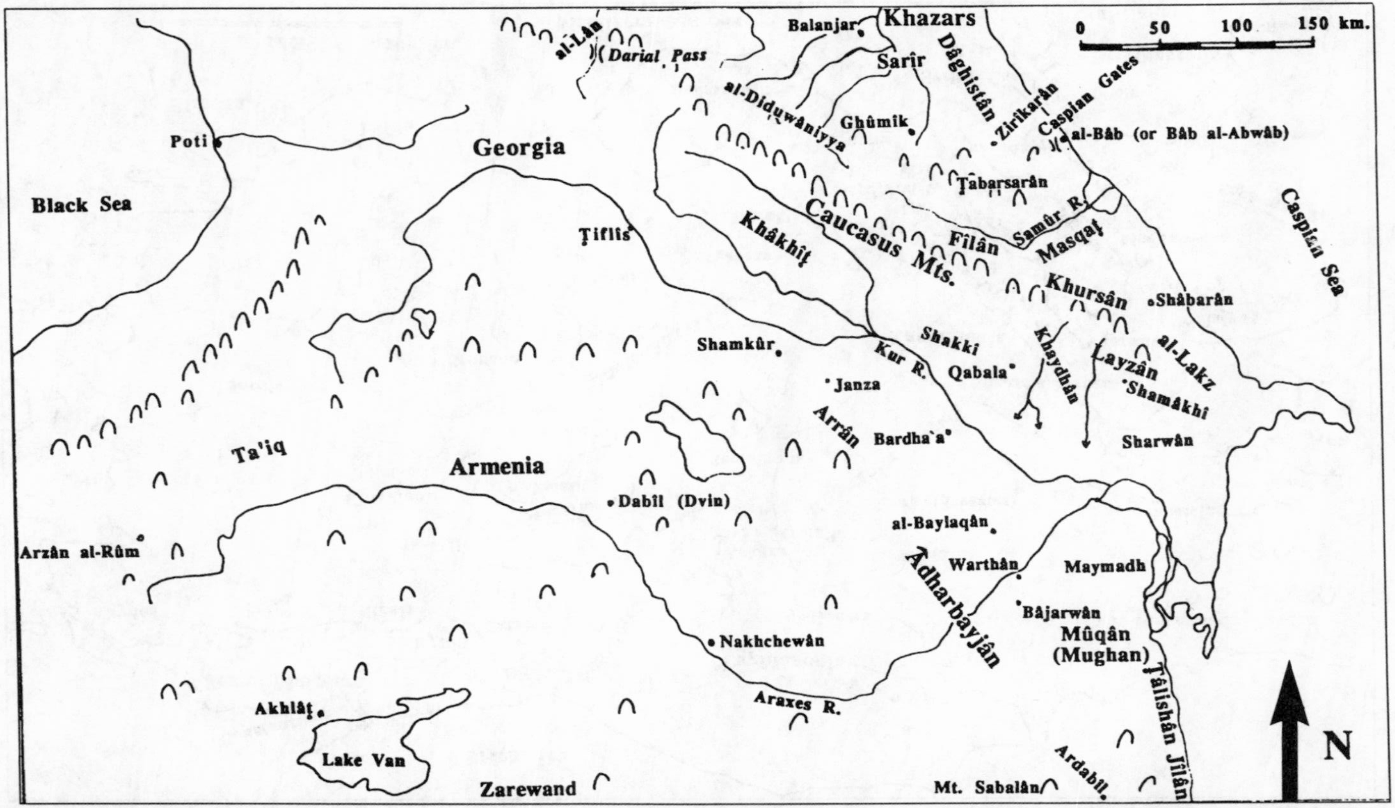
0 50 100 150 km.
Khazars
Balanjar
Sarîr
Dâghistân
al-Lân
(Darial Pass
al-Diduwâniyya
Ghûmik
Zirikarân
Caspian Gates
al-Bâb (or Bâb al-Abwâb)
Poti
Georgia
Black Sea
Ṭabarsarân
Caspian Sea
Khâkhîṭ
Caucasus Mts.
Filân
Samûr R.
Masqaṭ
Ṭiflis
Khursân
Shâbarân
Shamkûr
Shakki
Kur R.
Qabala
Khaydhân
Layzân
al-Lakz
Shamâkhî
Janza
Arrân
Bardha`a
Sharwân
Ta'iq
Armenia
Dabîl (Dvin)
al-Baylaqân
Arzân al-Rûm
Warthân
Maymadh
Âdharbayjân
Bâjarwân
Mûqân
(Mughan)
Nakhchewân
Ṭâlishân Jîlân
Akhlâṭ
Araxes R.
Lake Van
Ardabîl
N
Zarewand
Mt. Sabalân

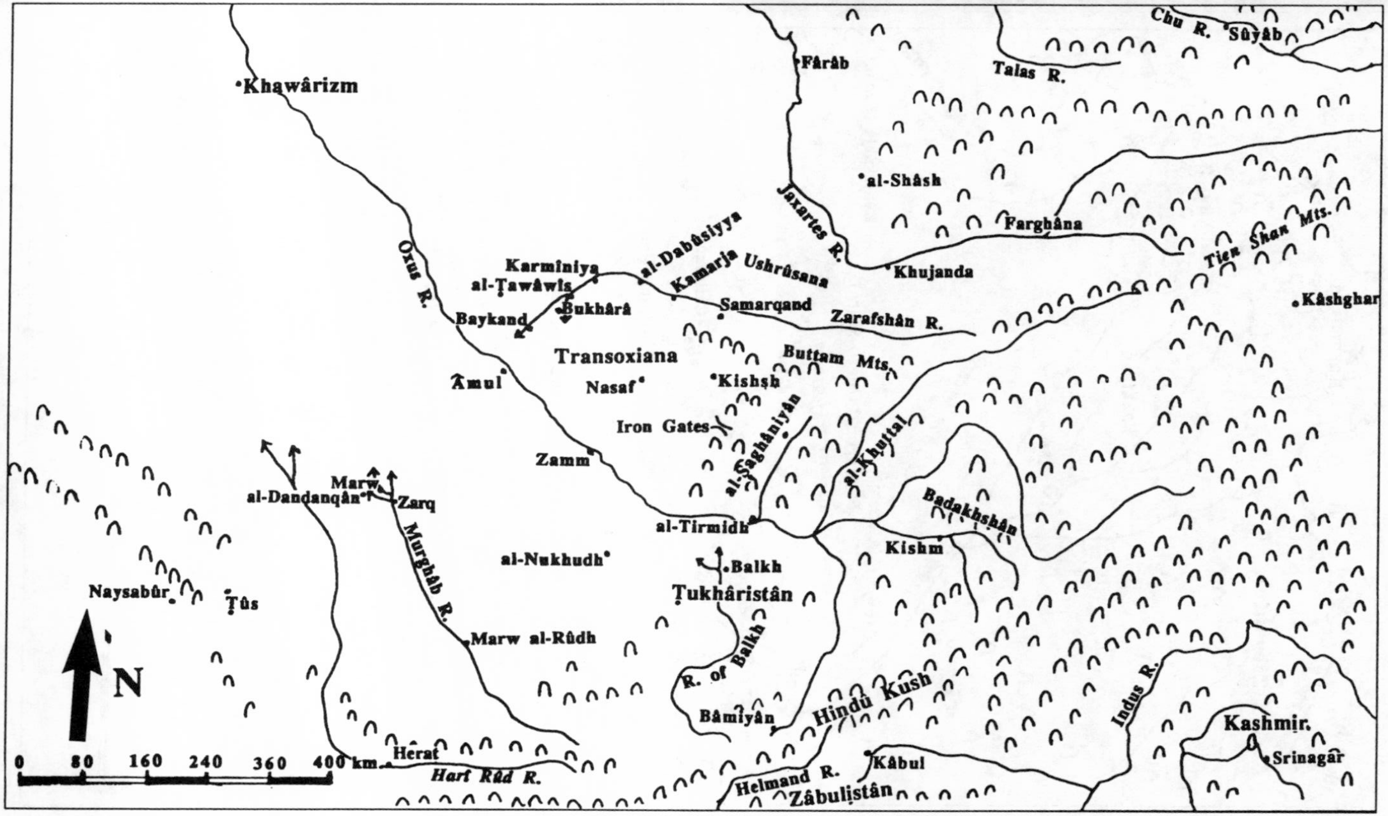

Map 6: Khurāsān and Transoxiana

Hindû Kush
Kâbul
Kashmir
Srinagar
Helmand R.
Indus R.
Zâbulistân
al-Kiraj
Himalayas
Jullundur
Takkiyân
Multân
K. of Yasovarman
Qîqân
Qandabil
Indus R.
Hakra R.
Great Thar Desert
Ganges R.
al-Rawr (Alor)
Bhattis
Kânyakubja (Kanauj)
Marmad (Maru-Mâra)
Jaisalmer
Rajasthan
Sind
Jodhpur
Châhmânas
Brahmanâbâd
al-Manşûra
al-Maḥfûza
Nirûn
Tatar (Tatta)
Bhillamâla
Gurjara States
Guhilas
Chitrakûta
Madhya Pradesh
Daybul
Mauryas
Gurjaratra
Gurjara-Pratîhâras
Châpas
Ujjayini
Kaccha (Cutch)
Mandal
al-Midh (Meds)
Gujarat
Mâlava (Mâlwâ)
Valabhi
Bhûmilkâ
Saurâshtra
Râshtrakûtas
Barawş (Broach)
Saindhavas
Maitrakas
Lâta
Acalapura
Kathiawar Pen.
Navasârikâ (Navsari)
Arabian Sea
Châlukya Empire
N
0
500 km.
Vâtâpi
(Badami)

Map 7: India

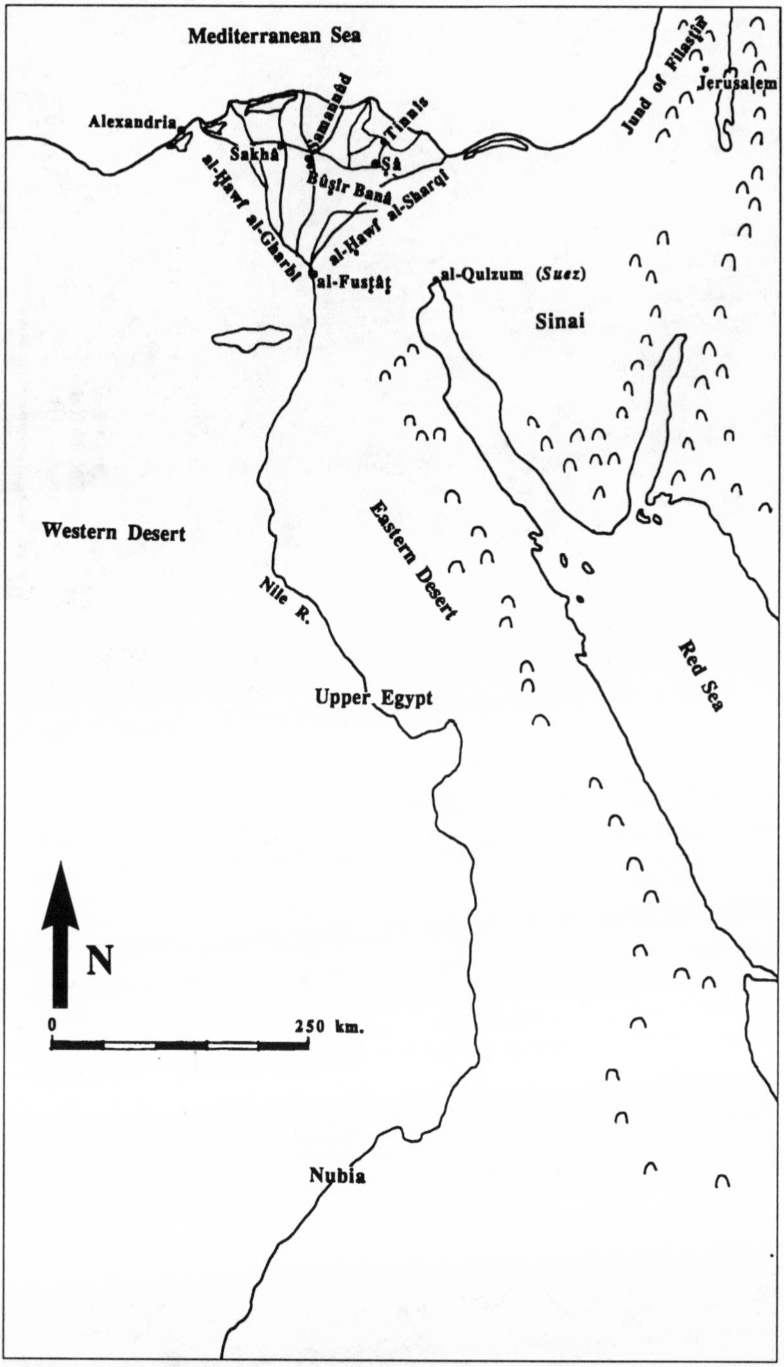
Mediterranean Sea
Alexandria
Sakhâ
Samannûd
Tinnis
Şâ
Bûşîr Banâ
al-Ḥawf al-Gharbî
al-Ḥawf al-Sharqî
al-Fusţâţ
al-Qulzum (Suez)
Jund of Filasţîn
Jerusalem
Sinai
Western Desert
Eastern Desert
Nile R.
Red Sea
Upper Egypt
Nubia
N
0
250 km.

Map 8: Egypt

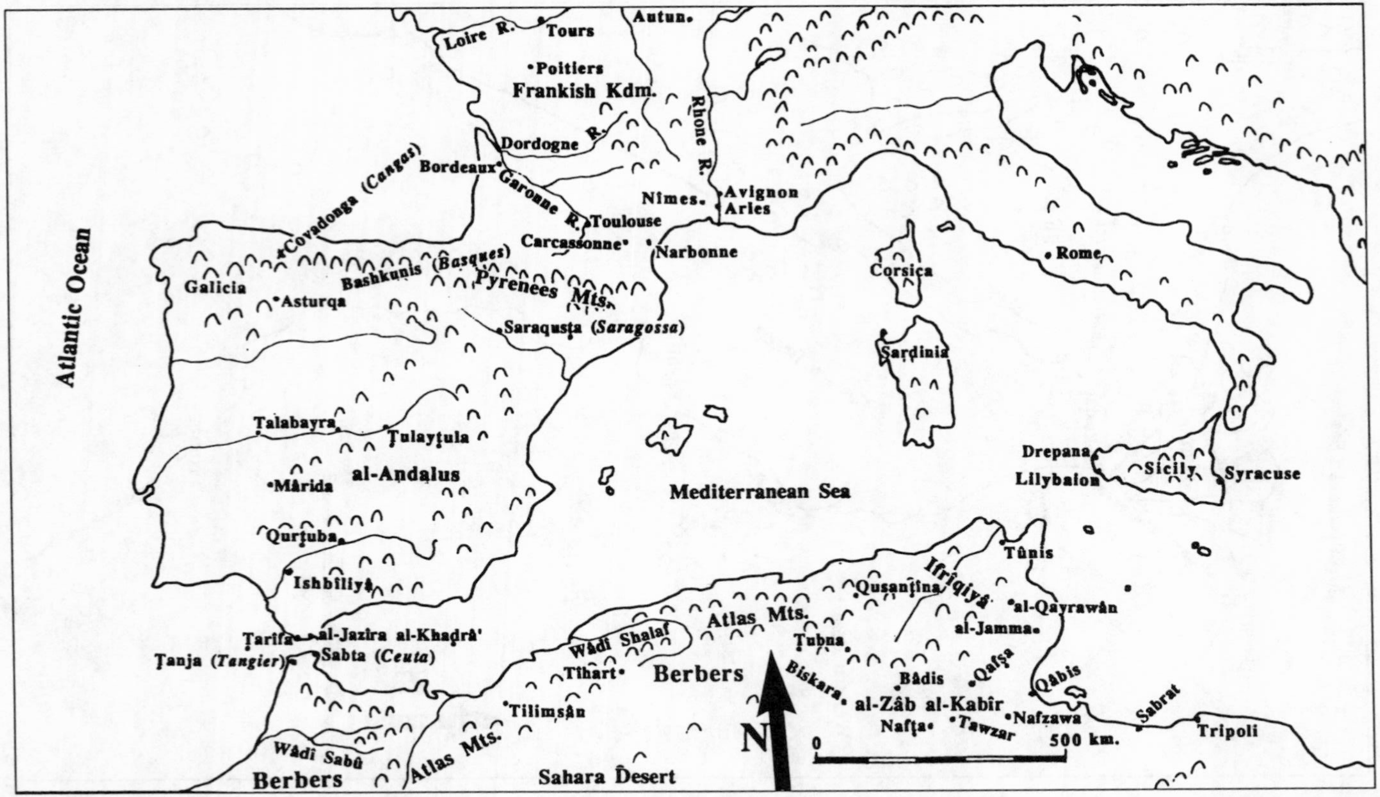

Atlantic Ocean
Loire R.
Tours
Autun
Poitiers
Frankish Kdm.
Rhone R.
Dordogne R.
Bordeaux
Garonne R.
Covadonga (Cangas)
Nîmes
Avignon
Arles
Toulouse
Carcassonne
Narbonne
Galicia
Asturqa
Bashkunis (Basques)
Pyrenees Mts.
Saraqusṭa (Saragossa)
Corsica
Rome
Sardinia
Ṭalabayra
Ṭulayṭula
al-Andalus
Mârida
Qurṭuba
Ishbîliyâ
Mediterranean Sea
Drepana
Lilybaion
Sicily
Syracuse
Tûnis
Ifrîqiyâ
Qusanṭina
al-Qayrawân
al-Jamma
Atlas Mts.
Ṭarifa
al-Jazira al-Khaḍrâ'
Ṭanja (Tangier)
Sabta (Ceuta)
Wâdi Shalaf
Tihart
Berbers
Ṭubna
Biskara
Bâdis
Qafṣa
Qâbis
al-Zâb al-Kabîr
Tilimsân
Nafṭa
Tawzar
Nafzawa
Sabrat
Tripoli
N
0
500 km.
Wâdi Sabû
Atlas Mts.
Berbers
Sahara Desert

Appendix A

Sources for the Reign of Hishām b. 'Abd al-Malik

Historical-Critical Considerations

History consists of facts and interpretations. The facts are the agreed-upon material realities relating to the past. They are the memory of things that once were that are generally agreed to have existed. However, they no longer exist, at least not in the same form. The ever-forward movement of time, of which we are directly conscious of only the portion that is the present moment, transforms everything, such that the very rock that was a second ago is no longer the same. Its context, as well as perhaps its form and its content, have already changed or moved. In this way, looking at the realities of the past is always looking through a distorting filter. Not only that, but we can sometimes be mistaken about the facts. Thus, the past can never be reexperienced *wie es eigentlich gewesen* (how it really was).[1]

But this does not mean that certain facts about the past cannot be ascertained. It would be difficult for anyone to dispute, for example, that John Kennedy was shot on 22 November 1963, or that Germany was occupied by the Allies after the Second World War. And, presumably, it will not be possible to dispute such facts even after a hundred years, although that will depend on their preservation and transmission, as well as the form such preservation and transmission takes. That is, the preservation and transmission must be not only accurate, but also convincing. But when we turn to long bygone eras, such as that of the early Islamic caliphate dealt with in this book, we are on much less certain ground. Such facts as can be regarded as established tend to be few and far between. There are certain facts, of course, which can be ascertained by the agreement of independent sources, including the death dates of various rulers or which empire controlled which places at which times. But overall, these stand out like occasional chronological signposts in a desert of uncertainty.

This leaves interpretation, the other, rather larger and more important component of history, which itself may be divided into parts. Perhaps the most obvious of these is interpretation of evidence in order to establish facts. Thus, contradictory versions of the same event may be collated from different sources and compared to establish the most probable reconstruction of the facts. The operative words here are 'most probable,' because the realm of certainty gets farther away as we become more removed from the facts, the body of agreed-upon truth. Nevertheless, with enough sources of ascertainable quality it is possible to establish a framework of likely facts in which to operate. Establishing such an agreed framework must be the first step for any special study of a particular period, for without a framework of probable facts, further interpretations become uncontrolled speculations.

For early Islamic history, a framework of probable facts is established by information found in the Arabic literary tradition, without whose existence such an exercise would be impossible. Though this tradition contains hundreds of separate works, we might now consider just one work as an example, the *Ta'rīkh* of Khalīfa Ibn Khayyāṭ al-'Uṣfurī (d. 240/854), which is one of the works most often cited in this book. Ibn Khayyāṭ's history consists of two slim volumes of mostly dry chronicles recording events, especially military campaigns fought against both foreign opponents and internal rebels, as well as successions to the caliphate, officials and governors of the caliphs, and sundry political information. The entries are most often extremely brief, but are full of names and dates and are arranged by year. Now, the limitations of such a work are obvious. It is event-oriented, deals with the elite, but almost completely lacks narratives explaining the events. Yet without this work, the task of writing this book would have been considerably more difficult. For many events it records are recorded nowhere else, and many other events may only be related by one or two other sources. Nothing in it can be automatically accepted without considering whatever other sources may exist, as well as the general emerging picture of its time based on our total reading and impression of early Islamic history. But what we can get from the events recorded in, or the probable facts that can be derived from, Ibn Khayyāṭ's accounts is material for the necessary bare framework within which various longer narratives may be arranged and understood.

Beyond the interpretation of evidence to establish a framework with a high degree of probable accuracy, there remains the other outstanding aspect of interpretation. This aspect is the assessment of the meaning of the ascertained facts, and in particular, the understanding of the causes and effects, including the motives for the behavior of the actors. Such an assessment does not mean an overt qualitative value judgement on conduct, declaring motives 'good' or 'evil', for this is where history passes over the border into panegyric or diatribe. Such value judgements would be recognized even by amateurs as biased, subjective, and probably worthless. However, subtler judgements would remain harder to detect. But even if it becomes possible to avoid making value judgements and inserting them in one's text, interpreting the facts still will be a far less objective and certain exercise than that of establishing the framework of past reality itself. For contemporary ideological commitments on the part of the historian tend to enter into his or her interpretations in a way not found so overtly in the bare cataloguing of the facts themselves. Indeed, while such subtle and insidious commitments may be conscious or unconscious, they are of necessity *always* present. That is because no writer can free himself from the environment in which he or she writes, a milieu whose structures will *always* affect the product.

Such commitments can be detected to some extent or other in all writers, ancient and modern. Regarding the sources for the early wars of Islam, one is immediately struck how the early historians, both Muslim and Christian, chronically fail to mention their own defeats, but all too willingly tout their victories over the other side. This is done, often to the point of exaggeration and sometimes to the point of fabrication. If one adds the scanty relevant Hindu inscriptions,[2] they do the same. This is hardly surprising, considering that they were set up to extol and commemorate the rulers credited with the victories. Naturally, these rulers would not want to record their own defeats. Since medieval history writing most often took place under various kinds of royal patronage, it is also not surprising that Muslim and Christian historians celebrated the victories and played down or failed to mention the defeats of their own side. However, some Muslim histories seem not to have been written under royal patronage, for it is far from clear that such writers as Ibn Khayyāṭ or al-Ṭabarī served their rulers. But what they may have lacked in service to their rulers, especially the defunct Umayyads, they made up for in ideological commitment to Islam. Thus, as far as battles with non-Muslims are concerned, Muslim writers celebrate or exaggerate Muslim victories and omit or belittle Muslim defeats.

This tendency is manifest in a writer like al-Ṭabarī, who prefers long narrative passages with clear ideological impact. Thus, the travails of the Khurāsānīs at the Battle of the Defile in 113/731 are brought out with poignant detail, but the battle is still described as a victory,[3] which it hardly was. At the same time, the catastrophic defeats of the siege of Constantinople of 98–99/717–18[4] and Ardabīl in 112/730,[5] though mentioned, are glossed over quickly. Other events, such as the Muslim siege of Nikaia in 109/727,[6] are not mentioned by any Muslim source. Certain other Muslim sources besides al-Ṭabarī are much worse, such as the sagas reported by Sayf b. 'Umar and Ibn A'tham, where defeats are turned into victories. On the other hand, while this tendency also affects even better sources like Ibn Khayyāṭ, it does so to a lesser extent because his chronicles contain few actual narratives with their tendentious explanations and excuses. And it remains a fact that the Muslim sources do usually mention Muslim defeats, however briefly.

Generally, the failure to mention or the belittling of one's own defeats is a manifestation of selective omission, which is a powerful historical weapon, for it eliminates what is omitted from consideration altogether. Sometimes early historians rather honestly, perhaps naively, state that this is what they are going to do. Thus, Ibn Hishām states that he will omit what it is undignified to discuss, or what would hurt the feelings of certain people, or what al-Bakkā'ī would not have approved of.[7] On the other hand, al-Ṭabarī, after significantly saying he is only reporting what he was told without adding any distorting interpretation, apologizes for anything the reader may find offensive, since he merely transmitted the reports as he found them,[8] thus in effect denying omission. But whatever the historians said, their omissions probably extend far beyond what they consciously intended to omit, as their works concentrate on wars, kings, and nobles, while making relatively little mention of non-Muslims, women, slaves, the lower social orders, and country-dwellers, except when any of these obtruded into the consciousness of the elites, usually through violent action. It should be noted that such omissions through concentration on a particular subject permeate all historical works even down to the present, and that the Muslim historians are in no way inferior to their contemporary non-Muslim historians. Rather, the Muslims often offer more detailed information.

In defense of historians' selectivity, it must be said that it is unavoidable. The raw historical material of the sources is almost always too much to be utilized entirely or fully. Even if it is fully cited, it is inevitable that some parts of the material will be emphasized more than others. This is because a historian, especially in the thesis-oriented writing of modern academia, will be trying to prove a point and will naturally emphasize those pieces of evidence that support his thesis, while belittling those that contradict it, relegating them to marginal comments or the footnotes. This is not necessarily harmful, for every piece of historical writing will eventually be evaluated on its merits, especially once the ideologically charged atmosphere in which it was originally created has vanished with time. If a greater variety of writings and opinions exist, so much the better. Only persons with programmatic, neo-totalitarian views who insist that there is but *one* correct interpretation will disapprove.

Aside from the slanting caused by selective omission of information, a problem that can sometimes be overcome by the introduction of other information from other sources, there is also the subtler and very pervasive slanting that results from the literary emplotment of the narrative, a kind of bias perhaps dependent on ideological commitment or personal world view. Although emplotment by historians has been discussed extensively by Hayden White in his *Metahistory*,[9] as well as in his other writings, it was referred to also by Marshall Hodgson in his discussion of al-Ṭabarī. Hodgson shows that al-Ṭabarī related the murder of ʻUthmān b. ʻAffān without introducing any narratives of his own. By the mere selection and arrangement of his material, he was able to direct his overall narrative, and not without drama, toward a particular result laden with ideological implications.[10]

Considering the limitations of selectivity and emplotment that characterize most historical writings, one may ask whether anything can be known or called true in history. Above I suggested there are incontrovertible facts, that is, those that are generally agreed on at the present, even if they do not have completely universal assent and even if they prove later to be wrong. I have also suggested that it is possible to establish other facts based on evidence, even if the interpretation of the facts will always be tentative. The facts themselves are not to be confused with the emplotment of the narrative, nor are they to be considered necessarily ambiguous, though they may be.[11] Therefore, some information is to be considered more accurate than other information. Historical facts should not to be equated with myth, however much the emplotments of historians may be related to poetry or myth,[12] and even though a continuum of relative truthfulness rather than a sharp border exists between fact and myth.

Some Aspects of Methodology

The purpose of this book is twofold: first, to establish the historical framework of the caliphate Hishām b. ʻAbd al-Malik (reigned

105–25/724–43), and second, to examine the evidence located in that framework to assess the causes of the collapse of Umayyad rule shortly after Hishām's death.

To accomplish these purposes, it has been necessary first to gather data from the sources noted in the bibliography so that as much of the background of Hishām's reign as possible could be reviewed. In doing this, I have not only looked at those pages in the histories dealing with the time of Hishām, but also those relating to al-Walīd II, Yazīd III, and Ibrāhīm b. al-Walīd, as well as some of those relating to Marwān II. This is necessary, because, while little information is available about Syria under Hishām himself, the situation is suddenly reversed with the multiple Syrian coups and civil wars as well as four caliphal successions in only two years after his death. During these years, the sources pay much attention to Syria, which now commands the center stage. Many new Syrian personages are mentioned, and many of these were doubtless active under Hishām as well, though mostly unmentioned in the reports referring to his time. Also, the uniquely interesting reform program presented by Yazīd III and his Qadarī supporters reflects developments under Hishām, as I have shown. Furthermore, to establish the background of the reign, I have had to examine the whole process of the Islamic *jihād* before Hishām as well, particularly in the time of his two immediate predecessors 'Umar II and Yazīd II.

After gathering data, I have tried to reconstruct the framework of probable facts for Hishām's reign. First, this consists of the geographical background of the caliphate, with attention to the relationships of the different provinces to each other, along with their relative importance in the state. With this, I examine the distribution of the various tribal groups and their respective roles and relative power in the state. Next, I have tried to establish the events of Hishām's caliphate and the involvement of the various participants in a probable sequence. The accuracy of this sequence then is confirmed by dates well established in the sources or other synchronisms, which gives us an absolute chronology as well. The chronology for Hishām's reign, being fairly close in time to the writing down of the sources, presents fewer problems than do the chronologies of earlier periods. But first, it is necessary to have an outward framework in which to place developments.

Besides the establishment of the factual framework, I have offered an interpretation of the facts making explicit the connections and interrelationships among the numerous developments that took place under Hishām, in particular, how these connections enlighten us about the reasons for the Umayyads subsequent collapse. While interpretations naturally are what remain most open for dispute, I offer mine without apology in the hope that they will receive acceptance because of my extensive use of available sources. For one of the main problems of medieval Islamic history is the tendentiousness of the sources, which has not yet been assessed by the kind of historiographical effort devoted to classical Greek and Roman historians. While such an investigation must be undertaken, it is often possible to compensate for the sources' tendencies by comparing different, conflicting versions. Such contradictory versions abound in the Muslim sources, even within the same source. For example, al-Junayd b. 'Abd al-Raḥmān al-Murrī is alternatively praised and condemned for his generalship in sundry, probably contemporary, reports.[13]

But the most significant comparison of versions, which I have made with great frequency and whenever possible, is that between sources from completely different national and religious traditions. For these traditions are, on the whole, completely independent of each other, as shown by their lack of parallelism and high rate of disagreement with one another. Owing to this independence, it is often possible to establish facts where agreement of separate traditions can be shown. Aside from the Muslim historical tradition, clearly the most voluminous of its time by far, I have used the Syriac Monophysite,[14] the Greek Orthodox,[15] the Near Eastern Orthodox ('Melkite'),[16] the Coptic,[17] the Armenian Monophysite,[18] the Georgian,[19] the Chinese,[20] the Frankish Catholic,[21] and the Spanish Catholic[22] literary historical traditions, as well as Indian Hindu inscriptions.[23] Presumably this list is exhaustive, although more varieties of literary evidence may eventually come to light.

Another method that produces results is that of reading between the lines to get to the facts through what the sources do not say. That is how Gibb surmised that Samarqand must have been lost about 113/731,[24] and it is also how we can measure the effects of the disastrous Battle of the Defile in the same year. This method has validity because the words of historians are meant to conceal as often as to enlighten. I am not speaking of an *argumentum ex silentio*, which may be based on a mere guess, but rather where something can be logically deduced from what is said.

Even when the strategies I have outlined are fully applied, considerable uncertainty will remain, especially with regard to motives of individuals, the workings of social forces and other intangibles. These are exactly the areas that usually are passed over in silence by the sources. But I hope the overall picture of Hishām's reign and its consequences can be greatly clarified.

The Nature of the Sources

Quite apart from the limitations of historical writing that I have already enumerated, deliberate bias, fabrication, selectivity, and subconscious literary emplotment, the nature of the source material constitutes another limitation of sweeping effects. Indeed, the nature of the source material could be described as the major constraint that the historian faces, for unless new material is fabricated out of nothing to fill in the empty spaces, the content of those spaces can hardly be discussed at all, and the historian can only discuss what is available. This will inevitably affect his product most deeply. Different periods will receive different treatments because the amount, quality, and type of the source material changes according to the epoch toward which we direct our attention.

All human existence may be conveniently divided into four periods by the type of source material available: the prehistoric, the reconstructed, the literary-traditional, and the archival, each of which will necessarily be attached to different dates in different geographical areas. The prehistoric is basically the preliterate societies that never had writing, as well as whose writing remains completely undeciphered, such as the Indus Valley civilization, for the sources for these are also non-written. The reconstructed consists of those societies where literacy once existed but whose languages became extinct and had to be reconstructed in modern times. Examples include Pharaonic Egypt and cuneiform Iraq. The literary-traditional category contains those societies whose literary tradition has been preserved, handed down, and studied in every generation in an unbroken chain to the present day, but for which there is no other deliberately preserved written evidence. They include the ancient Hebrews, Greeks, Romans, and the early medieval Muslims and West Europeans. The archival period indicates those societies which have not only preserved an unbroken written literary tradition, but also have continuously maintained archives down to the present. Therefore, modern societies are now, and have been for the better part of a millenium, archival.

The distinction between the literary-traditional and the archival is crucial, for archives contain contemporary documents whereas literary traditions do not. A piece of literature is a contemporary document of sorts for the time it is produced. But most of the contents of such documents refer to earlier times, sometimes hundreds of years earlier. This is especially the case with ancient and medieval historians, upon whom modern historians often rely.

While such literary sources can clearly be used as evidence, their testimony is not the same as that of archival documents, which may also not be disinterested, but are at least contemporary. Thus, the literary sources give us the evidence from one or more removes farther away than the archival sources. On the other hand, the quantity of evidence from literary sources is usually finite, whereas that from archives is endless. Thus, while there is some hope of perusing much or most of the evidence covering a literary-traditional period in a single lifetime, that becomes impossible with archival evidence, which heightens the crisis caused by selectivity for the latter. Finally, let us note that although contemporary documentary evidence for literary-traditional periods exists, for example in the form of Egyptian papyri, such documents do not represent what that society chose to preserve, but rather what it chose to throw out. Thus such documents, while priceless as evidence, do not constitute archival evidence.

This discussion is necessary because Umayyad times, in particular, represent a literary-traditional period, whose sources' most salient feature, to which attention has frequently been drawn,[25] is the fact that they are mainly literary sources often recorded in their present form considerably later than the events they report. Thus, as I have shown, the field of early Islamic history resembles that of the classical world: later literary sources with no archival evidence along with a great paucity of documents except for papyri from Egypt. In this situation, little contemporary evidence exists to control the literary sources. Furthermore, such physical evidence for Hishām's reign as does exist at present tends to have little bearing on political and military history, thereby forcing us to rely all the more on literary records. Only for economic matters is the primary physical evidence of much help, and even so it is somewhat ambiguous.

But, although one must exercise caution in using them, it is not the case that the literary sources are wholly invalid or that we cannot recover substantial information from them. This is true because these sources exist in great variety and abundance and include several independent national and religious traditions. Furthermore, the value of some of the literary sources for Hishām's time is enhanced by their having been written down within a reasonably short time after his reign. The earliest extant historical works relating to that reign, such as the genealogies of Ibn al-Kalbī (d. 204–06/819–21),[26] were recorded within a couple of generations of it. For his extensive accounts of Hishām's reign, al-Ṭabarī (d. 310/923), one of the chief sources, mainly quotes from now-lost written works by al-Madā'inī (d. 215/830), al-Wāqidī (d. 207/822), Abū 'Ubayda (d. 210/825) and al-Haytham b. 'Adī (d. 207/822).[27] Interestingly, all of these sources used by al-Ṭabarī belong to the same generation, dying, along with Ibn al-Kalbī, within ten years of one another.

Although al-Ṭabarī often additionally cites the sources behind these writers' reports, it is hard to tell if these earlier sources were also written ones. Probably in many cases they were,[28] but this matter is of less consequence for the reign of Hishām than for earlier history. In any case, there is a gap of only a couple of generations between Hishām and the written sources quoted by al-Ṭabarī. This is not necessarily too long for accurate oral transmission to occur, especially if it is attested by a number of different sources.[29] Fortunately, for Hishām's reign, an enormous number of such sources exist, some written by non-Muslims, allowing a considerable measure of control over the material.

Sometimes the reliability of the literary sources for Hishām's reign can also be shown by evidence of a continuous written transmission from his time onward. Certain written works now lost probably related to his reign, such as that of 'Awāna b. al-Ḥakam (d. 147/765),[30] the son of one of Hishām's governors, who can be considered a contemporary of at least some of the events he records. Though his own work is lost, some of 'Awāna's reports probably found their way into later sources which are still extant.[31] Likewise, Dennett's work on taxation in the Islamic state shows that accurate data may appear in literary works of a considerably later date, as their information about Egypt is strongly confirmed by papyri, mostly from Hishām's reign or earlier.[32] This suggests a written transmission from at least the time of Hishām which was continuous but whose details are now obscure.[33] Such a probability is further confirmed by the high accuracy of lists of Muslim governors extending as far back as the time of the Rāshidūn caliphs but generally not existing now in literary sources earlier than Khalīfa b. Khayyāṭ (d. 240/854).[34]

Indeed, one should allow the possibility of substantially accurate written transmission even when the mechanism of that transmission cannot be documented now, as with the lists of Ibn Khayyāṭ. Though desirable when possible, it is not necessary to be able to trace the transmission of literary historical records back to the beginning in order to use them, provided that they can be shown reliable by some other means. Also, it should be noted that in dealing with Hishām, we are talking about a much shorter period of doubtful transmission than is the case with early Republican Rome and can expect the sources to yield us a greater degree of detail as a result.[35] And, indeed, such is the case.

This then is the general situation regarding the sources for Hishām. In light of the attack on the reliability of the early Islamic literary sources by some scholars,[36] let us now review the sources in order to examine the limitations of the evidence in detail, starting with the currently available material contemporary to Hishām's reign.

The Limitations of the Material Evidence

Material evidence available at present for the reign of Hishām falls into three main categories: coins, Egyptian papyri and archaeological remains. While these are of relatively less importance in analyzing Hishām's reign than the literary sources, each still makes a considerable contribution and is important when it can provide relevant material proof about the situation under Hishām. This is because every piece of such material evidence constitutes a fact relating directly to that time, however much interpretations of the piece may differ. It is only this type of evidence that truly deserves to be called 'primary evidence.'

The most plentiful and accessable type of material evidence is the numismatic. Coins datable to the reign of Hishām consist of gold dinars, silver dirhams existing in vast quantities, and copper *fulūs*. Though these coins are nearly all aniconic and always follow the same pattern in their inscriptions, the dinars and dirhams usually give the date of minting, while the dirhams always and the *fulūs* often provide the mint name. This information helps establish that a centralization of mints took place under Hishām as is also indicated in the literary sources.[37]

Egyptian papyri, mostly in Greek but with some in Arabic, played a crucial role in clinching Dennett's argument about the system of taxation in the early caliphate.[38] According to the literary sources, this system underwent a certain tightening and change in assessments in Hishām's reign. The testimony of the papyri vindicates the literary sources on this question and also provides further details to help us understand these developments. Furthermore, the papyri provide a witness for social conditions at that time and in this respect are somewhat controlled by their continuous presence since the pharaonic period, thus permitting comparisons to be made with other times. Hence, it can be seen that the farmers making up the majority of Egypt's people were frequently in financial difficulties in other epochs as well.[39] Therefore, indications of this in papyri for Hishām's reign would not necessarily mean that conditions were especially bad or that the Umayyad government was extraordinarily oppressive.

The archaeological remains for Hishām's reign may ultimately prove to be the most impressive of the material evidence as well as the most relevant to the question of Umayyad government. This is because so much probably remains to be discovered, in view of the limited scope of the archaeological excavations so far undertaken, especially in those sites that were the main centers of early Islam.[40] For this book, the most important archaeological evidence is perhaps that of mosques dating to Umayyad times, though perhaps not to the reign of Hishām himself. Their importance lies in establishing some of the features of the early *jihād*, with which the mosque was intimately connected. Otherwise, most of what has been investigated to the present relating directly to Hishām's reign or near it in time concerns the numerous Umayyad 'desert palaces' scattered through Syria and Jordan. But, unfortunately, what has so far come to light is extremely ambiguous as evidence. Inscriptions, which would speak most directly, are very few. One of the most significant (although now lost) established that Qaṣr al-Ḥayr al-Sharqī in the Syrian desert was built in 110/729 under Hishām. Even such a dated inscription is very ambiguous as evidence, however, for it does not prove that this foundation was Hishām's desert capital of al-Ruṣāfa, as has been assumed, nor does it indicate the structure's purpose. The evidence of the 'palaces' themselves, which are mostly undated, is also difficult to interpret. It is unclear whether they served as way stations on caravan routes or merely as extravagant retreats for Umayyad caliphs and their kin. Thus, one must approach the archaeological as well as the other kinds of material evidence with a consciousness of their limitations and frequent ambiguity.

The Muslim Literary Sources and Their Geographical Limitations

While the available Muslim literary sources for Hishām's reign are vastly more plentiful than the material evidence, they nevertheless have many limitations and must be used cautiously. One of their biggest limitations is the great unevenness of their coverage. This is especially clear in the unbalanced coverage of al-Ṭabarī, whose narrative, despite its pretensions to universality, concentrates almost exclusively on Iraq and Khurāsān in this period.[41] This is a flaw that comes out most clearly in studying the foreign wars of the caliphate under Hishām, where al-Ṭabarī only constitutes the main source for the Khurāsānī front, is very disappointing on other fronts, and almost totally ignores India and the West. Most other early sources, including, for example, al-Dīnawarī (d. 282/895),[42] al-Ya'qūbī (d. 284/897),[43] and the anonymous *al-'Uyūn wa al-hadā'iq*,[44] tend to reflect the same selective geographical bias in greater or lesser degree.

Akhbār al-quḍāh by Wakī' (d. 306/918) is particularly illuminating in this respect. Covering the history of the judiciary in various places, it deals successively with al-Madīna, Makka with al-Ṭā'if, al-Baṣra, al-Kūfa, Damascus,[45] Filasṭīn,[46] Ifrīqiya, al-Urdunn,[47] al-Andalus, Ḥarrān, al-Mawṣil, Egypt, Baghdad, al-Madā'in, Khurāsān, and al-Ahwāz, followed by some brief appendices. Despite this impressive list, the book is most unbalanced. The first four jurisdictions through al-Kūfa take up almost nine-tenths of the book, and most of the rest of it is devoted to Baghdad, so that the other places named receive only a cursory treatment. Thus, the far West is notably shortchanged, Ifrīqiya and al-Andalus rating only a brief paragraph each, while the concentration on Iraq is almost total. Sometimes other areas are brought in only to show their relationships with Iraqi jurists.

In large part, this overwhelming geographical emphasis on Iraq and Khurāsān merely exemplifies a general metropolitan bias often found in ancient sources. The importance of events is only measured by their nearness to and impact in the capital city. Thus, contemporary Byzantine chroniclers such as Theophanes (d. 201/817) and Nicephorus (d. 214/829) rarely mention developments in the farther Byzantine provinces, concentrating instead on Constantinople, its vicinity, and the court.[48]

The 'Abbāsid writers do the same for the Islamic caliphate by concentrating on the Muslim metropolis of Baghdad and its province, Iraq. When dealing with the period before the establishment of the 'Abbāsid dynasty in Iraq, these writers naturally trace their heritage back to al-Kūfa, the precursor of Baghdad, and to Khurāsān. As the rebels who established the 'Abbāsid dynasty came mainly from Khurāsān, works from 'Abbāsid times dealing with Hishām's reign tend to concentrate on the portentious developments in that province, to the exclusion of much else. As these same rebels tended overwhelmingly to derive from Yamanī tribes, the grievances of the Yaman receive much more coverage in 'Abbāsid sources than the complaints of their Muḍarī opponents.[49] Al-Kūfa, as the great Yamanī center and crucible of early Shī'ism, of which the 'Abbāsid revolution was a reflection, receives, after Khurāsān, the best coverage for the period of Hishām in the principal sources. But it is a coverage limited to certain famous episodes, such as the rebellion of Zayd b. 'Alī, the dismissal of Khālid al-Qasrī and some Khārijite revolts. Other areas, such as al-Baṣra, the Ḥijaz, the Caucasus, and Syria receive only minimal mention in Hishām's reign in the principal universal histories, while the considerable remainder of the Islamic lands is hardly mentioned at all.

It should be emphasized that a similar metropolitan Iraqi bias pervades most of the nonchronological literary sources as well. For example, the works of al-Jāḥiẓ (d. 255/869) strongly reflect an Iraqi viewpoint[50] and contain subject matter best known by and of most interest to the inhabitants of the 'Abbāsid capital. Thus, al-Jāḥiẓ presents a fair amount of material about Khurāsān and Khurāsānīs.[51] Ibn Qutayba (d. 276/889) likewise covers much of the same ground in his numerous works while including comparatively little about other areas. Abū al-Faraj al-Iṣbahānī (d. 356/967) in his *al-Aghānī* adds only al-Madīna, the old cultural capital, to the areas of interest. Syria and North Africa he still largely ignores, except for occasional attention to the Umayyad caliphal court. Even the Andalusian Ibn 'Abd Rabbih (d. 328/940), living under an Umayyad dynasty hostile to the 'Abbāsids, reproduces the general eastern, that is Iraqi, historical tradition in his *al-'Iqd al-farīd*.[52]

The earliest literary works relevant to Hishām's reign, namely the *dīwāns* of various poets, are virtually contemporary documents and thus are of the greatest importance as evidence. Unlike the more prosaic material evidence already described, the poetry declares the feelings and opinions of its creators and their patrons. The most important poets for Hishām's reign are al-Farazdaq (d. 110–12/728–30),[53] who wrote many poems for and against Hishām and his famous contemporaries, and Jarīr (d. 110/728 or later), who also has many relevant poems.[54] Both seem to have died early in Hishām's reign, which considerably limits their value, as its most dramatic events happened after their deaths. Other important poets include Dhū al-Rumma (d. 117/735),[55] who, though his interest in political figures is small, still has some uniquely relevant verses, and Ru'ba b. al-'Ajjāj (d. 145/762),[56] who sang the praises of numerous important figures of Hishām's reign. More important is al-Kumayt b. Zayd al-Asadī (d. 126/744),[57] a most interesting and outspoken Muḍarī poet with Shī'ī sympathies.

With these early poets, the geographical selectivity of the sources once more manifests itself, as all of the five named above, whose works are the most extensively preserved of all the poets of Hishām's time, are Iraqis. However, they do balance the later literary sources somewhat in that at least the first four are generally favorable to the Umayyads. These four, al-Farazdaq, Jarīr, Dhū al-Rumma, and Ru'ba, interestingly all had desert backgrounds, all migrated to al-Baṣra, where they were all part of the Tamīm army division (*khums*), and all but Ru'ba died during Hishām's reign. The fifth, al-Kumayt, however, exemplifies a change taking place, as he had a Kūfan city background, was highly political and outspoken, almost openly favored the 'Alids, and was often in trouble with the authorities. Only he and Ru'ba out of the five lived to see the end of the reign. Works of other poets, such as al-A'war Ḥakīm b. 'Ayyāsh al-Kalbī, who was Syrian, defended the Umayyads vigorously, and engaged in poetic exchanges with al-Kumayt, unfortunately, have not survived. Considerable Khurāsānī poetry is preserved, however, in al-Ṭabarī's history, and is the only poetry to give much information about the struggles with the non-Muslims on the frontiers.

Fortunately, the geographical gaps in the universal histories and other literature surviving from 'Abbāsid times are to a large extent filled in by local histories, though these are frequently later in date and, in the case of North Africa and Spain, much later indeed. Nevertheless, local histories covering Hishām's reign exist for Spain,[58] North Africa,[59] Egypt,[60] al-Mawṣil,[61] and Sijistān,[62] not to mention Khurāsān[63]. Furthermore, considerably detailed local traditions are found in al-Ya'qūbī for Sind, and in Ibn A'tham (d. 314/926)[64] for the Caucasus. Sind is also chronicled for the period immediately before Hishām's reign, by the detailed if somewhat romanticized conquest narrative, *Fatḥnāmah-i Sind*, which exists in an early seventh/thirteenth-century Persian translation. Curiously omitted from the list of local histories is Syria, the metropolitan province of the Umayyads. This gap not only bespeaks a Kūfan lack of interest in eulogizing their erstwhile oppressors, but also bad luck in transmission, for a local historical tradition existed at one time. Its existence is proven by the traditions contained in certain late local chronicles of Syria, which, as they are now, give only sparse details about the Umayyad period.[65] More usefully, however, it is represented by the massive and still largely unpublished biographical dictionary of Ibn 'Asākir (d. 571/1176), *Ta'rīkh madīnat Dimashq al-kabīr*, which unfortunately is poorly accessible in its present unindexed condition.

A variety of other sources also help to fill in the gaps by offering much unique information. Foremost among these are the works of al-Balādhurī (d. 279/892). His *Futūḥ al-buldān* describes the struggles to widen the Islamic state's area of control and hence is very useful for the conditions on the frontiers in Hishām's time, when those efforts were still going on.[66] In particular, it enlightens us regarding the Caucasus and Sind, where we would have gaps otherwise. His other work, *Ansāb al-ashrāf*, is a genealogically organized history of the Islamic state through the early 'Abbāsids. However, the section relating to Hishām's reign, which remains unpublished, closely adheres to the interests of the Iraqi tradition, though it does add some genealogical material about the Umayyad family.[67]

More valuable for this reign is the *Ta'rīkh* of Khalīfa b. Khayyāṭ, a source at once early and very broad in its coverage, full of information about the Caucasus and North Africa and provided with priceless lists of governors and other officials. But its narratives are very brief.[68] It should be noted, however, that Ibn Khayyāṭ was also an Iraqi, a fact clearly demonstrated by his very brief *Ṭabaqāt*,[69] where al-Kūfa and al-Baṣra plainly take precedence over all other areas. Nevertheless, Ibn Khayyāṭ gives a more comprehensive coverage to areas outside of Iraq and Khurāsān than other early Muslim historians. Indeed, Ibn Khayyāṭ constitutes perhaps the single most useful work for the research embodied in this book.

Another most interesting work concentrating on the political history of the caliphate is *al-Imāma wa al-siyāsa*, which was attributed to the polymath Ibn Qutayba (d. 276/889), but is now considered the work of the Andalusian Ibn al-Qūṭiyya (d. 367/977). The last events mentioned in it are of 198/813. This work seems to contain pro-Umayyad and other exceptional material, for example, a very long saga of Mūsā b. Nuṣayr.[70] The inclusion of pro-Umayyad material with a North African interest would not be surprising if Ibn al-Qūṭiyya is indeed the author. Unfortunately, for the external relations of Hishām's reign, the work proves less valuable.[71]

Later general histories are often more inclusive in their concept of what constitutes universal history but nevertheless are significantly affected by the Iraqi historical tradition for the period we are studying. Thus, Ibn al-Athīr (d. 630/1233) in his *al-Kāmil* attempts to balance the Iraqi tradition with reports from North Africa, Spain, and other areas. Though for Hishām's reign he still tends to concentrate on Iraq and Khurāsān, doubtless owing to his use of al-Ṭabarī as the main source, he also gives valuable information for other areas, some of it unique.[72] Similarly, al-Nuwayrī (d. 733/1333), who includes a large section about early Islamic history in his encyclopedia,[73] follows the Iraqi tradition while adding some North African material. This suggests a dependence on al-Ṭabarī and possibly on Ibn al-Athīr as well.

Perhaps the richest of all the genres of Islamic historical writing is the biographical dictionary, several examples of which are relevant to the reign of Hishām. Among those devoted to obituary notices of the famous is the well-known work of Ibn Khallikān (d. 681/1282). Though its author is a Syrian, it conforms to the pattern of emphasizing the Iraqi historical tradition with its long articles on Khālid al-Qasrī[74] and Yūsuf b. 'Umar,[75] Hishām's two governors of Iraq. The caliph himself, and the rest of his house, are ignored, except for his brother Sulaymān, who is inexplicably included. Next, the enormous compendium of al-Ṣafadī remains incompletely published. It contains some data apparently not found elsewhere. However, its notices on Umayyad political personalities are usually very brief. Like Ibn 'Asākir's work, it is also difficult to use owing to its huge size.

However, the most common type of biographical dictionary is that devoted exclusively to religious figures, especially transmitters of traditions. These also form great compendia. Among those containing information on persons alive under Hishām we may list the early but strongly Iraq-centered *Ṭabaqāt* of Ibn Sa'd (d. 230/845), *Siyar a'lām al-nubalā'*[76] and *Mīzān al-i'tidāl* of al-Dhahabī (d. 748/1348), and *Tahdhīb al-tahdhīb* and *Lisān al-mīzān* of Ibn Ḥajar al-'Asqalānī (d. 852/1449). There are also the Islamic histories of al-Dhahabī[77] and Ibn Kathīr (d. 774/1373),[78] both of which contain rather abridged historical narratives and mostly consist of biographies of religious figures. All these works too are strongly affected by the predominance of the Iraqi historical tradition.

Though they are useful in assessing the reliability of transmitters of historical reports, the direct historical value of these biographical works for the period in question is less. Partly, this is because the same facts often are given in much greater detail elsewhere. It is also because much of the information given in long biographies is anecdotal and has been preserved either for the purpose of proving a legal point or for enhancing the reputation of the transmitter by citing testimony about his honesty. However, some, especially the works of al-Dhahabī, contain biographies of disreputable persons as well, including political figures. But the religious personages whom these biographical dictionaries are mainly concerned with often played little military or political role, to the extent that the religious and the political history sometimes seem to revolve in totally separate spheres isolated from each other. Thus, it is particularly significant when a figure is cited who played a historical as well as a religious role, thereby providing some meshing between the two spheres. Such is the case, for example, with Ibn Kathir's long biography of the Jazīran Maymūn b. Mihrān.[79]

Other Muslim sources that must be mentioned are the genealogical works. These are of the utmost importance, because the social identification of the Muslims in Umayyad times was entirely tribal and hence based on genealogy. As is abundantly attested by the sources, every Arab Muslim had a tribal surname (*nisba*) consisting of *-ī* appended to the name of the tribe. A non-Arab would be called a *mawlā* or client of a certain tribe, which formula, added to his name, performed the same function as the tribal surname. This system of identification worked whether the genealogies were fictitious or not. Sometimes, their fictitious character may have been known, but they still formed the underlying basis of the social and, most significantly, of the military organization.

A number of useful works catalogue the tribes alphabetically according to *nisba*. Probably the best known of these is al-Samʿānī's (d. 562/1166) *al-Ansāb*, an enormous compendium containing many genealogies of famous religious figures along with fewer of tribal and political leaders. Its abridgement by Ibn al-Athīr, entitled *al-Lubāb fī tahdhīb al-ansāb*, is in many ways more useful. While Ibn al-Athīr omits some of the individual genealogies, he corrects al-Samʿānī's mistakes with extensive commentaries and additions, showing himself on the whole far more discerning than the earlier scholar. The fact that he has personally researched and thought about the issues he deals with, rather than merely compiling reports from others, greatly enhances his work's authority, as well as his reputation as a scholar in general. Another work to be mentioned here is *al-Ishtiqāq* of Ibn Durayd (d. 321/933), which provides much incidental information about the tribes while providing etymologies for their names.

But the most comprehensive and authoritative of the genealogical works is Ibn al-Kalbī's great *Jamharat nasab Maʿadd wa al-Yaman al-kabīr*.[80] Unlike al-Balādhurī's incomplete *Ansāb al-ashrāf* already mentioned, this work gives a complete genealogy of all the Arab tribes. It shows the specific lineages of many important individuals with their supposed blood connections right back to the two eponymous aboriginal ancestors of all the Arabs, ʿAdnān, ancestor of the Muḍar and the Rabīʿa, and Qaḥṭān, ancestor of the Yaman. Thus, the work not only enables us to trace close blood relationships of certain individuals to each other, but also allows us to see the tribes in their greater groupings, with the political alignments that these implied. These connections are only occasionally explained in the other sources, yet they often help us to understand the background of various events. Similar to Ibn al-Kalbī's work and partly derived from it is *Jamharat ansāb al-ʿArab* by Ibn Hazm (d. 456/1064). In another similar work, *Nasab Quraysh*, al-Zubayrī (d. 236/851) provides the most specific genealogical information available about the Umayyad house, especially because he alone of early genealogists gives full details about marriages and women. Unfortunately, his work is limited to the tribe of Quraysh.

We must also make reference to the Muslim geographical works. These suffer some of the same limitations as the other literary sources in that they are much later in date than the reign of Hishām. Thus, some doubt exists about their relevance for certain facets of that reign, particularly in regard to the provincial boundaries and administrative arrangements they describe. The oldest Muslim geographical works describe the roads across the caliphate and include descriptions of the provinces as well. These are by al-Ya'qūbī (d. 284/897), Ibn Khurdādhbih (d. 300/913), Ibn Rustah (wrote c. 301/914), Ibn al-Faqīh, Qudāma b. Ja'far (d. 320/932), and al-Iṣṭakhrī (fl. c. 350/961). Besides these, there is the slightly later, completer geography of al-Muqaddasī (d. 375/985) and the very extensive geographical dictionary of Yāqūt (d. 626/1229). Though all of these considerably postdate Hishām's caliphate, they often contain apparently anachronistic information that may relate to somewhat earlier times than those in which they were written. Still, they need to be supplemented from what is known about the provincial arrangements earlier on in the defunct empires, particularly the East Roman Empire, for which considerable material exists.

Christian Literary Sources

Aside from the Muslim literature, many Christian chronicles exist which are of inestimable historical value for Hishām's reign. These chronicles seem without exception to have been written by Christian churchmen, usually of high rank in the episcopate. Thus, they are mainly devoted to Christian church history. But when they relate Muslim affairs, they do provide a hostile check on information that otherwise comes from Muslim sources. It has to be remembered, though, that just because these works are not by Muslim believers does not give them any guarantee of either objectivity or of accuracy. Quite to the contrary, as Kennedy points out, the non-Muslim writers were both biased and ignorant of internal Muslim developments.[81] Still, the Christian chronicles do offer other points of view and, frequently, new information as well. Furthermore, they represent different sects with their own traditions which are not all tied to the Byzantine viewpoint but are usually independent of it as well as of each other. Indeed, it is precisely the Byzantine tradition represented by the chronicle of Nicephorus that we have already mentioned which is of the least use for us for the period of Hishām, because its chief interest centered heavily in faraway Constantinople. On the other hand, the Byzantine chronicle of Theophanes is frequently valuable for the caliphate's Byzantine front as well as others.[82]

Probably the Syrian Monophysite chronicles are the most important Christian sources relevant to the reign of Hishām. For despite the shortness of their entries, there are half a dozen of them to compare. Also, they were recorded in Syria, the seat of the caliphate, so that they mainly provide information about the Byzantine front and internal affairs in Syria. All are in Syriac, which sets them off as part of an independent linguistic as well as national tradition. Perhaps the oldest of them is the substantial chronicle attributed wrongly to Dionysius of Tell Maḥré (d. 230/845), now dated as early as c. 184/800.[83] Despite its earliness in comparison to most of the Muslim tradition, however, its chronology does not inspire confidence. Indeed, most Christian chronicles have frequent errors or inexactness in chronology. Nevertheless, pseudo-Dionysius constitutes an important source. Next is the very sketchy *Chronicon anonymum ad A.D. 819 pertinens*. It has, however, only a couple of useful references for the reign.[84] Another fragmentary early chronicle, *Chronicon ad A.D. 846 pertinens*, adds little more.[85] Elias of Nisibis wrote a Syriac chronicle in 410/1019 which has a number of useful references.[86] The later Syriac Monophysite chronicle of Michael, the Bishop of Edessa (d. 595/1199) is very large but devotes little space to Hishām.[87] The latest major Syriac Monophysite chronicle, a substantial book, is the anonymous *Chronicon ad A.D. 1234 pertinens*, which contains many references.[88]

Besides the Syrian Monophysite chronicles, there are two fourth/tenth-century Orthodox or Malkite chronicles. Both of these are written in Arabic rather than Syriac and are considerably detailed, substantial works. One, written in Egypt, is that of Sa'īd b. al-Biṭrīq (Eutychius), the Orthodox Patriarch of Alexandria (d. 328/940).[89] The other and far more useful of the two for Hishām's reign is that of Agapius (Maḥbūb) b. Constantine of Manbij from northern Syria.[90] Because the Malkites recognized the primacy of Constantinople, their interest in the Byzantine empire and the Muslim campaigns against it is paramount.

Another completely independent Monophysite tradition is the Armenian. Very important is the chronicle of Lewond (written c. 174/790), without which a reconstruction of the history of the Caucasus at this period would be far less complete.[91] There are also a few important bits of information in the later Armenian history of Movses Dasxurançi (Moses Kalankatuaçi) (written c. 493/1100).[92] The royal chronicle of Georgia provides another Christian view of Caucasian history in a different language and appears to record a considerable Muslim campaign against Georgia not on record elsewhere.[93]

Yet another independent Monophysite tradition is that of the Coptic church of Egypt. Although this church has only one work to offer, the massive Arabic chronicle of Sāwīrus b. al-Muqaffa', the bishop of al-Ashmūnayn (fl. fourth/tenth century),[94] Sāwīrus's work is probably the single most important Christian chronicle for this book. Not only does he provide information on Egypt, but he also devotes more space to social conditions. He is surprisingly favorable to the Caliph Hishām, but nonetheless portrays a time of dire financial difficulties under his rule. Despite his bias and the frequent divine interventions in his work, Sāwīrus gives much information not found elsewhere.

Finally, far to the west, we find two useful works in Latin. One, the anonymous *Continuatio Isadori*, a chronicle written by a Spaniard in Seville, is a main source for Muslim Spain at this period.[95] Its value is all the greater because it was apparently written shortly after 136–37/754, the date at which it breaks off, and is thus extremely early. Furthermore, its information, though not without flaws, is on the whole very valuable. Of value only for the Muslim invasion of France is the anonymous Frankish *Chronicon Moissiacense*.[96]

Naturally, each of the writers of these Christian works tends to center his interest on his own locale, which further enhances their value, since none is Iraq-centered. Though their notices about Muslim and general affairs are short, they do not seem to derive their information from the existing Muslim sources and thus appear to provide an independent witness. One of their major deficiencies is their weakness on chronology, which on the whole affects them to a greater extent than the Muslim sources.

Social and Structural Limitations in the Muslim Literary Sources

Aside from their heavy geographical bias in favor of Iraq and Khurāsān, the Muslim literary sources also display several other limitations. First, they concentrate almost exclusively on the upper classes, especially the political leadership. Thus, except for occasional references, they describe an elite rather than the people as a whole.

The exception to this would appear to be the religious leadership, which often had humble origins. But this group, on close examination, also turns out to be an elite, whatever the *mawlā* derivation of many of its members may be. Thus, we find Abū Zinād[97] and al-Zuhrī[98] associated with the Caliph Hishām, which would necessarily mark them out as part of the elite. Other religious figures such as al-Qāsim b. Muḥammad b. Abū Bakr and Sālim b. 'Abd Allāh b. 'Umar[99] are also members of the old Qurashī aristocracy. When we speak of that area where the political and religious worlds touched the most, namely the judiciary and the men who held charge of it, we are also talking about an elite. This even seems true when we discuss rebels and heretics. Ghaylān al-Dimashqī, the originator of ideas called Qadariyya, though a Copt *mawlā*, seems to have held the position of a secretary in the government and was quite influential.[100] Bukayr b. Māhān, the 'Abbāsids' chief agent for the East at this period, was quite well-to-do after working as an interpreter (*tarjumān*) for the Umayyad governor of Sind.[101] Muqātil b. Ḥayyān, who seems to have been one of the chief religious leaders of Marw under Hishām, was the son of an important *mawlā* commander of the *mawālī* army division, and had also served, while still very young, as a secretary for one of the governors of Khurāsān.[102] Perhaps the most genuinely popular rebels were the *khawārij*. But the leaders even of these probably came from noble lineages in disadvantaged tribes.[103]

This brings up a related bias in the sources: some tribes receive better coverage than others. This imbalance not only reflects the pro-Yaman bias in the Kūfa-centered sources, but also numerous other factors. Each large tribal grouping tended to regard certain of its clans as possessors of greater nobility. Hence, there was a concentration on those clans such as the Quraysh's associates, the Thaqīf, who reappear under Hishām, or the Kinda, the Ṭayyi', and the Bal-Ḥārith among the Yaman. Even more important, certain tribal groups won much more attention when they had a governor in office. Hence we know much about the Bajīla under Hishām, owing to Khālid al-Qasrī's long term in office, and about the Layth, owing to the prominence of Naṣr b. Sayyār in Khurāsān. Another variation of this kind of distortion is that certain lineages in a single tribe receive more attention than others whose members are hardly ever named. This is especially true of the 'Adī al-Ribāb in Khurāsān, whose historian Abū al-Dhayyāl frequently describes the exploits of his relatives, thereby giving them as well as his tribe a prominence they probably did not enjoy at the time, as they were somewhat marginal members of the Tamīm.[104]

Besides this unevenness in the coverage of Arab Muslim groups, it must be noted that the non-Arab Muslims, the *mawālī*, receive less attention, perhaps even less than the non-Muslim subjects (*dhimmī*s), who, as we have seen, at least to some extent have their own sources. Although the majority of the histories and other literary works in Arabic were written by *mawālī*, this has left little trace in Umayyad history, where the prominent actors were Arabs, particularly those belonging to Arab tribal army regiments. Though the *mawālī* were probably beginning to form a major part of the Muslim population by Hishām's reign, individual *mawālī* receive scant treatment in the sources unless they were recorded as religious figures. Thus, the several *mawlā* secretaries of Hishām, who perhaps possessed great influence, are but little known. The exception that proves the rule is Ḥassān al-Nabaṭī, Hishām's estate manager, who is dealt with in detail only because of his possible role in the downfall of Khālid al-Qasrī.[105] On the other hand, Hishām's intimate friend and adviser al-Abrash al-Kalbī, although a prominent Syrian Arab, also is rarely mentioned.

Another important weakness prevalent among ancient historical works generally is that they place too much emphasis on events while ignoring peaceful developments. The fourteen peaceful years of Hishām's reign during which Khālid was the governor of Iraq should form, as we have seen, a very major theme for our Iraq-centered and pro-Yaman historical tradition. And in fact, these do get a certain amount of attention in the major sources such as al-Ṭabarī. However, for Khālid's governorship, this attention is almost exclusively expressed in the recording of what were seen as significant events, such as the change of subordinate governors or the arrest and execution of rebels. Indeed, the vast majority of narrative material in the sources generally deals with only two kinds of events, battles and transfers of power. Khālid's peaceful pursuits, such as his vast land reclamation projects, whatever their true worth, get almost no space. Importantly, what space they do receive is only part of the explanation for his downfall in 120/738. In contrast to the long years of his governorship, that single event merits an extremely long, detailed account in the pages of al-Ṭabarī.[106] Though Khālid's downfall was a significant event which added fuel to the Muḍar-Yaman controversy that played a large role in the Umayyad collapse, it is doubtful whether it was so pivotal a change as the sources would have it. Despite the attention it is given, its causes are obscure.

Just as they are event-oriented, the early Islamic historical sources are also episodic in nature, which consititutes another difficulty. Rather than consisting of a more or less unified narrative directed toward a single purpose by one author, as do most ancient historical sources from Herodotus onward, the Islamic sources cite their versions of events in independent, separately quoted and often overlapping and contradictory individual reports. Each of these is vouched for by at least a partial chain of transmitters in the case of major historians like al-Ṭabarī and al-Balādhurī. While the individual reports have been ordered chronologically by the annalistic historians whose works we have, the separate, independent nature of the reports remains clear from the way they are cited. Thus, there is little immediate sense of an overall view or direction to them, as a chronicler jumps from one topic to another in his narrative. As a result, for the reign of Hishām in particular, there is no feeling for the contemporaneity of certain events or of their possible effects on each other. Perhaps this is just as well, for the sources then express more bare information and less narrative development and literary emplotment. Thus, the interconnection of the various events as well as peaceful developments has to be established by careful research and reconstruction based on the sources. This work has been first of all an attempt to do just that.

Modern Scholarship

Modern Western scholars have dealt with the reign of Hishām mainly in their general histories of the Umayyads or Islam, Thus, they have not been able to give it special attention for the most part, with one significant exception: F. Gabrieli's *Il califfato di Hishām*, which has been neglected because of its relative inaccessability in Italian. Gabrieli's views are summed up, however, in his article on Hishām in *EI*². Though Gabrieli carefully assesses the results of the reign's military campaigns, especially the loss of most of North Africa and Spain, he feels on the whole that these campaigns were a success. He characteristically tends to blame al-Walīd II for "the beginning of the *fitna*, which was fatal for the dynasty."[107] He does not analyze the reign in a chronological sequence, preferring a topical treatment by geographical area. Nevertheless, while he does not put the reign in the greater context of Umayyad history, Gabrieli's work remains the best single treatment of the subject.

Turning to more general studies, the seminal work on the Umayyads is J. Wellhausen's *The Arab Kingdom and Its Fall*, which, though it follows al-Ṭabarī closely, provides an intelligent commentary on that work that has never been wholly replaced. Wellhausen tends to emphasize the difficulties with the *mawālī* as well as the Arab intertribal conflict.[108] Nowadays, his views are often challenged but still frequently taken as the starting point for discussion.

The most significant attempt to modify Wellhausen's thesis has been in M. Shaban's *The 'Abbāsid Revolution* and *Islamic History: a New Interpretation* A.D. *600–750* (A.H. *132)*, in which the author contends that the tribal strife was the more significant of the two factors emphasized by Wellhausen, the *mawālī* not having yet become politically important. However, he feels that the great competing tribal groupings, the Muḍar and the Yaman-Rabī'a, which were found more or less across the whole Islamic state, were tantamount to political parties with fully elaborated, conflicting political programs.[109]

P. Crone has scorned Shaban's ideas in her *Slaves on Horses*,[110] in which she contends that the competing groups were merely factions greedy for power with neither political programs nor any ethnic basis.[111] She does not, however, explain the source of their cohesion, and her attempt to retroject the considerably later concept of slave soldiery developed under the 'Abbāsids back to Umayyad times[112] is poorly supported.[113] As has already been pointed out in the introduction, none of the three writers just mentioned considers outside enemies to have been anything but a constant and therefore all ignore possible ups and downs on the frontiers as causes for internal change.[114]

Other than these, some significant monographs and articles relating to the period have been written in modern times. Several of these deal with specific provinces and their war fronts. Among these, H. A. R. Gibb's *The Arab Conquests in Central Asia* stands out for its clear description of the Turkish onslaught in Transoxiana, a description which is fully justified by the sources. In the same vein for the Caucasus front, D. M. Dunlop's *The History of the Jewish Khazars* presents a detailed scholarly discussion of the the Khazars' great war with the caliphate, which filled Hishām's reign.[115] C. E. Bosworth's *Sīstān under the Arabs, from the Islamic Conquest to the Rise of the Ṣaffārids (30–250/651–864)* provides similar coverage of the Sijistan front against the Zunbīls.[116] The Byzantine front is dealt with in R.-J. Lilie's *Die byzantinische Reaktion auf die Ausbreitung der Araber*.[117] 'Abdulwāḥid Dhanūn Ṭaha's *The Muslim Conquest and Settlement of North Africa and Spain* mostly covers Spain.[118] The

Spanish front is also the subject of R. Collins' *The Arab Conquest of Spain 710–797*.[119]

A number of other studies are concerned with various aspects of the internal situation in the caliphate. J. Van Ess' article "Les Qadarites et la Gailānīya de Yazīd III"[120] is a most helpful study of the background of Qadarī support among the Syrian Kalb, which is very crucial to the background and nature of the tribal parties or factions. D. Dennett's *Conversion and the Poll Tax in Early Islam* is full of material relating to Egypt in the time of Hishām and has solidly established the basis for discussion of Islamic taxation. Egypt is also the subject of I. Lapidus' article "The Conversion of Egypt to Islam,"[121] which also contains much relating to the reign of Hishām and shows that the conversion of the Copts had not yet become a significant factor.

Certain recent Arab scholarship is also of value. Most useful is Sa'd Zaghlūl 'Abd al-Ḥamīd's excellent *Ta'rīkh al-Maghrib al-'Arabī min al-fatḥ ilā bidāyat 'aṣr al-istiqlāl*, which intelligently and adequately covers the North African theater in a way not yet available in any Western language.[122] Supplementing this is Maḥmūd Ismā'īl 'Abd al-Rāziq's detailed study on the North African *khawārij*, *al-Khawārij fī bilād al-Maghrib ḥattā muntaṣaf al-qarn al-rābi' al-hijrī*.[123] Ḥusayn 'Aṭwān's *Sīrat al-Walīd b. Yazīd*, despite an anti-Yaman bias, is of great value in elucidating the relations between Hishām and his nephew al-Walīd II and in debunking some of the sensational charges against the latter (though confirming others). The author's ideas have been further elaborated in his *al-Walīd b. Yazīd: 'arḍ wa naqd*, which encompasses the first work. In particular, 'Aṭwān effectively and extensively employs literary criticism to analyze the Arabic poetry of the time, which is a source too often overlooked in Western scholarship. Another work exclusively devoted to Hishām's reign is 'Abd al-Majīd al-Kubaysī's *'Aṣr Hishām b. 'Abd al-Malik 105–125/724–743*, which is most interesting perhaps for its explanation of the revenue system. Umayyad administrative arrangements are catalogued by Najda Khammāsh in *al-Idāra fī-l-'aṣr al-Umawī*.

Appendix B

On the Population of the Umayyad Caliphate

Guessing the size of premodern populations means entering an area where certainty vanishes and speculation is rife. The estimates of Russell and McEvedy, referred to above in chapter 2, are open to considerable doubt on several grounds. First, both use average probable densities of known arable lands to arrive at them, but the controversy over the population of pre-Columbian America shows that this method, which tends to produce minimal estimates, has not won acceptance.[1] After all, considerable variations in density are likely, and a mistake as small as a factor of two could make a whopping difference.

Second, wide variations in the relative distribution of population in the provinces, according to the two writers, raise doubts about the accuracy of their estimates even as approximations. Thus, while Russell gives only one million as the population of Arabia, McEvedy has about five-and-one-quarter million.[2] On the other hand, Russell has more for Iraq, nine million, a figure McEvedy scoffs at while giving his own estimate of perhaps one-and-one-half million for Hishām's day.[3] Again, Russell has four million for Syria, though only three million in Hishām's time, while McEvedy allows only two-and-one-half million.[4]

McEvedy's distribution seems particularly faulty. It is scarcely believable that the dominant provinces in the empire, particularly Iraq, had so little demographic weight in what was their medieval heyday, especially compared to the backwater of Arabia. Surely if Arabia had been so comparatively populous, it would have exerted more influence on the course of events, and the capital would probably not have been removed from it in the first place. Indeed, even a cursory examination of the *kharaj* income from agricultural lands shows that Iraq must have been relatively densely populated.[5]

In fact, the wildly divergent estimates for Iraq seem to fly in the face of what rare population data there are. A figure of five hundred thousand to five hundred fifty thousand non-Muslim taxpayers in the districts belonging to al-Kūfa is cited in the sources for the reign of 'Umar I.[6] This has yielded estimates for the total non-Muslim population in al-Kūfa's territory of one million five hundred thousand and two million five hundred thousand.[7] Taking an averaged estimate of two million for the *sawād* of al-Kūfa, which would agree with the principle of four members per household,[8] we still have to add the non-Muslim peasant populations of the *sawād*s of al-Baṣra and al-Mawṣil. Also, the not inconsiderable Muslim population of the cities of al-Kūfa, al-Baṣra, and al-Mawṣil must be added, in addition to the non-Muslims having tax-exempt status or those evading payment, to get a total for Iraq. This would likely reach five million persons, far exceeding McEvedy's paltry esimate, though still far below that of Russell. Naturally, owing to the large number of unknown variables, such estimates must be approached with only the greatest reserve.

However, it would appear that McEvedy's and Russell's estimates, except perhaps for Russell's guess for Iraq, are on the whole too low. While it is theoretically possible to make estimates based on figures for tax income, as Russell has tried to do, there are too many uncertainties to arrive at even approximate population figures. Russell, relying on Dennett, reiterates several times that the head tax can be taken as about half the total tax cited for a province. But Dennett is only talking about a certain locale in Egypt, and it is very doubtful that such a general rule can be adduced from so little evidence.[9] Probably there was plenty of variation, as Dennett himself shows by demonstrating that each area was taxed differently owing to the varying circumstances in which Islamic rule was established in it.[10] In some areas only a lump sum was paid, without regard to the current population. An unknown, possibly large, segment of the population was tax exempt. A possibly larger proportion of the population may have escaped taxation illegally, especially in relatively inaccessable areas or those with few Arab Muslims. As elsewhere at different times, the tax collectors themselves may have surreptitiously pocketed a part of the proceeds. All these factors tend to make tax figures a hazardous basis for population estimates. Estimates based on such figures would generally make the population appear smaller than it was in reality. Thus, on the whole, Russell's and McEvedy's figures may be taken as low, minimum estimates, which shows that the caliphate under Hishām was in any case impressive in terms of population as well as area.

Glossary of Arabic Technical Terms

'amal (pl. *a'mâl*): An administrative province, region, or district. Especially refers to the civil administrative and tax-gathering duties of its governor.

'âmil (pl. *'ummâl*): A governor of a province, region, or district. In particular, one having civil administrative and financial responsibilities.

amîr: A governor of a province, usually one having command of troops. Also, a commander of a separate military force.

'asabiyya: The intense group feeling uniting a clan or tribe in mutual loyalty.

asâwira: Cavalry units of the defunct Persian Empire adopted into the Arab tribal system as a tribal regiment and a subdivision of the Tamîm tribal army division.

'ashîra (pl. *'ashâ'ir*): A clan, a subdivision of a tribe. The same as a *batn*.

baṭn (pl. *buṭûn*): A clan, a subdivision of a tribe. These formed the real basis for tribal loyalty in the Arab social system and also the basis for the organization of army regiments.

dâniq: A weight, roughly half a gram.

dhimmî: A non-Muslim subject of the caliphate, normally also a non-Arab.

dihqân: A non-Muslim local notable in any of the eastern provinces that had formerly belonged to the Sāsānian Empire. Often responsible for collecting taxes and usually friendly to the caliphal government.

dînâr: The standard gold coin of the caliphate, usually struck in Damascus.

dirham: The standard silver coin of the caliphate, struck in only a limited number of mints under Hishâm, usually one per super-province. About fifteen dirhams equalled a dinar, though the exchange rate was probably subject to fluctuation.

dîwân: The tribally arranged army register. Also, the collection of poetry of a particular poet. Also, a government office or ministry.

fitna: Discord, normally meaning civil war when used in political contexts.

fils (pl. *fulûs*): The copper coins of the caliphate, struck in many mints.

iqlîm: A region. Term used by al-Muqaddasî over two hundred years after Hishâm to refer to the geographical provinces of the caliphate.

jihâd: Literally, 'striving,' but generally refers to fighting in God's path in war against the non-Muslims.

jizya: Originally a general term for tribute paid by non-Muslims within the caliphate in return for the military protection afforded to them by the Muslim armed forces. Later it came to mean specifically the capitation tax paid only by non-Muslims.

jund (pl. *ajnâd*): A force of troops, or troops in general. Also, an administrative subdivision of Syria belonging to and supporting a particular army division of the same name. There were five Syrian *ajnâd*, to which the army of al-Jazira was added as a sixth *jund*. All these were the home troops of the Umayyad caliphate.

katîba (pl. *katâ'ib*): A tribal army regiment. Each of these usually was made up of the arms-bearing men of only one clan.

kharâj: Originally interchangeable with *jizya* in certain contexts, *kharâj* later came to specify the tax on lands originally held by non-Muslim landowners. With the passage of time, both Muslims and non-Muslims holding such lands came to pay it.

khârijî (pl. *khawârij*): Lit. 'a rebel.' Though these later developed into separate religious groups, now collectively known as Khârijites to Western scholars, under Hishâm the designation still mainly referred to their violent political rejection of the Umayyad caliphate. Many diverse groups having little or no relation to one another were identified with this broad label.

khums (pl. *akhmâs*): Lit. 'a fifth,' *khums* refers to one of the five tribal army divisions of al-Baṣra and Khurâsân. Each of these was composed of smaller kindred Arab tribal groupings and some of their non-Arab clients or *mawâlî*. *Khums* can also refer to the caliphal fifth of the spoils from military campaigns or to the not always acknowleged caliphal right to a fifth of the tax income of a province.

kûra (pl. *kuwar*): A district of a province, usually centering around a large town or city.

madîna: A city or town.

mawlâ (pl. *mawâlî*): A client of an Arab tribe. In the context of Hisham's reign, usually a non-Arab Muslim.

miṣr (pl. *amṣâr*): An Arab Muslim military settlement and metropolis of a province or superprovince. Under the Umayyads a city became a *miṣr* only if it had Arab troops settled in it. The largest *amṣâr* were new foundations by the Arab Muslims, but some were older cities partially settled by Arab troops.

muqâtil (pl. *muqâtila*): The Muslim troops enrolled in the army register and receiving regular pay from the government. The same as *jund* when the latter means troops.

nâḥiya (pl. *nawâḥî*): A country district containing a number of villages, possibly equivalent to a *rustâq*.

nisba: A tribal surname formed with an appended -î. This has been imported into English in such terms as Sa'udi, Israeli, Somali, etc. In Umayyad times, it usually meant that its possessor was an Arab, and it most often identified his clan (*baṭn*) rather than any larger tribal grouping.

qabîla (pl. *qabâ'il*): An Arab tribe.

qarya (pl. *qurâ*): A village or a town.

qaṣaba: The capital of a district.

ridda: Apostasy from Islam, especially the resistance to Islam that the first caliph, Abû Bakr, met with in Arabia in 11/632.

rub' (pl. *arbâ'*): One of the army divisions of al-Kûfa. Unlike the tribally based divisions of al-Baṣra and Khurâsân, the Kufan divisions were made up of antithetical tribal groups on government order.

rustâq (pl. *rasâtîq*): A country district containing a number of villages. Used mainly in provinces formerly belonging to the defunct Persian Empire.

ṣadaqa: Lit. 'charity,' but also the tax paid by Muslims to the caliphate, more generally known as *zakâh* or *zakât*.

sunna: A trodden path, hence the 'way' of the Prophet Muḥammad embodied in his normative practice, which was an example for the Muslims to follow. This later become codified in a vast literature of reports attributed to the Prophet and his companions.

wâlî: A provincial governor.

wilâya (pl. *wilâyât*): A province or superprovince of the caliphate governed by a *wâlî*.

Notes

Introduction

1. On this, see Appendix B.

2. Some Muslims may be surprised by or take exception to the description of the expansion of empires other than the caliphate, particularly that of the Mongols, as an ideological imperative justified on moral grounds, lest this seem to equate these various empires with each other. But I intend no value judgement. I am merely observing that each of these empires did indeed justify its expansion in moral terms. In most cases, these took the form of a claim by the imperial people that it had a greater fitness to rule because it was specially chosen by God. In the Muslim case, this was accompanied by a mandate to propagate God's law and rule by it, a mandate not exactly paralleled in the other cases, especially not that of the Mongols. The Mongols, according to a more recent view, did not establish a law to regulate the moral behavior of themselves or their subjects. Morgan, 96–99; *pace* Crone, 20.

3. Although Cornell, 19, points out that none of the Qur'ānic occurrences of the word *jihād* or its relatives derived from the same root *j-h-d* is necessarily connected with fighting, and while *jihād* certainly can be used in the general sense of "struggle," warfare is nevertheless enjoined frequently in the Qur'ān under *qitāl* ("fighting") or related terms. Since Muslim usage for centuries has agreed upon the usage of *jihād* to refer to Muslim fighting in God's path, I will use it for this meaning throughout this work.

4. The Mongol concept of being destined for universal dominion existed as early as the time of Genghis Khan. Ratchnevsky, 140, 159–60; Morgan, 14; Saunders, *Mongol Conquests*, 95, 98; Komroff, 44, 189–90.

5. Indeed, a well-known *ḥadīth* attributed to the Prophet states that the only true *jihād* is that waged to exalt God's word. Bukhārī, I, 42–43. Martyrs in the *jihād* are promised paradise. Qur'ān, iii, 169. And those who fight in God's path (and survive) are also promised a share of the spoil (*innamā ghanimtum*). Qur'ān, viii, 41.

6. E.g., Qur'ān, iii, 103; xlix, 9–10.

7. The 'Abbāsids managed to recover al-Qayrawān and its neighborhood only by 144/761. They also held Ṭubna (now Baṭna) in eastern Algeria, which represented their farthest known western advance. 'Abd al-Ḥamīd, 346, 348. In 184/800, 'Abbāsid North Africa was turned over to the quasi-independent Aghlabid dynasty.

8. First mentioned by Constantine Porphyrogenitus c. 340/950, though

he attributed it to Umayyad times over two hundred years earlier. It seems to have served both Arab prisoners and envoys sent to ransom them. By 585/1189, there may have been two mosques serving a considerable population of resident merchants and others. Canard, 94–99.

9. Qur'ān, xlix, 13; Shaban, *Revolution*, 168.

10. As in the noncanonical but well-known *ḥadīth* that the greater *jihād* is the struggle of a Muslim against himself. Cornell, 22.

11. *EI*[2], s. v. Hishām.

12. Ṭabarī, II, 1730–39; for a very favorable view, see pseudo-Ibn Qutayba, *Imāma wa siyāsa*, II, 104–8.

13. Kennedy, 112.

14. Kennedy, 116.

15. Wellhausen, *Kingdom*, 497–500, 557–59.

16. Shaban, *History*, 170–71, 174–79, *Revolution*, 158.

17. Crone, 46–48, 55–57, 61.

18. Shaban, *History*, 138.

19. Qur'ān, ix, 29.

20. On the change in the attitude of the Muslim troops toward fighting about the time of Hishām, see the sarcastic remarks of a contumacious non-Muslim princeling in Balādhurī, *Futūḥ*, 493.

Chapter 1

1. Qur'ān, iv, 59, 64–65, 105; v, 44–45, 47–50; Khadduri, 8–9, 16–17.

2. On the concept of *jihād* according to modern Western scholars, see *EI*[2], s. v. Djihād; Khadduri, 55–82; Shaybānī (Khadduri's introduction), 11–19; Bernard Lewis, 71–90; Armstrong, 31, 34–36, 40–43. For modern Muslim viewpoints, compare 'Umarī, II, 11–15; Hamidullah, 165–72, 191; Muḥammad 'Alī, 529–81; Cornell, 18–23; Ayoub, 205–32.

3. This is the dating of al-Wāqidī; Ibn Isḥāq puts the date in Ṣafar 2/August 623. Ibn Hishām, I, 590; Ṭabarī, I, 1265–66. The earliest verses prescribing *jihād* are said to be Qur'ān, xxii, 39–40. This is actually said to have been revealed precisely at the moment of the Prophet's migration to al-Madīna in 1/622, which is certainly plausible given the context. Wāḥidī, 177; Qurṭubī, XII, 46–49; Ibn Kathīr, *Tafsīr*, III, 225–26. Qur'ān, ii, 216, which is considered to be the verse enjoining the general *jihād* against the unbelievers, is found in a context with the next verse, ii, 217, which relates to the specific expedition of Nakhla, in which the first blood was shed by Muslims in war. That expedition is said to have fought on 1 Rajab 2/23 December 623. Ibn Hishām, I, 601–04; Ṭabarī, I, 1273–79; Muqātil, I, 184–87; Wāḥidī, 35–38; Qurṭubī, III, 27–32; Ibn Kathīr, *Tafsīr*, I, 252–55.

4. *Doctrina Iacobi*, 86.

5. pseudo-Sebêos, 123–31, 134, 141–45, 154–55, 157, 168–78, 180–82.

6. For example, the term *ghazw* is often used with the same meaning, as in Balādhurī, *Ansāb*, V, 50.

7. Qur'ān, ii, 190, 244; ix, 38–41.

8. Qur'ān, lvii, 10.

9. Qur'ān, ii, 245; lvii, 11, 18; lxiv, 17.

10. Qur'ān, xlix, 15.

11. Qur'ān, ix, 42–52; xlviii, 16.

12. Verse xlviii, 16, uses the word "to obey" (*tuṭī'ū*) with reference to the summons to fight, indicating that it was at that time a universal command. This seems to have been particularly applicable toward the end of the Prophet's life, when the Muslim state had become a large one. All able-bodied Muslim males were conscripted to go out on the very large Tabūk expedition. Those who did not were punished, the sanction being ostracism. See Qur'ān, ix, 117–18; Ibn Hishām, II, 516–19, 525, 529, 531–37. Otherwise, Muslim exegetes have usually, but not always, interpreted the enjoinment of *jihād* as a universal command. Some sought to restrict it to the Prophet's companions, while others regarded it as voluntary. Ibn Kathīr, *Tafsīr*, I, 252; Qurṭubī, III, 27. Note that the Qur'ān makes an exception for religious specialists who are to stay home and preach to the troops when they return. Qur'ān, ix, 122; Qurṭubī, VIII, 186–88. This assignment of a special group for religious instruction shows a considerable level of ideological sophistication.

13. Qur'ān, iv, 74. This verse is the source of the later designation of *khārijīs* as *shurāh*, "purchasers" of paradise.

14. Qur'ān, iii, 169–71, 195.

15. Qur'ān, xxxiii, 27; lix, 7–8. Qur'ān, iv, 95, specifies that both those who stay at home and those who fight have goodly reward, but the reward of those who fight is greater.

16. Qur'ān, viii, 41.

17. Qur'ān, xxii, 39–40. 'Umarī, II, 12–13, stresses that an important purpose of *jihād* is to defend the freedom of God's worship.

18. Qur'ān, ii, 190.

19. Qur'ān, ii, 191, 246.

20. Qur'ān, ii, 193; viii, 39.

21. Qur'ān, ix, 33; xlviii, 28; lxi, 9.

22. Qur'ān, ii, 15, 258; iv, 75; vii, 186; xx, 24, 43, 45; lxxix, 37; lxxxix, 11; Ibn Khayyāṭ, *Ta'rīkh*, 626, 639; Balādhurī, *Futūḥ*, 222; Ya'qūbī, *Ta'rīkh*, II, 257, 321; Ibn Khurdādhbih, 109.

23. Qur'ān, iv, 90; viii, 61.

24. Qur'ān, ix, 29.

25. The division of spoil taken in battle is laid down only in Qur'ān viii, 41.

26. Qur'ān, ii, 62; v, 69; ix, 29; xxii, 17.

27. Qur'ān, ii, 193; ix, 1–8. However, it was often pointed out that these verses refer only to actively hostile idolaters. Peaceful populations are not to be disturbed and may pay *jizya*, according to the Ḥanafīs and some of the Mālikīs. But some Mālikīs, the Shāfi'īs and the Ḥanbalīs take a stricter line. Qurṭubī, VIII, 70–71; Ibn Kathīr, *Tafsīr*, II, 347.

28. Qur'ān, ii, 256.

29. Qur'ān, xlix, 9.

30. Qur'ān, iii, 146, 173, 186.

31. Qur'ān, lxi, 4.

32. Qur'ān, iii, 152–59.

33. Qur'ān, iii, 172–74.

34. Bukhārī, IV, 18, 27, 62, 92; Muslim, II, 141; Ibn Kathīr, *Tafsīr*, I, 252.

35. Bukhārī, IV, 87.

36. Bukhārī, IV, 32–33; Muslim, II, 152–53.

37. Bukhārī, IV, 18. When considering this tradition, one should keep in mind how arduous the pilgrimage was to perform in premodern times.

38. Bukhārī, IV, 39.

39. Bukhārī, IV, 40–41; Muslim, II, 116–18. However, according to Shaybani, 81–82, 92–93, they were nevertheless given something as compensation.

40. Qurṭubi, VIII, 188.

41. Ibn al-Mubārak, 143, where it is noted that it also occurs in the canonical collection of al-Tirmidhī.

42. Cornell, 22.

43. Mālik, xxi, 2; Bukhārī, IV, 18–19; Muslim, II, 145–46.

44. Mālik, xxi, 27–33, 39–43; Ibn al-Mubārak, 37–45, 48–54, 59–61, 68, 72, 125; Bukhārī, IV, 19–22, 24–25, 29, 39–40; Muslim, II, 147–48, 150–51, 154–56.

45. Ibn al-Mubārak, 170–71; Bukhārī, IV, 27.

46. Ibn al-Mubārak, 30–31, 46; Muslim, II, 149.

47. Ibn al-Mubārak, 105–06, 108; Bukhārī, IV, 24.

48. Ibn al-Mubārak, 55, 62.

49. Ibn al-Mubārak, 140–42, 146, 149; Bukhārī, IV, 42–43; Muslim, II, 150–51, 160.

50. Ar. *maṭ'ūn*.

51. Ibn al-Mubārak, 54, 64, 155; Bukhārī, IV, 29; Muslim, II, 160–61.

52. Ibn al-Mubārak, 64, 155.

53. Bukhārī, IV, 17.

54. Ibn al-Mubārak, 44.

55. Ibn al-Mubārak, 28–29, 137, 139, 146–47; Bukhārī, IV, 18.

56. Ibn al-Mubārak, 32, 93; Bukhārī, IV, 27–28.

57. Ibn al-Mubārak, 32–33, 169; Bukhārī, I, 42–43, IV, 25; Muslim, II, 156–57; Hamidullah, 191.

58. Bukhārī, IV, 51; Shaybani, 76.

59. Bukhārī, I, 13; Muslim, I, 30 (near bottom). However, Muslim, I, 30, first *ḥadīth*, attributes the universal requirement of *ṣalāh* and *zakāh* only to Abū Bakr.

60. Bukhārī, IV, 85.

61. Muslim, II, 86–87. However, although Christianity eventually disappeared in Arabia, tens of thousands of Jews continued to live in Yaman until the present century, and some are still there.

62. Bukhārī, IV, 51, 73; Shaybani, 76, 95 n.

63. Muslim, II, 69.

64. Muslim, II, 71, 100.

65. Mālik, xxi, 8–11; Bukhārī, IV, 74; Muslim, II, 69, 73, 117–18; Shaybani, 76, 87, 92. However, the Prophet had burnt the date palms of the Banū al-Naḍīr. Qur'ān, lix, 5; Bukhārī, IV, 76; Muslim, II, 74. Abū Bakr, however, is said to have forbidden destruction of trees, flocks, and herds. Ṭabarī, I, 1850. But the *fuqahā'* seem to have permitted the destruction of inanimate enemy property that cannot by taken or carried off by the Muslims. Khadduri, 102–03.

66. Shaybani, 98–102; Hamidullah, 202–32, 237–51, 254–78.

67. Mālik, xxi, 15–26; Bukhārī, IV, 37, 65, 89, 91, 95–99, 102–16; Muslim, II, 75–81, 84; Shaybani, 84, 94. *Fiqh* ordained a host of rules for further subdividing and assigning the government's fifth. Shaybani, 77–79, 106.

68. Bukhārī, IV, 30; Muslim, II, 72.

69. Muslim, II, 69.

70. Bukhārī, IV, 66–67.

71. Bukhārī, IV, 60; Muslim, II, 129–32.

72. Compare Muslim, I, 186 (crowding to be in the first row in the mosque), and II, 158 (seeking a martyr's death on the battlefield).

73. Qur'ān, lxi, 4.

74. Jandora, 51.

75. Ṭabarī, I, 2489; Creswell and Allan, 10.

76. Oleg Grabar, 107, states that "the masjid was supposed to contain the whole Muslim population of a given city." Ṭabarī, I, 2489, states *al-murabba'a li-ijtimā' al-nās li-allā yazdaḥimū*, meaning, "the square (of the mosque) was for the meeting of the people that they might not be crowded together," implying that it was for the collective gathering of all the people (i. e., all the adult males) there at the same time.

77. Only one mosque is attested at each Islamic settlement in the early period. Ettinghausen and Grabar, 35–36.

78. This may represent a change from the very beginning at al-Madīna, where each clan sought to establish its own mosque. Balādhurī, *Futūḥ*, 1–2,

4–5. That may have arisen because of the distances between the different settlements of the oasis. However, small local mosques for other devotions than the congregational prayer may always have continued to exist. Oleg Grabar, 107, states that smaller mosques existed "from the very beginning in the early Muslim cities of Kufah and Baṣrah," but does not specify his evidence. While secondary mosques were no doubt a fairly early development, there is no certain evidence that they were present "from the very beginning."

79. Creswell and Allan, 5, 7. Ṭabarī, I, 2489, states that this trench was dug to keep the neighboring habitations from encroaching on it. While this is a plausible explanation, it very likely had a military purpose too, especially at first when the Muslims had only just settled in a potentially hostile environment. Interestingly, the Ṭabarī report uses the word *khandaq*, the same word used for the military trench at al-Madīna.

80. Raqīq, 120, referring to a battle fought in the reign of Hishām.

81. Creswell and Allan, 8–9, 96; Hoag, 14–16. Indeed, Ziyād b. Abī Sufyān is even said to have kept a standing force of five hundred troops in the mosque. Ibn al-Athīr, *Kāmil*, III, 451.

82. On the *principia* and *praetorium*, see Webster, 193–95; Connolly, 242–43, especially the drawing of the complex at the bottom left of p. 243.

83. Creswell and Allan, 8–9.

84. However, the *principia*'s basilica appears not to have been open as is the case with some early mosques' *qibla*-wall colonnades. On the other hand, some were walled off from the courtyard, such as the mosque of al-Walīd I at Damascus. The Damascus mosque also has exactly three naves. Oleg Grabar, 107–08, 117.

85. Actually, at the Roman legionary camp at Chester, the *principia* was 76 m. by 100 m. Webster, 193.

86. Hoag, 13.

87. Oleg Grabar, 107; Hoag, 13.

88. Oleg Grabar, 105, 116; Ettinghausen and Grabar, 36.

89. Balādhurī, *Futūḥ*, 338.

90. Abū Yūsuf, 15.

91. The Islamic tradition dates this to 6/628, when the Prophet is said to have sent out letters to the rulers of Byzantium, Persia, Abyssinia, and others, summoning them to embrace Islam. Ibn Hishām, II, 606–07; Ṭabarī, I, 1559–75; 'Umarī, II, 127–32; Watt, 345–47. However, the new policy of universal *jihād* is most clearly shown by the revelation of the ninth *sūra* of the Qur'ān, which repudiated treaties with idolaters and demanded that people of the book pay tribute as a sign of submission. This is plausibly dated to 9/631. Qur'ān, ix, 1–12, 28–29; Ibn Hishām, II, 543–54; Ṭabarī, I, 1720–21.

92. Assyrians: Roux, 264, 273–74, 320; Hallo and Simpson, 127. Romans: Harris, 9–10.

93. This history has generally been told a number of times, notably by Wellhausen, *Kingdom*, 4–325; Shaban, *History*, 11–137; Kennedy, 33–108, 116–23; Hawting, 21–81; Crone, 22–45. It is also available at last in an original source in English translation, *The History of al-Ṭabarī*, vols. VII–XXIV. Therefore, I will only here document to original sources points I consider particularly novel or controversial.

94. Because the state was never united under one rule again, the state of civil war might be considered to have become permanent with the fourth hiatus.

95. Ya'qūbī, *Ta'rīkh*, II, 370; Wellhausen, *Kingdom*, 311.

96. This expedition is the one indicated in pseudo-Sebêos, 123–24; Theophanes, 36 (under the year 631–32 C.E.). The Muslim sources are unanimous in dating it to 8/629. Wāqidī, 755–69; Ibn Hishām, II, 373; Ṭabarī, I, 1610, all probably relying on Ibn Isḥāq. It seems, however, owing to the dating of the retaliatory expedition of Usāma b. Zayd to 11/632, that the Mu'ta expedition has been displaced by as much as two years and should by dated to 10/631, after the Tabūk expedition of 9/631. The writer is preparing a separate study of this subject.

97. Theophanes, 53, 59, 61–63.

98. Probably the truce was renewed more than once. Mu'āwiya had to pay as much as one hundred thousand dinars for a single year. Ibn Khayyāṭ, *Ta'rīkh*, 236 (41/662); Ya'qūbī, *Ta'rīkh*, II, 258 (early 42/662); Theophanes, 46 (38–39/658–59).

99. Qur'ān, v, 51–52, 55–56; lx, 9, prohibiting pacts or alliances that in any way subordinate the Muslims. Also Qur'ān, ii, 249; iii, 146, emphasizing how disparity of numbers or resources should not make the Muslims afraid of fighting. Qur'ān, iii, 28, could be used to justify truces on grounds of expediency; however, the *tafsīrs* give no support to such an interpretation. Muqātil, I, 270; Qurṭubī, IV, 38; Ibn Kathīr, *Tafsīr*, I, 357.

100. Crone and Hinds, 6–7.

101. Creswell and Allan, 9, 15.

102. Ya'qūbī, *Ta'rīkh*, II, 283.

103. 'Abd al-Ḥamīd, 203–28, 240–45.

104. Shaban, *Revolution*, 3, 5–6, 28–29, 31–32, 48, 59, 64, 66–67.

105. Balādhurī, *Futūḥ*, 278–79; Ṭabarī, II, 157, 163. The island "Arwād" is probably the same as "Rūdis," which is Rhodes.

106. Theophanes, 51–53; Nikephoros, 84–87, 193–94; Lilie, 75–76; Stratos, 29–39. The only direct early references to Muslims reaching Constantinople are to the years 49/669 in Ṭabarī, II, 86, 54/674 in Theophanes and Nikephoros, and 56/676 in Ya'qūbī, *Ta'rīkh*, II, 285. Both Muslim accounts attribute the successful penetrations to the crown prince, Yazīd, which looks like a doublet and is also suspect of exaggeration to exalt the ruling house. The seven years referred to in the Greek sources are suspiciously

similar to the seven-year occupation of Rhodes in the Muslim sources. Most of the campaigning mentioned seems rather to be associated with Crete, Lykia and Pamphylia, places near Rhodes. Therefore, it appears that only occasional raids reached the neighborhood of Constantinople. These may have caused a scare, but the Muslims do not seem to have contemplated any assault on Constantinople itself at this time, let alone conducted a siege. The seven-year campaign must refer to Rhodes and southwestern Anatolia.

107. Ibn Khayyāṭ, *Ta'rīkh*, 272; Ya'qūbī, *Ta'rīkh*, II, 286; Ṭabarī, II, 188.

108. Ibn Khayyāṭ, *Ta'rīkh*, 280, 288; Ya'qūbī, *Ta'rīkh*, II, 302; Ṭabarī, II, 196; Theophanes, 53–54, 59; Agapius, *PO*, VIII, 492–3, 497; Michael, II, 455, 469. Almost all campaigning during the three years 60–62/680–82 was in Syria. This shows that Mu'āwiya did not make peace or pay tribute as asserted by Theophanes, 53–54, alone among all the historical sources. Theophanes' version is a doublet of the actual truce concluded by 'Abd al-Malik b. Marwān in 65/685.

109. Balādhurī, *Futūḥ*, 279; Ṭabarī, II, 157.

110. Balādhurī, *Futūḥ*, 278.

111. Dozens of prominent men were killed. Ibn Khayyāṭ, *Ta'rīkh*, 293–314.

112. They were now to some extent merged with the Madīnan Anṣār, with whom they were united by shared antipathy toward the Sufyānids.

113. Theophanes, 59, 61–62; Agapius, *PO*, VIII, 497; Michael, II, 469. This appears to be the second truce signed with the Byzantines in which the Muslims had to pay tribute, the first being that agreed to in the first civil war. Wellhausen, *Kingdom*, 168, seems to be in error in assigning this truce to Yazīd. See note 108, above.

114. The son of the independent governor of Khurāsān managed to hold out in al-Tirmidh until 85/704, however. Ṭabarī, II, 1145.

115. Raqīq, 64, 69.

116. In 92–93/711–12. Ibn Khayyāṭ, *Ta'rīkh*, 404; Balādhurī, *Futūḥ*, 273; Ibn 'Idhāri, II, 7–9; *Akhbār majmū'a*, 18–19; Collins, 28–31.

117. In 93–95/712–14. Ibn Khayyāṭ, *Ta'rīkh*, 405–06, 408–09; Balādhurī, *Futūḥ*, 535–39; Ya'qūbī, *Ta'rīkh*, II, 345–47; Pathan, 44–49; Lambrick, 184–91; Nadwi, 12–14.

118. For pre-Islamic Sind, see Lambrick, passim.

119. Ṭabarī, II, 1283–1304.

120. Ya'qūbī, *Ta'rīkh*, II, 359.

121. Wellhausen, *Kingdom*, 269, says, "He appointed new men to the most important official posts." A perusal of the list of his appointees in Ibn Khayyāṭ, *Ta'rīkh*, 463–69, reveals a considerable policy reversal from those of 'Abd al-Malik and al-Walīd I. Already under Sulaymān, the family and followers of al-Ḥajjāj, members of the Umayyad family, and many Muḍarīs associated with al-Jazīra had been excluded. This change was furthered

along by 'Umar II with his arrest of the unreliable and power–hungry Iraqi Yaman leader Yazīd b. al-Muhallab, as well as by his appointment of men like 'Adī b. Arṭāh and 'Abd al-Ḥamīd b. 'Abd al-Raḥmān, who had no power base of their own.

122. Dhahabī, *Siyar*, V, 53, 149.

123. Theophanes, 91; Lewond, 70–105; Agapius, *PO*, VIII, 502–03.

124. Ya'qūbī, *Ta'rīkh*, II, 366–67; *'Uyūn wa ḥadā'iq*, 60–63.

125. Ṭabarī, II, 1346, 1365; Balādhurī, *Futūḥ*, 196, 198, 221, 519; Ya'qūbī, *Ta'rīkh*, II, 362–63; *Akhbār majmū'a*, 30; Ibn al-Qūṭiyya, 38; Ibn 'Idhāri, II, 26. The opinion of Livermore, 306, that 'Umar considered withdrawing from Spain because of a dispute with the Muslim settlers there, finds no justification in the sources. It should be noted that this new policy was not implemented immediately, but after almost a year, as a summer campaign was carried out in 100/718. Ibn Khayyāṭ, *Ta'rīkh*, 468; Ṭabarī, I, 1349. This campaign may, however, have been by way of a diversion to cover the retreat of Maslama's expedition from Constantinople.

126. Wellhausen, *Kingdom*, 268–69.

127. Shaban, *History*, 121–24, 128, 131.

128. Ṭabarī, II, 1053–54; Shaban, *History*, 110, 122, 126. Possibly as early as 34/655 in 'Uthmān's caliphate. Ṭabarī, I, 2932.

129. Ṭabarī, II, 1314–17, 1346; *'Uyūn wa ḥadā'iq*, 24–33; Ibn al-Athīr, *Kāmil*, V, 27–28, 43; Theophanes, 82–85, 88–91; Canard, 80–94.

130. Theophanes, 88, n. 166.

131. Michael, II, 484–86.

132. However, *'Uyūn wa ḥadā'iq*, 30, 32–33, does mention the dimensions of the debacle, which it even calls "the mightiest catastrophe" (*al-dāhiya al-'uẓmā*).

133. That they did lose control of the sea is shown by the report claiming the Muslims feared the sea more than the Bulgars. Michael, II, 485. It is also strongly suggested by the Byzantines' ability to mount destructive seaborne raids against al-Lādhiqiyya on the Syrian coast in 100/719 right after the Muslims' withdrawal from Constantinople and against Tinnīs in Egypt in 101–02/720–21. Balādhurī, *Futūḥ*, 157; Kindī, 70; Maqrīzī, *Khiṭaṭ*, I, 177. Ya'qūbī, *Ta'rīkh*, II, 359, puts the al-Lādhiqiyya raid, probably erroneously, in Sulaymān's reign.

134. Balādhurī, *Futūḥ*, 196, 221.

135. For 99/718, see Ibn Khayyāṭ, *Ta'rīkh*, 432; Ya'qūbī, *Ta'rīkh*, II, 370. Although Ṭabarī, II, 1349, reports a campaign for 100/718–19, it is clear from a comparison of the names mentioned in his account to those in Ibn Khayyāṭ and al-Ya'qūbī that he is referring to 99/718; since the lunar year ended in the summer, that campaign probably extended into 100. See also Theophanes, 91, dating the raising of the siege to 15 August 718, which accords with 13 al-Muḥarram 100.

136. For example, the settlement of fifty thousand Iraqi families in Khurāsān in 51/671 and the attempt to settle the Iraqi army of Ibn al-Ash'ath in Sijistān. Shaban, *History*, 88, 109–10. This policy is also clearly stated in advice given by 'Abd Allāh b. 'Āmir to the Caliph 'Uthmān in 34/655. Ṭabarī, I, 2932.

137. Shaban, *History*, 110–11.

138. For the resumption of summer campaigns against the Byzantines in 102/720–21, see Ibn Khayyāṭ, *Ta'rīkh*, 473.

Chapter 2

1. Russell, 89.
2. McEvedy, 21–22, 126–28, 167, 171–72.
3. McEvedy, 99, 101–05, 135–36, 138–40, 142–43, 145–47,159, 162–63, 182–83, 185, 220–27, 229. The difference probably owes to the smaller size of the 'Abbāsid dominions after the loss of Spain, Morocco, and Algeria.
4. For a fuller discussion of the difficulties in making estimates of the population of the caliphate, see the Appendix B.
5. Walker, II, pp. liii–lv.
6. Khammāsh, 277; Rayyis, 229.
7. Morony, 163–64.
8. *EI*^{2}, s. v. Kūra; Morony, 129.
9. For different usages of terms in the same source, see Ibn Khurdādhbih, who decribes Iraq as divided into twelve *kuwar*, sixty *ṭasāsīj*, and many more *rasātīq* and *bayādira* (5–6, 8–14), but then describes the *kuwar* of Iṣbahān as consisting of seventeen *rasātīq* (20), while the *kuwar* of al-Ahwāz are either seven or eleven (42). In Syria, the *ajnād*, which are themselves described as *kuwar*, each consist of a number of *kuwar* or *aqālīm*: Qinnasrīn has fifteen, Ḥimṣ about thirty-six, Damascus twenty, al-Urdunn thirteen, and Filasṭīn twelve (75–79), while Egypt appears to have seventy-five *kuwar* (81–83). These examples should suffice to show that different terms may have had different meanings in different areas, the small, secondary *kuwar* of Syria and Iṣfahān being in no way equivalent to the much larger ones in Iraq.
10. The word *wilāya* implies sovereign authority, whereas the word *'amal* suggests subordination. See Ibn Manzur, s. v. w-l-y and '-m-l. Morony's claim that an *'amal* is only for fiscal administration is not borne out by the sources for Hishām's reign. See Morony, 129.
11. Ṭabarī, II, 1622–23.
12. Gabrieli, 121–22.
13. In Persian usage, these were originally known as *shahrs*. Morony, 129.

14. Muqaddasī, 47–57, esp. 47–48.

15. Maqrīzī, *Nuqūd*, 16.

16. Walker, II, pp. lix, lxi, lxiii–iv, 302–04.

17. For this term, see Khammāsh, 33–35. The original *amṣār* were defined by their being Arab Muslim military settlements built to watch over the new territories of the Islamic state. The first ones were al-Jābiya (soon dissolved), al-Kūfa, al-Baṣra, and al-Fusṭāṭ, while subordinate *amṣār* founded later included Marw and al-Qayrawān. Hishām's reign also saw attempts to found what amounted to new *amṣār* at Balkh in Ṭukhāristān and al-Maḥfūẓa and al-Manṣūra, the twin cities of Sind. For these latter, see Ṭabarī, II, 1490, 1591; Balādhurī, *Futūḥ*, 542–43; Pathan, 56, 65–70.

18. This is perhaps reflected in the story of Ziyād b. 'Ubayd Allāh al-Ḥārithī, who was told in 105/724 that the viceroy had never sent an Arab before to take over the fiscal administration of al-Rayy. This appears to indicate an arabization of the administration as the Muslims picked up administrative skills. Ṭabarī, II, 1470–71. See also Abbott, 30.

19. Crone, 32.

20. Kindī, 74–76; Ibn Taghrībirdī, I, 259, 264, 266; Abbott, 28–29, 32.

21. On the other hand, the separation of military and fiscal offices also could have been influenced by the desire to weaken the former in order to discourage revolts. What militates against such a view, however, is that the fiscal governors, being *mawālī*, were often too weak to resist the dictates of the Arab military governors.

22. Except in North Africa.

23. Ṭabarī, II, 1470; Gabrieli, 121–22.

24. Examples, aside from Khālid al-Qaṣrī's fourteen-year rule in Iraq (105–20/724–38), include the tenures of Yūsuf b. 'Umar in Yaman (106–20/725–38) then Iraq (120–26/738–44), 'Ubayd Allāh b. al-Ḥabḥāb in Egypt (107–16/726–734) then North Africa (116–23/734–41), al-Junayd al-Murrī in Sind (104–08/723–26) then Khurāsān (111–16/729–34), Ḥanẓala b. Ṣafwān al-Kalbī in Egypt (102–05/721–24 and 119–24/737–42) then North Africa (124–26/742–44), not to mention Marwān b. Muḥammad in al-Jazīra, Armenia and Ādharbayjān (114–15/732–33 and 117–27/735–44). See Gabrieli's chart between pp. 124–25.

25. A comparison with the similar practice of the Roman emperor Tiberius is possible. Tacitus, 77, 220.

26. For example, see Ṭabarī, II, 1480, 1494, 1505, 1513, 1543, 1553–59, 1581–82, 1596–97, 1602–03, for criticism of the military leadership of the governors of Khurāsān alone.

27. Hishām's agonizing over the appointment of Naṣr b. Sayyār to Khurāsān in 120/738 is illustrative. Ṭabarī, II, 1660–63. Also the story, perhaps apocryphal, that al-Junayd al-Murrī bought the governorship of Khurāsān in 111/729 for a pair of necklaces. Ṭabarī, II, 1527. It nevertheless

is indicative of what scholarly circles were wont to believe about such appointments.

28. This is actually stated in the sources regarding the governors of Khurāsān Qutayba b. Muslim (86–96/705–15) and Naṣr b. Sayyār (120–31/738–49). Wellhausen, *Kingdom*, 429–30; Ṭabarī, II, 1660, 1662–63.

29. On the tendency of governors to see their office as a chance to enrich themselves or their retainers, see Ṭabarī, II, 1468–71, 1641–42, 1648, 1654–55.

30. Under Hishām, this fate befell at least 'Umar b. Hubayra, Muslim b. Sa'īd, Haytham b. 'Ubayd al-Kilābī, 'Umāra b. Ḥuraym al-Murrī, 'Āṣim b. 'Abd Allāh al-Hilālī, and Khālid al-Qaṣrī. Ṭabarī, II, 1485, 1488, 1565, 1581, 1654–55; *Continuatio*, 360; Wolf, 142.

31. Crone, 40–41, 44.

32. Ṭabarī, II, 1812, 1814.

33. McEvedy, 146, 148.

34. Many Yamanī tribes, such as the Jurash and the Ḥaḍramawt, bore the names of places rather than of eponymous ancestors, but such names were always rationalized into eponymous ancestors who had given their names to the places. This process is nonetheless late enough in some cases to be traceable in the sources. Ibn al-Athīr, *Lubāb*, I, 221, 303.

35. Crone, 30, 224 n. 206.

36. For the Arab genealogists' attempt to order these and other terms describing tribal groups into a descending hierarchy, see Ibn 'Abd al-Barr, 44–45.

37. Balādhurī, *Futūḥ*, 460–61; Morony, 197–98, 207–08, 272–73; Crone, 38. Subject allies who did not embrace Islam, however, retained their own organization and fought without pay other than a share of the booty. These allied forces were often of significant size, e. g., fifteen thousand Armenians. Pseudo-Sebêos, 158–59; Lewond, 178 n. 9; Laurent, 55.

38. For example, the Habaṭ, a *baṭn* of the 'Amr branch of the Tamīm army division, had less than five hundred warriors. Balādhurī, *Futūḥ*, 487.

39. For example, the Rabī'a b. Ḥanẓala of the Tamīm joined the larger Yarbū' b. Ḥanẓala. Ibn Ḥazm, 222.

40. This seems to be the case with the Barājim, which originally united owing to the smallness of each of the five separate components. Ibn Ḥazm, 222.

41. Ṭabarī, II, 131, 664, 701; Morony, 245.

42. Except at al-Kūfa, where mutually hostile groups had deliberately been mixed to reduce the threat of revolution.

43. Morony, 250. The Baṣran Azd came from 'Umān, but were added by a genealogical fiction to a few of the original Azd (Azd al-Sarāh) who had previously migrated from 'Asīr. The Bakr represented mostly settled people from eastern and northeastern Arabia. The allied 'Abd al-Qays were

shore dwellers from the vicinity of Qaṭar and al-Baḥrayn. The Tamīm, the nomads' nomads, were from the Najdī interior. The Ahl al-'Āliya were from predominantly nomadic tribes from west-central Arabia. See *EI*² articles on these tribal groups.

44. Shaban, *History*, 87.

45. Crone, 32; Shaban, *History*, 88.

46. Ibn 'Abd al-Barr, 58.

47. Wellhausen, *Kingdom*, 180, citing Dozy. Still supporting this view, Kennedy, 92.

48. Wellhausen, *Kingdom*, 69–71, 180; Shaban, *History*, 120–21; Hawting, 36–37. However, Wellhausen considers the next-largest tribal groupings to be pre-Islamic. Wellhausen, *Kingdom*, 27.

49. Shaban, *History*, 120; Crone, 34–35.

50. Shaban, *History*, 121.

51. Crone, 42–48, and especially 233 n. 310.

52. That was the transfer of the large Quḍā'a group to the Yaman, which was done for political reasons in the Second *Fitna*.

53. Balādhurī, *Futūḥ*, 548–65, especially 549–50, 556, citing the overall order. Although stipends varied according to the earliness of one's Islam and one's participation in certain battles such as Badr, recipients appear to have been listed from the outset according to their clans.

54. Crone, 38.

55. Nevertheless, tribally organized regiments under the broad groups of Muḍar, Yaman, and Rabī'a remained important long into 'Abbāsid times, and their factional struggles continued to be significant. Omar, 22, 37–38,41–42.

56. *EI*², s. v. Ḳays 'Aylān.

57. For an enumeration of many of the numerous instances of tribal feeling and intertribal hostility expressed by Umayyad poets, especially in the later period and in the reign of Hishām, see al-Nuss, 365–632.

58. Crone, 44.

Chapter 3

1. Wellhausen, *Kingdom*, 230–31, 248–49; Shaban, *History*, 111.

2. *EI*², s. v. Djund; Le Strange, *Palestine*, 24.

3. For the principle that the army in each province is entitled to its province's income, see Ṭabarī, I, 2414.

4. For the boundaries of the Syrian *ajnād* under the Umayyads, see Balādhurī, *Futūḥ*, 134, 139, 156, 164, 166, 173, 176–77; Ya'qūbī, *Buldān*, 323–29; Ibn al-Faqīh, 102–03, 105, 109–12, 116; Ibn Khurdādhbih, 75–79; Qudāma, 246, 255; Iṣṭakhrī, 55–59, 61–63, 65–67; Muqaddasī, 154–55, 162, 172; Yāqūt, s.

v. al-Urdunn, al-Balqā', Qinnasrīn; *EI*^{2}, s. v. al-Balḳā'; Filasṭīn; Ḥimṣ, Ḳinnasrīn. Map 3 is based on a comparison of these sources and attempts to get back to the earliest boundaries for the *ajnād*. These remain somewhat speculative, however, owing to the lateness of the existing sources.

5. For the Romano-Byzantine provincial boundaries, see Van der Meer and Mohrmann, map 15a. This is the most detailed map of Byzantine Syria I could find. This and other maps showing the Romano-Byzantine provincial boundaries are based on the sources listed in Jones, 1451. Le Strange finds rather more correspondence with the Roman-Byzantine provincial scheme than seems warranted. Le Strange, *Palestine*, 26.

6. Balādhurī, *Futūḥ*, 156, supports Yazīd I, but Ibn Khayyāṭ, *Ta'rīkh*, 222, already has Qinnasrīnī divisions present at Ṣiffīn in 38/657.

7. The enormous size of the *jund* of Damascus may have posed somewhat of an administrative problem, for it seems that al-Balqā', though subordinated to Damascus, was practically governed as a separate unit. Yāqūt, s. v. al-Balqā'; *EI*^{2}, s. v. al-Balḳā'. This is attested for both before and after Hishām's reign by indications of a separate administration for al-Balqā'. Under 'Umar II, al-Balqā' is listed with its governor as if it were a full *jund* by Ibn Khayyāṭ, *Ta'rīkh*, 465, but it must never have been, for under al-Walīd I in 95/714 and later under Marwān II, it is clearly subordinate to Damascus, although it has its own governor. Ya'qūbī, *Ta'rīkh*, II, 347; *Akhbār al-dawla*, 392, 399. Therefore, it was presumably with Damascus under Hishām as well.

8. Ibn al-Faqīh, 103; Ibn Khurdādhbih, 79; Qudāma, 247, 251. Also the most fertile *jund*. See Iṣṭakhrī, 56–57, quoted by Le Strange, *Palestine*, 28.

9. Ya'qūbī, *Ta'rīkh*, II, 277–78; Balādhurī, *Futūḥ*, 230; Jahshiyārī, 286–87; Qudāma, 246–47, 251; Le Strange, *Palestine*, 44–46. A separate list given by Ibn Khaldūn is probably only a corrupt variant of that of al-Jahshiyārī and thus is of no separate merit. Rayyis, 517–22.

10. This heavier Arab concentration in Jordan at the outset is also suggested by its having five separate tribal divisions listed at Ṣiffīn, while no other group has but two. Ibn Khayyāṭ, *Ta'rīkh*, 222.

11. Kennedy, 92.

12. *'Uyūn wa hadā'iq*, 5.

13. These latter still numbered sixty thousand in 132/750 even after the defeat of their champion Marwān b. Muḥammad by the 'Abbāsids. Ṭabarī, III, 57.

14. Balādhurī, *Futūḥ*, 507; Ṭabarī, II, 81.

15. Ṭabarī, II, 1290–91; Balādhurī, *Futūḥ*, 520.

16. Their largest tribe, the Kalb, were possibly there as early as 1200 B.C.E., if their identification with the Hebrew subtribe of Caleb is entertained.

17. Shaban, *History*, 40–43, 74.

18. Al-Walīd I lived at several widely scattered places including Khunāṣira in Qinnasrīn and died at his estate at Dayr Murrān in the Ghūṭa outside Damascus. *'Uyūn wa ḥadā'iq*, 12; Creswell and Allan, 113.

19. Ṭabarī, II, 1281, 1336, 1340; Ya'qūbī, *Ta'rīkh*, II, 359. According to one report, he actually began his caliphate in al-Raqqa in Diyār Muḍar, but this could be a copyist's error for al-Ramla. *'Uyūn wa ḥadā'iq*, 16.

20. Ya'qūbī, *Ta'rīkh*, II, 361; *'Uyūn wa ḥadā'iq*, 43, 63. Probably he had an estate at Dayr Sam'ān, where he was buried. Ṭabarī, II, 1361–62.

21. Ṭabarī, II, 1463; 'Aṭwān, *Walīd*, 273–74; Creswell and Allan, 113.

22. Ṭabarī, II, 1463.

23. 'Aṭwān, *Walīd*, 275–76, 453, 457, 459–60.

24. Balādhurī, *Futūḥ*, 156; Kennedy, 99.

25. Wellhausen, *Kingdom*, 191–92; Kennedy, 98.

26. Yāqūt, s. v. Diyār Bakr, Diyār Rabī'a, Diyār Muḍar; Segal, 142–45.

27. For a definition of Diyār Muḍar, see Ibn al-Faqīh, 136; Ibn Khurdādhbih, 73–74; Qudāma, 246; Muqaddasī, 137; Yāqūt, s. v. Diyār Muḍar; *EI*^{2}, s. v. Diyār Muḍar; Le Strange, *Lands*, 101–08 and map III. For Osrhoene before Islam, see Segal, 9–17, 35–38, 96, 99, 150–52, 165–68, 261(map).

28. For a definition of Diyār Rabī'a, see Ibn al-Faqīh, 133; Ibn Khurdādhbih, 95; Qudāma, 245; Muqaddasī, 137; Yāqūt, s. v. Diyār Rabī'a; *EI*^{2}, s. v. Diyār Rabī'a.

29. Le Strange, *Lands*, 86–87.

30. Azdī, 24; Ibn Taghrībirdī, I, 259.

31. However, it might still have been sometimes subordinate to al-Jazīra under Hishām, but no evidence exists for that. For its administrative history in this period, see Azdī, 3–53. Earlier, it may have been subordinate to al-Jazīra under 'Abd al-Malik. Shaban, *History*, 106–07. Morony makes the subordination of al-Mawṣil to al-Jazīra a result of the Second *Fitna*. Morony, 136.

32. Ibn Khayyāṭ, *Ta'rīkh*, 393. Ibn Khayyāṭ, *Ta'rīkh*, 374, also dates Muḥammad's expedition to Armenia to 82/701, however.

33. Ibn Khayyāṭ, *Ta'rīkh*, 485.

34. For this history, see Ibn Khayyāṭ, *Ta'rīkh*, 492, 541–42; Gabrieli, 75–77.

35. Ya'qūbī, *Ta'rīkh*, II, 278; Jahshiyārī, 285–6; Qudāma, 246, 250–51; Ibn Khurdādhbih, 73–74, 94–95; Ibn al-Faqīh, 133.

36. In areas usually attributed to Diyār Rabī'a. The higher figure is more likely to be correct, as it includes Āmid, which was omitted from Qudāma's other list.

37. This strip of land along the Euphrates seems to have been separately administered in 'Abbāsid times, but earlier much of it probably had belonged to Diyār Muḍar, judging by the tribal names associated with the

city of al-Qarqīsiyā' under the Umayyads. See Qudāma, 246; Wellhausen, *Kingdom*, 170, 175–76, 184, 186, 191–92, 202, 393.

38. In areas usually attributed to al-Mawṣil.

39. In an area attributed to Armenia.

40. Possibly meant to include Armenia, as no separate figure for that province is cited.

41. Ṭabarī, III, 57.

42. This figure, or rather even a larger one, is suggested by the size of Marwān b. Muḥammad's army in the Caucasus in 114/732, one hundred twenty thousand, though this also contained some non-Jazīran elements. But other Jazīrans must have been garrisoning the upper Euphrates frontier at the same time. Ibn al-Athīr, *Kāmil*, V, 178.

43. Ibn Khayyāṭ, *Ta'rīkh*, 347.

44. Theophanes, 64–85; Ostrogorsky, 140–44, 152–56.

45. Shaban, *History*, 146.

46. Wellhausen, *Kingdom*, 70, 210–11.

47. Except for the large Muḍarī group of the Tamīm, who seldom held high office.

48. See, for example, the Caliph Hishām's opinion that they were incapable of holding an important governorship. Ṭabarī, II, 1662. Also a verse attributed to a Bakrī:

> "Don't you see that God has made His religion victorious,
> so that Quraysh has prayed behind Bakr b. Wā'il?"

The implications are very humiliating for the Bakr if one of their own poets regarded it as miraculous that Qurashīs would deign to be led by a Bakrī. Ṭabarī, II, 1913. Other verses pour scorn on the Bakr's warmaking capabilities. Ṭabarī II, 449, 1480.

49. Wellhausen, *Kingdom*, 209–10, 250, 399.

50. *EI*[2], s. v. Khawāri*dj*. Despite much scholarly writing among medieval Muslim and modern scholars about the beliefs of numerous named sects of *khawārij*, the term simply means 'rebels' and was so applied by the Umayyads to all who went out against their rule. Although Khārijism was expressed in religious terms, it was mainly a kind of political behavior at this period, as emphasized by Wellhausen, *Factions*, 20–23. This is also emphasized in the lengthy discussion in Dabashi, 121–45.

51. Wellhausen, *Kingdom*, 388, 417; *Factions*, 16, 79. Some persons described as *khawārij* like al-Mughīra b. Sa'īd and Bayān, neither of whom was from the Rabī'a, were actually Shī'īs. The *khawārij* in the Maghrib, where there were no Rabī'a, were mostly Berbers.

52. For Raba'ī *khawārij* under Hishām, see Ṭabarī, II, 1622–28, 1633–34; Balādhurī, *Ansāb*, Istanbul Ms., II, 261–66; Ibn Qutayba, *'Uyūn*, II, 147. Mentioned are the clans of Shaybān, 'Ijl, Yashkur, and 'Anaza.

53. Ṭabarī, I, 2032–33.

54. For the Jazīran Taghlib, see Balādhurī, *Futūḥ*, 216–18. For al-Akhṭal's Christianity, see Iṣbahānī, *Aghānī*, VIII, 3036, 3052, 3056.

55. "Among us are the mosques and the imam, but you won't see
among the Taghlib any mosque frequented (by worshippers)."
See Isbahānī, *Aghānī*, VIII, 3063.

56. For all these areas except the last three named, see Le Strange, *Lands*, passim. The entire book is virtually a description of the Iraqi super-province.

57. See table 3 below.

58. Shaban, *History*, 36–37.

59. Shaban, *History*, 40–42.

60. Morony, 245–50; Shaban, *History*, 51–52.

61. For some of these, see Ṭabarī, I, 2495; also, Morony, 239–45.

62. They were prevented from entering other areas both by the governors, who did not want even more disturbance-prone heterogeneity than they already had in their *amṣār*, and by the tribesmen who were already settled, who did not want rivals with a weak record in Islam to share the spoils. Shaban, *History*, 36, 40, 42–43, 45–46, 51–52, 54–55.

63. Shaban, *History*, 66–67.

64. Ṭabarī, I, 2411–13, 2496. Morony, 256, is mistaken in saying the system of stipend differences was abolished by 'Umar I, based on Ṭabarī I, 2633. The text says only that those who fought at Nihāwand were treated equally with those who had been at al-Qādisiyya, not that all latecomers now received two thousand dirhams, a step that is nearly impossible to imagine having taken place. See also Shaban, *History*, 54–55.

65. Wellhausen, *Kingdom*, 230–31.

66. Balādhurī, *Futūḥ*, 355; Ma'āḍīḍī, 14, 76–79; Wellhausen, *Kingdom*, 249; Walker, II, p. xcii; Kennedy, 101–02. Baḥshal (d. 292/905), the early historian of Wāsiṭ, dates its foundation to 75–78/694–97. See Baḥshal, 22, 43.

67. Shaban, *History*, 111.

68. Ḥusayn, 21–31; Morony, 487.

69. Morony, 491.

70. Blankinship, "Tribal Factor," 589–91, 600.

71. Al-Kūfa was the single most important intellectual center of early Islam, surpassing al-Madīna both in scholarly output and sophistication. This is demonstrated by its leading role in the recording of early Muslim law exemplified by such jurists as Abū Hanīfa b. al-Nu'mān (d. 150/767), Sufyān al-Thawrī (d. 161/778), Abū Yūsuf al-Qāḍī (d. 182/798), and Muḥammad b. al-Ḥasan al-Shaybānī (d. 189/805). That it was also a major center for historical studies is shown by writers such as Muḥammad b. al-Sā'ib al-Kalbī (d. 146/763), 'Awāna b. al-Ḥakam (d. 147/764), Abū Mikhnaf (d. 157/774), and the notorious Sayf b. 'Umar (d. c. 180/796). Works or cita-

tions from all of these exist. How long before their time a Kūfan written tradition can be discerned is a matter of dispute, and after 145/762 it was gradually transferred to Baghdād, where the Kūfan tradition to a large extent was continued. But al-Kūfa influenced the main formative period of Islam, so that its effect was all out of proportion to the shortness of its duration. See Ibn al-Nadīm, *Fihrist*, 103, 105–08, 255–58, 281; Schacht, 29, 31, 40, 57–58. A perusal of Ibn al-Nadīm will show the predominance of al-Kūfa in the early Muslim literary tradition.

72. Wellhausen, 209–10; Morony, 247.

73. Ṭabarī, II, 1379–1416; Wellhausen, *Kingdom*, 314–15, 318–19; Kennedy, 107–08; differently, Shaban, *History*, 136.

74. Ibn Khayyāṭ, *Ta'rīkh*, 247; Shaban, *History*, 87.

75. They were united 50–53/670–73, 60–64/680–84, 67–72/687–91, 74–95/693–714, 96–99/715–17, 102/721– end of Umayyad rule. Ibn Khayyāṭ, *Ta'rīkh*, 247, 260, 281, 321, 334, 340, 345, 347, 384–85, 414, 428–29, 463, 482–83.

76. Ibn Khayyāṭ, *Ta'rīkh*, 546.

77. Ṭabarī, II, 1651, 1653.

78. Ṭabarī, I, 2414.

79. Ṭabarī, I, 2836. Balādhurī, *Futūḥ*, 411, 499.

80. After this, Kūfans and Syrians began to be introduced to the lands of the Baṣran patrimony and share their fruits, but the original Baṣrans remained dominant in areas where they had settled in any numbers, such as Khurāsān.

81. They were already participating in its conquest by 24/645. They had clashed with the Jazīrans over it as early as 32/653. Ṭabarī, I, 2804–08, 2889–94.

82. Not even all of this belonged to the Kūfans, as the important district of Shahrazūr remained a part of the province of al-Mawṣil until 'Abbāsid times. Balādhurī, *Futūḥ*, 410.

83. Ṭabarī, I, 2836–38.

84. Ṭabaristān was subdued by the 'Abbāsids. Balādhurī, *Futūḥ*, 415–17. The Kūfans had suffered a classic disaster trying to reduce Ṭabaristān in the reign of Mu'āwiya. Balādhurī, *Futūḥ*, 411–12. Qūmis was subdued by Qutayba b. Muslim. Ṭabarī, I, 2839; II, 1322. Jurjān was reduced by Yazīd b. al-Muhallab in 98/716–17. Balādhurī, *Futūḥ*, 412–14.

85. Balādhurī, *Futūḥ*, 507; Tabari, II, 156.

86. Indeed, a strong Kūfan military presence is not felt in Khurāsān until the governorship of Yazīd b. 'al-Muhallab in 97–99/716–18. See Blankinship, "Tribal Factor," 589–91. In more detail, see Blankinship, "Al-'Arab fī Khurāsān," passim.

87. Ṭabarī, II, 1109–10.

88. From Sind; however, there is a possibility they had been with

Qutayba as early as 90/709 and were only returning to Khurāsān. Ṭabarī, II, 1203, 1257.

89. Ṭabarī, II, 1290–91.

90. Ṭabarī, II, 1318–34. That the conquest was essentially for the Kūfans can be deduced from Ibn al-Muhallab's appointment of the Khurāsāni Kūfans' commander Jahm b. Zaḥr al-Ju'fī as governor of Jurjān. Ṭabarī, II, 1332–33. Kūfan dominance in Jurjān is also shown by the prevalence there later on of tribal names associated with al-Kūfa.

91. This can be seen not only from mention of them in the campaign of 98/716–17, but also from the appearance shortly thereafter in Khurāsān of tribal *nisba*s associated with al-Kūfa. Ṭabarī, II, 1318, 1320, 1324.

92. Balādhurī, *Futūḥ*, 530–33; Pathan, 36–40. Note the prominence of the men of 'Abd al-Qays, a Baṣran Rabī'a tribe. The governors of Makrān mentioned as well as the Sulamī appointed by al-Ḥajjāj to conquer Sind also seem from their tribal *nisba*s to have been Baṣrans.

93. Balādhurī, *Futūḥ*, 534, 537–38; Pathan, 44–50.

94. Balādhurī, *Futūḥ*, 540, 542; Pathan, 54–56, 59.

95. Balādhurī, *Futūḥ*, 539–43; Ya'qūbī, *Ta'rīkh*, II, 356, 379–80.

96. Crone, 130, 133, 135–36, 138–41. Apparently the last time a governor of al-Yamāma was appointed directly by a caliph was by 'Abd al-Malik. Crone, 144.

97. Crone, 133, 136, 138–39, 140–41, 148, 151–52. For an exception, Crone, 148.

98. Crone, 133–35, 136–38, 141–43.

99. Ya'qūbī, *Ta'rīkh*, II, 277; Jahshiyārī, 281–86; Qudāma, 236, 239–40, 242–45, 248–51. However, some of Qudāma's figures are a few years later than the reign of al-Ma'mūn.

100. Qudāma presents two separate versions of provincial tax income which are usually, but not always, in agreement.

101. Ṭabaristān has been omitted, as it was not part of the caliphate in Umayyad times.

102. This territory, the bulk of Iraq, belonged mostly, but not entirely, to al-Kūfa. Kaskar and Kuwar Dijla are deemed subdivisions of it but belonged to al-Baṣra, which is why al-Jahshiyārī lists them separately. Thus, perhaps about thirty million dirhams on their account should be deducted from Qudāma's totals for al-Kūfa and added to those for al-Baṣra.

103. On the dividing line between the conquests of al-Kūfa and al-Baṣra in al-Jibāl, see Balādhurī, *Futūḥ*, 375, 377, 383–85.

104. This was the district in which Wāsiṭ was located. That Yūsuf b. 'Umar in 120/738 required Abān b. al-Walīd, Khālid al-Qaṣrī's governor of Wāsiṭ, to pay ten million dirhams could indicate that the district of Kaskar by then belonged to and was taxed from Wāsiṭ. Ya'qūbī, *Ta'rīkh*, II, 388. On the other hand, Abān's earlier willingness to pay twenty million dirhams to

cover a year's arrears in taxes suggests that this was the amount of Wāsiṭ's annual *kharāj*. Ṭabarī, II, 1651; Jahshiyārī, 63.

105. That Yūsuf b. 'Umar required Ṭāriq b. Abī Ziyād, Khālid al-Qasrī's administrator of Fārs, to pay a fine of twenty million dirhams in 120/738 suggests that this was the amount of Fārs' annual *kharāj* under Hishām. Ya'qūbī, *Ta'rīkh*, II, 388.

106. For Khurāsān and Transoxiana, see Le Strange, *Lands*, 382–489. Compare the smallness of Jurjān, Le Strange, *Lands*, 376–81.

107. Balādhurī, *Futūḥ*, 538.

108. *Fatḥnāmah-i Sind*, 148.

109. Ya'qūbī, *Ta'rīkh*, II, 380; Balādhurī, *Futūḥ*, 541.

110. Afterwards, Bukayr returned to al-Kūfa and significantly contributed to the finances of the 'Abbāsid movement. See *Akhbār al-dawla*, 194, 200–01; Ṭabarī, II, 1467.

111. Ṭabarī, II, 1334.

112. Morony, 239.

113. Ḥusayn, 84–88, 149–60.

114. Also exemplified in the work of al-Kumayt, who sympathized with Zaydī rather than extreme Shī'ī views. Ḥusayn, 77–84, 125–36, 167–95.

115. Ṭabarī, II, 1648.

116. Shaban, *History*, 103.

117. For the fewness of the Arabs in Egypt, see Kennedy, 65, 87, 93, 309. For a contrary opinion, estimating the Arabs in Egypt to have numbered thirty to forty thousand, see Shaban, *History*, 113.

118. Most of the Berbers are alleged to have embraced Islam through the efforts of Ismā'īl b. 'Abd Allāh b. Abī al-Muhājir, the *mawlā* of the Makhzūm, governor of North Africa for 'Umar II in 100–02/718–20. Balādhurī, *Futūḥ*, 273; 'Abd al-Ḥamīd, 264–66. But al-Walīd I's governor Mūsā b. Nuṣayr is also said to have provided Arab missionaries to instruct the new Berber troops in Islam as early as 89/708. Raqīq, 69–70.

119. Ibn Ḥazm, 495ff. However, at first there was a tendency to subordinate them individually to various Arab tribes as *mawālī*. That probably did not work owing to their numbers.

120. Some of these were adopted into the Arab military system in the East, namely the Asāwira, Ḥamrā', Zuṭṭ, and Sayābija. See Balādhurī, *Futūḥ*, 192, 459–63; Morony, 197–98, 207–08, 271–72. Generally, however, even the Iranian troops who formed an important division of Qutayba b. Muslim's army continued to be *mawālī* or clients of different Arab tribes. Ṭabarī, II, 1291.

121. These included the governors in 55–62/675–82, 69–73/688–92, 79–102/698–721, and 116–123/734–41. 'Abd al-Ḥamīd, 188–89, 214, 239, 259, 263, 266–67, 269, 278.

122. Yazīd b. Abī Muslim, the *mawlā* of the Thaqīf, was a Jazīran

attached to al-Ḥajjāj. He had also served as acting governor of Iraq when al-Ḥajjāj died, but was only appointed governor in his own right in North Africa. Ibn Khallikān, VI, 309–12; Ibn 'Idhāri, I, 48; Ibn 'Abd al-Ḥakam, *Futūḥ*, 213–14. 'Ubayd Allāh b. al-Ḥabḥāb, the *mawlā* of the Salūl, was also a Jazīran and had been fiscal governor of Egypt, but was only made a governor in his own right in North Africa. Abbott, 25–35. Mūsā b. Nuṣayr, the *mawlā* of the Lakhm, was of obscure origin, but probably his ancestor had been captured at 'Ayn al-Tamr in Iraq. Balādhurī, *Futūḥ*, 272; *Akhbār majmū'a*, 14; Ibn 'Idhāri, I, 39. Thus, the ancestral background of all these men is likely to have been Syriac Christian.

123. The governor of Egypt appointed or influenced the appointment of the governor of North Africa in 55/675, 69/688–89, and 86/705. 'Abd al-Ḥamīd, 188, 214, 235–38.

124. Spain was officially subordinate to the governor of North Africa. *Akhbār majmū'a*, 29.

125. In fact, Khurāsān's subordination to Iraq was recommended to Hishām by 'Āṣim b. 'Abd Allāh al-Hilālī, who cited its remoteness from the caliph as the reason for such a step, although that was to his own detriment. Ṭabarī, II, 1574.

126. The humiliation inflicted on Mūsā b. Nuṣayr by Sulaymān is well known.'Abd al-Ḥamīd, 253–56.

127. Ibn Khayyāṭ, 357, 359, 392–93; pseudo-Ibn Qutayba, *Imama wa siyāsa*, II, 50; Ibn 'Abd al-Ḥakam, 203–04; Kindī, 38, 40, 52, 60–62, 71–72, 82; *Akhbār majmū'a*, 14–15; Ibn 'Idhārī, I, 39; Ibn Taghrībirdī, I, 198; Abbott, 30–32, 34; Abun-Naṣr, 31–32. The accounts of Raqīq, 68, Ibn al-Athīr, *Kāmil*, IV, 369–72, 539–40, and Ibn 'Idhārī, I, 41, are confused and not to be preferred, *pace* 'Abd al-Ḥamīd, 235–38, etc. The question of the date of the start of Mūsā b. Nuṣayr's governorship is complex, but it appears to have begun in 79/698 rather than 89/708, as asserted by the latter sources.

128. Maqrīzī, *Khiṭaṭ*, I, 297.

129. Indeed, it contributed only three thousand men to Kulthūm b. 'Iyāḍ's army in 122/740, which probably represented a major proportion of its fighting strength. *Akhbār majmū'a*, 36.

130. Bishr b. Ṣafwān (102–09/721–27), 'Ubayd Allāh b. al-Ḥabḥāb (116–23/734–41), and Ḥanẓala b. Ṣafwān (124–27/742–45). Kindī, 71, 82; Ibn Taghrībirdī, I, 244, 250, 291; Abbott, 31–32.

131. 'Abd al-Ḥamīd, 187.

132. Ibn 'Abd al-Ḥakam, *Futūḥ*, 204–05, 217–19; Balādhurī, *Futūḥ*, 272.

133. Ibn 'Abd al-Ḥakam, *Futūḥ*, 200, 216, 218–19, 221, 223–25; Kindī, 52; Balādhurī, *Futūḥ*, 266.

134. Just as Spain was subordinate to North Africa, Egypt, and the caliph, Transoxiana was subject to Khurāsān, Iraq, and the caliph in turn. Spain is said to have been made independent of North Africa by 'Umar II,

but its dependence on the older province reappeared under Yazīd II. Ibn 'Idhāri, II, 26–27.

135. As well as his fear in the case of Spain of being cut off by the Byzantines by sea. Ibn 'Idhāri, II, 26; Ibn al-Qūṭiyya, 38.

136. Ibn 'Idhāri, II, 9–15, 24; Ibn al-Qūṭiyya, 35–36.

137. Ibn 'Idhāri, II, 24–25; Collins, 43–44.

138. Balādhurī, *Futūḥ*, 253, 256. Higher figures cited by Maqrīzī, *Khiṭaṭ*, I, 98, are exaggerations.

139. Ya'qūbī, *Ta'rīkh*, II, 277.

140. Kindī, 73; Balādhurī, *Futūḥ*, 262.

141. Maqrīzī, *Khiṭaṭ*, I, 99.

142. Jahshiyārī, 287. Libyan Barqa, usually considered part of Egypt, is reported by Jahshiyārī to have produced an annual income of one million dirhams.

143. Ibn Khurdādhbih, 84; Maqrīzī, *Khiṭaṭ*, I, 99, has 2.18 million.

144. Qudāma, 248, 251.

145. Maqrīzī, *Khiṭaṭ*, I, 99.

146. Balādhurī, *Futūḥ*, 268.

147. Jahshiyārī, 287.

148. Ibn 'Idhāri, I, 52; Ibn al-Athīr, *Kāmil*, V, 191.

149. Notably Abū Ja'far al-Mansūr and 'Abd al-Raḥmān al-Dākhil. Ibn Hazm, 20; Ibn 'Idhāri, II, 41.

150. Mūsā b. Nuṣayr is said to have taken one hundred thousand captives in campaigns in the central and western Maghrib. These would count as booty rather than tribute, but the effect must have been great. 'Abd al-Ḥamīd, 241.

151. *Continuatio*, 359–60.

152. On the Egyptian navy, see Shaban, *History*, 81–82, 123, 157–58.

153. Shaban, *History*, 149.

154. However, a few Syrians probably accompanied the Syrian governors of North Africa when they set out to take up their duties in the province, beginning with Ḥassān b. al-Nu'mān al-Ghassānī in 74/693. 'Abd al-Ḥamīd, 214–15.

155. For example, the two areas can be represented respectively by Mālik's *Muwatta'* and al-Isbahānī's *Aghānī*, both having roots in late Umayyad times.

156. As shown in the rather elaborate story about Hishām's correspondence with Yūsuf b. 'Umar, the governor of Yaman in 120/738. Ṭabarī, II, 1649, 1652.

157. Under Hishām, it was separate 114–18/732–36. Ṭabarī, II, 1561–62, 1586, 1592–93; Ibn Khayyāṭ, *Ta'rīkh*, 534.

158. Ya'qūbī, *Ta'rīkh*, II, 278.

159. Jahshiyārī, 287.

160. Qudāma, 249.
161. Jahshiyārī, 288.
162. Qudāma, 248.
163. Ṭabarī, II, 1777; Isbahānī, *Aghānī*, IV, 1453, 1460, 1469.
164. Jahshiyārī, 64–66.

Chapter 4

1. Especially Qur'ān ii, 30, where the reference to the *khalīfa*'s shedding of blood in the earth was sometimes sarcastically thrown back in the face of the caliphs. Although Qur'ān xxxviii, 26, portrays David as a ruler and judge in the earth, it immediately follows a passage (vv. 21–25) which shows him in a less favorable light making a mistake for which he has to ask God's forgiveness. Nevertheless, it is possible that the title of caliph derives from xxxviii, 26.

2. Crone and Hinds, 6–11, 24–42; Bernard Lewis, 43–46.

3. Abū Yūsuf, 3–6.

4. Bukhārī, IX, 96.

5. Bukhārī, IX, 78; Muslim, II, 120–22.

6. This principle is derived from, though not literally explicit in, *ḥadīth*s cited in Abū Yūsuf, 10, and Muslim, II, 136 (*man māta wa laysa fī 'unuqihi bay'atun māta maytatan jāhiliyya*). That such an oath was customarily made and taken very seriously by the authorities is shown, for example, by *'Uyūn wa ḥadā'iq*, 9, where al-Ḥajjāj is portrayed as executing Sa'īd b. Jubayr for breaking his oath of allegiance to the caliph. Like examples abound in the histories. However, the necessary oath of allegiance that every Muslim must acknowledge in his life is also otherwise explained in a *ḥadīth* as allegiance to God alone, as derived from Qur'ān ix, 111. Ibn Kathīr, *Tafsīr*, II, 391.

7. Qur'ān lx, 12, though referring only to women, is usually taken as the model example of such an oath. Otherwise, the importance of taking an oath of allegiance to the Prophet is mentioned in Qur'ān xlviii, 10, 18. Model oaths of allegiance to the Prophet are also cited in the *ḥadīth*. Mālik, 608; Bukhārī, IX, 96–99; Muslim, II, 138–42. However, a *ḥadīth* cited in Muslim, II, 140, suggests a refusal to pay to later rulers the same obligations offered to the Prophet.

8. Mālik, 608; Bukhārī, IX, 96–98.

9. Abū Yūsuf, 10–11; Bukhārī, IX, 77–78; Muslim, II, 129–31, 133, 135. Obedience to an undefined "those in authority among you" (*ūlū al-amri minkum*) is also enjoined in Qur'ān iv, 59, the only Qur'ānic verse commanding obedience to other than God and His Prophet.

10. Abū Yūsuf, 11; Bukhārī, IX, 78–79, 91–92; Muslim, II, 131, 133. In

Muslim, II, 132, however, only open apostasy on the part of the ruler justifies disobedience.

11. Muslim, II, 135–37.
12. Abū Yūsuf, 11; Muslim, II, 134, 136.
13. Muslim, II, 137–38.
14. Muslim, II, 137.
15. Abū Yūsuf, 11; Muslim, II, 133, 137.
16. Muslim, II, 132–33. The vagueness of the wording suggests a double meaning.
17. Abū Yūsuf, 4–6, 8–9; Bukhārī, IX, 80; Muslim, II, 124–26.
18. Ṭabarī, II, 1482–83, 1635, 1811.
19. Jāḥiẓ, *Bukhalā'*, 15, 150; Ṭabarī, II, 1730–33; *Continuatio*, 360, 363; Wolf, 140–41, 146–47. For an opposite view suggesting a love for fine clothes in great quantity, see Ibn 'Abd Rabbih, IV, 446. The incident referred to, the six hundred camel loads of clothes for himself and his entourage on his pilgrimage, would however have taken place in the first year of his reign, when the financial problem had perhaps not yet intensified.
20. Especially see his careful supervision of military expenditures reported in Ṭabarī, II, 1732–33.
21. The five hundred dirhams awarded to a poet as reported in Ṭabarī, II, 1737, does not seem like a very generous amount, while the raise in the poet's stipend by an unspecified amount tended to delay the actual disbursement of the further reward.
22. Ṭabarī, II, 1658.
23. On the significance of this border, see Toynbee, I, 75–76.
24. Jahshiyārī, 67.
25. Morony, 18, 97–98.
26. In fact, it seems that Hishām came to Damascus, the nominal capital, only rarely during his reign if at all, except for his investiture, which is recorded in Ṭabarī, II, 1467. Otherwise only Sāwīrus, *PO*, V, 74, clearly records Hishām as residing in a palace in Damascus during his reign.
27. Ṭabarī, II, 1826.
28. On the Euphrates at Bālis as well as elsewhere in Qinnasrīn. Balādhurī, *Futūḥ*, 176, 178; Yāqūt, s. v. Bālis.
29. Ibn Khayyāṭ, *Ta'rīkh*, 545; Ṭabarī, II, 1750; Jahshiyārī, 62, 68.
30. Ṭabarī, II, 1649–50; Jahshiyārī, 62.
31. Ṭabarī, II, 1468, 1614–16; pseudo-Ibn Qutayba, *Imāma wa siyāsa*, II, 105.
32. Only of local importance.
33. Later combined with the department of the privy seal.
34. Ibn Khayyāṭ, *Ta'rīkh*, 544–46.
35. Jahshiyārī, 59.
36. Jahshiyārī, 60. How exactly *ṣadaqa* may have differed from *kharāj*

here is not clear. Perhaps the former office was in charge of social welfare, or perhaps it collected the taxes of the metropolitan province of Syria as opposed to the rest of the caliphate.

37. Ibn Khayyāṭ, *Ta'rīkh*, 487.

38. These figures are based on a number of suppositions we have presented above. If the Syrian troops were around one hundred seventy-five thousand, the Jazīrans seventy-five thousand, and the Khurāsānis fifty-five thousand, we are already dealing with three hundred five thousand, without considering North Africa, Spain, and Sind, which even if allotted only thirty thousand apiece will still bring us near four hundred thousand. Other provinces too had some, though fewer, troops in them. A number of one hundred seventy-five thousand as opposed to four hundred thousand will also give the proper ratio of Syrians to others in the caliph's armies. Possibly, a considerable portion of the Syrians may have been on the military roles only to draw stipends, but this is far from clear.

39. In al-Madīna, this began in 88/707. Ṭabarī, II, 1192–94; *'Uyūn wa ḥadā'iq*, 4–6; Ibn al-Athīr, *Kāmil*, V, 9.

40. Ṭabarī, II, 1195–96, 1271–73; *'Uyūn wa ḥadā'iq*, 11.

41. *'Uyūn wa ḥadā'iq*, 5–6.

42. Jahshiyārī, 60; Ibn 'Abd al-Ḥakam, *Sīra*, 51–52.

43. Ibn 'Abd al-Ḥakam, *Sīra*, 49–50, 54, 112.

44. For Hishām, see Balādhurī, *Futūḥ*, 213; Ṭabarī, II, 1467, 1909; Jahshiyārī, 60–61; *'Uyūn wa ḥadā'iq*, 60; Yāqūt, s. v. al-Hanī wa al-Marī; Jarīr, 6, 150. For Sulaymān, see Yāqūt, s. v. al-Ramla. Note that he must have worked on al-Ramla mainly in the reign of al-Walīd I. He could hardly have undertaken the whole project while caliph, for he spent most of his caliphate in Qinnasrīn. Ṭabarī, II, 1336, 1340; Ya'qūbī, *Ta'rīkh*, II, 359; Ibn al-Athīr, *Kāmil*, V, 27, 293; *'Uyūn wa ḥadā'iq*, 16; Yāqūt, s. v. Dābiq; Le Strange, *Palestine*, 303–08. For Maslama's extensive estates, see Balādhurī, *Futūḥ*, 176, 178; Yāqūt, s. v. Bālis; Ṭabarī, III, 52. For Sa'īd, one of whose estates was granted by al-Walid I, see Balādhurī, *Futūḥ*, 213; Ṭabarī, III, 1913.

45. Kindi, 73.

46. Creswell and Allan, 113.

47. Ibn 'Abd al-Ḥakam, *Sīra*, 40–41.

48. Ājurī, 58.

49. Balādhurī, *Futūḥ*, 214.

50. Ṭabarī, III, 52.

51. E.g., Hishām granted estates to Sa'īd b. 'Amr al-Ḥarashī. Ibn A'tham, VIII, 60.

52. On these generally, see Creswell and Allan, 91–126, 131–216.

53. Creswell and Allan, 93, 95–96, 104–05, 112–13, 121, 124, 134, 142, 149, 158, 169, 173–74, 176, 199–200, 211–12, 215.

54. *Répertoire*, I, 23–4; Creswell and Allan, 93, 112, 134, 158, 199–200.

55. Creswell and Allan, 113.

56. The principle of generosity toward relatives was the Umayyads' ultimate justification for their extravagant allowances. Ibn 'Abd al-Ḥakam, *Sīra*, 126; Ājurī, 59.

57. For the tremendous fertility of the Marwānids, see Zubayrī, 160–69; Ibn Ḥazm, 87–108. 'Abd al-Malik and his sons who became caliphs each had between ten and twenty sons. 'Umar b. al-Walīd I, known as the 'Stallion of the Banū Marwān,' alone is said to have sired sixty sons. *'Uyūn wa ḥadā'iq*, 13.

58. Ṭabarī, II, 1834.

59. Balādhurī, *Futūḥ*, 538.

60. Two thousand four hundred sixty, according to Theophanes, 88–89; five thousand, according to Michael, II, 484; one thousand from Egypt and al-Maghrib alone, according to Dhahabī, *Siyar*, IV, 501.

61. *'Uyūn wa ḥadā'iq*, 19–20; Jahshiyārī, 49.

62. Ṭabarī, II, 1365; Wellhausen, 268–69; Shaban, *History*, 131.

63. Wellhausen, 313; Shaban, *History*, 133.

64. Ṭabarī, II, 1367.

65. Ibn 'Abd al-Ḥakam, *Sīra*, 79–80.

66. Ṭabarī, II, 1346, 1365; Balādhurī, *Futūḥ*, 196, 198, 519; Ya'qūbī, *Ta'rīkh*, II, 362–63; *Akhbār majmū'a*, 30; Ibn al-Qūṭiyya, 38; Ibn 'Idhāri, II, 26.

67. Balādhurī, *Futūḥ*, 540; Ibn al-Athīr, *Kāmil*, 54–55, 135.

68. Ibn 'Abd al-Ḥakam, *Sīra*, 44, 49–50, 132, 140–1; Ājurī, 58–62.

69. Ibn 'Abd al-Ḥakam, *Sīra*, 51–52, 54, 125–28; Ājurī, 57.

70. This is not to deny, though, that a few of them, such as Maslama b. 'Abd al-Malik, had plenty of influence.

71. Ibn 'Abd al-Ḥakam, *Sīra*, 45–46, 52–53. It appears that the distinction between the caliph's private purse and the state treasury was not yet entirely clear even under Hishām. Kubaysī, 348.

72. Ibn 'Abd al-Ḥakam, *Sīra*, 106.

73. Ibn 'Abd al-Ḥakam, *Sīra*, 133.

74. Ṭabarī, II, 1367.

75. Ibn 'Abd al-Ḥakam, *Sīra*, 79.

76. Ṭabarī, II, 1354.

77. Shaban, *History*, 132, 135.

78. Ṭabarī, II, 1367; Ibn 'Abd al-Ḥakam, *Sīra*, 48.

79. Ṭabarī, II, 1364; *'Uyūn wa ḥadā'iq*, 63.

80. Possibly implied by Ṭabarī, II, 1367.

81. Although in 100/719 he commanded an expedition against certain *khawārij* in Iraq. But note that he received no position of authority in the province such as he obtained under Yazīd II. Ṭabarī, II, 1348.

82. Ya'qūbī, *Ta'rīkh*, 359–60; Dhahabī, *Ta'rīkh*, IV, 177; *Siyar*, IV, 501. Michael the Syrian has him in charge of the supplies, a crucial role, and one that probably had a lot to do with the fleet. Michael, II, 484.

83. Indeed 'Umar b. Hubayra had already been rewarded by 'Umar II for his failure by being appointed governor of al-Jazīra in 100/718–19. This testifies to the rising political and military strength of the Jazīran element. Ṭabarī, II, 1349.

84. Kindī, 70.

85. Ibn 'Abd al-Ḥakam, *Sīra*, 51.

86. Shaban, *History*, 138.

87. Ṭabarī, II, 1432–33.

88. Ṭabarī, II, 1433; Crone, 107.

89. Crone, 144.

90. Ṭabarī, II, 1439–49; Gibb, 62–64; Shaban, *Revolution*, 101–02.

91. Ṭabarī, II, 1456, 1459–60; Shaban, *Revolution*, 102.

92. Crone, 138.

93. Ibn Khayyāṭ, *Ta'rīkh*, 484, 538.

94. Ibn Khallikān, VI, 309–11; Jahshiyārī, 42–43, 52, 55–57; Ibn 'Abd al-Ḥakam, *Futūḥ*, 213–14; Ya'qūbī, *Ta'rīkh*, II, 348, 353–54, 376; Ṭabarī, II, 1435; Balādhurī, *Futūḥ*, 273.

95. Ibn Khallikān, VI, 311; Jahshiyārī, 57; Ibn 'Idhāri, I, 48; Ya'qūbī, *Ta'rīkh*, II, 376; Ṭabarī, II, 1435; Raqīq, 99–101; 'Abd al-Ḥamīd, 267–68.

96. Balādhurī, *Futūḥ*, 274.

97. *Continuatio*, 359–60.

98. Kindī, 70.

99. Kindī, 78–79.

100. Jahshiyārī, 42.

101. Walker, II, lx–lxi, 301–04.

102. Al-Maqrīzī's statement is probably drawn from eastern sources and refers only to Iraq and the East. Even so, some dirhams were minted elsewhere than at Wāsiṭ or at Khālid al-Qaṣrī's adjunct estate of al-Mubāraka. Maqrīzī, *Nuqud*, 16.

103. Walker, II, 302–04. The list of other dirham mints besides Wāsiṭ and Damascus after 106/725 is highly instructive. Al-Mubāraka was simply the estate of Khālid near Wāsiṭ and therefore is not really distinct from the latter. Ifrīqiya, al-Andalus, Irmīniya, al-Bāb, Marw, and Balkh represent the centralized mints of superprovinces, though West's two mints did operate simultaneously, possibly owing to the loose structure of the West and the great distance between al-Qayrawān and Qurṭuba. Specimens alleged to be from al-Kūfa in Hishām's reign are not especially convincing. Walker, II, 174. The unique specimen from Sābūr for 123/741 is probably a mistake of some kind, ancient or modern. Walker, II, 80, 159.

104. Walker, II, lxviii, 241, 260, 279, 285.

105. Walker, II, lix.

106. Maqrīzī, *Nuqūd*, 16–17.

107. Balādhurī, *Futūḥ*, 575–76.

108. Jones, 411–27; Haldon, 173–74.

109. *Khāṣṣa* literally means *res privata*.

110. First mentioned under Hishām. Ibn Khayyāṭ, *Ta'rīkh*, 545.

111. Michael, II, 490; Pseudo-Dionysius, 23–24. The record of Hishām's estates according to the Arabic sources is assembled in Kubaysī, 58–61.

112. This group is already mentioned in 95/714. It, like the Dhakwāniyya, is associated with the Jazīran and Qinnasrīnī forces facing the Byzantines. Its commander was a *mawlā* of 'Abd al-Malik, but the unit was attached to several different Umayyads, including Maslama b. 'Abd al-Malik, Mu'āwiya b. Hishām, and Marwān b. Muḥammad. They numbered at least three thousand. Ibn Khayyāṭ, *Ta'rīkh*, 423, 492, 567, 597; Ṭabarī, II, 1268, 1306, 1397, 1401–02, 1893.

113. Ṭabarī, II, 1830, 1833, 1842, 1852–3, 1892, 1909. Michael, II, 505, mentions Sulaymān losing twelve thousand men of those called *zabounayé*; this latter term should be read *zakwanayé*, i. e., Dhakwāniyya as written in the Syriac language, in which the letters 'b' and 'k' look nearly alike.

114. Wellhausen, 372; Shaban, *History*, 147, 157, 161–62; Crone, 38, 53, 55.

115. The issue of the extent of caliphal authority is discussed at length by Crone and Hinds, passim. While I am content to acknowledge that the caliph bore the title *khalīfat Allāh* or 'God's deputy,' their arguments for caliphal legislative authority and against the existence of the Prophet's *sunna* are inconclusive, though space does not permit me to examine them here (pp. 19–80). For a critique of Crone and Hinds, see my review in the *MESA Bulletin* 21 (1987), 185–87. In any case, even Crone and Hinds admit that the Prophet's *sunna* was already an existing concept before the reign of Hishām (pp. 71–72, 78).

116. Ṭabarī, I, 2951–54, 2985, 2994, 2997.

117. Hawting, 42–43.

118. Ṭabarī, II, 111–35; Wellhausen, 124–25; Shaban, *History*, 89.

119. For the swiftness and completeness of the Umayyad collapse on the death of Yazīd, see Ṭabarī, II, 430–32, 434, 437, 439, 467–71, 488–89.

120. Ibn Khayyāṭ, *Ta'rīkh*, 234–35, 241, 246, 249, 251, 260–64; Wellhausen, *Factions*, 29–42; Haji Yahaya, 134–51.

121. Ṭabarī, II, 534, 546, 606–08, 610–11, 633, 638, 722; Wellhausen, *Kingdom*, 502, 504–06; Shaban, *History*, 94–95; Kennedy, 95–97.

122. This latter point is mostly evidenced in the increasingly ideological character of the opposition. This is the case not only with the Shi'i revolts of al-Mukhtār and Zayd b. 'Alī, but also in new underground movements preached for the first time by *mawālī*, such as the revolutionary Khārijism of 'Ikrima, the *mawlā* of Ibn 'Abbās, or the revolutionism of the 'Abbāsid movement.

123. See following notes 125–37.

124. Ya'qūbī, *Ta'rīkh*, II, 311; Oleg Grabar, 49–50.

125. Oleg Grabar, 62–65.

126. André Grabar, 47, 72–77, 95, 106.

127. Sāwīrus, *PO*, V, 25.

128. Sāwīrus, *PO*, V, 52; Kindī, 54.

129. Balādhurī *Futūḥ*, 574–75; Maqrīzī, *Nuqūd*, 6–7; Theophanes, 63; Walker, II, liv–lv, lvii, lix, lxii; Grierson, 97–98, 147; André Grabar, 77, 80–82; Bates, 245–55. According to Bates, 253, the dating of the Quinisext Council and its exact connection with the issue of coins depicting Jesus remains to be precisely determined.

130. Balādhurī, *Futūḥ*, 230. These records included especially the fiscal records, which were still in the hands of non-Muslim or *mawālī* secretaries. The military roll (*dīwān*) and the caliphal correspondence, both of which concerned the Muslim Arab rulers directly, had already been in Arabic from an early period. Jahshiyārī, 38.

131. Walker, II, liv.

132. Ibn 'Abd al-Ḥakam, *Sīra*, 136; Abū Yūsuf, 262; Michael, II, 488–89; Theophanes, 91; André Grabar, 128.

133. Agapius, *PO*, VIII, 503; Theophanes, 91.

134. This decree was applied thoroughly in Egypt. Kindī, 71–72; Ibn Taghrībirdī, I, 250; Michael, II, 489; Sāwīrus, *PO*, V, 72–73; pseudo-Dionysius, 17; André Grabar, 128–29; Barnard, 14, 16–18, 21–22.

135. André Grabar, 122–23.

136. André Grabar, 123, 129; Barnard, 18.

137. André Grabar, 122, 129.

138. Ibn Ḥabīb, *Muḥabbar*, 305–06; Ibn Rustah, 213.

139. Pseudo-Ibn Qutayba, *Imāma wa siyāsa*, II, 107–08.

140. Kubaysī, 78–79. The reports that say he did drink wine seem hostile propaganda, as his adversary al-Walīd II never makes the charge in his poems.

141. Balādhurī, *Ansāb*, Istanbul Ms., II, 238–39; 'Aṭwān, *Walīd*, 181–82, *Sīra*, 130.

142. 'Aṭwān, *Walīd*, 182, *Sīra*, 130.

143. Ṭabarī, II, 1731.

144. Walīd, 66.

145. Although he is said to have been ignorant of Umm Ḥakīm's wine drinking. Iṣbahānī, *Aghānī*, XVII, 6088, 6094–98.

146. Dhahabī, *Siyar*, V, 340–42, 447; Ibn Ḥajar, *Tahdhīb*, IX, 445–51. For al-Zuhrī's aristocratic attitude toward the *mawālī*, see Dhahabī, *Siyar*, V, 344.

147. Ṭabarī, II, 1482–83; Dhahabī, *Siyar*, V, 447; Ibn Ḥajar, *Tahdhīb*, V, 203–05.

148. Ṭabarī, II, 1482.

149. The scholars were Ṭā'ūs, the *mawlā* of the Ḥimyar, and Sālim b. 'Abd Allāh b. 'Umar b. al-Khaṭṭāb. Ṭabarī, II, 1472.

150. Ṭabarī, II, 1483. He may even have claimed to love the family of ʻAlī. Pseudo-Ibn Qutayba, *Imāma wa siyāsa*, II, 104.

151. In this regard, the career of ʻIkrima, the *mawlā* of Ibn ʻAbbās, is instructive. See *EI*², s. v. ʻIkrima; Ibn Ḥajar, *Tahdhīb*, VII, 263–73.

Chapter 5

1. The majority of the pages of the works of Wellhausen, Shaban, and Crone are devoted to the caliphal government's relations with the internal opposition.
2. Pseudo-Ibn Qutayba, *Imāma wa siyāsa*, II, 104.
3. *EI*², s. v. Hishām; Shaban, *History*, 152; Kennedy, 112, 116–17; Kubaysī, 4. But see the accurately unfavorable view of Wellhausen, *Kingdom*, 350.
4. Ṭabarī, II, 1485, 1488, 1565, 1581, 1654–55.
5. Ṭabarī, II, 1823–24.
6. Shaban, *History*, 135–7, 154; Wellhausen, *Kingdom*, 322.
7. In 71/691. Kennedy, 99; Shaban, *History*, 115.
8. Shaban, *History*, 139.
9. Wellhausen, *Kingdom*, 232–49, 313–19; Shaban, *History*, 110–11, 136.
10. Wellhausen, *Kingdom*, 248–49.
11. Ṭabarī, I, 2934–36.
12. Wellhausen, *Kingdom*, 70. Note especially the case of the Numayr, who had divisions in Qinnasrīn in Syria, in al-Baṣra, and in Khurāsān, but always stuck together. The close connections of the great Khurāsāni Muḍarī leader Naṣr b. Sayyār with the family of Mālik b. Sāriya al-Numayrī is especially notable in showing how the Muḍarī Syrians got along fine with the original Muḍarīs in Khurāsān. See Ṭabarī, II, 1473, 1583, 1590, 1721, 1723, 1991, 1994–95; Ibn Ḥazm, 279; Blankinship, "al-ʻArab fī Khurāsān," 88–90.
13. Blankinship, "Tribal Factor," 589–601.
14. Wellhausen, *Kingdom*, 278–79, 294, 308–09; Shaban, *History*, 168–71.
15. Ṭabarī, II, 1507–09.
16. Ṭabarī, II, 1290–91, 1354.
17. For examples, see Ibn al-Athīr, *Kāmil*, V, 402; Ṭabarī, II, 1605 (Jabala b. Abī Rawwād, the *mawlā* of the ʻAtīk), 1661, 1995 (al-Bakhtarī b. Mujāhid, the *mawlā* of the Shaybān), 1998 (Muqātil b. Ḥayyān al-Nabaṭī, the *mawlā* of the Shaybān).
18. Shaban, *History*, 178–79, 184.
19. *Akhbār majmūʻa*, 42; Ibn ʻIdhāri, II, 30.
20. Arabic names such as Maysara, Khālid b. Ḥumayd, and Ṣāliḥ b. Ṭarīf. Ibn ʻIdhāri, I, 52–57.
21. Hishām was surrounded by *mawlā* ministers and assistants. Other

mawālī held important posts elsewhere, even governorships. Ibn Khayyāṭ, *Ta'rīkh*, 539–40, 545–46, 556; Jahshiyārī, 60–62, 64–67.

22. Ṭabarī, II, 1986; Ya'qūbī, *Ta'rīkh*, II, 391–92; Wellhausen, *Kingdom*, 338–39, 499–500.

23. This particular point is adequately documented by Crone and Hinds, 4–11.

24. Wellhausen, *Factions*, 20.

25. Crone and Hinds, 129–32.

26. Indeed, Wellhausen, *Factions*, 22, even states, "The religion of the Khawārij is certainly political."

27. *'Uyūn wa ḥadā'iq*, 41–46.

28. Ṭabarī, II, 1622–23.

29. On the role of 'Ikrima, the Berber *mawlā* of Ibn 'Abbās, see Ibn Ḥajar, *Tahdhīb*, VII, 267, 269, 271; Dhahabī, *Siyar*, V, 15, 20–22, 27, 30, 33, *Ta'rīkh*, IV, 158–60.

30. Wellhausen, *Factions*, 21.

31. For his program, see Ṭabarī, II, 1687.

32. For the program of Yazīd III, see Ṭabarī, II, 1834–35.

33. Isbahānī, *Maqātil*, 92.

34. Ṭabarī, II, 1680–81, 1685, 1699–1709; Iṣbahānī, *Maqātil*, 92–96, 99–101.

35. In the case of Iran, the battles of al-Qādisiyya (16/637) and Nihāwand (19–21/640–42) were decisive. Balādhurī, *Futūḥ*, 314, 316–18, 374; Donner, 204–05. In that of Byzantium's Near Eastern provinces: al-Yarmūk (15/636). Balādhurī, *Futūḥ*, 160, 162; Donner, 133–35, 142, 144–45. In that of Gothic Spain: al-Buḥayra and Istija (92/711). *Akhbār majmū'a*, 18–19; Balādhurī, *Futūḥ*, 273; *Continuatio*, 352. In that of Sind: Rāwar (93/713). Balādhurī, *Futūḥ*, 536–37; Pathan, 45–46. It is notable that in the cases of both Spain and Sind, resistance tended to collapse as soon as the enemy's king was slain.

36. *Historical Atlas of South Asia*, 31; Majumdar, 150, 156–57, 173.

37. In fact, these mountain fastnesses hardly entered into the greater stategic equation at all. Mostly they had been bypassed by the original conquerors owing to the uninviting roughness of the terrain and the poverty of their inhabitants. Such areas included part of Asturias in Spain, Zābulistān and Ghūr in Afghanistan, areas that remain harsh enough to outsiders even in the late twentieth century, Ṭabaristān by the Caspian, and occasionally parts of Armenia and Georgia. The peoples of each of these areas had harshly handled one or more Umayyad armies when attacked, but constituted little threat to the anyone outside of their own upland territories and could thus be ignored by the caliphate. Balādhurī, *Futūḥ*, 411–12, 489–93; *Akhbār majmū'a*, 34, 61; Toumanoff, 400 n. 42, 405.

38. This is, however, an exception of vital significance.

39. Its impregnability is noted in Ibn A'tham, VII, 194.

40. Theophanes, 64.

41. Byzantine land expeditions into Syria for the rest of Umayyad times are recorded only for 82/701 and 128/746. Theophanes, 69, 112.

42. Gabrieli, 86, n. 1, quite properly lays great emphasis on this point, going so far as to say that the conquest of Constantinople at that time was materially impossible owing to the Muslims' bases being so far away in Syria and Mesopotamia.

43. Ṭabarī, II, 1315–17, 1346; Ya'qūbī, *Ta'rīkh,* II, 359–61, 363; Ibn Kathīr, *Bidāya,* IX, 174, 184; *'Uyūn wa ḥadā'iq,* 30, 32–33, 39; Theophanes, 88–91; Michael, II, 485–6; Guilland, 129; Kaegi, xvi, 44.

44. This appears to have been the case, as the Byzantine fleet retired to the Golden Horn. Theophanes, 89.

45. Theophanes, 89.

46. Theophanes, 88–89, 91, alleges only five Muslim ships escaped out of 2,460! Michael the Syrian records five thousand as the number of ships in the Muslim fleet. Michael, II, 484. However that may be, the magnitude of the Muslim naval debacle is suggested by the reticence of the Muslim sources to speak about naval actions and the failure of the Muslim writers to make any mention of their naval commanders mentioned by Theophanes. Guilland, 121, 124. Also, the only Byzantine retaliation was the seaborne raids on al-Lādhiqiyya in Syria in 100/719 and Tinnīs in Egypt in 101–02/720–21. Balādhurī, *Futūḥ,* 157; Kindī, 70; Maqrīzī, *Khiṭaṭ,* I, 177.

47. Lewond, 54–70; Dasxuranci, 207–09; Ibn Khayyāṭ, *Ta'rīkh,* 378–79, 393, 399, 403, 409–10, 416, 426, 431.

48. Dunlop, 7, 22, 25, 37, n. 29; Chavannes, *Documents,* 4.

49. Theophanes, 70, 72, 75–76, 101; Dunlop, 45.

50. Dunlop, 170.

51. Dunlop, 59–60. For example, the Muslims are said to have attacked the Turks at Bāb in 88/707 and 90/709 or 91/710. Ibn Khayyāṭ, *Ta'rīkh,* 403; *'Uyūn wa ḥadā'iq,* 3, 6.

52. Ibn Khayyāṭ, *Ta'rīkh,* 409; Dasxuranci, 209; Lewond, 69–70, offering three dates 95–97/714–16. Theophanes, however, has Maslama elsewhere engaged except in 96/715 (pp. 80–81). The Armenian versions suggest a doublet of his later campaign to al-Bāb in 113/731, but the fact that both Muslim and Christian writers report Maslama's role here suggests that it is factual.

53. Theophanes, 70.

54. Golden, 62.

55. Chavannes, *Documents,* 44, 81.

56. Chavannes, *Documents,* 34, 44, 284–85.

57. Chavannes, *Documents,* 45, 78, 81–82, 284–85.

58. Ṭabarī, II, 1421–28; Gibb, 61.

59. Appeals were sent by the princes of Bukhārā, al-Qūmidh, and Samarqand. Chavannes, *Documents*, 203–05.

60. Balādhurī, *Futūḥ*, 489–93.

61. The Zunbīl sarcastically commented that the Muslims had lost their fighting qualities and grown lazy. Balādhurī, *Futūḥ*, 493.

62. Until the time of al-Ma'mūn. Balādhurī, *Futūḥ*, 495.

63. For these kingdoms in general, see *Historical Atlas of South Asia*, 26, 28, 31, 33; Vaidya, I, 48–57 (Hsüan-tsang's list).

64. For example, on the sources for the Chalukyas, see Dikshit, 6–13, for Yasorvarman of Kanauj, see Mishra, 21–35.

65. Mishra, 57–58; Majumdar, III, 132–36.

66. See especially the scholarly monograph on Yasovarman by Mishra, 61–103, 117, 146–51. See also Tripathi, 188–208, 211–12; Majumdar, III, 128–31; Dikshit, 153.

67. Mishra, 45–46; Majumdar, III, 153–55.

68. Mishra, 46–47; Majumdar, IV, 19–21.

69. Mishra, 47–48; Majumdar, III, 161–62.

70. Mishra, 48; Majumdar, III, 157–60.

71. Majumdar, III, 154.

72. Mishra, 47; Majumdar, III, 162–63.

73. Mishra, 49–50, 53–54; Majumdar, III, 147–52.

74. Majumdar, IV, 98.

75. Majumdar, III, 161.

76. Mishra, 48–50; Majumdar, III, 155–7.

77. Mishra, 50–53; Majumdar, III, 246–47; Dikshit, 192.

78. Majumdar, III, 227, 246–7; Dikshit, 1–2, 190–3.

79. Majumdar, IV, 1–2; Dikshit, 186–87.

80. Archibald Lewis, 3–4, 12–13; Bord, 189–99; Lot, *Naissance*, 211.

81. The governor was al-Samḥ b. Mālik al-Khawlānī. *Continuatio*, 358; Ibn 'Idhāri, II, 26; Maqqarī, I, 235; III, 15; Ṭaha, 188; Arslān, 95–96. *Akhbār Majmū'a*, 31, wrongly states that al-Samḥ was dismissed from office rather than killed. Arslān, 69, 88, indicates that Odo had occupied Septimania first, thus giving provocation for the Muslim attack on Toulouse, but this is disproven by the sources and also Collins, 87, who emphasize that the Aquitainians were taken unprepared. There does not seem to be much evidence about when Septimania was lost to Gothic rule, but coins from the Narbonne mint record a Visigothic king Achila as late as c. 91–94/710–13. Collins, 32, 231.

82. Ibn 'Abd al-Ḥakam, *Futūḥ*, 213; Ibn 'Idhāri, I, 48; Ibn Khayyāṭ, *Ta'rīkh*, 466; 'Abd al-Ḥamīd, 264–66.

83. Ibn Khallikān, VI, 311; Ibn 'Idhāri, I, 48; Ibn 'Abd al-Ḥakam, *Futūḥ*, 213–14; Balādhurī, *Futūḥ*, 273–74.

84. Ibn 'Abd al-Ḥakam, *Futūḥ*, 188–89; Balādhurī, *Futūḥ*, 280–81;

Ṭabarī, I, 2593. Ibn Khayyāṭ, *Ta'rīkh*, 138, and Cuoq, 24–25, mention the original truce under the year 20/641, which is too early.

85. Ṭabarī, I, 2593.

86. Balādhurī, *Futūḥ*, 280–81.

87. Now flooded by the High Dam Lake.

88. Dombrowski, 55; Trimingham, 46.

89. Wāqidī, 983.

90. Ya'qūbī, *Ta'rīkh*, II, 178–79; Ṭabarī, I, 2595; Ibn al-Athīr, *Kāmil*, II, 569. According to Ibn al-Athīr, *Kāmil*, II, 497, 501, 536, 'Alqama participated in the conquest of Palestine, was settled in Jerusalem, and was governor of the province. His expedition against Abyssinia would then have sailed from Ayla on the Gulf of 'Aqaba.

91. Cuoq, 36–37; Trimingham, 46–47.

Chapter 6

1. Gabrieli, 85, adds the front's religious significance, owing to the clear division between Muslim and non-Muslim lands on it.

2. The terms 'left' and 'right' expeditions are first encountered in reference to the campaigns of 104/723. 'Uthmān, II, 100.

3. Ibn Khayyāṭ, *Ta'rīkh*, 475, 481. There is no evidence that Marwān b. Muḥammad, the governor of the Jazīran superprovince, ever led the summer expedition of the left.

4. Balādhurī, *Futūḥ*, 193.

5. Ibn Khurdādhbih, 105–08, names only five places in Anatolia surviving in his time as cities: Nikaia, Ephesos, Amorion, Ankyra, and Sarmalia. However, it is possible that he uses the term for city (*madīna*) loosely. See also Mango, 69, 71–73; Haldon, 92–124, both of whom emphasize the deurbanization of Anatolia.

6. Ibn Khurdādhbih, 105–08; Mango, 73.

7. Al-Ṭabarī puts this in 103/721. Al-Ya'qūbī adds a raid by an unidentified al-Walīd b. Hishām which took al-Makhāḍa (the ford) near Antioch. This may be a confusion with or a part of al-'Abbās's campaign. Ibn Khayyāṭ, *Ta'rīkh*, 473; Ya'qūbī, *Ta'rīkh*, II, 378; Ṭabarī, II, 1437; Agapius, *PO*, VIII, 505; Ibn al-Athīr, *Kāmil*, V, 101. Ibn Taghrībirdī, I, 251–52, records al-'Abbās' campaign under the year 103. Thebasa is to be identified from the map in Lilie facing p. 187. See also Ramsay, 339–41.

8. Ya'qūbī gives 'Abd al-Raḥmān b. Salīm al-Kalbī as leader of the summer expedition of 103/721 instead of Marwān. Ibn Khayyāṭ, *Ta'rīkh*, 475; Ya'qūbī, *Ta'rīkh*, II, 378; Elias, 163; Lilie, 145. Ibn al-Athīr, *Kāmil*, V, 105, repeats al-'Abbās's conquest of Dabasa of the previous year, no doubt a doublet.

9. Arabic Sībura, ancient Severias, in Armenia I north of Kaisareia Mazaka. Van der Meer and Mohrmann, map 16a.

10. Qaysara is unidentified. Ibn Khayyāṭ, *Ta'rīkh*, 478; Ya'qūbī, *Ta'rīkh*, II, 378. Lilie, 145, reverses the positions of 'Uthmān and 'Abd al-Raḥmān given by al-Ya'qūbī.

11. The earlier sources, however, omit all mention of this expedition. Ibn al-Athīr, *Kāmil*, V, 125; Lilie, 145. 'Uthmān, II, 100, states that this expedition was to prevent the Byzantines from exploiting the Khazar onslaught in the Caucasus.

12. *Chronicon ad 1234*, 309, is the only source which dates this raid and also states that it left Kilikia devastated, which would plausibly connect it with his earlier raids in 102–03/721–22. Michael, II, 489, also mentions this raid, but without a date, while Agapius, *PO*, VIII, 504, is rather muddled, though his text seems to imply al-'Abbās reached Paphlagonia. See also Lilie, 145.

13. As the Syrians in the expedition were commanded by Sa'īd b. Hishām, and as Marwān is specifically named Hishām's governor, the expedition must have taken place after Hishām ascended the throne in Sha'bān 105/January 724. Ibn Khayyāṭ, *Ta'rīkh*, 481; *'Uyūn wa ḥadā'iq*, 89; Ibn Taghrībirdī, I, 254; Brooks, 198; Le Strange, *Lands*, 118; Lilie, 145–46.

14. Sa'īd lost a whole raiding party of one thousand men. Ibn Khayyāṭ, *Ta'rīkh*, 491; Ya'qūbī, *Ta'rīkh*, II, 378; *'Uyūn wa ḥadā'iq*, 89; Theophanes, 95; Ibn al-Athīr, *Kāmil*, V, 134; Lilie, 145–46. Ibn Taghrībirdī, I, 254, reports only success. Although Ṭabarī, II, 1462, 1472, reports two expeditions by Sa'īd, in 105 and 106, it is likely that it is a doublet of the same expedition, which may have been underway in both years, as the lunar year division then fell at the beginning of the summer.

15. Agapius, *PO*, VIII, 505.

16. Ya'qūbī, *Ta'rīkh*, II, 394. However, 'Uthmān, II, 101, suggests that Mu'āwiya commanded the left flank expedition in 106/724, while Sa'īd commanded that of the right.

17. Ibn Khayyāṭ's *Arūliya* should be emended to *Darūliya* (Dorylaion). Ibn Khayyāṭ, *Ta'rīkh*, 492–93; Ya'qūbī, *Ta'rīkh*, II, 394; Ṭabarī, II, 1472, 1487–88; Azdī, 26; *'Uyūn wa ḥadā'iq*, 89; Ibn Taghrībirdī, I, 261; Theophanes, 96; Agapius, *PO*, VIII, 506; Elias, 164; *Chronicon ad 1234*, 309; Ibn Khurdādhbih, 102–03, 109, 113. According to pseudo-Dionysius, 24, the Jews betrayed Kaisareia to the Muslims, and Maslama enslaved the Christians there but took the Jews with him to safety when he retreated. Agapius and *Chronicon ad 1234* state that the Kaisareia taken was Neokaisareia Pontika, now Turkish Niksar, far to the north, but this is scarcely creditable in view of both Theophanes and the Muslim sources specifying Kappadokian Kaisareia.

18. Al-Ṭabarī and Ibn Taghrībirdī date Maslama's capture of Kaisareia to this year, but as Ibn Khayyāṭ gives the exact date and is generally more

detailed and reliable, his dating of Kaisareia's fall to the previous year is perhaps more accurate. Ibn Khayyāṭ, *Ta'rīkh*, 494; Ya'qūbī, *Ta'rīkh*, II, 394–95; Ṭabarī, II, 1491; Ibn Taghrībirdī, I, 262; Lilie, 146.

19. Agapius, *PO*, VIII, 506; Elias, 164; *Chronicon ad 1234*, 309.

20. That Theophanes, 97, has 'Amr as the name of the commander suggests that al-Baṭṭāl's personal name was indeed 'Amr. 'Abd Allāh could be simply an honorific, as in its being prefixed to 'Abd al-Malik's name in the Dome of the Rock.

21. Ṭayba or al-Ṭayna of the Arabic sources might be read as Ṭataya, which Conrad, 8, identifies with the ancient Tataion as well as with Theophanes' Ateous. The fall of Ateous/Ṭataya can be dated between Jumādā I 109/September 727 and Dhū al-Ḥijja 109/March–April 728, with a date in the early fall most likely. Ibn Khayyāṭ, *Ta'rīkh*, 495–96; Ya'qūbī, *Ta'rīkh*, II, 395; Ṭabarī, II, 1495; Azdī, 28; Ibn al-Athīr, *Kāmila*, V, 145; Ibn Taghrībirdī, I, 262, 266–67; Nikephoros, 128–29; Theophanes, 97–98; Michael, II, 501; Agapius, *PO*, VIII, 507; *Chronicon ad 1234*, 310; EI^2, s. v. al-Baṭṭāl, 'Abd Allāh; Lilie, 147; Ramsay, 439; Pauly-Wissowa, 2nd ser., VIII, 2462 (Tataion). Khanjara=Janjara is to be identified with Gangra, though Ibn Khayyāṭ and Ibn Taghrībirdī both put its fall in the previous year. This only means it fell before the beginning of the year 109 on 28 April 727. Gabrieli, 87, casts doubt on the expedition to Nikaia, claiming the supposed silence of the Muslim sources, but the Muslims often do not record their failures.

22. Al-'Aṭāsīn is also given in an itinerary in Ibn Khurdādhbih, 103, so that it can scarcely be a simple error. This itinerary reveals it as lying near Nakoleia on the northern road around the Anatolian plain and thus in Phrygia. See Ibn Khayyāṭ, *Ta'rīkh*, 496. It is not impossible that Ateous, Ṭayba, and al-Ṭayna of the various texts could also be identified with at 'Aṭāsīn, rather than Tataion, but the latter identification of Ateous seems best on linguistic grounds. Pauly-Wissowa, 2nd ser., VIII, 2462.

23. Ṭabarī, II, 1495; Lilie, 147.

24. *Al-'Uyūn wa al-ḥadā'iq* has al-Baṭṭāl in charge of Mu'āwiya's vanguard, but this may be a confusion with his role in 108/726, as this source is not very precise. Ibn Khayyāṭ, *Ta'rīkh*, 497; Ṭabarī, II, 1506; *'Uyūn wa ḥadā'iq*, 90; Ibn Taghrībirdī, I, 267; Lilie, 148. Ṣamāluh is Semalouos in the Armeniakon theme southeast of Ankara. See Lilie, map opposite p. 187.

25. Ṭabarī, II, 1507. These names emphasize the Egyptian character of the navy.

26. Ibn Khayyāṭ, *Ta'rīkh*, 500–01; Ya'qūbī, *Ta'rīkh*, II, 395; Ṭabarī, II, 1526; Ibn Taghrībirdī, I, 270; Lilie, 148.

27. Ṭabarī, II, 1526; Ibn Taghrībirdī, I, 270; Ibn Ḥajar, *Tahdhīb*, VI, 26. Al-Ṭabarī also makes al-Ḥakam b. Qays b. Makhrama commander of all the men of Syria and Egypt, perhaps meaning the land forces carried in Ibn Abī Maryam's fleet.

28. This is exactly the course allegedly suggested by Mūsā b. Nuṣayr to Sulaymān b. 'Abd al-Malik before the ill-fated siege of Constantinople. Dhahabī, *Siyar*, IV, 501.

29. The commander is called Thubayt al-Bahrānī in all the sources except Ibn Khayyāṭ and al-Balādhurī, but as Thubayt reappears later whereas the disgraced Mi'laq does not, it would seem that Ibn Khayyāṭ's and al-Balādhurī's version is the right one. There were also Jazīrans present in Mi'laq's army, however. The Khazars are reported to have been thirty thousand strong and to have overrun the Muslims' camp, routing the Muslim army all the way back to Syria. Nevertheless, the commander denied cowardice before the caliph, which shows that the Muslim generals viewed the Khazars as a very formidable enemy. Ibn Khayyāṭ, *Ta'rīkh*, 475, 485; Balādhurī, *Futūḥ*, 243; Ibn A'tham, VIII, 26, 28–29; Ibn al-Athīr, *Kāmil*, V, 110–11; Ibn al-Kalbī, II, 407; Dunlop, 62. However, Ṭabarī, II, 1437, Ya'qūbī, *Ta'rīkh*, II, 378, and Ibn Taghrībirdī, I, 251 scarcely notice the campaign, avoiding all mention of the Muslims' defeat.

30. Ibn al-Athīr claims the total of Muslim troops at Balanjar was thirty thousand, which appears to be an exaggeration of the figures in Ibn A'tham. The claim that each horseman received three hundred dinars in booty may also be exaggerated, as Dunlop hints, but it should be remembered that the horsemen were only a minority of the army and that their shares were much larger than the infantry's. Ibn Khayyāṭ, *Ta'rīkh*, 477–78; Ibn A'tham, VIII, 29–34; Ibn al-Athīr, *Kāmil*, V, 111–13, 125; Ibn Taghrībirdī, I, 253; Dunlop, 62–65. Perhaps it was in the wake of this campaign that al-Jarrāḥ ravaged Ghūmīk and settled prisoners from Khamzīn farther south in Khaydhān. Balādhurī, *Futūḥ*, 243.

31. In fact, the mountain princes (*mulūk al-jibāl*) are actually said to have revolted, threatening to cut off al-Jarrāḥ's possible route of retreat. The sources other than Ibn Khayyāṭ give Shakkī or Rustāq Millī as the place where al-Jarrāḥ wintered. Ibn Khayyāṭ, *Ta'rīkh*, 478; Balādhurī, *Futūḥ*, 243; Ibn A'tham, VIII, 34–35; Ibn al-Athīr, *Kāmil*, V, 113; *Chronicon ad 1234*, 309; Dunlop, 66. Elias, 163, makes Shakka (Shakkī) the major conquest of the campaign.

32. Ibn Khayyāṭ, *Ta'rīkh*, 480; Ya'qūbī, *Ta'rīkh*, II, 378; Ṭabarī, II, 1462; Azdī, 17; Ibn al-Athīr, *Kāmil*, V, 125. The chronology of these campaigns through 105/723 is somewhat confused because for a number of years until then the summer campaigning season spread over parts of two different Islamic lunar years, as the year's end then fell in midsummer. I have tried to assign a distnct campaign to each summer season, which leaves a problem only if we assume that the fall of Balanjar must have been in the summer immediately preceding Hishām's enthronement. This is implied but not necessitated by the sources, which are in any case hazy on chronology at this point. See Ibn al-Athīr, *Kāmil*, V, 113; Ibn A'tham, VIII, 35,38.

33. Ibn Khayyāṭ, *Ta'rīkh*, 480; Azdī, 22; Ibn Taghrībirdī, I, 254.

34. Balādhurī, *Futūḥ*, 239.

35. *Histoire de la Géorgie*, I, 258. However, Theophanes, 85, reports the Muslim conquest of Abasgia, Lazika, and Iberia under 98/716–17. Probably a number of expeditions, none of them finally decisive, took place, but Muslim control gradually increased.

36. An Iranian people, the Alans belonged to the same language group and occupied the same terrritory as the modern Ossetians, north and south of the Darial Pass. Presumably the Ossetian nationality is thus derived from the Alans.

37. Al-Balādhurī's and Ibn A'tham's accounts have lost the events of 105–11/724–29 through telescoping. Al-Ṭabarī incongruously attributes the campaign of 106/724 to al-Ḥajjāj b. 'Abd al-Malik, but this is unlikely, as we know that al-Jarrāḥ was the governor at this period. It is also unlikely that a brother of 'Abd al-Malik would serve as a subordinate commander for a general not of the Umayyad house. It is worth noting that the names al-Ḥajjāj and al-Jarrāḥ could easily be confused in the Arabic script. Ibn Khayyāṭ, *Ta'rīkh*, 490; Balādhurī, *Futūḥ*, 243; Ya'qūbī, *Ta'rīkh*, II, 394; Ibn A'tham, VIII, 35, 38; Ṭabarī, II, 1472; Ibn al-Athīr, *Kāmil*, V, 113, 134; Dunlop, 66–67. Azdī, 22, says he attacked Khazaria. Ibn Taghrībirdī, I, 254, misplaces this campaign under the year 105.

38. Ibn Khayyāṭ, *Ta'rīkh*, 492; Azdi, 25; Ibn al-Athīr, *Kāmil*, V, 137.

39. Ibn Khayyāṭ, *Ta'rīkh*, 492; Azdi, 25; Ibn al-Athīr, *Kāmil*, V, 137–38.

40. Balādhurī, *Futūḥ*, 243; Azdī, 25, gives the latter as Khasdān.

41. Lewond, 106–07; Dasxurançi, 209; Laurent, 159 n 1; Grousset, 315.

42. Evidence for these will be presented in the section below devoted to each area.

43. Ibn Khayyāṭ and al-Azdī report that al-Ḥārith was slain in the battle, but he reappears later in several other sources. Ibn Khayyāṭ, *Ta'rīkh*, 494; Azdī, 27; Ibn al-Athīr, *Kāmil*, V, 140–41; Dunlop, 67.

44. Ibn Khayyāṭ, *Ta'rīkh*, 496; Azdī, 29; Ibn al-Athīr, *Kāmil*, V, 145; Elias, 164; Dunlop, 67–68.

45. The campaign of 110/728 was even called 'the mud campaign.' Ibn Khayyāṭ, *Ta'rīkh*, 497; Ya'qūbī, *Ta'rīkh*, II, 395; Ṭabarī, II, 1506, 1526; Ibn al-Athīr, *Kāmil*, V, 155, 158; Ibn Taghrībirdī, I, 267, 270; *Chronicon ad 846*, 235; Elias, 165; Michael, II, 501; *Chronicon ad 1234*, 310; Dunlop, 68. It is probably the disaster referred to by Agapius, *PO*, VIII, 507.

46. Ṭabarī, II, 1421, 1439; Gibb, 61.

47. Ṭabarī, II, 1421–28.

48. Ṭabarī, II, 1438–49; Gibb, 61–64.

49. Ṭabarī, II, 1453–55; Shaban, *Revolution*, 102. Although Ibn A'tham, VIII, 27, says the caliphal fifth was forwarded to Yazid II, the more detailed

text of al-Ṭabarī makes certain that displeasure with the amounts being received was a major factor in Sa'īd's removal.

50. Ṭabarī, II, 1478. This is quite apart from the initial refusal of still others to campaign, which led to a violent clash at al-Barūqān to force them into the field. Ṭabarī, II, 1473–77.

51. Balādhurī, *Futūḥ*, 525–26; Ya'qūbī, *Ta'rīkh*, II, 374; Ṭabarī, II, 1478–79. The whole of the Farghāna Valley is only about 310 km. in length from Khujanda to modern Jalālābād in Kyrgyzstan. Since the Muslims were said to be besieging the Farghānan capital, presumably they were not much more than 150 km. from the fords in the Jaxartes they had to cross. That it took them eight days to complete their flight shows how much their progress was impeded by the Turks.

52. Balādhurī, *Futūḥ*, 525–26; Ya'qūbī, *Ta'rīkh*, II, 374; Ṭabarī, II, 1478–81, 1485.

53. Gibb, 65–6; Shaban, *Revolution*, 106.

54. Ṭabarī, II, 1489, 1493, 1496; Balādhurī, *Futūḥ*, 526. Ṭabarī, II, 1492–94, also reports a campaign in al-Khuttal, but this is partly confused with a campaign there in Asad's second governorship of 117–20/735–38.

55. Ibn A'tham, VIII, 98. This report might, however, be confused with events of his second governorship.

56. Ṭabarī, II, 1485–86, 1497–1501; Balādhurī, *Futūḥ*, 526; Shaban, *Revolution*, 107–08.

57. Shaban calls these Syrian troops, but, as Ashras was a Jazīran commander from a Jazīran tribe, his troops were probably also Jazīrans. There is no reason to believe Ibn A'tham's claim that he was accompanied by a great army, for Ibn A'tham's accounts are often popularized as well as pro-Jazīran. Ibn A'tham, VIII, 99; Shaban, *Revolution*, 109. Contrary to Shaban's statement, these were also not the first Syro-Jazīran troops in Khurāsān, as Ṭabarī, II, 1318, shows the opposite. One of those attested with Ibn al-Muhallab in 98/716–17 was Abū al-Jahm b. Kināna al-Kalbī, who was the cousin of the infamous Syrian general Manṣūr b. Jumhūr and had long served Syrian interests in al-Kūfa, even having served as an executioner for al-Ḥajjāj. Ṭabarī, II, 1020, 1098, 1328.

58. Probably the Muslims also retained control of areas such as al-Tirmidh and al-Ṣaghāniyān, as these were strongly pro-Qaysī places not mentioned as having been lost nor later retaken. Ṭabarī, II, 1504–05, 1507–10; Balādhurī, *Futūḥ*, 526; Wellhausen, *Kingdom*, 456–58; Gibb, 69–70. A letter from the *yabghū* of Ṭukhāristān, south of the Oxus, dating from 109/727 and appealing to the Chinese emperor for aid against the Arabs and asking him to command the *khāqān* also to intervene is translated in Chavannes, *Documents*, 206–07. That the anti-Arab revolt would even spread south of the Oxus to territory that had been firmly in Muslim hands much longer is elo-

quent evidence for the disintegration of the Arab position in Khurāsān's eastern appendages.

59. Ṭabarī, II, 1512–16; Wellhausen, *Kingdom*, 458–59.

60. Ṭabarī, II, 1516–25. Wellhausen, *Kingdom*, 459, is in error regarding the garrison of Kamarja, which was not part of Ashras' army, but was an isolated outpost holding out against the Turks. See Gibb, 71.

61. Ṭabarī, II, 1473–77.

62. Balādhurī, *Futūḥ*, 490–92; Bosworth, 44, 51, 54–55.

63. Bosworth, 58–59.

64. Balādhurī, *Futūḥ*, 493.

65. Balādhurī, *Futūḥ*, 493; Ya'qūbī, *Buldān*, 284.

66. Bosworth, 50–51, 72.

67. *Ta'rīkh-i Sīstān*, 125–26; Ya'qūbī, *Buldān*, 284; Ibn Khayyāṭ, *Ta'rīkh*, 537.

68. Ya'qūbī, *Ta'rīkh*, II, 383.

69. *Ta'rīkh-i Sīstān*, 126; Ibn al-Kalbī, I, 285; Ibn Khayyāṭ, *Ta'rīkh*, 537; Ya'qūbī, *Buldān*, 284, *Ta'rīkh*, II, 383. Regarding the tribal identity of al-Aṣfaḥ, Ibn al-Kalbī's genealogical testimony is decisive in deciding he was a Kalbī, despite the preference of Crone, 146, for a Baṣran Kindī identification for him. The Kindī identification in Ibn Khayyāṭ stems from a confusion of al-Aṣfaḥ's name with that of his Kindī successor, who does not appear in Ibn Khayyāṭ's list of governors. The Shaybanī identification in *Ta'rīkh-i Sīstān* probably owes to a substitution by local transmitters of the Sijistānī historical tradition seeking to glorify their tribal group. The Raba'ī Shaybān were among the earlier settlers of Sijistān, whereas the Syrian Kalb were not. The point is important, for it shows how the caliphate was tending to appoint Syrians as governors everywhere at that time, even in comparatively minor provinces.

70. Arabicization of the Indian Jaisimha. Majumdar, III, 170–72.

71. *Fatḥnāmah-i Sind*, 178.

72. Balādhurī, *Futūḥ*, 540; Ibn al-Athīr, *Kāmil*, IV, 589, V, 54–55, 135.

73. Al-Junayd must have been accompanied by ample military forces in view of his subsequent accomplishments. Ibn Khayyāṭ, *Ta'rīkh*, 464, 472, 484, 538; Balādhurī, *Futūḥ*, 540; Ya'qūbī, *Ta'rīkh*, II, 373; Ibn al-Athīr, *Kāmil*, V, 55, 86. Wellhausen, *Kingdom*, 459, is mistaken in saying that al-Junayd was in India until 111/729–30.

74. Daybul's importance in this period is evidenced by the large congregational mosque dedicated there in 109/727. Panhwar, 150.

75. According to a variant version, it was al-Junayd who attacked Jaysinh first. Balādhurī, *Futūḥ*, 540–41; Ibn al-Athīr, *Kāmil*, IV, 589–90, V, 55, 135; Pathan, 55. Panhwar, 148, points out that Chach would not have tried to go to Iraq had Jaysinh really apostatized, so the claim that he had must be false.

76. Majumdar, III, 172.

77. Balādhurī, *Futūḥ*, 541; Ya'qūbī, *Ta'rīkh*, II, 380.

78. Identifying al-Kīraj is a serious problem, for the sources are equivocal. *Fatḥnāmah-i Sind*, 166, places it near Qaṣṣa, which is Cutch, and therefore probably in Gujarat, while p. 122 includes it in a list with Baylamān in southern Rajasthan and Cambay in Gujarat. Also, al-Junayd's campaigns could be geographically more compressed if al-Kīraj is also placed in Gujarat like his other campaigns. On the other hand, Jaysinh fled from the Arabs to Chitor, then sent his helper Muḥammad al-'Ilāfī ahead to Punjab and Kashmir, presumably to seek asylum for him. Following this, Jaysinh journeys to al-Kīraj, then to Jullundur and the border of Kashmir. *Fatḥnāmah-i Sind*, 153–54, 174, 178. If al-Kīraj is in Gujarat, as suggested by the editor of *Fatḥnāmah-i Sind*, English notes, pp. 123–24, it becomes difficult to explain why Jaysinh sent al-'Ilāfī to Kashmir and then indeed followed himself, or how the harried prince could have gone from the region of Cambay to Jullundur with no intervening stages. Besides this, Ya'qūbī, *Ta'rīkh*, II, 379, recording the expedition of al-Junayd against al-Kīraj, reports the presence of the king of Kashmir, Chandrapīda, and gives his correct name, as verified by Indian and Chinese sources. This means either that al-Junayd persuaded the king of Kashmir to join him on an expedition near to his kingdom or else summoned him from a distance of over a thousand km. to campaign in Gujarat, trusting him not to ravage the Muslim province of Sind on the way. Such a possibility seems improbable, so that a northern location for al-Kīraj, if not necessarily Kangra, seems far more probable. According to Cunningham, 79, Kīra is a name for the valleys of Kashmir.

79. Balādhurī, *Futūḥ*, 539; *Fatḥnāmah-i Sind*, 185.

80. *Fatḥnāmah-i Sind*, 178.

81. Al-Junayd was accompanied by Chandrāpīda, the king of Kashmir (reigned at least 94–106/713–24), and his forces. Balādhurī, *Futūḥ*, 541; Ya'qūbī, *Ta'rīkh*, II, 379–80; Ibn al-Athīr, *Kāmil*, IV, 590, V, 135; Majumdar, III, 132–33, 173, IV, 244; Tripathi, 196; Vaidya, I, 236, 240.

82. Balādhurī, *Futūḥ*, 539; *Fatḥnāmah-i Sind*, 122, mentions earlier acceptance of Islam, including payment of tribute, by certain princes, including those of Cambay and Baylamān in Gujarat and southern Rajasthan.

83. Balādhurī, *Futūḥ*, 541; Ya'qūbī, *Ta'rīkh*, II, 380; Ibn al-Athīr, *Kāmil*, IV, 590, V, 135; Majumdar, III, 150–55, 161–62, 172; Tripathi, 227; *Historical Atlas of South Asia*, 33.

84. Majumdar, III, 150–52, 154–55, 157, 158–59, 162.

85. Balādhurī, *Futūḥ*, 541; Ya'qūbī, *Ta'rīkh*, II, 380; Ibn al-Athīr, *Kāmil*, IV, 590.

86. Panhwar, 150; Pathan, 112, citing *Fatḥnāmah-i Sind* for the statement that the ruler of Cutch actively helped Muḥammad b. al-Qāsim in the

original conquest of Sind. It seems that he is referring to the ruler of Bīt, an island in the Indus delta near Cutch. *Fatḥnāmah-i Sind*, 94, 98–99, 101, 105, 108, 110, 114, 117–18, 120, 124–26, 130, 136, 153, 155, 163. The same family are called rulers of Cutch in Balādhurī, *Futūḥ*, 536. Perhaps *Bīt* is etymologically related to *Mīdh* or *Med*, the name for the fierce seafarers from Cutch who may have assisted the later Muslim campaigns in Gujarat.

87. Ya'qūbī, *Ta'rīkh*, II, 380.

88. Balādhurī, *Futūḥ*, 541; Ibn al-Athīr, *Kāmil*, IV, 590.

89. Ya'qūbī, *Ta'rīkh*, II, 380.

90. Jarīr, 51; Balādhurī, *Futūḥ*, 541–42; Ṭabarī, II, 1565.

91. The cost is demonstrated both by the original sixty million–dirham price of the original invasion of Sind by Muḥammad b. al-Qāsim as well as by the attested later reluctance of troops to serve in India. Balādhurī, *Futūḥ*, 538, 542; Ṭabarī, II, 1624.

92. Ya'qūbī, *Ta'rīkh*, II, 379.

93. Ibn 'Abd al-Ḥakam, *Futūḥ*, 189. Balādurī, *Futūḥ*, 282, mentions only a later pact made by al-Mutawakkil with the Buja after an expedition in 241/855.

94. E.g., Sāwīrus, *PO*, V, 48–52, 54–62, 64–65, 67–73, 75–79, covering the years 96–112/705–30. Note however the praise lavished by Sāwīrus, *PO*, V, 73–74, on Hishām b. 'Abd al-Malik, despite his denunciation of Hishām's governors.

95. Places named as rebelling include Banā, Ṣā, Samannūd, Tanū, Tumayy, Qurbayṭ, Ṭurābiya, and all of al-Ḥawf al-Sharqī, which is the eastern edge of the Delta. Thus, the revolt was limited in scope. Kindī, 73–74; Ibn Taghrībirdī, I, 259; Maqrīzī, *Khiṭaṭ*, I, 79, II, 261; Sāwīrus, *PO*, V, 76, the only source to mention forced labor, also states that 'Ubayd Allāh doubled the taxes, but this is probably exaggerated.

96. Sāwīrus, *PO*, V, 86. However, this report may be merely a doublet of the original tax raise.

97. Kindī, 76–77.

98. Ibn Khayyāṭ, *Ta'rīkh*, 471–72; Ya'qūbī, *Ta'rīkh*, II, 376; Ibn 'Abd al-Ḥakam, *Futūḥ*, 213–14; Raqīq, 99–101; Ibn 'Iḍhārī, I, 48; Ibn Khallikān, VI, 309–11; 'Abd al-Ḥamīd, 267–68.

99. These include specifically Tripoli, Sabrat, and Sirt in Libya, al-Qayrawān, Qābis, and Tūnis in Tunisia, and Tangier and Ceuta in Morocco. Ibn 'Abd al-Ḥakam, *Futūḥ*, 205, 215–19, 221–25.

100. Including Tilimsān in Algeria. Ibn 'Abd al-Ḥakam, *Futūḥ*, 218.

101. Raqīq, 69–70; Ibn 'Idhārī, I, 48; 'Abd al-Ḥamīd, 265–66.

102. 'Ikrima's opposition to the Umayyads is demonstrated not only by his reputation for Khārijism but also by the fact that he died in hiding from the governor of the Ḥijāz. Ibn Ḥajar, *Tahdhīb*, VII, 267, 269, 271; Dhahabī, *Siyar*, V, 15, 20–2, 27, 30, 33, *Ta'rīkh*, IV, 158–60. Schacht's suggestion in

EI[2], s. v. 'Ikrima, that 'Ikrima traveled widely but not to North Africa seems only an unsupported speculation.

103. Ibn Khayyāṭ, *Ta'rīkh*, 485, 539; Ibn 'Abd al-Ḥakam, *Futūḥ*, 215–16; Ya'qūbī, *Ta'rīkh*, II, 382; Kindī, 72; Raqīq, 102–03; Ibn 'Idhārī, I, 49.

104. Apparently he killed one of Ibn Nuṣayr's sons. Ibn 'Abd al-Ḥakam, *Futūḥ*, 215.

105. Raqīq, 104–05; Ibn 'Idhārī, I, 50.

106. Ibn 'Abd al-Ḥakam, *Futūḥ*, 216–17. In the text, the object is called a *rijl*, or leg, which may be interpreted as a table leg according to the connected story of Solomon's table, which was captured by Ṭāriq b. Ziyād in 94/713. Ṭāriq seems to have broken off an inlaid table-leg (also *rijl*), which he then apparently withheld for himself, so that Mūsā had to have another leg made to replace it. When Mūsā claimed in front of the caliph to have captured Toledo, Ṭāriq was able to produce the leg as evidence in order to refute him. Ibn 'Abd al-Ḥakam, *Futūḥ*, 209; Raqīq, 80, 89; Ibn 'Idhārī, II, 16–18. The recurrence of the word *rijl* to represent gem-studded table-legs in the two stories, coupled with the theme of withholding part of the spoil from the government, suggests a confusion of two stories or a possible doublet. Thus, 'Abd al-Raḥmān here seems to have smashed up a table, forwarding only a leg of it to his superior, who held that the whole table should have been forwarded as part of the *ṣawāfī*. Perhaps when the story was abridged, the word *rijl* was incongruously substituted for *mā'ida*.

107. Finley, *Ancient Sicily*, 155–56, 161–62, 180, 182.

108. In 84/703. 'Abd al-Ḥamīd, 232–34.

109. E.g., in 86/705 (Sicily) and 87/706 (Sardinia). Ibn Khayyāṭ, *Ta'rīkh*, 381, 397.

110. Ibn Khayyāṭ, *Ta'rīkh*, 471.

111. Ibn Khayyāṭ, *Ta'rīkh*, 475.

112. Ibn Khayyāṭ, *Ta'rīkh*, 479.

113. Ibn Khayyāṭ, *Ta'rīkh*, 490.

114. Ibn 'Abd al-Ḥakam, *Futūḥ*, 216; Raqīq, 102; Ibn 'Idhārī, I, 49; 'Abd al-Ḥamīd, 272.

115. Ibn Khayyāṭ, *Ta'rīkh*, 494.

116. Ibn Khayyāṭ, *Ta'rīkh*, 496.

117. Ibn Khayyāṭ, *Ta'rīkh*, 498.

118. Ibn Khayyāṭ, *Ta'rīkh*, 501; Ibn 'Abd al-Ḥakam, *Futūḥ*, 216; Ibn al-Athīr, *Kāmil*, V, 174.

119. *Akhbār majmū'a*, 31, 34; Maqqarī, III, 17; Arslān, 67.

120. Ibn 'Idhārī, II, 26; Ibn Taghrībirdī, I, 251; *Continuatio*, 358; Wolf, 137–38; *Chronicon Moissiacense*, 290; Livermore, 306; Lot, *Naissance*, 102; Archibald Lewis, 21; Taha, 188; Arslān, 95–96; Sālim, 137–38.

121. Wolf, 167; Livermore, 307–09; Ṭaha, 189.

122. *Akhbār majmū'a*, 31, 34; Maqqarī, III, 17.

123. *Continuatio*, 359; Wolf, 139. This indicates another effort to get more income for the state.

124. Ibn 'Idhārī, II, 27.

125. Ibn al-Athīr, *Kāmil*, V, 136; *Chronicon Moissiacense*, 290; Lot, *Naissance*, 102; Archibald Lewis, 21.

126. *Chronicon Moissiacense*, 290.

127. This expedition is said also to have taken many other places, including Lyon and Valence, and to have split north of Autun into two groups which reached as far as Dijon and Sens. *Chronicon Moissiacense*, 291; Lot, *Naissance*, 102; Taha, 190; Sālim, 139. There is an indication in *Continuatio*, 359, of a disorderly retreat. See also Wolf, 140.

128. Ibn al-Athīr, *Kāmil*, V, 136; Ibn 'Idhārī, II, 27; Maqqarī, I, 235, III, 16; Wolf, 140; Ṭaha, 190; Arslān, 113; Aḥmad, 50; Gabrieli, 106. The evidence of *Continuatio*, 359, that he died a natural death cannot be gainsaid.

129. Maqqarī, I, 235, III, 18.

130. *Continuatio*, 359; Wolf, 140; Gabrieli, 106.

131. *Akhbār majmū'a*, 31; Ibn al-Qūṭiyya, 38; Maqqarī, I, 235–36, III, 17–18; Ibn 'Idhārī, II, 27–28; *Continuatio*, 360; Wolf, 141–42.

132. *Continuatio*, 360; Livermore, 311; Arslān, 108–09, 113–14; Sālim, 138.

133. Ṭaha, 190–91.

134. Sālim, 140.

135. The Berber leader's name is variously given as Munnuza, Maqrasha, Maqūsha, or Manūsa, the latter being preferred. *Continuatio*, 361; Ibn 'Idhārī, II, 28; Ibn Khaldūn, IV, 258; Maqqarī, I, 235; Ṭaha, 191–92; Wolf, 142–43.

Chapter 7

1. The only Muslim revolt against Hishām to this point had been that of 'Abbād al-Ru'aynī (or al-Ma'āfirī), who rebelled in Yaman around 106–08/724–26 with only three hundred men. Ṭabarī, II, 1487; Ibn Khayyāṭ, *Ta'rīkh*, 495; Balādhurī, *Ansāb*, Istanbul Ms., II, 263; *'Uyūn wa ḥadā'iq*, 109; Ibn al-Athīr, *Kāmil*, V, 141; Nuwayrī, 435. Curiously, Jarīr, 153–54, has a long polemic against this rebel but hardly ever mentions the massive military efforts going on against the non-Muslim powers.

2. Kindī, 73; *Continuatio*, 359–60.

3. *Ta'rīkh-i Sīstān*, 126; Ya'qūbī, *Ta'rīkh*, II, 383–84.

4. 'Abd Allāh's brother was Khālid's subgovernor of al-Baṣra.

5. Ibn Khayyāṭ, *Ta'rīkh*, 437; *Ta'rīkh-i Sīstān*, 127; Ya'qūbī, *Ta'rīkh*, II, 384.

6. Ṭabarī, II, 1527.

7. The dates of his governorship are unknown, but he followed al-Junayd, who was in office until c. 108/726 and was in office while al-Farazdaq (d. 110/728) was still alive. See next note.

8. Balādhurī, *Futūḥ*, 542; Ya'qūbī, *Ta'rīkh*, II, 380. I do not know what Ṭāṭarī dirhams are. Ṭāṭarā was probably a place in Sind at the mouth of the Indus, probably the same as modern Tatta. Perhaps al-Junayd minted dirhams there for his troops out of the spoils from India. But no such mint is recorded by Walker, and it would be strange if no copies at all had survived. Why this kind of dirham should be singled out for special mention by the literary texts is unclear. See Ibn al-Athīr, *Lubāb*, II, 76; Yāqūt, s. v. Ṭāṭrā; Panhwar, map facing p. 136 and map of Habbārīs, etc., between pp. 184–85.

9. In another version, Tamīm did not know whom to send back, as the poet had only mentioned the soldier's first name in the poem. Therefore, Tamīm sent all the men he had with like names to al-Farazdaq. However, this version is less likely to be the correct one. Farazdaq, 94–95; Balādhurī, *Futūḥ*, 542; Mubarrad, II, 87–88; Iṣbahānī, *Aghānī*, XXV, 8622–23; Ibn Manẓūr, s. v. ḥ-w-b.

10. For the identification of Takkayān with Punjab, see *Historical Atlas of South Asia*, 26, 28; Majumdar, III, 111, 601; IV, 111, 117; Tripathi, 86.

11. *Wa fī ayyām Tamīm kharaj al-Muslimūn 'an bilād al-Hind wa rafaḍū marākizahum falam ya'ūdū ilayhā ilā hādhih al-ghāya*. Balādhurī, *Futūḥ*, 542. This is curiously reminiscent of the refusal of Alexander the Great's troops to go farther into India and their insistence on going home.

12. The date of this disaster is unknown, but may fall around 113/731, if not earlier. Balādhurī, *Futūḥ*, 542; Ya'qūbī, *Ta'rīkh*, II, 380; Ibn al-Athīr, *Kāmil*, IV, 590; Panhwar, 150. Ibn Khayyāṭ, *Ta'rīkh*, 538, states that Tamīm was removed from office.

13. Lewond, 107; Dasxurançi, 209. Dasxurançi and Arabic sources state that this commander was the *khāqān*'s son, but that is unlikely in view of Lewond's information that the *khāqān* had died recently, so that the Khazars were ruled by his widow, perhaps as regent for an infant. The commander's name in Bal'amī is given as Bārjīk or variants thereof, but it would appear that the Armenian is more trustworthy, the initial "b" here perhaps being a mistake for "t" or "th", an easy error in the Arabic script.

14. Ibn al-Athīr, *Kāmil*, V, 159.

15. Lewond, 107, traces the Khazar route in great detail through al-Bāb, down the Caspian coast, and via al-Baylaqān to Ardabīl.

16. Ibn Khayyāṭ, *Ta'rīkh*, 502; Ṭabarī, II, 1530–31; Ibn A'tham, VIII, 38; Azdī, 30, 32; *Histoire de la Géorgie*, I, 257, n. 1; Dunlop, 69–70.

17. Ibn Khayyāṭ, *Ta'rīkh*, 502; Balādhurī, *Futūḥ*, 243; Ṭabarī, II, 1530–31; Ibn A'tham, VIII, 38; Azdī, 32; Lewond, 107; Elias, 165. Theophanes, 98,

records the battle but dates it wrongly, as does Dasxuranḉi, 209–10, and *Chronicon ad 1234*, 309–10.

18. Ibn A'tham, VIII, 41.

19. Agapius, *PO*, VIII, 506. But he has placed the event wrongly in the fourth year of Hishām, i. e., 108–09/726–27.

20. Ibn A'tham, VIII, 39–40.

21. Ibn Khayyāṭ, *Ta'rīkh*, 504; Ṭabarī, II, 1531; Ibn al-Athīr, *Kāmil*, V, 159.

22. Ibn Khayyāṭ, *Ta'rīkh*, 502; Ibn A'tham, VIII, 42.

23. Agapius, *PO*, VIII, 506.

24. Lewond, 107.

25. *Histoire de la Géorgie*, I, 257, n. 1; Lewond, 107.

26. Ibn Khayyāṭ, *Ta'rīkh*, 502; Ibn A'tham, VIII, 42; Azdī, 32; Ibn al-Athīr, *Kāmil*, V, 159; Ibn Taghrībirdī, I, 271; Theophanes, 98.

27. The Khazars besieged the fortress of Ampriotik there. Lewond, 107; *Histoire de la Géorgie*, I, 257, n. 1; Grousset, 316.

28. Balādhurī, *Futūḥ*, 243; Dunlop, 72. Ibn A'tham, VIII, 38, says the Khazars took Warthān and slew its people, but this is uncertain and perhaps improbable, as his account in general is less reliable.

29. Ibn A'tham, VIII, 41–42; Ibn al-Athīr, *Kāmil*, V, 177.

30. The first battle fought by the Muslims and a great victory over the pagans (2/624).

31. Ibn A'tham, VIII, 42–45; Ṭabarī, II, 1531; Azdī, 32; Ibn al-Athīr, *Kāmil*, V, 159–60.

32. *Histoire de la Géorgie*, I, 257, n 1.

33. Ibn A'tham, VIII, 59.

34. Ibn Khayyāṭ, *Ta'rīkh*, 503; Balādhurī, *Futūḥ*, 243; Ya'qūbī, *Ta'rīkh*, II, 381; Ibn A'tham, VIII, 45–58; Azdī, 32; Ibn al-Athīr, *Kāmil*, V, 160–62; Lewond, 107; *Histoire de la Géorgie*, I, 257, n 1; Elias, 165. The various battles fought and rescues of Muslim prisoners achieved by Sa'īd in these sources seem to all go back to a single battle near Bājarwān.

35. Ibn Khayyāṭ, *Ta'rīkh*, 504–05; Balādhurī, *Futūḥ*, 243–44; Ya'qūbī, *Ta'rīkh*, II, 381; Ibn A'tham, VIII, 58–60; *Histoire de la Géorgie*, I, 257, n1; Dunlop, 74–75.

36. Lewond, 108.

37. Those districts named as surrendering include Jurzān (easternmost Georgia), Sharwān, Masqaṭ, Lakz or Layzān, Ṭabarsarān, Fīlān, and Khursān. Some of these may have been submitting to the Muslims for the first time. Ibn Khayyāṭ, *Ta'rīkh*, 505; Balādhurī, *Futūḥ*, 244; Ya'qūbī, *Ta'rīkh*, II, 381; Ibn A'tham, VIII, 60–1; Dunlop, 77.

38. Ibn Khayyāṭ, *Ta'rīkh*, 504; Ṭabarī, II, 1531–32; Ibn A'tham, VIII, 61, 68; Azdī, 32; *'Uyūn wa ḥadā'iq*, 90; Ibn al-Athīr, *Kāmil*, V, 162; Dunlop, 75–76.

39. Ya'qūbī, *Ta'rīkh*, II, 381; Ṭabarī, II, 1560; Ibn A'tham, VIII, 61–67;

'Uyūn wa ḥadā'iq, 90; Ibn al-Athīr, *Kāmil*, V, 173–74, 177; Theophanes, 98, 101(probably a doublet); Dunlop, 77–79. Elias, 166, erroneously states that the *khāqān* himself was slain.

40. Ibn Khayyāṭ, *Ta'rīkh*, 505–06.

41. Ṭabarī, II, 1562; Ibn A'tham, VIII, 68–69. Differently, Dunlop, 79, who names al-Kūfa in place of Filasṭīn. The establishment of the new base at al-Bāb is also noted by Dasxuranci, 210.

42. It can be seen from the names of those with Sa'īd and Maslama that most in command positions were either Jazīran Muḍarīs or Umayyads with Jazīran Muḍarī connections, e. g., Marwān b. Muḥammad, 'Abd al-Malik b. Muslim al-'Uqaylī, Ibrāhīm b. 'Āṣim al-'Uqaylī, an 'Absī, al-Hudhayl b. Zufar b. al-Ḥārith al-Kilābī. Ibn A'tham, VIII, 47, 50, 52, 57. Also all those named by Balādhurī, *Futūḥ*, 243: Isḥāq b. Muslim al-'Uqaylī, Ja'wana b. al-Ḥārith b. Khālid al-'Āmirī, Dhufāfa b. 'Umayr b. al-Ḥubāb al-Sulamī and his brother Khālid, al-Furāt b. Salmān al-Bāhilī, all Jazīrans, and al-Walīd b. al-Qa'qā' al-'Absī, a Qinnasrīnī Qaysī. Commanders for Maslama in Ibn A'tham, VIII, 65, all have Jazīran or Qinnasrīnī connections except the Ḥimṣī-linked prince al-'Abbās b. al-Walīd, who may have also had connections farther north. Thubayt al-Bahrānī, Ibn A'tham, VIII, 66–67, is a Ḥimṣī, however.

43. Balādhurī, *Futūḥ*, 244.

44. However, the Khazars retained a legendary record of the capture of Ardabīl, showing its significance to them as well. Dunlop, 76.

45. Ibn Khayyāṭ, *Ta'rīkh*, 507. Marwān b. Muḥammad may have urged Hishām to remove Maslama because of the latter's lack of success at the front. Ibn al-Athīr, *Kāmil*, V, 177.

46. Lewond, 114–15.

47. Ibn A'tham, VIII, 69–70.

48. Ibn Khayyāṭ, *Ta'rīkh*, 507.

49. Ibn A'tham, VIII, 70.

50. Lewond, 113–14, 117; Toumanoff, 347, 349; Grousset, 316.

51. Lewond, 114; Grousset, 316.

52. Theophanes, 101.

53. Dunlop, 177–79.

54. Besides al-Jarrāḥ, al-Azdī, 32, names the Yamanī Ṣāliḥ al-Hamdānī.

55. Wellhausen, *Kingdom*, 340, entirely ignores the significance of al-Jarrāḥ's defeat, to which he devotes part of a sentence. Shaban, *History*, 144, also gives this defeat only a sentence, though he does call it an 'absolute disaster.'

56. Ṭabarī, II, 1527–29; Ibn A'tham, VIII, 99; Wellhausen, *Kingdom*, 459–60; Gibb, 72–73.

57. Ṭabarī, II, 1532–33. According to Ibn A'tham, VIII, 100, twenty-eight thousand were with al-Junayd.

58. Ṭabarī, II, 1532–33; Gibb, 73. In Ibn A'tham, VIII, 100, it is Naṣr b. Sayyār who warns al-Junayd against rashness.

59. Ṭabarī, II, 1533–34, 1546; Ibn A'tham, VIII, 101, 103; Gibb, 73–74.

60. Working back from the dated Battle of al-Ṭawāwīs, it can be calculated that this battle took place in Rabī' II 113/12 June–11 July 731. Ṭabarī, II, 1550.

61. Ṭabarī, II, 1534–39; 1546–47.

62. Ṭabarī, II, 1539–40.

63. Or, according to a less probable version, two thousand. Ṭabarī, II, 1541. According to Ibn A'tham, VIII, 103, twenty thousand men were with Sawra and all were killed. Perhaps this represents an estimate of the total Muslim dead rather than of Sawra's force.

64. Ṭabarī, II, 1541–44, 1546; Ibn A'tham, VIII, 103–05. Ibn Khayyāṭ, *Ta'rīkh*, 505, and Balādhurī, *Futūḥ*, 527, inaccurately call it a victory. Ibn Kathīr, *Bidāya*, IX, 303–04, despite his tendency to minimize Muslim defeats, gives an overall accurate assessment of the battle at greater length than he usually devotes to such matters.

65. Neither Wellhausen, *Kingdom*, 460–61, nor Shaban, *Revolution*, 113, seem to realize this. Gibb, 75, is better.

66. Ibn Khayyāṭ, *Ta'rīkh*, 505; Ibn A'tham, VIII, 103; Ibn Taghrībirdī, I, 272.

67. Ṭabarī, II, 1559.

68. Ibn A'tham, VIII, 10–14.

69. Ṭabarī, II, 1545; Balādhurī, *Futūḥ*, 527. Shaban's extensive argument that the order really meant to drop all but fifteen thousand Khurāsānīs from the army register is not convincing, because he did not realize the full extent of the disaster of the Defile. Probably not more than fifteen thousand Khurāsānī troops were left alive in any case. The caliphate now needed all the troops it could get. Certainly, the caliph preferred to employ rustic Khurāsānīs to mobilizing the dangerous and highly politicized Iraqis, yet he still had had to rush twenty thousand Iraqis to Khurāsān to plug the gaping hole in the realm's defenses. Contrary to Shaban's claim that these were "fresh, unassimilated tribesmen" and therefore more pliable than the Khurāsānīs, these Iraqis, especially the Kūfans among them, were actually the most turbulent, dangerous element in the empire and were perceived by the Umayyads as such. Shaban, *Revolution*, 113–17, *History*, 140–41.

70. Balādhurī, *Futūḥ*, 527.

71. Ṭabarī, II, 1539.

72. Ṭabarī, II, 1543.

73. Ṭabarī, II, 1545–46.

74. Ṭabarī, II, 1534.

75. Ṭabarī, II, 1536.

76. Ṭabarī, II, 1544–45.

77. Ṭabarī, II, 1548–49

78. The poets are Naṣr b. Sayyār al-Laythī, Ibn al-Sijf al-Mujāshi'ī, Ibn 'Irs al-'Abdī, and al-Shar'abī al-Ṭā'ī. These represent all the major Khurāsānī tribal groupings: the Ahl al-'Āliya, Tamīm, Rabī'a, and Yaman. Ṭabarī, II, 1546–48, 1553–59. There are also three lines by an anonymous poet in Ibn A'tham, VIII, 104.

79. Ṭabarī, II, 1554–56. My translation has been revised in light of Beeston and Conrad, 9–10. I have stuck to my wording of the last line here because I feel that the overall gist of the poem conveys broken-hearted despair.

80. That is, the Muslim fighters.

81. Khālid al-Qasrī, governor of the superprovince of the East.

82. Ambiguous reference to the Muslim leadership, even implying criticism of the caliphal policy of expansion.

83. Ṭabarī, II, 1557–59; Beeston and Conrad, 10. Again, I stand by my rendition of Ṭabarī, II, 1558, line 1, because it fits a context of defeat and despair, not boasting.

84. Ṭabarī, II, 1544, 1548–52; Gibb, 75. Differently Ibn A'tham, VIII, 106, whose account is vaguer and seems less reliable.

85. Some of these he may have already evacuated. Ṭabarī, II, 1544, 1550, 1552–53. Shaban overstates the case in saying that no Iraqis went to Samarqand even temporarily. Shaban, *Revolution*, 114–15.

86. The only figure cited, which cannot be considered reliable, is that of more than ten thousand Turks killed in the Defile. Ibn A'tham, VIII, 105.

87. Ṭabarī, II, 1561–64. Shaban cannot understand why al-Junayd did not undertake any expeditions in these years despite the arrival of reinforcements. This only underlines Shaban's failure to grasp the full extent of the disaster of the Defile. Shaban, *Revolution*, 114.

88. Ibn Khayyāṭ, *Ta'rīkh*, 507.

89. Gibb, 76.

90. Ṭabarī, II, 1585; Gibb, 78–79.

91. Gibb, 79.

92. Unidentified place.

93. Ibn Khayyāṭ, *Ta'rīkh*, 504; Ṭabarī, II, 1530; Ibn Taghrībirdī, I, 271–72; Michael, II, 501; *Chronicon ad 1234*, 310; Yāqūt, s. v. Kharshana; Ramsay, 248–49.

94. Theophanes, 101.

95. Al-Ya'qūbī attributes this to 112/730, but that is impossible. Al-'Amq can mean merely 'the valley' beside Mar'ash. Ya'qūbī, *Ta'rīkh*, II, 395; Lilie, 148.

96. Ṭabarī, II, 1559–60; Ibn al-Athīr, *Kāmil*, V, 173; Ibn Kathīr, *Bidāya*, IX, 304–05; Lilie, 149.

97. Mu'āwiya's role is only mentioned by *Chronicon ad 1234*, 310.

98. Ibn Khayyāṭ, *Ta'rīkh*, 507–08; Ṭabarī, II, 1561; Ibn Taghrībirdī, I, 274; Elias, 166; *Chronicon ad 1234*, 310; Lilie, 149. Ya'qūbī, *Ta'rīkh*, II, 395, substitutes Maslama b. 'Abd al-Malik for Sulaymān as commander, but is confused on the point, for he names Mu'āwiya, Sulaymān, and al-Baṭṭāl and mentions the capture of Constantine under 115/733.

99. Gibbon, III, 223; Arslān, 118. Lot, *Naissance*, 103, considers it prevented the islamization of Aquitaine; however, Lot, *Recueil*, II, 264–65, is more restrained. Gabrieli, 110, criticizes the tendency to award so much importance to a mere failed raid.

100. Maqqarī, I, 235–36, III, 16; Ibn al-Athīr, *Kāmil*, V, 174–75; Ibn 'Idhārī, II, 28; Theophanes, 94–95; Gabrieli, 108; Ṭaha, 192–93. There is considerable doubt about the date; Collins, 90–91 argues for 115/733.

101. The main ones are *Continuatio Isadori* and *Chronicon Mossiacense*, both used by Gabrieli, 109, etc.

102. Ibn 'Idhārī, II, 28; *Continuatio*, 361; Wolf, 142–43 (cf. 164–65, 168); Ṭaha, 189–90. The identification of this man with 'Uthmān b. Abī Nis'a al-Khath'amī, who had been governor for a few months in 110/728, which is found in Arslān, 114–17; Wolf, 142 n. 151, and in other works, is wholly unjustified. Even the cautious Lot, *Naissance*, 102–03, is deceived. Ibn Abī Nis'a was an Arab, not a Berber. Ibn Ḥazm, 392.

103. Gabrieli, 108–09.

104. *Continuatio*, 361; *Chronicon Moissiacense*, 291; Gabrieli, 109; Wolf, 143–44; Ṭaha, 192–93; Arslān, 117–19; Lot, *Naissance*, 103, *Recueil*, II, 258, 261; Archibald Lewis, 22. The *Continuatio* says only that 'Abd al-Raḥmān desired to plunder Tours, not that he reached it. The belief of Ṭaha that the Muslims had brought their families along with them to settle is inadmissible. Even if settlement was eventually contemplated, it would never have been carried out on a long-distance raid that was the very first reconnoitering of the area.

105. *Continuatio*, 361–62; *Chronicon Moissiacense*, 291; Gabrieli, 109; Lot, *Naissance*, 103; Archibald Lewis, 22.

106. "...ibique rex Abderaman cecidit cum exercitu suo in praelium." *Chronicon Moissiacense*, 291.

107. Theophanes, 94–95, 98. Both are wrongly dated.

108. Ibn Khayyāṭ, *Ta'rīkh*, 504.

109. Ibn Khayyāṭ, *Ta'rīkh*, 506.

110. Ibn Khayyāṭ, *Ta'rīkh*, 507. He gives 'Abd Allāh for 'Abd al-Malik, an obvious error.

Chapter 8

1. It should be noted once more, however, that actual, though not official, truces were in effect not only with the Berbers, who had accepted

Islam, but also perhaps with the Christian king of Abyssinia and certainly with the pagan Zunbīl of Zābulistān, who had refused to pay tribute since 101/720 or earlier. Balādhurī, *Futūḥ*, 493. Thus it was possible for the caliphate to take a practical view on occasion, but it had taken much sacrifice of blood and treasure on the Sijistān front to come to such a view.

2. Ibn Khayyāṭ, *Ta'rīkh*, 509–10; Ṭabarī, II, 1562; Ibn al-Athīr, *Kāmil*, V, 181; Agapius, *PO*, VIII, 507; Theophanes, 101, dates this before Sha'bān/September. Agapius, the only source to mention the capture of a town, relates the event to 114/732, as does Lilie, 149. The reference of *Chronicon ad 1234*, 310, records this year's expedition, but incorrectly states that Mu'āwiya died on it.

3. Ya'qūbī, *Ta'rīkh*, II, 395; Ṭabarī, II, 1564; Ibn al-Athīr, *Kāmil*, V, 182; Elias, 167; Lilie, 150.

4. Ibn Khayyāṭ, *Ta'rīkh*, 514; Ya'qūbī, *Ta'rīkh*, II, 395; Ṭabarī, II, 1573; Ibn al-Athīr, *Kāmil*, V, 195; Theophanes, 102; Elias, 167; Lilie, 150. Agapius, *PO*, VIII, 507, says Mu'āwiya captured 'a great number of fortresses,' but this is vague and doubtful in view of the silence of the other sources.

5. Ibn Khayyāṭ, *Ta'rīkh*, 515; Ṭabarī, II, 1588; Ibn al-Athīr, *Kāmil*, V, 196; Theophanes, 102; Elias, 167; Lilie, 150.

6. Kindī, 79–80; Ibn Taghrībirdī, I, 277; Maqrīzī, *Khiṭaṭ*, I, 303.

7. Ibn Khayyāṭ, *Ta'rīkh*, 517; Agapius, *PO*, VIII, 508; Theophanes, 102; Elias, 167. Balūniya is unidentified, unless it is the same as the fortress of Balansa in Kappadokia mentioned in Ibn Khurdādhbih, 108. Lilie, 150–51, opines that Sulaymān reached Pergamon, because a Pergamonian prisoner was taken, but this is unlikely, as the capture of the man seems to have been a long time before. See on this *Chronicon ad 1234*, 311–12.

8. Ṭabarī, II, 1593; Ibn al-Athīr, *Kāmil*, V, 214.

9. Ibn Khayyāṭ, *Ta'rīkh*, 519; Ṭabarī, II, 1635; Ibn al-Athīr, *Kāmil*, V, 228; Agapius, *PO*, VIII, 508; Theophanes, 103; *Chronicon ad 1234*, 312. The fall of Sideroun/Sindara, by synchronization of al-Ṭabarī with Theophanes, must have occurred in Ramaḍān-Dhū al-Ḥijja 120/September–December 738.

10. Ibn Khayyāṭ, *Ta'rīkh*, 524; Ya'qūbī, *Ta'rīkh*, II, 395. Ibn Khayyāṭ's report is mostly erroneous, however. Maslama b. 'Abd al-Malik is an error for Maslama b. Hishām, for the former had already died. The death of al-Baṭṭāl and the visit of the Caliph Hishām to Malaṭya, which Ibn Khayyāṭ puts in this year and *Chronicon ad 1234*, 312, a year earlier, must be placed in 122/740 and 123/741 respectively. See below.

11. Ṭabarī, II, 1667; Ibn al-Athīr, *Kāmil*, V, 240; Ibn Khurdādhbih, 108 (in the Theme of al-Qabāduq=Kappadokia); Lilie, 151. Agapius, *PO*, VIII, 508, has Maslama beseige and capture Ankyra. On Maṭāmīr, see Lilie, 151–52.

12. Agapius, *PO*, VIII, 508. But he misdates it to the year 13 of Hishām

= 117–18/735–36 and erroneously calls the commander Maslama b. 'Abd al-Malik.

13. Ibn Khayyāṭ, *Ta'rīkh*, 526; Theophanes, 102. Pseudo-Dionysius, 25, has b. Shabīb in place of b. Shu'ayb.

14. Ibn Khayyāṭ, *Ta'rīkh*, 526; Ṭabarī, II, 1716; *'Uyūn wa ḥadā'iq*, 100; Ibn al-Athīr, *Kāmil*, V, 248; Theophanes, 102. The figures given by Theophanes seem reasonable, except for those for Sulaymān's force at Tyana. *Al-'Uyūn wa al-ḥadā'iq* has compressed some of the events of 114/732 into its account of al-Baṭṭāl's death. Pseudo-Dionysius places the battle at Synnada and the Arab losses at forty-five thousand, a clear exaggeration. According to Lilie, 152–54, the results of this battle have been exaggerated and it is merely accidental that it coincides with the Umayyad collapse, whereas I view it as part of a pattern of defeats that greatly contributed to that collapse.

15. Agapius, *PO*, VIII, 509.

16. Ṭabarī, II, 1814.

17. Dunlop, 71.

18. Ibn Khayyāṭ, *Ta'rīkh*, 507; Wellhausen, *Kingdom*, 340.

19. Ibn A'tham, VIII, 70; Balādhurī, *Futūḥ*, 244; Lewond, 113. Confusion has arisen about Sa'īd's second governorship owing to the belief that Marwān became permanently ensconced from 114/732. The text of Ibn A'tham is unequivocal, however, and provides nice agreement with all seemingly contradictory versions. Marwān did succeed Maslama, but only for a year. Sa'īd then did hold the governorship for two years, 115–17/733–35, which are a complete blank as far as Marwān is concerned. Gabrieli, 81, missed this. Dunlop, 80, though he mentions the possibility, is noncommittal. It is conceivable, though unlikely, that Sa'īd was only governor under Marwān's auspices.

20. Michael, II, 501; Agapius, *PO*, VIII, 507. The latter, however, improbably has Maslama b. 'Abd al-Malik making peace with the Khazars owing to a defeat in the year 8 of Hishām 112–13/730–31. As Agapius is weak on chronology, this could be a reference to the later lull.

21. Ibn al-Athīr, *Kāmil*, V, 178.

22. Ibn Khayyāṭ, *Ta'rīkh*, 513; Ṭabarī, II, 1573.

23. Ibn Khayyāṭ, *Ta'rīkh*, 515.

24. This appears from Ibn A'tham, VIII, 70–71 and Ibn al-Athīr, *Kāmil*, V, 177–78, where it can be seen that Marwān went directly forth from Syria with his great army and a special commission from Hishām to fight the Khazars. But this could not have been at the beginning of his second governorship, as this great expedition is dated two years later to 119/737 by the most reliable chronology, which is that of Ibn Khayyāṭ, *Ta'rīkh*, 517. Tabari, II, 1635, would place the campaign still later by a year, but Ibn Khayyāṭ's dating is supported by Elias, 167. In any case, it appears that Marwān made

a special visit to Hishām in order to convince him to back the expedition and provide extra troops.

25. Balādhurī, *Futūḥ*, 244; Ibn A'tham, VIII, 71; Ibn al-Athīr, *Kāmil*, V, 178; Grousset, 317.

26. This information is from the Georgian historian Juanṣher, who is cited in Toumanoff, 400, n. 42, 405, nn. 52–54.

27. Al-Balādhurī and Ibn al-Athīr do not mention al-Bayḍā'/Itil nor any battle. Ibn Khayyāṭ, *Ta'rīkh*, 517; Balādhurī, *Futūḥ*, 244; Ibn A'tham, VIII, 71; Ibn al-Athīr, *Kāmil*, V, 178. Ṭabarī, II, 1635, seems to place this campaign in 120/738.

28. Iṣṭakhrī, 220–26; Yāqūt, s. v. Khazar; Dunlop, 91–93.

29. Ibn A'tham, VIII, 71–74.

30. Ibn A'tham, VIII, 74.

31. Balādhurī, *Futūḥ*, 245.

32. Dunlop, 84, 86, 116–21, 142, 148, 170.

33. Balādhurī, *Futūḥ*, 244; Ibn A'tham, VIII, 74; Lewond, 114, alone states that he returned beyond al-Bāb to Bardha'a, that Ashot Bagratouni and his Armenian forces had accompanied him, and that he sent a fifth of the booty to Hishām, occasioning the latter's outburst against his brother Maslama.

34. Dunlop, 85.

35. Ṭabarī, II, 1635.

36. Ibn al-Athīr, *Kāmil*, V, 240, treats Ghūmīk as the fortress where the prince of al-Sarīr had his capital, while Khīzaj is another fortress.

37. It had to pay an annual tribute of one thousand slaves and one hundred thousand measures of grain.

38. Ibn Khayyāṭ, *Ta'rīkh*, 523; Balādhurī, *Futūḥ*, 245; Ibn al-Athīr, *Kāmil*, V, 178, 240. The two accounts of Marwān's activities in 121–22/739–40 in Ibn al-Athīr, though recorded under 114 and 121, are clearly a doublet. Dunlop, 85, n. 123.

39. Amounting to one hundred slaves and ten thousand or twenty thousand measures of grain annually. Balādhurī, *Futūḥ*, 245; Ibn al-Athīr, *Kāmil*, V, 178.

40. Amounting to fifty slaves and ten thousand measures of grain annually. Zirūbkarān, which appears in place of Zirīkarān, is a mistake. Balādhurī, *Futūḥ*, 245.

41. Their tribute was five hundred slaves sent as a single payment and thirty thousand measures of grain to be paid annually. Balādhurī, *Futūḥ*, 245.

42. Or Sughdān or Masdār. Unidentified, but on the Caspian coast. Its tribute was one hundred slaves handed over only once and five thousand measures of grain sent annually. Balādhurī, *Futūḥ*, 245; Ibn al-Athīr, *Kāmil*, V, 178.

43. Their prince tried to flee to the Khazars but was killed. Kayrān is a mistake for Layzān in some sources. Its tribute was twenty thousand measures of grain. Khashram al-Sulamī was made their governor. Balādhurī, *Futūḥ*, 245–46; Ibn al-Athīr, *Kāmil*, V, 179.

44. Its tribute was ten thousand measures of grain delivered annually to al-Bāb, plus military service in the rear. Ṭabaristān and Ṭīrshān for Ṭabarsarān are copyists' mistakes. Balādhurī, *Futūḥ*, 245–46; Ibn al-Athīr, *Kāmil*, V, 178.

45. Fīlān seems to have been required only to give military help in time of need. Balādhurī, *Futūḥ*, 245–46.

46. Its tribute was ten thousand measures of grain annually, plus military service in the vanguard. Balādhurī, *Futūḥ*, 246.

47. Marwān seems to have gotten nothing from them. Balādhurī, *Futūḥ*, 246. For their identification with the modern Didos, see *EI*², s. v. al-Ḳabḳ.

48. Ibn Khayyāṭ, *Ta'rīkh*, 523–24; Balādhurī, *Futūḥ*, 245–46; Ṭabarī, II, 1667; Ibn al-Athīr, *Kāmil*, V, 178–79, 240.

49. Ya'qūbī, *Ta'rīkh*, II, 395.

50. Ṭabarī, II, 1564–65; Gardīzī, 256–57. Ibn Khayyāṭ, *Ta'rīkh*, 537, reports that Hishām removed al-Junayd from office in 115/733, but is less detailed and accurate than al-Ṭabarī for matters pertaining to Khurāsān.

51. Ṭabarī, II, 1564–65.

52. Ṭabarī, II, 1567.

53. Ṭabarī, II, 1567, 1570–71, 1577, 1583, etc.; Gardīzī, 257–58, says that 'Āṣim had hardly taken up his duties when the revolt broke out.

54. Shahristānī, I, 139–46; *EI*², s. v. Mur*dj*i'a.

55. Ṭabarī, II, 1575–76.

56. Gardīzī, 258. Al-Ḥārith also undertook to collect taxes and pay stipends to his own forces. Ibn A'tham, VIII, 106.

57. These elements had been led by the reformer Abū al-Ṣaydā' Ṣāliḥ b. Ṭarīf, the *mawlā* of the Ḍabba, who had complained to 'Umar II on behalf of the *mawālī* (Ṭabarī, II, 1353), fought for reform under Ashras in 110/728 (Ṭabarī, II, 1507–09), but since disappeared from the scene. The survival of his party can be deduced from the participation of his followers of 110/728 in al-Ḥārith's revolt in 116–17/734–35. These include Bishr b. Jurmūz al-Ḍabbī (Ṭabarī, II, 1566, 1568, 1583), Khālid b. 'Ubayd Allāh al-Hajarī (Ṭabarī, II, 1572, 1582—he is mistakenly referred to as al-Naḥwī, which is a copyist's error for al-Hajarī, in Ṭabarī, II, 1508), Abū Fāṭima al-Azdī (Ṭabarī, II, 1568, 1583, 1585), and al-Qāsim al-Shaybānī (Ṭabarī, II, 1584–85—al-Haytham is a copyist's error for al-Qāsim). It is very notable that Khālid al-Hajarī was present at the Defile, where he urged al-Junayd to hurry to safety in Samarqand to escape from the Turks, which suggests that disgust resulting from that disaster may have been a motivation for al-Ḥārith's

revolt. Ṭabarī, II, 1543. The survival of Abū al-Ṣaydā''s party was noted by Wellhausen, *Kingdom*, 465, but in less detail.

58. The leading supporters of al-Ḥārith mentioned in the previous note all had been long in Khurāsān and belonged to clans which had migrated early to Khurāsān from al-Baṣra.

59. Ibn Khayyāṭ, *Ta'rīkh*, 509; Ṭabarī, II, 1566–69. Ibn Khayyāṭ places al-Ḥārith's revolt and apparently al-Junayd's demise in 115/733, probably wrongly.

60. Ṭabarī, II, 1569–72.

61. Ṭabarī, II, 1570, 1572.

62. Shaban, *Revolution*, 119–20.

63. Ibn Khayyāṭ, *Ta'rīkh*, 509; Ṭabarī, II, 1579–80. Ibn Khayyāṭ reports that al-Ḥārith gained control of Marw.

64. Ibn Khayyāṭ, *Ta'rīkh*, 509; Ṭabarī, II, 1577; Gardīzī, 258. Ibn Khayyāṭ, however, avoids mention of the terms except that it was stipulated that al-Ḥārith had to withdraw to Balkh. This explains his location when Asad arrived in Khurāsān.

65. Shaban, *Revolution*, 120.

66. Ṭabarī, II, 1582.

67. Ṭabarī, II, 1573–74.

68. Ṭabarī, II, 1581.

69. Ṭabarī, II, 1573, 1581; Gardīzī, 258; Wellhausen, *Kingdom*, 467. If 'Āṣim's governorship was seven months, Asad must have arrived about Ramaḍān 116/September 734; if it was just under a year, he may have arrived about al-Muḥarram 117/January 735, probably not later.

70. Gardīzī, 258.

71. Ṭabarī, II, 1590 (four thousand Syrians and only two thousand Khurāsānīs from Balkh), 1609 (five Syrian and only four Khurāsānī divisions named).

72. Ṭabarī, II, 1581.

73. Ṭabarī, II, 1583.

74. Notice, however, their complaints about the ingratitude of the Umayyads toward them. Ṭabarī, II, 1577–79.

75. Ibn Khayyāṭ, *Ta'rīkh*, 509; Ṭabarī, II, 1582–85.

76. Ṭabarī, II, 1585–86, 1591.

77. Ṭabarī, II, 1589–91.

78. Reports occur in Ṭabarī, II, 1593–1608 and 1629–32. Probably both reports refer to this one campaign. The speculations of Wellhausen, *Kingdom*, 470–73, and Gibb, 81, about this passage in al-Ṭabarī requiring a second campaign in al-Khuttal in either 118/736 or 120/738 cancel each other out. The campaign described in Ṭabarī, II, 1629–32 is best assigned to the summer of 119/737, before the *khāqān* had mobilized.

79. Ṭabarī, II, 1593–95. Shaban, *Revolution*, 126–27, speculates that the

baggage train (*al-athqāl*) consisted of valuable trade goods being sent to China. But it is unlikely that Asad was thinking much of trade in the middle of a serious war and seems far simpler to suppose that the baggage consisted of the spoils of al-Khuttal.

80. Ṭabarī, II, 1598.

81. Ṭabarī, II, 1596–97.

82. Ṭabarī, II, 1598–1602.

83. Ṭabarī, II, 1603.

84. Ṭabarī, II, 1492, 1494, 1602–03. Though the text of al-Ṭabari is in Arabic, he makes occasional citations in Persian, as is the case with these verses.

85. Ibn Khayyāṭ, *Ta'rīkh*, 513; Ṭabarī, II, 1603–08. Ibn Khayyāṭ puts this in 117/735, which is most unlikely.

86. Gibb, 84.

87. Ṭabarī, II, 1609–12.

88. Ṭabarī, II, 1614–16.

89. Chavannes, *Documents*, 83, 285.

90. Ṭabarī, II, 1613–14; Gibb, 85.

91. Wellhausen, 473, n 2.

92. Ṭabarī, II, 1639, 1660–64, 1666; Gardīzī, 258–59.

93. Note the distaste with which Hishām ratifies an agreement concluded by Naṣr that he dislikes for containing too many concessions to an enemy in Ṭabarī, II, 1718.

94. Ṭabarī, II, 1664–65; Ibn A'tham, VIII, 146. For four years, Naṣr did not appoint any but Muḍarīs to office.

95. Ṭabarī, II, 1664; Gardīzī, 259.

96. Ṭabarī, II, 1688–89.

97. Ibn A'tham, VIII, 107.

98. Ṭabarī, II, 1689.

99. Gibb, 90.

100. Ṭabarī, II, 1694. Probably this is the same as the failed raid on Ushrūsana by Naṣr attributed by Balādhurī, *Futūḥ*, 527, to the caliphate of Marwān II. See Gibb, 92.

101. Ṭabarī, II, 1689–92.

102. Chavannes, *Documents*, 286, n 1.

103. Gibb, 91.

104. Ṭabarī, II, 1694.

105. Ibn A'tham, VIII, 107.

106. Ṭabarī, II, 1695.

107. Ṭabarī, II, 1717–18.

108. Ṭabarī, II, 1694–95.

109. Ṭabarī, II, 1691.

110. Ṭabarī, II, 1695–97.

111. Ṭabarī, II, 1688–89, is quite specific in saying Naṣr campaigned only three times, which were 121–23/739–41.

112. In fact, no further Turkish attacks worthy of note took place in Transoxiana until 291/904. Barthold, 256.

113. Ibn Khayyāṭ, *Ta'rīkh*, 537–38; *Ta'rīkh-i Sīstān*, 127–28; Ya'qūbī, *Buldān*, 284; Bosworth, 74.

114. All of the Muslim holdings in India, apparently even Sind, had been lost except Cutch. Balādhurī, *Futūḥ*, 542; Ya'qūbī, *Ta'rīkh*, II, 380.

115. Balādhurī, *Futūḥ*, 542; Ya'qūbī, *Ta'rīkh*, II, 380.

116. Archaeology has most recently shown the sites of al-Maḥfūẓa and al-Manṣūra to lie at Dalor Jo Bhiro about fourteen kilometers east of the modern city of Shahdadpur in Central Sind, while the site of Brahmānābād lies about ten kilometers further to the northeast at Depar Ghānghro. Pathan, 65–79, contains the most up-to-date and extensive discussion of this question, including his own investigations in person at the sites. See also Balādhurī, *Futūḥ*, 542–43; Ya'qūbī, *Ta'rīkh*, II, 380.

117. The fact that the leaders of the Yamanī Kalb argued over what to name al-Maḥfūẓa suggests that it was indeed a mainly Yamanī settlement. Balādhurī, *Futūḥ*, 542–43.

118. Mishra, 49–50, 54. Differently Majumdar, III, 150, 152, 156–57.

119. Dikshit, 166; Mishra, 50, 54, 56; Majumdar, III, 150, 173, IV, 98.

120. Dikshit, 166.

121. Dikshit, 311; Mishra, 52.

122. Mishra, 52; Majumdar, III, 173.

123. Majumdar, IV, 2.

124. Dikshit, 167.

125. Mishra, 48; Majumdar, III, 158–59.

126. Mishra, 46–47; Majumdar, IV, 19–20; Tripathi, 228.

127. Mishra, 92–93; Majumdar, III, 130; Panhwar, 153–55.

128. Mishra, 73–74, 84–85.

129. The report in Panhwar, 154, that al-Ḥakam conquered al-Kīraj seems to be a repetition of al-Junayd's conquest there and thus a doublet.

130. Of the same clan as the previous governor Tamīm b. Zayd.

131. Ṭabarī, II, 1623–24.

132. Ibn Khayyāṭ, *Ta'rīkh*, 526, 538; Balādhurī, *Futūḥ*, 539; Pathan, 109.

133. Ya'qūbī, *Ta'rīkh*, II, 388–89.

134. The others were al-Aṣfaḥ b. 'Abd Allāh al-Kalbī in Sijistān, al-Jarrāḥ al-Ḥakamī in Ādharbayjān, and 'Abd ar-Rahmān al-Ghāfiqī in France. All were Yamanīs.

135. Dikshit, 187.

136. Ṭabarī, II, 1658; Ibn al-Athīr, *Kāmil*, V, 220; Kubaysī, 111, 125.

137. Farazdaq, 365–66, 601–02

138. These were the *khawārij* Ṣubayḥ and Khālid. Though their belong-

ing to the Rabī'a is not specified, it is possible in view of their starting their rebellions around the Raba'ī centers of Herat and Bushanj and then going on to attack the Tamīmī center of Marw al-Rūdh afterwards. Alternatively, either or both could be dissident Tamīmīs. Balādhurī, *Ansāb*, Istanbul Ms., II, 261–63; *'Uyūn wa ḥadā'iq*, 108–09; Bosworth, 73.

139. However, it is uncertain whether all the rebels mentioned, al-Mughīra, Bayān, Bahlūl, al-Ashhab, Wazīr, and al-Ṣuḥārī, really belong to only 119/737 or whether they have merely been lumped together there by al-Ṭabarī because he is ignorant of the actual dates of their revolts. Balādhurī, *Ansāb*, Istanbul Ms., II, 263–66; Ṭabarī, II, 1619–29, 1633–34.

140. Ṭabarī, II, 1667–88, 1698–1716; Iṣbahānī, *Maqātil*, 90–101.

141. The claim that the Umayyads poisoned Abū Hāshim is presumably legendary. Iṣbahānī, *Maqātil*, 83–85.

142. Kindī, 81.

143. Ya'qūbī, *Ta'rīkh*, II, 391–92; Ṭabarī, II, 1986; *Akhbār al-Dawla*, 167, 241–42, 383–84.

144. Ṭabarī, II, 1687.

145. Its leaders were from the Yamanī Yaḥṣub and Tujīb. Kindī, 77–78.

146. Kindī, 78–79.

147. The name, given as Qarīja (or equivalent) by al-Kindī and Tarūja by al-Maqrīzī, is unidentifiable to me. Kindī, 79; Maqrīzī, *Khiṭaṭ*, I, 303.

148. Kindī, 79–80; Ibn Taghrībirdī, I, 277; Maqrīzī, *Khiṭaṭ*, I, 303. Though the latter two sources say that the Byzantines attacked and besieged a place in Egypt, Kindī's account with its reference to the commander of the expedition would appear to be more accurate. Probably it was easy to misunderstand that a governor of Egypt was cashiered for an attack on Egypt rather than a failed overseas expedition.

149. Kindī, 81; Ibn Taghrībirdī, I, 281. Sāwīrus has nothing to say about this rebellion, probably because it took place in Upper Egypt, which he often ignores.

150. Ibn Khayyāṭ, *Ta'rīkh*, 510. This report indicates that 'Ubayda was in office in 115/733. However, Raqīq, 106, says that he was dismissed in Shawwāl 114/about December 732.

151. The sources suggest other reasons. Raqīq, 105–06, and Ibn 'Idhārī, I, 50–51, suggest that Hishām removed him because of a Yamanī complaint about his partisanship for the Qaysīs, of whom he was one. But this is unlikely, as Hishām appointed another Qaysī and as the complaint refers to 110/728. Ibn 'Abd al-Ḥakam, *Futūḥ*, 217, and Ya'qūbī, *Ta'rīkh*, II, 382, state that 'Ubayda asked to be relieved of his post, which 'Abd al-Ḥamīd, 275, 278, agrees is most likely. But he still may have been under pressure to resign.

152. Ya'qūbī, *Ta'rīkh*, II, 382.

153. Ibn 'Abd al-Ḥakam, *Futūḥ*, 217.

154. 'Abd al-Ḥamīd, 279.

155. Ibn 'Idhārī, I, 51; Abbott, 21–32.

156. This is noted by Ibn 'Idhārī, II, 29.

157. This despite Ibn Khayyāṭ's description of the battle as a victory. He may merely mean that the Byzantines withdrew and did not annihilate the Muslim fleet. Ibn Khayyāṭ, *Ta'rīkh*, 511.

158. Ibn Khayyāṭ, *Ta'rīkh*, 511; Ibn 'Abd al-Ḥakam, *Futūḥ*, 217; Raqīq, 108. Ibn Khayyāṭ's mention of Ḥabīb's son 'Abd al-Raḥmān as commander of this expedition seems to be a mistake.

159. Raqīq, 108; Ibn 'Idhārī, I, 51.

160. 'Abd al-Ḥamīd, 282.

161. Ibn Khayyāṭ, *Ta'rīkh*, 514; Ibn 'Abd al-Ḥakam, *Futūḥ*, 217.

162. Ibn Khayyāṭ, *Ta'rīkh*, 515. The identification of Ūliya would be difficult to make if it were not identified in Ibn Khayyāṭ, *Ta'rīkh*, 381, as the nearest point in Sicily to Africa. This, coupled with the sufficient parallel of the sounds of "Ūliya" and "Lilybaion," makes the identification certain. "Ūliya" could also be read "Ūliba," though that seems unnecessary.

163. Ibn Khayyāṭ's wording here perhaps implies a storm rather than enemy action as the cause of the debacle. Ibn Khayyāṭ, *Ta'rīkh*, 517.

164. Ibn Khayyāṭ, *Ta'rīkh*, 524.

165. Ibn Khayyāṭ, *Ta'rīkh*, 526; Raqīq, 108–09; Ibn 'Idhārī, I, 51.

166. Ibn al-Athīr, *Kāmil*, V, 181; Maqqarī, I, 236, III, 18–19; *Continuatio*, 362; Wolf, 144–45. *Continuatio* gives 116–19/734–37 as the dates for 'Abd al-Malik's governorship, which appears wholly irreconcilable with the Muslim chronology which I have followed here. See note 168.

167. Ṭaha, 194.

168. There is some doubt about this date. Al-Wāqidī, cited in Maqqarī, I, 236, gives 'Abd al-Malik a term of four years rather than two. Maqqarī, III, 19–20, suggests that 'Uqba governed for either five years and two months or six years and four months. The end of his governorship can be fairly certainly placed in Ṣafar 123/January 741, shortly after the outbreak of the great Berber revolt (see below). Several sources seem to prefer a governorship of five years or so for him. *Akhbār majmū'a*, 34; Ibn 'Idhārī, I, 53, II, 29; Maqqarī, I, 236. *Continuatio*, 362, has his rule start in 119/737, which is contradicted by all the Muslim sources. Counting back five years and two months from Ṣafar 123, we get Dhū al-Ḥijja 117. Since 'Abd al-Malik's governorship began in Ramaḍān 114, this counting would give him a term of three years and three months, which al-Wāqidī may have rounded up to four years. *Continuatio*'s Muslim dates may partly be confused owing to the overlapping of the Christian and Muslim years.

169. *Continuatio*, 362–63; Wolf, 145.

170. Unidentified place near Astorga in Leon.

171. *Akhbār majmū'a*, 33–34; Ibn 'Idhārī, II, 29; Maqqarī, I, 236, III, 19.

172. *Chronicon Moissiacense*, 291; Ṭaha, 196.

173. Archibald Lewis, 23; Ṭaha, 196.

174. Archibald Lewis, 23.

175. *Chronicon Moissiacense*, 292. Though the text of this chronicle specifies that the defeated forces had 'come out of Syria,' which seems to be good evidence for yet another overextension of the already overburdened Syrian army, the point cannot be pushed too far, for the Frankish chronicler cannot be expected to have known much about the internal composition of the Muslim forces. He gives the Muslim commander as 'Amr b. Khālid, who is otherwise unknown.

176. Maqqarī, I, 236.

177. Archibald Lewis, 24.

178. Ibn 'Abd al-Ḥakam, *Futūḥ*, 217, shows that he perished in office. See also Ibn 'Idhārī, II, 30; Ṭāha, 197. According to *Continuatio*, 363; Wolf, 146, however, he resigned for reasons of ill health and died shortly afterwards of disease.

Chapter 9

1. This is the only direct reference in the sources to the plague ravaging Muslim army units under Hishām (Agapius, *PO*, VIII, 509), but there are many references to outbreaks of plague in Hishām's reign in the sources, especially in Syria (Ṭabarī, II, 1488 for 107/725, 1563 for 115/733, 1564 for 116/734) and in places with concentrations of Syrian troops, such as Wāsiṭ (Ṭabarī, II, 1561 for 114/732, 1564 for 116/734). Possibly the Syrian army units would have been especially susceptible to the plague, as they were for the most part a standing army living in camps and in urban concentrations even when not on campaign. This would be in contrast particularly to their rustic barbarian nemeses. However, the subject deserves further study, for it would be necessary to learn whether Hishām's reign suffered an increase in the incidence of the plague or whether it was equally present at most other times as well. In the former case, the plague may have been yet another cause contributing to the decline of the Syrian army.

2. Ibn Khayyāṭ, *Ta'rīkh*, 528; Ya'qūbī, *Ta'rīkh*, II, 395; Agapius, *PO*, VIII, 509. Elias, 168–69 nevertheless describes this campaign as a victory for Sulaymān but offers no details. Probably his account is confused with the expedition of the following year.

3. Balādhurī, *Futūḥ*, 221–22; Ibn Taghrībirdī, I, 289–90, gives twenty-five thousand as the size of the Byzantine force. Ibn Khayyāṭ, *Ta'rīkh*, 524, erroneously puts Hishām's own sortie in 121/739.

4. Agapius, *PO*, VIII, 510.

5. Theophanes, 105; Michael, II, 501; *Chronicon ad 1234*, 313.

6. Ya'qūbī, *Ta'rīkh*, II, 395; Theophanes, 106; Agapius, *PO*, VIII, 510. Elias, 169, states that Sulaymān killed Leo's son! Presumably this is mixed up with the much earlier killing in 114/732 of a Roman commander named Constantine, who was then misidentified with Leo's son and successor. Ibn al-Athīr, *Kāmil*, V, 259, states that the Byzantines whom Sulaymān encountered were led by the Emperor Leo, which is a mistake, as the latter had died the previous year.

7. Ibn Khayyāṭ, *Ta'rīkh*, 546; Ya'qūbī, *Ta'rīkh*, II, 395; Ṭabarī, II, 1769; Ibn al-Athīr, *Kāmil*, V, 274; Theophanes, 107; Agapius, *PO*, VIII, 511. Lilie, 155, has unnecessarily doubled this expedition into two falling in successive years.

8. Theophanes, 107.

9. Theophanes, 110.

10. Balādhurī, *Futūḥ*, 183–6; Theophanes, 108; Agapius, *PO*, VIII, 510. Ṭabarī, II, 1769, and Ibn al-Athīr, *Kāmil*, V, 274, say that the transfer was carried out by a fleet commanded by al-Aswad b. Bilāl al-Muḥāribī, and that the inhabitants of Cyprus were given the choice of whether to live in Syria or not, which implies that those evacuated were Muslims.

11. Balādhurī, *Futūḥ*, 543; Ya'qūbī, *Ta'rīkh*, II, 389, 399–400. The probabilty that the four thousand troops were Iraqis is based on the names of two commanders mentioned in al-Ya'qūbī who probably came with them: Ma'n b. Zā'ida al-Shaybānī and Marwān b. Yazīd b. al-Muhallab. The latter is clearly an Iraqi with Baṣran conections; for the former, Crone favors a Jazīran origin, but he could well be an Iraqi. Crone, 169.

12. Note that as recently as seven years before, in 115/733, Hishām had decided to dismiss or even execute al-Junayd al-Murrī for simply marrying Yazīd b. al-Muhallab's daughter. Ṭabarī, II, 1564.

13. Ya'qūbī, *Ta'rīkh*, II, 389–90.

14. Ya'qūbī, *Ta'rīkh*, II, 400.

15. Raqīq, 109, and Ibn 'Idhārī, I, 51–52, blame 'Umar b. 'Abd Allāh al-Murādī, but it is unlikely that this subgovernor undertook such drastic fiscal changes without approval of higher authority. Ibn 'Idhārī also explicitly states that this was the cause of the revolt. See also Sāwīrus, *PO*, V, 87; *Continuatio*, 360, 363; Wolf, 140–41, 146–47.

16. Ṭabarī, I, 2816; *Akhbār majmū'a*, 37; Sāwīrus, *PO*, V, 87.

17. For their character, see *Akhbār majmū'a*, 32–33; Ibn 'Idhārī, I, 53.

18. Ibn 'Idhārī, I, 52.

19. Ṭabarī, I, 2816.

20. Raqīq, 109; Ibn 'Idhārī, I, 52.

21. Ṭabarī, I, 2816.

22. Ṭabarī, I, 2816.

23. Ṭabarī, I, 2815–16. Khleifat, 139–40, denies the story of the delegation. However, even if Maysara himself was not a participant, there is no

reason to doubt that there were delegations that went to complain and that they were generally ignored by the caliph.

24. See above.

25. E.g., 'Abd al-A'lā b. Jurayj and 'Abd al-A'lā Zurzur. Though these are possibly the same person, the first was supposedly killed before the time in which the second is mentioned. See below in this chapter for both.

26. *Akhbār majmū'a*, 37, in attempting to prove that the Berber rebels were really *khawārij* in doctrine, is only able to cite their raising of Qur'āns and their shaving of their heads, which do not seem to be very convincing as doctrinal differences or distinctive characteristics. No doubt the *khārijī* doctrine that rebellion is justified led to religious implications, and it may be that they were partly or largely inspired by religious fervor. But neither of these implies that they were not also, perhaps mainly, a political movement or movements, for religion and politics are often intertwined. For the *khawārij* in general, see Shahristānī, I, 114–38; Wellhausen, *Factions*, 1–91, especially 20–23, emphasizing their political nature. For the Ṣufriyya in particular, see Shahristānī, I, 137. Unfortunately, Wellhausen has nothing to say about the North African Ṣufriyya. Shaban, *History*, 151–52, and Ṭāha, 200, concur in concluding that the North African Berber revolt had little if anything to do with eastern Khārijism. Indeed, it seems the attempt of *Akhbār Majmū'a* and whoever follows its lead to paint the Berber revolt in such terms bears much similarity to modern governmental attempts to denigrate the motives of dissident movements by blaming them on outside agitators and outside ideological poison, typical governmental propaganda unworthy of any credence.

27. Ibn Khaldūn, IV, 404–05.

28. Ibn al-Athīr, *Kāmil*, V, 191.

29. Raqīq, 109; Ibn al-Athīr, *Kāmil*, V, 191; Ibn 'Idhārī, I, 52.

30. Ibn Khayyāṭ, *Ta'rīkh*, 525.

31. Ibn 'Abd al-Ḥakam, *Futūḥ*, 218; Raqīq, 110; Ibn al-Athīr, *Kāmil*, V, 191; Ibn 'Idhārī, I, 53.

32. Ibn Khayyāṭ, *Ta'rīkh*, 525; Ibn 'Abd al-Ḥakam, *Futūḥ*, 217–18. Ibn Khayyāṭ calls the governor 'Amr b. 'Abd Allāh al-'Absī.

33. Raqīq, 109; Ibn al-Athīr, *Kāmil*, V, 191; Ibn 'Idhārī, I, 52.

34. *Akhbār majmū'a*, 35.

35. Ibn 'Abd al-Ḥakam, *Futūḥ*, 218; *Akhbār majmū'a*, 34–35; Ibn 'Idhārī, I, 52. According to Ibn Khayyāṭ, *Ta'rīkh*, 525, Maysara started his revolt in al-Sūs in cooperation with 'Abd al-A'lā, who was at Tangier.

36. Ibn Khayyāṭ, *Ta'rīkh*, 525.

37. Raqīq, 110; Ibn al-Athīr, *Kāmil*, V, 191–92; Ibn 'Idhārī, I, 53.

38. Raqīq, 110; Ibn al-Athīr, *Kāmil*, V, 192; Ibn 'Idhārī, I, 53; Ibn Khayyāṭ, *Ta'rīkh*, 529, reports that Maysara only died in 124/741–2. Ibn 'Abd al-Ḥakam, *Futūḥ*, 218, says that Maysara defeated Khālid b. Abī Ḥabīb

and then was killed at Tangier because he was not upholding the terms he had sworn to on taking office.

39. Ibn 'Abd al-Ḥakam, *Futūḥ*, 218; Raqīq, 110–11; Ibn al-Athīr, *Kāmil*, V, 192; Ibn 'Idhārī, I, 53–54; Ibn Khayyāṭ, *Ta'rīkh*, 525–26, lists some of the North African Muslim nobility who perished there.

40. Ibn Khayyāṭ, *Ta'rīkh*, 525–26; Ibn 'Abd al-Ḥakam, *Futūḥ*, 218.

41. Ibn Khayyāṭ, *Ta'rīkh*, 526.

42. Ibn Khayyāṭ, *Ta'rīkh*, 526.

43. Ibn 'Abd al-Ḥakam, *Futūḥ*, 218.

44. *Continuatio*, 363; Wolf, 146. although *Continuatio* shows his expedition a success, the actual outcome shows differently.

45. Ibn al-Athīr, *Kāmil*, V, 192.

46. Ibn al-Athīr, *Kāmil*, V, 250–51; Maqqarī, III, 19–20.

47. *Akhbār majmū'a*, 35; Raqīq, 111; Ibn 'Idhārī, I, 54.

48. Ibn 'Abd al-Ḥakam, *Futūḥ*, 220.

49. Ibn 'Abd al-Ḥakam, *Futūḥ*, 218; Raqīq, 111; Ibn al-Athīr, *Kāmil*, V, 192; Ibn 'Idhārī, I, 54.

50. Ibn 'Idhārī, I, 53. Raqīq, 110, already has them stationed there from an earlier stage.

51. Ibn 'Abd al-Ḥakam, *Futūḥ*, 218.

52. The problem of this man's tribal identification is vexed and important, for the Qushayr are a prominent Qaysī Muḍarī clan concentrated in Qinnasrīn, while the Qasr are a subclan of the Yamanī Bajīla to whom also belong the famous Khālid al-Qasrī, Hishām's governor of the East. Crone, 128, presents a useful survey of the sources' contradiction. While the Qushayrī identification is supported by the genealogists, the Qasrī connection would seem more logical for a Damascene, for Khālid al-Qasrī also hailed from there (Ibn 'Asākir, V, 70). Furthermore, it would be somewhat surprising that a Qushayrī with Muḍar connections would be put in charge of an army that was overwhelmingly Yamanī Syrian in composition, especially at this critical juncture which represented the height of the Muḍar-Yaman factional split. In addition, the fact that the Muḍar faction now controlled the entire East would make the appointment of yet another Muḍarī to the West leave the Yaman entirely out in the cold. All these arguments favor the Yamanī identification for Kulthūm.

53. Hārūn al-Qurnī, the *mawlā* of Mu'āwiya b. Hishām, and Mughīth, the *mawlā* of al-Walīd b. 'Abd al-Malik. *Akhbār majmū'a*, 37.

54. *Akhbār majmū'a*, 36.

55. Theophanes, 103.

56. Raqīq, 112, and Ibn 'Idhārī, I, 54, give twelve thousand, while Ibn 'Idhārī, I, 55, and II, 30, gives a total of thirty thousand troops including North Africans, of whom ten thousand were Umayyads. Again, the ten thousand probably refers to the forces surviving with Balj later. That they

should be described as Umayyads probably reflects a later attempt to show that the Spanish Umayyads had already entered Spain before 'Abd al-Raḥmān al-Dākhil.

57. Ibn 'Abd al-Ḥakam, *Futūḥ*, 218; Raqīq, 112; Ibn 'Idhārī, I, 54.

58. *Akhbār majmū'a*, 36; Ibn 'Idhārī, II, 30.

59. Raqīq, 112; Ibn 'Idhārī, I, 54; Ibn Khayyāṭ, *Ta'rīkh*, 528, gives the date of the beginning of Kulthūm's governorship as 1 Sha'bān 123/ 21 June 741.

60. Ibn 'Abd al-Ḥakam, *Futūḥ*, 218; *Akhbār majmū'a*, 37.

61. Ibn 'Abd al-Ḥakam, *Futūḥ*, 218–19; Raqīq, 112–13; Ibn al-Athīr, *Kāmil*, V, 192; Ibn 'Idhārī, I, 54–55.

62. Ibn al-Athīr, *Kāmil*, V, 192; Raqīq, 112–13; Ibn 'Idhārī, I, 54–55.

63. Raqīq, 113; Ibn 'Idhārī, I, 55; Ibn 'Abd al-Ḥakam, *Futūḥ*, 219, lays all the blame on Kulthūm rather than Balj, but Kulthūm's other actions show that he made at least some concessions to local feeling. The same source also blames Kulthūm for losing the battle.

64. Ibn Khayyāṭ, *Ta'rīkh*, 528.

65. *Akhbār majmū'a*, 37. This number is probably somewhat exaggerated. It would include all the troops in North Africa, not merely those with Kulthūm. On the other hand, the sober and nearly contemporary *Continuatio*, 363, reports that Kulthūm's force numbered one hundred thousand! See also Wolf, 147.

66. Al-Azdi is possibly a mistake for some Berber tribal name, for no other Azd are attested in the West at this time, except for Syrians with Kulthūm. Ibn Khayyāṭ, *Ta'rīkh*, 529.

67. Gabrieli, 101. Ibn Khayyāṭ, *Ta'rīkh*, 529, dates Kulthūm's disaster to 124, which could also be correct. But in that case it would have to have been at the start of al-Muḥarram/November–December 741, as Kulthūm was definitely dead by Ṣafar/December 741–January 742. Ibn Khayyāṭ, *Ta'rīkh*, 532. Ibn 'Idhārī, II, 31, dates Balj's entry to Spain to Dhū al-Qa'da 123/September–October 741, which seems much too early, though it is just conceivable that the Battle of Wādī Sabū could have been that early, but no earlier. Thus, Gabrieli's date seems the best compromise.

68. Ibn 'Abd al-Ḥakam, *Futūḥ*, 220; Ibn 'Idhārī, I, 55.

69. These included of the North Africans Sulaymān b. Abī al-Muhājir, Mughīth al-Rūmī, and Hārūn al-Qurnī (*Akhbār majmū'a*, 37–39; Ibn 'Idhārī, I, 55) and of the Syrians Muḥammad b. 'Ubayd Allāh al-Azdī and Yazīd b. Sa'īd b. 'Amr al-Ḥarashī (Ibn Khayyāṭ, *Ta'rīkh*, 529). See also Ibn 'Abd al-Ḥakam, *Futūḥ*, 220. Maqqarī, III, 20–21, reports that Kulthūm survived the battle, retreating with Balj to Sabta, where he died. *Continuatio*, 363, says that Kulthūm was beheaded by his own allies. See also Wolf, 147.

70. *Akhbār majmū'a*, 39. *Continuatio*, 363–64, also contains the motif of three parts without saying they were thirds. Its parts, however, consisted of

those taken prisoner, those who escaped eastward, and those with Balj who ended up in Spain. See also Wolf, 147–48.

71. Ibn ʿIdhārī, I, 55, II, 31.

72. *Akhbār majmūʿa*, 40.

73. *Akhbār majmūʿa*, 40. The caliph must have heard the news by Ṣafar 124/December 741–January 742. See Ibn ʿAbd al-Ḥakam, *Futūḥ*, 221.

74. *Akhbār majmūʿa*, 40–1.

75. Ibn ʿAbd al-Ḥakam, *Futūḥ*, 221.

76. *Akhbār majmūʿa*, 41.

77. Kindī, 82; Shaban, *History*, 149.

78. Ibn Khayyāṭ, *Taʾrīkh*, 531.

79. Raqīq, 114.

80. ʿUkkāsha found support among the Zanāta Berbers with whom he may have had a special relationship by birth or marriage. Ibn ʿAbd al-Ḥakam, *Futūḥ*, 219.

81. Ibn Khayyāṭ, *Taʾrīkh*, 531; Ibn ʿAbd al-Ḥakam, *Futūḥ*, 219; Raqīq, 114.

82. Ibn ʿAbd al-Ḥakam, *Futūḥ*, 221.

83. Ṣafwān b. Abī Mālik.

84. Ibn ʿAbd al-Ḥakam, *Futūḥ*, 221.

85. Commanding at Qābis were ʿAbd al-Aʿlā b. ʿUqba and Saʿīd b. Bajra al-Ghassānī. The latter seems to have succeeded Maslama as military commander at al-Qayrawān as well. Perhaps he had set out from there to relieve Qābis. Ibn Khayyāṭ, *Taʾrīkh*, 531; Ibn ʿAbd al-Ḥakam, *Futūḥ*, 219.

86. The great valley south of the various Atlas ranges is meant, especially its easternmost part in modern Tunisia. Yāqūt, s. v. al-Zāb, reports that the Great Zāb contains Biskara, Tawzar, Qusantīna, Tawlaqa, Qafṣa, Nafzāwa, Nafṭa, and Bādis, which generally fits this description. Ṭubna appears to be identical to the modern Baṭna, by metathesis.

87. Ibn Khayyāṭ, *Taʾrīkh*, 531–2; Ibn ʿAbd al-Ḥakam, *Futūḥ*, 221; Raqīq, 114. The latter places the victory at al-Miknasa, part of the borders of Tahūda, adjacent to Sabība, which was near al-Qayrawān.

88. Kindī, 82.

89. Raqīq, 115; Ibn al-Athīr, *Kāmil*, V, 193; Ibn ʿIdhārī, I, 58.

90. Ibn Khayyāṭ, *Taʾrīkh*, 532.

91. Ibn Khayyāṭ, *Taʾrīkh*, 529–30.

92. Conceivably the same as the present-day al-Faḥṣ halfway between al-Qayrawān and Tūnis.

93. Ibn Khayyāṭ, *Taʾrīkh*, 530; Ibn ʿAbd al-Ḥakam, *Futūḥ*, 221–22.

94. Ibn Khayyāṭ, *Taʾrīkh*, 530; Ibn ʿAbd al-Ḥakam, *Futūḥ*, 221–22; Raqīq, 115–16; Ibn ʿIdhārī, I, 58.

95. Ibn Khayyāṭ, *Taʾrīkh*, 504, 530; Ibn ʿAbd al-Ḥakam, *Futūḥ*, 222.

96. Ibn al-Athīr, *Kāmil*, V, 193–94.

97. Raqīq, 118.

98. Ibn Khayyāṭ, *Ta'rīkh*, 530–31.

99. Ibn Khayyāṭ, *Ta'rīkh*, 531; Ibn 'Abd al-Ḥakam, *Futūḥ*, 222.

100. Ibn 'Abd al-Ḥakam, *Futūḥ*, 222; Raqīq, 116–22; Ibn al-Athīr, *Kāmil*, V, 194; Ibn 'Idhārī, I, 58–59. The last three sources say that the number of Berber dead at al-Aṣnām were one hundred eighty thousand, which is an exaggeration not to be trusted even in a vague way, as it may have been invented by the caliphal tradition to counterbalance the earlier record of utter failure in the Berber war.

101. Raqīq, 119–22.

102. Ibn 'Abd al-Ḥakam, *Futūḥ*, 222–23; Raqīq, 122; Ibn 'Idhārī, I, 59.

103. Mu'āwiya b. Ṣafwān.

104. Ibn 'Abd al-Ḥakam, *Futūḥ*, 223.

105. Ibn 'Abd al-Ḥakam, *Futūḥ*, 223–24.

106. Ibn Khayyāṭ, *Ta'rīkh*, 529; Ibn 'Abd al-Ḥakam, *Futūḥ*, 220.

107. *Akhbār majmū'a*, 40, 42; Ibn 'Idhārī, II, 30.

108. *Akhbār majmū'a*, 42; Ibn 'Idhārī, I, 55–56. Maqqarī, III, 20, reports that 'Abd al-Malik tortured and executed the man who sent supplies to Balj, Ziyād b. 'Amr (or 'Abd al-Raḥmān b. Ziyād) al-Lakhmī.

109. Ibn al-Athīr, *Kāmil*, V, 252, and Ibn 'Idhārī, II, 31, put Balj's entry into Spain in Dhū al-Qa'da 123/September–October 741, which seems impossibly early, and he is also credited with an eleven-month governorship ending the following Shawwāl/August. It would appear that the date of Balj's entry into Spain would have to be a long time after the date cited and his governorship consequently much shorter.

110. *Akhbār majmū'a*, 42–43; Maqqarī, III, 20; *Continuatio*, 364; Ṭāha, 208; Wolf, 148.

111. *Akhbār majmū'a*, 42–43; Ibn 'Idhārī, I, 56, II, 30; Maqqarī, III, 20–21.

112. Ibn 'Idhārī, II, 31.

113. *Akhbār majmū'a*, 43–44; Ibn 'Idhārī, II, 31.

114. *Akhbār majmū'a*, 44; Ibn 'Idhārī, II, 31; Maqqarī, III, 21.

115. If Balj's governorship was indeed six months, as reported by Ibn 'Idhārī, II, 32, and if he indeed died in Shawwāl 124/August 742, then the Syrians' coup against 'Abd al-Malik must be dated to about Rabī' II–Jumādā I 124/February–March 742. This barely gives enough time for the Syrians to be defeated at Wādī Sabū in Dhū al-Ḥijja 123/ October–November 741, to suffer in Sabta, fighting a number of battles near there, to be brought over by 'Abd al-Malik, and to defeat the Berbers, all in a period of no more than three or four months. Gabrieli, 116, has Rabī' I/January for this coup; though he admits it is purely hypothetical, it seems too early to me.

116. *Akhbār majmū'a*, 44; Ibn 'Idhārī, II, 32; Maqqarī, III, 19, 21.

117. *Akhbār majmū'a*, 46.

118. *Akhbār majmūʻa*, 44–45; Ibn ʻIdhārī, II, 32; Maqqarī, III, 21.

119. *Akhbār majmūʻa*, 46–47; Ibn ʻIdhārī, I, 56. Ibn ʻIdhārī, II, 32, says Balj's army was less than one fifth that of the sons of ʻAbd al-Malik.

120. Ibn ʻIdhārī, II, 33. *Continuatio*, 364, also emphasizes the carnage. See also Wolf, 148–49.

121. Maqqarī, III, 22. Ibn ʻIdhārī, II, 33, and Maqqarī, I, 237, credit Thaʻlaba with at least ten months of rule, but that is impossible, as Balj died in Shawwāl 124/August 742 and Abū al-Khaṭṭār arrived in al-Muḥarram 125/November 742, which limits Thaʻlaba to about three or at most four months.

122. Although Berber Muslims had been enslaved in North Africa (refer to relevant section), the victims here were mostly Arabs, which compounded the outrage. *Akhbār majmūʻa*, 47–48; Ibn ʻIdhārī, II, 33; Maqqarī, III, 22.

123. *Akhbār majmūʻa*, 48. According to Raqīq, 105–06, Abū al-Khaṭṭār had long been an intimate associate of the family of Ḥanẓala, for he had served his brother Bishr during the latter's governorship of 102–09/721–27. Abū al-Khaṭṭār was tortured in 110/728 by Bishr's successor ʻUbayda al-Sulamī, wrote to al-Abrash, the Kalbī adviser of Hishām to complain, and thereby helped to precipitate the recall of ʻUbayda in 115/733.

124. Maqqarī, III, 24. The report on p. 22 that he came in Rajab/May, after Hishām's death, is a corruption based on the date of his overthrow.

125. *Akhbār majmūʻa*, 48–49; Ibn ʻIdhārī, II, 33; Maqqarī, I, 237. According to Raqīq, 123, ʻAbd al-Raḥmān took ship secretly to Tūnis for fear of Abū al-Khaṭṭār in Jumādā I 127/March–April 745.

126. He was deposed at the end of Rajab 127/May 745. Maqqarī, III, 24–25.

Conclusion

1. Ibn Khayyāṭ, *Ta'rīkh*, 546; Yaʻqūbī, *Ta'rīkh*, II, 395; Ṭabarī, II, 1769; Ibn al-Athīr, *Kāmil*, V, 274; Theophanes, 107; Agapius, *PO*, VIII, 511. The governor of Sind is said by one source to have undertaken eighteen campaigns under al-Walīd II, but such campaigns will have been on his own initiative and in any case amounted to little. Yaʻqūbī, *Ta'rīkh*, II, 400.

2. Ṭabarī, II, 1754–55.

3. Ṭabarī, II, 1825.

4. E.g., the probability that the extravagant palace of al-Mushattā, which was never completed, was built by al-Walīd II. Creswell and Allan, 211–12.

5. Ṭabarī, II, 1765–67.

6. Ṭabarī, II, 1778–80, 1819–22. He also sold control of Khurāsān back to Yūsuf b. ʻUmar. Ṭabarī, II, 1764.

7. Ṭabarī, II, 1781–84.

8. The Defile in 113/731 and Poitiers in 114/732 are omitted because most of the casualties were not Syrians.

9. Yazīd III's forces in Damascus were only fifteen hundred or two thousand. Ṭabarī, II, 1794, 1797. Note that the majority of the Damascus *jund* are said to have sworn allegiance to Yazīd III. Ṭabarī, II, 1788. This would imply that the rather miserable force he was able to send against al-Walīd II was most of what was left of that *jund*. Al-Walid himself had only two hundred men. Wellhausen, *Kingdom*, 364.

10. *'Uyūn wa ḥadā'iq*, 5.

11. Indeed, the great general al-'Abbās b. al-Walīd was able to come to al-Walīd II's succour from Ḥimṣ with only one hundred fifty troops from his household, while another Ḥimṣī set out with five hundred. Ṭabarī, II, 1798, 1802–03.

12. Wellhausen, *Kingdom*, 363.

13. It still numbered sixty thousand even after the 'Abbāsids had defeated it. Ṭabarī, III, 57.

14. Theophanes, 103.

15. Though certain of the reforms were associated with earlier Iraqi Yamanī rebels, there is no evidence associating any of them with Syrian Yamanīs before this.

16. Ṭabarī, II, 1353, 1507–10; Gardīzī, 258; *Continuatio*, 358.

17. Ṭabarī, II, 1687.

18. Ṭabarī, II, 1834–35. Other versions with slight differences are found in Ibn Khayyāṭ, *Ta'rīkh*, 551; Jāḥiẓ, *Bayān*, II, 142; Ibn Qutayba, *'Uyūn*, II, 248–49; Ibn 'Abd Rabbih, IV, 96, 463; *'Uyūn wa ḥadā'iq*, 150.

19. I have dealt with this above.

20. This is corroborated by stories like that found in Ṭabarī, II, 1731–32.

21. Balādhurī, *Futūḥ*, 214.

22. Shaban, *History*, 155–56.

23. Ṭabarī, I, 2815–16.

24. Ṭabarī, II, 1813.

25. Ṭabarī, II, 1688–89.

26. In fact, the Syrians called for a *shūrā* during their overthrow of al-Walīd II. Ṭabarī, II, 1804.

27. Ṭabarī, II, 1755–64.

28. Ṭabarī, II, 1776–77, 1784–85.

29. According to Yazīd III's point six.

30. Ṭabarī, II, 1788–1810.

31. Shaban, *Revolution*, 133, *History*, 155.

32. Iṣbahānī, *Aghānī*, VII, 2442, 2462, 2487, 2489, 2499, 2512; 'Aṭwān, *Walid*, 218–53.

Appendix A

1. The famous phrase of Leopold von Ranke, quoted in Stern, 57.

2. Mishra, 46, 50, 54; Dikshit, 166–67.

3. Ṭabarī, II, 1532–59. Note that *Shi'b 'Iṣām*, mentioned only in a poem on p. 1554, appears to refer to a Muslim defeat not otherwise recorded.

4. Ṭabarī, II, 1314–17; 1346.

5. Ṭabarī, II, 1530–31.

6. Theophanes, 97–98.

7. Ibn Hishām, I, 4.

8. Ṭabarī, I, 6–7.

9. White, 1–42, etc.

10. Hodgson, 352–56.

11. On this point, I agree with F. R. Ankersmit in his disagreement with Barthes over the latter's finding ambiguities in the simplest statements. F. R. Ankersmit, "Reply to Professor Zagorin," *History and Theory* 29 (1990), 278 n. 7.

12. The relationship of history to myth has exercised historians for millenia. See, for example, Livy, i, 1.

13. Ṭabarī, II, 1529, 1532–33, 1539, 1543, 1549–50, 1555, 1557–59.

14. Consulted in French and Latin translations.

15. Consulted both in the original Greek and in English translations.

16. Written in Arabic.

17. Written in Arabic.

18. Consulted in English translations.

19. Consulted in a French translation.

20. Consulted in French translations.

21. Written and consulted in Latin.

22. Written and consulted in Latin.

23. Reported in English-language research.

24. Gibb, 79.

25. Crone, 3–17.

26. Ibn al-Nadīm, 108–11.

27. In descending order of their importance in Ṭabarī. See Ṭabarī, *The History of al-Ṭabarī*, v. XXV, xii; Ibn al-Nadīm, 58–60, 111–17.

28. Dūrī, 43.

29. Kennedy, 352.

30. Ibn al-Nadīm, 103; Dūrī, 45–46.

31. For example, it is possible that al-Ya'qūbī's rather detailed treatment of Sind under Hishām may derive ultimately from 'Awāna, whose father was then governor of that province and met his end there.

32. Dennett, 88–115.

33. Kennedy, 354.

34. Crone, 213–14, n. 101.

35. For early Roman Republican history from about 500 B.C.E., the main extant literary sources date from the beginning of the 1st century C.E.; surviving inscriptions containing lists of the consuls are of nearly the same date. Though a historical tradition is known to have existed from about 200 B.C.E., with a poetic tradition a generation or two older, earlier sources are impossible to discern, except for a very primitive annual record displayed by the priests on boards. Since this must have been destroyed in the sack of Rome by the Gauls in 387 B.C.E., it is hard to understand how even the names of the consuls before that could have survived, yet they appear to have done so almost back to the beginning of the Republic. Huergon, 158–60, 165–66, 245, and especially 249; Finley, *Ancient History: Evidence and Models*, 9.

36. E.g., Crone, 3–15.

37. Maqrīzī, *Nuqūd*, 16–17; Walker, II, lix–lxiv.

38. Dennett, 65–115.

39. *Select Papyri*, I, 367, 379–81, 387–89, 391–93; II, 93, 101–05, 111, 173, 227–29, 253, 267, 273, 277, 281, 301–03.

40. E.g. in Iraq. Morony, 554.

41. Ṭabarī, II, 1466–1740.

42. Dināwarī, 336–47.

43. However, despite his brevity, al-Ya'qūbī gives much broader coverage than al-Ṭabarī. Ya'qūbī, *Ta'rīkh*, II, 378–96.

44. *'Uyūn wa ḥadā'iq*, 81–111.

45. Only 14 pages. See Wakī', III, 199–213.

46. Wakī', III, 213–4.

47. Wakī', III, 215.

48. However, Theophanes does give considerable information about the Muslim campaigns of Hishām's reign against the Byzantines. See Theophanes, 95–107.

49. K. Blankinship, "Tribal Factor," 589–603.

50. Jāḥiẓ, "Risāla fī al-nābita", in *Rasā'il al-Jāḥiẓ*, II, 7–23.

51. Jāḥiẓ, "Manāqib al-Turk", in *Rasā'il al-Jāḥiẓ*, I, 5–86 and III, 163–220.

52. Ibn 'Abd Rabbih, IV, 445–52.

53. *EI*², s. v. al-Farazdaḳ.

54. *EI*², s. v. Djarīr.

55. *EI*², s. v. Dhu'l-Rumma.

56. Iṣbahānī, *Aghānī*, XXIII, 8047–61; *EI*, s. v. Ru'ba b. al-'Adjdjādj

57. *EI*², s. v. al-Kumayt b. Zayd al-Asadī.

58. *Akhbār majmū'a*, 32–48; Ibn al-Qūṭiyya, 39–44; Ibn 'Idhāri, II, 27–33; Maqqarī, I, 235–7, 299, III, 15–23.

59. Ibn 'Idhāri, I, 49–59; Ibn 'Abd al-Ḥakam, *Futūḥ*, 215–23.

60. Ibn Taghrībirdī, I, 254–97; Kindī, 72–83, 340–51; Maqrīzī, *Khiṭaṭ*, I, 202–3.

61. Azdī, 21–51.

62. *Ta'rīkh-i Sistān*, 125–8.

63. Gardīzī, 255–65.

64. Ibn A'tham, VIII, 35–130.

65. Ibn Ṭūlūn, 7–10; Ibn Muhannā, *passim*; 'Aẓīmī, 203–11; Ibn al-'Adīm, I, 48.

66. Balādhurī, *Futūḥ*, 63, 140, 183, 196–97, 213, 221–22, 243–46, 270, 274, 356, 359, 404, 415, 452–53, 525–27, 541–43.

67. Balādhurī, *Ansāb*, Ms. Istanbul, II, 235–309.

68. Ibn Khayyāṭ, *Ta'rīkh*, 481–547.

69. E.g., only 20 pp. on Syria. See Ibn Khayyāṭ, *Ṭabaqāt*, 297–317.

70. Pseudo-Ibn Qutayba, *Imāma wa siyāsa*, II, 48–86.

71. Pseudo-Ibn Qutayba, *Imāma wa siyāsa*, II, 104–110.

72. Ibn al-Athīr, *Kāmil*, V, 123–264.

73. For Hishām, see Nuwayrī, 402–62.

74. Ibn Khallikān, II, 226–31.

75. Ibn Khallikān, VII, 101–12.

76. Dhahabī, *Siyar*, V.

77. Dhahabī, *Ta'rīkh*, IV–V.

78. Ibn Kathīr, *Bidāya*, IX, 233–354.

79. Ibn Kathīr, *Bidāya*, IX, 314–9.

80. Ibn al-Kalbī, I, 117–22.

81. Kennedy, 357–58.

82. Theophanes, 95–107.

83. Pseudo-Dionysius of Tell Maḥré, 18–30. Also called *The Chronicle of Zuqnīn*.

84. *Chronicon ad 819*, 16–18.

85. *Chronicon ad 846*, 235–36.

86. Elias, 163–69.

87. Michael the Syrian, II, 490–91, 500–2.

88. *Chronicon ad 1234*, 309–14.

89. Ibn al-Biṭrīq, II, 45–46.

90. Agapius, *PO*, VIII, 505–10.

91. Lewond, 115–17.

92. Dasxurançi, 209–10.

93. *Histoire de la Géorgie*, I, 256–58; Toumanoff, 345, 347, 351, 395, 399–401, 405–406, 412, 486 n. 215.

94. Sāwīrus, *PO*, V, 73–114.

95. *Continuatio*, 359–64. Its value is strongly and rightly emphasized by Collins, 26–36 and *passim*. It was also frequently quoted by Wellhausen and has been translated into English in Wolf.

96. *Chronicon Moissiacense*, 291–93.

97. Ṭabarī, II, 1482–3; Dhahabī, *Siyar*, V, 447.

98. Dhahabī, *Siyar*, V, 331, 339, 341–42.

99. Ṭabarī, II, 1472.

100. *EI*², s. v. Ghaylān b. Muslim.

101. Ṭabarī, II, 1467

102. Ṭabarī, II, 1330, 1364, 1504, 1566, 1570–71, 1615–16; Ibn Ḥajar, *Tahdhīb*, X, 277–79.

103. As shown by the full genealogies reported for some in the *nasab* books; e. g., for al-Ḍaḥḥāk b. Qays al-Shaybānī, see Ibn Ḥazm, 322.

104. Ṭabarī, II, 1528–29, 1534–36. Other accounts mentioning 'Adawīs are also probably derived from him in Ṭabarī, II, 1501, 1513.

105. Ṭabarī, II, 1641–42; Jahshiyārī, 59–67, has some unique information on Hishām's secretaries, but concentrates mostly on Iraq, also devoting more space to the downfall of Khālid than any other matter.

106. Ṭabarī, II, 1641–58.

107. *EI*², s. v. Hishām.

108. Wellhausen, *Kingdom*, 497–500, 557–59, and passim.

109. Shaban, *History*, 120–24, 136, 141–42, 155, 170–71, 178.

110. Crone, 209, n. 71, 211, n. 88.

111. Crone, 42–45.

112. Crone, 55–57.

113. Crone, 89–91.

114. More recently, Crone's view has been supported to some extent by G. Hawting in *The First Dynasty of Islam*, while Shaban's has received some qualified support from H. Kennedy in *The Prophet and the Age of the Caliphates*. Hawting, xix–xx, 53–55, 76, 90, 126; Kennedy 104–05.

115. Dunlop, 58–87. However, he did not use Ibn A'tham's *Futūḥ*, the most detailed source, except what another scholar has quoted of it.

116. Bosworth, 72–74.

117. Lilie, 143–55.

118. Ṭāha, 189–218.

119. Collins, 82–95 and *passim*. This work is limited by a lack of awareness of the full extent of the Arabic sources and a failure to utilize them. What it lacks on the Arabic sources is partly made up by a good command of the Latin sources.

120. In *Studia Islamica* (1970), 269–86.

121. In *Israel Oriental Studies* 2 (1972), 248–62.

122. 'Abd al-Ḥamīd, 271–314.

123. 'Abd al-Rāziq, 46–81.

Appendix B

1. For references, see McEvedy, 289, 292, 298, 312.
2. Russell, 89; McEvedy, 145.
3. Russell, 89; McEvedy, 151.
4. Russell, 89–90; McEvedy, 139, 143.
5. Ya'qūbī, *Ta'rīkh*, II, 277–8. The data refer to Mu'awiya's reign and are the closest extensive financial data we have to the time of Hishām.
6. Giving five hundred fifty thousand, Balādhurī, *Futūḥ*, 332; giving five hundred thousand, Ibn Khurdādhbih, 14, and Ibn Rustah, 105.
7. Cited in Morony, 175.
8. Russell, 52–9. It should be noted, however, that he allows the possiblity of multiplying by six for Muslim poll–tax figures. See Russell, 50.
9. Russell, 89–90; Dennett, 86–7, 107.
10. Dennett, 12.

Bibliography

Abbott, Nabia. "A New Papyrus and a Review of the Administration of 'Ubaid Allāh b. al-Ḥabḥāb." In *Arabic and Islamic Studies in Honor of Hamilton A. R. Gibb*. Ed. George Makdisi. Cambridge, Mass.: Dept. of Near Eastern Languages and Literatures, Harvard Univ., 1965, pp. 21–35.

'Abd al-Ḥamīd, Sa'd Zaghlūl. *Ta'rīkh al-Maghrib al-'Arabī min al-fatḥ ilā bidāyat 'uṣūr al-istiqlāl*. Alexandria: Munsha'at al-Ma'ārif, 1978.

'Abd al-Rāziq, Maḥmūd Ismā'īl. *al-Khawārij fī bilād al-Maghrib ḥattā muntaṣaf al-qarn al-rābi' al-hijrī*. 2nd printing. Casablanca: Dār al-Thiqāfa, 1406/1985.

Abun-Nasr, Jamil M. *A History of the Maghrib in the Islamic Period*. Cambridge: Cambridge University Press, 1987.

Abuswa, Mahmud Ahmed. "The Arabization and Islamization of the Maghrib: a Social and Economic Reconstruction of the History of the Maghrib during the First Two Centuries of Islam." UCLA Ph.D. Thesis, 1984.

Abū Yūsuf, Ya'qūb b. Ibrāhīm (d. 182/798). *al-Kharāj*. Ed. Muḥammad Ibrāhīm al-Bannā. Cairo: Dār al-I'tiṣām, 1981.

Agapius (Maḥbūb) de Menbidj (fl. 330/942). *Kitāb al-'unvān (histoire universelle)*. Part II, 2. Ed. and tr. Alexandre Vasiliev. In *Patrologia Orientalis*, VIII, 399–550.

Aḥmad, Muṣṭafā Abū Ḍayf. *al-Qabā'il al-'Arabiyya fī al-Andalus ḥattā suqūṭ al-khilāfa al-Umawiyya (91–422 h./710–1031 m.)*. Casablanca: Les Editions Maghrébines, 1983.

al-Aḥwaṣ al-Anṣārī, 'Abd Allāh b. Muḥammad (d. c. 110/728). *Shi'r al-Aḥwaṣ al-Anṣārī*. Ed. 'Ādil Sulaymān Jamāl. Cairo: al-Hay'a al-Miṣriyya al-'Āmma li al-Ta'līf wa al-Nashr, 1390/1970.

al-Ājurī, Abū Bakr Muḥammad b. al-Ḥusayn b. 'Abd Allāh (d. 360/971). *Akhbār Abī Ḥafṣ 'Umar b. 'Abd al-'Azīz*. Ed. 'Abd Allāh 'Abd al-Raḥīm 'Usaylān. Beirut: Mu'assasat al-Risāla, 1399/1979.

Akhbār al-dawla al-'Abbāsiyya wa fīhi akhbār al-'Abbās wa wuldih. Ed. 'Abd al-'Azīz al-Dūrī and 'Abd al-Jabbār al-Muṭṭalibī. Beirut: Dār al-Ṭalī'a li al-Ṭibā'a wa al-Nashr, 1971.

Akhbār majmū'a. Ed. Ibrāhīm al-Abyārī. Beirut: Dār al-Kutub al-Islāmiyya, 1401/1981.

al-'Alī, Ṣāliḥ Aḥmad. *al-Tanẓīmāt al-ijtimā'iyya wa al-iqtiṣādiyya fī al-Baṣra fī al-qarn al-awwal al-hijrī*. Baghdad: Maṭba'at al-Ma'ārif, 1953.

Ankersmit, F. R. "Reply to Professor Zagorin." *History and Theory* 29 (1990), 275–96.

Armstrong, Karen. *Holy War: The Crusades and Their Impact on Today's World*. New York: Doubleday (Anchor Books), 1991.

Arslān, al-Amīr Shakīb (d.1365/1946). *Ta'rīkh ghazawāt al-'Arab fī Faransā wa Sawīsarā wa Iṭāliya wa jazā'ir al-Baḥr al-Mutawassiṭ*. Beirut: Dār Maktabat al-Ḥayāh, 1966.

'Aṭwān, Ḥusayn. *al-Shi'r al-'Arabī fi Khurāsān fī al-'aṣr al-Umawī*. 'Ammān: Maktabat al-Muḥtasib, and Beirut: Dār al-Jīl, 1974.

———. *Sīrat al-Walīd b. Yazīd*. Cairo: Dār al-Ma'ārif, 1980.

———. *al-Walīd b. Yazīd: 'arḍ wa naqd*. Beirut: Dār al-Jīl, 1401/1981.

Ayoub, Mahmoud. "*Jihād*: A Source of Power and Framework of Authority in Islam." *Bulletin of the Institute of Middle Eastern Studies, International University of Japan* 6 (1992), 205–32.

al-Azdī, Abū Zakariyyā Yazīd b. Muḥammad (d. 334/946). *Ta'rīkh al-Mawṣil*. Ed. 'Alī Ḥabība. Cairo: al-Majlis al-A'lā li al-Shu'ūn al-Islāmiyya, 1387/1967.

al-'Aẓīmī, Muḥammad b. 'Alī al-Ḥalabī (d. 556/1161). *Ta'rīkh Ḥalab*. Ed. Ibrāhīm Za'rūr. Damascus: n. p., 1984.

Baḥshal, Aslam b. Sahl al-Razzāz (d. 288/900). *Ta'rīkh Wāsiṭ*. Ed. Jurjis 'Awwād. Baghdad, 1387/1967.

al-Balādhurī, Aḥmad b. Yaḥyā b. Jābir (d. 279/892). *Ansāb al-ashrāf*. Ms. Istanbul, Süleymaniye Kütüphanesi (Reisulküttap Mustafa Efendi), nos. 597–8. 2 vols. Also Vol. V. Ed. S. D. F. Goitein. Jerusalem: Hebrew University, 1936.

———. *Futūḥ al-buldān*. Ed. Ṣalāḥ al-Dīn al-Munajjid. Cairo: Dār al-Nahḍa al-Miṣriyya, 1956–57.

Barnard, L. W. *The Graeco-Roman and Oriental Background of the Iconoclastic Controversy*. Leiden: E. J. Brill, 1974.

Barthold, Vasilii Vladimirovich (d. 1349/1930). *Turkestan down to the Mongol Invasion*. 3rd ed. Tr. Mrs T. Minorsky. London: Luzac, 1968.

Bates, Michael. "History, Geography and Numismatics in the First Century of Islamic Coinage." *Revue Suisse de Numismatique* 65 (1986) 231–262.

Beeston, A. F. L., and Lawrence I. Conrad. "On Some Umayyad Poetry in the History of al-Ṭabarī." *JRAS*, forthcoming.

Blankinship, Khalid Yahya. "al-'Arab fī Khurāsān min 31 ilā 132 h." Unpublished MA thesis, Cairo University, 1983.

———. "The Tribal Factor in the 'Abbāsid Revolution: The Betrayal of the Imam Ibrāhīm b. Muḥammad." *JAOS* 108 (1988), 589–603.

Bord, Lucien-Jean. *Les Mérovingiens: les rois inconnus*. Chiré-en-Montreuil: Editions de Chiré, 1981.

Bosworth, C. E. *Sīstān under the Arabs, from the Islamic Conquest to the Rise of the Ṣaffārids (30–250/651–864)*. Rome: Istituto Italiano per il Medio ed Estremo Oriente (IsMEO), 1968.

Brooks, E. W. "The Arabs in Asia Minor 641–750, from Arabic sources." *Journal of Hellenic Studies* 18 (1898), 182–208.

Brosset, M. *Additions et éclaircissements à l'histoire de la Géorgie, depuis l'antiquité jusqu'en 1469 de J.-C.* St. Petersburg: Imprimerie de l'Académie Impériale des Sciences, 1851.

al-Bukhārī, Abū 'Abd Allāh Muḥammad b. Ismā'īl (d. 256/870). *Ṣaḥīḥ al-Bukhārī*. Cairo: Dār al-Sha'b, n. d. (1970's). 9 vols.

Canard, Marius. "Les expéditions des Arabes contre Constantinople dans l'histoire et dans la légende." *Journal asiatique* 208 (1926) 61–121. Reprinted in *L'expansion arabo-islamique et ses répercussions*. London: Variorum Reprints, 1974.

Chavannes, Edouard. *Documents sur les Tou-kiue (Turcs) Occidentaux*. Paris: Librarie d'Amérique et d'Orient, n. d. Includes *Notes Additonelles* with separate pagination.

Chronicon ad A.C. *1234 pertinens*. Vol. I. Ed. I.-B. Chabot. *Corpus Scriptorum Christianorum Orientalium*, Vol. LXXXI. *Scriptores Syri*, Vol. XXXVI. Louvain, 1920. Reprint Louvain: Imprimerie Orientaliste, 1953.

Chronicon ad A.D. *846 pertinens*. Ed. E. W. Brooks. Part IV in *Chronica Minora*, Vol. II. *Corpus Scriptorum Christianorum Orientalium*, Vol. III. *Scriptores Syri*, Vol. III. Louvain, c. 1904. Reprint Louvain: CSCO, 1960.

Chronicon anonymum ad A.D. *819 pertinens*. Ed. Aphram Barsaum. In *Chronicon ad* A.C. *1234 pertinens*. Vol. I. Ed. I.-B. Chabot. *Corpus Scriptorum Christianorum Orientalium*, Vol. LXXXI. *Scriptores Syri*, Vol. XXXVI. Louvain, 1920. Reprint Louvain: Imprimerie Orientaliste, 1953.

Chronicon Moissiacense. In *Monumenta Germaniæ Historica: Scriptorum*. Vol.I (pp. 280–313). Ed. Georg Heinrich Pertz. Hanover: Hahn, 1826.

Collins, Roger. *The Arab Conquest of Spain 710–797*. Oxford: Basil Blackwell, 1989.

Connolly, Peter. *Greece and Rome at War*. Englewood Cliffs, NJ: Prentice-Hall, 1981.

Conrad, Lawrence. "Notes on al-Ṭabarī's History of the Caliphate of Hishām ibn 'Abd al-Malik." *JRAS*, 3rd Ser., III (1993), 1–31.

Continuatio Isadori (Continuatio Byzantia Arabica et Continuatio Hispana). In *Monumenta Germaniæ Historica: Auctorum Antiquissimorum* (written c. 137/754). Vol. XI, (pp. 323–69). Ed. Theodore Mommsen. Berlin: Weidmann, 1894.

Cornell, Vincent J. "Jihad: Islam's Struggle for Truth." *Gnosis*, no. 21 (1991), 18–23.

Creswell, K. A. C., and James W. Allan. *A Short Account of Early Muslim Architecture*. Cairo: American University in Cairo Press, 1989.

Crone, Patricia. *Slaves on Horses: the Evolution of the Islamic Polity*. Cambridge: University Press, 1980.

——— and Martin Hinds. *God's Caliph: Religious Authority in the First Centuries of Islam*. Cambridge: University Press, 1986.

Cunningham, Alexander (d. 1311/1893). *The Ancient Geography of India*. Vol. I. *The Buddhist Period, Including the Campaigns of Alexander, and the Travels of Hwen-Thsang*. London, 1871. Reprint Varanasi: Indological Book House, 1963.

Cuoq, Joseph. *L'Islam en Ethiopie des origines au XVIe* siècle. Paris: Nouvelles Editions Latines, 1981.

Dabashi, Hamid. *Authority in Islam from the Rise of Muḥammad to the Establishment of the Umayyads*. New Brunswick, NJ: Transaction Publishers, 1989.

Dasxurancị, Movsês. *The History of the Caucasian Albanians* (London Oriental Series, Vol. VIII). Tr. C. J. F. Dowsett. London: Oxford University Press, 1961.

Dennett, Daniel C. (d. 1366/1947). *Conversion and the Poll-tax in Early Islam* (Harvard Historical Monographs Vol. XXII). Cambridge, Mass.: Harvard University Press, 1950.

al-Dhahabī, Shams al-Dīn Abū 'Abd Allāh Muḥammad b. Aḥmad b. 'Uthmān (d. 748/1348). *Siyar a'lām al-nubalā'*. Ed. Shu'ayb al-Arna'ūṭ. Beirut: Mu'assasat al-Risāla, 1981. 23 vols.

———. *Ta'rīkh al-Islām*. Cairo: Maktabat al-Qudsī, 1367–9. 6 vols.

Dhū al-Rumma, Ghaylān b. 'Uqba al-'Adawī (d. 117/735). *Dīwān Dhī al-Rumma*. Commentary of Aḥmad b. Ḥātim al-Bāhilī. Ed. 'Abd al-Quddūs Abū Ṣāliḥ. Damascus: Majma' al-Lugha al-'Arabiyya, 1393/1973. 3 vols.

Dikshit, Durga Prasad. *Political History of the Chalukyas of Badami*. New Delhi: Abhinav Publications, 1980.

al-Dīnawarī, Abū Ḥanīfa Aḥmad b. Dā'ūd (d. 282/895). *al-Akhbār al-ṭiwāl*. Ed. V. Guirgass. Leiden: E. J. Brill, 1888.

pseudo-Dionysius of Tell Maḥré (written c. 158/775). *Chronique* (Bibliotheque de l'Ecole des Hautes Etudes Vol. 112). Ed. and tr. J.-B. Chabot. Paris: Émile Bouillon, 1895.

Doctrina Iacobi nuper baptizati. Ed. N. Bonwetsch. *Abhandlungen der Königlichen Gesellschaft der Wissenschaften zu Göttingen, Philologisch-Historische Klasse*. Neue Folge Band XII, Nro. 3. Berlin: Weidmannsche Buchhandlung, 1910.

Dombrowski, Franz Amadeus. "The Growth and Consolidation of Muslim Power in the Horn of Africa: Some Observations." *Archív Orientální* 51 (1983) 55–67.

Donner, Fred McGraw. *The Early Islamic Conquests*. Princeton: University Press, 1981.

Dunlop, D. M. *A History of the Jewish Khazars*. New York: Schocken Books, 1954.

al-Dūrī, 'Abd al-'Azīz. *The Rise of Historical Writing among the Arabs*. Tr. Lawrence Conrad. Princeton: Princeton University Press, 1983.

Elias of Nisibis (fl. 410/1019). *Eliae metropolitae Nisibeni opus chronologicum*.

Vol. I. Ed. E. W. Brooks. *Corpus Scriptorum Christianorum Orientalium,* Vol. LXII. *Scriptores Syri,* Vol. XXI. Louvain, c. 1910. Reprint Louvain: CSCO, 1962.

Ettinghausen, Richard, and Oleg Grabar. *The Art and Architecture of Islam: 650–1250.* Harmondsworth: Penguin (Pelican History of Art), 1987.

al-Farazdaq, Tammām b. Ghālib (d. 112/730). *Sharḥ dīwān al-Farazdaq.* Ed. 'Abd Allāh Ismā'īl al-Ṣāwī. Cairo, 1936. 2 vols.

Fatḥnāmah-i Sind (Chachnāmah). Tr. 'Alī b. Ḥāmid b. Abī Bakr al-Kūfī (d. 613/1216). Ed. N. A. Baloch. Islamabad: Institute of Islamic History, Culture and Civilization, 1403/1983.

al-Fayrūzābādī, Majd al-Dīn Muḥammad b. Ya'qūb (d. 817/1414). *al-Qāmūs al-muḥīṭ.* 2nd printing. Cairo: Muṣṭafā al-Babī al-Ḥalabī, 1371/1952. 4 vols.

Ferrill, Arther. *The Fall of the Roman Empire: the Military Explanation.* London: Thames and Hudson, 1986.

Finley, Moses I. *Ancient History: Evidence and Models.* New York: Elizabeth Sifton Books, Penguin Books, 1987.

———. *Ancient Sicily.* Revised ed. London: Book Club Associates, 1979.

Fragmenta chronici anonymi auctoris ad A.D. 813 pertinenta. Ed. E. W. Brooks. Part I in *Chronica Minora,* Vol. III. *Corpus Scriptorum Christianorum Orientalium,* Vol. V. *Scriptores Syri,* Vol. V. Louvain, c. 1906. Reprint Louvain: CSCO, 1960.

Gabrieli, Francesco. *Il Califatto di Hishām: Studi di storia omayyade* (Mémoires de la Société Royale d'Archéologie d'Alexandrie Vol VII, No. 2). Alexandria: Société de Publications Egyptiennes, 1935.

Gardīzī, Abū Sa'īd 'Abd al-Ḥayy b. Ḍaḥḥāk b. Maḥmūd (fl. 442–3/1050–2). *Ta'rīkh-i Gardīzī (Zayn al-akhbār).* Ed. 'Abd al-Ḥayy Ḥabībī. Tehran: Dunyāy-i Kitāb, 1363.

Gibb, H. A. R. *The Arab Conquests in Central Asia.* London: Royal Asiatic Society, 1923.

Gibbon, Edward (d. 1208/1794). *The Decline and Fall of the Roman Empire.* Ed. Oliphant Smeaton. New York: The Modern Library, n. d. 3 vols.

Golden, Peter B. *Khazar Studies: An Historico-Philosophical Inquiry into the Origins of the Khazars.* Budapest: Akademiai Kiadó, 1980.

Grabar, André. *L'iconoclasme byzantin: le dossier archéologique.* 2nd ed. Paris: Flammarion, 1984.

Grabar, Oleg. *The Formation of Islamic Art.* New Haven: Yale University Press, 1973.

———, Renata Holod, James Knustad and William Trousdale. *City in the Desert: Qaṣr al-Ḥayr East* (Harvard Middle Eastern Monographs XXIII/XXIV). Cambridge, Mass.: Harvard University Press, 1978. 2 vols.

Grierson, Philip. *Byzantine Coins.* London: Methuen, 1982.

Grousset, René. *Histoire de l'Arménie, des origines à 1071*. Paris: Payot, 1947.

Guilland, Rodolphe. "L'expédition de Maslama contre Constantinople (717–718)." In *Études byzantines*. Paris: Presses Universitaires de France, 1959, pp. 109–33.

Haji Yahaya, Mahayudin. *The Origins of the Khawarij*. Subang Jaya, Selangor, Malaysia: Penerbitan Sarjana (M) Sdn. Bhd., 1984.

Haldon, J. F. *Byzantium in the Seventh Century: The Transformation of a Culture*. Cambridge: Cambridge University Press, 1990.

Hallo, William W., and William Kelly Simpson. *The Ancient Near East: A History*. San Diego: Harcourt Brace Jovanovich, 1971.

Hamidullah, Muḥammad. *The Muslim Conduct of State*. 7th ed. Lahore: Shaykh Muhammad Ashraf, 1397. Reprinted 1987.

Hammond, Nicholas G. L., ed. *Atlas of the Greek and Roman World in Antiquity*. Park Ridge, N. J.: Noyes Press, 1981.

Harris, William V. *War and Imperialism in Republican Rome 327–70 B. C.* Oxford: Clarendon Press, 1979.

Hawting, G. R. *The First Dynasty of Islam: The Umayyad Caliphate, A.D. 661–750*. Carbondale: Southern Illinois University Press, 1987.

Histoire de la Géorgie, depuis l'antiquité jusqu'au xixe siècle. Part 1. *Histoire ancienne, jusqu'en 1469 de J.-C.* Tr. M. Brosset. St. Petersburg: Imprimerie de l'Académie Imperiale des Sciences, 1849.

A Historical Atlas of South Asia. Ed. Joseph E. Schwartzberg. Chicago: University of Chicago Press, 1978.

Hoag, John D. *Islamic Architecture*. New York: Harry N. Abrams, 1975.

Hodgson, Marshall G. S. *The Venture of Islam*. Vol. I. *The Classical Age of Islam*. Chicago: University of Chicago Press, 1974.

Huergon, Jacques. *The Rise of Rome to 264 B.C.* Berkeley and Los Angeles: University of California Press, 1973.

Ḥusayn, Muḥammad Ḥājj. *al-Kumayt: ḥayātuh wa shi'ruh*. Damascus: Dār al-Ajyāl, n. d.

Ibn 'Abd al-Barr, Abū 'Umar Yūsuf b. 'Abd Allāh al-Nimarī al-Qurṭubī (d. 463/1071). *al-Qaṣd wa al-imam fī al-ta'rīf bi-uṣūl ansāb al-'Arab wa al-'ajam* and *al-Inbāh 'alā qabā'il al-ruwāh*. Cairo: Maktabat al-Qudsī, 1350.

Ibn 'Abd al-Ḥakam, Abū al-Qāsim 'Abd al-Raḥmān (d. 257/871). *Futūḥ Miṣr wa akhbāruhā* (Yale Oriental Series, Vol. III). Ed. C. C. Torrey. New Haven: Yale University Press, 1922.

Ibn 'Abd al-Ḥakam, Abū Muḥammad 'Abd Allāh (d. 214/829). *Sīrat 'Umar b. 'Abd al-'Azīz*. Ed. Aḥmad 'Ubayd. Reprint Cairo: Maktabat Wahba, 1983.

Ibn 'Abd Rabbih, Aḥmad b. Muḥammad (d. 328/940). *al-'Iqd al-farīd*. Ed. Aḥmad Amīn, Aḥmad al-Zayn and Ibrāhīm al-Abyārī. Cairo: Lajnat al-Ta'līf wa al-Tarjama wa al-Nashr, 1367–93/1948–73. 7 vols.

Ibn al-'Adīm, Kamāl al-Dīn 'Umar b. Aḥmad (d. 660/1262). *Zubdat al-ḥalab min ta'rīkh Ḥalab*. Vol. I. Ed. Sāmī Dahhān. Damascus: al-Ma'had al-Faransī li al-Dirāsāt al-'Arabīyya, 1951.

Ibn 'Asākir, Abū al-Qāsim 'Alī b. Abī Muḥammad al-Ḥasan (d. 571/1176). *Tahdhīb ta'rīkh madīnat Dimashq al-kabīr*. Ed. 'Abd al-Qādir Badrān and Aḥmad 'Ubayd. Damascus, 1911–32. 7 vols.

Ibn A'tham al-Kūfī, Abū Muḥammad Aḥmad al-Kindī (fl. 204/819). *al-Futūḥ*. Ed. Muḥammad 'Abd al-Mu'īd Khān and others. Ḥaydarābād: Dā'irat al-Ma'ārif al-'Uthmāniyya, 1388–95/1968–75. 8 vols.

Ibn al-Athīr, 'Izz al-Dīn Abū al-Ḥasan 'Alī b. Muḥammad b. Muḥammad al-Shaybānī al-Jazarī (d. 630/1233). *al-Kāmil fi al-ta'rīkh*. Ed. C. J. Tornberg. Leiden: Brill, 1851–76. 13 vols. Reissue Beirut: Dār Ṣādir, 1385–87/1965–67, with different pagination used here.

———. *al-Lubāb fī tahdhīb al-ansāb*. Cairo: Maktabat al-Qudsī, 1356–69. 3 vols.

Ibn al-Biṭrīq, Sa'īd (Eutychius, Melkite Patriarch of Alexandria) (d. 328/940). *al-Ta'rīkh al-majmū' 'alā al-taḥqīq wa al-taṣdīq*. Beirut, 1909.

Ibn Durayd, Abū Bakr Muḥammad b. al-Ḥasan (d. 321/933). *al-Ishtiqāq*. Ed. 'Abd al-Salām Muḥammad Hārūn. Cairo: Mu'assasat al-Khānjī, 1378/1958.

Ibn al-Faqīh, Abū Bakr Aḥmad b. Muḥammad al-Hamadhānī. *Mukhtaṣar kitāb al-buldān*. Leiden: E. J. Brill, 1885.

Ibn Ḥabīb, Abū Ja'far Muḥammad al-Baghdādī (d. 246/860). *al-Muḥabbar*. Ed. Ilse Lichtenstadter. Hyderabad: Dā'irat al-Ma'ārif al-Niẓāmiyya, 1942.

Ibn Ḥajar al-'Asqalānī, Abū al-Faḍl Aḥmad b. Nūr al-Dīn 'Alī (d. 852/1449). *Tahdhīb al-tahdhīb*. Hyderabad: Dā'irat al-Ma'ārif al-Niẓāmiyya, 1325–27. 12 vols.

Ibn Ḥazm, 'Alī b. Aḥmad (d. 456/1064). *Jamharat ansāb al-'Arab*. Ed. 'Abd al-Salām Muḥammad Hārūn. Cairo: Dār al-Ma'ārif, 1382/1962.

Ibn Hishām, 'Abd al-Malik (d. 218/833). *al-Sīra al-nabawiyya*. Ed. Muṣṭafā al-Saqqā, Ibrāhīm al-Abyārī, and 'Abd al-Ḥafīẓ Shalabī. 2nd printing. Cairo: Muṣṭafā al-Bābī al-Ḥalabī, 1375/1955. 2 vols.

Ibn 'Idhārī, Aḥmad b. Muḥammad al-Marrākushī (fl. c. 706/1306). *al-Bayān al-mughrib fī akhbār al-Andalus wa al-Maghrib*. Ed. G. S. Colin and E. Levi-Provençal. Leiden: Brill, 1948–51. 4 vols.

Ibn al-Kalbī, Abū-al-Mundhir Hishām b. Muḥammad (d. 204/819). *Ǧamharat an-nasab: das genealogische Werk des Hišām b. Muḥammad al-Kalbī*. Tr. and rearranged by W. Caskel and G. Strenziok. Leiden: Brill, 1966. 2 vols.

Ibn Kathīr, 'Imād al-Dīn Ismā'īl b. 'Umar al-Dimashqī (d. 774/1373). *al-Bidāya wa al-nihāya fi al-ta'rīkh*. Cairo: Maṭba'at al-Sa'āda, 1932–?. 14 vols. Ed. Beirut: Maktabat al-Ma'ārif, 1966. 8 vols.

———. *Tafsīr al-Qur'ān al-aẓīm*. Cairo: 'Isā al-Bābī al-Ḥalabī, n. d. [1970's], 4 vols.

Ibn Khaldūn, Abū Zayd 'Abd al-Raḥmān b. Muḥammad (d. 808/1406). *al-'Ibar wa dīwān al-mubtada' wa al-khabar fī ayyām al-'Arab wa al-'Ajam wa al-Barbar wa man 'āṣarahum min dhawī al-sulṭān al-akbar*. Beirut: Dār al-Kitāb al–Lubnānī li al-Ṭibā'a wa al-Nashr, 1959. 7 vols.

Ibn Khallikān, Shams al-Dīn Abū al-'Abbās Aḥmad b. Muḥammad b. Abī Bakr (d. 681/1282). *Wafayāt al-a'yān wa anbā' anbā' al-zamān*. Ed. Iḥsān 'Abbās. Beirut: Dār al-Qalam, 1968–71. 8 vols.

Ibn Khayyāṭ, Khalīfa al-'Uṣfurī, nicknamed "Shabāb" (d. 240/854). *al-Ṭabaqāt*. Ed. Akram Ḍiyā' al-'Umarī. Baghdad: Maṭba'at al-'Ānī, 1967.

———. *al-Ta'rīkh*. Ed. Suhayl Zakkār. Damascus: Wizārat al-Thiqāfa wa al-Siyāḥa wa al-Irshād al-Qawmī, 1967–8.

Ibn Khurdādhbih, Abū al-Qāsim 'Ubayd Allāh b. 'Abd Allāh (d. 300/913). *al-Masālik wa al-mamālik* (Bibliotheca Geographorum Arabicorum Vol. VI). Ed. M. J. De Goeje. Leiden: E. J. Brill, 1306/1889.

Ibn Manẓūr, Jamāl al-Dīn Abū al-Faḍl Muḥammad b. Mukarrim (d. 711/1311). *Lisān al-'Arab*. Ed. 'Abd Allāh 'Alī al-Kabīr, Muḥammad Aḥmad Ḥasab Allāh and Hāshim Muḥammad al-Shādhilī. Cairo: Dār al-Ma'ārif, 1980's. 6 vols.

Ibn al-Mubārak, 'Abd Allāh (d. 181/797). *al-Jihād*. Ed. Nazīh Ḥammād. Tunis: al-Dār al-Tūnisiyya li-al-Nashr, 1972.

Ibn Muhannā, Abū 'Alī 'Abd al-Jabbār b. 'Abd Allāh al-Khawlānī (fl. 365/976). *Ta'rīkh Dārayyā*. Ed. Sa'īd al-Afghānī. Damascus: al-Majma' al-'Ilmī al-'Arabī, 1369/1950.

Ibn al-Nadīm, Abū al-Faraj Muḥammad b. Abī Ya'qūb Isḥāq al-Warrāq (d. 380/990). *al-Fihrist*. Ed. Riḍā-Tajaddud b. 'Alī b. Zayn al-'Abīdīn al-Ḥā'irī al-Māzandarānī. Tehran: n. p., 1391/1971.

Ibn Qutayba, 'Abd Allāh b. Muslim al-Dīnawarī (d. 276/889). *al-Ma'ārif*. Ed. Tharwat 'Ukkāsha. Cairo: Dār al-Ma'ārif, 1960.

———. *'Uyūn al-akhbār*. Ed. Aḥmad Zakī al-'Adawī. Cairo: Dār al-Kutub al-Miṣriyya, 1343–49/1925–30. 4 vols. Reprint al-Hay'a al-Miṣriyya al-'Āmma li al-Kitāb, 1973–74.

(pseudo-)Ibn Qutayba. *al-Imāma wa al-siyāsa*. Ed. Ṭaha Muḥammad al-Zaynī. Cairo: Mu'assasat al-Ḥalabī, 1967. 2 vols.

Ibn al-Qūṭiyya, Abū Bakr b. 'Umar al-Qurṭubī (d. 367/977). *Ta'rīkh iftitāḥ al-Andalus*. Ed. Ibrāhīm al-Abyārī. Cairo and Beirut: Dār al-Kutub al-Islāmiyya, 1982.

Ibn Rustah, Abū 'Alī Aḥmad b. 'Umar. *al-Mujallad al-sābi' min kitāb al-a'lāq al-nafīsa* (Bibliotheca Geographorum Arabicorum Vol. VII). Ed. M. J. de Goeje. Leiden: E. J. Brill, 1892.

Ibn Taghrībirdī, Jamāl al-Dīn Abū al-Maḥāsin Yūsuf al-Atābikī (d. 874/1470). *al-Nujūm al-zāhira fī mulūk Miṣr wa al-Qāhira*. Vol. I. Cairo: al-Mu'assasa al-Miṣriyya al-'Āmma li al-Ta'līf wa al-Tarjima wa al-Ṭibā'a wa al-Nashr, 1383/1963.

Ibn Ṭūlūn, Shams al-Dīn Muḥammad (d. 953/1546). *al- Thaghr al-bassām fī dhikr man waliya qaḍā' al-Shām*. Ed. Ṣalāḥ al-Dīn al-Munajjid. Damascus: al-Majma' al-'Ilmī al-'Arabī, 1956.

al-Iṣbahānī, Abū al-Faraj ʻAlī b. al-Ḥusayn b. Muḥammad al-Qurashī (d. 356/967). *al-Aghānī*. Cairo: Dār al-Shaʻb, 1389–99/1969–79. 31 vols. (indexes still incomplete).

———. *Maqātil al-Ṭālibiyyīn*. Ed. Kāẓim al-Muẓaffar. al-Najaf: al-Maktaba al-Ḥaydariyya, 1385/1965.

al-Iṣṭakhrī, Abū Isḥāq Ibrāhīm b. Muḥammad al-Karkhī. *al-Masālik wa al-mamālik*. Leiden: E. J. Brill, 1927.

al-Jāḥiẓ, ʻAmr b. Baḥr (d. 255/869). *al-Bayān wa al-tabyīn*. Ed. ʻAbd al-Salām Muḥammad Hārūn. Cairo: Maktabat al-Khānjī, 1380–81/1960–61. 4 vols.

———. *al-Bukhalā'*. Ed. Ṭaha al-Ḥājirī. Cairo: Dār al-Maʻārif, 1958.

———. *Rasā'il al-Jāḥiẓ*. Ed. ʻAbd al-Salām Muḥammad Hārūn. Cairo: Maktabat al-Khānjī, 1399/1979. 4 vols. Ed. Ḥasan al-Sandūbī. Cairo, 1352/1933.

al-Jahshiyārī, Abū ʻAbd Allāh Muḥammad b. ʻAbdūs (d. 331/943). *al-Wuzarā' wa al-kuttāb*. Ed. Muṣṭafā al-Saqqā, Ibrāhīm al-Abyārī and ʻAbd al-Ḥafīẓ Shalabī. Cairo: Muṣṭafā al-Bābī al-Ḥalabī, 1938.

James, Edward. *The Origins of France: from Clovis to the Capetians, 500–1000*. London: Macmillan, 1982.

Jandora, John W. *The March from Medina: A Revisionist Study of the Arab Conquests*. Clifton, N. J.: Kingston Press, 1990.

Jarīr b. ʻAṭiyya b. al-Khaṭafa (d. 110/728). *Dīwān*. Ed. Muḥammad Ismāʻīl ʻAbd Allāh al-Ṣāwī. Cairo, 1353/1934. Reprint Beirut: Dār Maktabat al-Ḥayāh, 1965.

Jones, Arnold Hugh Martin. *The Later Roman Empire 284–602*. London: Basil Blackwell Ltd., 1964. 3 vols. Reprint Baltimore: The Johns Hopkins University Press, 1986. 2 vols. with same pagination as original.

Kaegi, Walter E. Jr. *Army, Society and Religion in Byzantium*. London: Variorum Reprints, 1982.

Kaḥḥāla, ʻUmar Riḍā. *Aʻlām al-nisā' fī ʻālamay al-ʻArab wa al-Islām*. 3rd ed. Beirut: Mu'assasat al-Risāla, 1977, 5 vols.

Kennedy, Hugh. *The Prophet and the Age of the Caliphates*. London: Longman, 1986.

Khaddūrī, Majid. *War and Peace in the Law of Islam*. Baltimore: Johns Hopkins Press, 1955.

Khammāsh, Najda. *al-Idāra fī al-ʻaṣr al-Umawī*. Damascus: Dār al-Fikr, 1400/1980.

Khleifat, Awad Mohammad. "The Caliphate of Hishām b. ʻAbd al-Malik (105–125/724–743), with Special Reference to Internal Problems." Ph. D. Thesis. University of London, May 1973.

al-Kindī, Abū ʻUmar Muḥammad b. Yūsuf al-Miṣrī (d. 256/870). *al-Wulāh wa al-quḍāh* (Gibb Memorial Series Vol. XIX). Ed. Rhuvon Guest. Leiden: E. J. Brill and London: Luzac, 1912.

Komroff, Manuel, ed. *Contemporaries of Marco Polo, Consisting of the Travel Records to the Eastern Parts of the World of William of Rubruck [1253–1255]; The Journey of John of Pian de Carpini [1245–1247]; The Journal of Friar Odoric [1318–1330] & The Oriental Travels of Rabbi Benjamin of Tudela [1160–1173]*. Reprint, New York: Dorset Press, 1989.

al-Kubaysī, 'Abd al-Majīd Muḥammad Ṣāliḥ. *'Aṣr Hishām b. 'Abd al-Malik 105–125/724–743*. Baghdad: Maṭba'at Salmān al-A'ẓamī, 1975.

Lambrick, Hugh Trevor. *Sind before the Muslim Conquest*. Hyderabad: Sindhi Adabi Board, 1973.

Lane-Poole, Stanley. *Historical Atlas*. Oxford: Clarendon Press, 1902.

Lapidus, Ira M. "The Conversion of Egypt to Islam". *Israel Oriental Studies* 2 (1972), 248–62.

Laurent, J. *L'Arménie entre Byzance et l'Islam, depuis la conquête arabe jusqu'en 886* (Bibliothèque des Ecoles Françaises d'Athènes et de Rome, Vol. CXVII). Paris: Fontemoing et Cie, Editeurs, 1919.

Le Strange, Guy (d. 1352/1933). *The Lands of the Eastern Caliphate*. Cambridge: University Press, 1905.

———. *Palestine under the Muslims: A Description of Syria and the Holy Land from A.D. 650 to 1500*. Cambridge: Riverside Press, 1890.

Lewis, Archibald R. *The Development of Southern French and Catalan Society, 718–1050*. Austin: University of Texas Press, 1965.

Lewis, Bernard. *The Political Language of Islam*. Chicago: University of Chicago Press, 1988.

Lewond (fl. c. 172/788). *The History of Lewond, the Eminent Vardapet of the Armenians*. Tr. Rev. Zaven Arzoumanian. Philadelphia: St. Sahag and St. Mesrob Armenian Church, 1982.

Lilie, R.-J. *Die byzantinische Reaktion auf die Ausbreitung der Araber* (Miscellanea Byzantina Monacensia XXII). Munich, 1976.

Livermore, Harold V. *The Origins of Spain and Portugal*. London: George Allen & Unwin, Ltd., 1971.

Livy, Titus (d. 12 C.E.). *The Early History of Rome*. Tr. Aubrey de Sélincourt. Harmondsworth: Penguin Books, 1960.

Lot, Ferdinand. "Etudes sur la bataille de Poitiers de 732." In *Recueil des travaux historiques de Ferdinand Lot*. Vol II. Geneva: Librairie Droz, 1970, pp. 243–67.

———. *Naissance de la France*. Paris: Fayard, 1970.

al-Ma'āḍīḍī, 'Abd al-Qādir. *Wāsiṭ fī al-'aṣr al-Umawī 81–132/700–49*. Baghdad: Dār al-Ḥurriyya li al-Ṭibā'a, 1396/1976.

McEvedy, Colin, and Richard Jones. *Atlas of World Population History*. Harmondsworth: Penguin, 1978.

Majumdar, R. C., and others. *The History and Culture of the Indian People*. Vol. III, *The Classical Age*. Vol. IV, *The Age of Imperial Kanauj*. Bombay: Bharatiya Vidya Bhavan, 1954–55.

Mālik b. Anas (d. 179/795). *al-Muwaṭṭa'*. Recension of Yaḥyā b. Yaḥyā al-Maṣmūdī. Ed. Muḥammad Fu'ād 'Abd al-Bāqī. Cairo: Dār al-Sha'b, 1371/1951.

Mango, Cyril. *Byzantium: The Empire of New Rome*. New York: Charles Scribner's Sons, 1980.

al-Maqqarī, Aḥmad b. Muḥammad al-Tilimsānī (d. 1041/1632). *Nafḥ al-ṭīb min ghuṣn al-Andalus al-raṭīb*. Ed. Iḥsān 'Abbās. Beirut: Dār Ṣādir, 1388/1968. 8 vols.

al-Maqrīzī, Taqī al-Dīn Aḥmad b. 'Alī (d. 845/1442). *al-Mawā'iẓ wa al-i'tibār bi dhikr al-khiṭaṭ wa al-āthār*. Reprint Baghdad: Dār al-Muthannā, 1970. 2 vols.

———. *al-Nizā' wa al-takhāṣum fīmā bayn Banī Umayya wa Banī Hāshim*. Ed. G. Vos. Leiden: E. J. Brill, 1888.

———. *al-Nuqūd al-Islāmiyya, al-musammā bi-shudhūr al-'uqūd fī dhikr al-nuqūd*. 5th printing. al-Najaf: al-Maktaba al-Ḥaydariyya, 1387/1967.

al-Mas'ūdī, 'Alī b. al-Ḥusayn (d. 346/957). *Murūj al-dhahab*. Ed. Charles Pellat. Beirut, 1966–79. 7 vols.

Michael the Syrian (d. 595/1199). *Chronique*. Ed. and tr. J.-B. Chabot. Paris, 1899–1910. 4 vols.

Mishra, Shyam Manohar. *Yasovarman of Kanauj: A Study of Political History, Social and Cultural Life of Northern India during the Reign of Yasovarman*. New Delhi: Abhinav Publications, 1977.

Morgan, David. *The Mongols*. Oxford: Basil Blackwell, 1986.

Morony, Michael. *Iraq after the Muslim Conquest*. Princeton: University Press, 1984.

al-Mubarrad, Muḥammad b. Yazīd (d. 285/898). *al-Kāmil fī al-lugha wa al-adab*. Ed. Muḥammad Abū al-Faḍl Ibrāhīm and al-Sayyid Shaḥāta. Cairo: Dār Nahḍat Miṣr. 4 vols.

Muḥammad 'Alī, Maulānā. *The Religion of Islām: A Comprehensive Discussion of the Sources, Principles and Practices of Islām*. 5th ed. Lahore: Aḥmadiyya Anjuman Ishā'at Islām, 1983.

al-Muqaddasī, Shams al-Dīn Abū 'Abd Allāh Muḥammad b. Aḥmad b. Abī Bakr al-Bashshārī (d. 375/985). *Aḥsan al-taqāsīm fī ma'rifat al-aqālīm* (Bibliotheca Geographorum Arabicorum Vol. III). Ed. M. J. De Goeje. Leiden: E. J. Brill, 1877 and 1906.

Muqātil b. Sulaymān al-Balkhī (d. 150/767). *Tafsīr Muqātil b. Sulaymān*. Ed. 'Abd Allāh Maḥmūd Shaḥāta. Vols. I and II. Cairo: al-Hay'a al-Miṣriyya al-'Āmma li-al-Kitāb, 1980–84.

Muslim b. al-Ḥajjāj al-Qushayrī al-Naysābūrī, Abū al-Ḥusayn (d. 261/875). *Ṣaḥīḥ Muslim*. Cairo: 'Īsā al-Bābī al-Ḥalabī, n. d. 2 vols.

Nadwi, Syed Sulaiman. *Indo-Arab Relations*. Tr. M. Salahuddin. Hyderabad, Deccan: The Institute of Indo-Middle East Cultural Studies, 1962.

Naqā'iḍ Jarīr wa al-Farazdaq. Ed. Anthony Ashley Bevan. Leiden: E. J. Brill, 1905–12. 3 vols.

Nikephoros Patriarch of Constantinople (d. 214/829). *Short History* (Corpus Fontium Historiae Byzantinae Vol. XIII). Ed. and tr. Cyril Mango. Washington: Dumbarton Oaks Research Library and Collection, 1990.

al-Nuṣṣ, Iḥsān. *al-'Aṣabiyya al-qabaliyya wa āthāruhā fī al-shi'r al-Umawī*. Beirut: Dār al-Yaqaẓa al-'Arabiyya, 1963.

al-Nuwayrī, Shihāb al-Dīn Aḥmad b. 'Abd al-Wahhāb (d. 732/1331). *Nihāyat al-arab fī funūn al-adab*. Vol. XXI. Ed. 'Alī Muḥammad al-Bajāwī. Cairo: al-Hay'a al-Miṣriyya al-'Āmma li al-Kitāb, 1976.

Omar, Farouk. *'Abbasiyyat: Studies in the History of the Early 'Abbasids*. Baghdad: University of Baghdad, 1396/1976.

Ostrogorsky, George. *History of the Byzantine State*. Revised ed. New Brunswick, N. J.: Rutgers University Press, 1969.

Panhwar, M. H. *Chronological Dictionary of Sind*. Jamshoro, Pakistan: Institute of Sindhology, 1983.

Pathan, Mumtaz Husain. *Arab Kingdom of al-Mansurah in Sind*. Sind, Pakistan: Institute of Sindhology, 1974.

Paulys Realencyclopädie der classischen Altertumswissenschaft. Stuttgart: J. B. Metzlersche Verlagtsbuchhandlung, 1894–1980.

Pipes, Daniel. "Mawlas: Freed Slaves and Converts in Early Islam." *Slaves and Slavery in Muslim Africa*. Vol I. *Islam and the Ideology of Enslavement*. Ed. John Ralph Willis. London: Frank Cass, 1985.

Qudāma b. Ja'far, Abū al-Faraj al-Kātib al-Baghdādī (d. 320/932). *Nabdh min kitāb al-kharāj wa ṣan'at al-kitāba* (Bibliotheca Geographorum Arabicorum Vol. VI). Leiden: E. J. Brill, 1306/1889.

al-Qurṭubī, Abū 'Abd Allāh Muḥammad b. Aḥmad al-Anṣārī (d. 671/1273). *al-Jāmi' li-aḥkām al-Qur'ān*. Beirut: Dār al-Kutub al-'Ilmiyya, 1408/1988. 20 vols. in 10, plus index vol.

Ramsay, W. M. *The Historical Geography of Asia Minor*. Reprint, Amsterdam: Adolf M. Hakkert, 1962.

al-Raqīq al-Qayrawānī, Abū Isḥāq Ibrāhīm b. al-Qāsim (fl. fifth/eleventh centuries). *Ta'rīkh Ifrīqiya wa al-Maghrib*. Ed. al-Munjī al-Ka'bī. Tūnis: Rafīq as-Saqṭī, 1968.

Ratchnevsky, Paul. *Genghis Khan: His Life and Legacy*. Tr. and ed. by Thomas Nivison Haining. Oxford: Basil Blackwell, 1991.

al-Rayyis, Muḥammad Ḍiyā' al-Dīn (d. 1397/1977). *al-Kharāj wa al-nuẓum al-māliyya li-al-dawla al-Islāmiyya*. 3rd ed. Cairo: Dār al-Ma'ārif, 1969.

Répertoire chronologique d'épigraphie arabe. Vol. I. Cairo: Institut Français d'Archéologie Orientale, 1931.

Roux, Georges. *Ancient Iraq*. 2nd ed. Harmondsworth: Penguin Books, 1980.

Ru'ba b. al-'Ajjāj al-Tamīmī. *Sammlungen alter Arabischer Dichter: der Diwan des Regezdichters Ruba ben Elaggag*. Ed. W. Ahlwardt. Berlin: Verlag von Reuther & Reichard, 1903.

Russell, J. C. "Late Ancient and Medieval Populations." *Transactions of the American Philosophical Society*. New Series. 48, No. 3 (1958).

al-Ṣafadī, Ṣalāḥ al-Dīn Khalīl b. Aybak (d. 764/1363). *al-Wāfī bi al-wafayāt*. Ed. Sven Dedering et al. Leipzig, Istanbul, Damascus and Wiesbaden: Franz Steiner Verlag, 1931– . 18+ vols. to date.

Sālim, al-Sayyid 'Abd al-'Azīz. *Ta'rīkh al-Muslimīn wa āthārihim fī al-Andalus: min al-fatḥ al-'Arabī ḥattā suqūṭ al-khilāfa bi-Qurṭuba*. Beirut: Dār al-Ma'ārif-Lubnān, 1962.

al-Sam'ānī, Abū Sa'īd 'Abd al-Karīm b. Muḥammad (d. 562/1166). *al-Ansāb*. Ḥaydarābād: Dā'irat al-Ma'ārif al-'Uthmāniyya, 1382–1402/1962–82. 13 vols.

Saunders, John J. *A History of Medieval Islam*. London: Routledge and Kegan Paul, 1965.

———. *The History of the Mongol Conquests*. New York: Barnes and Noble, 1971.

Sāwīrus b. al-Muqaffa'. *History of the Patriarchs of the Coptic Church of Alexandria (Siyar al-ābā' al-baṭārika)*. Part 3. Ed. and tr. B. Evetts in *Patrologia Orientalis*, V (1910), 3–215.

Schacht, Joseph. *An Introduction to Islamic Law*. Oxford: Clarendon Press, 1964.

pseudo-Sebêos (fl. c. 40/661). *Sebêos' History*. Tr. Robert Bedrosian. New York: Sources of the Armenian Tradition, 1985.

Segal, J. B. *Edessa, 'the Blessed City'*. Oxford: Clarendon Press, 1970.

Select Papyri. Vol. I. Tr. A. S. Hunt and C. C. Edgar. London: William Heinemann, Ltd., 1932.

Shaban, Muhammad 'Abd al-Hayy. *The 'Abbasid Revolution*. Cambridge: University Press, 1970.

———. *Islamic History: a New Interpretation. Vol. I, A.D. 600–750 (A.H. 132)*. Cambridge: University Press, 1971.

al-Shahristānī, Abū al-Fatḥ Muḥammad 'Abd al-Karīm b. Abī Bakr Aḥmad (d. 548/1153). *al-Milal wa al-niḥal*. Ed. 'Abd al-'Azīz Muḥammad al-Wakīl. Cairo: Mu'assasat al-Ḥalabī, 1387/1968. 3 vols.

al-Shaybānī, Muḥammad b. al-Ḥasan (d. 189/805). *The Islamic Law of Nations: Shaybani's Siyar*. Ed. and tr. Majid Khadduri. Baltimore: Johns Hopkins Press, 1966.

Stern, Fritz, ed. *The Varieties of History from Voltaire to the Present*. Cleveland: The World Publishing Co. (Meridian Books), 1956.

Stratos, Andreas N. *Byzantium in the Seventh Century*. Tr. Harry T. Hionides. Vol. IV (668–685). Amsterdam: Adolf M. Hakkert, 1978.

al-Ṭabarī, Abū Ja'far Muḥammad b. Jarīr (d. 310/923). *Ta'rīkh al-rusul wa al-mulūk*. Ed. M. J. De Goeje et al. Leiden: E. J. Brill, 1879–1901. 13 vols. in

3 series plus index and supplements. Also *The History of al-Ṭabarī. Vol. XXV. The End of Expansion.* Tr. Khalid Yahya Blankinship. Albany: SUNY Press, 1989.

Tacitus, Cornelius. *The Annals of Imperial Rome.* Tr. Michael Grant. Rev. ed. Harmondsworth: Penguin Books, 1977.

Ṭāha, 'Abdulwāḥid Dhanūn. *The Muslim Conquest and Settlement of North Africa and Spain.* London: Routledge, 1989.

Talbi, Mohamed. "Un nouveau fragment de l'Histoire de l'Occident Musulman (62–196/682–812), l'épopée d'al-Kahina." *Cahiers de Tunisie,* 1971.

Ta'rīkh al-khulafā'. Facsimile reproduced by P. Griyaznevitch. Moscow: Dār al-Nashr "al-'Alam," 1967.

Ta'rīkh-i Sīstān. Ed. Malik al-Shu'arā' Bahār. Tehran: Muḥammad Ramaḍānī, 1314/1935.

Theophanes (d. 201/817). *The Chronicle of Theophanes.* Tr. Harry Turtledove. Philadelphia: University of Pennsylvania Press, 1982.

Toumanoff, Cyril. *Studies in Christian Caucasian History.* Washington: Georgetown University Press, 1963.

Toynbee, Arnold J. *A Study of History.* Oxford: University Press, 1934–61. Reprint New York: Galaxy Books, 1962. 11 vols.

Trimingham, J. Spencer. *Islam in Ethiopa..* London: Oxford University Press, 1952.

Tripathi, Rama Shankar. *History of Kanauj to the Moslem Conquest.* Delhi: Matilal Banarsidass, 1959.

al-'Umarī, Akram Ḍiyā'. *Madīnan Society at the Time of the Prophet.* Vol. II. *The Jihād Against the Mushrikūn.* Tr. Hudā Khattāb. Herndon, VA: International Institute of Islamic Thought, 1411/1991.

'Uthmān, Fatḥī. *al-Ḥudūd al-Islāmiyya al-Bīzanṭiyya bayn al-iḥtikāk wa al-ittiṣāl al-ḥaḍārī.* Cairo: al-Dār al-Qawmiyya li-al-Ṭibā'a wa al-Nashr, 1966. 2 vols.

al-'Uyūn wa al-ḥadā'iq fī akhbār al-ḥaqā'iq. Vol. III (Fragmenta Historicorum Arabicorum I). Ed. P. De Jong and M. J. De Goeje. Leiden: E. J. Brill, 1869.

Vaidya, C. V. *History of Mediæval Hindu India.* Poona: the Oriental Book-supplying Agency, 1921–4. 5 vols.

Van der Meer, F., and Christine Mohrmann, *Atlas of the Early Christian World.* Ed. and tr. Mary F. Hedlund and H. H. Rowley. London: Nelson, 1966.

Van Ess, Josef. "Les Qadarites et la Gailāniyya de Yazīd III". *Studia Islamica.* 1970.

al-Wāḥidī, Abū al-Ḥusayn 'Alī b. Aḥmad al-Naysābūrī (d. 468/1076). *Asbāb al-nuzūl.* Beirut: Dār al-Kutub al-'Ilmiyya, 1402/1982.

Wakī', Muḥammad b. Khalaf b. Ḥayyān (d. 306/918). *Akhbār al-quḍāh.* Ed. 'Abd al-'Azīz Muṣṭafā al-Marāghī. Cairo: al-Maktaba al-Tijāriyya al-Kubrā, 1366–9/1947–50. 3 vols.

al-Walīd b. Yazīd b. 'Abd al-Malik (d. 126/744). *Shi'r*. Ed. Ḥusayn 'Aṭwān. 'Ammān: Maktabat al-Aqṣā, 1979.

Walker, J. *A Catalogue of the Arab-Byzantine and Post-Reform Umayyad Coins*. Vol. II, *Arab-Byzantine and Post-reform Umayyad Coins*. London, 1956.

al-Wāqidī, Muḥammad b. 'Umar (d. 207/822). *al-Maghāzī*. Ed. Marsden Jones. London: Oxford University Press, 1966.

Watt, W. Montgomery. *Muḥammad at Medina*. Oxford: Clarendon Press, 1956.

Webster, Graham. *The Roman Imperial Army of the First and Second Centuries* A.D. 3rd ed. Totowa, NJ: Barnes & Noble Books, 1985.

Wellhausen, Julius. *The Arab Kingdom and Its Fall*. Tr. Margaret Graham Weir. Calcutta: University of Calcutta, 1927.

———. *The Religio-Political Factions in Early Islam* (North-Holland Medieval Translations Vol. III). Ed and tr. R. C. Ostle and S. M. Walzer. Amsterdam: North-Holland Publishing Co., 1975.

White, Hayden. *Metahistory: The Historical Imagination in Nineteenth-Century Europe*. Baltimore: The Johns Hopkins University Press, 1973.

Wolf, Kenneth Baxter, tr. *Conquerors and Chroniclers of Early Medieval Spain* (Translated Texts for Historians, Vol. IX). Liverpool: University Press, 1990.

al-Ya'qūbī, Abū al-'Abbās Aḥmad b. Isḥāq b. Wāḍih (d. 284/897). *al-Buldān* (Bibliotheca Geographorum Arabicorum Vol. VII). Ed. A. W. T. Juynboll. Leiden: E. J. Brill, 1892.

———. *al-Ta'rīkh*. Ed. M. Th. Houtsma. Leiden: E. J. Brill, 1883. 2 vols.

Yāqūt al-Ḥamawī, Abū 'Abd Allāh Ya'qūb b. 'Abd Allāh (d. 626/1229). *Mu'jam al-buldān*. Ed. F. Wüstenfeld. Leipzig, 1866–73. 5 vols.

al-Zubayrī, Abū 'Abd Allāh al-Muṣ'ab b. 'Abd Allāh b. al-Muṣ'ab (d. 236/851). *Nasab Quraysh*. Ed. E. Lévi-Provençal. Cairo: Dār al-Ma'ārif, 1953.

Index

This is primarily an index of proper names, although the reader will also find certain italicized technical terms and a very few other words. All of the proper names and significant technical terms of the main text are indexed except those of extremely frequent occurrence, such as "Hishām," "Islam," "Muslim," and "Umayyad," which have been indexed only selectively. Book titles are also omitted except those of anonymous works. The notes have been similarly dealt with, except that all references to authors and titles are omitted unless they are important in the note text. Also, modern names have been mostly omitted from the indexing of the notes. The glossary is not indexed. The maps have been thoroughly indexed in a separate section following this one.

In the alphabetizing, the definite article "al-" has always been ignored, regardless of whether it appears at the beginning of an item or in the middle. Some Umayyad caliphs are designated by Roman numerals, but these are ignored in alphabetizing. Tribal groups are distinguished by the article "the"; names of countries have no article.

Abān b. al-Walīd al-Bajalī, 297
Abasgia, 316
'Abbād al-Ru'aynī (or al-Ma'āfirī), 322
al-'Abbās b. al-Walīd I b. 'Abd al-Malik, 80, 83, 119, 312–13, 325, 346
'Abbāsid revolution: forces, 5, 56, 59–60, 62, 66, 100, 206, 230, 259; foreshadowing of, 185; ideology, 97–99, 101, 191, 230, 260, 306; organization, 268, 298; sources for, 259; victory, 2, 54, 292, 346
'Abbāsids: administration, 41, 51, 63, 100, 293; Arab tribes under, 45, 57, 231, 291; finance, 41, 53, 71; maintain caliphate, 3, 7, 230; population under, 37; Qurashī lineage, 77; sources written under, 13, 21, 125, 259–60, 262; weakness of, 3, 20, 53, 71; western limit of rule, 3, 9, 212, 279, 288; conquer Zābulistān, 110
'Abd al-A'lā b. Jurayj al-Ifrīqī, the *mawlā* of Mūsā b. Nuṣayr, 207, 340
'Abd al-A'lā b. 'Uqba, 343
'Abd al-A'lā Zurzur, the *mawlā* of Mūsā b. Nuṣayr, 217, 340
'Abd Allāh b. 'Abd al-Malik b. Marwān I, 69
'Abd Allāh b. Abī Burda b. Abī Mūsā al-Ash'arī, 147, 185–86, 322
'Abd Allāh b. Abī Maryam, the *mawlā* of the Anṣār, 121, 314
'Abd Allāh b. 'Amr (or 'Amr b. 'Abd Allāh) al-Baṭṭāl, 120–21, 162–63, 169, 234–35, 314, 328–30
'Abd Allāh b. 'Uqba b. Nāfi' al-Fihrī, 120–21
'Abd Allāh b. Ziyād al-Anṣārī, 165
'Abd Allāh b. al-Zubayr b. al-'Awwām al-Asadī al-Qurashī, 21, 27, 93
'Abd al-'Azīz b. Ḥātim b. al-Nu'mān al-Bāhilī, 107
'Abd al-'Azīz b. Marwān I b. al-Ḥakam, 69
'Abd al-Ḥamīd, Sa'd Zaghlūl, 272

'Abd al-Ḥamīd b. 'Abd al-Raḥmān b. Zayd b. al-Khaṭṭāb al-'Adawī al-Qurashī, 287
'Abd al-Malik b. Hishām b. Ayyūb al-Ḥimyarī, 250
'Abd al-Malik b. Marwān I b. al-Ḥakam: administration, 48–49, 51–52, 69, 77, 80, 98, 293, 297; builds Dome of the Rock, 93–94, 314; favoritism for Muḍar, 56, 286; ideological policy, 28, 38, 78, 93–96; progeny, 304; revolts against, 58; subordinates, 306; truce with Byzantines, 27, 286
'Abd al-Malik b. Muslim b. Rabī'a al-'Uqaylī, 151, 325
'Abd al-Malik b. Qaṭan b. Nahshal al-Fihrī, 165, 196, 208–9, 218–20, 337, 344; sons, 345
'Abd al-Qays, the, 67, 290, 297
'Abd al-Raḥmān b. 'Abd Allāh b. Makhashsh al-Ghāfiqī, 138, 142, 163–65, 196, 234–35, 321, 328, 335
'Abd al-Raḥmān b. Ḥabīb b. Abī 'Ubayda al-Fihrī, 211, 218, 220–21, 337, 345
'Abd al-Raḥmān b. Mu'āwiya b. Hishām al-Dākhil, 300, 342
'Abd al-Raḥmān b. Mu'āwiya b. Ḥudayj al-Sakūnī, 121
'Abd al-Raḥmān b. al-Mughīra al-'Abdarī, 208
'Abd al-Raḥmān b. Muḥammad b. al-Ash'ath al-Kindī, 34, 62, 98–99, 288
'Abd al-Raḥmān b. Na'īm b. Zuhayr al-Ghāmidī, 127
'Abd al-Raḥmān b. 'Uqba al-Ghifārī, 211, 214–16
'Abd al-Raḥmān b. Salīm al-Kalbī, 119, 312–13
'Abd al-Raḥmān b. Ziyād al-Lakhmī, 344
'Abd al-Rāziq, Maḥmūd Ismā'īl, 272
'Abd al-Wahhāb b. Bukht, 162
'Abd al-Wāḥid b. Yazīd al-Hawwārī al-Madhamī, 216–17
Abkhazia, 172
al-Abrash. *See* Sa'īd al-Abrash b. al-Walīd (or Bakr) al-Kalbī
'Absīs, 325
Abū Bakr b. Abī Quḥāfa b. 'Āmir al-Taymī al-Qurashī, 22, 24, 283
Abū al-Dhayyāl. *See* al-Hunayd b. Iyās b. Zuhayr al-'Adawī, Abū al-Dhayyāl
Abū Fāṭimah al-Azdī, 332
Abū Ḥanīfa b. al-Nu'mān, 295
Abū Hāshim 'Abd Allāh b. Muḥammad b. 'Alī b. Abī Ṭālib, 336
Abū 'Imrān al-Hudhalī, 165
Abū al-Jahm b. Kināna al-Kalbī, 317
Abū al-Khattār. *See* Ḥusām b. Ḍirār al-Kalbī, Abū al-Khaṭṭār
Abū Mikhnaf Lūṭ b. Yaḥyā, 295
Abū al-Ṣaydā'. *See* Ṣāliḥ b. Ṭarīf (2), the *mawlā* of the Ḍabba, Abū al-Ṣaydā'
Abū Sufyān b. Ḥarb b. Umayya, 24
Abū 'Ubayda Mi'mar b. al-Muthannā, the *mawlā* of the Taym, 255
Abū Yūsuf. *See* Sālim al-Azdī, Abū Yūsuf
Abū Yūsuf Ya'qūb b. Ibrāhīm al-Qāḍī, 295
Abū Zinād 'Abd Allāh b. Dhakwān, 78, 96, 268
Abyssinia, 74, 114–16, 284, 312, 329
Abyssinians, 74, 115–16
Achila, 311
Ādharbayjān, 8, 39–40, 52–54, 58, 61, 107–8, 122–25, 149–51, 154, 171, 289, 335
'Adī b. Arṭāh al-Fazārī, 287
'Adī al-Ribāb, the, 268, 350
'Adnān, the, 45, 264
Adulis, 116
Aegean Sea, 25
Afghanistan, 309; central, 38; eastern, 129
Africa, 67, 114, 200, 337
Agapius (Mahbūb) b. Constantine of Manbij, 149–50, 170–71, 200–201, 266
Aghlabids, 279
Ahl al-'Āliya, 291, 327
Ahl al-balad, 220
Ahl al-Madīna, 73
Aḥmad b. A'tham al-Kindī al-Kūfī, 122, 157, 171, 173, 250, 261
Aḥmad b. Faḍlān b. al-'Abbās, the *mawlā* of Muḥammad b. Sulaymān, 173
Ahmadabad, 133
al-Ahwāz, 40, 57, 61, 63–64, 259, 288
'Ā'isha bt. Hishām b. 'Abd al-Malik, 83
Ajnād (sing. *jund*): army divisions, 179,

210, 219, 221; districts, 47–50, 80, 84, 224, 288, 291–92
Akhbār majmū'a, 210
Akhlāṭ, 151
Akhmās, 42, 44
al-Akhṭal, Ghiyāth b. Ghawth al-Taghlibī, 56
Akroinon (Aqrun), 20, 162, 169–70, 200–201, 210, 224, 232, 235
Alan Gates, 106. *See also* Darial Pass, the
Alans, 123, 316
Aleppo, 95
Alexander the Great, 323
Algeciras. *See* al-Jazīra al-Khaḍrā'
Algeria, 3, 9, 114, 214, 216, 279, 288, 320
'Alī b. Abī Ṭālib b. 'Abd al-Muṭṭalib, 20–21, 23–24, 32, 73, 92, 96, 191
'Alids, 77, 92, 101, 190–91, 226, 229, 308
Allies, the, 247
'Alqama, 141
'Alqama b. Mujazzaz, 115, 312
Amanus Mountains, 23
America, pre-Columbian, 273
Amid, 293
Amorion, 312
Ampriotik, 324
al-'Amq, 162, 327
'Amr b. Fātik al-Kalbī, 139
'Amr b. Khālid, 234, 338
'Amr b. Muḥammad b. al-Qāsim al-Thaqafī, 186, 202–3
'Amr b. Muslim b. 'Amr al-Bāhilī, 131–32
Amṣār (sing. *miṣr*): on Caucasus front, 108, 150, 154; characteristics, 17, 26, 40–41; in Egypt, 70; founding of, 26, 289; geography distribution, 104, 115; in Iraq, 57–60, 63; in North Africa, 70, 72, 210; provinces of, 61; in Sind, 186; troops of, 34, 44, 74–75
Āmul, 155
Anahilapataka, 112
Anakopia, 172
Anatolia: geography, 104, 312, 314; southeast, 34; southwest, 286; war in, 25, 105, 118, 120–21, 176, 200–201, 224, 234–35; west, 162, 168
'Anaza, the, 294
'Anbasa b. Suḥaym al-Kalbī, 89, 141–42
al-Andalus, 40, 67, 90, 197, 259, 305. *See also* Spain
Andalusia. *See* al-Andalus
Andalusians, 260
Ankara. *See* Ankyra
Ankyra, 168–69, 312, 314, 329
Anṣār, the, 286
Antioch, 33–34, 48, 120, 312
'Aqaba, Gulf of, 312
Aqrun. *See* Akroinon
al-Aqṣā Mosque, 82
Aquitaine, 113, 141, 164, 328
Aquitanians, 164, 311
Aqwā Burtūra, 220
Arabia: conquest of, 19, 22; eastern, 24, 58, 63–64, 75, 290; geography, 40, 74, 104, 115; as metropole of caliphate, 14, 17, 138; northern, 136; population, 42, 44, 273, 283; Roman province of, 48; in Second *Fitna*, 27–28; southern, 50; western, 1, 22, 73–75, 291
Arabic: language, 28, 38–39, 80, 94, 257, 307; names, 205, 207, 264; sources written in, 197, 248, 253, 266–67, 269
Arabs: administrative roles, 41, 289; in Caucasus, 150; earliest Muslims, 113; Egyptian, 69, 135–36, 213, 274, 298; expansion, 1, 57–58, 68; genealogies, 264, 290; individual named, 182, 185, 219; intertribal conflict, 5, 48, 98, 271; Iraqi, 58, 61; Jazīran, 51–52, 54–55; Khurāsānī, 62, 126–28, 156, 177, 179, 185, 317; military methods, 13, 15, 17, 72, 104; modern scholars, 272; North African, 30, 67–69, 73, 114, 136–37, 139, 164–65, 195, 204–8, 211–12, 215, 217; old settlers, 5, 57, 99–100, 209, 226; prisoners, 170, 280; rights to spoils and stipends, 31, 68, 86, 99–100, 225; Sijistānī, 130; Sindī, 131, 134, 148– 49, 186, 319; sources on, 269; Spanish, 73, 142, 164, 196, 219–21, 328, 345; Syrian, 5, 24, 49–50, 73, 142; tribal organization, 24, 42, 45; Yamanī, 24
Aramaeans, 23
Araxes River, 122, 124, 151, 175
Arbā', 42, 44
Ardabīl, 40, 53, 108, 149–51, 154, 157, 212, 224, 233, 250, 323, 325
Arelate, 197
Arles, 197

Armenia: administrative organization, 52–54, 107, 123–24, 153–54, 294; Armenia I (former Roman province), 119, 313; Armenia IV (former Roman province), 27, 119; geography, 40, 106–7, 309; governors, 122, 149–50, 171, 289; Irmīniya as mint, 40, 305; Islam in, 108; Khazar invasion, 122; Muslim expeditions in, 68, 107, 151, 169, 172, 293; strategic position, 31, 107
Armeniakon theme, 314
Armenian sources, 253, 266–67, 310
Armenians, 23, 107–8, 153–54, 172, 290, 331
Arrān, 149–50
Arzān al-Rūm, 150
'Aṣabiyya, 55, 66
Asad b. 'Abd Allāh b. Asad al-Qasrī al-Bajalī, 123, 127–28, 179–82, 185, 233–34, 317, 333–34
Asāwira, the, 43, 298
al-Aṣbagh b. 'Abd al-'Azīz b. Marwān I, 94
al-Aṣfaḥ b. 'Abd Allāh al-Kalbī, 130, 146–47, 231, 233, 318, 335
'Ashā'ir. *See buṭūn*
al-Ashhab, 336
al-Ashmūnayn, 267
Ashot Bagratouni. *See* Bagratouni, Ashot
Ashras b. 'Abd Allāh al-Sulamī, 124, 127–28, 141, 155, 177, 181, 317–18, 332
Asia, 67
Asia Minor, 146, 169. *See also* Anatolia
Asīd b. Zafir (or Zufar) al-Sulamī, 172
'Aṣim b. 'Abd Allāh b. Yazīd al-Hilālī, 120, 176–79, 181, 183, 290, 299, 332–33
'Asīr, 290
al-Asnām, 217, 344
Assyrians, 18
Astorga. *See* Asturqa
Asturias, 141, 309
Asturqa, 219, 337
al-Aswad b. Bilāl al-Muḥāribī, 339
Aswān, 114–15
al-'Aṭāsīn, 120, 168, 314
Ateous, 120, 168, 314. *See also* Ṭataya
Atlas Mountains, 114, 343
'Aṭwān, Husayn, 272
Autun, 141, 322
Avignon, 197
'Awāna b. al-Ḥakam b. 'Awāna al-Kalbī, 186, 256, 295, 347
Ayla, 312
'Ayn al-Tamr, 299
Azd, the, 57, 60, 62, 157, 177, 290, 342
Azd 'Umān, the, 67
Azerbaijan, 106. *See also* Adharbayjān
Azraqīs, 206

al-Bāb: geography, 106; in Khazar war, 108, 122, 151–52, 157, 171, 310, 323, 331; mint, 40, 305; as a *miṣr*, 151–54, 172, 174–75, 186, 224, 325. *See also* Caspian Gates
Bāb al-Abwāb. *See* al-Bāb
Bāb al-Lān, 106. *See also* Darial Pass, the
Badakhshān, 180
Badami, 112
Bādis, 343
Badr, Battle of, 150
Baghdad, 40, 259–60, 296
Bagratids, 153, 172
Bagratouni, Ashot, 153, 172, 331
Baharīmad, 133
Bahlūl, 101, 336
al-Bahrayn, 57, 63, 291
Bāja, 216
Bājarwān, 149–51, 324
Bajīla, the, 268
al-Bakhtarī b. Mujāhid, the *mawlā* of the Shaybān, 308
al-Bakkā'ī, 250
Bakr b. Suwayd, 193, 234
Bakr b. Wā'il, the, 56, 62, 67, 290, 294
al-Balādhurī, Ahmad b. Yaḥyā b. Jābir, 48–49, 71, 115, 134, 173, 261–62, 264, 270
Balanjar, 122, 152, 315
Balansa, 329
Balāṭ al-Shuhadā', Battle of. *See* Poitiers, Battle of
Bal-Ḥārith, the, 268
Bālis, 302
Balj b. Bishr al-Qushayrī (or al-Qasrī), 211–13, 218–21, 235, 341–42, 344–45
Balkh, 40, 155, 176–77, 180–81, 183, 289, 305, 333

al-Balqā', 48, 51, 80, 292
Balūniya, 169, 329
Banā, 320
Bappa, 188
Baqdūra, 211
Barājim, the, 290
Barawṣ. *See* Barūṣ
Barcelona, 141
Bardha'a, 149, 151, 172, 174, 331
Barmer, 133
Barqa, 210, 300
Barunj, 133. *See also* Broach
al-Barūqān, 128, 317
Barūṣ (Barawṣ), 133. *See also* Broach
Barwān, 40
al-Bashkuns. *See* Basques
Basques, 196
al-Baṣra: administration, 57, 60, 84; dependencies, 58, 61–64, 297; geography, 18, 29, 59; governors, 322; as a *miṣr*, 289; migration from, 61–63, 333; mosques in, 17, 284; politics, 24, 60; population, 274; sources for, 259–60, 262; tribes, 44, 57, 60, 67, 308
Baṣran superprovince, 61
Baṣrans, 60–63, 66–67, 75, 126, 147, 296–97, 339
Baṭna, 343
al-Baṭṭāl. *See* 'Abd Allāh b. 'Amr al-Baṭṭāl
Bay'a, 77
Bayān b. Sam'ān al-Tamīmī, 294, 336
al-Bayḍā', 149, 172, 331. *See also* Itil
Baykand, 128, 155; Battle of, 124, 128
al-Baylamān, 133, 319. *See also* Bhillamala
al-Baylaqān, 149–51, 323
Beja, the. *See* Buja, the
Berar, 112
Berbers, 228, 232; in Muslim army, 31, 68, 195, 204–5, 228; break unity of caliphate, 19, 232; embrace Islam, 29, 68, 72, 113–14, 137–38, 193, 298, 328–29; enslaved, 71, 89, 137, 193–94, 204, 345; grievances, 204–5, 226, 228; Khārijism among, 100–102, 114, 193, 206, 208, 214, 294, 340; in North Africa, 68, 86, 114, 136–40, 145, 164–65, 328; resist caliphal expansion, 6, 23, 25, 73, 100, 103–4, 113; course of great revolt, 164, 170, 195, 199–200, 203–18, 228, 231, 236, 337, 344; in Spain, 68, 100, 114, 142, 164, 196, 209, 219–21, 322–28, 344; tribes, 343; warfront against, 72, 139, 165
Bhattis, 111, 133
Bhillamala, 111, 133, 187
Bhinmal, 133
Bhumilka, 112, 187
Bilāl b. Abī Kabsha, 130
Bishr b. Jurmūz al-Ḍabbī, 332
Bishr b. Ṣafwān b. 'Amr al-Kalbī, 138–39, 233, 299, 345
Biskara, 343
Bīt, 320
Bithynia, 120
Black Sea, 106
'Blacks, Land of the,' 194
Booty: in Anatolia, 54–55, 118, 168; taken by Byzantines, 201; in Caucasus, 125, 151, 153, 171, 232, 315, 331; importance as income, 58, 65–66, 82, 84, 87, 103, 167, 194; in India, 65, 134; in Jurjān, 66; monopolized by Arabs, 68; in North Africa, 194, 204, 300; in Nubia, 115; principles for dividing, 12, 14, 279, 281, 290; in Sicily, 140; in Sind, 65, 84; in Spain, 72, 138; in Transoxiana, 232
Bordeaux, 164
Bosphorus, 105
Bosworth, C. E., 271
Brahmānābād, 186, 335
Brahmins, 30
Broach, 111–12, 133
Buddhists, 30
Buerre River, 197, 234
al-Buḥayra, Battle of, 309
Buja, the, 135, 320
Bukayr b. Māhān al-Hurmuzfarrahī, the *mawlā* of the Musliya, 65, 268, 298
Bukhārā, 128, 155, 160–61, 311
Bulgars, 287
Bushanj, 336
Buṭūn, 42–44, 58, 63, 66
Byzantines: administration, 48, 80; in Armenia, 107; in Caucasus, 172; civil wars, 31, 54, 201, 223; coins, 28, 94, 307; counteroffensives by, 26, 28, 31, 33–34, 170, 192–93, 200–202, 287, 310, 336–38; defeat Muslims, 19–20, 119, 169–70, 200, 232; frontier zone,

Byzantines (*continued*)
49–50, 57, 117–19, 163, 224; geography, 104–5; historical tradition, 33–34, 259, 265–66; iconoclasm, 95, 173; invited to accept Islam, 32, 95, 284; Khazar alliance, 108–9, 153–54, 174, 313; Muslim campaigns against, 20, 22, 25, 31, 38, 55, 87, 118–21, 162–63, 168–69, 200–201, 216, 223, 288, 339, 348; Muslim forces against, 306; navy, 22, 105, 169–70, 192, 194–95, 199, 202, 232, 300, 310, 337; in North Africa, 25, 29, 114, 116, 137; organized opponents of Muslims, 2, 6, 25, 54– 55, 93–94, 104, 117; prisoners, 163, 169, 201; provinces, 48, 52, 103, 259, 292, 309; in Sicily and Sardinia, 139–40, 165, 194–95; strategy against Muslims, 105, 167, 170; trade with Muslims, 94; truces with Muslims, 23, 27, 286; warfront, 8, 25, 29, 31, 54–55, 107, 117–21, 123, 145, 162–63, 167–70, 199–201, 203, 266, 271; in West Mediterranean, 72. *See also* Greek sources; Greeks
Byzantium. *See* Byzantines

Caesarea Palestinae, 48
Caleb, the, 292
Cambay, 319
Cappadocia. *See* Kappadokia
Carcassonne, 141
Carthage, 25
Caspian coast, 172, 175, 323, 331
Caspian Gates, 106, 149. *See also* al-Bāb
Caspian Sea, 106, 309
Caucasians, 172; North, 171
Caucasus: central, 123; eastern, 151; expeditions against Khazars in, 4, 34, 108, 122, 124–25, 149–55, 171–74, 232–33, 294; geography, 1, 106; Khazars in, 103, 106, 108; mountains, 37, 106, 108, 122, 171, 175; local Muslim campaigns in, 122–23, 145, 171–72, 174–75, 202; Muslims stationed in, 224, 229, 236; northern, 171–72, 174; offensive of Khazars in, 109, 117, 122, 124–25, 149–51, 154, 161–63, 231, 233, 313; sources for, 165, 186, 260–62, 266–67; truce with Khazars, 171; warfront, 106–7, 109, 121–25, 149–54, 170–75, 180, 199, 202–3, 271. *See also* Transcaucasia
Central Asia, 6, 25
Central Asians, 109. *See also* Turks, Central Asian
Cerdanya. *See* Cerritania
Cerritania, 164
Ceuta. *See* Sabta
Chach (Ṣaṣ) b. Dāhir b. Ṣaṣ, 132, 318
Chach dynasty, 85, 131
Chahamanas, 111
Chalukyas, 103, 112, 148, 187, 189, 311
Chandrapīda, 319
Chapas (Chapotakas), 112
Charles Martel, 112, 164, 197, 208
Chavotakas, 187
China, 1, 37, 334
Chinese, the: emperor, 110, 188, 317; empire, 1–2, 37; people, 109, 182; sources, 109, 184, 253
Chinese Turkistan. *See* Xinjiang
Chitor (Chitrakuta), 111, 133, 187–89, 319
Christians: Abyssinian, 329; in Arabia, 283; Armenian, 106, 153–54, 266– 67; Cypriot, 202; Georgian, 106; Jazīran, 56; Mardaites, 27; Middle Eastern, 93, 253; Monophysite, 52, 266–67; Muslims become, 200; Muslim ideological campaign against, 93–96; Muslim laws concerning, 13–14, 28–29; Nubian, 114; Orthodox (and Malkite), 25, 104, 154, 173, 253, 266, 313; sources, 120, 196, 200, 208, 249, 253, 265–66, 310; Spanish, 141–42, 196; Syrian, 26–28, 299; Western European, 72; Egyptian. *See* Copts
Chronicle of Alfonso III, The, 141
Chronicon ad A. D. 846 pertinens, 266
Chronicon ad A. D. 1234 pertinens, 201, 266
Chronicon anonymum ad A. D. 819 pertinens, 266
Chronicon Moisssiacense, 267
Cilicia. *See* Kilikia
Civil wars. *See Fitna*
Colchis. *See* Kolkhis
Collins, R., 272
Constantine (Byzantine commander), 162–63, 328, 339

Constantine V, 153–54, 169, 339
Constantinople: earlier expeditions against, 20, 22, 25–26, 285–86; geography, 105–6; mosque in, 3; siege by Maslama, 19–20, 31, 33– 34, 38, 72, 78, 84, 86–87, 104, 117–18, 121, 139, 250, 287, 310, 315; source of gold coins, 94; in the sources, 259, 266
Continuatio Isadori, 89, 164, 196, 208, 267
Copts (Egyptian Christians): conversion to Islam, 272; historical tradition, 253, 267; individual named, 268; manned Muslim navy, 72, 105, 139; peaceful character, 23, 70; revolts, 135–36, 165, 192, 194, 204
Cordoba. *See* Qurtuba
Corsica, 139
Crete, 286
Crone, Patricia, 5, 45, 271
Cushites, 135
Cutch (Kaccha), 111, 133–34, 148, 186–87, 319–20, 335
Cypriots, 202
Cyprus, 120, 202, 339

Dabasa, 119, 168, 312. *See also* Thebasa
Dabīl, 107, 153
al-Dabūsiyya, 128
Dāghistān, 106
al-Ḍaḥḥāk b. Qays b. al-Ḥuṣayn al-Shaybānī, 350
Dahlak Islands, 74, 116
Dahnaj, 133
Dalisandos, 119
Damascenes, 210, 223
Damascus: army division, 49–50, 82, 152, 170, 224, 346; as capital, 24, 40, 51, 112, 302; district of, 47–50, 80, 170, 288, 292–93; mint, 90, 305; mosque of, 82, 95, 284; sources for, 259; tribes, 341
al-Dandanqān, 178
Dantidurga, 187
Darband, 106
Darial Pass, the, 106, 123–24, 149, 172, 233, 316
Dasxuranči, Movses, 267
David, 301
Day of Thirst, 126–27, 146, 180
Daybul, 132, 148, 186, 318
Dayr Murrān, 293
al-Daylam, 40
Dead Sea, 22
Defile, Battle of the, 156–57, 159–60, 176, 185, 212, 249, 253, 326–27, 332, 346
Dennett, Daniel, 256–57, 272, 274
al-Dhahabī, Shams al-Dīn Muḥammad b. Aḥmad, 263
Dhakwāniyya, the, 91, 306
Dharmsala, 132
Dhāt al-Ṣawārī, Battle of, 22
Dhimmīs, 96, 269. *See also* non–Muslims
Dhū al-Rumma, Ghaylān b. ʻUqba b. Buhaysh al-ʻAdawī, 260–61
Dhufāfa b. ʻUmayr b. al-Ḥubāb al-Sulamī, 325
Didos, the, 332
al-Didūwāniyya, 175
Dihqāns, 149
Dijon, 322
al-Dīnawarī, Abū Ḥanīfa Ahmad b. Dāwūd, 259
Dionysius of Tell Mahré, pseudo-, 266
Dīwān: military rolls, 87, 307; poetry collection, 260; as for government department, see each under its own Arabic name, e. g., *dīwān al- rasā'il*, see under *al-rasā'il, dīwān*
Diyār Muḍar, 51–55, 80, 293
Diyār Rabīʻa, 51–54, 293
Doctrina Iacobi nuper baptizati, 12
Dome of the Rock, 93–94, 314
Don River, 108
Dordogne River, 164
Dorylaion, 120, 313
Drepana (Trapani), 193, 234
Dunlop, D. M., 174, 271
Dvin. *See* Dabīl

East, Diocese of the, 51
East, the. *See* Eastern superprovince
Eastern superprovince: ʻAbbāsids in, 268; administration, 60–61, 69, 93, 202, 305; income, 63–65, 71; governors, 29, 88, 98, 123, 126, 194, 341; *khawārij*, 56, 60, 190; *mawālī* from, 68, 138; sources for, 67, 97; territories of, 52, 57–58, 61–64, 103–4; tribes, 52–53, 56–58, 66–67, 123, 222. *See also* Iraqi superprovince

East Roman Empire, 2
Egypt: administration, 38, 40–41, 47, 67, 69–74, 89, 98, 288, 299; ancient, 254; Arabs in, 58, 298; army of, 210, 214; Byzantine raid on, 287, 310; conquest, 19, 22; dependencies, 69, 300; geography, 103; governors, 194, 204, 210, 213, 289, 299, 336; income from, 71, 124; naval contribution, 72, 192, 304, 314; receives Zayd's head, 191; relations with Christians in, 23, 70, 94, 307; revolts in, 135–36, 165, 192; in Second *Fitna*, 27–28; sources for, 255–57, 261, 267, 272, 274; sources written in, 261, 266–67; tribes, 57, 73, 236; Upper, 46, 192, 336
Egyptians, 87, 105, 192, 211–13, 234–35, 314. *See also* Copts
Elburz Mountains, 61
Elias of Nisibis, 266
English political parties, 45
Ephesos, 312
Ethiopia, 135. *See also* Abyssinia
Ethiopian sources, 116
Eudo, Duke of Aquitaine. *See* Odo, Duke of Aquitaine
Euphratensis, 48
Euphrates River, 18, 47, 50–51, 107, 119, 225, 293–94, 302
Europe, Western, 112–13, 163
European scholars, 72, 163, 270–72
Europeans, West, 254
Eustathios, 169
Eutychius, Patriarch of Alexandria. *See* Sa'īd b. al-Bitrīq

al-Faḥṣ, 343
Fārāb, 184
Farandiyya, 162, 168
al-Farazdaq b. Ghālib b. Ṣa'ṣa'a al-Mujāshi'ī, 46, 67, 148, 190, 260–61, 323
Farghāna, 126, 128, 156, 184, 317
Farghānans, 184
Fārs, 40, 57, 61, 64, 298
Fās, 211, 235
al-Fath, Wādī, 219
Fatḥnāmah-i Sind, 65, 261
Fay', 226
Fertile Crescent, 19, 26, 55, 68, 104
Field of Martyrs, Battle of the. *See* Poitiers, Battle of
Fīlān, 175, 324, 332
Filasṭīn, 47–49, 51, 80, 152, 259, 288, 325. *See also* Palestine
Fiqh, 283
Fitna: First, 19–20, 23, 27, 29, 78, 92; Second, 19–21, 26–27, 29, 47, 51, 78, 82, 92–93, 98, 291; Third, 5, 19–20, 270; Fourth, 49
France, 4, 72, 115, 124, 140–43, 146, 163–65, 196–97, 203, 231, 234, 267, 335
Franks, 6, 103–4, 112–13, 140, 163–64, 167, 197, 203; Frankish frontier, 219–220; kingdom, 112–13, 164, 197; sources, 163–64, 253, 267; warfront, 142, 163, 196–97
Friday worship, 16, 32
Fuqahā', 283
al-Furāt b. Salmān al-Bāhilī, 325
al-Fusṭāṭ, 18, 40, 70, 192, 289
Futūḥ, futūḥāt, 1

Gabrieli, Francesco, 163–64, 270
Galicia, 141, 196–97, 219
Ganges River, 111
Gangra, 120–21, 168, 314
Ganza, 150
Garonne River, 164
Gaul, 103
Gauls, 348
Genghis Khan, 279
Georgia, 106, 122–23, 172, 309, 324
Georgian sources, 253
Georgians, 108, 331
Germany, 247
Geyve, 120
al-Ghamr b. Yazīd II b. 'Abd al-Malik, 83, 169, 201–2
Gharjistān, 127
al-Ghaṭāsīn. *See* al-'Aṭāsīn
Ghaylān al-Dimashqī, 268
Ghazāla, 152
Ghazwat al-ashrāf. *See* Nobles, Battle of the
Ghevond. *See* Lewond
Ghūmīk, 174, 315, 331
Ghūr, 127, 309
al-Ghūṭa, 293

Gibb, H. A. R., 161, 182–83, 253, 271
Gibraltar, Strait of, 208
God, 1–3, 11, 14, 16, 18, 24, 27, 77–79, 86, 92, 94, 101, 232, 279, 294, 301
Goldziher, Ignaz, 45
Gothic kingdom of Spain, 103–4, 113, 142–43, 309
Goths, 70, 141. *See also* Visigoths
Great Thar Desert, 111, 148
Greece, 34, 104
Greeks, 34, 207, 254; chronology, 162; fire, 193; language, 28, 38, 94, 104, 257; sources, 105, 162, 165, 253, 259. *See also* Byzantines
Guhilots, 111, 133, 188
Gujarat, 132–33, 147, 187–89, 202–3, 234, 319–20
Gulf, the, 58
Gurjara–Pratiharas, 103, 111, 148, 188
Gurjaras, 111–12, 133, 187
Gurjaratra, 133

Ḥabaṭ, the, 290
Ḥabīb b. Abī 'Ubayda b. 'Uqba al-Fihrī, 194–95, 206–9, 211–12
Ḥadīth, 13–15, 77, 206, 279–80, 301
Ḥaḍramawt, 73
Ḥaḍramawt, the, 290
al-Ḥājib, 81
al-Ḥajjāj b. 'Abd Allāh b. al-Ḥakam al-Ḥakamī, 150
al-Ḥajjāj b. 'Abd al-Malik b. Marwān I, 316
al-Ḥajjāj b. Yūsuf b. al-Ḥakam al-Thaqafī, 29, 63, 65, 84, 87–88, 90, 129, 136, 286, 297, 299, 301, 317
al-Ḥakam b. 'Awāna b. 'Iyād al-Kalbī, 134, 186–89, 202, 235, 335
al-Ḥakam b. Qays b. Makhrama al-Muttalibī al-Qurashī, 314
Ḥakīm b. 'Ayyāsh al-Kalbī, al-A'war, 261
Hamadhān, 40
Hamdān, the, 66
Hamites, 68
Ḥamrā', the, 298
Ḥanafīs, 282
Ḥanbalīs, 282
Ḥanẓala b. Ṣafwān b. 'Amr al-Kalbī, 95, 210, 213–18, 221, 224, 289, 299, 345
al-Ḥaras, 81
Ḥarb b. Qaṭan b. Qabīṣa b. Mukhāriq al-Hilālī, 185–86
Ḥāriq b. Abī Ziyād, 298
Ḥarīsh, the, 151
al-Ḥārith b. 'Amr al-Tā'ī, 123–25, 151, 316
al-Ḥārith b. Surayj b. Zayd al-Mujāshi'ī al-Tamīmī, 176–84, 191, 332–33
al-Ḥarra, Battle of, 73, 78
Ḥarrān, 51, 83, 259
Hārūn al-Qurnī, the *mawlā* of Mu'āwiya b. Hishām, 341–42
Ḥassān b. Ghunāba (or 'Atāfa), 218
Ḥassān b. Muḥammad b. Abī Bakr, the *mawlā* of the Jumaḥ, 139
Ḥassān b. al-Nu'mān al-Ghassānī, 29, 300
Ḥassān al-Nabaṭī, 269
al-Ḥawf al-Sharqī, 320
Ḥawrān, 83
al-Haytham b. 'Adī b. 'Abd al-Raḥmān al-Ṭā'ī, 256
al-Haytham b. 'Ubayd al-Kilābī, 290
Hebrews, 254, 292
Hellespont, 34
Hephthalites, 25
Heraclian dynasty, 31
Herat, 336
Herodotus, 270
High Atlas. *See* Atlas Mountains
Ḥijāz, the, 21, 24, 73–75, 115, 260, 320
Ḥijāzīs, 120
Ḥīla b. Ḥammād al-Ghaṭafānī, 130
Hilāl b. Aḥwaz b. Arbad al-Māzinī, 131
Himachal Pradesh, 132
Ḥimṣ, 8, 47–49, 51, 80, 83, 118, 152, 288, 346
Ḥimṣīs, 52, 122, 182, 325, 346
Ḥimyar, the 66
Hindū Kush, 129
Hindu literature, 133
Hindus, 30, 103–4, 110–11, 148, 190
al-Ḥīra, 61
Hishām b. 'Abd al-Malik b. Marwān I: adherence to doctrine of *jihād*, 4, 6, 34, 78–79, 102, 124, 213, 230; administrative behavior and policy, 4, 41–42, 52–53, 57, 80–81, 85, 122–23,

Hishām b. ʻAbd al-Malik b. Marwān I: *(continued)* 125, 138, 142, 151–53, 176, 182, 193, 196, 205, 209, 223, 227–28, 294, 336, 339, 350; appointments to office, 41, 171, 182, 192, 194, 209, 330; Christians favorable to, 267, 320; concept of caliphal office, 77; estates, 79, 81, 91, 190, 227; fiscal policy, 4, 40, 71–72, 79, 82–83, 87, 89–91, 124, 135, 145, 228, 230–32; ideological policy, 78, 93, 95–96, 184, 268; military activity and policy of caliph, 150–51, 157, 160, 172, 192, 200–02, 209–10, 213, 329, 331, 338; personal traits and behavior, 4– 5, 79, 95–96, 150, 152, 182, 201, 209, 213, 217, 227, 331, 334; relations with al-Walīd II, 272; residence and movements, 51, 302, 329

Hishām b. Muḥammad b. al-Sāʼib al-Kalbī, 255–56, 264

Hodgson, Marsall, 251

al-Hudhayl b. Zufar b. al-Ḥārith al-Kilābī, 325

al-Hunayd b. Iyās b. Zuhayr al-ʻAdawī, Abū al-Dhayyāl, 269

al-Ḥurr b. Yūsuf b. Yahyā al-Umawī al-Qurashī, 52, 135

al-Ḥusām b. Ḍirār b. Salāmān al-Kalbī, Abū al-Khaṭṭār, 215, 221, 345

al-Ḥusayn b. ʻAlī b. Abī Ṭālib, 21, 26–27, 191

Iberia (in Caucasus), 316

Iberian peninsula, 196

Iberians, 104

Ibn ʻAbd Rabbih, Yūsuf b. ʻAbd Allāh al-Nimarī al-Qurṭubī, 260

Ibn Abī Muslim. *See* Yazīd b. Abī Muslim, the *mawlā* of the Thaqīf

Ibn ʻAsākir, ʻAlī b. al-Ḥasan, 261, 263

Ibn al-Ashʻath. *See* ʻAbd al-Raḥmān b. Muḥammad b. al-Ashʻath

Ibn Aʻtham. *See* Aḥmad b. Aʻtham al-Kindī al-Kūfī

Ibn al-Athīr, ʻIzz al-Dīn ʻAlī b. Muḥammad al-Shaybānī al-Jazarī, 171, 216, 262, 264

Ibn Durayd, Muḥammad b. al-Ḥasan, 264

Ibn Faḍlān. *See* Aḥmad b. Faḍlān b. al-ʻAbbās, the *mawlā* of Muḥammad b. Sulaymān

Ibn al-Faqīh, Aḥmad b. Muḥammad al-Hamadhānī, 53, 265

Ibn Ḥajar al-ʻAsqalānī, Aḥmad b. ʻAlī, 263

Ibn Ḥazm al-Andalusī, ʻAlī b. Aḥmad, 264

Ibn Hishām. *See* ʻAbd al-Malik b. Hishām b. Ayyūb al-Ḥimyarī

Ibn Ḥumayd. *See* Khālid b. Ḥumayd al-Zanātī

Ibn ʻIdhārī, Aḥmad b. Muḥammad al-Marrākushī, 219, 221

Ibn ʻIrs al-ʻAbdī, Khālid b. al-Muʻārik, 159, 327

Ibn al-Kalbī. *See* Hishām b. Muḥammad b. al-Sāʼib al-Kalbī

Ibn Kathīr, ʻImād al-Dīn Ismāʻīl b. ʻUmar al-Dimashqī, 263

Ibn Khallikān, Aḥmad b. Muḥammad, 263

Ibn Khayyāṭ. *See* Khalīfa b. Khayyāṭ al-ʻUsfurī

Ibn Khurdādhbih, ʻUbayd Allāh b. ʻAbd Allāh, 53, 265

Ibn al-Muhallab. *See* Yazīd b. al-Muhallab b. Abī Ṣufra

Ibn Nuṣayr. *See* Mūsā b. Nuṣayr, the *mawlā* of the Lakhm

Ibn Qutayba, ʻAbd Allāh b. Muslim al-Dīnawarī, 260, 262

Ibn al-Qūṭiyya, Abū Bakr b. ʻUmar al-Qurṭubī, 262

Ibn Rustah, Aḥmad b. ʻUmar, 265

Ibn Saʻd. *See* Muḥammad b. Saʻd

Ibn Shihāb al-Zuhrī. *See* Muḥammad b. Muslim b. Shihāb al-Zuhrī

Ibn al-Sijf al-Mujāshiʻī, 327

Ibn al-Zubayr. *See* ʻAbd Allāh b. al-Zubayr b. al-ʻAwwām

Ibrāhīm b. ʻAṣim al-ʻUqaylī, 185–86, 325

Ibrāhīm b. Hishām b. Ismāʻīl al-Makhzūmī, 120

Ibrāhīm b. al-Walīd I b. ʻAbd al-Malik, 252

Iconoclasm, 94–95

Idolaters, 13–14

Ifrīqiya, 39–40, 90, 99, 138–39, 219, 259, 305. *See also* North Africa, Tunisia

'Ijl, the, 294
Ikonion, 119, 168
'Ikrima, the *mawlā* of Ibn 'Abbās, 138, 193, 206, 306, 308–9, 320–21
al-Imāma wa al-siyāsa, 97, 262
India, 202, 224, 231–33, 259; central 103; Friday mosques in 16; inscriptions, 111, 187–88, 249, 253; Muslim campaigns in, 4, 65, 131–34, 143, 147, 186–90, 320, 323, 335; Muslim defeat in, 148, 163, 167, 187–90, 202, 224, 231–33; northern 111, 188; northwestern 132; ignored by sources, 259; southern, 112, 187; states of, 6, 110–13, 133, 187–88, 202; warfront, 115, 162; wealth of, 65, 134, 175; west coast 103; western 145, 160. *See also* Sind
Indian Ocean, 186
Indians, 6, 66, 104, 111, 148, 187–89
Indus River, 62, 131–32
Indus Valley civilization, 254
Iqṭā', 82
Iran, 19, 22, 30, 58, 61, 103, 309
Iranians, 110, 178, 184, 298, 316
Iraq: administration, 40, 57–67, 69, 90, 288, 297; 305; ancient, 254; capital of 'Abbāsids, 51; capital of Eastern superprovince, 318; caliphal estates in, 91, 190; conquest, 19, 22; dependencies, 61–67, 126, 130, 179, 299; in First *Fitna* , 21; in Second *Fitna* , 28; geography, 50, 125; governors, 88, 129, 179, 185, 189, 191, 202, 263, 269, 289, 299; grievances against Umayyads, 25, 58–59, 61–62, 98, 177, 190; historical tradition, 60, 79–80, 259–63, 267, 269, 295–96; *khawārij* in, 60, 188, 190, 304; northern, 150; population of, 23, 203, 273–74; revolts against Umayyads, 58, 177, 190–91; source of recruitment, 231; sources on, 258–63, 350; tribes, 57–58, 60, 66–67; Umayyads control by force, 29, 47, 84–85, 87, 191, 229, 236; wealth, 53, 63–65, 71, 175
Iraqi superprovince, 40, 57, 63, 126–27, 295. *See also* Eastern superprovince
Iraqis: in Caucasus, 172; demobilized by Umayyads, 29, 59, 78, 84, 154, 191, 226; in India, 233; individuals named, 261–62, 339; in Khurāsān, 146, 157, 161, 176–77, 179, 288, 326–27; in North Africa, 68; in Sijistān, 288; in Sind, 202–3, 339; Umayyads contemplate recruitment of, 154, 179, 203, 213; oppose Umayyads, 23, 26, 78, 84, 161, 190–91; Yaman seek support of, 225; Yamanī, 346
Irbid, 51
Irene, 153–54
Irmīniya. *See* Armenia
Iṣbahān, 288
al-Iṣbahānī, Abū al-Faraj, 260
Iṣfahān. *See* Iṣbahān
Isḥāq b. Muslim al-'Uqaylī, 174, 325
Ishbīliyā (Seville), 267
Islam: little spread in Armenia, 68, 108; many Berbers embrace, 29–30, 68, 113–14, 193, 328–29; caliphate propagates to Berbers, 137, 193, 205, 298; Berber *khawārij* propagate, 100, 137–38, 193; early Berber resistance to, 89; some Berbers not yet Muslim, 72, 103, 194; Byzantines invited to accept, 32, 95, 284; slow spread among Copts, 272; disaffection from government, 3; financial officials embrace, 41; Franks resist, 112; heroes, 21; historians' commitment to, 249; official ideology of caliphate, 11, 92–96, 153; Indians embrace, 319; Khazars avoid, 173; Kūfan influence on, 296; mass appeal, 4, 15; mountainous areas resist, 68; Prophet propagates, 284; Sindīs embrace, 131–32, 136; little spread among Spanish, 70; Taghlib resist, 56; universalism, 59; Transoxianans embrace, 136; volunteers fight for, 172
Islamic coins, 28, 38, 40, 90–91, 94, 145, 147, 257, 323
Islamic law, 15, 60, 77–78, 96, 295
Islamic worship. *See ṣalāh*
Ismā'īl b. Abd Allāh b. Abī al-Muhājir, the *mawlā* of the Makhzūm, 298
Ismā'īl b. 'Ubayd Allāh b. al-Ḥabḥāb, the *mawlā* of the Salūl, 207, 235
al-Iṣṭakhrī, 173, 265
Istija, Battle of, 309

Italian language, 270
Italy, 104
Itil, 172, 174, 331. *See also* al-Baydā'.

Jabala b. Abī Rawwād, the *mawlā* of the 'Atīk, 308
al-Jābiya, 289
Ja'far b. Ḥanẓala al-Bahrānī, 182
al-Jāḥiẓ, 'Amr b. Baḥr, 260
Jahm b. Zaḥr al-Ju'fī, 297
al-Jahshiyārī, 48–49, 53–54, 63–64, 71, 81
Jaisalmer, 111, 133
Jalālābād, 317
al-Jamma, 215
Jarāwa, 217
Jarīr b. 'Atiyya al-Tamīmī, 46, 56, 67, 260–61
al-Jarrāḥ b. 'Abd Allāh al-Ḥakamī, 8, 108, 122–23, 149–50, 154, 157, 165, 233, 315–16, 325, 335
Ja'wana b. al-Ḥārith b. Khālid al-'Āmirī, 325
Jaxartes River, 103, 126–27, 183–84, 233, 317
Jayabhata IV, 187
Jaysinh b. Dāhir b. Ṣaṣ, 131–32, 137, 318–19
al-Jazīra: administration, 40, 50–54, 80; army division, 88, 152, 224; base against Byzantines, 168; dependencies, 52–54, 123, 293; governors, 289, 305; tribes, 8, 50, 52, 54–57, 126; wealth, 53–54, 58
al-Jazīra al-Khaḍrā', 209
Jazīran superprovince, 40, 50, 52–53, 69
Jazīrans: army, 50–51, 54–55, 179, 229, 303; on Byzantine front, 8, 55, 118–20, 170, 224–25, 235, 306; in the Caucasus, 54, 124, 151–52, 170–72, 294, 315; defeated by Khurāsānīs, 9, 99; defeat Yamanīs, 218; excluded from office, 286; in Khurāsān, 127, 178, 185, 317; clash with Kūfans, 61, 296; individual named, 87, 88, 131, 176, 185, 263, 298–99, 325; in North Africa, 68; political-military weight, 8, 51, 54, 154, 224–25, 229, 305; provinces ruled by, 52–54, 123, 154; reluctance to campaign, 150; in Sind, 202; tribal conflict, 55–57, 225; warfronts near home, 146, 225
Jerusalem, 17, 82, 312
Jesus Christ, 94, 307
Jewish sources, 173
Jews, 13–14, 173, 283, 313
al-Jibāl, 40, 57, 61, 64, 297
Jidda, 116
Jihād: connection with mosque, 16–17, 258; definition, 1, 279–80; end of, 3–4, 20, 203, 228; in France, 196; hiatus in, 23; ideology, 2, 15, 18, 31, 96, 279; legimates Umayyad rule, 78–79, 232; non–Muslims' view, 187; in North Africa, 193–95, 213; against oppressors, 226; policy of state, 1, 6, 11, 18–19, 35, 96, 252, 284; retrenchment of 'Umar II, 78; rules, 11–16, 115, 280–81, 284; in Spain, 205; strengthened by success, 7, 20, 22, 29
Jīlān, 175
Jizya, 6, 11, 13, 15, 31, 86–88, 114, 125, 127–28, 132, 137, 183, 191, 282
Jodhpur, 133
Jordan (modern country), 83, 95, 258. *See also* al-Balqā' and al-Urdunn
Jordan River, 48
Juansher, 331
Judaism, 108, 173–74
Juhayna, the, 66
Jullundur, 131, 319
al-Junayd b. 'Abd al-Raḥmān al-Murrī: campaigns in India, 65, 132–34, 147–48, 187, 189, 318–19, 335; campaigns in Transoxiana, 155–61, 165, 233, 325–27, 332; governor of Khurāsān, 161, 176, 181, 253, 289, 332–33; 339; governor of Sind, 88, 131–32, 289, 318, 323
Jurash, the, 290
Jurjān, 30, 57, 61–62, 64, 66, 297
Jurz 133. *See also* Gurjaratra
Jurzān, 106, 324. *See also* Georgia
Justinian II, 31, 105, 109

Kabul, 23
Kaccha. *See* Cutch
Kachchhellas, 133, 187
Kadar River, 208, 235
Kaisareia Mazaka, 119–21, 162, 168, 313–14
Kalankatuaci, Moses. *See* Dasxuranci, Movses

Kalb, the, 66, 272, 292, 318, 335, 345
Kamakh (Kamakhon), 119
Kamarja, 128, 318
Kamarja, Battle of, 124, 128
Kanarese, the, 112
Kanauj (Kanyakubja), 111, 148, 188
Kangra Valley, 132, 319
Kappadokia, 119–20, 162, 169, 329
Karkotas, 111, 134
Karmīniya, 160
Karnataka, 112, 148
Kasāk, 172
Kasāl, 172
Kashmir, 111, 132–34, 188, 319
Kaskar, 64, 297
Katā'ib, 42–43
Kathiawar Peninsula, 111–12, 133–34, 187, 234–35
Kathīr b. Rabī'a, 119
al-Kawthar b. al-Aswad al-'Anbarī, 173
Kennedy, Hugh, 4, 265
Kennedy, John F., 247
Khākhīṭ, 174
Khālid (*khārijī*), 335
Khālid b. 'Abd Allāh b. Asad al-Qasrī al-Bajalī: dismissal, 67, 185, 228, 260, 269, 350; estates, 190, 305; family, 95, 127; prominence of, 194, 268; rule in Iraq and East, 90, 126, 158, 188, 190, 269, 289, 327; seat of government, 61; sold to enemy, 223, 225; sources on, 263; subordinates, 130, 147, 185, 189, 297–98, 322; tortured, 223, 290; tribal connections, 98, 341
Khālid b. Abī Ḥabīb al-Fihrī, 207, 209, 235, 340
Khālid b. Ḥumayd al-Zanātī, 207, 211–12, 216–18, 308
Khālid b. 'Ubayd Allāh al-Hajarī, 332
Khālid b. 'Umayr b. al-Ḥubāb al-Sulamī, 325
Khalīfa, 77
Khalīfa b. Khayyāṭ al-'Uṣfurī, 81, 88, 120, 153, 171, 174, 185–86, 195, 248–49, 256, 262
Khammāsh, Najda, 272
Khamzīn, 152, 172, 175, 315
Khāqān, Khazar, 109, 124, 151–53, 171, 173–74, 323, 325
Khāqān, Turgesh, 109–10, 123, 125, 128, 155–56, 158, 177; 180–84, 317, 333. *See also* Sülü
Kharāj, 53, 65, 70–71, 74, 88–89, 122–23, 141, 177, 183, 194, 273, 298, 302
al-kharāj wa al-jund, dīwān, 81
Khārijīs. See khawārij
Khārijism, 102, 138, 206, 294, 306, 320, 340
Khārijites. *See khawārij*
Kharīstān, Battle of, 182
Kharsianon, 162, 168
Khashram al-Sulamī, 332
Khasmadān, 123
al-Khātam, dīwān, 81
al-Khātam al-ṣaghīr wa al-khāṣṣa, dīwān, 81, 91
Khawārij (sing. *khārijī*): in al-Basra, 60; Berbers, 100–01, 206, 208, 211, 236, 340; campaigns against, 188, 208, 211, 304; in Egypt, 192; in Iraq, 188, 190; in Khurāsān, 190; leaders, 101, 206, 268; missionaries, 96, 100; as political opposition, 24, 101–2, 206, 294, 309, 340; from Rabī'a, 24, 56, 190, 294; in Sijistān, 130, 147, 185; from Tamīm, 24, 56, 67, 190; revolts of, 74, 92, 102, 114, 130, 188, 208, 335–36; sources on, 260, 272; from Yaman, 192
Khaydhān, 151, 315
al-Khazā'in wa buyūt al-amwāl, dīwān, 81
Khazar khanate, 54, 103, 108, 167, 173
Khazaria, 152, 154, 172, 233, 316
Khazars: allied with Byzantines, 106, 108–9, 153–54; danger to Muslims, 53, 106, 150; history, 108; Muslim campaigns against, 122–25, 149– 55, 167, 170–74, 330; offensives by, 108, 122, 124–25, 149–50, 313, 315, 323–25; opponents of Muslims, 6, 104, 108, 332; royal family, 323; peace with, 171, 330; sources for, 271; warfront, 54, 87, 106, 108–9, 117, 167, 170, 175; campaign in winter, 122, 150, 181
Khīraj, 174
Khīzaj, 174, 331
Khosroïds, 172
Khujanda, 126–27, 317
Khunāsira, 293

Khurāsān: administration, 38–40, 62, 124, 142, 228; bias in favor of, 258, 267; as dependency of al-Basra, 57, 62–64, 296; conquest, 19, 25, 61– 62; eastern 25; in Second *Fitna*, 28; governors, 124, 127, 132, 155, 161, 179, 209, 268, 289–90, 333, 345; revolt of al-Ḥārith b. Surayj, 176–82, 184, 191; under Iraq, 69, 98, 299; independent province, 127; Iraqis in, 29, 62–63, 157, 176–77, 179, 288, 296–97; Jazīrans in, 127, 178, 185; *khawārij*, 190; struggle over *mawālī*, 5, 86–88, 99– 100, 177, 205, 226; provincial army, 44, 50, 99–100, 146, 157, 177, 230; source of recruits, 231; sources for, 259–62, 332; Syrians in, 178–80, 182, 185, 224, 228–29, 317; resents Syrians, 98–99, 130, 211; tribes in 5, 268, 308, 333; struggle against Turks, 156–57, 176, 180–84; 318; dislike of Umayyads, 191, 194, 197, 206; warfront, 7, 66, 123, 125, 179, 259; wealth, 64

Khurāsānī superprovince, 40

Khurāsānīs: in ʻAbbāsid revolution, 5, 9, 99, 102, 230; army size, 303; conscription of, 157, 326; hostility to governors, 127, 157, 161, 179; individual named, 156, 176, 182, 185, 308; Kūfan, 297; military disasters, 155, 157, 180–81, 185, 233–34, 249, 326; low morale among, 128, 156, 161, 185, 195; poetry, 158–60, 261; replaced by outsiders, 176; revolt, 176–79, 185; sources on, 260; tribal groupings, 177, 333, 327; support Umayyads, 180, 182

Khursān, 324

al-Khuttal, 180–81, 317, 333–34

Khuttalān. *See* al-Khuttal

Khuzāʻa, the, 206

Khūzistān, 40

Kilikia, 33–34, 85, 118–19, 313

Kinda, the, 66, 268

Kīra, 132, 319

al-Kīraj, 132–34, 147, 319, 335

Kirmān, 40, 57, 61, 64

Kishsh, 156, 161

Köl-chür. *See* Kūrsūl

Kolkhis, 107

al-Kubaysī, ʻAbd al-Majīd, 272

al-Kūfa: administration, 57, 290, 305; army division of, 62, 325; bias in favor of, 261, 268; capital, 73; dependencies, 58, 61, 296–97; geography, 18, 29, 58; income, 63–64; intellectual center, 59–60, 295– 96; as a *miṣr*, 58, 60, 63, 289; mosques in, 16–17; 284; population, 274; Shīʻī revolutionism in, 21, 24, 27, 59, 66, 92, 102, 190, 226; sources for, 259, 262; Syrians in, 67, 317; tribes, 24, 44, 57–58, 62, 66, 147

Kūfans: demilitarized, 59–60, 66, 84, 226; discontent, 58–61, 66, 99, 102, 179, 226; ideological sophistication, 59–60, 62; individual, 101, 261; in Khurāsān, 62–63, 326; migration to Baṣran lands, 296, 326; revolts, 58, 101, 191; in Sind, 62–63. *See also* Iraqis

Kulthūm b. ʻIyāḍ b. Waḥwaḥ al-Qushayrī (or al-Qasrī), 170, 209–15, 218, 224, 235, 299, 341–42

al-Kumayt b. Zayd b. al-Akhnas al-Asadī, 46, 66, 260–61, 298

Kur River, 122, 151

Kur Valley, 123

Kūrṣūl, 183–84

Kuwar Dijla, 64, 297

Kyrgyzstan, 317

Kyzikos, 25

al-Lādhiqiyya, 170, 287, 310

Lake Van, 151

Lake Urmiya, 150

Lakhmīs, 216

al-Lakz, 123, 173–75, 324

al-Lān, 171

Lapidus, Ira, 272

Lata, 112, 187

Latin language, 163

Latin sources, 267

Layth, the, 268

Layzān, 175, 324

Lazika, 316

Lebanon, 170

Lebanon Mountains, 23

Leo III, 32, 95, 153, 169, 201, 339

Leo IV, 154

Leon, 337

Lewond, 151, 266
Libya, 70, 104, 217, 320
Lilie, R.-J., 271
Lilybaion, 195, 337
Lykia, 286
Lyon, 322

Ma'add, the, 50
Ma'āfirīs, 192
McEvedy, Colin, 37, 273–74
al-Madā'in, 259
al-Madā'inī, 'Alī b. Muḥammad, 255
Madhya Pradesh, 133
al-Madīna, 1, 16, 19, 22–23, 27, 73–74, 78, 82, 120, 283–84, 303
al-Maghrib. *See* North Africa
al-Mahdī, Muḥammad, 115
al-Maḥfūẓa, 186–87, 289, 335
Maitrakas, 111, 133, 187
al-Makhāḍa, 312
Makka, 13, 24, 40, 74, 82, 259
Makka, Great Mosque of, 93
Makrān, 30, 38, 64, 297
Mālaba, 133. *See also* Malwa
Malaṭya, 34, 118–20, 162, 169, 200–01, 329
Mālava. *See* Malwa
Mālik b. Sāriya al-Numayrī, 308
Mālik b. Shu'ayb, 169, 235
Mālikīs, 282
Malwa, 111, 133, 148, 188
Mamikonians, 153, 172
al-Ma'mūn, 'Abd Allāh b. Hārūn, 48, 53, 63, 71, 74, 311
Ma'n b. Zā'ida al-Shaybānī, 339
Manbij, 150
al-Mandal, 133
al-Manṣūr, Abū Ja'far 'Abd Allāh b. Muḥammad, 300
Manṣūr b. Jumhūr b. Ḥiṣn al-Kalbī, 317
al-Manṣūra, 40, 186–87, 202, 289, 335
Manūsa, 164, 322
al-Maqqarī, 221
al-Maqrīzī, Taqī al-Dīn Aḥmad b. 'Alī, 90
Mar'ash, 162, 327
Mardaites, 20, 27–29, 31
Mardān Shāh, 150
Marianos, 169
Mārida, 219–21
Marj Rāhiṭ, 8, 27, 224–25
Marj al-Sabalān, 149
Marmad, 133
Marsala. *See* Lilybaion
Martyrs, 14
Maru–Mala. *See* Marmad
Marw, 25–26, 40, 100, 155, 160, 177–79, 183, 268, 289, 333
Marw al-Rūdh, 181, 336
Marwān I b. al-Ḥakam b. Abī al-'Āṣ, 27, 56
Marwān II b. Muḥammad b. Marwān I: advises Hishām, 325; campaigns against Byzantines, 119, 312–13; as caliph, 51, 80, 218, 230, 252, 292; campaigns in Caucasus, 152–53, 170–75, 294, 325, 330–32; defeat and death, 292; forces under, 172, 306; governor of Jazīran superprovince, 53, 88, 289, 312, 330
Marwān b. Yazīd b. al-Muhallab al-'Atakī al-Azdī, 202, 339
Marwānids, 20–21, 27–29, 31–32, 56, 70, 82, 93, 96, 177, 182, 204, 223, 304
Masdār, 331
Maslama b. 'Abd al-Malik b. Marwān I: in Anatolia, 120–21, 162, 313, 328–30; in Caucasus, 108, 123–25, 151–53, 233, 310, 330; siege of Constantinople, 287; death, 329; dismissal, 125, 149; estates, 80, 82, 303; failures of, 86–87, 124–25, 152–53, 171, 176, 233, 325, 331; forces under, 151–52, 306, 325; governor of East, 87–88; influence, 88, 304; protégés, 87–88, 151
Maslama b. Hishām b. 'Abd al-Malik, 169, 329
Maslama b. Sawāda al-Fihrī (or al-Judhāmī), 211, 214–15, 343
Masqaṭ, 324
al-Maṣṣīṣa, 33
Maṭāmīr, 168–69, 329
Maurontius, Patrician of Provence, 197
Mauryas, 111, 133, 187–88
al-Mawa, 121, 168
Mawālī (non-Arab Muslims): advisers, 210; Arab attitude toward, 59, 100, 307; in army, 88, 99, 205, 298; complaints lodged by, 99, 117, 177, 203, 205, 332; conflict with Umayyads, 99–102, 179, 271, 306; control fiscal

Mawālī (continued)
posts, 41, 135, 194, 289, 307–8; control government departments, 80, 100; denied rights in army, 31, 86–87, 99, 205; dissatisfaction with status, 5; hold governorships, 68, 88, 135, 194, 309; Ibn Nuṣayr's family protect, 205–6; *jizya* taken from, 31, 86–88, 128, 204–5, 228; military commanders, 120; naming convention, 264; in navy, 87; private armies of, 91; religious leaders, 268; reforms sought for, 33, 177, 191, 225–26; revolts, 100, 117, 128, 137, 178, 207; sources on, 269; subordinated to Arab tribes, 298; 'Umar II favors, 31, 86, 117; not united, 100
Mawāsā, 119, 168
al-Mawṣil, 24, 40, 52–53, 150, 259, 261, 274, 293–94, 296
Maymūn b. Mihrān, the *mawlā* of the Naṣr, 120, 263
Maysara al-Faqīr al-Madgharī, 205, 207, 211, 308, 339–40
Mediterranean Sea, 18, 22, 103, 118, 200; eastern, 120, 139, 169, 199, 234; western, 118, 136, 139, 193, 199, 231
Meds, the, 186, 189, 235, 320
Mérida. *See* Mārida
Merovingians, 112
Mesopotamia, 310; Upper, 50. *See also* al-Jazīra
Mewar, 133
Michael the Syrian, Bishop of Edessa, 33, 124, 171, 266
Mīdh. *See* Meds, the
Miḥrāb, 17
Mihrān River, 131–32
al-Miknasa, 343
Mi'laq b. Ṣaffār al-Bahrānī, 122, 315
Minbar, 17
Mongols, 1–2, 279
Mopsuestia. *See* al-Massīsa
Morocco, 3, 9, 38, 70, 72, 114, 194, 207, 211, 288, 320
Moroccans, 219–20
Mu'āwiya b. Abī Sufyān b. Ḥarb, 24–27, 47–48, 51, 53, 58, 60, 63–64, 71, 74, 92, 285, 296, 351
Mu'āwiya b. Hishām b. 'Abd al-Malik, 119–21, 162–63, 168–69, 306, 313–14, 327–29
Mu'āwiya b. Ṣafwān, 344
al-Mubāraka, 305
Muḍar, the: under 'Abbāsids, 291; on Byzantine front, 50, 55; caliphal policy toward, 286; cohesion of, 55, 308, 334; connection with Rabī'a, 56; in Egypt, 135, 236; eponymous ancestor, 264; favor expansion, 123; hold most offices before Hishām, 32, 55; individual named, 176, 179, 182, 260, 308, 325; in al-Jazīra, 8, 54, 146, 154, 224; in Khurāsān, 182–83, 259; in al-Kūfa, 66; in North Africa, 73, 210; in Qinnasrīn, 50, 224; in Sind, 187; in Spain, 142; struggle with the Yaman, 8, 45–46, 73, 223, 269, 271, 341; tribes linked to, 50, 68, 341. *See also* Qays 'Aylān, the
Mughān Steppe, the, 151. *See also* Mūqān
al-Mughīra b. Sa'īd, 294, 336
Mughīth al-Rūmī, the *mawlā* of al-Walīd b. 'Abd al-Malik, 341–42
Muhallabids, 63, 88, 131, 202
Muḥammad b. 'Abd Allāh, the Prophet of God, 11–13, 18–22, 24, 26, 77, 94, 115, 280–81, 283–84, 301
Muḥammad b. 'Abd al-Malik b. Marwān I, 83
Muḥammad b. Abī Bakr, the *mawlā* of the Jumaḥ, 139
Muḥammad b. 'Amr b. 'Uqba, 217
Muḥammad b. Aws al-Anṣārī, 139
Muḥammad b. al-Ḥasan b. Farqad, the *mawlā* of the Shaybān, 295
Muḥammad b. Hishām b. 'Abd al-Malik, 169
Muḥammad b. Ḥijr b. Qays al-'Abdī, 185
Muḥammad b. Ḥujr al-Kindī, 147
Muḥammad b. Marwān I b. al-Ḥakam, 52, 107, 293
Muḥammad b. Muslim b. Shihāb al-Zuhrī, 78, 96, 268, 307
Muḥammad b. al-Qāsim b. Muḥammad al-Thaqafī, 63, 65, 84, 132–33, 319–20
Muḥammad b. Sa'd b. Manī', Kātib al-Wāqidī, 263
Muḥammad b. al-Sā'ib b. Bishr al-Kalbī, 295
Muḥammad b. 'Ubayd Allāh al-Azdī, 342

Muḥammad al-'Ilāfī, 319
al-Mujashshir b. Muzāḥim al-Sulamī, 156–57
al-Mukhtār b. Abī 'Ubayd b. Mas'ūd al-Thaqafī, 21, 59, 92, 306
Multān, 111
Munnuza. *See* Manūsa
al-Muqaddasī, 40, 265
Mūqān, 175. *See also* Mughan Steppe, the
Muqātil b. Ḥayyān al-Nabaṭī, the *mawlā* of the Shaybān, 268, 308
Muqātila, 84, 100, 127
Murji'a, 60, 176
Mūsā b. Abī Khālid, the *mawlā* of Mu'āwiya b. Ḥudayj al-Sakūnī, 208
Mūsā b. Nuṣayr, the *mawlā* of the Lakhm: background, 299; caliphal adviser, 315; campaigns, 300; dismissal, 299, 321; family, 205–6, 321; governor of North Africa, 29, 69, 88, 262; *mawālī*, 205–7; propagates Islam, 29, 137, 205, 298; subordinates, 138
al-Mushattā, 345
Muslim b. 'Amr al-Bāhilī, 63
Muslim b. Sa'īd al-Kilābī, 88, 126–27, 181, 231, 233, 290
Muslim chronology, 162
Muslim navy: at Constantinople, 26, 87, 105, 304, 309; campaigns in east Mediterranean, 22, 25, 31, 121; Egyptians in, 72, 87, 105, 139, 192, 314; defeats in east Mediterranean, 20, 26, 34, 105–6, 139, 169, 192, 199, 232; at Rhodes, 25–26; in west Mediterranean, 72, 139–40, 165, 193–95, 199, 216, 233
Muslim prisoners, 147, 150–51, 170, 184, 201, 221, 324
Muslim sources: biographical dictionaries, 263; compared to Chinese sources, 184; compared to Christian sources, 141, 162–65; 196, 201, 208–9, 253, 265, 267, 310; compared to Indian sources, 133, 187; genealogical works, 264–65; geographical works, 265; literary compilations, 260; local histories, 261; poetry, 260–61, 272; tendencies, 249–50; universal histories, 258–59, 261–62
Muslim women, 200
al-Mustanīr b. al-Ḥārith al-Ḥarashī (or al-Ḥuraythī), 140, 165, 216, 233
Mu'ta, 22, 285
al-Mutawakkil, Abū Ja'far b. Muḥammad, 320

al-Naḍīr, Banū, 283
Nāfi' b. Abī 'Ubayda b. 'Uqba al-Fihrī, 169, 192, 234
Nafṭa, 343
Nafzāwa, 217, 343
Nagabhata I, 188
Najdīs, 206, 291
Nakhla, 280
Nakoleia, 120, 314
Nandipuri, 112, 133, 187
Narbonne, 113, 141–42, 196–97, 203, 220, 311
Naṣr b. Sayyār b. Rāfi' al-Laythī, 176–77, 182–85, 209, 228, 268, 289–90, 308, 326–27, 334–35
Navarre, 164
Navasarika, 187–89, 234
Navies. *See* Byzantines, navy; Muslim navy
Naysābūr, 40, 178
Near East, 103–4
Neokaisareia Pontika, 313
Nihāwand, Battle of, 295, 309
Nikaia, 120–21, 250, 312, 314
Nikephoros, 259, 266
Niksar, 313
Nile: cataracts, 115; delta, 135, 320; river, 18, 114; valley, 115, 135
Nīmes, 141
Nisba, 264
Nizār, the, 56
Nobles, Battle of the, 208
non-Arabs, 29, 43, 68, 80, 86, 99, 131, 136, 264, 269
non-Muslims: as allies of caliphate, 172; early conquests of, 22; not forced to be Muslims, 13; as frontier enemies, 9, 20, 25, 34, 45, 54, 194, 249, 261, 322; in Muslim government, 41, 307; population, 273–74; rebels among, 207; sources, 250, 256, 269; as subjects of caliphate, 23, 59, 89, 95–96, 136, 141, 176–77, 183, 199, 227–28; tribal peoples, 72

North Africa: administration, 40, 69–71, 117, 299; Arabs in, 73, 136, 139, 221; army of, 68, 136–37, 139, 205, 207, 303, 341–42; Berbers accept Islam, 29–30, 68, 114, 136–38, 193; Berbers mistreated, 86–88, 114, 135–37, 164, 194, 205–6; Berbers revolt, 100, 170, 195, 207–19, 224–25, 235; conquest, 19, 25, 29–30, 69; dependencies, 196; geography, 38, 103–4, 114; governors, 68, 138, 163, 193–94, 204, 209–10, 215–16, 221, 289, 298–99; *khawārij*, 101, 138, 206, 294, 321, 340; later Muslim campaigns, 34, 72, 140, 194; sea campaigns from, 72, 116, 165, 193–95, 233–34; sources for, 67, 73, 260–62, 270, 272; Syrians in, 8–9, 229, 236, 341–42; western, 207, 212; 300. *See also* Ifrīqiya
North African superprovince. *See* Western superprovince
Nubians, 114–15
al-Nukhudh, 177
Numayr, the, 308
al-Nuwayrī, Shihāb al-Dīn Aḥmad b. 'Abd al-Wahhāb, 262

Odo, Duke of Aquitaine, 113, 141–42, 164, 311
Osrhoene, 52, 293
Ossetians, 316
Oviedo, 197
Oxus Basin, 127
Oxus River, 127, 155–56, 160–61, 180–81, 234, 317

Pacific Ocean, 1
Palaestina Prima, 48
Palaestina Secunda, 48
Palestine, 46, 312. *See also* Filastīn
Palmyra, 51
Pamphylia, 286
Pamplona, 196
Paphlagonia, 119–20, 168, 201, 313
Papyri, 28, 38, 94, 255–57
Parasikas, 188
Pelayo (Pelagius), 141, 197
Pepin of Héristal, 112
Pergamon, 329
Persia, 2, 17, 22, 104, 284. *See also* Iran, Sāsānian Empire
Persian Gulf. *See* Gulf, the
Phoenice Libanensis, 48
Phoenice Prima, 48
Phrygia, 120, 314
Pilgrimage, 13
Poetry: Khurāsānī, 158–60; Umayyad, 260–61, 291
Poitiers, 164, 196, 234
Poitiers, Battle of, 163–65, 346
Polytheists. *See* Idolaters
Pontic Mountains, 104
Portugal, 3
Poti, 107
Praetorium, 17
Pratiharas. *See* Gurjura-Pratiharas
Principia, 17, 284
Prophet. *See* Muḥammad b. 'Abd Allāh
Prophet, house of, 191, 226
Provence, 197
Pulakesirāja, 187
Punjab, the, 111, 133, 147–48, 319, 323
Pyrenees Mountains, 72, 113, 141–42, 164, 196

Qabala, 151
Qābis, 214–15, 320, 343
Qadarīyya, the, 252, 268, 272
al-Qādisiyya, Battle of, 295, 309
Qafṣa, 215, 343
Qaḥṭān, the, 45, 264
Qandabīl, 131
al-Qarn, 217
al-Qarqīsiyā', 294
al-Qāsim b. Muḥammad b. Abī Bakr al-Taymī al-Qurashī, 96, 268
al-Qāsim b. 'Ubayd Allāh b. al-Ḥabḥāb, the *mawlā* of the Salūl, 194
al-Qāsim al-Shaybānī, 332
Qasr, the, 341
Qaṣr al-Bāhilī, 109, 126
Qaṣr al-Ḥayr al-Gharbī, 227
Qaṣr al-Ḥayr al-Sharqī, 227, 258
Qaṣṣa, 133, 319. *See also* Cutch
Qaṭar, 291
Qaynīs, 188
al-Qayrawān: administration, 40, 69, 305; in Berber revolt, 199, 209–12, 214–18, 232, 343; founding, 25–26,

al-Qayrawān *(continued)*
70; governors, 138; as a military base, 25, 70, 72, 289, 320; mint, 40, 90; Syrians in, 224
Qayrawānīs, 217
Qays 'Aylān, the: 336; 'Abbāsid attitude toward, 99; in al-Basra, 57; on Byzantine front, 49; in Caucasus, 124, 152; dominant position, 55–56, 98; governors, 88, 98, 181, 336; individuals, 88, 127, 139, 150, 157, 185, 187, 192, 214, 325, 336; in al-Jazīra, 54–57, 152; in Khurāsān, 178; in Qinnasrīn, 57, 152; in Syria, 57; struggle with Yaman, 8, 45–46, 98, 224, 336; tribes, 341. *See also* Muḍar, the
Qays b. Sa'd b. 'Ubāda al-Khazrajī al-Anṣārī, 24
Qaysara, 119, 168, 313
Qinnasrīn: city of, 47; district of, 47–48, 288; Qays/Muḍar in, 8, 50, 57, 224, 308, 341; as seat of caliphs and princes, 51, 80, 83, 293, 302–3;
Qinnasrīnīs: on Byzantine front, 118, 224, 306; in Caucasus, 124, 152; individuals named, 88, 126, 150, 169, 171, 325; in North Africa, 210; at Ṣiffīn, 292
Quḍā'a, the, 50, 57, 66, 291
Quḍā'īs, 57
Qudāma b. Ja'far, 48–49, 53, 63–64, 265
Quinisext Council, 94, 307
al-Qūmidh, 311
Qūmis, 57, 61, 64, 296
Qūniya, 119. *See also* Ikonion
Qur'ān, the: application demanded, 176–78, 191, 226; basis of law, 92; on caliphal office, 77; coin inscriptions, 28; Dome of the Rock inscriptions, 94; on *jihād*, 6, 11–13, 15, 279; on *jizya*, 6, 11, 13; raising of in battle, 340; recited on battlefield, 16; taught to Berbers, 137; motivates 'Umar II, 31; on Muslim unity, 3; Walīd II accused of shooting, 229
Qurashīs, 58, 73, 96, 268, 294
Qurbayt, 320
Qurrā', 16
Quraysh, the, 20, 23–24, 27, 77, 268, 294
Qurṭuba, 40, 70, 90, 219–20, 235, 305
Qusanṭīna, 343
Qushayr, the, 341
Quṣṣāṣ, 16
Qutayba b. Muslim b. 'Amr al-Bāhilī, 30, 126, 128–29, 183, 290, 296–98
Qutham b. 'Awāna al-Kalbī, 139, 195, 234

Raba'īs, 56, 185
al-Rabī' b. Ziyād al-Ḥārithī, 62
Rabī'a, the: under 'Abbāsids, 291; in al-Basra, 57, 60, 67, 297; Christianity among, 56; eponymous ancestor, 264; in al-Jazīra, 54–56; *khawārij* from, 24, 56, 67, 190, 294, 336; in Khurāsān, 177, 179–80, 327; marginality, 55–56; struggle with the Muḍar, 45, 60, 67, 190, 271; in Sijistān, 129, 318
Rabī'a b. Ḥanẓala of the Tamīm, the, 290
Rajasthan, 133, 147, 187, 189, 319
Rajputana, 111
al-Ramla, 47–48, 51, 293, 303
al-Ramm River, 153
al-Raqīq al-Qayrawānī, Ibrāhīm b. al-Qāsim, 214, 216–17
al-Raqqa, 150, 293
Ra's Kayfā, 83
al-Rasā'il, dīwān, 81
al-Rashīd, Hārūn, 48–49, 53, 63, 71, 74
Rāshidūn caliphs, 18, 20, 22, 77, 256
Rashtrakutas, 112, 187, 189
Rāwar, Battle of, 309
al-Rawr, 186
Raysūn, 83
al-Rayy, 57, 61, 289
Red Sea, 115, 135
Rhodes, 25–26, 285–86
Rhône River, 197
Rhône Valley, 141, 197
Ridda wars, 58
Roman camps, forts, 16–17, 284
Roman Empire, 1–2, 17, 37, 91, 114, 265
Roman historians, 253
Roman Republic, 45, 72, 256, 348
Romans, 1, 18, 72, 114, 232, 254; Hispano–Romans, 30, 70, 141
Ru'ba b. al-'Ajjāj b. Ru'ba al-Sa'dī al-Tamīmī, 260–61
al-Rusāfa, 51, 150
Russell, J. C., 37, 273–74

Russia, 106
Rustāq Millī, 315

Ṣā, 320
Sabeans, 13
al-Sabība, 210, 343
Sābiqa, 58
Sabrat, 214, 320
Sabta (Ceuta), 212, 218, 220–21, 320, 342, 344
Sabū, Battle of Wādī, 211–12, 218, 221, 224, 235, 342, 344
Sābūr, 305
al-Ṣadaqa, 81, 302
al-Ṣafadī, Khalīl b. Aybak, 263
al-Ṣaghāniyān, 160–61, 183, 317
Sa'īd al-Abrash b. al-Walīd (or Bakr) al-Kalbī, 81, 269, 345
Sa'īd b. 'Abd al-Malik b. Marwān I, 82, 119, 303
Sa'īd b. 'Amr b. Aswad al-Ḥarashī, 88, 126, 150–51, 171, 303, 317, 324–25, 330
Sa'īd b. Bajra al-Ghassānī, 215, 343
Sa'īd b. al-Biṭrīq (Eutykhios), 266
Sa'īd b. Hishām b. 'Abd al-Malik, 121, 313
Sa'īd b. Jubayr b. Hishām, the *mawlā* of the Asad b. Khuzayma, 301
al-Ṣā'ifa al-yumnā, 118–20, 168–69, 312–13
al-Ṣā'ifa al-yusrā, 118–21, 168, 312–13
Saindhavas, 111–12, 187
Ṣalāh, 14, 78, 283
Ṣāliḥ b. Ṭarīf (1), 308
Ṣāliḥ b. Ṭarīf (2), the *mawlā* of the Ḍabba, Abū al-Ṣaydā', 183, 332–33
Ṣāliḥ al-Hamdānī, 325
Sālim b. 'Abd Allāh b. 'Umar I b. al-Khaṭṭāb, 268, 307
Sālim b. 'Abd al-Raḥmān, 81
Sālim al-Azdī, Abū Yūsuf 211, 218
Salīṭ, Wādī, 219
Ṣamāluh, 121, 314. *See also* Semalouos
Samandar, 152, 172
al-Sam'ānī, 'Abd al-Karīm b. Muḥammad, 264
Samannūd, 320
Samarqand, 40, 126–28, 155–56, 158–61, 180, 183–84, 233, 253, 311, 327, 332
al-Samḥ b. Mālik al-Khawlānī, 141, 165, 311
Samūr River, 174
Sangarios River, 120
Saraqusṭa, 208, 219–20
Sardinia, 139, 165, 195, 204, 234, 321
Sardis, 168
al-Sarīr, 174, 331
Sarmalia, 312
Sāsānian administrative system, 80
Sāsānian Empire, 52
Sāsānian military formations, 68
Sāsānids, 2, 22, 25, 30, 38, 94, 103–04, 106–07
Saurashtra, 112, 133, 187; North, 189
Sawād, the, 63–64, 274
ṣawāfī, 64, 83, 321
Sāwīrus b. al-Muqaffa' al-Ashmūnī, 267
Sawra b. al-Ḥurr b. Nāfi' al-Abānī, 156–57, 326
Sayābija, the, 298
Sayf b. 'Umar al-Usayyidī, 250, 295
(Pseudo-)Sebêos, 12
Second Punic War, 232
Second World War, 18, 247
Semalouos, 121, 168, 314
Semites, 68
Sens, 322
Septimania, 113, 197, 311
Severias, 313. *See also* Sibora
Seville. *See* Ishbīliyā
Shaban, Muḥammad 'Abd al-Ḥayy, 5, 33, 98, 178, 229, 271
al-Shābarān, 174
Shadhūna, 219
Shāfi'īs, 282
Shahrazūr, 296
Shakkī (Shakka), 315
Shalaf, Wādī, 209, 211
al-Shar'abī al-Ṭā'ī, 158, 327
Sharwān, 151, 175, 324
al-Shāsh, 155–56, 183–84
Shāshīs, 184
Shaybān, the, 294, 318
Shi'b 'Iṣām, 347
Shī'īs, 16, 21, 24, 27, 56, 190, 260, 294, 306
Shī'ism, 59, 66, 102, 191, 259
Shīrāz, 40
Shīza, 119
Shūrā, 229, 346
al-Shuraṭ, dīwān, 81
Sibora (Ar. Sībura), 119, 168, 313
Sicily, 72, 104, 139–40, 165, 193–95, 204, 206–8, 216, 233–34, 321, 337

Sideroun, 168–69, 329
Sidonia. *See* Shadhūna
Ṣiffīn, 292
Sijistān: geography, 110; governors, 129–30, 147, 185–86; income from, 64; inhabitants, 129, 228, 318; under Iraq, 57, 61, 64; Iraqis in, 29, 63, 288; *khawārij*, 130, 147, 185; sources, 146–47, 261, 271; Syrians in, 130, 229; truce with Zunbīl, 129, 186, 202, 228; wars with Zunbīl, 110, 129–30, 146–47, 231, 233, 335
Sijistānīs, 146, 233
Sind: administration, 40, 65, 87–88; army of, 303; base for Muslims, 110, 148, 167, 186, 189; campaigns in, 132, 186, 202–3, 345; Chach dynasty restored by 'Umar II, 32, 85, 131–32, 137; conquest of, 2, 19, 29–30, 38, 82, 84, 297; 309, 320; disliked by troops, 112, 148; geography, 103–4, 110–11, 116, 323, 335; governors, 65, 131, 186, 268, 289; under Hishām, 117, 319, 335; income from, 64, 82, 84, 103; under Iraq, 57, 62, 64, 202; Iraqis in, 29, 62–63, 202–3; nearly lost by Muslims, 148, 202, 232; *miṣrs* of, 289; Muslim navy in, 134; included Punjab, 133, 148; revolts in, 148, 190, 202; sources for, 261–62, 347; Syrians in, 63, 228–29, 236; warfront, 66, 148
Sindān, 175
Sindara. *See* Sideroun
Sindīs, 132, 136, 202, 234
al-Sīrjān, 40
Sirt, 320
Sīza, 119
Slavs, 153, 173–74
Smbat, sons of, 172
Solomon's table, 321
Spain: administration, 40, 67, 69–70, 87, 89, 124, 141–42, 196, 299; army of, 303; base against France, 113, 140; Berbers in, 68, 100, 114, 142, 164, 204–5, 219, 221; campaigns in north, 70, 72, 140–42, 164, 196– 97, 272; civil strife, 142, 209, 219–21; conquest, 2, 19, 29–30, 38, 68– 70, 82, 114, 141, 309; geography, 1, 67, 103–4, 309; ; governors, 113, 138, 141, 163, 165, 196, 208–9, 218, 344; income from, 71–72, 82; Islam in, 70; lost to caliphate, 3, 9, 221–22, 232, 288; Muslims settled in, 142, 145, 197, 209, 220–21, 234–35, 287, 342–43; native Christians, 196, 267; opposition to Umayyads, 197; reforms sought, 226; sources for, 163, 253, 261–62, 267, 270–71; Syrians in, 9, 73, 210, 212, 219–22, 224, 228–29, 236; tribes, 73; under 'Umar II, 33– 34, 70, 85, 287, 300; western, 219
Spanish, the modern, 1
Ṣubayḥ (*khārijī*), 335
Ṣufrīs, 206, 208, 214, 340
Sufyān al-Thawrī, 295
Sufyānids, 20, 24, 26–28, 286
Sughd, 128, 155–56, 233
Sughdān, 331
Sughdīs, 110, 126–27, 184
Ṣuḥārī b. Shabīb b. Yazīd al-Shaybānī, 336
Sulamīs, 297
Sulaymān b. 'Abd al-Malik b. Marwān I, 8, 31, 51, 80, 82, 90, 93, 95, 263, 286, 299
Sulaymān b. Abī al-Muhājir, 342
Sulaymān b. Hishām b. 'Abd al-Malik, 91, 163, 168–70, 200–01, 235, 306, 328, 330, 338–39
Sülü, 109, 126, 183. *See also khāqān*, Turgesh
Sunna, 77, 92, 176, 178, 191, 226, 306
Sunnīs, 16, 21, 206
Surast, 133. *See also* Saurashtra
al-Sūs al-Aqṣā, 194, 207, 235, 340
Synnada, 170, 330
Syracuse, 140, 195, 206–7
Syria: administration, 28, 39–40, 47–48, 51, 69, 71, 288; 302; *amṣār*, 18, 47; Arabs in before Islam, 52; army sent against Berbers from, 210; Byzantine, 292; Byzantine and Mardaite attacks on, 20, 28, 139, 170, 286, 310; Byzantine prisoners killed in, 201; base against Byzantines, 117, 169–70, 310; caliphal residences, 80; coast, 170, 202, 287; conquest, 19, 22; Cypriots settled in, 202, 339; estates in, 83, 91, 258; Second *Fitna* in, 26–27, 51, 98; geographical position, 50–51, 57, 70, 103–4, 123, 125, 225; home of Syrian army, 229; income from, 48– 49, 54, 58, 71; base against

Syria *(continued)*
Khazars, 315, 330; metropolitan province, 1, 47, 50, 69, 79, 99; opposes 'Alī, 23; plague in, 338; political consciousness, 59; population size, 273; power vacuum in after Hishām, 8, 213, 218, 222, 224–25, 229; sources for 252, 260–61; sources written in, 266; tribes, 50, 56–57, 272, 308; truce with Byzantines in, 23, 27; Umayyad collapse in, 217; Umayyad stronghold, 24, 34, 93, 154
Syria Prima, 48
Syria Secunda, 48
Syriac: language, 266, 306; speakers, 68
Syrian (Christian) sources, 120, 162, 253, 266
Syrian Desert, 258
Syrians: alienated by caliphal extravagance, 83; alienated by defeats, 26, 188–89; in Caucasus, 53, 122–23, 150, 152, 154, 172, 224, 229, 233, 236; army of, 47, 49–50, 54, 71, 82, 303, 338; fight Byzantines, 118–19, 170, 234–35, 313–14; Christians of, 23, 27–28; coup against al-Walīd II, 229–30; in Egypt, 236; exhausted by campaigning, 8, 145–46, 214, 222, 224; in Second *Fitna*, 27; in France, 197; hegemony of, 8, 24, 47, 58–59, 98, 199, 225; individuals named, 130, 147, 165, 186, 214–17, 261, 263, 269, 317–18, 342; in India, 134, 149, 189, 224, 233–35; in Iraq, 29, 47, 58–59, 85, 87, 188, 229, 236; in Khurāsān, 128, 155, 157, 178–82, 185, 224, 229, 317, 333; losses, 8–9, 99, 119, 122, 146–47, 149, 154, 170, 185, 212–13, 224, 228–36, 346; mainstay of Umayyads, 154, 191, 223–24, 230; migration of, 296; monopolize offices, 25, 32, 63, 123; in North Africa, 9, 73, 200, 210–14, 218–19, 224–25, 229, 235–36, 300, 342, 344; in provinces, 7, 47, 50, 99, 190, 229, 236; reform program, 8, 225–29; resented, 158; scattering of, 99, 102, 190, 224–25, 228–30, 236; in Sijistān, 130, 147, 229, 233, 236; in Sind, 63, 148, 203, 229, 236; in Spain, 9, 73, 142, 210, 212, 219–22, 224, 229, 235–36, 338, 344; struggle with Iraqis, 23; in Syria, 229, 236, 346; in Transoxiana, 233–34, 236; Yaman-Mudar struggle, 8, 50, 224; predominantly Yamanī, 8, 66
Syro-Jazīran army, 98, 121, 170, 175, 200, 233, 235, 317
Syro-Palestinians, 46

al-Ṭabarī, Abū Ja'far Muḥammad b. Jarīr, 67, 128, 204, 249–51, 255–56, 258–59, 261–62, 269–71
Ṭabaristān, 30, 38, 61, 66, 68, 296–97, 309
Ṭabarsarān, 175, 324, 332
Tabūk, 281, 285
Taghlib b. Wā'il, the, 56, 295
Ṭaha, 'Abd al-Wāḥid Dhanūn, 271
Tahūda, 343
al-Ṭā'if, 74, 82, 259
Ta'iq, 107
Tajmīr al-bu'ūth, 148, 226–27
Takkayān 148, 323. *See also* Punjab
Takrīt, 64
Talabayra, 219
Talavera. *See* Talabayra
Tamīm, the: in al-Basra, 57, 60, 67, 75, 261; excluded from office, 294; *khawārij*, 24, 56, 67; in Khurāsān, 177, 180, 190, 327, 336; opponents of Rabī'a, 56, 60, 67; origin, 291; in Sijistān, 129; tribal composition, 269
Tamīm b. Zayd b. Ḥamal al-Qaynī, 147–48, 186–87, 189, 233, 323, 335
T'ang dynasty, 37
Tangier, 70, 72, 137, 194, 207, 217–18, 235, 320, 340–41
Tanjā. *See* Tangier
Tanū, 320
Ṭarīfa, 208
Ta'rīkh-i Sīstān, 146
Ṭāriq b. Ziyād, the *mawlā* of Mūsā b. Nuṣayr, 321
Ṭarīq al-Furāt, 53
Tataion. *See* Ṭataya
Ṭāṭarā, 323
Ṭāṭarī dirhams, 147, 323
Ṭataya (Tataion), 120, 314
Tatta, 323
Taurus Mountains, 104, 118
Ṭā'ūs, the *mawlā* of the Ḥimyar, 307
al-Ṭawāwīs, 160; Battle of, 326

Tawlaqa, 343
Tawzar, 343
Ṭayba or al-Ṭayna. *See* Tataya
Ṭayyi', the, 268
Thābit b. Khaytham al-Lakhmī, 165, 216, 235
Tha'laba b. Salāma b. Jaḥdam al-'Āmilī, 221, 345
Thaqīf, the, 55, 67, 268
Thar Desert. *See* Great Thar Desert
Tharmach, 149
Thebasa, 119; 312. *See also* Dabasa
Theodosiopolis, 106
Theophanes, 33, 119, 162, 169, 201, 210, 259, 266
Thubayt al-Bahrānī, 315, 325
Tiberias, 47
Tiberius, 289
Tibet, 110
Tibetans, 188
Ṭiflīs, 122–23, 149, 172
Tigris River, 50, 52
Tilimsān, 208, 211, 320
Tilimsān, Wādī, 208–9
Tinnīs, 287, 310
al-Tirmidh, 286, 317
Tlemcen. *See* Tilimsān
Toledo. *See* Tulaytula
Toulouse, 113, 141, 311
Tours, 164, 328
Tours, Battle of. *See* Poitiers, Battle of
Transcaucasia, 108, 125. *See also* Caucasus
Transoxiana: administration, 62, 128, 142, 185, 299; campaigns in, 35, 125–28, 155–61, 182–84, 202, 232, 335; conquest, 19, 29–30, 38, 62, 82; defeats of Muslims in, 122, 140, 155–57, 163, 165, 231, 233; geographical situation, 70, 103–04, 116, 194; governors, 147, 176; income from, 64, 82; Iraqis in, 66; lull in, 171, 176; *mawālī* in, 100; rebellion in, 125; sources on, 106, 125, 271; Turgesh power in, 110, 117; under 'Umar II, 33–34, 70, 85; warfront, 66, 110, 145, 156, 162, 167, 181, 185, 199
Transoxianans, 88, 110, 127–28, 136, 181
Trapani. *See* Drepana
Tribunal, 17
Tripoli in Libya, 70, 72, 140, 210, 214–15, 217, 320
Tripolitans, 217
Ṭubna, 215–16, 235, 279, 343
Tujīb, the, 336
Ṭukhāristān, 100, 155, 161, 176–77, 180–81, 289
Ṭulayṭula (Toledo), 219, 321
Tūmān, 175
Tūmān Shāh, 172, 174–75
Tumayy, 320
Tunis, 139, 216–17, 219, 221, 320, 343, 345
Tunisia, 3, 19, 25, 70, 104, 113–14, 199, 212, 214–17, 232, 235, 320, 343
Ṭurābiya, 320
Turgesh, the 103–4, 109–10, 117, 125, 128, 155, 167, 182, 184. *See also* Turks
Turks: defeated by Muslims, 182–84, 232; geographical situation, 103–4; Khazars, 103–4, 108, 122, 310; opponents of caliphate, 6, 33, 66, 104, 109; attack in Transoxiana, 109, 125–28, 155–61, 180–82, 271, 317–18, 327, 332, 335; settled in Transoxiana, 110; West Turkish khanate, 108–9. *See also* Turgesh, the
al-Ṭuruz, 81
Tyana, 169, 330

'Ubayd Allāh b. 'Alī al-Sulamī, 131
'Ubayd Allāh b. al-Ḥabḥāb, the *mawlā* of the Salūl: provokes Copt revolt, 135; dismissed from North Africa, 209, 211; fiscal governor of Egypt, 41, 135, 236, 289, 299, 320; tries to conquer Morocco, 114, 194; governor of North Africa, 69, 194–95, 204, 206–8, 289, 299; appoints subgovernor of Spain, 196; subordinates, 214; taxation policies, 135, 204, 228
'Ubayda b. 'Abd al-Raḥmān al-Sulamī, 138–40, 163, 193–94, 336, 345
Uḥud, Battle of, 13
Ujjayini, 111, 133
'Ukkāsha b. Ayyūb al-Fazārī, 214–17, 343
'Ulamā', 268
Ūliya. *See* Lilybaion
'Ulūj, 59
Ulya, 196
'Umān, 57, 63

'Umar b. 'Abd Allāh al-Murādī, 207, 235, 339
'Umar II b. 'Abd al-'Azīz b. Marwān: administration, 31–35, 292, 299; centralization of minting, 90; debates *khawārij*, 101; defeat at Constantinople, 31, 33–34, 78, 86, 117; equity, 32; estates, 83; governors, 127, 298, 305; hears *mawālī*, 177; ideological measures, 32, 78, 93, 95; pact with Nubians, 115; piety, 33, 86; policy on *mawālī*, 31, 33, 86, 114, 131, 140, 191, 332; policy of tribal balance, 21, 31–32, 287; propagates Islam, 68, 137, 193; public works, 86; reduces expenditures, 85; reforms reversed, 87, 117; restores Chach dynasty in Sind, 85, 131–32, 137; seat of rule, 51, 80; suspends *jihād*, 19, 32–33, 38, 78, 85, 103; Syrian Yaman political program, 8, 98; wants withdrawals, 33–34, 70, 131, 287; withdraws Syrians from Iraq, 85
'Umar b. Hubayra b. Mu'ayya al-Fazārī, 87–88, 119, 126, 131, 290, 305
'Umar I b. al-Khaṭṭāb b. Nufayl al-'Adawī al-Qurashī, 17, 22, 26, 45, 82, 115, 229, 274, 295
'Umar b. al-Walīd I b. 'Abd al-Malik, 304
'Umāra b. Ḥuraym al-Murrī, 176, 290
Umayyad Mosque (Damascus), 82, 95
Umayyad palaces, 227, 258
Umayyad princes: as commanders, 162, 306, 325; cooperate with Yaman revolutionaries, 229; as governors, 88, 171; estates, 80, 82–83, 227, 304; stipends, 82, 85, 87; excluded from office, 88, 286
Umm Ḥakīm bt. Yaḥyā b. al-Ḥakam, 52, 96, 307
United States of America, 18
'Uqba b. al-Ḥajjāj al-Salūlī, 196–97, 208–9, 337
'Uqba b. Nāfi' b. 'Abd Qays al-Fihrī, 25, 73
al-Urdunn, 47–49, 51, 80, 83, 130; army division, 292; district of, 288; sources for, 259
Urdunnīs, 165, 216
Urmiya, Lake. *See* Lake Urmiya
Usāma b. Zayd b. Hāritha al-Kalbī, the *mawlā* of the Prophet, 285
Ushrūsana, 183, 334
'Uthmān b. Abī Nis'a al-Khath'amī, 328
'Uthmān b. Abī 'Ubayda b. 'Uqba al-Fihrī, 139–40, 194, 234
'Uthmān b. 'Affān b. Abī al-'Āṣ, 22–23, 27, 51, 58, 71, 77, 82, 92, 99, 179, 251, 287
'Uthmān b. Ḥayyān al-Murrī, 119, 313
al-'Uyūn wa al-ḥadā'iq, 259
Uzayn, 133. *See also* Ujjayini

Vaḷabhi, 111, 187, 189, 234
Valence, 322
Vallamandala, 133. *See also* Bhillamala
Van, Lake. *See* Lake Van
Van Ess, J., 272
Vascones. *See* Basques
Vatapi. *See* Badami
Vikramāditya II, 187
Visigoths, 2, 30; 311. *See also* Goths
Volga River, 108, 149, 172–73

Waddā' b. Ḥumayd al-Azdī, 131
Waḍḍāḥiyya, the, 91, 120
Wakī', Muḥammad b. Khalaf b. Ḥayyān, 259
al-Walīd I b. 'Abd al-Malik b. Marwān I: administration, 38, 61, 292; army, 50; building projects, 82, 86, 303; Christian poet of, 56; conquests under, 29–30, 38, 82, 128; estates granted by, 82–83, 303; favoritism for Muḍar, 286; governors, 298; ideological policy, 93; income from conquests, 82, 84; mosques of, 82, 95, 284; North Africa pacified, 70; residences, 51, 80, 293; social welfare, 82, 86; stipends for Umayyad princes, 82–83, 85
al-Walīd b. Hishām, 312
al-Walīd b. al-Qa'qā' al-'Absī, 169, 325
al-Walīd II b. Yazīd II b. 'Abd al-Malik: administration, 345; alienates Umayyads, 229; alienates Yaman, 223; blamed for Umayyads' fall, 4, 270; campaigns under, 345; disastrous situation as caliph, 26, 201–2, 223, 229; estates, 83, 227; expeditions under, 201–3; relations with Hishām,

al-Walīd II b. *(continued)*
96, 307; residences, 51, 80; overthrow, 5, 8, 51, 98, 218, 223–24, 229–30, 346; transfers Cypriots to Syria, 202
al-Wāqidī, Muḥammad b. 'Umar b. Wāqid, 255
Wartanīs, 172
Warthān, 122, 124, 149–51, 324
Wāsiṭ, 29, 40, 59, 61, 84, 90, 295, 297–98, 305
Wazīr al-Sakhtiyānī, 336
Wellhausen, Julius, 5, 33, 45, 55, 271
West Turkish Khanate, 108–9
Western scholars, 13
Western superprovince, 40, 67–69, 71–73, 97–98, 103–4, 123, 136, 209, 259, 305, 341
White, Hayden, 251

Xerxes, 34
Xinjiang, 37

Yabghū of Tukhāristān, 317
Yaḥṣub, the, 336
Yaḥyā b. Salama al-Kalbī, 89, 141–42
Yahyā b. Zayd b. 'Alī b. al-Ḥusayn, 101
al-Yamāma, 57, 63, 297
Yaman (country), 1, 21, 37, 73–75, 153, 283, 289, 300, 322
Yaman, the (people): under 'Abbāsids, 99, 259, 291; allied with Rabī'a, 55–56; basis of Umayyad power, 8, 154, 223–24; Berber links, 68; bias in favor of, 268–69; on Byzantine front, 8; in Caucasus, 8, 53, 123, 154; coup against al-Walīd II, 8; dominate Syrian army, 8; in Egypt, 57, 71, 73, 192; eponymous ancestor, 264; exhaustion, 146; governors, 123, 181; individuals 122–23, 127, 139, 147, 179, 187, 192, 195, 223, 325, 335, 341; in Iraq, 24, 66–67, 259, 346; in Khurāsān, 126, 179, 327; losses, 9, 146, 154; in North Africa, 8–9, 210; political program, 8, 33, 225–29, 346; Quḍā'a joins, 50, 291; in Sind, 187, 335; in Spain, 9, 220; struggle with Qays/Muḍar, 45–46, 73, 98, 142, 223–24, 269, 271, 336; in Syria, 50, 57, 71, 213, 218, 225, 346; tribes, 50, 66, 290, 336, 341, Umayyads' attitude toward, 32, 66, 98; in Yaman, 75
al-Ya'qūbī, Aḥmad b. Isḥāq b. Wāḍiḥ, 48–49, 53–54, 63–64, 119, 134, 146, 162, 259, 261, 265
Yāqūt al-Ḥamawī al-Rūmī, 265
Yarbū' b. Ḥanẓala of the Tamīm, the, 290
al-Yarmūk, Battle of, 309
Yashkur, the, 294
Yasovarman, 111, 148, 188, 311
Yazīd II b. 'Abd al-Malik b. Marwān I: administration, 81, 123, 129, 300, 304; booty, 66; campaigns under, 65, 117–19, 122, 131; finance, 316; governors, 88–89, 114, 131, 136, 138; ideological policy, 32, 93, 95; internal discord, 98; introduces Syrians in Caucasus, 52; Jazīran ascendancy under, 57, 87–88, 123; *jihād* policy, 29, 34–35, 38, 87, 102, 104, 231; names Hishām to succeed, 79; residences, 51, 80; special treatment of North Africa, 137; undoes reforms of 'Umar II, 87–89, 125
Yazīd b. Abī Muslim Dīnār, the *mawlā* of the Thaqīf, 88–90, 114, 136–37, 139, 204–5, 298
Yazīd b. Ghurayf al-Hamdānī, 130
Yazīd b. Masrūq al-Yahsubī, 139
Yazīd I b. Mu'āwiya b. Abī Sufyān, 26–27, 48, 58, 92, 285–86, 306
Yazīd b. al-Muhallab b. Abī Ṣufra al-'Atakī al-Azdī: family, 176, 202, 339; not favored by 'Umar II, 32, 287; governor of Khurāsān, 30, 62, 66, 296, 317; revolt of, 34, 52, 57, 60, 87, 98–99, 131
Yazīd b. Sa'īd b. 'Amr al-Ḥarashī, 342
Yazīd III b. al-Walīd I b. 'Abd al-Malik, 21, 80, 83, 91, 102, 223, 226, 228, 230, 252, 346
Yūsuf b. 'Umar b. Muḥammad al-Thaqafī: governor of Iraq, 61, 66–67, 90, 185, 202, 289, 297–98, 345; governor of Yaman, 289, 300; sources on, 263

al-Zāb, 215–16, 235, 343
Zabīd, 40

Zābulistān, 23, 38, 68, 110, 116, 129, 231, 329
Zakāh, 14, 283
Zamīndāwar, 233
Zanāta Berbers, the, 343
Zarafshān Valley, 161
Zaragoza. *See* Saraqusta
Zarawand, 150–51
Zarmān, 155
Zarq, 178
Zayd b. ʻAlī b. al-Ḥusayn b. ʻAlī, 21, 101–2, 190–91, 226–29, 260, 306
Zayd b. ʻAmr al-Kalbī, 217
Zaydīs, 21, 298
Zirīkarān, 175, 331
Zirūbkarān. *See* Zirīkarān
Ziyād b. Abī Sufyān, 44, 60, 284
Ziyād b. ʻAmr al-Lakhmī, 344
Ziyād b. ʻUbayd Allāh b. ʻAbd al-Ḥijr al-Ḥārithī, 289
Zoroastrians, 13, 150
al-Zubayrī, al-Musʻab b. ʻAbd Allāh b. al-Muṣʻab, 265
Zubayrids, 24, 27, 60, 77, 92
al-Zuhrī. *See* Muḥammad b. Muslim b. Shihāb al-Zuhrī
Zunbīl, the, 110, 129–30, 146–47, 186, 231, 271, 311, 329
Zuṭṭ, the, 298

Map Index

Abydos, 240
Abyssinia, 237
Acalapura, 243
Adhana, 239–40
Ādharbayjān, 237–38, 241
Akhlāṭ, 239, 241
Akroinon, 240
Alexandria, 244
Amanus Mountains, 239–40
Amorion, 240
Āmul, 242
Anatolikon Theme, 240
al-Andalus, 238, 245
Ankyra, 240
Antioch, 239–40
Arabian Sea, 243
Araxes River, 241
Ardabīl, 237–38, 241
Arles, 245
Armenia, 237–39, 241
Arrān, 241
Arzān al-Rūm, 241
Asturqa, 245
Atlantic Ocean, 238, 245
Atlas Mountains, 245
Autun, 245
Avignon, 245

al-Bāb (or Bāb al-Abwāb), 241
Badakhshān, 242
Bādis, 245
Bājarwān, 241
Balanjar, 241
Balīkh River, 239
Bālis, 239
Balkh, 242
Balkh, River of, 242
al-Balqā', 239
Bāmiyān, 242
Barawṣ or Barūṣ (Broach), 243
Bardha'a, 241
Barqa, 237–38
Bashkunis (Basques), 245
al-Basra, 237
al-Bayḍā', 237–38
Baykand, 242
al-Baylaqān, 241
Berbers, 245
Bhattis, 243
Bhillamāla, 243
Bhūmilka, 243
Biskara, 245
Bithynia, 240
Black Sea, 237–38, 240–41
Bordeaux, 245
Brahmanābād, 243
Bukellarion Theme, 240
Bukhārā, 242
Būṣīr Banā, 244
Buttam Mountains, 242
Byzantine Empire, 237–38, 240

Carcassonne, 245
Caspian Gates, 241
Caspian Sea, 237–38, 241
Caucasus Mountains, 241
Chāhmānas, 243
Chalukya Empire, 237, 243
Chāpas, 243
China, 237
Chitrakūta, 243
Chu River, 242
Constantinople, 237–38, 240
Corsica, 238, 245
Covadonga (Cangas), 245
Crete, 237–38
Cyprus, 237–39

Dabīl (Dvin), 241
Dābiq, 239–40
al-Dabūsiyya, 242

Dāghistān, 241
Dahlak Islands, 237
Dalisandos, 240
Damascus, 237–39
Damascus, Jund of, 239
al-Dandanqān, 242
Darial Pass, 241
Daybul, 237, 243
Dayr Sam'ān, 239
Dead Sea, 239
al-Didwāniyya, 241
Diyār Mudar, 239
Diyār Rabī'a, 239
Dordogne River, 245
Dorylaion, 240
Drepana, 245

Eastern Desert (of Egypt), 244
Egypt, 237–38, 244
Egypt, Upper, 244
Euphrates River, 237–40

Fārāb, 242
Farghāna, 242
Fīlān, 241
Filasṭīn, Jund of, 239, 244
Frankish Kingdom, 238, 245
al-Fusṭāṭ, 237–38, 244

Galicia, 245
Ganges River, 243
Gangra, 240
Garonne River, 245
Georgia, 237–38, 241
Ghūmīk, 241
al-Ghūr, 237
Great Thar Desert, 243
Gujarat, 237, 243
Guhilas, 243
Gurjaratra, 243
Gurjura–Pratiharas, 243
Gurjura States, 243
Gurjuras, 237

Hakra River, 243
Harī Rūd River, 242
Ḥarrān, 239–40
al-Ḥawf al-Gharbī, 244
al-Ḥawf al-Sharqī, 244
Helmand River, 242–43
Herakleia, 240
Herat, 242
al-Ḥijāz, 237–38
Himalayas, 243
Ḥimṣ, 239
Ḥimṣ, Jund of, 239
Hindu Kush, 242–43

Ifrīqiyā, 245
Ikonion, 240
India, 243
Indian Ocean, 237
Indus River, 237, 242–43
Iraq, 237–38
Irbid, 239
Iron Gates, 242
Ishbīliyā, 245
Itil, 237–38

Jaisalmer, 243
al-Jamma, 245
Janza, 241
Jaxartes River, 242
Jayhān River, 240
al-Jazīra, 237–39
al-Jazīra al-Khaḍrā', 245
Jerusalem, 239, 244
al-Jibāl, 237
Jīlān, 241
Jodhpur, 243
Jordan River, 239
Jullundur, 243

Kābul, 242–43
Kaccha (Cutch), 243
Kaisareia Mazaka, 239–40
Kamarja, 242
Kamkh, 239–40
Kānyakubja (Kanauj), 243
Kappadokia, 240
Karmīniya, 242
Kāshghar, 242
Kashmīr, 237, 242–43
Kathiawar Peninsula, 243
Kharsianon Theme, 240

Kilikia, 239–40
Kilikian Gates, 240
Kirmān, 237
Khābūr River, 239
Khākhīt, 241
Khawārizm, 242
Khaydhān, 241
Khazar Khanate, 237–38
Khazars, 241
Khujanda, 242
Khunāṣira, 239
Khurāsān, 237, 242
Khursān, 241
al-Khuttal, 242
al-Kīraj, 243
Kishm, 242
Kishsh, 242
Kotyaion, 240
al-Kūfa, 237–38
Kur River, 241
Kyzikos, 240

al-Lādhiqiyya, 239
Lake Van, 239, 241
al-Lakz, 241
al-Lān, 241
Lāta, 243
Layzān, 241
Lilybaion, 245
Loire River, 245
Lykia, 240

Madhya Pradesh, 243
al-Madīna, 237–38
al-Maḥfūẓa, 237, 243
Maitrakas, 243
Makka, 237
Makrān, 237
Malaṭya, 239–40
Mālava (Mālwā), 243
Manbij, 239–40
Mandal, 243
al-Manṣūra, 237, 243
Mar'ash, 239–40
Mārida, 245
Marmad (Maru–Māra), 243
Marmara, Sea of, 240
Marw, 237, 242
Marw al-Rūdh, 242
Masqat, 241
al-Maṣṣīṣa, 239–40
Mauryas, 243
al-Mawṣil, 237–38
Maymadh, 241
Mediterranean Sea, 237–40, 244–45
al-Mīdh (Meds), 243
Mount Lebanon, 239
Multān, 243
Mūqān (Mughan), 241
Murghāb River, 242
Mu'ta, 239

Nafṭa, 245
Nafzāwa, 245
Nakhchewān, 241
Nakoleia, 240
Narbonne, 245
Nasaf, 242
Navasārikā (Navsari), 243
Naysābūr, 242
Neokaisareia Pontika, 240
Nikaia, 240
Nile River, 237–38, 244
Nīmes, 245
Nīrūn, 243
Nubia, 237–38, 244
al-Nukhudh, 242

Orontes River, 239
Oxus River, 242

Paphlagonia, 240
Podandos, 239–40
Poitiers, 245
Poti, 241
Pyrenees Mountains, 245

Qabala, 241
Qābis, 245
Qafṣa, 245
Qandabīl, 243
Qaṣr al-Ḥayr al-Gharbī, 239
Qaṣr al-Ḥayr al-Sharqī, 239
al-Qayrawān, 238, 245
Qinnasrīn, 239–40
Qinnasrīn, Jund of, 239

Qīqān, 237, 243
al-Qulzum (Suez), 244
Qurṭuba, 238, 245
Qusanṭīna, 245

al-Rabba, 239
Rajasthan, 243
al-Ramla, 239
al-Raqqa, 239–40
Rāshtrakūtas, 243
al-Rawr (Alor), 243
al-Rayy, 237
Red Sea, 237–38, 244
Rhodes, 237–38, 240
Rhône River, 245
Rome, 245
al-Ruṣāfa, 239

Ṣā, 244
Sabalān, Mount, 241
Sabrat, 245
Sabta (Ceuta), 245
Sabū, Wādī, 245
al-Ṣaghāniyān, 242
Sahara Desert, 237–38, 245
Saindhavas, 243
Sakhā, 244
Samandar, 237–38
Samannūd, 244
Samarqand, 242
Samūr River, 241
Sangarios River, 240
Saraqusta (Saragossa), 245
Sardinia, 238, 245
Sardis, 240
Sarīr, 241
Sarmalia, 240
Saurashtra, 243
Sayhān River, 240
Sebasteia, 239–40
Semalouos, 240
Shābarān, 241
Shakkī, 241
Shalaf, Wādī, 245
al-Shām, 237–40
Shamākhī, 241
Shamkūr, 241
Sharwān, 241
al-Shāsh, 242
Sibora (Severias), 239–40
Sicily, 238, 245
Sijistān, 237
Sinai, 244
Sind, 237, 243
Srinagar, 242–43
al-Sūs, 238
Sūyāb, 242
Synnada, 240
Syracuse, 245
Syria, 237–39
Syrian Desert, 239
Syrian Gates, 240

Ṭabaristān, 237
Ṭabarsarān, 241
Tadmur, 239
Ta'iq, 241
Takkiyān, 243
Ṭalabayra, 245
Talas River, 242
Ṭālishān, 241
Ṭanja (Tangier), 245
Ṭaranda, 239–40
Ṭarīfa, 245
Ṭarsūs, 239–40
Tataion, 240
Ṭaṭar (Tatta), 243
Taurus Mountains, 239–40
al-Ṭawāwīs, 242
Tawzar, 245
Thebasa, 240
Tiberias, 239
Tien Shan Mountains, 242
Tīhart, 245
Tigris River, 237–39
Tilimsān, 245
Tinnīs, 244
al-Tirmidh, 242
Toulouse, 245
Tours, 245
Transoxiana, 237, 242
Tripoli, 245
Ṭubna, 245
Ṭukhāristān, 242
Ṭulayṭula, 245
Tūnis, 245
Turgesh Khanate, 237
Ṭūs, 242

Ujjayinī, 243
'Umān, 237
al-Urdunn, Jund of, 239
Ushrūsana, 242

Valabhi, 243
Vātāpi (Badami), 243

Warthān, 241
Western Desert (of Egypt), 244

al-Yamāma, 237
Yaman, 237
Yasovarman, Kingdom of, 237, 243

al-Zāb al-Kabīr, 245
Zābulistān, 237, 242–43
Zamm, 242
Zarafshān River, 242
Zarewand, 241
Zarq, 242
Zirīkarān, 241